DEADBALL STARS
OF THE
NATIONAL LEAGUE

DEADBALL STARS
OF THE
NATIONAL LEAGUE

Written by the Deadball Era Committee of
THE SOCIETY FOR AMERICAN BASEBALL RESEARCH

Edited by Tom Simon

BRASSEY'S, INC.
WASHINGTON, D.C.

ON THE COVER: At West Side Grounds in Chicago, crowds ring the field on August 30, 1908, for the game between the Cubs and the New York Giants. Chicago wins 2-1 behind Jack Pfiester, pulling within a half-game of the first-place Giants.

Library of Congress Cataloging-in-Publication Data

Deadball stars of the National League / written by the Deadball Era Committee of the Society for American Baseball Research; edited by Tom Simon.-- 1st ed.
       p. cm.
  ISBN 1-57488-860-9
  1. Baseball players--United States--Biography. 2. National League of Professional Baseball Clubs. I. Simon, Tom (Thomas P.), 1965- II.

Society for American Baseball Research. Deadball Era Committee.
GV865.A1D3715 2004
796.357'092'2--dc22

2003025946

Brassey's, Inc.
22841 Quicksilver Drive
Dulles, Virginia 20166

The Society for American Baseball Research
812 Huron Rd., Suite 719
Cleveland, OH 44115

Text and cover designed by Glenn LeDoux

ISBN 1-57488-860-9

First Edition
10 9 8 7 6 5 4 3 2 1

I do not like the lively ball. I think the game far more interesting when the art of making scores lies in scientific work on the bases. Moreover, I am inclined to believe that the public does not like the lively ball all the time. It is true that the spectator likes to see home runs hit, but there are times when he gets weary of it.

John McGraw, from his 1923 autobiography,
My Thirty Years In Baseball

When I played baseball it was as much a battle of wits as a trial of strength and speed. Everything was trying to outguess the other fellow and we used to spend hours doping out plays, but I guess most of the current players have stopped thinking. All they have to do now is walk up to the plate, grip the bat at the end, and take a swing.

Johnny Evers, from a 1925
interview in the *New York Sun*

Back in my day batters were smart. They weren't trying to hit the ball out of the park on every trip. Their main idea was to get on base, no matter how. Yes, I'd love to be pitching today against those lively ball cow-tailers. I'm sure I'd have a lot of fun.

Mordecai Brown, from a 1941
interview in *The Sporting News*

Keith Olbermann

FOREWORD

I'm still not sure I didn't meet the reincarnation of Fred Merkle.

In 1990, the granddaughter of the ill-fated and unjustly-blamed Giants first baseman contacted me at the Los Angeles television station for which I then worked. Every September 23rd since 1976, I've done one kind of commemoration of the Merkle game or another, on radio, television, or in print. She and her husband had happened upon one of them.

Most of the Merkle family's memorabilia had been destroyed in a fire in Florida decades earlier. Thus, much of what his youngest daughter, and her daughter, could see of Fred Merkle's baseball career came from the fleeting and piercing misrepresentations of "Merkle's Boner" that cropped up every year around the anniversary of the game itself.

Understanding that I had a small collection of Merkleiana, and a large amount of sympathy for him, his granddaughter asked if she and her husband could visit my home and see the old baseball cards, photos, and documents pertaining to his career.

They did not mention that they were bringing their son with them.

He was a toddler then, just barely up on his feet, and while they thumbed through the clippings and pictures, he contented himself sitting cross-legged before a mirrored wall in my living room.

I was droning on about how the entire sport had literally changed the rules on their poor ancestor on that September day in 1908 when our attention was seized by a grunt coming from the little boy. He was pulling himself upright by grabbing a thin piece of ornamental wood stuck to the mirror.

The moment he managed to stand, a piece of the wood snapped off from the mirror. As he wobbled where he stood, the foot-long piece gripped tight in his hands, he looked at it in confusion for the briefest of moments, then squealed with delight and began to swing it, purposefully and with concise, exact motions.

Fred Merkle's great-grandson was taking a few practice swings in my living room. He even followed through correctly.

None of us spoke for a while after that.

My fascination with the Deadball Era began long before that seeming visitation in my sunny living room in Los Angeles, and even before the fundamental unfairness of the Fred Merkle story leaped out at a ten-year-old me from the pages of a long-lost copy of *Baseball Digest*.

After all, that time was the most ancient epoch in which the game would have been easily recognizable to the fans of today. The fluctuating numbers of strikes for an out and balls for a walk had been settled. Pitchers and hitters had adjusted to the repositioning of the mound. The leagues—the ancient clans of our society, American and National—were fixed and seemingly immutable. Some damn fools were already advocating the designated hitter, night games, and interleague play. Game strategy was identical to today's, except that home run hitters and the big inning were extinguished by the great pitchers on a year-round basis, not just in the post-season.

In short, that era and those men so exhaustively chronicled in these pages are merely the oldest memories of the game we know now. Honus Wagner's salary astonished his fans as surely as Alex Rodriguez's has astonished *his*. Ty Cobb's skills and sulks drew and alienated his admirers just as confoundingly as Barry Bonds' swings and mood swings have befuddled his. There were even goofball executives, matinee idols, and baseball card manufacturers who made too many cards of the over-publicized superstars at the expense of the workmanlike pillars of the sport.

But you already know about Wagner and Cobb, and Tinker, Evers, and Chance. Take some time to introduce yourself to Bill Dahlen and Sherry Magee, to Wilbur Cooper and Ed Reulbach.

And to Fred Merkle.

KEITH OLBERMANN
SABR MEMBER SINCE 1984

INTRODUCTION

By the time I was eight I knew that I'd been born 75 years too late. Ever since then I've been trying to go back in time to the so-called Deadball Era—a misnomer, as nearly all baseball historians now agree (it was the rules that changed in 1920, not the ball), but one that has become so accepted that it seems futile to use another term. Occasionally I feel like I've almost succeeded. The first time was in sixth grade, when I discovered Larry Ritter's classic _The Glory of Their Times_ on the library shelf. Since then I've gotten that feeling again while reading Mike Sowell's _The Pitch That Killed_, examining the Charles Conlon photographs in Neal McCabe's _Baseball's Golden Age_, studying the detailed ballpark diagrams in Marc Okkonen's _Baseball Memories 1900-1909_, and listening to the audio version of _Glory_.

Though I've been interested in the Deadball Era since childhood, the idea for this book can be traced to my New Year's resolution for the year 2000. That year my resolution, I kid you not, was to post more frequently to SABR-L, the list server for the Society for American Baseball Research. I figured it was a modest resolution that I had at least some chance of keeping. As it turned out, it had more of an impact on my life than any other, for it was what prompted me on January 8, 2000, to post the following: "Are there others out there whose primary interest is the Deadball Era, 1900-20? If so, I think we should give serious consideration to starting a SABR Deadball Committee."

The next day I received my first response, an e-mail from Brian Marshall: "I was reading your post on forming a Deadball Committee and thought it was one of the best ideas I've heard since I joined SABR." Then came an e-mail from David Jones ("1901-19 is my favorite era in baseball as well"), and one from Scott

Flatow (whose e-mail address is DEADBALL). Within a week I'd received similar messages from eight other SABR members around the country, including one from R. J. Lesch, who wrote: "Thanks for getting the lumpy, licorice-stained ball rolling!" We started calling ourselves the "Deadball Dozen," but we had an unusual problem: enough willing Indians but no willing Chief—or, as I wrote in an e-mail on January 13, "lots of willing Indians but no willing Speaker—or lots of willing Naps but no willing Lajoie." Having recently handed over the reins of the Gardner-Waterman (Vermont) Chapter of SABR, I just wanted to be a member of a Deadball Committee; I didn't want to be its chairman, and I especially didn't want to produce its newsletter.

Then on January 15 I received a timely e-mail from Bill Lamberty: "I'd like to help out with the Deadball Committee, and I'm particularly interested in helping with the newsletter. I'm the Sports Information Director at Montana State University, and if we could work our production schedule around my busiest times of year, I believe I could be of valuable assistance." If Bill were to serve as vice-chairman and produce the newsletter, I thought, then how much time could it possibly take to be chairman of such a small group?

Looking back on those early e-mails, some of which I printed and saved in a binder, I see that by January 17 we had our officers (Simon and Lamberty), a new name and different parameters (we had sandwiched "Era" into "Deadball Committee" and redefined the era as 1901 to 1919), an official mascot (Terry Turner, whose major league career spanned exactly 1901-19), a name for our newsletter (_The Inside Game_), and even the slogan that has appeared on the masthead since the first issue ("Let's get this lumpy, licorice-stained ball rolling!"). I really knew we were on to something when

I received an e-mail from Larry Ritter on January 20: "John Thorn tells me you are chairing an underground society devoted to the memory of such as Terry Turner, Dode Paskert and Germany Schaefer. What Rites of Passage must I undergo to join? If they are not too strenuous, please count me in."

Taking our inspiration from SABR's great Nineteenth Century Committee, we also had an idea from the very beginning for our first major group project, the result of which is the book you are now reading. We decided that to get beyond the Honus Wagners and Ty Cobbs to the Homer Smoots and Tilly Walkers, we needed to produce two separate volumes, one for the National League and another for the American (which is soon to follow). Within those volumes we decided to organize the chapters by team, in order of finish of the teams' cumulative records for the entire Deadball Era. Hence the chapters for the NL volume, after a chapter for league officials and umpires, are ordered as follows:

	W	L	Pct.
New York	1,652	1,165	.586
Chicago	1,640	1,185	.581
Pittsburgh	1,595	1,229	.565
Philadelphia	1,396	1,406	.498
Cincinnati	1,360	1,471	.480
Brooklyn	1,263	1,542	.450
Boston	1,187	1,620	.423
St. Louis	1,167	1,643	.415

Within those chapters the biographies appear chronologically, in order of the subject's debut with that team. We also tried to find a photo depicting each player in the uniform of the team in whose chapter he appears.

Perhaps the most enjoyable part of the entire project was selecting the subjects who made the cut. (It was during that process that David Jones branded Dick Egan as "The Anti-Dode" and I stirred up a McGraw-like storm of controversy by threatening to burn, as a sacrifice to DEC icon Dode Paskert, an off-condition T-206 of Egan at the DEC annual meeting.) As I wrote in the second issue of *The Inside Game*, our little subcommittee "resembled the admissions committee for the Hell's Angels: If you were a boozer with a good nickname who got into bar fights, allegedly threw games, and ultimately committed suicide at age 29, we liked you. If you were steady but unspectacular and went on to live a normal life, you were in danger of being branded another Dick Egan." My special thanks to the members of that subcommittee, who went on to serve as "team editors," keeping the pressure on contributors to submit drafts and performing the initial edits: David Anderson (Chicago and Cincinnati); Steve Constantelos (Boston and New York); David Jones (Philadelphia and Pittsburgh); and Lyle Spatz (Brooklyn and St. Louis).

The National League chapter begins with an introduction that includes a graph depicting the rises and falls in National League attendance over the Deadball Era; a chart listing the NL's leaders in 17 categories for the years 1901-19, which was compiled by Gary Namanny using MS-Access (minimum 1,200 at-bats for batting leaders and 1,000 innings for ERA leaders); and annual all-star teams as selected by our friends at STATS Inc., who were kind enough to allow us to reprint them. The introduction for each team chapter includes a graph depicting the rises and falls of the club's winning percentage over the Deadball Era; a chart, again by Gary Namanny, listing the franchise leaders in 17 categories for the years 1901-19; and an All-Era Team, as selected by DEC members in a poll conducted by Steve Constantelos.

Though Strat-O-Matic was my game of choice, I spent a good portion of my childhood studying the "suggested batting order" sheets produced by the APBA Game Company, especially those for seasons of the distant past. Perhaps that's why I love the pages of this book containing the most common batting orders for each Deadball Era season, which were compiled by Angelo Louisa (who handled 1912 himself) with the assistance of David Anderson (1908); Michael Foster (1902, 1910); Len Jacobson (1907); David Jones (1914-16); R. J. Lesch (1913); Jim Sandoval (1919); Gabriel Schechter (1911); Richard Smiley (1909, 1917); Jim Troisi (1903-06); Paul Wendt (1901); and Allan Wood (1918). Those who study the lineups closely—as I undoubtedly will—may notice a mysterious "R. Taggert," who batted second and played left field for the Boston Braves during the second half of the 1918 season. The man's real name was Robert Taggert, but he's listed in the baseball reference books as Jim Kelly, the name he played under in 1914-15. Why he chose to play under his real name in 1918 is unknown; maybe he no longer had the need for an alias, or perhaps he was merely trying to distinguish himself from the Joe Kelly who coincidentally played the same position for the Braves during the first half of 1918.

When I wasn't playing Strat-O-Matic, I spent the rest of my childhood writing to old-time baseball players, especially those few survivors of the Deadball Era like Rube Marquard, asking for autographs. Perhaps my favorite feature of this book, then, is the collection of autographs painstakingly assembled by Paul Esacove with the assistance of some of the hobby's leading dealers and collectors: Kevin Keating (whom I list first because of the extraordinary number of signatures he contributed); Doug Averitt; Harold Elsch; Mike Gutierrez; Dave Larson; Joe Murphy, and Jim Stinson. Paul did an incredible job considering that many of our subjects died long before autograph collecting became commonplace, and the handful of signatures he failed to find are thought not to exist in the hobby.

I'd also like to thank my friends in Cooperstown—Bill Burdick, Eric Enders, and Gabriel Schechter—for tracking down photographs, articles, and clippings, often on short notice. R. J. Lesch did the same for materials from *The Sporting News* in St. Louis. Steve Gietschier of *The Sporting News*, Piriya Metcalfe of the Chicago Historical Society, and Mary Brace of the George Brace Collection also assisted with photographs, as did Susan Dellinger (the granddaughter of Edd Roush), Paul Sallee (a descendant of Slim), Patty Sites (the granddaughter of Mike Mowrey), Cindy Thomson (the granddaughter of Mordecai Brown), Jim Schneider, and Steve Steinberg.

My thanks for writing the foreword to Keith Olbermann, who shares the passion, and to the authors of my all-time favorite books, Larry Ritter and Mike Sowell, for the back-cover blurbs, not to mention the inspiration. SABR treasurer F. X. Flinn, a fellow Vermonter, was an ardent supporter from the night we met in Montpelier and I first explained to him the idea for this book. My friend Mark Alvarez, SABR's former publications director, went above the call of duty, volunteering to help edit even when it was no longer his job to do so. His successor, Jim Charlton, is as steady and wise as Mark—which is high praise in my book. Chris Kahrl of Brassey's kept me involved in every deci-

sion, which I appreciate. Eric Enders and David Jones took on the difficult task of fact checking a fact-intensive book. Among the sources they found most useful were *Total Baseball* (7th ed.), *STATS All-Time Major League Handbook*, Neft & Cohen's *The World Series,* the Retrosheet Web site, and www.baseball-reference.com, which is updated whenever changes are made to the official record. A quick note on style: I took the liberty of clarifying some quotations with minor word changes and shortening others without the use of ellipses.

The Deadball Era Committee has grown to more than 200 members since that initial email in January 2000, and 75 contributed in various ways to this volume. I'd like to thank each and every one of them: David Anderson; Paul Andresen; Mark Armour; Dennis Auger; John Bennett; Sam Bernstein; Michael Betzold; Bill Bishop; Gilbert Bogen; Tommy Carrella; Frank Ceresi; David Cicotello; Steve Constantelos; Gene DeLiso; Joe Dittmar; Mark Dugo; Jon Dunkle; Eric Enders; Paul Esacove; Jan Finkel; Michael Foster; Cappy Gagnon; Phil Gawthrop; Don Geiszler; Dan Ginsburg; Irv Goldfarb; Peter Gordon; Jim Hekel; Len Jacobson; Don Jensen; David Jones; Bill Kirwin; Martin Kohout; Mike Lackey; Sean Lahman; Bill Lamberty; R. J. Lesch; Dan Levitt; Dick Leyden; Angelo Louisa; Norman Macht; Larry Mansch; Brian Marshall; Peter Maurice; Wayne McElreavy; Paul Mittermeyer; Jim Moyes; Gary Namanny; Dan O'Brien; Marc Okkonen; Larry Ritter; Greg Ryhal; John Saccoman; Eric Sallee; Paul Sallee; Jim Sandoval; Gabriel Schechter; Alex Semchuck; David Shiner; Richard Smiley; Lyle Spatz; Steve Steinberg; Mark Sternman; Brian Stevens; Troy Strecker; Bill Swank; Joan Thomas; Dick Thompson; Cindy Thomson; Zack Triscuit; Scott Turner; Michael Wells; Paul Wendt; and Allan Wood.

Finally, and most important, I thank my wife, Carolyn, who hates it when I say that I was born 75 years too late. Though I'd love to go back in time, I'd do it only if I could take her with me.

TOM SIMON
NOVEMBER 2003

CONTENTS

NATIONAL LEAGUE

This 1896 photo shows the New York City block where the National League had its headquarters for most of the Deadball Era.

Entering the 1901 season, the National League faced its most serious challenge in its 25 years of existence. During the off-season Ban Johnson's American League had declared itself a rival major league, establishing franchises in three NL cities (Boston, Chicago, and Philadelphia) and signing scores of former National Leaguers, including stars like Jimmy Collins, Nap Lajoie, John McGraw, and Cy Young.

Though McGraw returned to the NL in 1902, that year the AL invaded St. Louis and stole additional stars: Jesse Burkett, Ed Delahanty, Rube Waddell, and Bobby Wallace, to name a few. By that time some believed that the caliber of play in the junior circuit was higher, and AL attendance in 1902 outstripped the NL's by more

than a half-million paying customers. Making the situation worse for NL magnates, AL competition was driving "wartime" salaries for players higher than they had ever been before.

For years NL owners had fought amongst themselves, selfishly resisting a strong central authority, but by the winter of 1902-03 desperate measures were in order. That December they installed Harry Pulliam as league president and instructed him to make peace with the AL. In Cincinnati less than one month later a deal was struck, with the NL recognizing the AL as a separate but equal entity playing under common rules.

Though the agreement cost the NL additional stars in Jack Chesbro, Sam Crawford, and Willie Keeler, as

N.L. ATTENDANCE (in millions) 1901–1919

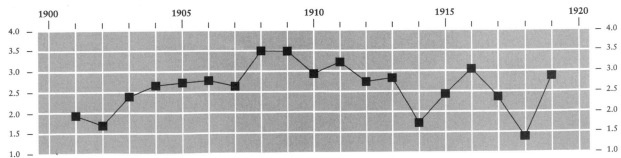

well as its monopoly in New York City, it nonetheless proved worthwhile; even though just three teams (Pittsburgh, New York, and Chicago) won pennants, the league enjoyed a decade of prosperity, with NL attendance peaking at over 3.5 million in 1908. Still, the NL frequently broke into bickering factions, driving Pulliam to suicide and causing his successor Thomas Lynch, as he left office, to state that the magnates would merit more dignified treatment if they showed some dignity themselves.

The NL faced another crisis in 1914 when the Federal League established itself as yet another rival major league. The Feds stole big-name players such as Joe Tinker, Mordecai Brown, Doc Crandall, and Mickey Doolan, and competed head-to-head against NL franchises in Brooklyn, Chicago, Pittsburgh, and St. Louis. Once again NL attendance and quality of play plummeted while player salaries skyrocketed.

This time the established leagues received an assist from U.S. District Judge Kenesaw Mountain Landis, an ardent baseball fan who delayed ruling on the Federal League's antitrust action filed in the Northern District of Illinois. Landis figured the longer he held off, the more likely the parties would come to a settlement. He was right. An agreement was reached to buy out the Feds in 1916, once again in Cincinnati, with new NL president John Tener playing an important role in the negotiations.

NL attendance rebounded in 1916 to exceed its 1913 total, and it reached that level again in 1919 after a two-year dropoff due to World War I. Again prosperity reigned, but yet another crisis loomed, this one brought on by rampant gambling in baseball during the Deadball Era.

National League magnates take a break from bickering to pose for a group photo at their meeting on December 8, 1914.

LEAGUE LEADERS
1901–1919

BATTING

GAMES
H. Wagner 2298
S. Magee 2087
T. Leach 1996

RUNS
H. Wagner 1414
T. Leach 1260
S. Magee 1112

HITS
H. Wagner 2766
S. Magee 2169
T. Leach 1991

RBI
H. Wagner 1375
S. Magee 1176
H. Zimmerman 796

DOUBLES
H. Wagner 506
S. Magee 425
J. Sheckard 296

TRIPLES
H. Wagner 210
S. Magee 166
T. Leach 164

HOME RUNS
G. Cravath 116
F. Schulte 92
F. Luderus 84

STOLEN BASES
H. Wagner 601
S. Magee 441
B. Bescher 425

BATTING AVERAGE
M. Donlin 333
H. Wagner 325
E. Roush 320

PITCHING

GAMES
C. Mathewson 629
R. Ames 533
S. Sallee 413

WINS
C. Mathewson 373
P. Alexander 208
M. Brown 208

LOSSES
C. Mathewson 185
R. Ames 167
V. Willis 167

INNINGS
C. Mathewson 4747
R. Ames 3198
V. Willis . . . . $3106\frac{1}{3}$

STRIKEOUTS
C. Mathewson 2487
R. Ames 1702
P. Alexander 1539

WALKS
R. Ames 1034
V. Willis 841
C. Mathewson 824

SHUTOUTS
C. Mathewson 79
P. Alexander 70
M. Brown 50

ERA
M. Brown 1.93
J. Pfiester 2.02
J. Vaughn 2.08

STATS INC. N.L. ALL-STARS, 1901-1919

1901
B. Donovan, P
N. Hahn, P
A. Orth, P
D. Phillippe, P
D. McGuire, C
J. Kelley, 1B
T. Daly, 2B
O. Krueger, 3B
H. Wagner, SS
J. Burkett, OF
E. Delahanty, OF
J. Sheckard, OF

1902
J. Chesbro, P
N. Hahn, P
J. Tannehill, P
J. Taylor, P
J. Kling, C
J. Beckley, 1B
H. Peitz, 2B
T. Leach, 3B
B. Dahlen, SS
G. Beaumont, OF
F. Clarke, OF
H. Wagner, OF

1903
S. Leever, P
C. Mathewson, P
J. McGinnity, P
D. Phillippe, P
J. Kling, C
F. Chance, 1B
C. Ritchey, 2B
H. Steinfeldt, 3B
H. Wagner, SS
R. Bresnahan, OF
F. Clarke, OF
M. Donlin, OF

1904
J. Harper, P
C. Mathewson, P
J. McGinnity, P
K. Nichols, P
M. Grady, C
F. Chance, 1B
M. Huggins, 2B
A. Devlin, 3B
H. Wagner, SS
M. Donlin, OF
H. Lumley, OF
C. Seymour, OF

1905
R. Ames, P
C. Mathewson, P
D. Phillippe, P
E. Reulbach, P
R. Bresnahan, C
F. Chance, 1B
M. Huggins, 2B
E. Courtney, 3B
H. Wagner, SS
M. Donlin, OF
C. Seymour, OF
J. Titus, OF

1906
M. Brown, P
J. McGinnity, P
J. Pfiester, P
V. Willis, P
R. Bresnahan, C
F. Chance, 1B
S. Strang, 2B
H. Steinfeldt, 3B
H. Wagner, SS
H. Lumley, OF
S. Magee, OF
R. Thomas, OF

1907
M. Brown, P
C. Mathewson, P
O. Overall, P
T. Sparks, P
R. Bresnahan, C
F. Chance, 1B
E. Abbaticchio, 2B
D. Brain, 3B
H. Wagner, SS
F. Clarke, OF
T. Leach, OF
S. Magee, OF

1908
M. Brown, P
N. Maddox, P
C. Mathewson, P
E. Reulbach, P
R. Bresnahan, C
F. Chance, 1B
J. Evers, 2B
H. Lobert, 3B
H. Wagner, SS
F. Clarke, OF
M. Donlin, OF
S. Magee, OF

1909
M. Brown, P
H. Camnitz, P
C. Mathewson, P
O. Overall, P
G. Gibson, C
E. Konetchy, 1B
L. Doyle, 2B
H. Steinfeldt, 3B
H. Wagner, SS
F. Clarke, OF
M. McCormick, OF
M. Mitchell, OF

1910
M. Brown, P
K. Cole, P
C. Mathewson, P
E. Moore, P
L. McLean, C
E. Konetchy, 1B
L. Doyle, 2B
B. Byrne, 3B
H. Wagner, SS
A. Hofman, OF
S. Magee, OF
F. Schulte, OF

1911
B. Adams, P
P. Alexander, P
R. Marquard, P
C. Mathewson, P
C. Meyers, C
E. Konetchy, 1B
L. Doyle, 2B
H. Lobert, 3B
H. Wagner, SS
S. Magee, OF
F. Schulte, OF
J. Sheckard, OF

1912
L. Cheney, P
C. Hendrix, P
R. Marquard, P
C. Mathewson, P
C. Meyers, C
E. Konetchy, 1B
L. Doyle, 2B
H. Zimmerman, 3B
H. Wagner, SS
D. Paskert, OF
J. Titus, OF
O. Wilson, OF

1913
R. Marquard, P
C. Mathewson, P
T. Seaton, P
J. Tesreau, P
C. Meyers, C
J. Daubert, 1B
J. Viox, 2B
H. Zimmerman, 3B
J. Tinker, SS
G. Cravath, OF
T. Leach, OF
S. Magee, OF

1914
P. Alexander, P
B. James, P
D. Rudolph, P
J. Tesreau, P
C. Meyers, C
J. Daubert, 1B
J. Evers, 2B
H. Zimmerman, 3B
R. Maranville, SS
J. Connolly, OF
G. Cravath, OF
S. Magee, OF

1915
P. Alexander, P
A. Mamaux, P
E. Mayer, P
F. Toney, P
F. Snyder, C
F. Luderus, 1B
L. Doyle, 2B
H. Groh, 3B
B. Herzog, SS
G. Cravath, OF
T. Griffith, OF
B. Hinchman, OF

1916
P. Alexander, P
L. Cheney, P
J. Pfeffer, P
E. Rixey, P
I. Wingo, C
H. Chase, 1B
L. Doyle, 2B
R. Hornsby, 3B
A. Fletcher, SS
G. Cravath, OF
B. Hinchman, OF
Z. Wheat, OF

1917
P. Alexander, P
F. Schupp, P
F. Toney, P
J. Vaughn, P
I. Wingo, C
H. Chase, 1B
L. Doyle, 2B
H. Groh, 3B
R. Hornsby, SS
G. Burns, OF
G. Cravath, OF
E. Roush, OF

1918
W. Cooper, P
B. Grimes, P
L. Tyler, P
J. Vaughn, P
M. Gonzalez, C
S. Magee, 1B
G. Cutshaw, 2B
H. Groh, 3B
R. Hornsby, SS
G. Burns, OF
D. Paskert, OF
E. Roush, OF

1919
J. Barnes, P
D. Ruether, P
S. Sallee, P
J. Vaughn, P
I. Wingo, C
F. Luderus, 1B
L. Doyle, 2B
H. Groh, 3B
R. Maranville, SS
G. Burns, OF
H. Myers, OF
E. Roush, OF

1901-1919
C. Mathewson, P
P. Alexander, P
M. Brown, P
R. Bresnahan, C
C. Meyers, C
F. Chance, 1B
L. Doyle, 2B
H. Groh, 3B
H. Wagner, SS
S. Magee, OF
F. Clarke, OF
G. Cravath, OF

LEAGUE STANDINGS 1901-1919

1901

Team	W	L	Pct.	GB
Pittsburgh	90	49	.647	--
Philadelphia	83	57	.593	7½
Brooklyn	79	57	.581	9½
St. Louis	76	64	.543	14½
Boston	69	69	.500	20½
Chicago	53	86	.381	37
New York	52	85	.380	37
Cincinnati	52	87	.374	38

1902

Team	W	L	Pct.	GB
Pittsburgh	103	36	.741	--
Brooklyn	75	63	.543	27½
Boston	73	64	.533	29
Cincinnati	70	70	.500	33½
Chicago	68	69	.496	34
St. Louis	56	78	.418	44½
Philadelphia	56	81	.409	46
New York	48	88	.353	53½

1903

Team	W	L	Pct.	GB
Pittsburgh	91	49	.650	--
New York	84	55	.604	6½
Chicago	82	56	.594	8
Cincinnati	74	65	.532	16½
Brooklyn	70	66	.515	19
Boston	58	80	.420	32
Philadelphia	49	86	.363	39½
St. Louis	43	94	.314	46½

1904

Team	W	L	Pct.	GB
New York	106	47	.693	--
Chicago	93	60	.608	13
Cincinnati	88	65	.575	18
Pittsburgh	87	66	.569	19
St. Louis	75	79	.487	31½
Brooklyn	56	97	.366	50
Boston	55	98	.359	51
Philadelphia	52	100	.342	53½

1905

Team	W	L	Pct.	GB
New York	105	48	.686	--
Pittsburgh	96	57	.627	9
Chicago	92	61	.601	13
Philadelphia	83	69	.546	21½
Cincinnati	79	74	.516	26
St. Louis	58	96	.377	47½
Boston	51	103	.331	54½
Brooklyn	48	104	.316	56½

1906

Team	W	L	Pct.	GB
Chicago	116	36	.763	--
New York	96	56	.632	20
Pittsburgh	93	60	.608	23½
Philadelphia	71	82	.464	45½
Brooklyn	66	86	.434	50
Cincinnati	64	87	.424	51½
St. Louis	52	98	.347	63
Boston	49	102	.325	66½

1907

Team	W	L	Pct.	GB
Chicago	107	45	.704	--
Pittsburgh	91	63	.591	17
Philadelphia	83	64	.565	21½
New York	82	71	.536	25½
Brooklyn	65	83	.439	40
Cincinnati	66	87	.431	41½
Boston	58	90	.392	47
St. Louis	52	101	.340	55½

1908

Team	W	L	Pct.	GB
Chicago	99	55	.643	--
New York	98	56	.636	1
Pittsburgh	98	56	.636	1
Philadelphia	83	71	.539	16
Cincinnati	73	81	.474	26
Boston	63	91	.409	36
Brooklyn	53	101	.344	46
St. Louis	49	105	.318	50

1909

Team	W	L	Pct.	GB
Pittsburgh	110	42	.724	--
Chicago	104	49	.680	6½
New York	92	61	.601	18½
Cincinnati	77	76	.503	33½
Philadelphia	74	79	.484	36½
Brooklyn	55	98	.359	55½
St. Louis	54	98	.355	56
Boston	45	108	.294	65½

1910

Team	W	L	Pct.	GB
Chicago	104	50	.675	--
New York	91	63	.591	13
Pittsburgh	86	67	.562	17½
Philadelphia	78	75	.510	25½
Cincinnati	75	79	.487	29
Brooklyn	64	90	.416	40
St. Louis	63	90	.412	40½
Boston	53	100	.346	50½

1911

Team	W	L	Pct.	GB
New York	99	54	.647	--
Chicago	92	62	.597	7½
Pittsburgh	85	69	.552	14½
Philadelphia	79	73	.520	19½
St. Louis	75	74	.503	22
Cincinnati	70	83	.458	29
Brooklyn	64	86	.427	33½
Boston	44	107	.291	54

1912

Team	W	L	Pct.	GB
New York	103	48	.682	--
Pittsburgh	93	58	.616	10
Chicago	91	59	.607	11½
Cincinnati	75	78	.490	29
Philadelphia	73	79	.480	30½
St. Louis	63	90	.412	41
Brooklyn	58	95	.379	46
Boston	52	101	.340	52

1913

Team	W	L	Pct.	GB
New York	101	51	.664	--
Philadelphia	88	63	.583	12½
Chicago	88	65	.575	13½
Pittsburgh	78	71	.523	21½
Boston	69	82	.457	31½
Brooklyn	65	84	.436	34½
Cincinnati	64	89	.418	37½
St. Louis	51	99	.340	49

1914

Team	W	L	Pct.	GB
Boston	94	59	.614	--
New York	84	70	.545	10½
St. Louis	81	72	.529	13
Chicago	78	76	.506	16½
Brooklyn	75	79	.487	19½
Philadelphia	74	80	.481	20½
Pittsburgh	69	85	.448	25½
Cincinnati	60	94	.390	34½

1915

Team	W	L	Pct.	GB
Philadelphia	90	62	.592	--
Boston	83	69	.546	7
Brooklyn	80	72	.526	10
Chicago	73	80	.477	17½
Pittsburgh	73	81	.474	18
St. Louis	72	81	.471	18½
Cincinnati	71	83	.461	20
New York	69	83	.454	21

1916

Team	W	L	Pct.	GB
Brooklyn	94	60	.610	--
Philadelphia	91	62	.595	2½
Boston	89	63	.586	4
New York	86	66	.566	7
Chicago	67	86	.438	26½
Pittsburgh	65	89	.422	29
Cincinnati	60	93	.392	33½
St. Louis	60	93	.392	33½

1917

Team	W	L	Pct.	GB
New York	98	56	.636	--
Philadelphia	87	65	.572	10
St. Louis	82	70	.539	15
Cincinnati	78	76	.506	20
Chicago	74	80	.481	24
Boston	72	81	.471	25½
Brooklyn	70	81	.464	26½
Pittsburgh	51	103	.331	47

1918

Team	W	L	Pct.	GB
Chicago	84	45	.651	--
New York	71	53	.573	10½
Cincinnati	68	60	.531	15½
Pittsburgh	65	60	.520	17
Brooklyn	57	69	.452	25½
Philadelphia	55	68	.447	26
Boston	53	71	.427	28½
St. Louis	51	78	.395	33

1919

Team	W	L	Pct.	GB
Cincinnati	96	44	.686	--
New York	87	53	.621	9
Chicago	75	65	.536	21
Pittsburgh	71	68	.511	24½
Brooklyn	69	71	.493	27
Boston	57	82	.410	38½
St. Louis	54	83	.394	40½
Philadelphia	47	90	.343	47½

NATIONAL LEAGUE

Henry O'Day

Henry Francis O'Day
Umpire 1888–89, 1895–1911, 1913, 1915–27

Hank O'Day remains the only man in history to play, umpire, and manage in the National League. A loner with no family life and little interest in anything but baseball, O'Day was best friends with fellow NL umpire Bob Emslie, and they spent their free time sitting together, seldom exchanging a word. "Look at O'Day," said AL umpire Silk O'Loughlin. "He's one of the best umpires, maybe the best today, but he's sour. Umpiring does something to you. The abuse you get from the players, the insults from the crowds, and the awful things they write about you in the newspapers take their toll." Bill Klem called O'Day a "misanthropic Irishman," while Christy Mathewson said that arguing with O'Day was like "using a lit match to see how much gasoline was in a fuel tank."

Born in Chicago on July 8, 1862, Henry Francis O'Day began his major league career as a right-handed pitcher in the American Association in 1884-85. He spent the next four years in the NL with Washington and New York before winding up his pitching career in the Players League with a 22-win season in 1890. O'Day's overall record was mediocre—he was 73-110 with a 3.74 ERA—but he made a great impression as a substitute umpire, filling in to avoid a postponement when illness, injury, or travel problems prevented the assigned umpire from officiating a game.

Hired as a full-time NL umpire in 1895, O'Day became known for his bravery to make the right call, no matter how unpopular. He's best remembered for his actions on September 23, 1908, at the end of a game between the Chicago Cubs and New York Giants at the Polo Grounds. O'Day was behind the plate, with his friend Emslie on the bases, when the Giants' Al Bridwell singled with Moose McCormick on third and Fred Merkle on first. Seeing McCormick score the apparent winning run, Merkle immediately ran for the Giant clubhouse. Cubs second baseman Johnny Evers screamed for the ball fielded by teammate Artie Hofman, but Giants pitcher Joe McGinnity intercepted it and threw it into the crowd. Evers found another ball, tagged second, and appealed to Emslie to call Merkle out. Emslie refused. Evers then appealed to O'Day, who made the call, negating an apparent Giant victory. Because of the chaos on the field, O'Day ruled the game a tie and left. After the NL upheld the ruling and the Cubs won the replay, John McGraw maintained that O'Day had robbed him of a pennant.

The most curious part of O'Day's career was his two tours of duty as a manager, first with the 1912 Cincinnati Reds and later with the 1914 Cubs. During his time with Cincinnati some opponents groused that his former colleagues gave the Reds an unfair edge. O'Day's managerial record was undistinguished: the Reds finished at 75-78 while the Cubs were 78-76. Both teams finished fourth. Hank returned to umpiring in 1915 and held on until 1927. The length of his 35-year career is second only to Klem's, as is his service in 10 World Series. When O'Day died in Chicago on July 2, 1935, former NL president John Heydler called him one of the greatest umpires ever in terms of knowledge of the rules, fairness, and courage to make the right call.

David Anderson

NATIONAL LEAGUE

ROBERT D. EMSLIE
UMPIRE 1891–1924

Tagged with the derisive nickname "Wig" because he suffered from premature baldness and wore a hairpiece, Bob Emslie nonetheless remained even-tempered with a pleasant smile, earning the respect and confidence of players and spectators alike. Emslie was known as the National League's most informed arbiter on the rules. With the permanent installation of the double-umpire system in 1911, he stopped working behind the plate and became exclusively a base umpire.

Robert D. Emslie was born on January 27, 1859, in Guelph, Ontario, Canada. He got his start in baseball as a right-handed curveball pitcher with various semipro teams in Ontario before turning professional with Camden, New Jersey, of the Interstate League in 1882. At midseason 1883 Emslie made his major league debut with the last-place Baltimore Orioles of the American Association, going 9-13 with a solid 3.17 ERA. In 1884 he completed all 50 games he started, winning 17 of his first 21 decisions en route to a 32-17 record and 2.75 ERA. The next year, however, Bob strained his arm from excessive use of the curveball. He retired as a player in June 1887 and returned home to Canada. Later that summer, while attending an International League game between Toronto and Hamilton, Emslie was asked to officiate when the assigned umpire fell ill. He spent the next four years umpiring in three leagues: the International League (1888-89), the American Association (1890), and the Western League (1891). Bob made his NL debut on August 17, 1891.

Emslie is best remembered as the base umpire on September 23, 1908, when controversy erupted at the end of the Giants-Cubs game at the Polo Grounds. Johnny Evers, who'd noticed "Merkle's Boner," tagged second and appealed to Emslie, who claimed he didn't see the play. Emslie later told NL president Harry Pulliam that he "had to fall to the ground to keep [Al Bridwell's] ball from hitting me." Plate umpire Hank O'Day declared Merkle out and the game a tie. Emslie's role marked him with another ignominious nickname, "Blind Bob," given him by John McGraw. Over the years Emslie ejected the New York manager 13 times, a mark exceeded only by Bill Klem. An international grandmaster at trap shooting, Bob once bet McGraw $500 in a contest to fire at apples placed at second base. McGraw declined, saying, "Maybe you can see apples, but you can't see baseballs."

Emslie served 33 years as an active-duty umpire, retiring at the end of the 1924 season. He then served as NL chief of umpires, inspecting, scouting, and coaching new umpires. During his retirement in St. Thomas, Ontario, Emslie coached youth baseball and enjoyed curling, bowling, and golf. Reticent to grant interviews because of an incident early in his career in which a New York reporter misquoted him, Emslie overcame his silence during retirement and declared Christy Mathewson the greatest pitcher of all time and Honus Wagner the greatest all-around player. He disdained the lively ball, observing, "There's less inside baseball, which I like." Emslie was 84 when he died in St. Thomas on April 26, 1943, with a son and daughter surviving him. He was inducted into Canada's Baseball Hall of Fame in 1986.

DAVID CICOTELLO

Harry C Pulliam

NATIONAL LEAGUE

HARRY CLAY PULLIAM
PRESIDENT 1902–09

Described as "an idealist, a dreamer, and a lover of solitude and nature," Harry Pulliam rose to high places in each of his chosen professions through hard work and a charming demeanor. Pulliam became a successful baseball executive with the Louisville and Pittsburgh National League franchises, and as NL president he was an innovative administrator who helped stabilize major league baseball at a critical juncture in its history. He was publicly lauded throughout his career for integrity and square dealing, but self-doubt and a nervous nature were at the core of his existence, and he took his own life at age 40.

The son of a tobacco farmer, Harry Clay Pulliam was born on February 9, 1869, in Scottsburg, Kentucky. After attending public schools in Louisville, Harry graduated from the University of Virginia School of Law before entering journalism, starting as a cub reporter at the *Louisville Commercial* and rising to become city editor. In that position he made the acquaintance of local entrepreneur Barney Dreyfuss— some credit Pulliam with teaching his German friend proper English—and soon was in Dreyfuss's employ, first as secretary and later president of the Louisville Colonels. During his time in the newspaper business Harry had become interested in politics; while with the Colonels he served in the Kentucky Assembly as a Democrat representing Louisville's sixth and seventh wards. Dubbed the "Red Bird Statesman" for successfully introducing a bill to protect that species, Pulliam was regarded as a capable legislator.

While serving as president of the Colonels, Pulliam was pestered relentlessly by a minor leaguer who was originally from Louisville about a stocky, bow-legged infielder playing minor league ball in Paterson, New Jersey. Though he resisted for some time, Harry finally went to see young Honus Wagner while the Colonels were playing in Brooklyn. With Dreyfuss's backing, the Colonels secured Wagner's services for $2,100, and Pulliam himself accompanied the young player on the train from New Jersey to the Bluegrass State. Undoubtedly Harry's gentle nature played a role in making Wagner feel comfortable, and it's telling that he allowed Wagner to stop in his hometown of Carnegie on the way to Louisville.

That same gentlemanly demeanor helped the Pittsburgh Pirates, run after 1900 by Dreyfuss and Pulliam once they consolidated with the Louisville organization, to retain the core of talent that became a National League dynasty. When Ban Johnson, later a Pulliam ally, announced that his upstart American League would be considered a second major league and would obtain talent by disregarding the NL's reserve clause, Dreyfuss and Pulliam visited or wired each Pirate player to assure his loyalty. Though it's sometimes written that Pittsburgh lost no players to the AL because Johnson masterminded a plot to leave the Pirates intact, there's evidence that at least one AL manager, Clark Griffith, and perhaps two others visited Pittsburgh to try to lure Wagner away. Pulliam's congeniality and proactive nature helped stave off raids.

NL magnates tabbed the 33-year-old Pulliam as president, secretary, and treasurer on December 12, 1902, replacing the clumsy three-man executive board, which just a year earlier had deposed ineffective president Nick Young. Dreyfuss reportedly wept at the news that his primary lieutenant was leaving him. Harry was a strong and decisive administrator, but he soon was at odds with New York Giants owner John Brush. Pulliam's first reelection was unanimous, and his next two were by 7-1 votes, but Cincinnati's Garry Herrmann formed an alliance with Brush, and thereafter Pulliam was elected by 6-2 margins.

Though he had his detractors—most notably in New York, where John McGraw accused him and his umpires of siding with Dreyfuss and the Pirates—his work was regarded highly enough by the majority of NL owners that his salary increased from $3,500 in 1903 to $10,000 by the end of 1906. In 1907 the owners appointed John Heydler as secretary and treasurer when Harry's health began to suffer under the strain of his multiple duties. As the years passed, Pulliam began to take attacks more personally. In his last years he secluded himself in his apartment on the third floor of the New York Athletic Club when not at his office.

Pulliam's tragic demise began when he was forced to rule on the 1908 Merkle Incident, declaring the game a tie that would have to be replayed if it had an effect on the outcome of the pennant race. "Much as I deplore the unfortunate ending of a brilliantly played game as well as the subsequent controversy, I have no alternative than to be guided by the law," he wrote. "I believe in sportsmanship, but would it be good sportsmanship to repudiate my umpires simply to condone the undisputed blunder of a player?" Pulliam's decision, of course, touched off an even greater controversy, especially when the Giants lost the one-game playoff, and his physicians later blamed the ensuing turmoil for his severe state of depression. At that year's winter meetings Pulliam suffered a nervous breakdown and was granted an indefinite leave of absence, with Heydler assuming his duties. After convalescing in Tennessee and Florida, Harry was back on the job as of June 28, 1909, but friends noticed that he was moody, uncommunicative, and lacked his usual effervescence.

At 9:30 A.M. on July 28, 1909, Pulliam arrived at his office in the St. James Building and started going through a stack of correspondence. He was halfway through when he stopped, and for a time he sat at his desk, staring out the window. At 1:00 P.M. Harry left the office, telling his stenographer that he didn't feel well. Apparently he went straight to his apartment, not saying a word to anyone at the NYAC clubhouse. At 9:30 P.M. Pulliam raised a revolver to his right temple and pulled the trigger, holding the gun so close to his head that the powder burned him severely.

The bullet blew out his right eye and passed completely through his skull. After lying in agony for some time, Pulliam struggled to the telephone and knocked the receiver off the hook. At 10:00 P.M. a club attendant, checking on Harry because his phone was tying up the NYAC's circuits, found the room unlocked and the young executive's body in a corner, lying in a pool of blood. He was alive, moaning feebly. A physician determined that Pulliam was too badly wounded to be moved to a hospital. The police from the West 51st Street Station were summoned, and Pulliam was quietly placed under arrest for attempted suicide.

When the coroner arrived, he leaned over the body and asked, "How were you shot?" Pulliam moaned, and then with an effort, as if every word caused extreme pain, said, "I am not shot." Then his head fell back and he lost consciousness. Harry Pulliam passed away on the floor of his apartment at 7:40 A.M. on July 29. He was buried in Cave Hill Cemetary in Louisville on August 2, the first time in history that both NL and AL games were postponed in tribute. After the funeral a special meeting of the NL Board of Directors appointed Heydler as Pulliam's successor.

BILL LAMBERTY

NATIONAL LEAGUE

WILLIAM J. KLIMM (KLEM)
UMPIRE 1905–41

Bill Klem was known as an innovator. Over the years he has received credit for developing the inside chest protector and the signals for safe, out, strike, and fair and foul ball, but he himself took credit only for developing the fair-foul signal during his 1904 stint in the American Association. Klem also accepted credit for teaching umpires to work the "slot," which he claimed gave them a better view of the strike zone by looking between the catcher and batter.

The son of Dutch immigrants, Klem was born William J. Klimm in Rochester, New York, on February 22, 1876. Like many of his umpiring contemporaries, Bill wanted to be a professional baseball player. In 1896 he tried out for catcher with Hamilton of the Canadian League, but a bum arm ended that hope. For the next few years he played semipro ball in New York and Pennsylvania, supplementing his pay by working construction.

Klem's life took a turn in 1902. In Berwick, Pennsylvania, he read a newspaper account about how his hometown friend Silk O'Loughlin was faring as an American League umpire. Having tried his hand at umpiring in a 1901 game between the New York Cuban Giants and a semipro team from Berwick, Klem decided to make it his career. He took a job with the Class D Connecticut League that paid him $7.50 for a single game and $10.50 for a doubleheader. "If the home team lost you got an awful amount of abuse with your money," Klem recalled.

The following year Klem moved up to the Class B New York State League, another circuit with a tough reputation. He was the only umpire to last the entire season. In 1904 Klem umpired in the American Association, which is where he received the nickname "Catfish" for his piscine mouth. Bill immediately ejected anyone who called him by the detested nickname.

During his year in the AA Klem started getting attention from the big leagues. Hank O'Day introduced him to NL president Harry Pulliam, who told him that he was watching him. Pulliam hired Klem to umpire a 1904 post-season exhibition between Cleveland and Pittsburgh. In 1905 Klem was offered $2,100 to umpire in the AL through the efforts of O'Loughlin. He held out for an offer from Pulliam, who eventually matched the AL offer. Klem remained a loyal National Leaguer for life, referring to the junior circuit as "the hucksters of the big leagues."

Many histories say Klem was so good at calling balls and strikes that he was plate umpire for the first 16 years of his career. That's untrue. Throughout his career Klem took his regular turn on the bases when he was with a partner. The NL didn't guarantee two-man crews until 1911, however, so during his first six years he often worked solo.

In 1940, his last full season, Klem was hit by a ground ball and realized that at age 66 he was finally slowing down. He worked a handful of games in 1941 but knew he was done when he missed a tag on a stolen base in a St. Louis-Brooklyn game. Klem said it was the first time he only thought, not knew, that a man was out. He served as the head of NL umpires until his death in Miami on September 1, 1951. Klem was elected to the Baseball Hall of Fame two years later.

DAVID ANDERSON

Chas. Rigler

NATIONAL LEAGUE

CHARLES "CY" RIGLER
UMPIRE 1906–22, 1924–35

With a reputation as the least thin-skinned of his contemporaries, Cy Rigler chose the role of peacemaker, refraining from profanity and seldom ejecting a player or manager. It's a good thing, too, because he stood nearly 6'0" and weighed 270 lbs. "It is a mistake to suppose I am in the game as a fighter," Cy once said. "It will be the fault of the player or spectator if I am called upon to exercise physical authority." Despite his massive size, Rigler was quick to move into position to make a call. His voice was unhesitant, clear, and boomed like a foghorn, and he insisted on having his eyes examined frequently.

The son of a fireman, Charles Rigler was born on May 16, 1882, in Massillon, Ohio. He began his athletic career as a semipro baseball player and right tackle for the Massillon Tigers professional football team. When a knee injury cut short his playing career, Rigler found himself on the officiating side of sports. He began as an umpire in the Central League in 1904, introducing the gesture of raising his right arm to denote a strike in 1905 (at approximately the same time, Bill Klem was popularizing the use of arm and hand signals in the majors). The following year NL president Harry Pulliam hired Rigler, and except for 1923 he worked continuously until his retirement from active duty in 1935.

Rigler was rarely called on to exercise physical authority, but there were exceptions. During a Reds-Cardinals game at Robison Field in 1915, Cy overruled a call involving Cincinnati's Tommie Leach, who'd been caught off second base as a result of the hidden-ball trick. Field umpire Bill Hart didn't see the play, but Rigler, who was behind the plate, did and called Leach out. Reds manager Buck Herzog argued vehemently, shoving Rigler in the chest protector and spiking him. Rigler decked Herzog with one punch. A riot ensued, with spectators and players from both teams crowding around the combatants. A dozen policemen were required to restore peace.

During the off-season Rigler made his home in North East, Pennsylvania, where he worked in the gas and oil fields for a subsidiary of Standard Oil Company. In his spare time he designed ballparks, cared for golf courses, and developed a vineyard. He also was a football referee and a multi-sport coach at the University of Virginia. Rigler amassed more than 6,100 games in his tenure as an umpire. At the time of his retirement he ranked second to Klem in seniority for those with service in the 20th century only. In an era when umpires were selected on merit, Rigler worked 10 World Series and was chosen to work the first All-Star Game in 1933 (along with Klem, Bill Dineen, and Bill McGowan).

Because of his understanding manner, Rigler was assigned many younger umpires over the years for tutelage and training. Following his retirement at the end of the 1935 season he was named NL chief of umpires. The assignment was short-lived. Rigler was 53 when he died in Philadelphia on December 21, 1935, following brain surgery. He was survived by his wife, Nellie, and her two daughters from a previous marriage. Albert "Dolly" Stark was the only major league umpire among the mourners.

DAVID CICOTELLO

NATIONAL LEAGUE

John Kinley Tener
President 1913–18

Many achieve success in their chosen field, but few match the versatility of John Tener. During the 30-year span from 1888 to 1918, this Horatio Alger figure was a major league pitcher, successful businessman, U.S. congressman, governor of Pennsylvania, and finally the ninth president of the National League.

The seventh of 10 children, John Kinley Tener was born in County Tyrone, Ireland, on July 25, 1863. His parents, George and Susan (Wallis) Tener, were well-to-do farmers. In 1873 they decided to emigrate to the United States to join their eldest daughter in Pittsburgh. Before they could leave, however, George contracted pneumonia and died. Despite the loss of her husband, Susan went ahead with the move. Shortly after the family's arrival she also died, leaving John an orphan at age 10. Largely due to the efforts of John's eldest brother, George Jr., the stricken family held together. John completed school and went to work for a local iron and steel manufacturer.

John's real love, however, was baseball. The 6'4", 180 lb. right hander left home in 1885 to pitch for Haverhill of the New England League, where his teammates included Wilbert Robinson. John met his future wife, Harriet Day, in Haverhill. In 1888 he returned to Pittsburgh where his pitching on local sandlots caught the attention of Chicago White Stockings manager Cap Anson, who signed him in August. Despite a disastrous first game (he lost to Indianapolis, 14-0), John posted a 7-5 record and 2.74 ERA. After the season he accompanied the White Stockings on a world tour, playing in New Zealand, Australia, Ceylon, Egypt, Italy, France, and England. In addition to his mound duties, Tener served as treasurer, a difficult task given the different currencies, and was chosen to help explain baseball to the Prince of Wales.

During the tour Tener became friendly with John Montgomery Ward, a friendship that resulted in his becoming secretary of the Baseball Brotherhood. Following another respectable season with Chicago, Tener joined his fellow Brotherhood members in jumping to the Players League in 1890, posting a disappointing 3-11 record and 7.31 ERA for the Pittsburgh entry. Afterward he left baseball to return to business, becoming the cashier of the First National Bank in the Pittsburgh suburb of Charleroi. By 1898 Tener had worked his way up to president of that institution. He also organized the Charleroi Savings and Trust Company, serving as its secretary and treasurer, and the Mercantile Bridge Company, serving as president for a time before accepting a position on the board of directors. He later served as a director of other companies, including two Pittsburgh–area street railways.

In 1908 John Tener was elected to the U.S. House of Representatives, defeating a seven-term incumbent. He was renominated for Congress in 1910, but the Republican Party had bigger plans for him: Tener was nominated for and subsequently was elected the governor of Pennsylvania. His successful term in office featured the passage of significant legislation to improve state roads and schools, a public utilities act, and the establishment of a pension program for widows decades before the introduction of Social Security.

During that time the National League, due largely to a lack of unity among its owners, was gradually becoming less powerful than the American League, united under Ban Johnson's leadership. Tired of the situation, NL owners voted not to renew the one-year contract of league president Thomas Lynch and to replace him with a more prestigious leader. New Philadelphia owner William Baker proposed Tener, and it was

agreed to offer the Pennsylvania governor a four-year contract, reportedly for $25,000 per year. Tener was amenable to the offer, provided that he could serve on a part-time basis without salary until the end of January 1915, when his term as governor expired (under Pennsylvania law, Tener could not succeed himself as governor). On December 9, 1913, Tener was unanimously elected NL president.

Soon after his election the Federal League war began. Though he remained in the background until his term as governor ended, Tener played a major role in battling and ultimately negotiating a settlement with the rival league. He publicly ridiculed the Feds' quality of play, an example of which was his reaction to a Federal League plan in 1915 to reduce the price of some seats to 10 cents. When asked for comment, Tener stated, "I believe most businessmen charge for their goods in due relation to the value of the goods that they have to offer, don't they?"

One of Tener's major initiatives during his term as NL president was his strong stand against umpire baiting and rowdy behavior. Like Ban Johnson, he strongly supported his umpires. Following a June 1917 incident in which Giants manager John McGraw struck umpire Bill Byron, Tener suspended McGraw for 16 days and fined him $500. After McGraw delivered an angry tirade against Tener to reporters, the former governor added $1,000 to the fine. Another contentious incident involved Cubs owner Charles Murphy, who frequently embarrassed the league with his ill-advised player transactions and outspoken comments. Tener had to step in when Murphy tried to void the contract of Johnny Evers before the 1914 season, and he later played an important role in forcing Murphy out of baseball by arranging for Cincinnati newspaper magnate Charles Taft to purchase Murphy's stock in the Cubs. Tener also played a prominent role in baseball's recognition of the Players Fraternity, but he later withdrew his support, charging that the group had adopted a policy "calamitous to the best interest of the sport."

When John Tener was chosen as NL president, Pittsburgh owner Barney Dreyfuss stated that the owners' goal was to rally behind him and "bring together the petty factions that now exist in our ranks." Despite that avowed intention, the politics and in-fighting continued among senior circuit owners and between the two leagues. Though unanimously reelected as NL president in November 1917, Tener deliberated for two months before agreeing to an additional one-year term.

The final straw for Tener resulted from a dispute over the rights of pitcher Scott Perry, who'd been sold by Atlanta to the Boston NL team in 1917 on a conditional basis, in essence a 30-day trial. After remaining with Boston a little over two weeks, Perry jumped to an outlaw team. The National Commission, which consisted of Tener, Ban Johnson, and Cincinnati owner Garry Herrmann, ruled that Boston retained the rights to Perry should the pitcher return to Organized Baseball, contingent on their paying the balance of the purchase price. In 1918, however, Atlanta sold Perry to the Philadelphia Athletics. When Perry started the season by pitching well, Boston exercised its rights to Perry and appealed to the National Commission, which supported Boston's claim. Connie Mack, however, refused to accept the verdict or Boston's offer of a compromise. With Ban Johnson's support, Mack went to court to secure an injunction to prevent the enforcement of the National Commission's ruling. Tener was furious. He urged NL owners to break off relations with the AL, including cancelling the World Series, unless the Athletics returned Perry to Boston. The NL owners refused to support such a stand, and Tener resigned on August 6, 1918.

After leaving baseball Tener devoted himself to his various business interests in Pittsburgh. He became involved with the Elks Club, both locally and nationally, and headed the Elks War Relief Commission during and after World War I. He remained active in politics but was unsuccessful in his bid to secure the Republican nomination for another term as Pennsylvania governor. The former NL president maintained his interest in baseball, regularly attending games at Forbes Field. Harriet Tener died in January 1935. In August 1936 John married Leone Evans, but she took ill and died in October 1937. John Tener died from heart disease on May 19, 1946, and was buried in Homewood Cemetery in Pittsburgh. Stating that "we have lost a dear friend and a great American," Pennsylvana governor Edward Martin ordered state flags flown at half-mast for 30 days.

DAN GINSBURG

NEW YORK

The old wooden grandstand at the Polo Grounds, which was replaced by a steel-and-concrete structure in 1911, sits beneath Coogan's Bluff in this circa 1905 photo.

Befitting the nation's biggest, richest, and most influential city, the New York Giants won six National League pennants during the Deadball Era, becoming the most successful, famous, and glamorous team in the world of sports. They owed their incredible success primarily to two men: John McGraw, their brilliant, brawling manager; and Christy Mathewson, their classy, clean-cut pitcher.

Ravaged by eight years under the abrasive ownership of Andrew Freedman, the once proud Giants reached their nadir in 1902, when they suffered their worst record ever, 48-88. Taking over as manager in the midst of that horrendous season, McGraw immediate-

ly jettisoned nine players and replaced them with rising stars he'd brought with him from Baltimore, among them Joe McGinnity, Roger Bresnahan, and Dan McGann. With holdover Mathewson and the additions over the next two seasons of Mike Donlin, Bill Dahlen, and Art Devlin, the Giants won the NL pennant in 1904, rising from the bottom of the standings to the top in only two seasons. That same club won a second pennant and a World Series in 1905; McGraw always considered it the best team he ever managed.

Losing out to the Chicago Cubs from 1906 to 1908, McGraw brought in a bumper crop of fresh, young talent: infielders Fred Merkle, Larry Doyle, Art Fletcher,

WINNING PERCENTAGE 1901-1919

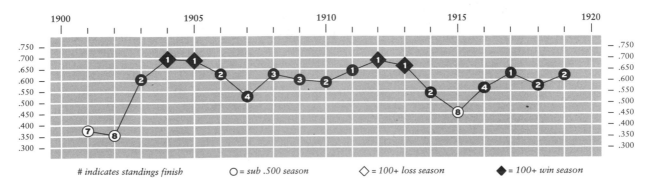

# indicates standings finish   ○ = sub .500 season   ◇ = 100+ loss season   ◆ = 100+ win season

and Buck Herzog; outfielders Red Murray and Fred Snodgrass; catcher Chief Meyers; and pitchers Rube Marquard and Doc Crandall. The youth movement culminated in a team built around speed—the Giants averaged over 300 stolen bases per season, including a record 347 in 1911—that won three consecutive pennants from 1911 to 1913, though no world championships. The core of that team remained together through 1915, when the Giants finished last due in part to the ineffectiveness of Mathewson and Marquard.

This time McGraw rebuilt largely with veterans acquired from other teams, obtaining center fielder Bennie Kauff from the Federal League and third baseman Heinie Zimmerman, second baseman Herzog (his third stint with the Giants), and pitchers Rube Benton and Slim Sallee in midseason trades. Along with holdovers like outfielder George Burns and pitchers Jeff Tesreau and Ferdie Schupp, that team compiled a record 26-game winning streak in September 1916, though it resulted in only a fourth-place finish. That same group returned in 1917 to win New York's final pennant of the Deadball Era.

Even as the Giants were finishing second in 1918 and 1919, McGraw, ever on the lookout for promising players, already was assembling the core of the team—right fielder Ross Youngs, first baseman George Kelly, and infielder Frankie Frisch—that went on to win four consecutive NL pennants in the early 1920s.

ALL-ERA TEAM

F. SNODGRASS, CF

G. BURNS, LF

R. MURRAY, RF

L. DOYLE, 2B

A. FLETCHER, SS

A. DEVLIN, 3B

F. MERKLE, 1B

C. MATHEWSON, P

C. MEYERS, C

TEAM LEADERS 1901-1919

BATTING

GAMES
L. Doyle	1485
A. Fletcher	1280
A. Devlin	1116

RUNS
L. Doyle	858
G. Burns	651
A. Fletcher	581

HITS
L. Doyle	1617
A. Fletcher	1267
G. Burns	1179

RBI
L. Doyle	675
A. Fletcher	560
F. Merkle	508

DOUBLES
L. Doyle	254
G. Burns	204
F. Merkle	192

TRIPLES
L. Doyle	115
G. Burns	64
R. Murray	63

HOME RUNS
L. Doyle	63
F. Merkle	48
D. Robertson	29

STOLEN BASES
G. Burns	293
L. Doyle	280
A. Devlin	266

BATTING AVERAGE
M. Donlin	.333
C. Meyers	.301
L. Doyle	.293

PITCHING

GAMES
C. Mathewson	628
H. Wiltse	339
J. McGinnity	300

WINS
C. Mathewson	372
J. McGinnity	151
H. Wiltse	136

LOSSES
C. Mathewson	185
D. Taylor	100
J. McGinnity	88

INNINGS
C. Mathewson	4738
J. McGinnity	2151⅓
H. Wiltse	2053

STRIKEOUTS
C. Mathewson	2484
R. Ames	1169
H. Wiltse	948

WALKS
C. Mathewson	823
R. Ames	620
J. Tesreau	572

SHUTOUTS
C. Mathewson	79
H. Wiltse	27
J. Tesreau	27

ERA
C. Mathewson	2.10
J. McGinnity	2.38
J. Tesreau	2.43

The 1912 Giants line up in batting order: Devore, Doyle, Snodgrass, Murray, Merkle, Herzog, Meyers, and Fletcher.

TYPICAL LINEUPS 1901–1919

Though some in the Deadball Era came pretty close, no major league team uses an identical lineup and batting order over the course of an entire season. That was especially true during the war-muddled 1918 season, when many players were forced to "work or fight." For that reason we present two lineups for 1918: one for the first half and another for the second half.

1901

1. G. Van Haltren, CF
2. K. Selbach, LF
3. S. Strang, 3B
   A. McBride, RF
4. C. Hickman, RF-INF
5. G. Davis, SS
6. J. Ganzel, 1B
7. R. Nelson, 2B
8. J. Warner, C

1902

1. G. Browne, LF
2. J. Dunn, RF-INF
3. D. McGann, 1B
   J. Jones, LF
4. S. Brodie, CF
5. F. Bowerman, C
6. B. Lauder, 3B
7. H. Smith, 2B
8. J. Bean, SS

1903

1. G. Browne, RF
2. R. Bresnahan, CF
3. D. McGann, 1B
4. S. Mertes, LF
5. C. Babb, SS
6. B. Lauder, 3B
7. B. Gilbert, 2B
8. J. Warner, C

1904

1. R. Bresnahan, CF
2. G. Browne, RF
3. A. Devlin, 3B
4. D. McGann, 1B
5. S. Mertes, LF
6. B. Dahlen, SS
7. B. Gilbert, 2B
8. J. Warner, C

1905

1. G. Browne, RF
2. M. Donlin, CF
3. D. McGann, 1B
4. S. Mertes, LF
5. B. Dahlen, SS
6. A. Devlin, 3B
7. B. Gilbert, 2B
8. R. Bresnahan, C

1906

1. R. Bresnahan, C-CF
   S. Shannon, LF
2. G. Browne, RF
3. D. McGann, 1B
   C. Seymour, CF
4. S. Mertes, LF
5. B. Dahlen, SS
6. A. Devlin, 3B
7. B. Gilbert, 2B
   S. Strang, 2B-OF
8. F. Bowerman, C

1907

1. S. Shannon, LF
2. G. Browne, RF
3. A. Devlin, 3B
4. C. Seymour, CF
5. R. Bresnahan, C
6. D. McGann, 1B
7. B. Dahlen, SS
8. L. Doyle, 2B

1908

1. F. Tenney, 1B
2. L. Doyle, 2B
3. R. Bresnahan, C
4. M. Donlin, RF
5. C. Seymour, CF
6. A. Devlin, 3B
7. M. McCormick, LF
8. A. Bridwell, SS

1909

1. F. Tenney, 1B
2. L. Doyle, 2B
3. M. McCormick, LF
4. R. Murray, RF
5. B. O'Hara, CF
6. A. Devlin, 3B
7. A. Bridwell, SS
8. A. Schlei, C

1910

1. J. Devore, LF
2. L. Doyle, 2B
3. F. Snodgrass, CF
4. R. Murray, RF
5. A. Bridwell, SS
6. A. Devlin, 3B
7. F. Merkle, 1B
8. C. Meyers, C

1911

1. J. Devore, LF
2. L. Doyle, 2B
3. F. Snodgrass, CF
4. R. Murray, RF
5. F. Merkle, 1B
6. A. Bridwell, SS
   B. Herzog, 3B
7. A. Devlin, 3B
   A. Fletcher, SS
8. C. Meyers, C

1912

1. J. Devore, LF
2. L. Doyle, 2B
3. F. Snodgrass, CF-LF
   B. Becker, CF
4. R. Murray, RF
5. F. Merkle, 1B
6. B. Herzog, 3B
7. C. Meyers, C
8. A. Fletcher, SS

1913

1. G. Burns, LF
2. T. Shafer, 3B
3. A. Fletcher, SS
4. L. Doyle, 2B
5. F. Merkle, 1B
6. R. Murray, RF
7. C. Meyers, C
8. F. Snodgrass, CF

1914

1. B. Bescher, CF
2. L. Doyle, 2B
3. G. Burns, LF
4. A. Fletcher, SS
   D. Robertson, RF
5. F. Merkle, 1B
6. F. Snodgrass, CF-RF
7. M. Stock, 3B
8. C. Meyers, C

1915

1. G. Burns, LF
2. D. Robertson, RF
3. L. Doyle, 2B
4. A. Fletcher, SS
5. F. Merkle, 1B
6. H. Lobert, 3B
7. F. Snodgrass, CF
8. C. Meyers, C

1916

1. G. Burns, LF
2. L. Doyle, 2B
3. D. Robertson, RF
4. B. Kauff, CF
5. A. Fletcher, SS
6. F. Merkle, 1B
7. B. McKechnie, 3B
8. B. Rariden, C

1917

1. G. Burns, LF
2. B. Herzog, 2B
3. B. Kauff, CF
4. H. Zimmerman, 3B
5. A. Fletcher, SS
6. D. Robertson, RF
7. W. Holke, 1B
8. B. Rariden, C

1918 (First half)

1. R. Youngs, RF
2. B. Kauff, CF
3. G. Burns, LF
4. H. Zimmerman, 3B
5. A. Fletcher, SS
6. W. Holke, 1B
7. L. McCarty, C
8. J. Rodriguez, 2B

1918 (Second half)

1. G. Burns, LF
2. R. Youngs, RF
3. A. Fletcher, SS
4. J. Wilhoit, CF
5. H. Zimmerman, 3B
6. W. Holke, 1B
7. E. Sicking, 2B
8. L. McCarty,
   B. Rariden, C

1919

1. G. Burns, LF
2. R. Youngs, RF
3. A. Fletcher, SS
4. L. Doyle, 2B
5. B. Kauff, CF
6. H. Zimmerman, 3B
7. H. Chase, 1B
8. L. McCarty
   M. Gonzalez, C

The Giants' "big four," circa 1911:
Mathewson, Ames, Wiltse, and Marquard.

NEW YORK

CHRISTOPHER MATHEWSON
RIGHT-HANDED PITCHER 1900–16

In the time when Giants walked the earth and roamed the Polo Grounds, none was more honored than Christy Mathewson. Delivering all four of his pitches, including his famous "fadeaway" (now called a screwball), with impeccable control and an easy motion, the right-handed Mathewson was the greatest pitcher of the Deadball Era's first decade, compiling a 2.13 ERA over 17 seasons and setting modern National League records for wins in a season (37), wins in a career (373), and consecutive 20-win seasons (12). Aside from his pitching achievements, he was the greatest all-around hero of the era, a handsome, college-educated man who lifted the rowdy world of baseball to respectability. Matty was the basis, many say, for the idealized athlete Frank Merriwell, an inspiration to many authors over the years, and the motivation for an Off-Broadway play based on his life and writings. "He gripped the imagination of a country that held 100 million people and held this grip with a firmer hold than any man of his day or time," wrote sportswriter Grantland Rice.

The oldest of six children of Minerva (Capwell) and Gilbert Mathewson, a Civil War veteran who became a post office worker and farmer, Christopher Mathewson was born on August 12, 1880, in Factoryville, Pennsylvania, a small town in the northeastern part of the state, not far from the New York border. His forebears, original followers of Roger Williams in Rhode Island, had settled in the region as the nation began to expand westward after the Revolutionary War. The blond-haired, blue-eyed Christy was always big for his age—he eventually grew to 6'1½" and 195 lbs.—and his playmates called him "Husk." At age 14 he pitched for the Factoryville town team. Christy continued pitching for area semipro teams while attending Keystone Academy, a Factoryville prep school founded by his grandmother. The summer after his graduation, Christy was pitching for the team from Honesdale, Pennsylvania, when Dave Williams, a left-handed teammate who later pitched three games for the Boston Americans, taught him the fadeaway.

In September 1898 Mathewson enrolled at Bucknell University. He pitched for the baseball team and played center on the basketball team, but football was his chief claim to fame at Bucknell, which played a rugged schedule that included national powerhouses such as Penn State, Army, and Navy. For three years Christy was the varsity's first-string fullback, punter, and drop kicker; Walter Camp, the originator of college football's All-America team, called him "the best all-around football player I ever saw." Majoring in forestry, Mathewson also was a top-flight student who excelled in extracurricular activities, serving as class president and joining the band, glee club, two literary societies, and two fraternities. Bucknell was also where he met his future bride, Jane Stoughton.

During the summer after his freshman year, Mathewson signed his first professional contract with Taunton, Massachusetts, of the New England League. He pitched in 17 games and went 2-13. To make a bad season worse, Taunton folded and the players had to arrange a Labor Day exhibition just to raise funds for their transportation home. Before the start of the

Bucknell-Penn football game that fall (in which Matty kicked two long-range field goals, then worth five points apiece, the same as touchdowns), an old major league pitcher named Phenomenal Smith signed him to a contract with Norfolk for the following summer. Reporting right after final exams, Mathewson became an immediate sensation in the Virginia League, amassing a 20-2 record by mid-July. After the last of those victories, Smith took Matty aside and offered him a choice between Philadelphia or New York of the National League. Christy chose New York, thinking the Giants needed pitching more than the Phillies, and made his major league debut on July 17, 1900, one month shy of his 20th birthday.

Mathewson did little more than pitch batting practice for the Giants, becoming so frustrated that he wrote a friend, "I don't give a rip whether they keep me or not." Toward the end of the season he received two starting assignments and lost both of them, ending the year winless in three decisions with a 5.08 ERA. The Giants returned him to Norfolk. That off-season the Cincinnati Reds drafted him for $100, then traded him back to the Giants for a washed-up Amos Rusie. It was part of a collusive plan to save $900; the Giants would have had to pay $1,000 to Norfolk if they'd kept Mathewson after the season, and Reds owner John T. Brush was negotiating to purchase the Giants from Andrew Freedman. In 1901, his first full season in the majors, Mathewson pitched a no-hitter against the St. Louis Cardinals on July 15 and went 20-17 with a 2.41 ERA for a seventh-place club. New York fans started calling him "The Big Six." Matty thought it was because of his height, but the nickname probably originated when sportswriter Sam Crane compared him to New York City's Big Six Fire Company, "the fastest to put out the fire."

The Giants floundered again at the start of 1902, prompting new manager Horace Fogel to play Mathewson in three games at first base and four in the outfield in addition to his pitching duties. Many have implied that this was a sign of Fogel's ineptitude, but years later Matty defended Fogel, explaining that the manager knew he was a good hitter and fielder and was willing to try anything to turn around his team. The experiment ended, however, when John McGraw took over as manager on July 19. To that point Mathewson had won only one game, but over the rest of the season

he won 13, eight of them shutouts, winding up at 14-17 with a 2.11 ERA as the Giants finished last. That winter Matty married Jane Stoughton while McGraw continued rebuilding his team. The Mathewsons honeymooned in Savannah, where the Giants held spring training. Blanche McGraw took the young pitcher's wife under her wing, while the McGraws treated Christy like the son they never had.

Christy Mathewson enjoyed a breakout year in 1903, the first of three consecutive 30-win seasons. That year he went 30-13 with a 2.26 ERA and a career-high 267 strikeouts, which stood as the modern NL record until Sandy Koufax struck out 269 in 1961. Matty was just as good in 1904, leading the Giants to the NL pennant with a 33-12 record and 2.03 ERA, but the following year he was even better. Mathewson was 31-9 with a miniscule 1.28 ERA, capping off his banner 1905 season with the best World Series any pitcher ever had. Opposing him in the opener on October 9 was Philadelphia's Eddie Plank, a fellow Pennsylvanian who'd pitched against him several times while attending Gettysburg College. Mathewson got the victory, as he had in each of their college matchups, shutting out the Athletics on four hits. After Chief Bender shut out the Giants in Game Two, Matty was ready to pitch again in Game Three but received an extra day's rest when the game was rained out. On October 12 he shut out the Athletics, 9-0, on another four-hitter. The next day Joe McGinnity defeated Plank, 1-0, and Mathewson returned on just one day's rest to clinch the Series with a 2-0 victory over Bender. Within a span of six days, he'd pitched 27 innings, allowing 14 hits, one walk, and no runs while striking out 18. The next week Matty and his catcher Frank Bowerman went hunting in Bowerman's hometown of Romeo, Michigan. Coaxed to pitch for Romeo in its final game of the season against archrival Lake Orion, Christy lost, 5-0, to an obscure group of semipros.

Mathewson was the toast of New York. Endorsement offers poured in, with Matty "pitching" Arrow shirt collars, leg garters (for socks), undergarments, sweaters, athletic equipment, and numerous other products. He received an offer to put his name on a pool hall/saloon but turned it down when his mother asked, "Do you really want your name associated with a place like that?" But in a pattern that haunted him for the rest of his life, disappointment and tragedy followed his greatest triumph. In 1906 Matty caught a dose of diphtheria and nearly died, struggling to a 22-12 record and an uncharacteristic 2.97 ERA. Late that season the Giants called up his brother Henry, who was only 19 years old. In his first start Henry set a modern NL record by walking 14 Chicago Cubs. Disappointing though the '06 season was, Matty experienced his greatest joy on October 6, when Jane gave birth to the couple's first and only child, a son they named Christopher Jr.

Mathewson's biggest year came in 1908, when he set career highs in wins (37), games (56), innings (390⅔), and shutouts (11). His control was rarely better, averaging less than one walk per nine innings. Matty's season ended in disappointment, however, when he took a no-decision in the "Merkle Game" and lost to Mordecai Brown, 4-2, in the one-game playoff. By his own admission he had "nothing on the ball" in that contest, and he also felt responsible that four people had lost their lives in falling accidents at the Polo Grounds that day (if he'd only said the word, the Giants would have refused to play and those tragedies would have been averted). Compounding his guilt, in January 1909 Christy found the body of his youngest brother, Nicholas, dead in his parents' barn of a self-inflicted gunshot wound. Two years earlier, Detroit Tigers manager Hughie Jennings had wanted to sign the 17-year-old Nicholas and bring him directly to the majors, but Christy had advised against it.

Mathewson nonetheless bounced back to go 25-6 with a career-best 1.14 ERA in 1909. He helped the Giants win three consecutive NL pennants from 1911 to 1913, leading the NL in ERA in both 1911 (1.99) and 1913 (2.06). In 1914, however, the 34-year-old Matty started experiencing a constant pain in his left side toward the end of the season. Doctors found nothing wrong and told him he was just getting old. It affected his performance, however; his ERA increased to 3.00 in 1914, even though he still managed to win 24 games, and the following year he was just 8-14 with a 3.58 ERA. By the midpoint of the 1916 season Matty had won just three games. Knowing that his days as an effective pitcher were behind him, he decided that he wanted to manage. On July 20 McGraw came through for his friend, trading him for Cincinnati Reds player-manager Buck Herzog on condition that Matty replace Herzog as manager.

Matty was a good manager who might have become a great one, but he could do little with Herzog's leftovers and finished tied for last in 1916. At least he added some interest to an otherwise dismal season, pitching one last game against his old rival on "Mordecai Brown Day" in Chicago. In the only major league game he ever pitched in a uniform other than New York's, the 36-year-old Matty yielded 15 hits but defeated a nearly 40-year-old Brown, 10-8, giving him the 373rd and final victory of his 17-year career. In 1917 Mathewson guided Cincinnati to a 78-76 record, its first winning season since 1909, but tragedy struck on July 1 when his brother Henry died of tuberculosis at age 30, leaving behind four young daughters. Matty's Reds continued their improvement in 1918, but on August 9 he suspended his notorious first baseman, Hal Chase, after confronting him about some suspicious-looking misplays and a $50 payment to pitcher Jimmy Ring. Cincinnati went on to finish third, but by that point Mathewson was in France, having been commissioned a captain in the Army's Chemical Warfare Division. While Matty was overseas, Chase's case came before the National Commission; without the star witness against him, Chase was exonerated.

While in France Mathewson endured a bad bout of influenza and was exposed to mustard gas during a training exercise. He was hospitalized and apparently had recovered by the time he returned to the United States in the spring. On his arrival, however, he discovered that Pat Moran was managing the Reds. When owner Garry Herrmann didn't hear from Matty that he'd be back in time for spring training (they had written each other, but neither had received the other's message), he did what he felt he needed to and hired a new manager. Mathewson resigned from the Reds and accepted a position from McGraw as assistant manager of the Giants. In 1919 New York finished second to the Matty-built Reds, and Matty covered the World Series for the *New York Times*. Before the first game he saw several Chicago White Sox conversing with Chase in the lobby of Cincinnati's Hotel Sinton. Doubting the legitimacy of the Series before a single pitch was thrown, Mathewson discussed the possibility of a fix with sportswriter Hugh Fullerton and agreed to circle suspicious-looking plays on his scorecard. Angry at what he witnessed, believing that "his" team would have won the Series on its own merit, Matty forwarded his findings to the National Commission.

Returning to the Giants in 1920-21, Mathewson was unable to shake the cough that had plagued him since joining the club in 1919, and the pain in his left side was back and worse than ever. The physicians who examined him in 1921 immediately diagnosed the condition as tuberculosis. It's possible that he'd contracted the disease from his brother Henry and had it since 1914, but the physicians who'd examined him then were looking for muscle strain, not lesions irritating his lung and rubbing the inside of his ribs. Along with his wife, Christy set off for the tuberculosis sanitarium in Saranac Lake, New York, where he initially received a prognosis of six weeks to live. For the next two years he fought to recover from the deadly disease. By the winter of 1922-23 Matty thought he was strong enough to return to baseball.

That winter McGraw urged Judge Emil Fuchs of New York to purchase the Boston Braves. "And if you buy them," McGraw said, "I've got the man who can run the club for you." On February 11, 1923, Fuchs announced that he'd bought the Braves and Christy Mathewson would serve as president. His physicians warned him that he couldn't undertake too much, but Matty nonetheless threw himself into the task of rebuilding the woeful Braves. Some reports say that his cough returned in 1925 after he was soaked in a spring training rain shower. Whether it was stress, the rain, or a disease that wouldn't give in, Matty's body began to fail, and he was forced to return to Saranac Lake, where he died on October 7, 1925. McGraw was in Pittsburgh, covering the World Series for a newspaper syndicate. When he received the news, he immediately left for New York to meet his wife. Together they went to Saranac Lake to be with Jane Mathewson and Christy Jr.

Three days later, with his manager, wife, and son standing graveside, Christy Mathewson was laid to rest in Lewisburg, Pennsylvania, in view of the Bucknell campus. Today there's a memorial gate at the entrance to the campus, built in 1927 with donations from every big-league team, and in 1989 the Bison football stadium was rededicated as Christy Mathewson Memorial Stadium.

EDDIE FRIERSON

NEW YORK

LUTHER HADEN "DUMMY" TAYLOR
RIGHT-HANDED PITCHER 1900–08

A gangly right hander with an unorthodox corkscrew delivery, Dummy Taylor first caught the attention of the New York Giants with his fastball, but he also had a good curve and developed what one called "the best drop ball delivered across the plate by any pitcher." While many viewed his lack of hearing as a handicap, Taylor believed that all it did was heighten his other senses. The 6'1", 160 lb. deaf mute was adept at stealing signs because of his keen eyesight, and he also believed that he could read a base runner's intentions by studying his facial expressions, helping him give up relatively few stolen bases. Dummy wasn't the first deaf player in the majors, or the last, but he became the most visible because he played in New York for baseball's most glamorous team. "Wherever Taylor goes he will always be visited by scores of the silent fraternity among whom he is regarded as a prodigy," observed the *Saturday Evening Post*.

One of three deaf children of hearing parents, Luther Haden Taylor was born on February 21, 1875, in Oskaloosa, Kansas. Growing up on the family farm, Luther attended the Kansas School for the Deaf in the nearby town of Olathe from 1884 to 1895. At the time new inventions such as the telephone and phonograph were changing the hearing world, but for the deaf those technological advances served only to isolate them further. Many turned to sports, where they could compete in ways that they couldn't off the field. Luther was an outstanding boxer but his father encouraged him to pursue baseball. When he finished high school in 1895, Taylor pitched for minor league teams in Missouri and Kansas. In subsequent years he played in Illinois and Georgia before making his major league debut with the New York Giants on August 27, 1900. Pitching for a last-place team, Taylor went 4-3 with a 2.45 ERA.

The Giants didn't just add Taylor to their roster; they embraced him as a member of their family. Player-manager George Davis learned sign language and encouraged his players to do likewise, as did John McGraw when he took over as Giants manager in mid-1902. Taylor had "a genial, humorous spirit that covets companionship," according to the *Saturday Evening Post*, and his presence had a profound effect on his teammates. "We could all read and speak the deaf-and-dumb sign language, because Dummy took it as an affront if you didn't learn to converse with him," said Fred Snodgrass in *The Glory of Their Times*. "He wanted to be one of us, to be a full-fledged member of the team. If we went to the vaudeville show, he wanted to know what the joke was, and somebody had to tell him. So we all learned. We practiced all the time. We'd go by elevated train from the hotel to the Polo Grounds, and all during the ride, we'd be spelling out the advertising signs." The Giants even did away with conventional baseball signs and used sign language for a while, at least until opponents caught on.

In 1901, their first full season in New York, Dummy Taylor and 20-year-old Christy Mathewson became the workhorses of a young pitching staff that was just starting to develop into one of baseball's best. Taylor led NL pitchers by making 45 appearances, finishing with 18 wins and a league-leading 27 losses for the seventh-place Giants. Interestingly, he wasn't the team's only deaf mute: the pitching staff also briefly included Dummy Deegan and Dummy Leitner. The following year Taylor jumped to the American League for more money, but none of his Cleveland teammates knew sign language and he became depressed. After pitching just four games in two months, Dummy rejoined the Giants, now managed by McGraw, and went 7-15 down the stretch despite a 2.29 ERA. If he suffered from a lack of run support in 1902, he enjoyed the opposite experience the following year, going 13-13 despite a horrible 4.23 ERA, the third-worst among NL pitchers with more than 200 innings.

As was the practice in those days, Taylor often served as first-base coach on days when he wasn't pitching. To the delight of the fans, he clowned around and made gestures behind the backs of the umpires. Dummy sometimes let loose a loud piercing noise—teammate Mike Donlin likened it to the "crazed shrieking of a jackass"—to rattle opposing pitchers or just to annoy the arbiters. Umpire Charlie Zimmer once got so irritated with the shrill sound that he ejected Taylor, perhaps the only instance of a deaf player being tossed for being too noisy. It wasn't the last time Dummy faced an umpire's wrath. One day it was pouring rain, but umpire Hank O'Day refused to call the game. Taylor ducked into the clubhouse and returned wearing huge rubber boots and twirling a bright yellow umbrella. O'Day yelled furiously at Dummy as he clowned around in the coach's box, but the deaf pitcher pretended not to notice. Taylor signed an unflattering description of the arbiter to McGraw, and was surprised when O'Day signed back, "You go clubhouse, pay $25." O'Day hadn't picked up everything Taylor had called him, but having been raised by deaf parents, he knew enough to know that it wasn't flattering.

In 1904 Taylor and his fellow pitchers led the Giants to their first pennant in 15 years. It was by far the best season of Dummy's career, as he finished with a 21-15 record and 2.34 ERA. The Giants repeated as NL champions the following year, with Taylor posting a 16-9 record, and the deaf pitcher was scheduled to start Game Three of the 1905 World Series against the Philadelphia Athletics. Rain cancelled the contest, however, and McGraw opted to start Mathewson when the game was rescheduled. Dummy continued to pitch well over the next three seasons, finishing with a winning record each year and remaining one of the most popular players on the Giants. He was the life of the camp at spring training, as is evident from this Sam Crane clipping from 1908: "Yesterday Taylor was more full of life, good nature and ginger than ever. Bresnahan began to spar with him, but Luther is pretty good with his hands and knocked off Bresnahan's dicer the first crack out of the box. This pleased the amiable Luther immensely, and then there was more finger lingo than could be furnished in a deaf-and-dumb asylum. All the old players are adept at the deaf-and-dumb language, especially Bresnahan. Needham tried to break in with it, but Luther looked at Tom's knotted digits and spelled out on his fingers: 'Another Bowerman; I'll bet he has a brogue.'"

The Giants released Taylor after the 1908 season. He was soon to turn 34, and McGraw wanted to give his job to a young lefty named Rube Marquard. Dummy pitched in the minors for seven more seasons, mostly with teams near his Kansas home, ending his career with Topeka in 1915. By then he was also working at his alma mater, the Kansas School for the Deaf, coaching five sports. In 1923 Taylor moved on to a deaf school in Iowa, and later he spent nearly two decades as a coach, teacher, and administrator at the Illinois School for the Deaf. Several of his students went on to play minor league baseball, and one, Dick Sipek, reached the majors with the Cincinnati Reds in 1945. After retiring in 1940, Taylor worked as a scout for the Giants and later opened a barbershop. Luther Taylor was married three times but didn't have any children. He died at age 82 on August 22, 1958, 11 days after suffering a heart attack.

Dummy Taylor's story reached a new audience in 2000 when SABR member Darryl Brock used him as the inspiration for his novel *Havana Heat*. The book is a first-person account of Taylor's fictional attempt to impress McGraw and return to the majors on a 1911 barnstorming tour of Cuba.

SEAN LAHMAN

John McGraw

NEW YORK

John Joseph McGraw
Manager 1902–32

John McGraw was perhaps the National League's most influential figure in the Deadball Era. From 1902 to 1932 he led the New York Giants to 10 NL pennants, three World Series championships, and 20 first- or second-place finishes in 29 full seasons at their helm. His 2,763 managerial victories are second only to Connie Mack's 3,731, but in 1927 Mack himself proclaimed, "There has been only one manager—and his name is McGraw." The pugnacious McGraw's impact on the game, moreover, was even greater than his record suggests. As a player he helped develop "inside baseball," which put a premium on strategy and guile, and later managed like he'd played, seeking out every advantage for his Giants. Known as "Muggsy" (a nickname he detested) and "Little Napoleon" (for his dictatorial methods), McGraw administered harsh tongue-lashings to his players and frequently fought with umpires; he was ejected from 118 contests during his career, more than any other manager. "McGraw eats gunpowder every morning for breakfast and washes it down with warm blood," said Giants coach Arlie Latham.

The oldest of eight children of Ellen (Comerfert) and John McGraw, an Irish immigrant who fought in the Civil War and later worked in railroad maintenance, John Joseph McGraw was born on April 7, 1873, in the village of Truxton, New York, about 25 miles south of Syracuse. During the winter of 1884-85 a diphtheria epidemic claimed Ellen and three of her children, leaving John Sr., a heavy drinker, alone to raise Johnny and the other four survivors. One night in the fall of 1885, 12-year-old Johnny received such a severe beating from

his father that he moved across the street to the Truxton House Inn, where a kindly widow named Mary Goddard took him in and raised him along with her own two sons. Besides attending school, Johnny performed chores around the hotel, delivered newspapers, and peddled candy, fruit, and magazines on the train from Cortland to Elmira.

At 16 years old, Johnny McGraw stood barely 5'7" and weighed little more than 100 lbs., but that didn't stop him from becoming the star pitcher for the local Truxton Grays. When Truxton's manager, Bert Kenney, became part owner and player-manager of the Olean franchise in the New York-Penn League in 1890, Johnny begged for and received a place on the team. In his first game on May 18, McGraw played third base and made eight errors in 10 chances. He was released after six games but caught on with Wellsville of the Western New York League, batting .364 in 24 games. Following the season, one of his teammates organized a winter tour of Cuba, and McGraw went along, playing shortstop for the "American All-Stars." On the way home the team stopped in Gainesville, Florida, to play a spring training exhibition against the NL's Cleveland Spiders. McGraw collected three doubles in five at-bats, receiving national publicity when the story made *The Sporting News*. From among the resulting offers he received for the coming season, he chose Cedar Rapids of the Illinois-Iowa League and batted .276 in 85 games as the club's regular shortstop.

That August McGraw made his major league debut with the American Association's Baltimore Orioles, filling in at various positions and hitting .270 in 33 games. In 1892 the AA disbanded and Baltimore was absorbed into the now 12-team National League. McGraw started the season as utility man but took over as the regular third baseman after Ned Hanlon was appointed manager in midseason. Under Hanlon's tutelage, McGraw became the NL's best leadoff hitter, batting over .320 for nine straight years, twice leading the league in runs and walks, stealing 436 bases, and compiling a career on-base percentage of .466, which ranks behind only Ted Williams and Babe Ruth. McGraw choked up on the bat and swung with a short, chopping motion that diminished his power, but he could place the ball anywhere he wanted. He also wasn't above cheating. "McGraw uses every low and contemptible method that his erratic brain can conceive to win a play by a dirty trick," wrote one reporter.

With players like Joe Kelley, Hughie Jennings, Wilbert Robinson, Steve Brodie, Sadie McMahon, and Dan Brouthers, all of whom were employed by or associated with McGraw in later years, Hanlon's Orioles won three consecutive pennants in 1894-96 and finished second in 1897-98. Concerned about slumping attendance in Baltimore, Orioles owner Henry Von der Horst tried to transfer most of his key personnel to Brooklyn in 1899, but McGraw and his friend Robinson refused to report, claiming business interests that demanded their attention in Baltimore. Von der Horst reluctantly let them stay, and the 26-year-old McGraw managed the Orioles to a surprising third-place finish, just behind Brooklyn. Baltimore might have done even better, but in late August McGraw's wife, Mary, died from a ruptured appendix; a grieving John missed much of September. The Orioles disbanded when the NL contracted to eight teams in 1900. After again refusing to report to Brooklyn, McGraw was sold to the St. Louis Cardinals along with Robinson. Agreeing to go only when the reserve clause was removed from his contract, he signed for a salary of $10,000—the highest in baseball history to that point—and hit .344 in 99 games.

In 1901 McGraw returned to Baltimore as manager and part owner of that city's franchise in Ban Johnson's new American League. Throughout that season and the next, he quarreled constantly with Johnson, who habitually supported his umpires in their frequent disputes with McGraw. Johnson finally suspended McGraw

indefinitely in July 1902, and at that point the temperamental manager jumped back to the NL as player-manager of the New York Giants, even though he'd recently married a Baltimore woman, Blanche Sindall. One of his first acts in New York was to release nine players, despite the protests of Giants owner Andrew Freedman. McGraw also brought six key players with him from Baltimore. The Giants finished last that season but rose to second in 1903, even though McGraw's much injured knee finally gave out for good during spring training, effectively ending his career as a player.

In 1904 the Giants became NL champions, finishing with a won-lost record of 106-47, 13 games ahead of the Chicago Cubs. McGraw and new Giants owner John T. Brush so detested Ban Johnson and his league that they refused to take on the Boston Americans in what would have been the second World Series. After winning again in 1905, however, they agreed to play the AL champion Philadelphia Athletics. New York triumphed in four out of five games, three of them Christy Mathewson shutouts. McGraw led the Giants to pennants again in 1911, 1912, 1913, and 1917, but lost the World Series each year. His regular-season success was due to his knack for evaluating and acquiring players who fit into his system, which stressed good pitching, sound defense, and aggressive base running. McGraw bought, sold, and traded players more than his counterparts, grooming prospects for years before letting them play regularly. He also was an innovator, using pinch-runners, pinch-hitters, and relief pitchers more than other managers.

Many commentators believed that McGraw's lack of World Series success was due to his strong preference for players who fit his system. The Giants were generally considered less talented than other top teams—they were a second-class team with a first-class manager, claimed Johnny Evers. Until left fielder Ross Youngs entered the league in 1917, catcher Roger Bresnahan was McGraw's only regular position player on the Giants during the Deadball Era who eventually made the Hall of Fame. McGraw's teams also seemed to make mental errors in big games, as though they didn't know what to do or were paralyzed at the thought of how the Old Man might react if they lost. After New York's 1913 World Series defeat by the Athletics, even the usually loyal Mathewson blamed McGraw for the team's setbacks in a ghostwritten article. The Giants, said the article, are a "team of puppets being manipulated from the bench on a string."

McGraw's fiery personality made him fascinating to contemporaries outside sports. Gamblers, show-business people, and politicians were drawn to him. As his celebrity grew, McGraw became increasingly involved in various, sometimes questionable, off-field activities. For a while McGraw owned a poolroom in Manhattan with gambler Arnold Rothstein, who later became the principal financial backer of the 1919 World Series fix, and he sometimes spent winters in Cuba, where he and Giants owner Charles Stoneham owned a share of a racetrack and casino. When Stoneham bought the Giants in 1919, McGraw became vice-president and minority owner of the club. Between 1912 and 1923 he helped resolve various ownership crises of the Boston Braves—which usually paid off in trades that helped New York more than Boston. Fatefully, McGraw also was instrumental in Colonel Jacob Ruppert's purchase of the Yankees and the decision to allow them to share the Polo Grounds when the Giants were on the road.

In 1920 Babe Ruth arrived to play for the Yankees. The team's attendance soared as Ruth began blasting home runs out of the Polo Grounds, prompting an enraged McGraw to instruct Stoneham to evict the upstart tenants. In what was widely viewed as a battle between inside baseball and the new power game, McGraw had the consolation of beating the Yankees in the World Series of 1921-22 ("I signaled for every ball that was pitched to Ruth during the 1922 World's Series," McGraw gloated). The tide turned for good in 1923, however, when the Yankees crushed the Giants, four games to two, for their first world championship, with Ruth clouting three home runs. In 1924 the Giants won a record fourth consecutive NL pennant but lost another World Series, this time to the Washington Nationals. Early in his career his teams emphasized the stolen base, but as the long ball came to dominate baseball, McGraw—despite his personal dislike of the home run—adapted to the change. For the rest of the decade and the early 1930s, the Giants fielded some fine teams but were never good enough to win. Plagued by health problems, McGraw resigned on June 3, 1932.

John McGraw made his last major public appearance at Comiskey Park in July 1933, managing the National League against Connie Mack's American Leaguers in baseball's first official All-Star Game. He

was 60 years old when he died at his home in New Rochelle, New York, on February 25, 1934, of prostate cancer and uremia—but mostly, according to one reporter, because he was no longer top dog. He was buried in New Cathedral Cemetery in Baltimore, near several of his old Oriole teammates, as well as his first wife, Mary.

McGraw was inducted into the National Baseball Hall of Fame in 1937. Blanche inherited her husband's stock in the Giants and carried on his memory, frequently attending games with Christy Mathewson's widow. Her most tragic time, at least according to the New York newspapers, was on that September day in 1957 when the Giants played their final game at the Polo Grounds before departing for San Francisco. She said the move would have broken John's heart. Nonetheless, she was present at Seals Stadium in April 1958 at the team's first game on the West Coast, and again when Candlestick Park opened two years later. Blanche McGraw died on November 5, 1962, only a few weeks after attending the New York games of the Giants-Yankees World Series.

DON JENSEN

Joseph J. McGinnity

NEW YORK

JOSEPH JEROME McGINNITY
RIGHT-HANDED PITCHER 1902–08

Joe McGinnity was an "Iron Man" in almost every sense. Though the nickname came from his off-season work in his wife's family business, an iron foundry in McAlester, Oklahoma, McGinnity became famous for pitching both ends of doubleheaders and led his league in innings pitched four times in the five seasons from 1900 to 1904. He was also an "Iron Man" in terms of longevity: he pitched professionally until age 54, racking up 246 wins in the major leagues and another 240 in the minors, a combined total topped only by Cy Young. A stocky 5'11" right hander, McGinnity for most of his career weighed a good deal more than the 206 lbs. listed in record books. He owed his durability to a style of delivery that saw him alternate between overhand, sidearm, and a wicked underhanded curve that he called "Old Sal." "I've pitched for 30 years and I believe I've averaged over 30 games a season, and in all my experiences I've never had what I could truthfully call a sore arm," Joe said.

Joseph Jerome McGinty (he changed his last name to McGinnity as an adult) was born on March 19, 1871, in the Quad City of Rock Island, Illinois, at the junction of the Rock and Mississippi rivers. His early minor league career gave no indication of the success to come: in 1893-94 he was a combined 21-29 for Montgomery of the Southern Association and Kansas City of the Western League, with more walks than strikeouts and far more hits than innings pitched. Returning to Springfield, Illinois, McGinnity operated a saloon and built a reputation as a tough character, serving as his own bouncer when the need arose. He also pitched at the semipro level for the next three years, and it was then that he discovered Old Sal, the pitch that changed his career. In 1898 McGinnity returned to professional baseball with Peoria of the Western

Association, going 9-4 with fewer hits (118) than innings (142) and more strikeouts (74) than walks (60) for the first time in his professional career.

The following year McGinnity made his National League debut with the Baltimore Orioles. The 28-year-old rookie was 28-16, leading the NL in wins and ranking second in games (48), third in ERA (2.68), and fourth in innings (366⅓). During one week in October McGinnity appeared in every game, winning five games in six days. In 1900 Joe joined the Brooklyn Superbas, as did several other Orioles, but the change in cities made no difference in his winning ways. His 28-8 record gave him the NL lead in wins for the second time in as many seasons, and for the first time he led the league in innings with 343. After the Superbas captured the NL pennant, McGinnity led them to a three-games-to-one victory over the Pittsburgh Pirates in the *Chronicle-Telegraph* Cup by pitching two complete games without allowing a single earned run.

Turning down an offer of almost twice as much to return to Brooklyn, Joe McGinnity signed for $2,800 with the Baltimore franchise in the new American League, managed by his old manager-teammate on the 1899 Orioles, John McGraw. McGinnity's career almost ended on August 21, 1901, when he spat tobacco juice in the face of umpire Tom Connolly, precipitating an on-field melee. McGinnity was arrested and hauled before a judge, but his bigger concern was AL president Ban Johnson, who wanted his league free from brawls, especially of the umpire-baiting variety. Initially Johnson announced that he was permanently suspending the burly pitcher, but he reduced the suspension to 12 days when a penitent McGinnity agreed to apologize to Connolly. Joe made up for lost time by pitching both halves of two September doubleheaders,

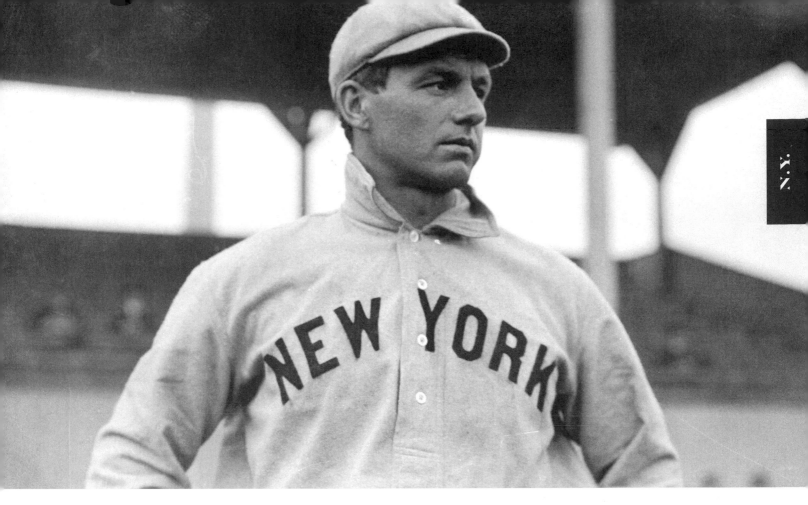

earning split decisions in each. He finished the season at 26-20 and led the AL in games (48), complete games (39), and innings (382).

McGinnity started 1902 in Baltimore but followed McGraw to New York in mid-July. The following year, his first full season with the Giants, he again led the National League with 31 wins and pitched an incredible 434 innings, a modern NL record that will probably stand forever. That August McGinnity recorded his most extraordinary feat by pitching complete games in both ends of three doubleheaders, winning all six games. After the last of the three, the *New York Times* reported that he showed "no signs of fatigue—in fact, he seemed fresh enough to tackle the visitors for a third contest if that were necessary." The rough-and-tumble McGinnity differed greatly from his refined teammate Christy Mathewson, but the two combined for 73% of the Giants' victories in 1903, making them the 20th century's most successful pitching tandem in that regard. The following year McGinnity enjoyed his greatest season, leading the Giants to the pennant by winning 14 consecutive games en route to a 35-8 record. Again he led the National League in games (51)

and innings (408), and he also paced the circuit in shutouts (9), saves (5), and ERA (a career-best 1.61).

Mathewson replaced McGinnity as the National League's best pitcher in 1905, but the Iron Man contributed 21 wins to another pennant-winning season. The Giants had five pitchers who won at least 15 games that season, but McGinnity started two of the five World Series games against the Philadelphia Athletics. He lost Game Two to Chief Bender by giving up three unearned runs on five hits, but he bounced back in Game Four to pitch a five-hit shutout, winning 1-0. In 1906 McGinnity reclaimed the NL lead in wins with 27 even though he missed 10 days in July while serving another suspension. This time his antagonist was Pittsburgh Pirates catcher Heinie Peitz, with whom he'd exchanged verbal insults for quite some time. After reaching his breaking point, McGinnity gave chase to Peitz, caught up with him, threw him to the ground, and began pummeling him. When the dust settled, National League president Harry Pulliam levied a series of fines and suspensions, the heaviest to McGinnity for what Pulliam called "attempting to make the ball park a slaughterhouse."

The 36-year-old McGinnity finished 1907 with an 18-18 record, his only non-winning season in the majors. His ERA increased almost a full run to 3.16, and he yielded more hits than innings for the first time since 1901, prompting reporters to speculate that he was past his days of big-league usefulness. McGinnity missed the start of the 1908 season, suffering from a severe fever at his home in McAlester. He didn't pick up his first win until May 30, and shortly thereafter John Brush, the Giants owner, put him on waivers in an unsuccessful attempt to rid himself of the big pitcher's "ironclad" $4,000 salary (he also received a $1,000 bonus). Brush tried again on August 22 but again found no takers. That afternoon McGraw called on McGinnity after Red Ames walked the first two Reds batters, "and the Iron Man performed in his 1903 style," wrote Jack Ryder in the *Cincinnati Enquirer*. "Isn't baseball a funny proposition? Here is a pitcher the Giants are trying to give away. Necessity forces his use a few hours after the gift proposition is made, and the old boy works like a Mathewson." McGinnity pitched well for the rest of the season, ending up at 11-7 with five shutouts, a league-leading five saves, and a 2.27 ERA.

Down the stretch of that 1908 season, McGinnity played interesting roles in two of the most famous games in history. In the Merkle Game, quickly recognizing what the Cubs were up to, he recovered the ball hit by Al Bridwell and threw it into the stands to prevent Johnny Evers from retrieving it and tagging second base. Evers obtained a loose ball from somewhere, probably the Cubs dugout, and umpire Hank O'Day ruled in favor of the Cubs, necessitating a one-game playoff at the end of the season. "Before the game we talked over in the clubhouse how in the world we could get [Frank] Chance out of there," recalled Fred Snodgrass. "Matty was to pitch for us, and Frank always hit Matty pretty well. So it was cooked up that Joe McGinnity was to pick a fight with Chance early in the game. They were to have a knockdown, drag-out fight and both would get thrown out. Of course, we didn't need McGinnity, but they needed Chance. McGinnity did just as he was supposed to. He called Chance names on some pretext or other, stepped on his toes, pushed him, actually spit on him. But Frank wouldn't fight. He was too smart. And they beat us, with Chance getting a key hit."

On February 27, 1909, the Giants finally released McGinnity, but that ended only phase one of his baseball career. He went on to spend another 14 seasons in the minors, becoming part owner and player-manager of teams in Newark, Tacoma, Butte, and Dubuque. At Newark the Iron Man went 29-16 in 1909 and set all-time Eastern League records for innings (422) and shutouts (11). He also continued his doubleheader pitching ways, winning both ends on August 27, 1909, and July 23, 1912. McGinnity racked up five 20-win seasons and one 30-win season in the minors before pitching his last game in Organized Baseball in 1925 at the grand old age of 54, hurling for Springfield, Illinois, where he'd discovered Old Sal some 30 years earlier. In 1926 he joined old teammate Wilbert Robinson as a coach with the Brooklyn Dodgers. In the spring of 1929 Joe was helping out with the Williams College baseball team when he became ill and returned to Brooklyn, where his daughter lived. He died there at age 58 on November 14, 1929, and was buried next to his wife in McAlester. Joe McGinnity was inducted into the National Baseball Hall of Fame in 1946.

MICHAEL WELLS

NEW YORK

Dennis Lawrence "Dan" McGann
First baseman 1902–07

Dan McGann's career closely paralleled that of John McGraw, his teammate, friend, and drinking companion in Baltimore, St. Louis, and New York. Some regarded the 6'0", 190 lb. McGann as the National League's finest first baseman; he batted .292 and averaged 71 RBI and 29 stolen bases in his first eight full seasons, led the NL in being hit by pitches six times, and ranked among the Top 10 in total bases and on-base percentage twice. McGann received even more attention for leading NL first basemen in fielding percentage six times from 1899 to 1906. As his career went into eclipse, however, the big switch-hitter feuded with McGraw and increasingly brooded over his family history of death and violence, eventually taking his own life in 1910 at the age of 39.

Dennis Lawrence McGann was born in Shelbyville, Kentucky, on July 15, 1871. He began his career in professional baseball with his hometown team in the Bluegrass League in 1891. In subsequent years he went on to that league's Harrodsville club, as well as Lexington and Marysville, both in the Kentucky League. McGann spent 1895 with Norfolk-Portsmouth of the Virginia League, playing everywhere except pitcher, catcher, and first base, the position at which he eventually settled. The following year he returned to the Virginia League as Lynchburg's second baseman and put together a tremendous season, batting .346 with 14 home runs and 30 stolen bases in 86 games. When second baseman Bobby Lowe went down with an injury, the Boston Beaneaters purchased McGann's contract in August. The 25-year-old rookie batted .322 with power but committed 21 errors in 43 games.

McGann earned a second chance at the National League after switching to first base and batting .354 with an Eastern League–leading 20 triples for Toronto

in 1897. Joining the legendary Baltimore Orioles, who were coming off a second-place finish after three consecutive NL pennants, Dan replaced Jack Doyle at first base and batted .301 with a career-high 106 RBI, the league's fifth-highest total. In 1899 he became one of many Orioles to transfer from Baltimore to Brooklyn, but he batted just .243 over the season's first half. The Superbas sent him to the Washington Nationals to make room at first base for Hughie Jennings, whose injured arm prevented him from playing shortstop. McGann bounced back to bat .343 for the second half, but after the season the soon-to-be-contracted Nationals sold him and pitcher Gus Weyhing to the St. Louis Cardinals.

In St. Louis McGann was reunited with McGraw. After a pair of solid seasons with the Cardinals, in 1902 the line drive-hitting first baseman jumped to the Baltimore Orioles of the American League, where his former teammate on the old Orioles was serving his second year as player-manager. In July McGraw, feuding with AL president Ban Johnson, jumped to the New York Giants, and McGann followed. In a fateful move, McGraw installed the big veteran at first base and moved Christy Mathewson, who'd playing that position, permanently back to pitcher. McGann won the first of four consecutive NL fielding titles in 1903 and finished the season with 36 stolen bases. The following year he tied for fourth in the NL with 42 steals. On May 27, 1904, McGann became the first player in the modern era to steal five bases in a single game—a feat not matched in the NL until Davey Lopes did it for the Los Angeles Dodgers in 1974, and not surpassed until Atlanta's Otis Nixon swiped six in 1991.

McGann helped McGraw bring to the Giants the rowdy brand of play for which the old Orioles had been famous. Characteristic was a brawl the big first base-man provoked during a 10-2 victory over the Phillies in April 1905. After McGann tried to score from second on a hit and was thrown out at the plate by Sherry Magee, he punched catcher Fred Abbott, who respond-ed by hitting McGann in the back with the ball. The umpire ejected both players. "How long will the National League stand for the hoodlum tactics of this New York team both on and off the field?" railed one Philadelphia newspaper. Hoodlum or not, McGann batted .299 that year with 14 triples as the Giants won their second consecutive NL pennant. In that year's World Series he batted only .235, but in Game Three he drove in four runs on three hits as New York defeated the Philadelphia Athletics.

In 1907 a pitch by Cincinnati's Andy Coakley broke McGann's wrist during spring training. When the veter-an first baseman returned to the Giants in midseason, he was out of shape and his relationship with McGraw became strained. That winter McGraw traded him to Boston in a blockbuster eight-player deal that brought first sacker Fred Tenney to New York. When a reporter pointed out that Tenney, like McGann, was 36 years old, McGraw said that Tenney had taken better care of himself. In 1908 McGann played 135 games for Boston and slumped to .240 with only eight doubles and nine stolen bases. During a game against the Giants in May he grounded into a ninth-inning double play to end a rally. As McGann ran toward first base, McGraw called him a "damned ice wagon!"—a vehicle known for its lack of speed. "That's how the Giants lost a lot of games last season," the Giants manager told reporters after the game, noting that there was no one left on his club who wouldn't have been safe at first on the play. Hearing of McGraw's criticism, McGann went to the Copley Square Hotel that evening and threw a punch at the Giants manager as he played a game of billiards. After Mathewson failed to separate the two, McGraw dashed to his upstairs room with McGann in hot pur-suit, locking himself in. Boston released the first base-man after the season.

McGann spent the next two seasons with Milwaukee of the American Association. One commen-tator called him "perhaps the best known of the men who have sought a refuge in the minor leagues after a thrilling career on the diamonds of the big circuits," but his hitting continued to deteriorate, with his batting average shrinking to a career-low .225 in 1910. According to one report, McGann intended to play for Oakland of the Pacific Coast League in 1911. According to another, he was planning to play for Louisville, near his home in Shelbyville, Kentucky, where he'd accumulated significant real estate and financial holdings.

On the night of December 13, 1910, McGann was found dead in his room in Besler's Hotel in Louisville, with a bullet in his chest and a revolver in his hand. The coroner ruled his death a suicide. Indeed, McGann was said to be preoccupied with the tragic deaths of several close family members. In 1909 one of his brothers had taken his own life. The previous New Year's Eve, another brother had died due to an infection resulting from an accidental shooting. McGann's sister commit-ted suicide in 1890 following the death of their mother. Despite that unfortunate family history, McGann's two surviving sisters believed that he'd been murdered. Missing from his hand was a dia-mond ring worth $800, which witnesses had noticed McGann wearing when he was last seen alive, but a diamond pin, $37 in cash, and a $1,000 promissory note were still on his body when it was found.

DON JENSEN

NEW YORK

LEON KESSLING "RED" AMES
RIGHT-HANDED PITCHER 1903–13

Red Ames's curveball was one of the Deadball Era's most dramatic pitches. "Players say no man who holds a place in the pitcher's box is able to curve the ball so far as he can," wrote *The Sporting Life* in 1906. "It is a fact that he doesn't always know himself where his curves are going to land." Ames carried a reputation for being "liberal with passes," often ranking among the NL leaders in walks per nine innings, and in 1905 he set a dubious modern record by uncorking 30 wild pitches. Despite his frequent bouts of wildness, the right hander managed to hang on for 17 seasons in the National League, compiling a 183-167 record with a 2.63 ERA. He had a knack for losing tough, close games, becoming known as the unluckiest man in baseball—to newspaper reporters and fans his middle initial stood for "Kalamity."

Leon Kessling Ames was born on August 2, 1882, in Warren, Ohio, the old capital of the Western Reserve in the days before Ohio became a state. Leon started pitching professionally in 1901 with Zanesville, Ohio, then went to Ilion of the New York State League for the 1902-03 seasons. In 1903 he was 12-12 with an eye-popping 221 strikeouts in 229 innings, earning a late-season trial with the New York Giants. Though the 5'10½", 185 lb. Ames was dwarfed by the strapping specimens on John McGraw's pitching staff, he made the most of his opportunity by tossing five hitless innings against the St. Louis Cardinals on September 14, 1903. The umpire called the game due to darkness and an impending storm, giving Ames an auspicious win in his major league debut. When he pitched a complete-game five-hitter in his next start, the 21-year-old rookie put himself in position to win a job the following season.

After a year as a spot starter for the 1904 pennant winners, Ames enjoyed one of his most successful sea-sons in 1905, posting a nine-game winning streak and a 22-8 record with a 2.74 ERA and 198 strikeouts in 262⅔ innings. In that year's World Series, however, he pitched only one inning of relief as McGraw went with his stalwarts, Christy Mathewson and Joe McGinnity. Though Ames continued to pitch effectively for the Giants through the beginning of 1913, he never again won more than 15 games in a single season. The only year from 1905 to 1917 in which he failed to reach double digits in victories, however, was 1908. That year Ames missed several months with a kidney ailment but returned late in the season and, in the words of one reporter, "pitched as no one imagined he would ever learn to do." Under the excruciating pressure of the most exciting pennant race in history, he won seven of eight decisions in September and October, giving the Giants a second reliable pitcher behind Mathewson. "When Ames has control—and he has it these days—there is no beating him," wrote one New York reporter. Another wrote: "It is safe to say that McGraw and his Giants would have been in a sorry case in the last 10 days of the desperate fighting had it not been for the splendid work of Leon Ames."

Ames was most effective in cold weather. That trait, combined with McGraw's reluctance to pitch Mathewson on Opening Day, led to Red receiving the honor of starting the season opener three years in a row. It was in those games, however, that his hard-luck streak emerged. On April 15, 1909, he held Brooklyn hitless for nine innings at the Polo Grounds, but Kaiser Wilhelm of the Superbas kept the Giants' bats almost as cold and the game went into extra innings. Ames gave up a hit to Whitey Alperman with one out in the 10th but kept the shutout going through the 12th. In the 13th, however, Brooklyn scored three runs to win the contest. In the 1910 opener, Ames matched up against Al Mattern, a Boston pitcher who always was tough on the Giants. Red held Boston hitless for seven innings and still held a 2-1 lead with two outs in the ninth and the bases empty. The Doves tied the game with a walk and two singles, then won it in the 11th on a Giant error. Ames' string of bad-luck openers continued on April 12, 1911, when he held the Phillies hitless for six innings and scoreless for eight. With two out in the ninth, Fred Luderus doubled home the only two runs of the game to win it for the Phils and Earl Moore, who'd stymied the Giants completely.

"Leon Ames stacks up against the toughest luck of any pitcher in the big show," claimed the *New York Times* on August 13, 1911. The day before, Ames had lost a tough game to Philadelphia, 2-0, at the Polo Grounds, dropping his record to 5-9. In four of those losses the Giants scored two runs or less. The *Times* pleaded: "Won't someone please send Mr. Ames the left hind foot of a churchyard rabbit, a few swastika pins and some old rusty horseshoes?" Ames was discouraged on the eve of the Giants' final road trip. "I don't see any use in taking me along, Mac," he told McGraw. "The club can't win with me pitching if the other guys don't even get a foul." Red went along anyway, and in his mail on September 11 he received a necktie and four-leaf clover sent by an unnamed "prominent actress." Ames was to wear the tie with his street clothes and conceal it under his uniform during games. He followed instructions and won his next start easily. That night at dinner Red pointed to the tie and declared, "I don't change her until I lose." The Giants posted a sparkling 19-4 record on that road trip, clinching the pennant, with Ames contributing four victories in five starts (the Giants won the fifth start, in St. Louis, in the 10th inning).

Ames was a solid contributor to the 1911-12 pennant winners, taking his turn in the rotation in cool weather and pitching in relief as temperatures rose. On May 22, 1913, the Giants sent him, Heinie Groh, Art Devore, and $20,000 to the Reds for Art Fromme and Eddie Grant. Red started regularly in Cincinnati and pitched well for a couple of years, hurling a career-high 297 innings in 1914, when he posted a 15-23 record and contributed a league-leading six saves. After a poor start in 1915 prompted his sale to St.

Louis on July 24, Ames became the Cardinals' most effective pitcher during the second half, going 9-3 with a 2.46 ERA. He remained a valuable member of their pitching staff through the end of the 1918 season, starting as well as relieving and leading the league in saves again with eight in 1916. Time finally caught up with the 36-year-old Ames in 1919, when he split the season between St. Louis and Philadelphia and was pounded for 114 hits in 86 innings.

Red caught on with Kansas City of the American Association, winning a combined 33 games in 1920-21 before drawing his release early in 1922. He pitched briefly for Daytona of the Florida State League in 1923 before retiring to his hometown of Warren. Leon and his wife, Rena, had one son, Leon Jr., who pitched in the minors until 1929. While working for a Warren dairy company, Red damaged his lungs when he accidentally inhaled ammonia fumes emanating from a defective drum. After a lingering illness, he died on October 8, 1936, at the age of 54.

R. J. LESCH

NEW YORK

John Tomlinson Brush
Owner 1903–12

A sufferer from locomotor ataxia, a painful disease of the nervous system that caused him to walk with two canes, John T. Brush overcame his infirmity to become a successful retail magnate and owner of the New York Giants from 1903 until his death in 1912. Though the Giants became the most valuable franchise in professional sports during his tenure, and he was generally regarded as the most influential magnate in the National League's executive sessions, Brush was not well liked by players or the press. "Chicanery is the ozone which keeps his old frame from snapping," wrote one critic, "and dark-lantern methods the food which vitalizes his bodily tissues."

John Tomlinson Brush (some suggested the T stood for "Tooth") was born in Clintonville, New York, on June 15, 1845. Orphaned at age four, John lived with his grandfather until going to Boston at age 17 to seek his fortune in the clothing business. After serving with the First New York Artillery during the Civil War, he opened a department store in Indianapolis when he was 30 years old. Brush's first contact with baseball came in 1887, when he bought into the upstart Indianapolis Hoosiers of the National League as a means of advertising his store. In 1889 he formulated the "Brush Classification Plan," under which players were placed into one of five groupings based on both on- and off-field performance. Each class had a corresponding salary cap—Class A players could earn $2,500 annually, and the salaries decreased $250 in each lower class so that Class E players could earn $1,500. The plan, which was approved by Brush's fellow owners, caused a backlash among the players, leading directly to the formation of John Montgomery Ward's Players League.

The NL dropped Indianapolis in 1890, so Brush bought stock in the New York Giants and became owner of the Cincinnati Reds the following year. In Cincinnati he came under fire from Ban Johnson, then a local sportswriter. When the newly formed Western League was searching for a president in 1894, Brush interceded to make sure Johnson got the job, thus ending criticism from the young reporter's pen. The two continued to lock horns, however. Brush still owned stock in the Indianapolis franchise of the American Association, and Johnson criticized his shady dealings involving the rosters of the AA Hoosiers and the NL Reds. The upshot was that the Cincinnati owner was forced to sell his stock in the Indy club. Prior to the 1898 season Brush floated another "Brush Rule" past his fellow owners, this one stating that any player who addressed an umpire or fellow player in a "villainously filthy" manner would be brought before a three-man disciplinary board and banished for life if found guilty. The players received the rule about as well as Brush's 1889 edict limiting their salaries, and it had about the same lasting impact.

In 1901 Brush attended a meeting with fellow NL owners Andrew Freedman of New York, Frank Robison of St. Louis, and Arthur Soden of Boston at Freedman's estate in Red Bank, New Jersey. Earlier that same quartet had decried syndicate baseball, but now they were formulating a plan for an even larger syndicate, the National League Base Ball Trust, which would hire all managers and assign players to teams that would no longer be individually owned. The four robber barons proposed that the former owners would hold shares in the trust, with Freedman receiving a 30% share, his three compatriots receiving 12% each, and those not present receiving less (the Brooklyn ownership would receive only 6%). The syndicate plan died on the vine because, not surprisingly, it didn't gain the fifth vote necessary for approval.

On August 12, 1902, Giants owner Freedman anounced, "I will turn the inside affairs of the business over to Mr. Brush, as I have little or no time to give to baseball, while Mr. Brush will be able to devote practically all his time to the game." In retrospect it seems clear that Brush favored New York all along. In 1900 the Giants purchased Christy Mathewson from Norfolk of the Virginia League. When the rookie did nothing to distinguish himself in three games, Freedman sent him back to Norfolk, where he went 21-2. After the season Brush drafted him for the Reds, then "traded" him to the Giants for sore-armed Amos Rusie, who hadn't pitched since 1898. Mathewson, of course, went on to win 372 games for New York, while Rusie didn't win a single game for Cincinnati.

Brush purchased the Giants outright from Freedman in 1903. At the time the department-store mogul still owned the Reds and also had shares in the American League's Baltimore Orioles, and the rash of personnel transactions that preceded the sale of his Cincinnati and Baltimore shares positioned New York to be a juggernaut for the first third of the 20th century. The most important of those moves was the signing of John McGraw away from his own Orioles to manage the Giants, but Brush also orchestrated the releases from their Baltimore contracts of future Hall of Famers Roger Bresnahan and Joe McGinnity, both of whom signed with New York. When the loaded Giants ran away with the NL pennant the following year, Brush (with prodding from McGraw) became responsible for the cancellation of the 1904 World Series. "There is nothing in the constitution or playing rules of the National League which requires its victorious club to submit its championship honors to a contest with a victorious club in a minor league," he announced.

Just after midnight on April 14, 1911, a night watchman on the elevated train tracks adjacent to the Polo Grounds saw flames in the bleachers in right cen-

ter field, probably the result of a cigarette discarded by a fan during the Giants' 6-1 loss to the Phillies the previous day. Before the horse-drawn fire engines arrived, the blaze spread into the main grandstand and enveloped the entire ballpark; nothing could be saved except a section of outfield bleachers. The next day, accompanied by a group of reporters and pushed along in a wheelchair by his second wife, stage actress Elsie Lombard, who was 25 years his junior, Brush showed up at the smoldering remains of his ballpark to assess the damage. "Elsie," he said, "I want to build a concrete stand. The finest that can be constructed. It will mean economy for a time. Are you willing to stand by me?" Brush's architects started working on the blueprints immediately, and in May the team held a press conference to unveil the plans for "Brush Stadium," a concrete-and-steel structure with a seating capacity of over 40,000.

Though the new name never caught on—everyone continued to call it the Polo Grounds—the new ballpark was hailed at its opening in August 1911 as a monument to the man who had built it. "As one amusement man of world-wide experience, who stood and marveled, remarked: 'Why, Mr. Brush, you have thrown 30 theatres into one and put them all into a 10-acre lot,'" wrote Baseball Magazine. "There is another effect about the new stadium which no theatre could ever have. This feature is its massive beauty. Take it away from the background of the lofty rocky bluff behind it, and stretch it on a plain, and it would command the same air of respect that is held by the pyramids built in all their silent grandeur on the shifting sand of the desert. There is nothing like it in baseball, and even New York, with all of its marvels, pauses a moment to take a fresh breath and brag about the 'biggest baseball yard in the world.'"

Brush lived to see his Giants play in three World Series (1905, 1911, and 1912). Shortly after the last of those fall classics, he was thrown from an automobile in Harlem and sustained a serious hip injury. On November 26, 1912, while aboard a train to a sanatorium in Southern California to recuperate, Brush died while passing through Missouri. His obituary in the New York Times described him as "one of the wisest and ablest counselors in the National League."

JOHN SACCOMAN

NEW YORK

ARTHUR McARTHUR DEVLIN
THIRD BASEMAN 1904–11

Art Devlin didn't create headlines, just wins. The feisty Devlin was an above-average base runner and solid right-handed hitter with a lifetime batting average of .269 who bunted well and executed the hit-and-run play to perfection. Generally considered the best third baseman of his day, the 6'0", 175 lb. former collegian led the National League in assists in three of his eight seasons as a regular, and in 1908 he also led the league in putouts and fielding percentage. Devlin ranks among the Top 20 third basemen of all time in total chances per game. Famed sportswriters Frank Graham and Grantland Rice both considered him the Giants' all-time greatest third baseman.

One of several children of Edward Devlin, an Irish immigrant who worked as a harness maker and locksmith, Arthur McArthur Devlin was born in Washington, D.C., on October 16, 1879. In the fall of 1899 Art enrolled at Georgetown University, showing early talent on both the baseball and football teams. In the latter sport he started at halfback but was switched to fullback to make better use of his size; football historian Morris Bealle named him the fullback on the all-time Georgetown team. Art also stood out for the baseball Hoyas, usually playing first base. After his sophomore year he left Georgetown to play professional baseball in Wilmington, North Carolina, appearing at every position except pitcher and catcher. In 1902 Devlin moved up to the high minors with Newark and settled in at third base, posting a breakout season the following year when he batted .287 and stole 51 bases to rank among the Eastern League's leaders in the latter category. New York Giants manager

John McGraw scouted him, liked what he saw, and purchased his contract.

Devlin joined the Giants in 1904 to a less than rousing welcome, with teammates and opponents initially dismissing him as "McGraw's college boy." He put together an impressive spring training, however, sparing his manager from having to play third base himself. Devlin made his major league debut in Brooklyn on April 14, going hitless but handling four chances at third base in a 7-1 victory. Many sources erroneously state that he hit a grand slam in his first major league at-bat. The 24-year-old rookie did connect for a bases-loaded home run at the Polo Grounds off John Brackenridge of the Phillies, but it occurred on April 22, after he'd already played a week with the Giants. Devlin made four hits in five at-bats that day; the grand slam was his only home run of the season and one of just 10 in his career, but Art helped the Giants win the pennant by batting .281 with 66 RBI and 33 steals.

Slipping a bit in his sophomore year, Devlin batted .246 but stole a league-leading 59 bases (tying Billy Maloney of the Cubs), the only time he ever led the NL in a significant offensive category. He bounced back to enjoy his best season in 1906, both on the field and off. Devlin posted career highs in batting average (.299), on-base percentage (.396), and slugging percentage (.390), and his 54 stolen bases ranked third in the NL behind Frank Chance and Sherry Magee. Besides fielding everything that came his way, Art snagged a bride—Ilma Wilk (the daughter of Frederick Wilk, the vice-president of the Union Trust Company), whom he'd met during his

Georgetown days. One newspaper announced: RICH BRIDE FOR PLAYER. The subheading specified: DEVLIN, OF NEW YORK GIANTS, TO WED WEALTHY CHICAGO GIRL. The couple married on Thanksgiving Day.

At the start of 1908, his fifth season with the club, Devlin was the senior member of the infield in terms of longevity with the Giants. On May 23 of that season he tied a record by handling 13 chances at third base, but his two errors helped the St. Louis Cardinals win, 6-2. The errors and the loss were bad enough, given the outcome of the season, but Art made one off the field, too. With the Giants seemingly in first place for good, Harry Niemeyer of the *New York Globe* reported from Pittsburgh on August 26 that the players were spending their World Series money before getting it, with Devlin promising his wife a Persian lamb coat. He played in all 157 games that season, batting .253 and stealing just 19 bases, but his wife went coatless when the Giants lost to the Chicago Cubs in a one-game playoff.

Like his manager and many of his Giant teammates, Devlin was frequently ejected. Perhaps the worst of his transgressions as a player occurred on June 23, 1910. The Giants were beating the Superbas at Washington Park in Brooklyn when a fan, according to *The Sporting Life*, hollered, "Devlin, you dog, will you never stop?" A nearby youngster translated the epithet as "Yellow Dog," bringing Devlin into the stands. Larry Doyle and Josh Devore followed. Everybody got into it, including McGraw, before Bill Klem "butted in as a peacemaker." All three players were thrown out of the game. Devlin was arrested and arraigned the next day, as one Bernard J. Rossier Jr. charged him with assault and planned to sue him for $5,000 in damages. NL president Thomas Lynch suspended Devlin and fined Doyle and Devore $50 each for being accessories.

Devlin played solid ball in 1909-10 but began to decline in 1911 as his legs started to go bad. He lost his starting position to Buck Herzog and appeared in just 95 games, not playing at all in that year's World Series. To make a bad year worse, Art and Ilma separated that December and eventually divorced. She moved back to Chicago, where her father said, "I have heard stories that Devlin has not been doing the right thing by her." That same month the Giants sold Devlin to the cellar-dwelling Boston Rustlers. He played a significant number of games at every infield position other than second base in 1912, batting .289 in 124 games. The following year the 33-year-old Devlin slumped to a career-low .229 in his final season in the majors, though he went out in style by slapping a game-winning single in the ninth inning to beat the Pittsburgh Pirates on August 25. That night manager George Stallings sent him to Rochester of the International League in exchange for a pitcher named George Davis. "I wonder where they would have sent me if I'd struck out—Medicine Hat?" quipped Devlin.

No playing record exists for Devlin in 1914, though he managed the last-place Oakland Oaks of the Pacific Coast League for part of that season. In 1915-16 he played third base for Montreal and Rochester in the International League, and the following two years he was player-manager for Norfolk of the Virginia League. Devlin held coaching jobs with the Giants, Braves, and Pirates from 1919 through 1935. While with the Giants in 1921, Art tried to convince McGraw to sign a Columbia University student named Louis Gehrig; when Gehrig failed to impress Mac in a brief tryout at the Polo Grounds, Art found the young slugger his first job in professional baseball with Hartford of the Eastern League. Accounts suggest that Devlin hardly mellowed as he grew older. Coaching third base for the Braves on July 25, 1926, he was riding Cincinnati Reds third baseman Babe Pinelli, who brushed against him while leaving the field after the third inning. The 46-year-old Devlin took a swing at the 30-year-old Pinelli, igniting one of the fiercest brawls in baseball history.

Devlin held a variety of jobs after leaving professional baseball, including a position with the Home Owners Loan Corporation in Washington during World War II. He also was involved in an executive capacity with a semipro baseball league in northern New Jersey. Toward the end of his life Art worked in a hospital in Hudson County, where one of his fellow employees was Danny Murphy, his opponent from the 1905 World Series. Art's second wife, the former Gertrude Griffin, died on August 16, 1948. Despondent and in ill health, Art Devlin died in Jersey City on September 18, 1948. He is buried in Congressional Cemetery in Washington.

JAN FINKEL

NEW YORK

George LeRoy "Hooks" Wiltse
Left-handed pitcher 1904–14

The only left hander who pitched regularly for John McGraw's Giants until Rube Marquard joined the rotation in 1909, George Wiltse was known as "Hooks," not for his ability to curve a baseball, or for his hook nose, but for his fielding prowess. One story credits catcher Frank Bowerman with saying "that's hooking 'em" after Wiltse used his long right arm to snare a shot hit back through the middle, while another says that it was a manager in Syracuse who said Wiltse had hooks for hands after watching him work out at first base. A lean six-footer with deep-set eyes and a wad of tobacco usually in his mouth (he pitched poorly against the Cincinnati Reds on June 19, 1905, reportedly because he swallowed a quid and suffered an upset stomach), Wiltse won in double figures each of his first eight seasons with the Giants, compiling a 139-90 record and 2.47 ERA over 12 seasons in the major leagues.

George LeRoy Wiltse was born on September 7, 1880, on the family farm in Pecksport, New York, but record books list his birthplace as Hamilton, the nearest town and the site of Colgate University. The youngest of nine children, seven of them boys, George got his start in baseball by joining his brother Lewis, also a left hander, in throwing baseballs against the barn door. Their father put a stop to barn damage by moving his family to Syracuse, where they entered the carpet business. In 1901 Lewis Wiltse became a major league pitcher, winning one game for the eventual National League champion Pittsburgh Pirates before his sale to Connie Mack's Philadelphia team in the new American League. Dubbed "Snake," Lewis went 13-5 for the Athletics and won eight more games for them in 1902 before being sent to the Baltimore Orioles. His major league career ended after four appearances for the New York Highlanders in 1903.

By that time George was a professional too, having launched his career with Scranton of the independent Pennsylvania State League in 1902. He was with the team a month and went 3-3, going home to Syracuse when the league disbanded in June. From there George signed with the visiting Troy team of the New York State League, receiving $25 to pitch against the Syracuse Stars on June 19, 1902. Wearing his Scranton uniform, he impressed his hometown crowd with flashy fielding and three hits (teammate Johnny Evers knocked out four), but Syracuse won the game with a ninth-inning rally. Torn between baseball and selling carpets, Wiltse opted to sign with Troy for $275 a month, playing the outfield part-time while compiling a 7-15 pitching record. In 1903 he improved to 20-8 with Troy, and that winter his contract was sold to the New York Giants.

Wiltse made one of the strongest first impressions in major league history, going 12-0 in his first 12 decisions with the 1904 Giants, a record that remains unbroken and wasn't even tied until San Diego Padres reliever Butch Metzger won his first dozen decisions in 1974-76. Wiltse debuted on Opening Day, April 21, but didn't receive his first start until May 29, when he contributed two hits to a 5-3 victory over Brooklyn. He shut out the Superbas on three hits in his second start on June 19, and from then on he took his regular turn, keeping his winning streak alive until a 7-3 loss to Cincinnati on September 22. Wiltse finished his rookie year with a 13-3 record and 2.84 ERA, continuing his good fortune by marrying Della Schaffer in November. The following season, as the number five pitcher on McGraw's staff, Hooks went 15-6 with a 2.47 ERA, then sat on the bench and watched his roommate, Christy Mathewson, pitch the Giants to the 1905 world championship. Over the next two years Wiltse won a combined 29 games, etching his name into the record book again on May 15, 1906, by striking out seven batters in two innings (after striking out three Reds in the fourth inning, he got four more in the fifth because catcher Roger Bresnahan dropped strike three on the leadoff hitter, Jim Delahanty).

Hooks Wiltse's best season was 1908, when he replaced Joe McGinnity as the Giants' number two starter behind Mathewson. Setting career highs in games (44), starts (38), complete games (30), and shutouts (7), Wiltse compiled a 23-14 record with a 2.24 ERA. On July 4, 1908, in the first game of a doubleheader against Philadelphia, he pitched one of the greatest games in baseball history. Hooks retired the first 26 Phillies in a row before facing the opposing pitcher, George McQuillan, who'd also pitched scoreless baseball. With a 1-2 count, Wiltse threw what appeared to be strike three, but umpire Cy Rigler, who later admitted he'd made a mistake, called it a ball. The next pitch hit McQuillan, and Hooks had to settle for a 10-inning no-hitter instead of a perfect game when the Giants scored a run for him in the top half of the inning. If that was the high point of 1908, the low point had to be September 23, when Fred Merkle's failure to touch second base on a game-winning hit cost the Giants a key victory over the Cubs. Wiltse was the first-base coach, and years later he told an interviewer, "There is no doubt that Merkle missed touching second base. Still, nobody knows whether the Cubs ever got the official baseball into second base to force Merkle because of the mass confusion."

In 1909 Wiltse went 20-11 with a 2.00 ERA but proved unable to maintain the workload of 1908, developing a reputation as a cold-weather pitcher who wore down as the summer went on. The year he turned 30, 1910, was the last time he pitched over 200 innings in a season, finishing with a 14-12 record and 2.72 ERA. Used judiciously

by McGraw, Hooks continued to make solid contributions. In 1911 he went 12-9 in the regular season and pitched twice in relief in the World Series, giving up seven runs to the winning Athletics in the Game Six finale. Hooks didn't play at all in the 1912 World Series but enjoyed one of his greatest moments in the 1913 Fall Classic. After pitching sparingly during the regular season (57⅔ innings with a 1.56 ERA but no decisions), Wiltse filled in at first base in Game Two at Philadelphia when injuries felled Merkle and Fred Snodgrass. In the bottom of the ninth inning of a scoreless game, Athletic baserunners reached second and third with nobody out. The next two batters slashed grounders at Wiltse, who both times snared the ball and cut down the potential winning run at the plate. The Giants won the game in the 10th inning, 3-0, but went on to lose the World Series for the third consecutive year.

In 1914 Wiltse was 1-1 in 20 games, all in relief, before the Giants released him on August 29. After starting the 1915 season with Jersey City of the International League, he finished out his major league career by making 18 appearances for Brooklyn of the Federal League, going 3-5 but with five saves. Hooks pitched, managed, and played first base in the minors through 1924, mainly with Buffalo of the International League. In 1925 Miller Huggins brought him back to New York as pitching coach for the Yankees, just in time for Babe Ruth's bellyache to mire the team in the second division. Wiltse retired from baseball after spending 1926 back in the International League with Reading. Returning to his home in Syracuse, he sold real estate and got involved in politics, serving as an alderman in 1932-33 and as deputy assessor from 1934 to 1944. Hooks Wiltse died from emphysema at age 78 on January 21, 1959, in Long Beach, New York.

GABRIEL SCHECHTER

NEW YORK

MICHAEL JOSEPH DONLIN
OUTFIELDER 1904–06, 1908, 1911, 1914

A flamboyant playboy and partygoer who dressed impeccably and had a quip and a handshake for everyone he met, Mike Donlin was "one of the most picturesque, most written-about, most likeable athletes that ever cut his mark on the big circuit." Donlin also could hit as well as anyone in baseball during the Deadball Era. Though he rarely walked, the powerfully built 5'9" left hander was a masterful curveball hitter with power to all fields. His career slugging percentage of .468 compares favorably to better-known contemporaries Honus Wagner (.466) and Sam Crawford (.452), and his .333 lifetime batting average might have earned him a spot in the Hall of Fame had he sustained it over a longer career. But Donlin wasn't serious about the game, and his love of the bottle and frequent stints in vaudeville limited him to the equivalent of only seven full seasons.

Michael Joseph Donlin was born on May 30, 1878, in Peoria, Illinois, but grew up in Erie, Pennsylvania. When he was eight his parents, railroad conductor John Donlin and his wife, Maggie, were killed in a bridge collapse. Forced to hustle for a living, young Mike worked as a machinist and was often in poor health, with a concave chest due to consumption. At 15 he got a job as a candy seller on a California–bound train. Mike remained in California, where he ran footraces and played baseball. Primarily a left-handed pitcher who also played some outfield, Donlin starred for Los Angeles in 1897 and the Santa Cruz Sandcrabs in 1898-99. Even early in his career he was mindful of the value of publicity. While with the Sandcrabs Donlin gave a photo of himself to San Francisco Examiner artist Hype Igoe, saying: "If you put a picture of me in the paper, I know I'll get a break." University of Oregon coach Tom Kelly recalled pitching against Mike a month after Admiral Dewey's victory at Manila Bay. Donlin's bat was painted red, white, and blue, and he called it "Dewey." Kelly described him as "the typical wild Irish kid, imbued with natural baseball sense and confidence."

Halfway through the 1899 season, Donlin had appeared in 29 games for Santa Cruz and was batting .402. A correspondent for The Sporting News sent clippings about him to editor Joe Flanner in St. Louis, who passed them on to Cardinals player-manager Patsy Tebeau. St. Louis acquired Donlin for little more than train fare. Mike learned he was going to the National League while locked up for drunkenness in a Santa Cruz jail. He reported to League Park in St. Louis wearing a newspaper photo of himself clipped to his lapel. When the gatekeeper refused him entry, he proclaimed, "I am Mike Donlin," and pointed to the clipping. In his debut on July 19, 1899, Donlin pitched in relief against Boston. Afterward, hearing Tebeau needed a shortstop, the left hander volunteered and handled a dozen chances in his first game. "I was swelled on myself at shortstop that first day," he recalled. The next day, in front of a big crowd, Donlin mishandled every chance and made several wild throws. He was moved to first base in the fifth inning and had trouble there, too. After a few days Tebeau put Donlin in the outfield, where he played for most of his career despite a continuing reputation for subpar defense. He batted .323 for the Cardinals in

1899 and .326 in 1900. Donlin went on to bat over .300 in 10 of his 12 seasons.

In 1901 Mike Donlin jumped to the American League with the Baltimore Orioles. He soon became friends with his new manager, John McGraw, who admired the young slugger's fiery temperament. One day in Detroit, Baltimore pitcher Harry Howell was ejected for arguing a call, and Donlin responded by firing a ball at the umpire's back. Of course Donlin's prowess at the plate also helped his standing with McGraw. On June 24, 1901, he got six hits in six at-bats: two singles, two doubles, and two triples. Donlin batted .340 in his first season as a regular, and his future seemed unlimited. But in March 1902 Mike went on a drinking binge in Baltimore, urinating in public and accosting two chorus girls. He was sentenced to six months in prison and the Orioles released him. Paroled a month early for good behavior, Donlin joined the Cincinnati Reds in August, appearing in 34 games and batting just .287.

In 1903 Mike Donlin stayed out of trouble and almost won the NL batting crown, hitting .351 to Honus Wagner's .355. He also finished second in the league in runs (110) and triples (18), and third in slugging (.516). The next spring Donlin and some teammates were carousing in a bar during spring training in Augusta, Georgia, when a customer, irritated by Donlin's singing, pulled a revolver on him. Manager Joe Kelley might have saved Mike's life by spiriting him away. That summer Donlin was hitting .356 when he went on another bender in St. Louis. Kelley suspended him for 30 days, then traded him to the New York Giants, reuniting him with McGraw.

Donlin asked New York sportswriters to give him an even break, promising: "If you treat me right, I'll be on the up and up." He had little need to worry. Slashing pitches into the gaps, running the bases with reckless abandon, and arguing incessantly with the umpires, Donlin became the baseball idol of Manhattan. Because of his strutting walk and red neck, he was dubbed "Turkey"—a nickname he hated, but he had such a following that kids imitated his strut. When the Giants won their first pennant of the Deadball Era in 1904, Donlin was the offensive star, his .329 average ranking second in the NL behind Wagner. The following year he was named captain and enjoyed his greatest season, batting a career-high .356, third best in the NL. Donlin

led the league with 124 runs and was second with 216 hits. The Giants won the pennant again, and Donlin hit .263 in the World Series.

On April 11, 1906, Donlin married actress Mabel Hite, a stunning Broadway musical-comedy sensation. Newspapers reported that marriage had tamed him, loosening his attachment to the bottle. Early that season Donlin broke his ankle sliding, finishing his season at 37 games and forever depriving him of his blazing speed. In the spring of 1907 he demanded the same $3,300 he'd been paid in 1906, plus a $600 bonus if he stayed sober all year. Owner John Brush declined. Mike held out and eventually went on the vaudeville circuit with his wife, missing the entire season. With characteristic confidence he proclaimed: "I can act. I'll break the hearts of all the gals in the country." Critics generally disagreed. One said that Donlin "never was the actor he thought he was or wanted to be."

Donlin returned to the Giants for the 1908 season. Huge ovations greeted him at the home opener, with bleacherites yelling, "Oh you Mabel's Mike!" In the ninth inning the Giants were down by a run with two outs and a man on second. Donlin worked the pitcher to a full count, then homered into the right-field bleachers to win the game. Thousands of fans mobbed the field, slapping him on his back as he rounded the bases, taking his cap and ripping the buttons off his shirt. It was the beginning of another great season for Donlin, who finished second in the NL in batting average (.334), hits (198), RBI (106), and slugging percentage (.452). After the season he received the *New York Journal* trophy as New York's most popular player. John Barrymore, one of Donlin's best friends, performed Hamlet's soliloquy at a dinner in his honor.

On October 26, 1908, Hite and Donlin's one-act play, *Stealing Home*, opened at the Hammerstein Theater in New York. Though the play was acclaimed, reviews for the ballplayer-turned-actor were mixed. *Variety* raved: "Mike Donlin as a polite comedian is quite the most delightful vaudeville surprise you ever enjoyed." But another critic wrote, "Hite was so good she could carry him." For the next three winters the pair performed *Stealing Home* in front of sold-out houses from Boston to San Francisco. Donlin vowed never to return to baseball because he was making more money in show business. One of the greatest players of his era missed two more seasons during his prime. By 1911, however, *Stealing Home* finally had run its course and Hite's other vaudeville ventures were floundering, so Donlin returned to baseball. His lengthy hiatus took its toll. Mike had as many arguments as hits for the Giants, and on August 1, 1911, he was sold to the lowly Boston Rustlers. Donlin played center field and batted .315, but the Rustlers didn't need an aging star and his salary demands, so they traded him to Pittsburgh. In 1912 Mike played 77 games for the Pirates, 51 of them in right field, and hit .316.

That fall Hite was diagnosed with cancer. She died in December 1912, the same month the Pirates put Donlin on waivers. Philadelphia claimed him but he announced his retirement. Late in the summer of 1913 Donlin attempted a comeback,

With his cap at a belligerent angle, a scar on his cheek from a knifing, and usually with a plug of tobacco in his jaw, Mike Donlin could look the part of a rugged Deadballer.

playing 36 games with minor league Jersey City. McGraw invited him on a post-season barnstorming tour through Europe, Asia, and Africa. Based on Donlin's hitting on the tour, McGraw decided to give his old friend another chance. "The Apollo of the whackstick is back with the Giants," exclaimed the *New York World*. But the erstwhile star was washed up at age 36, managing only five hits in 31 at-bats, all as a pinch-hitter.

In October 1914 Mike married Rita Ross, a member of the famed musical-comedy team Ross & Fenton. He returned to vaudeville, pairing up with New York Yankees pitcher Marty McHale, but their act flopped. In 1915 Donlin started his movie career, starring in a film about his own life called *Right Off the Bat*. In 1916 he managed a semipro team in New Jersey and the next winter ran a baseball clinic and a boxing tournament in Cuba. In 1917 Donlin managed the Memphis Chicks of the Southern Association. At first he was popular with the fans, but they booed him when he put himself in to pitch and made a farce of the game. He quit the Chicks—or by some accounts was fired—in midseason. Later that year the War Department appointed him to teach baseball to U.S. soldiers in France. In 1918 Donlin returned to California as a scout for the Boston Braves. He got into Hollywood movies, helped by his friend Barrymore. Mike appeared with the great actor in the 1918 film *Raffles*, and his later roles included parts in Buster Keaton's classic *The General*, in which he played a Union general, and *The Sea Beast*, a *Moby Dick* adaptation in which Barrymore played Ahab. He was always in demand as as a consultant for baseball movies.

Donlin had chronic money troubles and was constantly scraping for jobs in baseball and acting. In 1927 actors and movie stars staged a minstrel show to raise money to send him to the Mayo Clinic for a major operation. One of Mike's last movie roles was in 1933's *Air Hostess*. That spring he still wanted to get back into baseball, asking a friend if he could get a coaching job with the Giants. A heart attack took Turkey Mike Donlin in his sleep on September 24, 1933.

MICHAEL BETZOLD

NEW YORK

Larry Doyle

Lawrence Joseph Doyle
Second baseman 1907–16, 1918–20

A left-handed hitter with power and speed who batted .290 over 14 seasons in the National League, "Laughing Larry" Doyle carried an unusually potent bat for a Deadball Era second baseman, but he's as well-known today for his kindly nature and sunny disposition. "It's great to be young and a New York Giant," he famously remarked to Damon Runyon in 1911, when he helped his team to its first of three consecutive NL pennants. Popular with teammates and manager John McGraw, Doyle was the Giants field captain for more than five years, and filled in as the team's manager when McGraw was ejected or suspended. "Doyle is easily the best ball player on the Giants, a hustling, aggressive, McGraw style of player, full of nerve, grit and true courage," wrote Hugh Fullerton in 1912. "I think he is gamer than his manager, and in some respects a better baseball general."

The son of a coal miner, Lawrence Joseph Doyle was born on July 31, 1886, in Caseyville, Illinois. For five years Larry worked as a coal digger in the mines near Breese, Illinois, 39 miles east of St. Louis. "When you first go down into the earth there comes a sudden realization of what might happen to you," he wrote in 1908. "Nowadays the mines can be lighted by electricity, and it's comparatively simple to go through a mine. But when you get caught without a light in some deep labyrinth in the bowels of the earth, it's no picnic." Larry played semipro baseball on weekends, earning anywhere from nothing to $2 per game, depending on the size of the audience. In 1906 he quit mining to play professionally for Mattoon, Illinois, of the Kitty League. Larry gained an appreciation for the relative safety of his new profession when six miners lost their lives on Christmas Eve in what came to be known as the 1906 Breese Mining Disaster.

After a year in the Kitty League, Doyle spent the first half of 1907 playing third base for Springfield of the Three-I League, batting .290 in 66 games. The club president was Dick Kinsella, the portly proprietor of a Springfield paint shop. Kinsella parlayed Doyle's talents into a lively bidding war, with the Detroit Tigers and Washington Senators each offering $4,000. McGraw raised the bid to $4,500 after receiving a favorable report from old teammate Dan Brouthers, whom he'd dispatched to the Illinois capital to look over the 20-year-old Doyle. At the time $4,500 was the highest price ever paid for a minor leaguer, but the Giants shattered the record a year later by paying $11,000 for Rube Marquard, with Kinsella again brokering the transaction. "Sinister Dick," as he was called because of his dark complexion, went on to a long and successful career as a scout for the Giants, discovering Ross Youngs among others.

Doyle arrived in New York on July 21, 1907. "The train from Springfield dumped me off in Jersey City because Grand Central wasn't even built then," he recalled. "When I got off the ferry, I walked over to a cop. 'How do I get to the Polo Grounds?' I asked. 'See that El over there? Take it to the last stop,' he said. I got off at the last stop and looked around. I didn't see any Polo Grounds. All I saw was the ocean. I was at South Ferry, the wrong end of the line." Larry started his first major league game the next day against the Chicago Cubs, playing second base for the first time ever in his professional career. In the seventh inning, with Frank Chance on third base, the nervous rookie fielded Artie Hofman's slow roller and hesitated, unsure whether to throw to first or home. Chance scored, putting the Cubs ahead 2-0, which ended up the final score. Doyle wasn't charged with an error, and Chance's run was merely insurance, but later generations of sportswriters exaggerated Larry's performance into an almost mythical example of first-game jitters, with Larry booting the ball all over the field and costing the Giants a victory. Though he wasn't nearly that bad, he still was disappointed. McGraw patted him on the back and said, "Forget it. When you learn more about second, you won't make mistakes like that."

Replacing the 38-year-old Tommy Corcoran in the everyday lineup for the rest of the season, Doyle batted .260 with only three extra-base hits in 227 at-bats. He committed 26 errors in 69 games for a .917 fielding percentage, an extraordinarily poor record for a second baseman. With the hefty price the Giants had paid for his contract, New York fans and writers felt cheated. "This is the summer of 'Larry' Doyle's prosperity or discontent," wrote the *New York Evening Telegram* at the start of 1908. "Doyle was so streaky last year that it was almost out of the question to get any fixed line on his ability. One day he would be a dead wall which nothing could pass, and the next he wobbled on every hit that came to him, like a boxcar on a coal railroad. Some days he could hit the ball on both sides of the seams, and on other days he missed all sides. Some baseball men are confident that it is merely a question

of time when Doyle will establish himself as a sterling, dependable player. If they have failed to read the signs right they are willing to be sentenced to eat five-dozen hard-boiled eggs and 18 caviar sandwiches as punishment."

Nobody ended up eating any caviar sandwiches, though Doyle did struggle at the start of 1908; after his fielding error and base-running blunder cost the Giants a 1-0 loss to the Cardinals on May 20, the *St. Louis Post-Dispatch* wrote, "Mr. Doyle has been analyzed, assayed, dissected and microscopically scrutinized to the end that the peach part of him is entirely absent. In fact, even to the naked eye Mr. Doyle's appearance at League Park yesterday was positively citric. He contributed a bunch of fat-headed work that would drive a real manager like McGraw to the woods to think it over." As the season went on, developing into one of the most exciting in history, Larry suddenly became the team's hottest hitter, raising his batting average above .300. "I hung on to Doyle when the New York fans and critics were calling for his scalp," McGraw bragged, "and today I wouldn't trade him for any man playing baseball." On September 8, however, Doyle was badly spiked by John Hummel of the Brooklyn Superbas. He was on crutches for nearly the rest of the season, returning only to pinch-hit for Christy Mathewson in the one-game playoff against the Cubs. Larry lofted a foul to catcher Johnny Kling, who made the catch despite having two beer bottles, a drinking glass, and a derby hat thrown at him.

Over the next four years Larry Doyle averaged 36 stolen bases per season and established himself as one of the National League's greatest stars. In 1909 he led the NL with 172 hits and finished second in home runs (6), third in slugging (.419), and fourth in batting (.302). The next year Doyle batted .285 and ranked third in home runs (8) and fourth in runs (97). After showing up on time for spring training for the first time in three years, 10 lbs. lighter and in the best shape of his life, the 24-year-old captain of the Giants elevated his performance to an even higher level in 1911. Doyle batted .310 and was selected as the second baseman on *Baseball Magazine*'s NL All-America team, leading the league in triples (25) and finishing second in slugging (.527), fourth in home runs (13), fifth in runs (102), and seventh in on-base percentage (.397). In Game Five of that year's World Series, Larry tagged up and scored

the winning run on a fly ball in the bottom of the 10th inning, but umpire Bill Klem later stated that he never touched the plate and would have been called out had the Athletics tagged him before leaving the field.

At the height of his stardom Doyle earned an annual salary of $8,000, only $3,000 less than his road roommate, Mathewson. He invested in Florida real estate, and he and Matty studied the stock market intently. In 1912 Doyle again reached double figures in home runs and posted career highs in batting average (.330) and RBI (90), winning the Chalmers Award as the NL's most valuable player. The prize, of course, was a Chalmers automobile. "I didn't even know how to put gasoline into it," Larry recalled. The following season he might have wished he'd remained ignorant; a week before the end of the season he lost control of the car and crashed it into a tree, bruising his arm and shoulder. Doyle missed the end of the regular season but recovered sufficiently to play in the World Series, though he managed only three hits and committed three errors in the five games. Defense undoubtedly was the former third baseman's biggest weakness. Doyle shaded closer to second base than other second basemen, preventing him from covering as much ground on the first-base side, and he also reportedly had trouble coming in for slow grounders.

In the fall of 1913 Larry married Gertrude McCombs of Miami. After turning down a two-year contract from the Federal League that would have paid him $27,000, Doyle returned to the Giants in 1914 and batted .260, adding further evidence to McGraw's theory that a player always needs a year to adjust to marriage. The next year he rebounded to win the NL batting title with a .320 average, making *Baseball Magazine*'s All-America team for the second time. In 1916 Doyle slumped once again. This time the Giants traded him to the Cubs on August 28 in a five-player deal that was essentially Doyle for Heinie Zimmerman. Reunited with his old friend Fred Merkle on the right side of the Chicago infield, the veteran second baseman batted a career-low .254 in 1917. On January 4, 1918, the Cubs packaged him to the Boston Braves in a deal for pitcher Lefty Tyler, but four days later the Giants reacquired him, announcing that he'd assume pinch-hitting and utility duties. He missed much of 1918 with a broken leg but regained his starting position the next year, appearing in 100 games at second base and batting

.289 with seven home runs. The 33-year-old Doyle remained a regular in 1920, closing out his major league career by batting .285 in 137 games.

Over the next two decades Larry Doyle worked for the Giants in various posts, including managing their minor league affiliates in Toronto and Nashville. The Doyles raised a son, Larry Jr., and two daughters, Doris and Edith, before Gertrude passed away in 1937. A smoker and former coal miner, Larry was diagnosed with tuberculosis in 1942. Word of his illness reached Blanche McGraw and Jane Mathewson, and the widows of his former manager and roommate teamed with NL president Ford Frick to send him to the Trudeau Sanitarium in Saranac Lake, New York, where Matty had convalesced almost 20 years earlier. Larry and Mrs. Mathewson remained close over the years, with the old ballplayer referring to her as "my manager." Doyle not only survived tuberculosis, he outlived the sanitarium itself; it closed its doors in 1954, but Doyle remained in Saranac Lake until his death at age 87 on March 1, 1974.

R. J. LESCH

Fred Merkle

NEW YORK

CARL FREDERICK RUDOLF MERKLE
FIRST BASEMAN 1907–16

Due to a base-running blunder on September 23, 1908, Fred Merkle became known by such unflattering epithets as "Bonehead," "Leather Skull," and "Ivory Pate." Those who knew him, however, described him as a "gentleman and scholar" and "voracious reader"; Chief Meyers called him "the smartest man on the club." *Baseball Magazine* described the 6'1", 190 lb. Merkle as "a hard hitter who usually delivers in the pinches" and "the most finished fielder in his league," but what really set him apart from other first basemen was his base running. One of the few Deadball Era players who routinely slid headfirst, Merkle "was not what one could call a very fast man on a sprint," wrote John McGraw, "but he was adept at stealing third. He never started unless he had the right lead, and once he started he rarely missed."

The son of German immigrants Ernest and Amalie (Thilghman) Merkle, Carl Frederick Rudolf Merkle was born on December 20, 1888, in Watertown, Wisconsin. Fred grew up in Toledo, Ohio, where he went to school and earned recognition as a star halfback in football and pitcher in baseball, playing under the Americanized name he'd adopted, Frederick Charles Merkle. He pitched for Toledo semipro teams starting in 1905 and tried out with Newark in the Ohio-Pennsylvania League in 1906. Later that season Fred signed to play third base with Tecumseh of the South Michigan League but was quickly shifted to first base. Returning to Tecumseh in 1907, the 18-year-old right-handed hitter batted .271 and led the league with six home runs, prompting his purchase by the New York Giants for $2,500. Making

his major league debut on September 21, Fred appeared in 15 games and batted .255.

Fred played in 38 games in 1908, but he's best remembered for the only game in which he appeared in the starting lineup. On September 23, in the final two weeks of a sweltering three-way pennant race, Merkle substituted at first base for the injured Fred Tenney. In the bottom of the ninth inning at the Polo Grounds, the Giants and Chicago Cubs were tied, 1-1. With two out and Moose McCormick on first base, Merkle drove McCormick to third. The next batter, shortstop Al Bridwell, lined Jack Pfiester's offering up the middle, knocking umpire Bob Emslie from his feet. When McCormick scored the would-be winning run, the fans at the Polo Grounds went wild and swarmed onto the diamond.

According to his own affidavit, Merkle was about 15 feet from second base when he veered toward the clubhouse in center field. Chicago center fielder Artie Hofman fielded Bridwell's hit and threw the ball to second baseman Johnny Evers, but somehow Giants pitcher Joe McGinnity came up with the ball and fired it deep into the crowd. While Evers was trying to recover Hofman's throw, Merkle claimed he returned to second base and stood there while the Cubs protested. He remained there until Christy Mathewson came along and said, "Come on, let's go to the clubhouse. Emslie said he would not allow the claim." Evers, who eventually found another ball, clamored for the attention of home plate umpire Hank O'Day, claiming that Merkle had failed to touch second. O'Day called Merkle out on a force play. Judging that the spectators couldn't be cleared from the field to allow play to resume, O'Day declared the game a tie, a decision that was upheld on appeal. "Merkle was careless, to be sure," wrote *Baseball Magazine*, "but withal, he did only what many others had done without suffering criticism."

Arguably Merkle's "boner" cost the Giants the 1908 pennant, but McGraw always defended him, pointing out that his team had lost a dozen other games that it should have won. Nonetheless, the misplay haunted Merkle, who batted only .191 without a single home run in 79 games the next season. "Listen to them hoot," he said to his manager. "You're making a mistake to keep me here. They don't want me." McGraw replied, "I wish I had more players like you. Don't pay any attention to those weathercocks. They'll be cheering you the next time you make a good play." McGraw's patience was rewarded in 1910, when Merkle replaced Tenney and batted .292 with 70 RBI as the Giants' regular first baseman. The next year he batted .283 with career highs in home runs (12), RBI (84), and stolen bases (49), finishing seventh in the Chalmers Award voting. One of his dozen homers was reportedly the longest ever hit on the Cincinnati grounds.

Merkle enjoyed arguably his finest season in 1912, when he batted a career-high .309 with 11 home runs, 84 RBI, and 37 stolen bases. In Game Eight of that year's World Series against the Boston Red Sox, however, he figured in another luckless play. Fred was poised to be the hero when his single in the top of the 10th inning scored Red Murray from second to give the Giants the lead. The bottom half began with Fred Snodgrass's infamous muff in center field, allowing pinch-hitter Clyde Engle to reach second. After Harry Hooper flied out and Steve Yerkes walked, Tris Speaker hit a high foul near the first-base coach's box. Though most observers agreed that it was his ball, Merkle backed away when Mathewson reportedly called for the catcher, Meyers, to make the catch. The ball fell to the ground, giving Speaker another chance, and he slashed a long single to right that started the Sox's winning rally. In New York, the headlines the next day read BONEHEAD MERKLE DOES IT AGAIN.

Performing well as the regular first baseman through 1915, Merkle was batting an uncharacteristic .237 when the Giants traded him to the Brooklyn Robins for catcher Lew McCarty in August 1916. Filling in for the injured Jake Daubert, Fred played in 23 games for Brooklyn down the stretch and got into three games during the 1916 World Series. When Cubs first baseman Vic Saier broke his leg early in 1917, the Robins sold Merkle to Chicago for $3,500. He remained in Chicago's starting lineup for three years, playing in another World Series in 1918. Though he was only 31 years old, Merkle's National League career ended in 1920, after which he put up consistently huge numbers in four years as the first baseman for Rochester of the International League.

After the 1924 season, in which Merkle batted .351 and slammed 22 home runs, *The Sporting News* reported that Rochester manager George Stallings was willing to trade his star first baseman to the New York Yankees as backup insurance for Wally Pipp, but expected young Louis Gehrig in return. In June 1925 the Yankees did acquire Merkle, but they held onto Gehrig and parted with $6,000 instead. Fred remained as a coach and occasional player through 1926, when he became a member of his sixth losing World Series team. After the season the Yankees released him to make room for his former Giants teammate Art Fletcher as coach. Merkle started the 1927 season as player-manager of Reading in the International League but was dismissed in June. Two years later he managed in his new hometown of Daytona Beach, Florida but his tenure was short-lived. One day a player referred to him as a bonehead; Merkle walked off the diamond and never returned.

Over the course of his career, Merkle saved enough to move to Daytona Beach and purchase a farm where he raised fruit crops. The Depression hit him hard, forcing him to work on a WPA county bridge project. After World War II Fred became a partner in a firm that manufactured fishing lures. He shunned reporters, who usually only wanted to ask him about his bonehead play, but he was a regular at Daytona Beach Islanders games. He spent his retirement playing bridge, golf, and chess. The 67-year-old Merkle died in his sleep on March 2, 1956, in Daytona Beach.

TREY STRECKER

NEW YORK

RICHARD WILLIAM "RUBE" MARQUARD
LEFT-HANDED PITCHER 1908–15

Tall and gangly with a cannon for a left arm, Rube Marquard made headlines around the country in 1908 when the New York Giants purchased his contract for the unprecedented price of $11,000, by far the largest amount ever paid for a ballplayer. Initially the New York reporters called him the "$11,000 Peach," but two years later, when he was still in search of his 10th major league victory, they derided him as the "$11,000 Lemon." Just when John McGraw was about to give up on him, Marquard won a total of 73 games from 1911 to 1913, including a 19-game winning streak in 1912 that remains the record nearly a century later. With a wicked curveball to complement his blazing fastball, and a fine screwball learned from his friend Christy Mathewson, the 6'3", 180 lb. southpaw finally lived up to New York's high expectations.

The son of Lena and Fred Marquard, who worked for the city as an engineer, Richard William Marquard was born in Cleveland on October 9, 1886. His mother's death in 1899 gave rise to a stubborn independence in young Richard. To his father's dismay, he had no inclination toward schoolwork; all he wanted to do was play baseball. Richard became a standout pitcher, earning the nickname "Rube" because he reminded observers of Rube Waddell. His most notable success came with the Telling Ice Cream Company, which paid him $15 per week to deliver ice cream and $10 to pitch on Sunday afternoons for the company team. In his free time Rube hung around poolrooms and smoke shops, mingling with older players. Sometimes he served as batboy for the Cleveland Naps.

One night in June 1906, the 19-year-old Marquard stole out of the house and rode freight trains, hobo-style, to Waterloo, Iowa, where he had an invitation to try out for the local team in the Iowa State League. The trip took five days and nights, and he arrived hungry, broke, and exhausted. He pitched twice against Keokuk and beat them once, but to his disappointment he did not receive a contract. Marquard continued to shine in Cleveland semipro leagues and waited for another opportunity, which came the next spring when he signed with Canton of the Central League. For two years Rube dominated. He won 23 games at Canton in 1907 and 28 the next year for Indianapolis in the American Association, breaking league records at both stops. By late summer 1908 Rube had drawn the attention of several major league teams, including the Giants.

Marquard arrived in New York in September as the Giants were locked in a fierce three-way pennant race with the Cubs and Pirates. He arrived in time to witness the Merkle Game, making his first major league start just two days later at the Polo Grounds against the Cincinnati Reds. In what he later called the worst day of his life, Rube pitched miserably, giving up six hits and five runs (two earned) in the defeat. "I was so badly rattled I didn't get over it all winter," he recalled. "I lost confidence in myself completely and those calls, 'take him out,' '$11,000 lemon,' and so on, they ring in my ears yet." For the next two years Marquard continued to struggle, winning a total of only nine games. In 1911, however, Wilbert Robinson joined the Giants as an assistant coach and made Rube his special project. Under Robinson's tutelage, the 24-year-old left hander finally fulfilled his potential, posting a 24-7 record and leading the NL in strikeouts (237).

The following year Rube enjoyed his greatest season, going 26-11 and winning two more games in that year's World Series against the Boston Red Sox. His 19-game winning streak began with his first outing of the year on April 11, when he beat Brooklyn's Nap Rucker, 18-3. Nearly three months later he defeated Rucker again, 2-1, for the final game of the streak. In between Marquard beat every team in the league at least twice, including Brooklyn, Boston, and Philadelphia three times each. When he finally lost to Chicago on July 8, his record stood at 19-1; at the time only two other NL pitchers, Rube Benton and Larry Cheney, had as many as 10 wins. In the Chalmers Award voting Marquard finished eighth, first among pitchers.

Rube became an instant celebrity, advertising products, writing a newspaper column, and even starring in a silent movie called *Rube Marquard Wins*. He also appeared on the Broadway stage, singing, dancing and telling jokes, and there he met the beautiful Blossom Seeley, the so-called "hottest girl in town." Noticing the chemistry between Rube and Blossom, enterprising managerial agents booked them to appear as a duo at New York's Palace Theater. Audiences loved them and soon they were appearing on stages across America, each earning $1,500 per week. "Marquard & Seeley" sang, joked, and flirted onstage, performing their hit songs "Breaking the Record" and "The Marquard Glide." Though Blossom was married, she and Rube began a love affair. Blossom divorced her husband in January 1913 and married Rube in March; six months later she gave birth to Richard Marquard Jr.

Marquard posted his third consecutive 20-win season in 1913, finishing at 23-10 with only 49 walks in 288 innings, less than half as many as he'd walked in fewer innings only two years earlier. After that season Rube struggled. He went 12-22 with a 3.06 ERA in 1914 and got off to an even worse start the following year, though he pitched the only no-hitter of his career against Brooklyn on April 15. In August 1915 Marquard arranged his own sale to Brooklyn, managed by his old mentor Robinson. Once again Uncle Robbie helped him resurrect his career. Rube won 13 games with a career-best 1.58 ERA for the pennant-winning Robins in 1916, and posted a 19-12 record the next year. After slumping to 9-18 in 1918 and missing most of 1919 with a broken leg, Rube won 10 games in 1920 and appeared in his fifth World Series, this one against his hometown Indians. Before Game Four a Cleveland undercover policeman arrested him for scalping his box-seat tickets. The judge, believing that the negative publicity

was punishment enough, fined Marquard only $1 and court costs, for a grand total of $3.80, but Brooklyn owner Charles Ebbets wasn't as forgiving. On December 15 he traded Rube to Cincinnati for Dutch Ruether.

Marquard had his last winning season in 1921, going 17-14 with a 3.39 ERA. He hoped to finish his career with Cincinnati, but after the season the Reds traded him and infielder Larry Kopf to the Boston Braves for pitcher Jack Scott. Rube held on for four mediocre years, finally retiring in 1925. By that time he was divorced from Blossom Seeley. Marquard managed in the minors for a few years but tired of the constant travel. Eventually he remarried and lived quietly in Baltimore, working at horse racing tracks and spending his winters in Florida. One year after his wife Naomi died in 1954, he married for a third time, this time to a wealthy widow named Jane Hecht Guggenheimer.

In 1966 a New York University economics and finance professor named Larry Ritter traveled the country collecting oral histories from old-time ballplayers, including Rube. Ritter's resulting book, *The Glory of Their Times*, become an instant classic. A whole new audience came to know Rube and his exploits, and Cooperstown took notice, too. In 1971 Rube Marquard was elected to the National Baseball Hall of Fame. He died in Baltimore on June 1, 1980, at the age of 93.

LARRY MANSCH

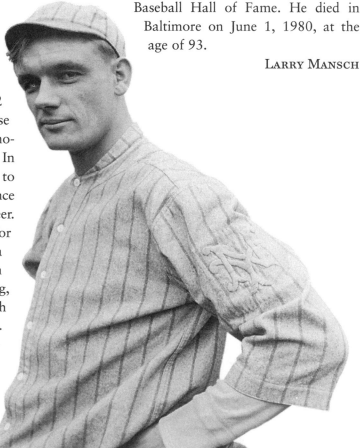

NEW YORK

FREDERICK CARLISLE SNODGRASS
OUTFIELDER 1908–15

A regular in the New York Giants outfield for six seasons, Fred Snodgrass was the "meteor" of 1910, leading the National League in batting average for most of the year before tailing off at the end. Despite his solid contributions to three pennant-winning clubs, the tenacious center fielder will forever be remembered for his infamous "muff" in the final game of the 1912 World Series. "Hardly a day in my life, hardly an hour, that in some manner or other the dropping of that fly doesn't come up, even after 30 years," Snodgrass said in a 1940 interview. "On the street, in my store, at my home . . . it's all the same. They might choke up before they ask me and they hesitate—but they always ask." Even death didn't spare Snodgrass; his 1974 obituary in the *New York Times* was headlined FRED SNODGRASS, 86, DEAD; BALL PLAYER MUFFED 1912 FLY.

Frederick Carlisle Snodgrass was born in Ventura, California, on October 19, 1887, the youngest of three children of Andrew and Addie Snodgrass. A Kentucky native who worked as a sheriff and later as a private patrolman, Andrew moved to the West Coast and married Addie, a California native, in 1874. One of Fred's brothers spent many years in the California Home for Feeble Minded Children, dying in 1912 at age 33. Fred attended St. Vincent's College, a Catholic school in Los Angeles that later merged with Loyola Marymount University. While he was catching for the St. Vincent's baseball team, his hustle caught the eye of John McGraw as the Giants were training in Los Angeles during the spring of 1907. In Los Angeles the following winter for the horse racing season, McGraw inquired after Snodgrass and offered him a contract. Fred joined the Giants after the school year ended in June 1908, making his debut as a catcher but collecting only four at-bats the entire season.

In 1909 it became apparent that Chief Meyers was going to succeed Roger Bresnahan as the Giants catcher, so McGraw tried the speedy Snodgrass all over the diamond, finally settling on the outfield. Still an apprentice, "Snow" logged only 70 at-bats that season but hit .300, stole 10 bases, and demonstrated a willingness to unleash his quick temper on opposing teams. In 1910 Snodgrass played most of the time in center field and quickly established himself as a coming star. His average peaked at .377, and as September began he led the NL at .362 and was in contention for a Chalmers automobile to be presented to the major leaguer with the highest batting average. In over his head while trying to keep pace with Ty Cobb and Nap Lajoie, Snodgrass stopped hitting and faded to .321, still good enough to rank fourth in the NL.

Snodgrass remained McGraw's center fielder for a half dozen years, joining the lineup at the same time as Meyers, Fred Merkle, and Josh Devore. Winners of three straight pennants in 1911-13, the team was built around speed; in 1910 Snodgrass stole 33 bases and was fourth on the team, behind Red Murray, Devore, and Larry Doyle. In 1911 Snodgrass was second with 51 steals, his career high. He also finished third on the team with 83 runs and 77 RBI. He made solid contributions to the next two pennant winners, scoring 91 runs in 1912 and hitting .291 in 1913.

Snodgrass ran into major problems in the World Series, beginning in 1911. In Game Three he led off the bottom of the 10th inning in a 1-1 game with his favorite maneuver, intentionally getting hit by a pitch. The umpire didn't buy it, but he did draw a walk, and after a sacrifice bunt he tried to advance on a short passed ball. The throw to Frank Baker at third base beat Snodgrass easily, so he leaped at Baker, hitting him spikes first as the tag was applied. He'd done the same thing earlier in the Series, but this time he inflicted a wound that took several minutes to treat. Baker had the last laugh when he scored the winning run in the 11th inning, but all of Philadelphia was scandalized by what they saw as a deliberate attempt by Snodgrass to injure the Athletics' star slugger. The next day, after Game Four was rained out in the Quaker City, Snodgrass felt the wrath of the fans. SNODGRASS HOOTED OUT OF PHILADELPHIA, read the front-page headline in the *New York Times*. As the rain and abuse continued, McGraw sent Snodgrass back to New York amid rumors that he'd been shot. When play resumed after a week of postponements, Fred went hitless in the final three games, batting .105 for the Series.

It got worse for Snodgrass in the 1912 World Series, when he made the misplay that became his albatross. With the Giants leading, 2-1, in the bottom of the 10th inning of the deciding game, Fred dropped an easy fly ball by leadoff batter Clyde Engle for a two-base error. The ball was hit more toward right fielder Red Murray, but on the Giants the center fielder was supposed to call for everything he could reach. Snodgrass made the call, Murray stepped aside, and, as Snodgrass explained in later years, "because of overeagerness, or over-confidence, or carelessness, I dropped it." He was forever blamed for the winning rally that ensued, but two events mitigate his fault. The next batter, Harry Hooper, drilled a long shot that Snodgrass speared for a spectacular catch. In a just world, he would have caught the first ball and the second would have gone for a double, yielding the same outcome. The key to the inning was a high foul pop by Tris Speaker on which Christy Mathewson made the mistake of calling for Chief Meyers to make the catch. Meyers couldn't reach the ball, while Merkle, who could have caught it easily, stood still as directed by Mathewson. Given a reprieve, Speaker singled to score the tying run and set up the Series winner.

Snodgrass stayed with the Giants until a mid-1915 trade to Boston, where he'd been involved in a rhubarb the previous season. During a Labor Day showdown for first place, Braves pitcher Lefty Tyler had knocked Snodgrass down four pitches in a row, then mocked his muffed catch. Snodgrass mouthed off, and when the fans kept on him, he thumbed his nose at everyone, bringing Boston mayor James Curley onto the field to demand an ejection. McGraw stood by Snodgrass that day, but a prolonged batting slump landed him in Braves Field in 1915. Fred's contract expired after the 1916 season. Rather than sign for a lower salary, he went home to California, spent 1917 in the Pacific Coast League, and retired to go into the appliance business.

If Snodgrass was hounded through the years by reminders of his biggest failure, it didn't prevent him from thriving. A successful businessman and banker in Oxnard, he was elected to the city council in 1930 and served three terms before being appointed mayor in 1937. He held the office for 11 months before resigning to move to Ventura, where he bought a ranch, grew lemons and walnuts, and continued to prosper with his wife, Josephine, and their daughter, Eleanor. In 1963 Larry Ritter visited Snodgrass. Their time together resulted in the longest chapter in *The Glory of Their Times*. Fred Snodgrass died in 1974 at age 86.

GABRIEL SCHECHTER

J.O. "Doc" Crandall

NEW YORK

JAMES OTIS "DOC" CRANDALL
RIGHT-HANDED PITCHER 1908–13

Doc Crandall is generally regarded as the premier relief specialist of the Deadball Era. Though he never led the National League in saves, he did lead the league in relief appearances each year in 1909-13 and relief victories in 1910-12, compiling a record of 45-16 over that three-year period. "Crandall is the Giants' ambulance corps," wrote Damon Runyon. "He is first aid to the injured. He is the physician of the pitching emergency, and they sometimes call him old Doctor Crandall. He is without an equal as an extinguisher of batting rallies and run riots, or as a pinch hitter." In the latter role the .285 lifetime hitter never really excelled, batting just .229 in 96 pinch at-bats over the course of 10 seasons, but one reporter nevertheless proclaimed him "the only pinch-hitting pitcher ever developed in the Big Leagues."

James Otis Crandall was born on October 8, 1887, in Wadena, Indiana, a town with fewer than 60 inhabitants but a long baseball history. Three Wadena residents, the Rowley brothers (Warren, Frank, and Tom), organized the town's first club in the late 1860s and later played with George and Harry Wright. Two generations later, four more Wadenans went on to play Organized Baseball. One of them was Fred "Cy" Williams. Like the Rowleys, the other three were brothers: Otis, Karl, and Arnold Crandall. Their father, Mark, had been part of the second generation of Wadena ballplayers in his youth and later owned a farm and co-owned the Crandall Mead & Company general store, which sponsored the town baseball team. Once the chores were done at the farm and store, he had no qualms about his sons taking off for an open pasture to

play ball with friends. The same went for young Williams, who also worked in the store as a clerk.

"Ote" made the jump from the town team to semi-pro ball before turning 15, pitching for the Brook club in 1902. The next year he tried out for Fowler, the county seat, but caught on with Frankfort, Indiana, when Fowler passed on him. In 1906 Crandall reached Cedar Rapids of the Three-I League, where he caught the attention of John McGraw, manager of the New York Giants. In *My Thirty Years in Baseball*, McGraw wrote that in reviewing the list of players available for the 1907 draft, he noticed a Crandall playing for Cedar Rapids. The Giants manager knew nothing about the player, but he'd played for Cedar Rapids early in his own professional career and decided to take Crandall on a whim.

When he arrived for spring training in 1908, Otis found that the Giants had no uniforms available that fit his stocky frame. Unfazed, he shagged flies in street clothes for a couple of days. McGraw eventually found him a uniform—and a place on the team when it went north. Crandall was a good ground ball pitcher, and McGraw had the infield to take advantage of that style. The 20-year-old rookie said little, listened intently, and learned quickly. In his first big-league season Crandall started 24 games, completing 13, and relieved in eight others. It was the only year in his six with the Giants in which he started more than he relieved. "Crandall was one of the coolest pitchers I ever saw," McGraw recalled. "He had no fear, no nerves."

Doc Crandall's career as a relief specialist began in 1909, when he started only seven games but relieved in

23. McGraw had experimented with relief pitchers earlier; in addition to sending in Christy Mathewson to extinguish rallies, he also used George Ferguson almost exclusively in relief in 1906-07 and Bill Malarkey in the same role in 1908. In an era when financial concerns prevented most clubs from carrying anywhere near the full 25-man roster permitted by league rules, some considered McGraw's use of relief pitchers an extravagance. Crandall posted a career-high six saves in 1909, and five in each of the next two seasons. His best overall year was 1910, when he went 17-4 in 42 games, relieving in 24 and starting 18. Seven of his starts came during September, when he filled in for the injured Red Ames. Proving that he was not just a "failed starter" converted to relief because of an inability to finish games, Crandall pitched seven complete games and won all but one of them.

Doc was at his most versatile in 1911, though the story he told later in life about playing every position except catcher was an exaggeration, at least as far as regular-season games are concerned. Coming off a season in which he'd batted .342 with power, Crandall filled in at shortstop in late June, when Al Bridwell came down with "malaria." As soon as Bridwell was able to take the field, Larry Doyle was injured in a baserunning collision, so Crandall moved to second base for three games. His defense was adequate at both positions, though he did make three errors in the nine games. Crandall also pitched in 41 games in 1911, posting a 15-5 record, but he saved his best for Game Five of that year's World Series. He pitched the last three innings, socked an RBI double, scored a run, and earned New York's second and last win of the Series.

Crandall turned in two more solid seasons as the Giants repeated as NL pennant winners in 1912-13. During the latter year he became the first pitcher to make over 30 relief appearances (32, against only three starts), but his campaign took an odd turn on August 6, when McGraw traded him to the last-place Cardinals for catcher Larry McLean. Twelve days later, after Doc had appeared in only two games as a pinch-hitter, the Giants paid cash to get him back. One source attributes the reversal to fan displeasure while another says the Giants players were the cause, nearly coming to blows with their manager. *The Sporting News* at the time

advanced a more credible theory, namely that St. Louis was unwilling to pay Crandall the same salary he'd earned in New York and the pitcher was threatening to go home to Wadena.

Crandall returned to St. Louis in 1914, this time with the Federal League's Terriers. He shed his reliever role, starting in 21 of his 27 appearances, and also played 63 games at second base, batting .309 with a .429 on-base percentage. In 1915 Crandall started in 33 of his 51 appearances, posting a 21-15 record and finishing second in the FL in innings pitched (312⅔). The St. Louis Browns acquired him in the Federal League dispersal draft. He was shelled in his first two appearances and the Browns cut him loose. Coming off a 20-win season, Crandall's career appeared to be over at age 28.

As it turned out, Crandall was just getting warmed up. Over the next 13 years he became a fixture in the Pacific Coast League, starting games instead of finishing them. In 1917 he was a 26-game winner for the Los Angeles Angels, good for second in the league. In the war-shortened 1918 season Crandall won 16 games for the PCL champion Angels, including a no-hit bid on April 7 that was spoiled with two outs in the ninth inning—by his brother Karl, playing for Salt Lake City, a fact that was featured in *Ripley's Believe It or Not*. After the PCL season ended in July, Doc got into five games with the Boston Braves, his last in the majors. With the Angels from 1917 through 1926 and again in 1929, Crandall rolled up a 224-147 record with a 2.92 ERA. He threw the first official pitch when Los Angeles' Wrigley Field opened in 1925.

Crandall tried ownership in 1927-28 with Wichita of the Western League, where he also hurled a few games. He then returned to the majors for a four-year stint as the pitching coach for the Pittsburgh Pirates. In 1935 Crandall managed Des Moines, where his roster included his son, Jim, a catcher who went on to a lengthy minor league career. Doc ended his days in baseball with two PCL coaching stints: Seattle in 1937 and Sacramento in 1938. In his later years he suffered a series of strokes that left him paralyzed. Doc Crandall died in Bell, California, on August 17, 1951, survived by his wife, Bertha, and his children Jim and Dorothy.

R. J. LESCH

Buck Herzog

NEW YORK

CHARLES LINCOLN "BUCK" HERZOG
INFIELDER 1908–09, 1911–13, 1916–17

Buck Herzog was one of the most versatile infielders in the history of the major leagues; his 1,493 games were divided almost equally between second base, shortstop, and third base. His motto, "When you get 'em down, choke 'em," earned him the nickname "Choke 'Em Charley." John McGraw signed Herzog for the New York Giants in 1908, beginning a baseball love-hate relationship exceeded perhaps only by George Steinbrenner and Billy Martin. No player better exemplified McGraw's ferocious fighting spirit than the 5'11", 160 lb. Herzog, yet the two generally couldn't stand each other. Over the course of a decade the Giants traded away the aggressive infielder three times and brought him back twice, both times experiencing immediate success when he reentered the fold. "I hate his guts," McGraw once said about Herzog, "but I want him on my club."

Charles Lincoln Herzog was born in Baltimore on July 9, 1885. When he was a child, his family moved to a farm near Ridgley, Maryland, where Buck grew much-acclaimed cantaloupes during his playing career. After attending the University of Maryland, playing shortstop alongside third baseman Frank Baker, Herzog spent the 1907 season in the minors and signed with the Giants the following year. His ancestry was German Presbyterian, but his large nose and ambiguous surname caused many New Yorkers—including the Yiddish newspapers—to assume he was Jewish. As a rookie Herzog hit .300 in 64 games. He slumped in 1909, however, batting a mere .185. Stuck on the bench, he antagonized McGraw and earned himself an exile to the last-place Boston Rustlers.

Herzog played third base in 1910 and shortstop the following year, developing managerial aspirations along the way. In 1911 he was leading the team with a .310 average when he ran afoul of manager Fred Tenney, who accused him and outfielder Doc Miller of "laying down" and fined them both. Herzog responded by going on strike, forcing a mid-July trade back to the Giants. McGraw's offense had faltered, but when he put Herzog at third base and young Art Fletcher at shortstop, the lineup jelled and marched to the pennant. Buck hit .290 for the season with career highs of 157 hits, 90 runs, 67 RBI, and 48 stolen bases.

Herzog was a mainstay of McGraw's pennant-winning teams of 1911-13. His 12 hits in the 1912 World Series set a record that stood for more than a half century. For the Series Buck hit .400, stole two bases, scored six runs, and drove in five. Ring Lardner wrote that Herzog "was more peppery than Captain Doyle himself and looked like an electric battery compared with Fletcher and Merkle. He played rings around any other man on the rival infields. He is a human illustration of the value of energy and application." But an injury early in 1913 caused Herzog to lose his regular third-base job; he wound up platooning with Tillie Shafer and suffering through a 1-for-19 nightmare in the 1913 World Series. That winter, while McGraw was on a world tour, Giants owner Harry Hempstead traded Herzog to Cincinnati for former stolen-base champion Bob Bescher. Hempstead knew that McGraw craved speed, but the temperamental manager was livid when he learned of the deal.

In Cincinnati Herzog was named manager and played shortstop; his Reds finished last, but the Giants suffered without him. In 1915 Buck brought his team in seventh, ahead of only McGraw's. Herzog's tenure as Cincinnati manager was rocky. He battled with the front office, followed the McGraw tradition of terrorizing umpires and earning suspensions, and became

frustrated by the failure of his players to match his overachieving style. Midway through 1916, a desperate McGraw sought to revive his floundering team by bringing back Herzog. This time he traded three future Hall of Famers—Christy Mathewson, Bill McKechnie, and Edd Roush—for Herzog and Red Killefer. McGraw put Herzog at shortstop, named him captain, and the Giants won a record 26 games in a row to climb to a fourth-place finish.

At 1917 spring training Herzog engaged in what writer Joe Williams dubbed "the Louis-Schmeling fight of baseball." When a golf outing caused Ty Cobb to arrive late for an exhibition game, the Giants razzed him so viciously that he threatened to "undress" them during the game. On a steal attempt, Cobb slid so high that he spiked Herzog above the knee. In the ensuing brawl, Cobb was grinding Herzog's face in the dirt when Jim Thorpe and others pulled them apart. After the game Herzog challenged Cobb to a fight. They met in Cobb's hotel room, with the furniture stacked up and only Eddie Ainsmith present as the third man. After a half hour of mayhem, a bloody Herzog emerged, eyes nearly swollen shut, and told teammates, "I got hell kicked out of me, but I knocked the bum down, and you know that swell head, he'll never get over the fact that a little guy like me had him on the floor."

Playing second base, Herzog had a statistically subpar 1917 but led the Giants to another pennant. He hit .250 in the World Series but made a key error in the pivotal Game Five, allowing the White Sox to tie the game. The Giants lost the Series and McGraw quickly jettisoned the once again hated Herzog back to Boston in a deal that returned former captain Larry Doyle to New York. In 1919 Herzog moved to Chicago, where he finished his career in 1920 amidst controversy. He was one of several Cubs suspected of throwing a game to the Phillies, and though no solid evidence implicated Herzog, he was released along with the others. Later Rube Benton accused him of an attempted bribe. Once waived out of the majors, Herzog never returned.

Known as a shrewd businessman who always negotiated more lucrative contracts than other players with similar talents, Herzog signed a record $12,000 minor league contract in 1920. He split the year between Columbus and Louisville but quit playing when the contract wasn't renewed. In 1924 Herzog briefly managed Newark of the International League, his last job in professional baseball. He then served as baseball coach at the U.S. Naval Academy, and when that post dried up he worked many years for the B & O Railroad. Later Herzog worked at a Maryland racetrack. Ironically, this man who'd prided himself on his negotiating acumen and enjoyed the trappings of wealth wound up destitute at the end of his life. In the winter of 1952-53 he was found penniless on the streets of Baltimore, ravaged by tuberculosis. Old baseball friends helped him out, but he died at age 68 on September 4, 1953.

GABRIEL SCHECHTER

NEW YORK

John Tortes "Chief" Meyers
Catcher 1909–15

As a Native American in the Deadball Era, Jack Meyers couldn't avoid being saddled with the nickname "Chief," but he did as much as any Native American of his generation to shatter the stereotypical image of the dumb Indian. Meyers was more sophisticated than nearly all of his fellow players. "A strong love of justice, a lightning sense of humor, a fund of general information that runs from politics to Plato, a quick, logical mind, and the self-contained, dignified poise that is the hallmark of good breeding—he is easily the most remarkable player in the big leagues," wrote one reporter. On the field, the strong but slow-footed Meyers was an excellent offensive catcher, retiring with a .291 average over his nine-year career.

A member of the Cahuilla tribe, also called the Mission Indians, John Tortes Meyers was born on July 29, 1880, in Riverside, California. His father died when he was only seven years old, making his mother, Felicite, the most important influence in his early life. Jack attended Riverside High School and played semi-pro baseball throughout the Southwest. In 1905 he was catching in a tournament in Albuquerque when he caught the attention of a rival player named Ralph Glaze, a baseball and football standout at Dartmouth College who later made the majors as a pitcher with the 1906-08 Boston Americans. Glaze thought the 5'11", 194 lb. catcher could help his college team on both the gridiron and the diamond. Pointing out that the school's charter provided for the education of Native Americans, Glaze convinced Dartmouth alumni in his hometown of Denver to equip Meyers with cash, railroad tickets, and an altered diploma because Meyers hadn't yet completed high school.

With the assistance of a tutor, Meyers attended classes at Dartmouth during the 1905-06 school year and enjoyed his time there immensely, but college administrators soon discovered that his high school diploma was a fake. They offered to admit him if he completed a preparatory program, but when school let out, the 25-year-old catcher instead signed a contract with Harrisburg of the independent Tri-State League. The Harrisburg team "certainly laid themselves to make me a happy Indian," Jack said sarcastically. "I went to the clubhouse and nobody paid more attention to me than they did to the bat bag." Finally getting into a game on Independence Day, Meyers was assigned to catch a spitballer named Frank Leary, who pitched a couple of games for the Cincinnati Reds the following season. "I was getting it everywhere but my glove," he recalled. "I had five passed balls in two innings." Leary was intentionally crossing up Meyers, who finally stopped putting down signs. "Do you know, that did me more good than anything that ever happened to me?" Chief recalled. "It made me mad. I had been timid and now I was mad enough to be brave."

At that point Meyers' career took off. After spending 1907 in the Northwestern League with Butte and 1908 with St. Paul of the American Association, Chief found himself in New York City as a 28-year-old rookie with the Giants at the end of the tumultuous 1908 season. He failed to appear in a single game, but that winter the Giants traded Roger Bresnahan to the St. Louis Cardinals. The following year Meyers shared the catching duties with Admiral Schlei. In 1910 he became the regular, batting .285 to establish himself as one of the best-hitting catchers in the game. The press, in New York and elsewhere, took an immediate liking to Meyers because he made more interesting copy than his teammates. During rainouts or off-days, while other players played cards or billiards, Meyers would do some historical sightseeing or watch a local college football team practice. In Boston, wrote Bozeman Bulger, Meyers made a point of visiting the art museums, where he spent hours touring the exhibits.

After two years in the majors, Meyers was popular enough for the vaudeville circuit. At Hammerstein's Victoria Theatre on October 23, 1910, Chief teamed up with Christy Mathewson in a vaudeville sketch entitled "Curves." Written by Bulger and produced by actress May Tully, the half-hour sketch featured Meyers and Mathewson in a scene set at the Polo Grounds, with Tully playing an ardent spectator. The players, in their home uniforms, demonstrated for Tully and the audience how to throw various pitches, and Meyers explained the workings of the catcher. Tully then returned the favor by teaching Mathewson and Meyers to act, which, according to *Variety*, "brings out a travesty drama with Meyers as the 'bad Indian.' Mathewson is the cowboy who comes to the rescue of the forlorn maiden and overcomes the 'bad Indian' by hitting him in the head with a baseball." Today it sounds as improper as a blackface minstrel show, but at the time *Variety* called it a "most satisfactory vehicle."

In 1911-13 Meyers finished in the Top 10 each year in Chalmers Award voting for the NL's most valuable player. In 1911 he led the Giants in batting for the first of three consecutive seasons with a .332 average, third highest in the National League. "Meyers has become the deepest student of batting on the team," wrote a *New York Times* reporter after watching him correctly predict the type of pitches thrown by Pirates phenom Marty O'Toole. The next year Chief hit for the cycle on June 10 en route to a career-high six home runs and a .358 average, second in the NL behind only Heinie Zimmerman's .372. His hot hitting continued in the 1912 World Series, when he started all eight games and batted .357. Meyers remained one of the Giants' best hitters through 1914, when he batted .286 in a career-high 134 games.

Playing in over 100 games for the sixth consecutive season, the 35-year-old Meyers batted just .232 in 1915 and the Giants placed him on waivers. Both Brooklyn and Boston claimed him, with the Robins winning his rights on a coin flip. In Brooklyn, Meyers was reunited with ex-Giants Rube Marquard, Fred Merkle, and his mentor Wilbert Robinson, the former Baltimore Orioles catcher. He remembered the 1916 Robins as "outsmarting the whole National League," but he batted .247 in 80 games and knew that he was nearing the end. "I cheated a little on my age so they always thought I was a few years younger," Chief recalled, "but when the years started to creep up on me I knew how old I was, even if nobody else did." He split 1917 between Brooklyn and Boston, on the latter club replacing Hank Gowdy, who'd enlisted for service in World War I. Meyers himself eventually joined the U.S. Marine Corps.

After receiving his honorable discharge in 1918, Meyers hooked on with the Buffalo Bisons, managed by former Giants teammate Hooks Wiltse, and batted .328 in 65 games. He started the following year as player-manager for New Haven in the Eastern League but was replaced in midseason. Chief was catching for a semipro team in San Diego in 1920 when the crowd booed him, making him quit baseball altogether.

Meyers returned to the Riverside area and became a police chief for the Mission Indian Agency. He also worked for the Department of the Interior as an Indian supervisor. His nephew, Jack Meyers, remembered his namesake performing "Casey at the Bat" for children's groups around the Santa Rosa reservation. "He could be very theatrical and entertaining," recalled his nephew. Meyers was a favorite at old-timers games for both the Dodgers and the Giants, especially after those teams moved to California. He passed away just short of his 91st birthday in San Bernardino, California, on July 25, 1971.

R. J. LESCH

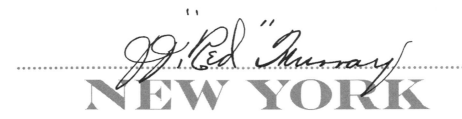

NEW YORK

JOHN JOSEPH "RED" MURRAY
RIGHT FIELDER 1909–15, 1917

Despite his impressive statistics in power hitting, baserunning, and fielding, Red Murray remains one of the least recognized stars of the Deadball Era. "Murray was for years noted as one of the greatest outfielders in the National League," wrote J. C. Kofoed in the April 1924 issue of *Baseball Magazine*. "His throwing arm was the best ever, his ground covering ability and sureness of eye were classic. Furthermore, he was remarkably fast as a base runner, and noted as a batter as well." In his seven seasons as a regular, Murray led NL outfielders in home runs, RBI, stolen bases, and assists a total of 16 times.

The son of Hanna (Sheehan) and William Murray, a coal miner originally from Edinburgh, Scotland, John Joseph Murray was born on March 4, 1884, in the north-central Pennsylvania town of Arnot, where Mother Jones led a famous strike of the United Mine Workers in 1899. After attending Arnot public schools, John (already known as "Red" for the color of his hair) played semipro baseball for the Father Mathew team in Elmira, New York, some 40 miles north of Arnot. There he met Joe Birmingham, an Elmira native and future major leaguer who became a lifelong friend. Following two years at Lock Haven College (now Lock Haven University of Pennsylvania), where he played football, basketball, and baseball, Murray moved on to the University of Notre Dame in 1904. For two years Red was the catcher and batting star of a Fighting Irish baseball team that also included Birmingham.

When the 1906 school year ended, Murray signed his first professional contract with the St. Louis Cardinals, for whom he batted .257 in seven games as a catcher and 34 in the outfield. The next year the Cardinals made him their regular left fielder. Murray displayed his trademark combination of power and speed, slugging seven homers (third in the NL) to go along with 23 stolen bases. On May 27 he hit a home run measured at 471 feet, then considered the longest blast in St. Louis history. Perhaps Murray's greatest season came in 1908. At age 24 he played in all 154 games and finished second in the NL in stolen bases (48) and third in hits (167), home runs (7), and total bases (237). That December the Cardinals traded him to the New York Giants in the deal for Roger Bresnahan, giving Bresnahan a chance to manage and Murray a chance to play for a winning team.

Red Murray became the cleanup hitter of John McGraw's juggernaut Giants of 1909-12. Over that same period Murray ranked third in the NL in total RBI, trailing only Honus Wagner and Sherry Magee. He and Wagner tied for the most home runs in the majors from 1907 through 1909 (21), with Red smacking a league-leading seven round-trippers in 1909. On one home run, according to an oft-reported story, McGraw ordered Murray to lay down a sacrifice bunt, but the independent-thinking slugger swung away instead. McGraw became so irate at Murray's refusal to follow orders that he fined him $50.

Those Giants, of course, were known mainly for their speed. A 1976 book entitled *A Baseball Century: The First Hundred Years of the National League* states, "On the legs of Josh Devore, Buck Herzog, Fred Snodgrass, Arthur Fletcher, and 'Laughing Larry' Doyle, the Giants raced to pennants in those years." Inexcusably, the author left out Murray and Fred Merkle, even though they tied Snodgrass for the team lead in stolen bases from 1911 to 1913. Similarly, Lee Allen slighted Murray in his 1950 book *100 Years of Baseball*. Allen wrote, "This [stolen-base] epoch extended roughly from 1910-1912," then listed "greyhounds" Bob Bescher of the Reds, Max Carey of the Pirates, and Doyle, Snodgrass, and Devore of the Giants as the "creators of this terror on the paths." Where was Red Murray? During that three-year span he pilfered 143 sacks, second only to Bescher's 218 and far surpassing Allen's other "greyhounds."

Murray's combination of power and speed places him in some heady company. Since 1900 only 13 players have finished in the top five in the major leagues in home runs and stolen bases during the same season. Willie Mays (1955) and Hank Aaron (1963) are the only players to accomplish that feat in the past 70 years. Only three men did it twice: Honus Wagner (1907-08), Red Murray (1908-09), and Ty Cobb (1909-10).

Murray was no slouch on defense, either. From his usual position in right field at the Polo Grounds, which some reporters called "Murray Hill," Red led all NL

outfielders in assists in 1909 (30) and 1910 (26). He was the only outfielder in the majors to accumulate more than 100 assists during the period 1907-10. On September 10, 1913, Murray threw out pitcher George McQuillan on what appeared to be a clean single to right field. In his 1924 article in *Baseball Magazine*, Kofoed wrote, "My general recollection of the powerful-whipped National League outfields of the comparatively recent past was that [Mike] Mitchell, Murray, and Owen 'Chief' Wilson were equipped with about as powerful arms as anyone in the league."

As for his glove work, Murray made six putouts in Game Six of the 1912 World Series, including two that were described as "spectacular," and his game-saving catch on August 16, 1909, has been called the greatest in the history of Forbes Field. Heavy thunderclouds threatened throughout the game, and at the moment of his leaping, fingertip catch, lightning lit up the sky and "the accompanying crash of thunder fairly jarred the earth." McGraw called it the "greatest and most dramatic" catch he ever saw, and it was later featured in *Ripley's Believe It or Not*. Lightning struck twice, as it were. On July 17, 1914, Murray was knocked unconscious by a bolt after catching a fly ball for the final out in a 21-inning contest.

During that 1914 season Murray slumped to a .223 batting average and lost his regular position in the outfield. The following year the Giants traded him to the Chicago Cubs. In 1916 Murray was coaxed out of retirement to play for Toronto of the International League, managed by his childhood friend Joe Birmingham. Red ended his major league career with 22 at-bats for the Giants in 1917.

Murray returned to the Elmira area, where he married Beatrice Riley in 1920. He owned and operated a battery and tire store for two decades, served as a Democratic alderman for three years, and was Elmira's recreation director for 18 years. In 1950 Murray was voted Elmira's greatest baseball player of the half century. Red died of leukemia on December 4, 1958, in Sayre, Pennsylvania, not far from his birthplace. His obituary ranked him "with Mel Ott as one of the two greatest right fielders in New York Giant history."

CAPPY GAGNON

NEW YORK

ARTHUR FLETCHER
SHORTSTOP 1909–20

In the early teens the New York Giants were hated all around the circuit, but no Giant other than John McGraw drew as much ire as Art Fletcher. "There was fighting everywhere they went," wrote Frank Graham, "and Fletcher always was in the thick of it. He fought enemy players, umpires, and fans. He was fined and suspended frequently." Fletcher's feistiness made him as popular at the Polo Grounds as he was unpopular on the road. Beginning in 1913, a lady with a large hat invariably sat in the front row of the center-field bleachers. As the Giants took the field at the start of each game, she shouted, "Come on, Artie!" Fletch waved his glove at her, all the fans applauded, and then the visiting leadoff hitter stepped to the plate.

Arthur Fletcher was born on January 5, 1885, in Collinsville, Illinois, just across the Mississippi River from St. Louis. A skinny, lantern-jawed youngster who was Collinsville's best ballplayer, Art traveled over an hour by trolley to play in more competitive games than he could find in his hometown. His parents opposed his dream of playing professional baseball, however, so he attended business college in St. Louis, graduating with a degree in stenography. In 1906 Art played shortstop for Staunton, Illinois, performing well enough to receive an offer from Dallas of the Texas League for 1907. His father pressured him to keep his full-time job at Ingersoll-Rand, the company that manufactured the drills that were digging the Panama Canal, so he remained at home and played for the Collinsville Reds. In March 1908 Art arranged a two-week vacation from work so he could attend spring training with Dallas. Because business was slow, his boss told him he could take the summer off and return in October if he made the Dallas club.

That very spring the New York Giants played a series of exhibition games against Dallas. Fletcher refused to be awed by the major leaguers (including McGraw, their pugnacious manager), and sassed them back as roughly as they sassed him. He slid into them, spikes high, and when their pitchers threw at him, he continued to crowd the plate. Fletcher's fearless attitude and play so impressed McGraw that he bought an option on his contract for $1,500. Years later Art admitted, "I was a pretty fresh busher." McGraw reportedly said of him, "That's my kind of ball player." After batting .273 with 35 stolen bases in 147 games as the Dallas shortstop, the 24-year-old Fletcher joined the Giants as part of an influx of rookies in the spring of 1909, serving as utility infielder during his first two years with the club. He was so self-conscious about his jutting chin that he had a collar sewn on his uniform that he wore turned up.

McGraw saw something—perhaps a mirror image of himself—in the brash youngster. At the start of 1911 he benched his veteran third sacker, Art Devlin, in favor of Fletcher. In mid-May the Giants traded their regular shortstop, Al Bridwell, back to the Boston Nationals for Buck Herzog. McGraw installed Herzog at third base and moved Fletcher to shortstop. Initially the fans couldn't believe that a former utility man was replacing the flashy and popular Bridwell, and they razzed Art unmercifully. But he soon won them over with his sterling defensive play and offensive skills that were far superior to Bridwell's. The gritty right-handed hitter finished fifth in the National League in batting average (.319) and sixth in on-base percentage (.400), while beginning a 10-year streak of ranking among the league leaders in times hit by pitch (with the exception of 1915, he led the league in that category each year from 1913 to 1918). He was also a notorious free-swinger; his 30 bases on balls in 1911 were a career high, and in 1915 he drew only six walks despite a career-high 562 at-bats.

Though Fletcher never again batted .300, he frequently finished just below that mark, compiling a .277 batting average over the course of his 13-year career. He also fielded brilliantly, drawing comparisons to Honus Wagner, Joe Tinker, and Mickey Doolan. With Art as their shortstop, the Giants won three pennants in a row—1911, 1912, 1913—and an additional one in 1917, the year McGraw named him team captain. Fletcher didn't distinguish himself in the Fall Classic, batting just .191 and committing a dozen errors in his 25 World Series games. Some of those miscues were costly. In Game Three of the 1911 World Series, for instance, Art's error in the top of the 11th inning helped the Philadelphia Athletics score twice and hand Christy Mathewson his first World Series defeat, 3-2. The following year Fletch committed two errors early in Game Two to give the Boston Red Sox a 4-2 lead. A third miscue in the eighth inning tied the game, which eventually ended in a 6-6 draw.

On June 8, 1920, McGraw sent the 35-year-old Fletcher (along with pitcher Bill Hubbell and $100,000) to the Philadelphia Phillies for 29-year-old Dave Bancroft, the National League's best shortstop. Fletch hit .296 in 102 games for the Phillies, but the team was hopeless. When his brother and father both passed away in the spring of 1921, Art went back to Collinsville and sat out the entire season. Despite the sabbatical, he returned in 1922 and batted .280 in 110 games. In one game that season Art thought that umpire Bill Klem was favoring the Giants. "Why don't you put on a New York uniform?" he suggested. That remark earned him an ejection, and a few minutes later a banner was hung from the center-field clubhouse that read "Catfish Klem." Klem halted the game until the sign came down. Fletcher always received credit for that sign, but years later he admitted that he didn't create it; he merely encouraged a teammate to do it. Regardless, the league fined Art $50 and suspended him for three days.

After the 1922 season Fletcher gave up playing and accepted the job as Phillies manager. His fiery leadership improved the team's record in two of his first three years, but never enough to please an old Giant who was accustomed to finishing in the first division. In 1924 Fletcher brought the seventh-place Phillies to New York for a year-end series with the Giants, who were locked in a pennant race with Brooklyn. Phillies shortstop Heinie Sand told Art that Giants outfielder Jimmy O'Connell had offered him $500 "not to bear down." Fletcher exposed the bribe attempt, and O'Connell and Giants coach Cozy Dolan were both banned from baseball. In 1925 the Phillies tied for sixth, their best finish since 1918, but the following year they regressed to last. Tired of losing and realizing that he might ruin his health if he continued his fighting ways, Art decided to resign.

The next year Miller Huggins, an old National League friend, persuaded Fletcher to take a coaching job with the New York Yankees. Art loved coaching for a winning team and turned down several managerial offers to remain with the Yanks. He did manage the Bronx Bombers for 11 games at the end of 1929, but only because Huggins was hospitalized. When Huggins died and was replaced by Joe McCarthy, reporters speculated that Fletcher would be fired because he and McCarthy had feuded in 1926, when they both were managing in the NL. McCarthy recognized Art's value, however, and the third-base coach and master heckler remained with the Yankees until heart problems forced him to retire in 1945. With more than $75,000 in World Series and first-division checks, Art and his wife, Irene, lived in extreme comfort in Collinsville, where they returned after every season. When Art Fletcher died in Los Angeles of a heart attack on February 6, 1950, it was reported that he'd cashed more World Series checks, 15, than anyone in history.

PETER GORDON

NEW YORK

GEORGE JOSEPH BURNS
LEFT FIELDER 1911–21

Not to be confused with the American League first baseman or the cigar-wielding comedian of the same name, who were roughly his contemporaries, George Burns of the National League was one of the most consistent hitters in major league history, batting .287 for his 15-year career, but never higher than .303 nor lower than .272 in a full season. John McGraw described Burns as "one of the most valuable ball players that ever wore the uniform of the Giants." Wielding a 42", 52-oz. bat (a tree trunk even by Deadball Era standards), he consistently ranked among the NL leaders in hits, runs, walks, and stolen bases. Though he stood just 5'7" and weighed 160 lbs., George was tremendously strong; an excellent boxer and wrestler, he was one of the Giants who challenged Jim Thorpe to wrestling matches before McGraw forbade the practice.

The son of John Burns, who ironically was a cigar maker, George Joseph Burns was born in Utica, New York, on November 24, 1889. The elder Burns also ran a pool hall, where George worked as a boy and learned how to handle a cue (in later years other Giants would not play him in billiards unless he played left-handed). The younger Burns also played sandlot baseball in the Utica area, usually pitching or catching to get as much action as possible. On October 18, 1908, George and his father were in the grandstand at the Utica Athletic Field for an exhibition between the Syracuse Stars and Utica Harps of the New York State League. Utica's catcher didn't show up, so Harps manager Charley Dooley asked George, a well-known semipro, to fill in. After the game Dooley signed him for the following year.

Burns played primarily catcher for the next two seasons before new manager Charlie Carr switched him to right field in 1911. McGraw's old Baltimore Orioles teammate Sadie McMahon, scouting for the Giants, spotted Burns and recommended the speedy outfielder, who batted .289 with 40 stolen bases that season. Utica and the Giants closed the deal for $4,000, and George made his major league debut on October 3, 1911. He got into five more games that fall, notching the first of his 2,077 hits on the last day of the season. The next year McGraw decided to keep Burns on the bench rather than farm him out to a minor league team. "You may not play much this year but I want you with me," explained McGraw during spring training. "You sit next to me on the bench and I'll tell you all I can about the way they play ball up here." The well-behaved, soft-spoken rookie played in 29 games, batting .294 with seven stolen bases.

In 1913 the 23-year-old Burns became McGraw's Opening Day left fielder, displacing speedy leadoff hitter Josh Devore, who'd fallen out of favor and soon was traded. Left field in the Polo Grounds was a notoriously difficult position on bright, sunny afternoons, and Devore had lost fly balls in the sun too frequently for McGraw's liking. Determined not to make the same mistake, Burns worked hard to become a specialist at playing the sun field, in time adopting a special cap with an extra long bill and blue sunglasses attached to it (at the plate he switched to a short-billed cap). Reporters dubbed the left-field bleachers "Burnsville," as the pint-sized speedster rapidly established himself as a fan favorite. Initially batting third in the order, George moved to leadoff at midseason and became known for his daring base running. Playing in 150 games, Burns batted .286 and finished second in the NL in doubles (37), third in hits (173), and fourth in stolen bases (40).

Moving back to the three-hole in 1914, Burns enjoyed his greatest season, finishing fourth in the Chalmers

Award voting and earning a spot on *Baseball Magazine*'s National League All-America team for the first time (he also made the team each season from 1917 to 1919). He batted a career-high .303 and led the NL in runs (100) and stolen bases (a career-high 62). Burns also ranked second in the NL in hits (tied with Zack Wheat at 170) and on-base percentage (.403), and third in doubles (35) and bases on balls (89).

Starting in 1915 George Burns was the Giants leadoff hitter for most of his stay in Manhattan. The denizens of Burnsville were rarely disappointed, as their hero almost never missed a game; from 1915 to 1917 he played in 459 consecutive contests, then a record for an outfielder. One of Burns' worst seasons was 1915, when he batted a career-low .272 and the Giants finished last. He bounced back to lead the NL in runs in 1916 and 1917, and during the latter season he also led the NL with 75 bases on balls. Burns went on to lead the league in walks five times in seven years, peaking with 101 in 1923. Apparently it took him several years to acquire his plate discipline; in his rookie season of 1913, sportswriter Hugh Fullerton wrote, "Burns looks odd on the New York team because of the quick, business-like manner he uses in batting. He walks right up and hits, as if in a hurry to get it over."

In 1919 Burns had the second-highest batting average of his career (.303) and led the NL in on-base percentage (.396) and stolen bases (40). George set career highs in runs (115) and hits (181) in 1920, and he remained a fixture in left field for the Giants until midseason 1921, when he moved to center to make room for Irish Meusel. His performance in that year's World Series was his best of the three in which he participated. Burns batted .333 for the victorious Giants, collecting 11 hits in all (four in Game Three alone), five of them for extra bases. Surprisingly, the 1921 World Series was his last appearance in the Giants lineup.

On December 6, 1921, McGraw traded Burns, catcher Mike Gonzalez, and $150,000 to the Cincinnati Reds for Heinie Groh. New York expressed its gratitude for George's decade of service by holding a "George Burns Day" on June 10, 1922. As part of the ceremonies, the Giants hoisted their 1921 world championship flag with Burns (in his Cincinnati uniform) leading the procession. Playing center and right, the sun fields at Redland Field, George continued to perform up to his customary standard in 1922-23, not missing a single game in either season. He slipped a notch in 1924, however, and in 1925 the Phillies acquired him for the waiver price. The 35-year-old outfielder batted .292 in 88 games in his final major league campaign.

Burns continued as an active player in the minor leagues through 1930. In 1926 he played in 163 games for Newark and led the International League in doubles (49) and stolen bases (38). The following two years he was player-manager for Williamsport of the New York-Penn League, finishing out the 1928 season with 18 games as player-manager for Hanover of the Blue Ridge League. In 1931, his last year in baseball, George returned to the Polo Grounds as a coach for McGraw's Giants. In retirement he returned to Gloversville, New York, just outside Utica, and ran his father's pool hall for a time, then became the payroll clerk at a tannery. Occasionally Burns played first base for local semipro teams. After retiring in 1957, he lived quietly in Gloversville until his death at age 76 on August 15, 1966.

R. J. Lesch

NEW YORK

CHARLES MONROE "JEFF" TESREAU
RIGHT-HANDED PITCHER 1912–18

At 6'2" and 225 lbs., Jeff Tesreau was big and strong, just the way John McGraw liked his pitchers. With a steady personality and solid work ethic, Tesreau leaped to stardom after developing a devastating spitball that he threw with the speed of a top fastball. Over the course of his seven-year career he compiled a 115-72 record and 2.43 ERA while holding opponents to a .223 batting average (for comparison's sake, Walter Johnson's career mark was .227, Christy Mathewson's was .236, and Pete Alexander's was .250, though each pitched considerably longer than Tesreau), leading the National League in that category in each of his first three seasons. "That big fellow has the best spitball in the league," said Johnny Evers. "I think he is as good with the spitter as Ed Walsh."

Charles Monroe Tesreau (TEZ-row) was born on March 5, 1889, on a farm near Ironton in the mining country of southeast Missouri (the encyclopedias list his birthplace as Silver Mine, a town that no longer exists). Charlie worked on the farm and completed eight years of school, setting off for nearby Perryville at age 17 to work in a lead mine and pitch for the mining company's team. His blazing fastball soon attracted the attention of the Perryville team of the independent Trolley League, which signed him for $50 a month. At Perryville in 1908 Tesreau won 37 of the 43 games he pitched, routinely striking out half the batters he faced. He signed with Austin of the Texas League, but when St. Louis Browns scout Charlie Barrett offered him a contract, he signed that one too. Austin appealed to the National Commission and won the rights to Tesreau.

Managing Houston of the Texas League in 1909, Barrett ended up with Tesreau anyway when Austin released him. The scout-turned-manager pitched Tesreau in a series of exhibitions against the Browns, but St. Louis manager Jimmy McAleer wasn't interested in the big right hander. After Houston dismissed Barrett, Tesreau went hopping from team to team around the Texas League and elsewhere, earning the nickname "Bullfrog." Scouts loved his fastball, but managers feared his inability to control it. During a tryout with the Detroit Tigers, Tesreau injured Germany Schaefer and Charley O'Leary with errant fastballs, earning him a trip back to the Texas League. In 1910 he pitched the whole season for Shreveport and posted a 15-14 record with 179 strikeouts against only 71 walks. The New York Giants purchased him and brought him to New York in September. Though Tesreau didn't get into any games, he did catch the eye of sportswriter Bill McBeth, who noticed the big pitcher's resemblance to heavyweight boxer Jim Jeffries and nicknamed him "Jeff."

At spring training in 1911, Giants special instructor Wilbert Robinson determined that Tesreau needed more control and an out pitch to go along with his fastball. Robinson suggested the spitter. Big Jeff worked on the pitch all spring while barnstorming throughout the South. One day in the lobby of the Hotel Murphy in Richmond, Virginia, after that day's exhibition was rained out, Damon Runyon reportedly overheard Tesreau say, "It would be a great day for bear hunting. Bears always bite best when it's raining." Runyon dubbed him "The Big Bear Hunter of the Ozarks," even though he technically wasn't from the Ozarks. Later Jeff told interviewers that he'd never hunted bear, either ("quail are my specialty"), so the nickname was shortened to "The Big Bear of the Ozarks," or simply "The Ozark Bear." With more nicknames than reliable pitches, Tesreau spent the 1911 season with Toronto of the Eastern League under the tutelage of yet another former

McGraw teammate, Joe Kelley. Continuing to work on his spitball, he compiled a 14-9 record but walked 96 batters in 213 innings.

Robinson again worked with Tesreau during spring training in 1912. This time Jeff opened the season with the Giants, starting the second game of the year on a dark, gloomy day at Brooklyn's Washington Park. He gave up only three hits and three walks, but Giant errors caused his demise, 4-2. "Tesreau has curves which bend like barrel hoops and speed like lightning," wrote the *New York Times*. "He's just the kind of a strong man McGraw has been looking for." Jeff remained a regular starter throughout the season, compiling a seven-game winning streak down the stretch that included a no-hitter against the Phillies on September 6. For the year the rookie posted a 17-7 record and led the NL in the brand-new category of earned run average, his 1.96 mark beating out teammate Mathewson's 2.12.

McGraw selected Tesreau, his most effective late-season pitcher, to start the World Series opener at the Polo Grounds, preferring that his rookie pitch in front of a home crowd. He ended up losing to Boston Red Sox ace Smoky Joe Wood, 4-3, and dropped the rematch in Game Four, 3-1, but McGraw turned to him once again in Game Seven, with the Giants down three games to two (with one tie). Tesreau rewarded his manager's confidence with an 11-4 win over Wood to tie the Series at three games apiece. "It was the worst game I pitched and the only one I won," he recalled.

After his eventful rookie year, Tesreau remained one of the Giants' top starters for the next five seasons. In 1913 he went 22-13 with a 2.17 ERA for another pennant-winning club, but he lost his only World Series start, 8-2. On May 16, 1914, Jeff was one out away from a second no-hitter when Joe Kelly of the Pirates lined a single for Pittsburgh's only hit of the game. While the rest of the Giants swooned late in the season to finish second to the Miracle Braves, Tesreau led the staff with a 26-10 record and 2.37 ERA. His eight shutouts were the most in the National League, and he also posted career highs in games started (40), complete games (26), innings (322⅓), and strikeouts (189). The following year Tesreau went 19-16 with a 2.29 ERA

despite pitching for a last-place club. Though he slipped a little in 1916-17, going a combined 27-22 even as the Giants rebounded to winning form, he reported to training camp in 1918 in excellent shape, ready to resume his past level of success.

Prior to spring training McGraw had asked Tesreau to take the pitchers, catchers, and some out-of-condition players and a few others down South for some early work. When the manager arrived later, he asked Jeff to report on the players' evening activities. The big pitcher refused, claiming that a man's behavior away from the ballpark was his own business. That touched off a feud between the stubborn manager and his equally stubborn pitcher. Tesreau got off to a tough-luck start, going 4-4 but with a 2.32 ERA in his first dozen games, and suddenly left the team. He was just 29 years old but he never pitched another game in Organized Baseball.

With World War I underway, Tesreau took a job with Bethlehem Steel and went 7-4 in 12 games in the Steel League that year. He made the acquaintance of Tom Keady, the company's recreational executive, who had connections at Dartmouth College. Dartmouth was looking for a new baseball coach, and Keady recommended Tesreau. Jeff refused to report to the Giants in 1919, and McGraw refused to release or trade him, so the big pitcher spent the year coaching Dartmouth.

Despite an offer from the Boston Braves, Tesreau ended up spending the rest of his life coaching at Dartmouth, though he occasionally pitched for New England semipro teams through 1925. He became a beloved figure as well as a successful coach on the Ivy League campus, frequently going up against his nemesis from the 1912 World Series, Joe Wood, who was coaching at Yale. Tesreau's career record from 1919 to 1946 was 379 wins, 264 losses, and four ties. His teams won the Quadrangular League championship in 1925 and the Eastern League championship in 1930, 1935, 1936, and 1938. In Tesreau's later years his weight ballooned to nearly 300 lbs. He was only 57 when he died in Hanover, New Hampshire, on September 24, 1946, five days after suffering a stroke during a fishing trip.

R. J. LESCH

NEW YORK

James Francis Thorpe
Outfielder 1913–19

Jim Thorpe was the Deadball Era's greatest all-around athlete. In addition to playing major league baseball for six seasons, the 6'1", 185 lb. Thorpe was an Olympic champion in the pentathlon and decathlon and the greatest American football player in history, according to a 1977 *Sport Magazine* poll. His disappointing baseball career—in 289 National League games he hit only .252 with seven home runs and 29 stolen bases—demonstrated what multi-sport athletes like Michael Jordan have since discovered, that mere possession of superb natural tools doesn't guarantee success on the diamond. "I can't seem to hit curves," Jim admitted. "I believe I could hit .300 otherwise."

Great-grandson of the famed warrior Black Hawk of the Sauk (sometimes called Sac) tribe, James Francis Thorpe was born on May 28, 1887, on the Sac and Fox Indian reservation near Prague, in the Oklahoma Territory. His father, Hiram, was a blacksmith who married at least five Native American women and fathered more than 20 children. Because of his early athletic prowess, Jim received the name Wa-tho-huck ("Path Lit by Lightning" in the Mesquakie-Sauk language) from his mother, Charlotte. The boy was a disciplinary problem, however, and his truancy finally angered his father so much that he sent him to the Carlisle Indian School in Pennsylvania in 1904. A vocational institution operated by the federal government to teach Indians industrial skills and integrate them into white society, Carlisle was, according to one of its former athletes, "nothing but an eighth-grade school, but they called us a college."

In the fall of 1907, Carlisle coach Glenn "Pop" Warner convinced Thorpe to try out for the football team. Jim excelled at halfback, punter, and kicker, but in 1909 he withdrew from Carlisle (one of several times he left the institution) and worked on a farm in North Carolina. During the summers of 1910-11 he accepted $60 per month to play baseball in the Eastern Carolina League for Rocky Mount and Fayetteville. Encouraged by Warner—and with an eye turned toward the 1912 Olympics—Thorpe returned to Carlisle in 1911-12. He was sensational on the gridiron against major collegiate foes, and Walter Camp selected him for the All-America football team in both years.

With his triumphs at the Stockholm Olympics in 1912, Thorpe's fame spread worldwide. "Sir, you are the greatest athlete in the world," declared Sweden's King Gustav. After the Games, however, Thorpe was forced to return his medals and trophies when the Amateur Athletic Union discovered that he'd played minor league baseball. "I did not play for money," he wrote in a letter to the AAU president. "I was not very wise in the ways of the world and did not realize this was wrong. I hope I will be partly excused by the fact that I was simply an Indian School Boy and did not know that I was doing wrong because I was doing what many other college men had done, except they did not use their own names."

Stripped of his amateur status, Thorpe signed a three-year contract in February 1913 for the staggering sum of $6,000 per season—the most ever paid to a major league rookie—to play baseball for the New York Giants, who beat out five other clubs to sign him. "There can be no denying that he is a great prospect," wrote one observer, "and many critics would not be surprised if, under McGraw's careful tutelage, he developed into another Ty Cobb." At the signing ceremony, however, the Giants manager admitted that he'd never seen Thorpe in action; he didn't know what position he played or even that Thorpe was right-handed.

Thorpe got off to a rocky start with the Giants by showing up late for a spring training exhibition. He received time at first base and the outfield, and his difficulty with breaking pitches soon became evident. During the season Thorpe was used primarily as a pinch-hitter and pinch-runner, compiling only 35 at-bats and hitting .143 with two stolen bases. "I felt like a sitting hen, not a ballplayer," he said. His roommate, Chief Meyers, remembered a night when Jim came in late and woke him up. "He was crying, and tears were rolling down his cheeks," Meyers recalled. "'You know, Chief,' he said, 'the King of Sweden gave me those trophies, he gave them to me. But they took them away from me, even though the guy who finished second refused to take them.'"

On the Giants' 1913-14 World Tour, Thorpe brought along his first wife (he eventually had three), but McGraw viewed his behavior as inappropriate for a married man and lectured him on the dangers of drinking. After playing most of the 1914 season in the American Association with Milwaukee, he spent most of 1915 in the Eastern League, hitting a combined .303 with 22 steals for Harrisburg and Jersey City; with the latter club he was sued for his involvement in a saloon brawl, while the former club had released him because of his "disturbing influence on the team." Thorpe was back in Milwaukee in 1916. In the press McGraw insisted that although Jim was still raw, he was a fast learner with the instincts to become a star. Privately, however, Mac was beginning to have doubts.

In 1917 McGraw loaned Thorpe to the Cincinnati Reds, then managed by Christy Mathewson. "Jim would take only two strides to my three," said Reds teammate Edd Roush. "I'd run just as hard as I could, and he'd keep up with me just trotting along." Recalled from Cincinnati on August 1, Thorpe appeared in 26 more games for the Giants and ended his only big-league season in which he appeared in over 100 games with a composite average of .237. In 1918 he appeared in only 58 games all year, and the following season he'd appeared in just two as of May 21. After Jim complained about his lack of playing time, the Giants traded him to the Boston Braves for washed-up pitcher Pat Ragan. Thorpe hit .327 in 60 games for the Braves, by far his best major league performance, but 1919 proved to be his last season in the majors.

Over the next three years Jim Thorpe played baseball for several minor league clubs but focused most of his energies on professional football, which he'd been playing during the off-season since founding the Canton Bulldogs in 1915. Jim had trouble adjusting to life after professional sports. In 1930 he traveled to Southern California as master of ceremonies for C. C. Pyle's cross-country marathon. He settled there, working as a ditch digger on a WPA project and an extra in 50 motion pictures (including the James Cagney classic, *White Heat*). Though past the age of enlistment, Thorpe joined the Merchant Marine in 1945 and served on an ammunition ship. Burt Lancaster played him in the 1951 movie *Jim Thorpe—All-American*. Thorpe tried to develop a nightclub act in the early 1950s. Newspapers reported that he was penniless.

Jim Thorpe was 65 years old when he died of a heart attack in his trailer home in Lomita, California, on March 28, 1953. Though he'd been operating a nearby bar, his death certificate listed his occupation simply as "Athlete." Jim's third wife had his body interred in Shawnee, Oklahoma, before she moved it to Tulsa. In 1957 the body was transferred once again to Mauch Chunk and East Mauch Chunk, Pennsylvania. Hoping to transform themselves into a tourist center, the towns merged and renamed themselves Jim Thorpe in his honor. After a long campaign led by Thorpe's daughter Grace, the International Olympic Committee reversed its 1912 decision on Thorpe's eligibility in 1983, reissuing his gold medals and adding his name to its list of Olympic champions.

DON JENSEN

NEW YORK

BENJAMIN MICHAEL KAUFF
CENTER FIELDER 1916–20

A flashy dresser and world-class trash talker, Bennie Kauff was the Deion Sanders of the Deadball Era. "I'll make them all forget that a guy named Ty Cobb ever pulled on a baseball shoe," the brash 26-year-old told reporters on his arrival with the New York Giants in 1916. Kauff's boastfulness wasn't without some justification. Dubbed "The Ty Cobb of the Federal League," Kauff was the most heralded young player of his generation, a five-tool star whose unique combination of speed and power defied his stocky 5'8" frame. Though he performed well in the National League's faster company, Kauff never matched the high expectations he and others had set for him, and his career ended prematurely in 1921 with his controversial banishment from the game.

Benjamin Michael Kauff was born on January 5, 1890, in Pomeroy, Ohio, the oldest child of William and Hanna Kauff. The Kauffs descended from German immigrants, and because of his name many sources incorrectly state that he was Jewish. William Kauff worked independently in the mines, and when Bennie turned 11 he quit school and went into partnership with his father. The younger Kauff was unusually strong. "Benny's shoulders and arms are out of proportion to his height," one reporter observed. "Despite this fact, he is not muscle-bound, can throw a ball like a shot out of a rifle, and is as fast and agile as a rabbit." Bennie credited his strength to his long hours in the mines. "The work was very hard," he told *Baseball Magazine*. "Seven years I worked in the dust and grime and baseball proved my way of escape from a lifetime spent in the same monotonous way."

Kauff got his start playing weekend baseball for local amateur teams. By 1909 he was a jack-of-all-trades for the Keystones, a neighborhood club. "In my first game I caught for three innings, pitched for three innings, and then caught for three more innings," Kauff recalled. His pitching was good enough to merit a professional gig with Parkersburg, West Virginia, of the Virginia Valley League in 1910. The league didn't keep official statistics, but sources indicate that Kauff compiled a 14-4 pitching record with a .417 batting average and 87 stolen bases.

Based on that stellar performance, the New York Highlanders invited Kauff to spring training in 1911. Noting the left hander's rifle arm and brilliance with the bat, manager Hal Chase projected him as an outfielder but decided that he was too green for the majors. New York sent him north to Bridgeport of the Connecticut State League, where Kauff established himself as one of the league's most promising players. The Yankees looked him over again in 1912, then farmed him out after he appeared in all of five games. This time he wound up with Hartford, where he led the Eastern Association with a .345 batting average in 1913. That performance caught the attention of the St. Louis Cardinals, who sent Kauff to Indianapolis of the American Association, hoping they could hide him there until they needed him.

Kauff did play for Indianapolis in 1914, but not in the American Association. Prior to the start of the season, the Hoosiers of the upstart Federal League swooped in and offered him double his previous salary. Understandably frustrated with his lack of progress in

Organized Baseball, Kauff accepted and quickly became the new league's top attraction. Playing primarily center field, he easily paced the circuit in runs (120), hits (211), on-base percentage (.447), and stolen bases (75), and his .370 batting average topped his nearest competitor by more than 20 points. As Kauff lifted the Hoosiers to the pennant, the press notices started piling up. "Kauff is the premier slugger, premier fielder, premier base stealer and best all-round player in the league," gushed *The Sporting Life*.

"He is being called a second Ty Cobb, yet there are many followers of the Federal clubs who say that within next season Kauff will play rings around the Georgia Peach." According to sportswriter Frank Graham, Kauff loved the publicity "and cheerfully agreed that he was at least Ty's equal, if not his superior, for he was not bound by false modesty."

Off the field, Kauff flaunted a wardrobe replete with diamond rings and fancy diamond tie pins to match his ego. "Having seen him in civilian array, we are undecided whether Benny Kauff is a better show on or off," Damon Runyon remarked. "In his working apparel he is a companion piece to Tyrus Raymond Cobb and Tris Speaker, while in his street makeup he is a sort of Diamond Jim Brady reduced to a baseball salary size." To his teammates, Kauff was renowned for his ability to chew tobacco, smoke a cigar, and drink a glass of beer all at the same time, without interruption to any of the three pursuits. In short, he was a hell of a lot of fun, and the New York Giants wanted him. After the 1914 season, the Federal League's Indianapolis franchise shifted to Newark, but Kauff found himself transferred to the Brooklyn Tip Tops as repayment of the outgoing Indianapolis owner's old debts. Kauff thought he should have been a free agent, so he negotiated a three-year contract with the Giants in April 1915. At the press conference announcing his signing, Kauff declared that he would "bunt a home run into that right-field stand every day." But when the Giants attempted to take the field against the Boston Braves with Kauff in center field later that afternoon, the Braves refused to play, arguing that Kauff was ineligible because he'd signed with an outlaw league. NL president John Tener agreed and voided the contract.

Exiled to Brooklyn, Kauff again played brilliantly, leading the Federal League with a .342 batting average, .446 on-base percentage, and .509 slugging percentage, all while swiping a league-best 55 bases. That performance did nothing to dissuade the Giants from their quest to land him. When the Federal League folded following the 1915 season, Kauff applied for and received reinstatement into Organized Baseball, then inked another contract with the Giants. It was, Kauff confided to a reporter, "the ambition of my life."

A half century later, Graham vividly recalled Kauff's first appearance in camp with the Giants in the spring of 1916: "He wore a loudly-striped silk shirt, an expensive blue suit, patent leather shoes, a fur-collared over-coat and a derby hat," Graham wrote. "He was adorned with a huge diamond stickpin, an equally huge diamond ring and a gold watch encrusted with diamonds, and he had roughly $7,500 in his pockets." The forgiving right-field porch of the Polo Grounds was still on Kauff's mind. "I'll hit so many balls into the grandstand that the management will have to put screens up in front to protect the fans and save the money that lost balls would cost," he bragged. The New York press loved his act, and soon headlines like ALL PITCHERS WILL BE EASY, KAUFF ADMITS graced the sports pages.

Judged against the hype, Kauff was a huge disappointment. Playing center field every day, he didn't set the league on fire, he didn't destroy NL pitching, he didn't reinvent the game; he was merely very good. His unimpressive .264 batting average masked other attributes: a knack for getting on base, a penchant for the long ball (he hit nine home runs and 15 triples that season), and an aggressive—though some called it reckless—baserunning style that produced 40 stolen bases. That package would have been a credit to any team, but alas, it didn't measure up to Ty Cobb. The fans never let him forget it. "Why, do you know, back in New York they jeer me if I don't knock the cover off the ball with every swing," Kauff groused during a June road trip. He also complained that he'd been treated unfairly by the media. "The newspaper men in New York are inclined to josh a fellow a little more than seems necessary," he said. "I have tried to treat everybody fairly. And while there is probably no ill feeling on their part, they have made me out a sort of swell-headed gink."

In the eyes of a public fixated on batting averages, Kauff played much better in 1917 and 1918, as he cleared the magic .300 barrier each season. But with more singles came fewer walks and extra-base hits, and as a result his cumulative offensive value remained more or less constant. He managed to steal some headlines in the 1917 World Series when his two home runs propelled New York to a Game Four victory. He was in the middle of another fine season in 1918 when he was drafted into the Army, helping train new recruits until the Great War ended that November. In retrospect, Kauff's wartime break from baseball was an important demarcation in his brief career. In his first two and one-half seasons in the NL, Kauff found himself at the cen-

ter of a swirling vortex of media hype and criticism, mostly of his own creation. Yet when he returned to the Polo Grounds in 1919, the prevailing atmosphere was far more somber—and scandalous.

Kauff put forth another good season in 1919, finishing second in the NL in home runs (10) and fourth in RBI (67). Despite his efforts, the Giants never seriously challenged for the pennant. By September New York's hopeless situation convinced at least two regulars, Hal Chase and Heinie Zimmerman, to start fixing games. During one western trip, Chase and Zimmerman tried to bribe several teammates to help them, including Kauff, who reported the attempt to McGraw. Despite that act of integrity, rumors of Kauff's own dishonesty soon began to surface. Billy Maharg, one of the conspirators who helped fix the 1919 World Series, later claimed that Kauff had taken part in that scheme, and Arnold Rothstein, the notorious gambler who had bankrolled the operation, reportedly told American

League president Ban Johnson that Kauff had asked him for $50,000 in bribe money to give to the players prior to the Series.

The most substantive allegation of wrongdoing emerged in February 1920 when Kauff was indicted on auto-theft charges in connection with the Manhattan auto-parts business he'd started the previous fall with his half-brother, Frank Home, and Giants teammate Jesse Barnes. Authorities alleged that in December Kauff and two associates stole a vehicle from a West End Avenue parking lot, then fitted it with a new paint job, new tires, and a new license before selling it to an unsuspecting customer for $1,800. Kauff denied the charges, contending that he was unaware the car was stolen when he resold it.

That's where matters stood when the bell rung on the 1920 season. Despite the ongoing criminal investigation, Kauff reported for duty with the Giants. With the ugly rumors surrounding Kauff and the entire sport that season, McGraw grew reluctant to play his talented center fielder and finally sent him to the Toronto Maple Leafs of the International League in early July. In the half season Kauff spent in Toronto, he batted .343 and stole 28 bases, even as he endured taunts from fans. The auto-theft case still hadn't gone to trial, but at season's end McGraw re-acquired Kauff anyway, telling reporters he expected to use him as his regular center fielder. "Kauff is innocent of the charge of buying stolen automobiles," McGraw contended. "He simply got in with evil companions who mixed him into the case before he knew it."

Commissioner Landis, however, had his own suspicions. After meeting with Kauff prior to the start of the 1921 season, Landis ruled that the Giant center fielder would be ineligible pending resolution of the criminal matter. The trial finally began in early May and lasted five days. The state's chief witnesses were Kauff's two evil companions, ex-cons who claimed they'd helped Kauff select and refit the stolen automobile. The defense countered that Kauff had been eating dinner with his wife at the time of the alleged incident, then brought out a series of character witnesses, including McGraw and teammate George Burns, to defend Kauff's reputation. The jury deliberated for less than an hour before returning a not-guilty verdict.

After his victory in court, Kauff had every expectation that he'd be quickly reinstated into the good graces of Organized Baseball. He was in for a surprise. Landis sat on Kauff's application for much of the summer, then refused to lift the ban. Despite the verdict, Landis insisted that the trial "disclosed a state of affairs that more than seriously compromises your character and reputation. The reasonable and necessary result of this is that your mere presence in the lineup would inevitably burden patrons of the game with grave apprehension as to its integrity." Landis later told Fred Lieb that the jury's verdict "smelled to high heaven" and was "one of the worst miscarriages of justice that ever came under my observation."

Kauff had never been formally accused of throwing games, but *The Sporting News* applauded Landis' decision and linked Kauff with the eight banned Black Sox. "They, too, like Kauff, are 'innocent' in the eyes of a trial court, but the court of public opinion has its own notions regarding them," the paper editorialized. "Presumably we have heard the last of Bennie Kauff in baseball. It is well." Stunned by Landis's decision, Kauff applied to the New York State Supreme Court for a permanent injunction against his banishment. "I say that I am every inch as much of a gentleman, and have as high a sense of ethics and character as this man Landis, who has no standing as far as I am concerned," Kauff said. But all hope for resuscitating his career ended in January 1922, when the court concluded it had no grounds to act on Kauff's request, though in his ruling Justice E. G. Whitaker agreed that "an apparent injustice has been done the plaintiff [Kauff]."

His playing career over, Kauff lived out much of the rest of his life in Columbus, Ohio, with his wife, Hazel, and the couple's only child, Robert. According to his obituary, the banned player worked for 22 years as a scout, and later, appropriately enough, as a clothing salesman. Kauff died on November 17, 1961, after suffering a cerebral hemorrhage. He is buried in Columbus's Union Cemetery.

DAVID JONES

CHICAGO

The home of National League baseball in Chicago from 1893 to 1915, West Side Grounds hosted four World Series from 1906 to 1910, the most successful period in the history of the Cubs franchise.

When the Chicago Orphans—so named in 1898 when Pop Anson was fired after 19 years at their helm—finished the 1901 season tied for sixth, it proved the low point of the most successful decade in franchise history. Over the next four years, new manager Frank Selee built the foundation of outstanding teams to come by acquiring pitchers Mordecai Brown and Ed Reulbach and forming the best-known double-play combination of all time by moving Joe Tinker to shortstop, signing Johnny Evers to play second, and turning Frank Chance into a first baseman. Tuberculosis forced Selee to take what turned out to be a permanent leave of absence in mid-1905, with Chance serving as his replacement, but by that time the Cubs—the team's new nickname, coined in 1902 because of the youthfulness of its players—were solid contenders.

Starting in 1906, the Chicago Cubs put together one of baseball's greatest dynasties, winning four pennants and two world championships in five seasons. New owner Charles Murphy added the finishing touches by acquiring Jimmy Sheckard, Harry Steinfeldt, Jack Pfiester, and Orval Overall. The Cubs won 55 of their last 65 games in 1906 to finish with a record 116 victories, thanks in large part to a 1.76 team ERA. Lowering that mark to 1.73 in 1907, Chicago won 107 games and swept Detroit in the World Series, the first

WINNING PERCENTAGE 1901–1919

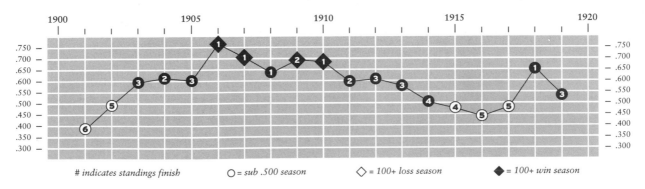

# indicates standings finish   ○ = sub .500 season   ◇ = 100+ loss season   ◆ = 100+ win season

of two consecutive wins over the Tigers in the fall classic, the last in team history. The Cubs completed their dynasty with 104 wins in each of the next two seasons, finishing second in 1909 and bringing their final pennant to West Side Grounds in 1910.

Despite a Chalmers Award–winning performance by Frank Schulte, whose 21 home runs set a modern record, Chance's great machine sputtered to second in 1911 and finally showed signs of breaking down: Steinfeldt was released, Overall retired with a sore arm, catcher Johnny Kling was dispatched to Boston, and Chance himself played in just 31 games. The following year Heinie Zimmerman batted .372, but the Cubs dropped to third place, after which Chance resigned, Tinker was traded to Cincinnati, and Brown and Sheckard were released. Reulbach was sold to Brooklyn in midseason 1913, and Evers was traded to Boston after managing the club to another third-place finish. By 1914 Schulte was the only regular left from the Cubs of 1906-10.

After the Federal League collapsed, Chicago Whales owner Charles Weeghman acquired a controlling interest in the Cubs in 1916 and moved them into his ballpark at Clark and Addison streets on the north side of Chicago, where they play to this day. Two years later the Cubs captured their fifth pennant of the Deadball Era—and last until 1929—behind the strong pitching of Jim Vaughn, Claude Hendrix, and Lefty Tyler.

ALL-ERA TEAM

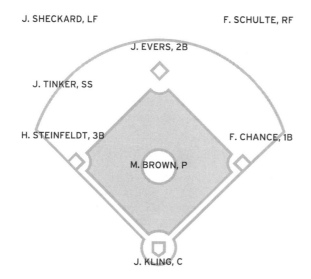

A. HOFMAN, CF

J. SHECKARD, LF   F. SCHULTE, RF

J. EVERS, 2B

J. TINKER, SS

H. STEINFELDT, 3B   F. CHANCE, 1B

M. BROWN, P

J. KLING, C

TEAM LEADERS 1901–1919

BATTING

GAMES
F. Schulte 1564
J. Tinker 1537
J. Evers 1409

RUNS
F. Schulte 827
J. Evers 742
F. Chance 699

HITS
F. Schulte 1590
J. Tinker 1436
J. Evers 1340

RBI
F. Schulte 712
J. Tinker 670
H. Zimmerman 561

DOUBLES
F. Schulte 254
J. Tinker 220
H. Zimmerman 210

TRIPLES
F. Schulte 117
J. Tinker 93
H. Zimmerman 80

HOME RUNS
F. Schulte 91
V. Saier 53
H. Zimmerman 48

STOLEN BASES
F. Chance 375
J. Tinker 304
J. Evers 291

BATTING AVERAGE
H. Zimmerman 304
F. Chance 298
F. Merkle 276

PITCHING

GAMES
M. Brown 346
E. Reulbach 281
J. Vaughn 248

WINS
M. Brown 188
E. Reulbach 136
J. Vaughn 129

LOSSES
M. Brown 86
J. Vaughn 78
J. Lavender 68

INNINGS
M. Brown 2329
E. Reulbach 1864⅔
J. Vaughn 1806

STRIKEOUTS
M. Brown 1043
J. Vaughn 977
E. Reulbach 799

WALKS
E. Reulbach 650
J. Vaughn 509
C. Lundgren 476

SHUTOUTS
M. Brown 48
E. Reulbach 31
J. Vaughn 31

ERA
M. Brown 1.80
J. Pfiester 1.85
O. Overall 1.91

The 1906 Cubs set a single-season record with 116 wins, which was unmatched until the 2001 Seattle Mariners tied it, playing 10 additional games.

TYPICAL LINEUPS 1901–1919

1901

1. T. Hartsel, LF
2. D. Green, CF
3. C. Dexter, INF
4. J. Doyle, 1B
   F. Chance, RF
5. C. Childs, 2B
6. F. Raymer, 3B
7. B. McCormick, SS
8. J. Kling
   M. Kahoe, C

1902

1. J. Slagle, LF
2. D. Jones, CF-RF
3. F. Chance, 1B
4. J. Dobbs, CF
   B. Congalton, RF
5. J. Tinker, SS
6. B. Lowe, 2B
7. J. Kling, C
8. G. Schaefer, 3B

1903

1. J. Slagle, LF
2. D. Casey, 3B
3. F. Chance, 1B
4. D. Jones, CF
5. J. Tinker, SS
6. D. Harley, RF
7. J. Evers, 2B
8. J. Kling, C

1904

1. J. Slagle, LF
2. D. Casey, 3B
3. F. Chance, 1B
4. J. McCarthy, CF
5. D. Jones, RF
6. J. Evers, 2B
7. J. Kling, C
8. J. Tinker, SS

1905

1. J. Slagle, CF
2. F. Schulte, LF
3. B. Maloney, RF
4. F. Chance, 1B
5. J. Tinker, SS
6. J. Evers, 2B
7. D. Casey, 3B
8. J. Kling, C

1906

1. J. Slagle, CF
2. J. Sheckard, LF
3. F. Schulte, RF
4. F. Chance, 1B
5. H. Steinfeldt, 3B
6. J. Tinker, SS
7. J. Evers, 2B
8. J. Kling, C

1907

1. J. Slagle, CF
2. J. Sheckard, LF
3. F. Schulte, RF
4. F. Chance, 1B
5. H. Steinfeldt, 3B
6. J. Tinker, SS
7. J. Evers, 2B
8. J. Kling, C

1908

1. J. Slagle, CF
2. J. Sheckard, LF
3. F. Schulte, RF
4. F. Chance, 1B
5. H. Steinfeldt, 3B
6. J. Evers, 2B
7. J. Tinker, SS
8. J. Kling, C

1909

1. J. Evers, 2B
2. J. Sheckard, LF
3. F. Schulte, RF
4. F. Chance, 1B
5. H. Steinfeldt, 3B
6. A. Hofman, CF
7. J. Tinker, SS
8. J. Archer, C

1910

1. J. Evers, 2B
2. J. Sheckard, LF
3. A. Hofman, CF
4. F. Chance, 1B
5. H. Steinfeldt, 3B
6. F. Schulte, RF
7. J. Tinker, SS
8. J. Kling, C

1911

1. J. Sheckard, LF
2. F. Schulte, RF
3. A. Hofman, CF
4. H. Zimmerman, 2B
5. J. Doyle, 3B
6. J. Tinker, SS
7. V. Saier, 1B
8. J. Archer, C

1912

1. J. Sheckard, LF
2. F. Schulte, RF
3. J. Tinker, SS
4. H. Zimmerman, 3B
5. T. Leach, CF
6. V. Saier, 1B
7. J. Evers, 2B
8. J. Archer, C

1913

1. T. Leach, CF
2. J. Evers, 2B
3. F. Schulte, RF
4. H. Zimmerman, 3B
5. V. Saier, 1B
6. M. Mitchell, LF
7. A. Bridwell, SS
8. J. Archer, C

1914

1. T. Leach, CF
2. W. Good, RF
3. V. Saier, 1B
4. H. Zimmerman, 3B
5. F. Schulte, LF
6. B. Sweeney, 2B
7. R. Corriden, SS
8. R. Bresnahan, C

1915

1. W. Good, RF
2. B. Fisher, SS
3. F. Schulte, LF
4. H. Zimmerman, 2B
5. V. Saier, 1B
6. C. Williams, CF
7. A. Phelan, 3B
8. J. Archer, C

1916

1. R. Zeider, INF
2. M. Flack, RF
3. L. Mann, LF
4. H. Zimmerman, 3B
5. C. Williams, CF
6. V. Saier, 1B
7. J. Archer, C
   O. Knabe, 2B
8. C. Wortman, SS

1917

1. M. Flack, RF
2. L. Mann, LF
3. L. Doyle, 2B
4. F. Merkle, 1B
5. C. Williams, CF
6. C. Deal, 3B
7. C. Wortman, SS
8. A. Wilson
   R. Elliott, C

1918 (First half)

1. M. Flack, RF
2. C. Hollocher, SS
3. L. Mann, LF
4. F. Merkle, 1B
5. D. Paskert, CF
6. C. Deal, 3B
7. P. Kilduff
   R. Zeider, 2B
8. B. Killefer, C

1918 (Second half)

1. M. Flack, RF
2. C. Hollocher, SS
3. L. Mann, LF
4. D. Paskert, CF
5. F. Merkle, 1B
6. C. Deal
   C. Pick, 3B
7. R. Zeider, 2B
8. B. Killefer, C

1919

1. M. Flack, RF
2. C. Hollocher, SS
3. L. Mann, LF
4. F. Merkle, 1B
5. D. Paskert, CF
6. C. Pick, 2B
7. C. Deal, 3B
8. B. Killefer, C

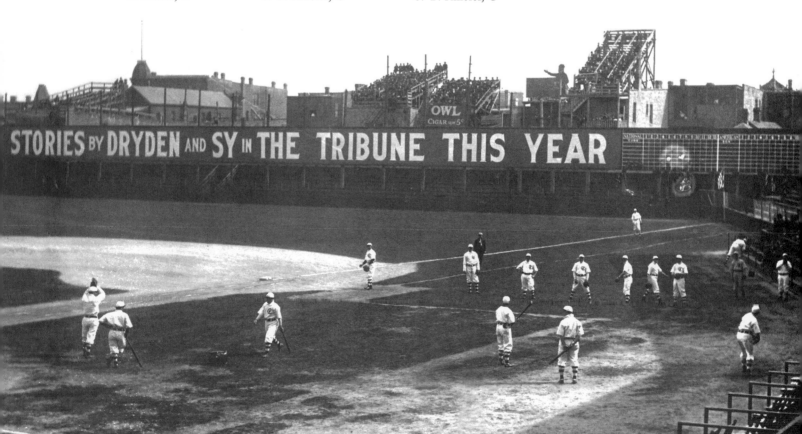

CHICAGO

Frank LeRoy Chance
First baseman 1898–1912, Manager 1905–12

Best known today for his role in Franklin P. Adams' poem "Baseball's Sad Lexicon," Frank Chance was the hardnosed and successful manager-first baseman of the Chicago Cubs from 1905 to 1912, achieving a .664 winning percentage in his seven and one-half seasons as the Cubs' "Peerless Leader." Also nicknamed "Husk" because of his physical stature (6'0", 190 lbs.), the diffident Chance transformed himself on the playing field, inspiring his players with his fighting spirit. "He is the personification of affability off the field and his Cubs like nothing better than to be invited to smoke, eat, or drink with him or to listen when he is in a conversational mood," wrote *Baseball Magazine*'s Richard Lardner, "but not even his best friend could say that he is a pleasant party to have around when a close game is in progress."

The son of William Harvey Chance, vice-president of the First National Bank of Fresno, Frank Leroy Chance was born in Fresno, California, on September 9, 1877. His parents wanted him to become a banker, and many sources state that he attended Washington College in Irvine, California, though college records don't confirm his attendance. Frank's break in baseball came in 1897 when he caught and played the outfield for the semipro Fresno Tigers, reportedly batting .386 with 45 stolen bases in just 34 games. Many sources credit his discovery to Chicago outfielder Bill Lange, a San Francisco native, but Chicago owner James Hart told a different story. Hart credited former San Francisco club owner Henry Harris, who had seen Chance catch in an amateur tournament in San Francisco in the fall of 1897. "Bill Lange had nothing to do with finding Chance," said Hart, "and never heard of him until I asked Bill to look the youngster over when he went back to the coast that fall."

Making his National League debut on April 29, 1898, the 20-year-old Chance played in 53 games as a rookie—33 at catcher, 17 in the outfield, and three at first base—batting .279 with 32 runs and 14 RBI. He continued to serve as a backup catcher through the 1900 season, and though he batted close to .300 each year, it became clear after Johnny Kling joined the team in September 1900 that he'd never become the regular backstop. Frank played mostly in the outfield in 1901, and the following year he was one of eight players who shared the first base position. Manager Frank Selee is often credited with turning Chance into a first baseman in 1903, but he did so only after rookie Bill Hanlon was a complete flop and ultimately abandoned the team. Even then Husk was considered nothing more than a temporary replacement, but he ended up playing 121 games at first base and batting .327 with a league-leading 67 stolen bases. He followed up that performance in 1904 by leading the team again with a .310 average and clouting six home runs, a career high.

Selee fell ill with tuberculosis midway through the 1905 season, leaving the Cubs with a 37-28 record. The players conducted a vote and selected Chance as his successor. After Hart ratified the choice, the 27-year-old player-manager led Selee's team to a strong 55-33 finish. On the field Chance led the team yet again in batting with a .316 mark, and he also led the National League with a .450 on-base percentage, mainly because he established career highs in walks (78) and times hit by pitch (17). New owner Charles Murphy made the easy yet brilliant decision to retain him as player-manager for 1906, and that year the Cubs won 116 games en route to an appearance in the World Series. Dubbed "The Peerless Leader" that season by Chicago sportswriter Charles Dryden, Chance batted .319 and led the

NL in runs (103) and stolen bases (57). A couple of years later, teammate Johnny Evers wrote, "I don't think any player in the game, with the exception of Ty Cobb, did more brilliant work for his team than Frank Chance. He was a great batter, a great fielder, and a great base runner."

In a 1906 game against the Cincinnati Reds, Chance broke a late-inning tie by stealing home all the way from second base, which he had also stolen on the previous pitch. It became known as "baseball's most expensive base" when Murphy, to show his appreciation, supposedly granted him 10% ownership of the club, but Frank later claimed that he'd had to purchase his Cubs stock. Despite his great success as a player and a leader, Chance was earning considerably less than his peers among NL managers. "The years we won pennants and when we set a record of 116 games won, I was getting $5,500 a season," he recalled. "At the same time John McGraw was getting $18,000 and Fred Clarke $15,000. I had to threaten to quit in order to get my salary lifted to $10,000. Murphy would argue that I had some stock in the club and ought to be satisfied with that. Well, I bought that stock and I worked hard for it."

Chance never again topped the .300-mark after 1906, nor did he lead the NL in any offensive category, but he remained the Cubs' top target for abuse. In 1907 he received an eight-day suspension for hurling a pop bottle into the bleachers at Brooklyn, but he did so only after numerous bottles had been thrown at him. Plagued by injuries throughout his career, most notably a barrage of beanings due to his propensity for crowding the plate, Chance played in fewer games each season starting in 1908. "There are pains that shoot through his head and other parts of his body too numerous to mention, and make it just about impossible for him to take an active, playing role in the game at which he is so expert," wrote Lardner. By 1911 Chance had phased himself out of the everyday lineup, appearing in only 31 games that season.

He'd lost his hearing in one ear and part of it in the other, causing him to talk in an annoyingly whiney tone.

Chance had also developed blood clots in his brain. While hospitalized for brain surgery in 1912, he became embroiled in a public dispute with Murphy, who'd denounced the Cubs for their drinking and poor play. Chance defended his players in the newspapers, and in private he chastised Murphy for failing to spend the money to provide him with sufficient talent. On September 28, 1912, Murphy announced that Chance wouldn't return as manager. The Cubs placed him on waivers, which were withdrawn when the Cincinnati Reds claimed him, and ultimately he ended up signing a three-year contract as player-manager of the New York Yankees at $20,000 per year. Chance spent just two seasons with the Yankees, playing in just 13 games. He hated managing that team; they were a second-division club, and he was convinced that Hal Chase was throwing games on him. Chance quit the team on September 14, 1914, with the Yankees buying out the remainder of his contract for $3,300.

In 1915 Chance returned home to his magnificent "Cub Ranch" in Glendora, California, where he operated an orange grove. Using the proceeds from the sale of his Cubs stock, he purchased a one-third interest in the Los Angeles Angels of the Pacific Coast League, serving as manager in 1916-17 and playing in a handful of games. He returned to the majors in 1923 as manager of the Boston Red Sox, but the team finished dead last. The following year Chance accepted a job managing his old crosstown nemesis, the White Sox, drawing the ire of Chicago's Northside loyalists, but he was spared that ignominy when he was struck down by bronchial asthma. Frank Chance was only 47 when he died at Good Samaritan Hospital in Los Angeles on September 15, 1924. He left behind an estate valued at more than $250,000. Twenty-two years later, the Committee on Baseball Veterans elected Chance to the National Baseball Hall of Fame, along with teammates Joe Tinker and Johnny Evers. Poetic justice.

GREGORY RYHAL

CHICAGO

John W. Taylor
Right-handed pitcher 1898–1903, 1906–07

Jack Taylor was the greatest "iron man" pitcher of the 20th century, hurling 187 consecutive complete games from June 20, 1901, to August 9, 1906. Often pitching for losing teams, Taylor relied on pitch location and guile to compile a lifetime record of 152-139 with a 2.66 ERA. "Corner working is his forte," wrote one reporter. "He mixes up pitches. Fast and slow come along with almost the same motion." Ed Reulbach, who played with Taylor on the 1906-07 Cubs, claimed that his veteran teammate had a mastery over Honus Wagner. "Had Wagner been obliged to bat against Old Jack Taylor all through a season his average would have shrunk to .150," said Reulbach.

John W. Taylor was born on January 14, 1874, in New Straightsville, Ohio, in the southeast corner of the state. He later moved to nearby Nelsonville and achieved baseball notoriety pitching for semipro teams in Marietta, Ohio, and Parkersburg, West Virginia. Late in the 1896 season, Connie Mack's Pittsburgh Pirates played an exhibition in Parkersburg and Taylor beat the big-league club. Mack was impressed. When he left Pittsburgh the following year to take the helm of the Western League's Milwaukee Brewers, he signed Jack to his first professional contract. Aided by Mack's guidance, Taylor blossomed into a star with Milwaukee. His 1897 season was cut short by a broken arm, but the following year he pitched in 44 games, compiling a 28-14 record with 41 complete games. Taylor tied for the league lead with four shutouts and finished third in wins.

The National League's Louisville Colonels held an option on Taylor, but in a move that puzzled observers at the time, the Colonels relinquished their rights and allowed him to go to the Chicago Orphans for a late-season trial. (It was later reported that Louisville received pitcher Walt Woods as compensation from Chicago.) In his NL debut against Pittsburgh on September 25, 1898, Taylor pitched a complete game to defeat Bill Hart, 7-4. The rookie appeared four more times that season, each a complete-game victory, two of them against Louisville. In light of his sensational 5-0 debut, Taylor's first full major league season was a bit disappointing. He ended up with an 18-21 record and a 3.76 ERA (the league ERA was 3.85), though his 39 complete games was just one behind the league leaders. One of the season's highlights occurred on April 16, when our Jack Taylor (known as "Jack Taylor II") outpitched Cincinnati's "Brewery Jack" Taylor (known as "Jack Taylor I") for an 8-4 victory.

The fortunes of the Chicago team continued to decline in 1900. Despite his record of 10-17, Taylor actually pitched well, finishing third in the NL with a 2.55 ERA. In 1901 he improved to 13-19, though his ERA rose to 3.36, slightly above the league average. On June 13 of that year, Taylor lasted only four innings against the Giants. It was the last time he was relieved until August 13, 1906. During that span Jack completed all 187 of his starts, including both ends of a doubleheader on one occasion, and finished an additional 15 games in relief. Given the changes in the game over the last century, it's a record that is sure to stand the test of time.

Jack Taylor was the National League's best pitcher in 1902. Finishing at 23-11 for a team with a losing record, Taylor led the NL in ERA (1.33) and ranked third in innings (324⅔), fewest hits per game (7.51), and shutouts (7). On June 22 he handed the Pittsburgh Pirates a rare defeat, holding Wagner hitless in eight at-bats and beating Deacon Phillippe, 3-2, in 19 innings, the second longest game in National League history to that point. Taylor had another fine year in 1903, going 21-14 for the rapidly improving Cubs even though his ERA rose to 2.45. Again he ranked third in the NL in fewest hits per game (7.98). That season marked the end of a three-year "war" between the rival leagues, and the Cubs agreed to play their American League counterpart, the Chicago White Sox, in a city series after the conclusion of the regular season. Coming off a fine year, Taylor naturally was the choice to start the first game, and he handily mastered the seventh-place White Sox by a score of 11-0. In his other three starts, however, he lost by scores of 10-2, 9-3, and 4-2.

Suspicious of Taylor's work during the series, Cubs president Jim Hart traded him and rookie catcher Larry McLean to the St. Louis Cardinals during the off-season for pitcher Mordecai Brown and catcher Jack O'Neill. In early 1904 Taylor made his first visit to Chicago as a Cardinal. Responding to jeers from the stands over his poor performance in the city series, Jack stated, "Why should I have won? I got $100 from Hart for winning and I got $500 for losing." At that point Hart went public with his charges of dishonesty, but no immediate action was taken against Taylor. In July, however, Jack was accused of throwing a game against the Pirates. This time Garry Herrmann, chairman of the National Commission, declared that Taylor was "not an honest ball player," but he was allowed to continue playing and finished the 1904 season with a 20-19 record and a league-leading 39 complete games.

After the season a hearing was held to consider the charges against Taylor. Jack testified that he and teammate Jake Beckley had been on a drinking and gambling spree the night before the game in question. He credited his poor performance to wildness brought on by lack of sleep rather than dishonesty. On February 15, 1905, the NL Board of Directors handed down its verdict: Taylor was acquitted of throwing games, but he was found guilty of bad conduct and fined $300. Jack angrily refused to pay, saying, "They had no case against me for crookedness over in Pittsburgh." In a letter to Herrmann discussing the case, Pittsburgh club secretary W. H. Locke made a prophetic statement: "If Taylor escapes punishment the crusade will be a difficult one, as gamblers will be convinced that the league is only bluffing."

The next month Taylor was called before the National Commission for a hearing on the charges from the 1903 Chicago city series. Hart submitted three affidavits from people who overheard Taylor's statement about being paid $500 to lose, and stated that he could provide many more along the same lines, but the commission held, "The evidence submitted, alleging that the player made certain remarks relative to the post-season games of 1903, is insufficient to find him guilty of conduct detrimental to the welfare and good repute of the game." After his acquittal Taylor resumed pitching for the Cardinals, finishing the 1905 season with a 15-21 record and a lousy 3.44 ERA. He was again accused of throwing games during the 1905 city series between the Cardinals and St. Louis Browns, won by the Browns, five games to two, but no action was taken and he returned to the Cardinals for 1906.

Taylor got off to a solid start that season, going 8-9 with a 2.15 ERA, but on July 1 St. Louis traded him to the Cubs, of all teams, for pitcher Fred Beebe, catcher Pete Noonan, and cash. (By then Hart was no longer connected with the Cubs.) Finally joining a pennant-winning outfit, the 32-year-old Taylor finished out 1906 in superb form, going 12-3 with a 1.83 ERA to give him a combined record of 20-12 for the season. It proved to be his last hurrah in the major leagues.

Taylor managed only a 7-5 mark with a 3.29 ERA for the 1907 Cubs before drifting back to the minors, appearing with Columbus, Grand Rapids, Kansas City, Dayton, Evansville, and Chattanooga. Retiring from baseball after the 1913 season, Jack returned to Ohio and settled in Murray City, where he worked as a coal miner until his health failed. The former "iron man" died of cancer at age 64 on March 4, 1938, at White Cross Hospital in Columbus.

DAN GINSBURG

CHICAGO

JOHN GRANSFIELD KLING
CATCHER 1900–11

Johnny Kling was generally considered the best defensive catcher of the Deadball Era's first decade. "Kling is a brilliant general who worked perfectly with pitchers and the infield, and his throwing was near perfect," wrote Johnny Evers. The career .271 hitter was a modest, clean-cut family man, but he was also adept at the psychological warfare that was part of baseball in his era; he was a master at bolstering his pitcher's confidence and working the umpire for favorable calls, and he earned the nickname "Noisy" for the steady string of chatter he kept up from behind the plate. "John Kling is a very bad man with youngsters," wrote Christy Mathewson, "and sometimes he can get on the nerves of older players in close games when the nerves are strung tight."

John Gransfield Kling was born in Kansas City on February 25, 1875. Some have claimed that Kling was among baseball's first Jewish stars, but a letter written by his wife states that he was a baptized Lutheran. At an early age Johnny started making deliveries for the family baking business, but he sometimes allowed a ball game to interrupt his rounds. In 1893-95 he was the pitcher-manager and leadoff hitter of the Schmeltzers, a Kansas City semipro outfit. In 1896 Kling made an impressive professional debut with Houston of the Texas League, batting .356 in 52 games in the outfield and at shortstop. He played those same positions the following year at Rockford of the Western Association, appearing in 14 games before returning to the Schmeltzers. Kling's big break came in 1900, when he moved behind the plate and batted .301 in 108 games for St. Joseph, Missouri, of the Western League. Dispatched by the Chicago Orphans to scout Sammy Strang, Ted Sullivan was so impressed with Kling that he also purchased the young backstop.

In his major league debut, Kling went 3-for-4 as the Orphans tied the second game of a doubleheader on September 11, 1900. The next day he proved his toughness in a seventh-inning collision with New York Giants pitcher Win Mercer; Johnny remained in the game while Mercer was carried off the field unconscious. That fall Kling caught 15 games for Chicago and batted .294, an early indication that his offensive ability exceeded that of most Deadball Era backstops. The next season he shared the catching duties with Mike Kahoe and Frank Chance, appearing in 69 games behind the plate and hitting a respectable .273. In 1902 new manager Frank Selee made Kling his full-time catcher. The 27-year-old backstop responded by hitting .285 with a career-high 24 steals in 114 games, leading the team with 57 RBI despite usually batting seventh. He also led the NL in putouts, assists, and double plays. Kling was even better the following year, when he caught 132 games and batted .297 with career highs in doubles (29), triples (13), and RBI (68).

Though Kling suffered an offensive drop-off in 1904-05, he played a crucial role as Chicago rode its pitching to an improved record each season. John's defense remained superb—from 1902 to 1908 he led NL receivers in putouts six times, fielding percentage twice, and assists and double plays once—but he made other contributions that didn't show up in statistics. "Kling is a master of the art of working umpires on balls and strikes, which is one of the duties of a catcher that is not suspected by the spectators," wrote Evers. "Kling's method is to be friendly with all umpires, siding with them, telling them they are right, and frequently whispering to them to be on guard for a certain curve that is coming. He urges them not to pay attention to other players, and while never openly criticizing

CIII.

umpires, he occasionally whispers that he thought the ball might have been over the corner." Cub pitchers appreciated Kling's efforts; Ed Reulbach called him "one of the greatest catchers who ever wore a mask."

Bouncing back to hit .312 in 1906, Kling entered the national spotlight as the Cubs won four pennants over the next five years. In the 1907 World Series he received great acclaim for gunning down five Detroit Tigers in 11 tries, preventing AL base-stealing champ Ty Cobb from pilfering a single base. When the Cubs beat the Tigers again in the 1908 World Series, Cobb joined the consensus that Kling was one of the best catchers ever. That off-season Johnny won another world championship, this one in pocket billiards. Deciding to earn a living in the pool hall, he sought and received—in writing—an indefinite leave of absence from Cubs president Charles Murphy, who said that the Cubs would go on without him, just as Marshall Field's Chicago department store had remained open after its founder's recent death. The star catcher remained in Kansas City for the entire season, shooting pool and catching occasionally for semipro teams.

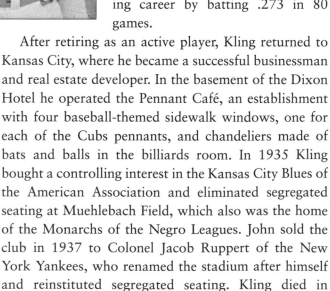

Perhaps the best indicator of Kling's importance to the great Chicago Cubs dynasty is this: 1909 was the only year in a five-year run that the Cubs failed to capture the pennant. The hiatus was costly for Kling as well. He failed to defend his billiards championship, and when he finally rejoined the Cubs in 1910, he was fined $700 by the National Commission. Kling maintained that players should learn a lesson from him and stay in the game until ready to retire. "Right now I am as good as ever, I believe," he said midway through the season, "but after my own experience in getting back into condition, I can readily understand why Jim Jeffries failed in his attempt to defeat Jack Johnson. I am not a drinking man—I don't even smoke—yet it was pretty tough for me to regain my old-time form, so I can see where these fellows who dissipate and carouse have their troubles after being out a while."

On June 10, 1911, the Cubs sent Kling to the Boston Rustlers in a trade involving eight players; aside from the 36-year-old catcher, the only player in the deal who amounted to anything was Wilbur Good, who became a regular outfielder for the 1914-15 Cubs. Some claimed that Kling was banished for his poor performance in the 1910 World Series, in which he batted just .077, while others erroneously believed that Kling had held out in 1909 and the trade was belated punishment. The most likely explanation is that Johnny had gotten off to a slow start (.175 in 27 games) and the Cubs had another catcher, Jimmy Archer, who was just as good and eight years younger. Kling played more frequently in Boston, appearing in 75 games, but batted just .224 to round out the worst season of his 13-year career.

That winter a consortium headed by James Gaffney and John M. Ward acquired the Boston franchise. Ward, the old-time Brotherhood leader, appointed Kling as manager to replace Fred Tenney. Appearing in 81 games as a player, Johnny batted a career-high .317 in 1912, but the Braves finished dead last at 52-101 and Ward resigned as president. Soon thereafter Gaffney announced that Kling would not return as manager. In February 1913 the Braves sold the soon-to-be 38-year-old catcher to the Cincinnati Reds, with whom he ended his playing career by batting .273 in 80 games.

After retiring as an active player, Kling returned to Kansas City, where he became a successful businessman and real estate developer. In the basement of the Dixon Hotel he operated the Pennant Café, an establishment with four baseball-themed sidewalk windows, one for each of the Cubs pennants, and chandeliers made of bats and balls in the billiards room. In 1935 Kling bought a controlling interest in the Kansas City Blues of the American Association and eliminated segregated seating at Muehlebach Field, which also was the home of the Monarchs of the Negro Leagues. John sold the club in 1937 to Colonel Jacob Ruppert of the New York Yankees, who renamed the stadium after himself and reinstituted segregated seating. Kling died in Kansas City at age 71 on January 31, 1947.

DAVID ANDERSON

CHICAGO

JOSEPH BERT TINKER
SHORTSTOP 1902–12, MANAGER 1916

Renowned for his ability to execute the hit-and-run play and deliver clutch hits in big games, Joe Tinker compiled a batting average of .262 and stole 336 bases in 13 full seasons in the majors, but he's best known for anchoring the defense of a team that many consider the greatest of all time. "It is impossible to speak of the great deeds which made the Cubs of 1906 the most formidable team in the history of the game without due mention of their peerless shortstop, Joe Tinker," wrote F. C. Lane in *Baseball Magazine*.

The son of a contractor, Joseph Bert Tinker was born on July 27, 1880, in Muscotah, Kansas, a tiny village 36 miles north of Topeka. Joe was two when his family moved to Kansas City. At age 14 he played for his school team, the Footpads. Two years later Joe joined a semipro club called the John Taylors, playing against future Cubs teammate Johnny Kling of the Schmeltzers. In June 1899 he left Kansas City and joined a semipro outfit called the Paragons from Parsons, Kansas. After that club disbanded, Tinker played for Coffeyville, a town on the border of Oklahoma Territory that soon became famous as Walter Johnson's off-season home.

Tinker started the 1900 season in the Western League with Denver, playing out of position at second base and batting just .219 in 32 games. In June Denver sold him to Great Falls of the Montana State League. With the team in financial straits, Great Falls sent Tinker to Helena for $200 and Joe Marshall, who also went on to the majors. After batting .322 in a combined 57 games for Great Falls and Helena, Tinker played the entire 1901 season for Portland, batting .290 with a league-leading 37 stolen bases for the Pacific Northwest League champions. Both the Cincinnati Reds and Chicago Orphans were interested in the young third baseman, but Joe requested that he be sold to the Orphans.

At 1902 spring training, new Chicago manager Frank Selee tried out a dozen shortstops in his quest to replace Barry McCormick, who'd jumped to the AL. Ultimately he settled on Tinker, who reluctantly agreed to switch from his preferred position at third base. Joe proved a surprisingly adept hitter, batting .261 as a rookie before reaching a mark of .291 with 70 RBI in 1903, but he also led the NL with 72 errors in his first season. His fielding improved dramatically over the next several years, however, and in 1906 he led all NL shortstops with a .944 fielding percentage. Joe went on to lead the league in that category five times, and he also led the NL in range factor four times and double plays once. He and Cubs second baseman Johnny Evers worked so well together that Lane called them the "Siamese twins of baseball" because "they play the bag as if they were one man, not two." Off the field, however, they didn't get along, though Joe always downplayed the problem.

In 1908 Joe Tinker became a household name. He played in all 157 games, holding the Cubs together during a rash of injuries that forced several teammates to miss significant portions of the season. He batted .266 and led the Cubs in hits (146), triples (14), home runs (6), RBI (68), and slugging percentage (.391), and his outstanding defense drew frequent mention. Joe also had key hits in the two biggest games of 1908. On

September 23, in the so-called Merkle Game, he hit a home run off Christy Mathewson for the only Cubs run in a game that was declared a 1-1 tie. In the one-game playoff against the Giants on October 8, the Cubs defeated Mathewson, 4-2, with Tinker's triple the key hit in a four-run third inning. The great Giants pitcher was at his best that season, winning a career-high 37 games, but Tinker was his personal nemesis. The Cubs shortstop hit over .350 against Matty for his career, but he hit over .400 against him in 1908.

While other key Cubs aged and fell victim to injuries over the next several seasons, Tinker was just entering his prime. Despite batting in the lower part of the order, he drove in 69 runs in both 1910 and 1911. In 1912 Joe batted .282 and set career highs in runs (80) and RBI (75), finishing fourth in the Chalmers Award voting for the National League's MVP. After the season, however, Cubs owner Charles Murphy appointed Evers to replace Frank Chance as manager. Tinker wasn't keen on playing under his double-play partner, and on December 15, 1912, the Cubs traded their shortstop of 11 years to the Cincinnati Reds in an eight-player deal.

The 32-year-old Tinker became Cincinnati's player-manager in 1913. The Reds got off to a poor start when the Ohio River flooded Redland Field early that season, but Joe excelled on a personal level. "I believe I am playing the best game of my career right now," he told Lane. Though the Reds finished with a 64-89 record, Tinker played in 110 games and established career highs in batting (.317), slugging (.445), and fielding (.968).

Tinker was a players' manager. "In my opinion a manager ought to be as lenient with his club as circumstances allow, and the less he interferes with the personal liberties of the men the better," he told Lane. When owner Garry Herrmann informed him that the Reds were sending a spy on road trips in 1914, Joe balked

and refused to sign a contract. The Reds tried to sell him to Brooklyn but Tinker ended up jumping to the Federal League, becoming the first big-name player to throw in with the upstart league. Joe enjoyed great success as player-manager of the Chicago Whales. Playing in their new ballpark, Weeghman Park, the Whales finished a close second in 1914 and won the pennant the following year, outdrawing the Cubs in both seasons.

When the Federal League folded after 1915, Whales owner Charles Weeghman purchased the Cubs and brought Tinker with him as manager. Joe lasted only one season, leading his old team to a fifth-place finish. In 1917 he became part owner and manager of the Columbus team in the American Association. Due to his wife's health problems, Joe sold his interest in 1920 and moved to Orlando, where he became owner-manager of the Gulls of the Florida State League.

Tinker became one of Orlando's leading citizens, investing in real estate and operating a number of businesses, but he lost much of his wealth during the Great Depression. In his remaining years Joe suffered from diabetes, but he lived long enough to learn of his induction into the National Baseball Hall of Fame in 1946. Joe Tinker passed away in Orlando on his 68th birthday, July 27, 1948. He is the namesake of Tinker Field, which remained the home of minor league baseball in Orlando until 2000.

LEN JACOBSON

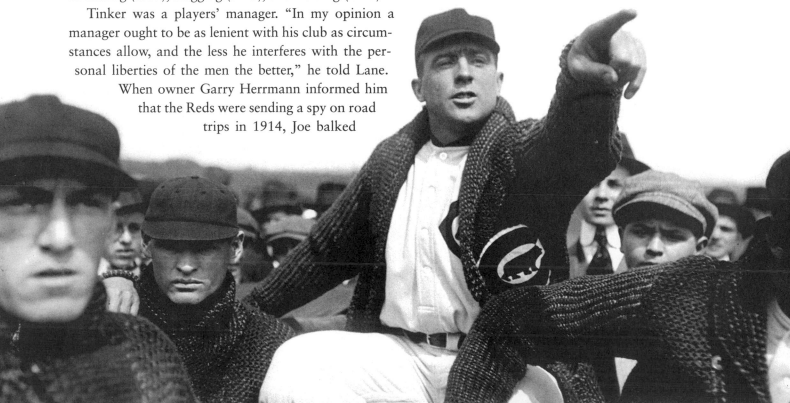

CHICAGO

JOHN JOSEPH EVERS
SECOND BASEMAN 1902–13, MANAGER 1913

An excellent bunter, accomplished base stealer, and pesky left-handed hitter who usually had the National League's best walk-to-strikeout ratio after his first few seasons, Johnny Evers was considered one of the Deadball Era's smartest and best all-around players. His nickname, "The Human Crab," was originally bestowed due to his unorthodox manner of sidling over to ground balls before gobbling them up, but most baseball men considered it better suited to his temperament than his fielding. A 5'9", 125 lb. pepper pot with a protruding jaw, Evers developed a reputation as a troublemaker by squabbling regularly with teammates, opponents, and especially umpires. "They claim he is a crab, and perhaps they are right," said Cleveland Indians manager Joe Birmingham. "But I would like to have 25 such crabs playing for me. If I did, I would have no doubts over the pennant. They would win hands down."

John Joseph Evers was born on July 21, 1881, in Troy, New York. The proper pronunciation of the family's surname has always been a source of confusion, but Johnny clarified the matter during a public appearance late in his career. According to a Boston sportswriter, he said, "Either way was right: that while Eh-vers was the correct pronunciation, everyone in Troy, his home, called him Ee-vers and always had done so." Johnny tipped the scales at just 100 lbs. when he signed with his hometown club in the New York State League in 1902. When he appeared in a game at Albany the fans reportedly assumed that he was some sort of comic act, but the 20-year-old shortstop fielded everything hit his way and won the game with a three-run double.

Later that summer the manager of the Chicago Cubs, Frank Selee, heard that a capable pitcher was toiling for Troy. He arranged an exhibition between his club and the Trojans, a common practice at the time. The pitching prospect, Alex Hardy, was impressive, so Selee offered the Troy ownership $1,000 for him. Hardy's employers countered by requesting $1,500. "I'll tell you what I'll do," Selee responded. "If you throw in that kid who played short today, I'll give you the $1,500." The Troy owners were quick to oblige.

Evers was batting .285 and leading the New York State League with 10 home runs (only two less than he hit in his entire 18-year major league career), but he was regarded as a nuisance because of his short temper. He also committed plenty of errors at short, though he had great range in the field.

Making his major league debut on September 1, 1902, Johnny played his customary position while Selee moved his regular shortstop, fellow rookie Joe Tinker, to third base. Three days later, however, the Chicago skipper rearranged the infield, moving Evers to second and returning Tinker to short, the positions at which they remained for the next decade. Despite occasional flashes of brilliance, Evers' 26-game trial during the final month of that season was a bust; he batted .222 without a single extra-base hit, drawing just three walks and stealing only a single base. But regular second baseman Bobby Lowe suffered a severe knee injury late in 1902, and by spring training the following year he still hadn't healed. Evers won the starting job by default. This time he was ready, batting .293, pilfering 25 bases, and contributing solid defense. At the beginning of 1904 Selee sold Lowe to the Pittsburgh Pirates. Johnny played in 152 games that season.

The scrappy Evers didn't hit his first major league home run until July 21, 1905, when he popped a Chick Fraser pitch over the fence in the right-field corner at Boston's South End Grounds. By that point he'd appeared in more than 350 big-league games. Johnny made up for his lack of power with his mastery of "inside baseball." In 1906 he stole a career-high 49 bases, and the next year he pilfered 46. Evers also generally increased his bases on balls each season, peaking at 108 in 1910, only eight behind league leader Miller Huggins. "I am convinced that in my own career I could usually have hit 30 points higher if I had made a specialty of hitting," said the man with a lifetime batting average of .270. "In my own case I have frequently faced the pitcher when I had no desire whatever to hit. I wanted to get a base on balls."

The mutual antipathy between Evers and his keystone partner, Tinker, has become legendary. The most common explanation is that they held a grudge against each other because of a dispute over cab fare, but some historians date their animosity to a highly publicized on-field brawl in 1905. Years later Evers told an entirely different story: "One day early in 1907, he threw me a hard ball; it wasn't any farther than from here to there," Evers claimed, pointing at a lamp about 10 feet from where he sat. "It was a real hard ball, like a catcher throwing to second." The throw bent back one of the fingers on Evers' right hand. "I yelled to him, you so-and-so. He laughed. That's the last word we had for—well, I just don't know how long." Whatever the reason for their bitterness, Evers and Tinker were an impeccable defensive tandem on the diamond. "Tinker and myself hated each other," Evers admitted, "but we loved the Cubs. We wouldn't fight for each other, but we'd come close to killing people for our team. That was one of the answers to the Cubs' success."

Evers batted an even .300 in 1908, the first of only two times in his career that he reached that magical number. He also played a crucial role in that year's pennant race, the closest and most exciting in history. On September 4 the Cubs were locked in a scoreless duel in Pittsburgh when the Pirates loaded the bases with two outs in the bottom of the ninth. On what appeared to be a game-winning hit to center, the runner at first,

Warren Gill, left the field without bothering to touch second base. Evers, standing on second, called for the ball and demanded that umpire Hank O'Day rule the play a force out, which would nullify the run and send the game into extra innings. Gill's maneuver was customary in those days, and O'Day refused to make the call. "That night O'Day came to look me up, which was an unusual thing in itself," Evers recalled many years later. "Sitting in a corner in the lobby, he told me that he wanted to discuss the play. O'Day then agreed that my play was legal and that under the circumstances, a runner coming down from first and not touching second on the final base hit was out." Evers' account may not be trustworthy, especially given O'Day's exceptionally reclusive nature and the lengthy period between the event and the retelling, but the incident undoubtedly had a pronounced effect on the umpire, as was demonstrated by subsequent events.

An almost identical situation arose on September 23, this time with the Cubs battling the Giants at the Polo Grounds. When New York's Al Bridwell hit an apparent game-winning single with two outs in the bottom of the ninth, the runner on first, Fred Merkle, headed for the clubhouse without touching second. Evers called for the ball, eventually got one (though probably not the one Bridwell hit), and stepped on second base. O'Day was again the umpire, and this time he called the runner out. Given the irregularity of the call, the critical nature of the game, the temperaments of the opposing managers, and the animosity between the Cubs and Giants, O'Day's verdict sparked a firestorm of controversy. Eventually NL president Harry Pulliam ruled the game a tie, to be replayed if it had any impact on the pennant race. It did. The Cubs went back to New York for a one-game playoff, winning 4-2 to secure their third consecutive NL pennant, and went on to thrash the Tigers in the World Series for the second straight year, with Evers batting .350 and leading all players with five runs scored. His headiness on the play that became known as "Merkle's Boner" was given due credit for the Cubs' triumph and cemented his reputation as one of baseball's brainiest players.

Evers was as high-strung as he was smart—one reporter described him as a "keen little umpire-fighting bundle of nerves." Though he was injured and unable to play in the 1910 World Series, he attended the games on crutches and sat on the bench for the sole purpose

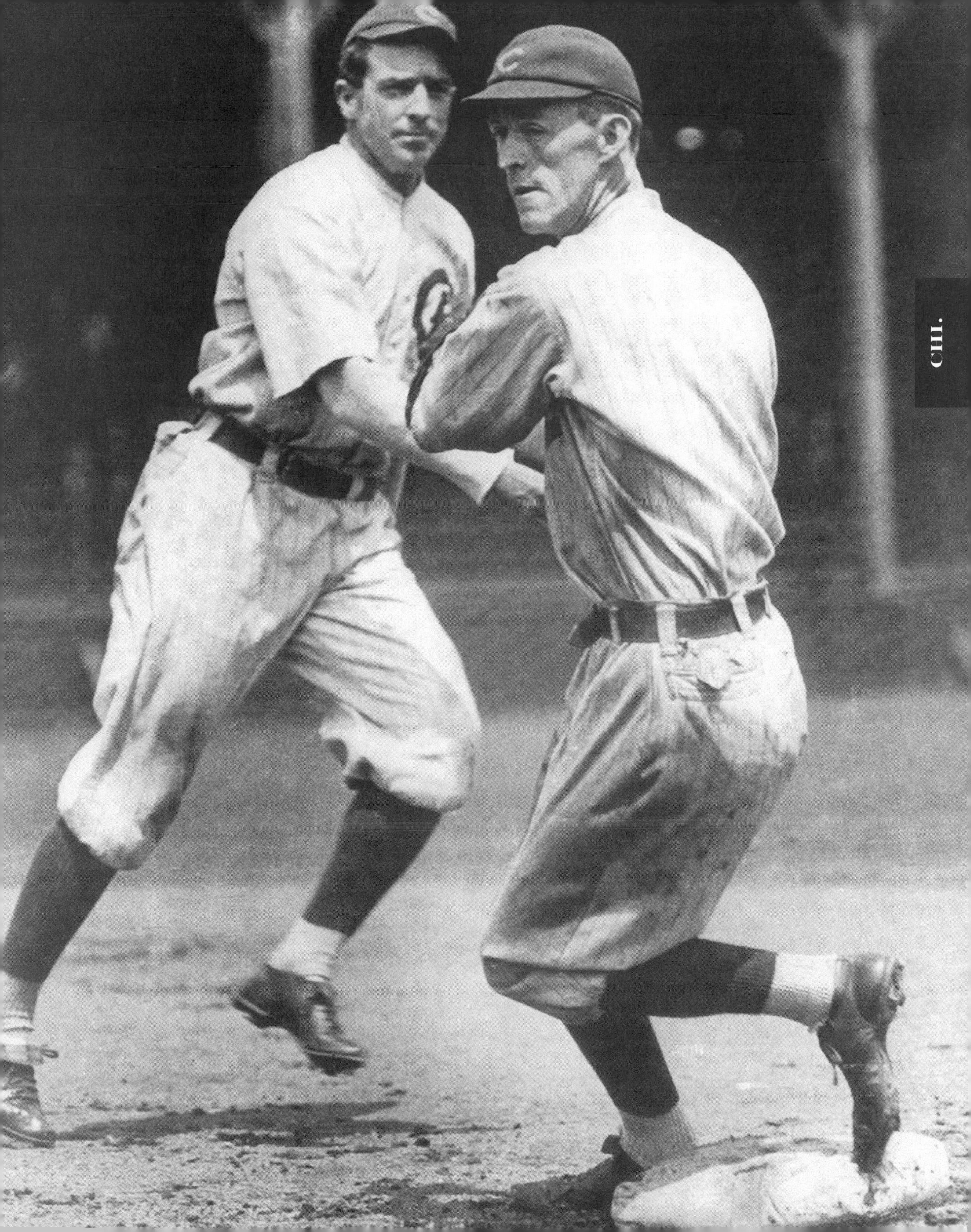

of baiting the umpires. In 1911 Johnny played in just 46 games when he was knocked out of commission for most of the season by a nervous breakdown; he claimed it was caused by the loss of his entire accumulated capital, $25,000, in a business venture. Evers bounced back to enjoy the best season of his career in 1912, batting a career-high .341 and finishing second in the NL with a .431 on-base percentage. At the end of that season Frank Chance resigned as manager (or was fired, depending on who you believe), and Cubs owner Charles Murphy gave the 31-year-old Evers a five-year contract as player-manager. On May 10, 1913, "Johnny Evers Day" at the Polo Grounds, a sizeable number of Troy residents journeyed to New York City to see their favorite son collect a single, double, and walk in four trips to the plate. Evers also scored the winning run as his Cubs (often called the "Trojans" in the newspapers that year) vanquished the Giants, 2-1. But the Cubs failed to improve on the previous year's third-place finish, and after the season Murphy summarily dismissed his manager despite the long-term contract.

The fallout was acrimonious. Murphy initially claimed that Evers had resigned. Johnny angrily disputed that, and the other NL owners unanimously sided with him. Murphy then tried to trade his ex-manager to the Boston Braves for two players and cash. Evers said he wouldn't report, and his refusal was made more piquant when the Federal League offered him $30,000 to forsake the NL altogether. Though Evers later claimed that he had no intention of jumping to the Feds, that was far from clear at the time. Disgusted by Murphy's tactics and afraid of losing one of their top stars, the NL owners nullified the trade and awarded Evers his release, permitting him to sell his own contract to the Braves for $25,000 plus bonuses and incentives of various sorts. His overall earnings for 1914 made him the highest-paid player in baseball.

The deal was risky for the Braves on several counts. Due to his age (32), slender frame (he spent off-days wolfing down candy bars to keep on as much weight as possible), hypersensitivity, and proclivity for getting ejected, Evers couldn't be counted on for everyday play. Nevertheless the unorthodox deal benefited a number of people, none more than Evers himself. His new man-

ager, the like-minded George Stallings, quickly appointed him team captain. Johnny took his duties seriously, running teammates ragged in practice and taking it as a personal insult when anyone put forth an effort that he regarded as subpar. "He'd make you want to punch him," teammate Rabbit Maranville recalled, "but you knew Johnny was thinking only of the team." After rocketing from last place to first over the last 10 weeks of the 1914 season, the "Miracle Braves" swept the Philadelphia A's to become world champions. Evers was sensational down the stretch and outstanding in the Series, batting .438 with several key hits. To cap off his spectacular season, he won the Chalmers Award as the NL's MVP.

That was Evers' last great year. Injuries and suspensions cost him almost half of the 1915 season. When healthy he performed at his usual level, but his disputes with umpires, never far from the sports headlines even in the calmest of times, became weekly fare. Johnny's nerves were frayed even beyond their usual state. In early August, with the Braves trying to catch the Phillies in the pennant chase, he announced that he needed to leave the team immediately or risk a recurrence of the nervous breakdown he'd suffered in 1911. Johnny managed to complete the 1915 campaign, but it was his last as a regular. He had a poor year in 1916, and after he batted a meager .193 over the first half of 1917, the Braves placed him on waivers. Evers spent the second half with the Phillies, who released him at season's end. The following year he earned a spot on the Opening Day roster of the Red Sox but was released before appearing in a single game.

Evers returned to the Cubs as manager in 1921 and skippered the White Sox three years later. He failed to complete either season, and both clubs performed less successfully under his direction than either before or after he took the reins. The White Sox assignment made him the first and so far the only man to manage both Chicago major league clubs. During the 1930s Evers ran a sporting-goods store in Albany, New York. In 1942 he suffered a stroke that debilitated him for the rest of his life. Johnny Evers died in Albany on March 28, 1947, one year after his induction into the National Baseball Hall of Fame.

DAVID SHINER

CHICAGO

MORDECAI PETER CENTENNIAL "THREE FINGERED" BROWN
RIGHT-HANDED PITCHER 1904–12, 1916

Mordecai "Three Fingered" Brown was one of the premier pitchers of the Deadball Era, but today he is remembered as much for his "handicap" as his on-field exploits. The stump that remained of Brown's index finger imparted an odd spin on the ball, causing unusual motion on his pitches. His fastball dropped right at the plate, similar to a modern split-finger fastball, while his curve, which was considered the best in the NL, broke in toward right-handed batters, like today's screwball. One reporter claimed that Brown's hand wasn't very flexible, making the act of throwing extremely painful, but he still managed to win 239 games while losing only 130. His career ERA of 2.06 is the third lowest of any pitcher with 2,000 innings pitched and the lowest of any pitcher who racked up 3,000 innings. Brown also retired as the all-time saves leader with 49, which wasn't surpassed until 1926 by Firpo Marberry.

The son of Peter and Jane "Lula" (Day) Brown, immigrants of English and Welsh descent, Mordecai Peter Centennial Brown was born on October 19, 1876, in the tiny farming and coal-mining community of Nyesville, Indiana, 26 miles north of Terre Haute. Mort (as his family called him) was seven when he caught his right hand in the grinding knives of a corn shredder on his uncle's farm, severing his index and part of his little fingers and mangling his middle finger. A few weeks later, while his hand was still in a cast, he fell chasing a rabbit and broke the rest of his fingers. Those accidents left Mort with a deformed hand, or "paw" as he called it. Due to his age at the time of his injuries, he never learned to throw a ball with a regular hand; all of his

throwing was done with his deformity. Nonetheless Brown took to baseball, and in 1898 he played third base for a semipro team in Coxville, a nearby town. Later he became known as a good-fielding pitcher—in 1908 he handled 108 chances without an error—which may have been due to the experience he gained with ground balls during his early days as a third baseman.

While playing semipro ball in Indiana, Brown also worked odd jobs in the coal mines of Parke County, leading to his second baseball nickname, "Miner." One day Coxville's regular pitcher was injured and Miner Brown took his place. He performed so well that he made the conversion to full-time pitcher. In 1901 a semipro player from Terre Haute, Frank Firman (the brother of NL umpire Cy Firman), recommended Brown to the Terre Haute Hottentots of the Illinois-Indiana-Iowa League. The club offered Miner a tryout and initially rejected him. Only after 600 local fans signed a petition threatening to boycott Hottentot games did the team give him another look. He compiled a 23-8 record as Terre Haute claimed the inaugural Three-I League pennant. That performance earned Brown a promotion to Omaha of the Western League, where he had a 27-15 season in 1902.

St. Louis Cardinals manager Patsy Donovan heard of Miner Brown's "freak ball" and signed him for 1903. The 26-year-old rookie's statistics don't look impressive on the surface, but his .409 winning percentage was considerably better than the Cardinals' .314, and his nine victories, 83 strikeouts, and 2.60 ERA led the St. Louis staff. Chicago Cubs manager Frank Selee saw beneath the surface. After the season he offered two talented but troublesome players, 21-game winner Jack Taylor and oversized catcher Larry McLean, for Brown and catcher Jack O'Neill. The Cardinals couldn't refuse, and after a slow start with his new team—he gave up 12 runs on 13 hits and seven errors to the Cincinnati Reds in his first start, and lost his second start as well—Brown recovered to post a 15-10 record with a 1.86 ERA in 1904. He continued to pitch well the next season, joining Jake Weimer and Ed Reulbach as 18-game winners on the Chicago staff.

In 1906 Mordecai Brown emerged as the Cubs ace, achieving star status with one of the best seasons ever. His 1.04 ERA not only led the National League that season, it was also the NL's lowest ERA of the 20th century and the third lowest in major league history. Brown also posted a 26-6 record and a league-leading nine shutouts. The 1906 World Series wasn't as kind to him. The heavily favored Cubs lost to the crosstown White Sox in six games, with Brown starting three of them. He split Games One and Four, a pair of pitchers' duels against Nick Altrock, winning the latter by spinning a two-hit shutout. Chance pitched Brown on one day's rest in Game Six. He was obviously tired—reports indicate that he wasn't picking his leg up high—and the Pale Hose pounded him for seven runs, ending the Cubs' hopes. The next season Mordecai pitched at the same high level, going 20-6 with a 1.39 ERA and leading the Cubs to another World Series. He started once in the '07 Series, in Game Five, and whitewashed the Detroit Tigers on seven hits.

Brown's role on the Cubs changed in 1908. Not only was he the ace of the staff, expected to start and win all the big games, but he also became the primary relief pitcher. Beginning that season, Brown led the NL in saves (calculated retroactively, of course) for four consecutive years. In 1911, working almost half of his games in relief, he set a new record for saves in a season (13) that lasted until 1924. At the end of his career, Brown had the most saves of any pitcher in major league history, though no one knew it until well after his death. In 1908 Brown won a career-high 29 games, including three victories over his chief rival, Christy Mathewson. He came up especially big during the final week of the season. On October 4, in front of a record-setting crowd of 30,247, Brown pitched his third game in six days but still managed to eliminate the Pirates

from the pennant race, 5-2, knocking in three of the runs himself. The Cubs then waited as the Giants won their last three games of the season, forcing a tie and a replay of the Merkle Game on October 8. The one-game playoff pitted Mathewson against Jack Pfiester, but the "Giant Killer" lasted only two-thirds of an inning, giving up one run and leaving two runners on base before giving way to Brown. Mordecai struck out Art Devlin to end the Giants rally. Two innings later the Cubs scored four runs off Matty. With the lead in hand, Brown allowed only one more run, which came in the seventh after he'd loaded the bases with no outs.

Two days later the Cubs began the World Series, a rematch against Detroit. In Game One Brown entered in the eighth inning with the game tied. He gave up one unearned run, but the Cubs unloaded on Ed Summers for five runs in the top of the ninth. Brown held the Tigers scoreless in the bottom half for a 10-6 victory, receiving credit for the win from the official scorer. He came back three days later to start Game Four and pitched his third shutout in World Series play, becoming the only pitcher in major league history to pitch a shutout in three consecutive World Series. The Cubs won the Series in five games, after which Ty Cobb called Brown's curveball "the most devastating pitch I ever faced."

Brown's success in 1908 earned him an even greater workload in 1909. That year he led the NL in wins (27), saves (9), innings pitched (342⅔), and complete games (32). Brown missed out on his second ERA title, posting a 1.31 mark to finish second behind Mathewson's 1.14. Despite his efforts, the Cubs failed to win the NL pennant for the first time since 1905. They returned to the World Series in 1910, however, and Mordecai again led the Cubs rotation with 25 victories and seven saves. In Game Two of the World Series against the Philadelphia Athletics, Brown suffered the loss after allowing nine runs in seven innings. He pitched two innings of relief to get the victory in Game Four, but the next day he started Game Five and gave up seven runs as Philadelphia clinched the Series. Brown never again appeared in World Series play, but he left with a 5-4 record and 2.81 ERA. Only Christy Mathewson has surpassed his three shutouts.

The effects of advancing age, years of hard work, and a pre-season knee injury finally began to show on Mordecai Brown in 1911. He put together a decent sea-

son, winning 21 games and saving another 13, but his ERA (2.80) was up nearly a run. The Cubs nevertheless signed him to a three-year deal for $7,000 a year, $5,500 from the Cubs and $1,500 from a personal contract with owner Charles Murphy. Still slowed by the knee injury, Mordecai appeared in only 15 games in 1912, starting eight and compiling a 5-6 overall record. With Brown's days as an effective major league pitcher apparently over, the Cubs sold him to Louisville of the American Association, which offered him a paltry $300 a month. At that point the Reds, under manager Joe Tinker purchased Brown and offered him a $4,000 contract, with the potential to gain two $1,000 bonuses solely at Tinker's discretion. Brown went 11-12 with a 2.91 ERA in his only season with the Reds.

One of 1914's biggest coups for the Federal League was the St. Louis Terriers signing Mordecai Brown to a three-year contract as player-manager for $7,500 a season. Brown's pitching clearly outshone his managing: he went 12-6 with a 3.29 ERA, but the Terriers went 50-63 and were in seventh place when Fielder Jones replaced Mordecai at the helm. Brown finished the season with the Brooklyn Tip Tops, going 2-5 for the fifth-place club. After the season Tinker, now managing the Chicago Whales, acquired Brown for the 1915 campaign. Once again Mordecai was an integral part of a pitching staff that brought a pennant to Chicago, contributing a 17-8 record and a team-best 2.09 ERA.

When the Feds folded, Brown followed Tinker back to the team of their glory days. Mordecai didn't pitch much for the Cubs in 1916, appearing in only 12 games and compiling a 2-3 record. His most important game occurred on September 4, when he made the last start of his major league career. The game matched Brown against his nemesis, Christy Mathewson, whom he'd beaten nine consecutive times from June 13, 1905, to June 3, 1909. Mathewson won this final duel, 10-8, cutting Brown's career advantage to 13-11 in the 24 games in which the NL's two premier pitchers of the first decade of the Deadball Era were the pitchers of record in the same game.

Rather than retire, the 40-year-old Brown once again followed Tinker, this time to Columbus of the American Association. He pitched there for the next two seasons, going a combined 13-14 in 42 games. In 1919 Brown became player-manager of Terre Haute of the Three-I League, where he'd begun his professional career 18 years earlier. He went 16-6 with a 2.88 ERA, and Indianapolis picked him up for the stretch run of the American Association season. Mordecai returned to the Terre Haute Browns (named for their celebrated manager) in 1920 for what turned out to be his final season in Organized Baseball.

Brown enjoyed a successful post-baseball career. He owned and operated a Texaco service station in Terre Haute, earning enough money to invest in the Terre Haute club of the Three-I League in the early 1940s. When he wasn't working he spent many hours at the local Elks club, telling baseball stories from the olden days. Mordecai Brown died at age 71 on February 14, 1948, of complications from diabetes. He and his wife, Sarah, are buried in Terre Haute's Roselawn Cemetery. A year after his death, Brown was elected to the National Baseball Hall of Fame.

BRIAN MARSHALL

CHICAGO

Frank M. Schulte

FRANK M. "WILDFIRE" SCHULTE
OUTFIELDER 1904–16

Eschewing the common Deadball Era technique of punching at the ball for singles, the left-handed–hitting Frank Schulte was a precursor of the modern, swing-from-the-heels slugger. He used a "switch"—an unusually thin-handled bat (though his weighed 40 oz.)—and held it all the way down at the end, breaking about 50 each season. "Schulte would stand with his bat over his shoulder until the ball was almost on top of him," said Johnny Evers. "Then he would make a lightning cut at it." Though remembered primarily for his distance hitting and droll sense of humor, the longtime Cubs right fielder had enough speed to steal home 22 times, and he also had the strongest outfield arm of the Deadball Era's first decade.

The son of a building contractor, Frank M. Schulte was born on September 17, 1882, in the western New York village of Cohocton. After developing his baseball skills at school, Frank played a variety of positions for a slew of independent teams, including Blossburg, Pennsylvania, and Waverly and Lestershire in his native state, as well as a team sponsored by the Endicott-Johnson Shoe Company. Sportswriter Hugh Fullerton once asked him for a complete history of his baseball career. "I think he gave me a list of seven towns before he got to one as large as Skaneateles," wrote Fullerton, "and never a smile as he recounted his averages and feats." In 1899 Frank's father, worried that his boy had found a dishonest profession, offered him $1,000 to burn his baseball suit and keep the books for the Schulte contracting interests. Frank declined.

Schulte left his semipro days behind in 1902 to begin a three-year run with the Syracuse Stars of the New York State League, where he batted between .280 and .307 each season and finally settled into his position in the "outer garden." Looking to shore up his dynamic but ailing outfield of Jimmy Slagle, Jack McCarthy, and Davy Jones, Chicago Cubs manager Frank Selee dispatched George Huff to upstate New York in 1904 to assess a youngster named Magee. Unlike Sherwood and Lee, this particular Magee passed into baseball oblivion, but Huff was taken with Schulte's talent and purchased his contract on August 21. Making his major league debut exactly one month later, four days after his 22nd birthday, Frank amassed five hits (including a double and a triple) in a doubleheader at Philadelphia, and three days later he hit the first of his 92 career home runs. Appearing in 20 games for the Cubs that fall, he hit .286 with two homers and 13 RBI.

After batting .274 and tying for the team lead with 14 triples as the Cubs regular left fielder in 1905, Schulte switched to right field the following year and established himself as one of the National League's most dangerous hitters, batting .281 and tying for the league lead in triples (13) while finishing fourth in home runs (7) and fifth in total bases (223). He was even better in 1910, when he batted .301 with 29 doubles, 15 triples, and 10 home runs, leading the NL in the last of those categories. Frank performed solidly during the regular season but saved his best for his four World Series appearances. He hit for a .309 average in the fall classic, batting safely in all 10 contests in the 1907 and '08 championships and in all but one game in '06 and '10. Sandwiched between those four Series was a 13-game hitting streak, which ranks fourth all-time.

Schulte and legendary sportswriter Ring Lardner shared a special appreciation for each other's sense of humor. "Frank Schulte hated anything false or tinged with 'bull,'" wrote Fullerton. "He was so modest and so self-effacing that he never, even in the days when he was leading the home run hitters of the country, ceased to dodge publicity and avoid the limelight." Another of Schulte's well-known admirers was the actress Lillian Russell, and the origin of his distinctive nickname can be traced to spring training 1908 when he and some teammates saw her perform in a play called *Wildfire* in Vicksburg, Mississippi. Frank, who participated in harness races on ice around Syracuse during the off-season, subsequently named one of his best trotters Wildfire. Before long the Chicago sportswriters got wind of it, and he too became known by the name.

Schulte had many eccentricities. One of them was combing the streets for hairpins, which he believed to be predictors of success in the batter's box. Frank believed that the bigger the hairpin, the greater the hit. He must have found a lot of big ones in 1911. That year, aided by a somewhat livelier ball, the lifetime .270 hitter mounted one of the Deadball Era's greatest assaults on National League pitching. Schulte batted an even .300 and led the NL in home runs (21), RBI (121), total bases (308), and slugging percentage (.534). He also was fourth in hits (173) and runs (105), and, perhaps most surprisingly to modern fans, second in sacrifices (31). Frank became the first player ever to top the 20 mark in home runs, triples (21), doubles (30), and stolen bases (23), a feat not duplicated until 1957 by Willie Mays. For good measure, Schulte became the first player ever to clout four grand slams in one season.

Though the Cubs dropped to second, his individual exploits earned him the NL Chalmers Award.

Though Schulte never again approached his 1911 numbers, he remained a productive power hitter for several seasons, hitting a dozen home runs in both 1912 and 1915 to rank among the NL's top three in each season. After eight years in right field, he moved back to left in 1914, the year that a feud with manager Hank O'Day nearly caused him to bolt to the Federal League. Schulte continued with the Cubs, however, until July 29, 1916, when they traded him to the Pittsburgh Pirates. Wildfire was one of the final players from Chance's 1906-10 champions to leave the Cubs.

At that point Schulte's career went into a steep decline. After batting .296 with five home runs in 72 games in 1916, he fell to .254 without a single homer in 55 games with the Pirates. Schulte also failed to hit a single home run in 1917 before going to the Phillies for the waiver price on June 14. After he batted .214 with just one home run for the season, the Phils sold him to the Washington Senators in December 1917. Again Schulte went homerless, though he raised his batting average to .288 in his final season as a major leaguer. After playing for the Baltimore Drydocks team during "Work or Fight," Wildfire played in the minors in 1919-22. Returning in 1920 to Syracuse, where his professional career had begun nearly two decades earlier, Schulte proved that he could still play at age 39 by hitting .309 with 35 doubles, 12 triples, and 16 home runs in 1921. He finished his playing career in 1923 in the Pacific Coast League with Oakland, where he lived for the rest of his life with his wife, the former Mabel Kirby. A 1918 fire burned down all of the buildings on a farm they owned near Orlando, Florida. Worst of all, Frank was stricken with paralysis for a time in 1930. He passed away at age 67 on October 2, 1949, at Merritt Hospital in Oakland.

SCOTT TURNER

CHICAGO

ARTHUR FREDERICK "SOLLY" HOFMAN
UTILITY MAN 1904–12, 1916

An above-average center fielder and one of the Deadball Era's finest utility men, Artie Hofman was a timely hitter and one of the fleetest men in the game. Known as "Circus Solly," a nickname some attributed to a comic-strip character from the early 1900s, while others swore it came from his spectacular circus catches in the outfield, Hofman garnered attention with his playing style and also his lively antics. "He is serious only when asleep," jibed *Baseball Magazine*. Along with fellow free spirits Frank Schulte and Jimmy Sheckard, Hofman completed what Ring Lardner once called "the best outfield I ever looked at."

Arthur Frederick Hofman was born in St. Louis on October 29, 1882. One of five ball-playing brothers—Louis, Oscar, George, and Erwin were the others—Arthur received encouragement from his father, Louis Sr., who managed the well-known Mound City Ice and Cold Storage team, which played its games at Lindell Park, then at the corner of Grand and Hebert, only a block north of the future site of Busch Stadium. His sister, Birdie, starred on the Central High School basketball team and was a teammate of novelist Fannie Hurst. All of the Hofman brothers played in the St. Louis Trolley League, and Oscar played briefly for Columbus in the American Association. An exceptional track star at Smith Academy, Arthur performed so well with the Belleville (Illinois) Clerks that he earned a contract with Evansville in the Three-I League, where he played third base in 1901-02.

After appearing in a handful of games with the Pittsburgh Pirates in 1903, Hofman and Hans Lobert were farmed out together to Des Moines of the Western League for the remainder of the season. In 1904 Artie hit .301 as Des Moines' regular shortstop, prompting his acquisition by the Chicago Cubs late that season.

The rookie found it difficult to break into the famous Cub infield. "I know I can play better than Steinfeldt, Tinker, or Evers—but you won't give me a chance!" Sid Keener recalled Hofman saying to Frank Chance. "Besides, I've been watching you around first base and I'm convinced you're slowing up, too. Give me that mitt and I'll show you how first base should be played." Admonished by Johnny Kling to keep his mouth shut, Hofman worked out at a different position each day until some of the infielders began worrying about their jobs. According to Keener, Evers took Chance aside and said, "I've been watching Slagle out in center field and he's slowing up. Why don't you try that kid Hofman?"

During his tenure with the Cubs, Hofman played every position except pitcher and catcher and was generally regarded as the game's best utility man before he became a regular in center field in 1909. Perhaps he's most famous as the outfielder who fielded the hit on which Fred Merkle failed to touch second base. Hugh Keough, a newspaper writer who was friendly with Hofman, claimed that the irrepressible Circus Solly fielded the ball and jokingly fired a curve to Johnny Evers, who missed it, allowing the ball to be picked up by Joe McGinnity, who lobbed it into the grandstand.

Before the 1908 World Series, Chance forbade Hofman's wedding to Miss Rae Looker and demanded for the good of the team that the ceremony be postponed until after the season. The Cubs won their second consecutive World Series in Detroit on October 14, 1908, and the Hofmans didn't dally, marrying the next day in Chicago. The couple moved to Akron, Ohio, where Hofman partnered with his brother-in-law, who owned two restaurants, and settled into family life. In 1909 Artie travelled to Cuba with A. M. McAllister's all-star team. Though the only man on the team who could play third base, Hofman abandoned the team when he received a letter reminding him that it was his six-month-old daughter's first Christmas. "He put up such a plea," *The Sporting News* reported, "that it melted even the Cuban soldiers, who couldn't understand a word he said."

In 1908-09 Hofman was named to *Collier's* All-American teams, picked by Billy Sunday and Cap Anson, but his best season was 1910, when he hit .325 with 86 RBI and 29 stolen bases. In 1912 Artie's legs began to give him trouble, and in June Chicago traded him and pitcher King Cole to Pittsburgh for pitcher Lefty Leifield and outfielder Tommie Leach. The next year Hofman was sent to Kansas City but refused the

assignment, asking to be sent to the Pacific Coast League, where he hoped to spend time with Chance and other old friends. A month later he was sold to Nashville. Still "a heavy batter and a quick thinker," loyal Chicagoans lamented "the passing of the famous Circus Solly, who was one of the strong gears of the now dismantled Cub machine."

In March 1914 Hofman signed a $7,000 per year contract with Brooklyn of the Federal League. "The Brooklyn fans will forget all about Jake Daubert's fancy first basing after they watch me for a while," he boasted. Hofman still maintained his old sense of humor. During the Brook Feds' 1914 training trip, he and outfielder Steve Evans volunteered to umpire an exhibition game against the University of South Carolina. Prior to the game the jokesters snuck a dozen baseballs into the hotel kitchen, where they put half of them on ice and baked the others. During their teammates' innings, the umpires gave them frozen balls to hit, but when the collegians were at bat, the lively baked balls were thrown in, and the college boys hit them a country mile.

In April 1915 Hofman clashed with manager Lee Magee because he failed to follow instructions to wait out the pitcher, instead hitting the first pitch. Artie made the dubious claim that he was playing "Johnny Evers style" baseball; Magee replied that Lee Magee style ball would be played as long as he was in charge. A $10 fine for smoking cigarettes brought the conflict to its climax. Hofman turned in his uniform and announced that he was going home to Akron. One week later, the "kicking player" was sent to Buffalo in a four-club deal that brought southpaw Nick Cullop to Brooklyn.

When the Federal League collapsed, Hofman quit baseball and settled in Chicago, where he owned a haberdashery and operated a youth baseball clinic on the abandoned West Side Grounds. He returned to the professional game briefly in 1916, filling emergency utility roles with the Cubs and New York Yankees before retiring with a .269 lifetime batting average. Hofman moved to St. Louis in 1918 but returned to Chicago seven years later and became a high school baseball coach. He was the uncle of Bobby Hofman of the New York Giants (1949-57). Artie Hofman died in his native St. Louis on March 10, 1956, less than two weeks after Fred Merkle.

TREY STRECKER

Ed Reulbach

CHICAGO

Edward Marvin Reulbach
Right-handed pitcher 1905–13

According to J. C. Kofoed of *Baseball Magazine*, Big Ed Reulbach was "one of the greatest pitchers that the National League ever produced, and one of the finest, clean-cut gentlemen who ever wore a big league uniform." A statuesque 6'1", 190 lb. right hander, Reulbach employed the technique of "shadowing"—hiding the ball in his windup—as well as a high leg kick that Chief Meyers later compared to Juan Marichal's. His curveball was generally regarded as the finest in either league, making him one of baseball's most difficult pitchers to hit. He hurled two one-hitters, six two-hitters, and 13 three-hitters, and in 1906 he yielded only 5.33 hits per nine innings, still the fifth-lowest ratio of all time.

Reulbach's weakness was his occasional lack of control. In 1920 he revealed to Hugh Fullerton that he had a weak left eye. "There were times when the eye was worse than usual, especially on hot, gray days, or when the dust was blowing from the field," he said. "Lots of times the sweat and heat would affect the good eye and I'd have to figure out where the plate was."

Edward Marvin Reulbach was born in Detroit on December 1, 1882. At age eighteen he was already a veteran of one minor league season with Sedalia of the Missouri Valley League when he enrolled at the University of Notre Dame in the fall of 1901. Reulbach played inter-hall football and basketball and was one of the varsity's top hitters in a pre-season exhibition series against the reigning AL champion Chicago White Sox, but the faculty declared him ineligible for 1902—not because he was a professional but because he was a freshman. After pitching for Sedalia for each of the next two summers, Ed became Notre Dame's star outfielder and pitcher, breaking the college's single-season record for strikeouts in 1904 and never yielding more than six

hits in a game that season. That June his teammates elected him captain for 1905.

Fate had something else in store for Ed Reulbach in 1905. While pitching in Vermont's outlaw Northern League for the Montpelier-Barre Hyphens, he met and fell in love with his future bride, Nellie Whelan of Montpelier. To be closer to Nellie, Ed passed on his senior year at Notre Dame and enrolled in medical school at the University of Vermont. In the spring he became the star of the UVM baseball team, batting cleanup and playing left field when he wasn't pitching. Newspapers called Reulbach the "greatest of all college pitchers," and on May 12, after winning his fourth start, 1-0, against Syracuse, he received an offer from the Chicago Cubs that "would take the breath away from an average person," according to the *Burlington Free Press*. That night, accompanied by a large group of students, Ed caught the train to New York. Four days later he made his debut at the Polo Grounds against the reigning NL champion New York Giants, tossing a complete game and giving up only five hits in a 4-0 loss.

Despite missing the first month of the 1905 season, the 22-year-old Reulbach posted an 18-14 record with a 1.42 ERA and only 208 hits allowed in 291⅔ innings (6.42 per nine innings). He remained one of the NL's most dominant pitchers through 1909. In 1906 he pitched 12 low-hit games (five hits or fewer), not including the one-hitter he threw against the White Sox in Game Two of that year's World Series, and started a 17-game personal winning streak that didn't end until June 29, 1907. It was the post-1900 record for consecutive victories until Rube Marquard broke it in 1912, and it remains the fifth-longest streak in history. On September 26, 1908, Reulbach became the only pitcher ever to throw a doubleheader shutout, also setting an

NL record with 44 consecutive scoreless innings. He led the league in winning percentage each season in 1906-08, a feat matched only by Lefty Grove. From May 30 to August 14, 1909, Reulbach went on a 14-game winning streak, becoming the only 20th-century NL pitcher with two winning streaks as long as 14 games. A November 1913 article in *Baseball Magazine* judged Reulbach's 1909 streak the most impressive in history; in 14 games he surrendered only 14 runs while pitching five shutouts and five one-run games. One of the wins came on June 30, 1909, in the first game ever played at Forbes Field.

Reulbach's magnificent five-year run finally ended in 1910, when he tailed off to 12-8 with a 3.12 ERA in only 173⅓ innings; he and Nellie had one child, a son whose diphtheria caused Ed to miss part of that season. Reulbach improved to 16-9 with a 2.96 ERA in 1911, but the following year his record dipped to 10-6 while his ERA ballooned to 3.78. In July 1913, with his record a mere 1-3 with a 4.42 ERA, the Cubs practically gave him to Brooklyn for cash and an undistinguished pitcher named Eddie Stack. In his first six days with his new team, Reulbach proved that he still could pitch by giving up only two hits in 16 innings. Over the second half he posted a 7-6 record and 2.05 ERA, but the most telling sign that he'd returned to form was his ratio of hits per nine innings, a typically Reulbachian 6.30 (77 hits in 110 innings). Reulbach's stellar second half earned him the starting assignment on Opening Day 1914, when he defeated that year's eventual world champions, the Boston Braves. Despite his 11-18 record, the veteran right hander was Brooklyn's second-best pitcher in 1914, compiling a 2.64 ERA in 256 innings.

Off the field, Reulbach was one of the founding members of the short-lived Baseball Players' Fraternity. One of his ideas was for major leaguers to sign a pledge of total abstinence from alcohol. His efforts to raise player salaries were more popular with his colleagues, but they may have cost him his job with Brooklyn. One day during the 1914 season, owner Charlie Ebbets offered team captain Jake Daubert a $500 raise for the coming year. Daubert told Reulbach while the team was en route to Chicago, but Ed advised Jake not to sign right away, figuring that the Federal League would offer even more when the train arrived. Daubert refused to sign until Ebbets increased his offer to $9,000 per year for five years, a whopping raise of $5,000 per year. Reulbach himself was offered a big contract by the Feds, possibly as an incentive to induce other teammates to sign, but Ed declined. He ended up signing with the Feds anyway because Ebbets released him after learning that he was a ringleader in the movement to raise salaries, and (perhaps not coincidentally) no other NL team offered him a contract.

With the Federal League's Newark Peps, Reulbach put together one last outstanding season in 1915, going 21-10 with a 2.23 ERA. Among that year's highlights were his Opening Day triumph over Chief Bender and his 12-inning win over former Cubs teammate Mordecai Brown. Reulbach also pitched and won the final game in Federal League history, defeating the Baltimore Terrapins, 6-0, in the second game of an October 3 doubleheader. The Pittsburgh Pirates acquired the rights to the big right hander in the Federal League dispersal draft but sold him to the Braves just before the start of the 1916 season. Reulbach pitched mostly in relief before ending his career in baseball with Providence of the International League in 1917.

Reulbach's post-baseball years generally weren't happy ones. He spent a fortune trying to save the life of his constantly ill son, who ended up dying anyway in 1931, and an article in the *Chicago Tribune* the following year referred to Ed at age 50 as a "sad and lonely man." Reulbach died at age 78 on July 17, 1961, in Glens Falls, New York.

CAPPY GAGNON

CHICAGO

CHARLES WEBB MURPHY
OWNER 1906–13

One of the most controversial figures of the Deadball Era, Charles Murphy owned the Chicago Cubs from 1906 to 1913, the period during which they reached their greatest heights. The Cubs won four National League pennants and two world championships under his ownership, making Chicago the center of the baseball universe. But instead of being revered by the fans, his players, and his fellow owners, the ambitious, energetic Murphy was generally despised. "When I had the Cubs I was too busy for entertaining, or cultivating people," he explained. "It is some task to run a championship ball club and cater to 25 'prima donna' ball players. When night comes you are all in and don't care for wine parties or bacchanalian revels—at least I did not." As for the baseball establishment, he had this to say: "Some I had refused to loan money to, others were not in love with me because my club had beaten theirs so often, and the Chief Executive [John Tener] was not pleased with me because I had refused to sign his contract—the only club owner who kicked on his compensation, which was more than we could afford."

The son of Irish immigrants, Charles Webb Murphy was born in Wilmington, Ohio, 60 miles northeast of Cincinnati. Moving to Cincinnati to study pharmacology, Murphy graduated from pharmacy school and worked for a while at Keenan's drugstore. Before long, however, he quit to become a writer for the *Cincinnati Enquirer*, a newspaper owned by Charles Phelps Taft, the older half brother of future president William Howard Taft. (President Taft later endorsed baseball in his speeches and frequently attended major league games; many credited Murphy for convincing the president to lend his presence to the national pastime.) Murphy became sporting editor, and in that position he became friendly with John T. Brush, owner of the Reds.

Charles left the *Enquirer* to become assistant city editor at the *Cincinnati Times-Star*, but he wasn't there long before Brush hired him in 1905 as press agent for the New York Giants. One day Murphy suggested to Brush that he should mix around more with people and increase his personal popularity. The elderly Giants owner, who was in poor health and didn't know 100 persons in greater New York, aside from his players, smiled and said: "If the Giants win, I will be popular. If they lose I will not be. All the personal popularity in the world gets the club owner nothing if his club is a loser." Charles remembered those words and made them his own philosophy when he became an owner.

That time came surprisingly soon. On his first western road trip with the Giants, Murphy overheard NL president Harry Pulliam tell Cincinnati Reds owner Garry Herrmann that Jim Hart was putting the Chicago Cubs up for sale. Taking the midnight train from Cincinnati to Chicago, the 37-year-old press agent obtained an option from Hart to purchase all of his Cubs stock for the bargain price of $105,000. Securing a $100,000 loan from his friend and former employer Charles Taft, Murphy closed the deal on July 31, 1905.

The Cubs were an up-and-coming team, and Murphy and new manager Frank Chance went to work during the off-season to make the team even stronger. Relying on Chance's knowledge and insights, Murphy acquired third baseman Harry Steinfeldt and pitcher Orvie Overall from the Cincinnati Reds, the team he used to cover, and outfielder Jimmy Sheckard, pitcher Jack Pfiester, and catcher Pat Moran from other sources. In their first full season under Murphy's ownership, the Cubs became the greatest team in the history of baseball, winning a record 116 games to finish 20 games ahead of Murphy's former employer, the defending world champion Giants. To cap off a nearly perfect year, the Cubs met their crosstown rivals, the White Sox, in the 1906 World Series. In his first season Murphy earned profits of $165,000, which he used to pay back all of the money he'd borrowed from Taft.

The Cubs continued their winning ways in 1907, again running away with the NL pennant and, according to some observers, achieving a triumph for "clean ball" over the dirty and underhanded methods favored by McGraw's Giants. Before long, however, Murphy began engendering ill will of his own. His Cubs continued traveling to visiting ballparks in horse-drawn carriages festooned with bells and banners, defying a league rule banning such parades. Murphy also ignored a league edict requiring him to build a clubhouse for the visiting team at West Side Grounds. But any bad feeling caused by those transgressions was minor compared to the maelstrom of ugliness Murphy stirred up over the Merkle Game. His behind-the-scenes machinations and bombastic comments in the press made him numerous enemies. "Charles Murphy, president of the Chicago club, has no sentiment for baseball, only for the money there may be in it for him," wrote Sam Crane in the *New York Evening Journal.* "In fact, the 'Chubby One' is considered a joke all over the National League, and nowhere more so than in Chicago."

Murphy got himself into even more hot water during the 1908 World Series by relegating his former brethren in the press to the back row of the grandstand for games at West Side Grounds. He also was reprimanded for selling World Series tickets to scalpers for a profit. By the end of the Series, Murphy rivaled McGraw as the most hated man in baseball. An even more serious malfeasance occurred in 1911 when he falsely accused St. Louis Cardinals manager Roger Bresnahan, a former Giant player and close friend of McGraw's, of conspiring to allow New York to win the pennant. Murphy induced Philadelphia Phillies owner Horace Fogel, another former sportswriter who was backed by Murphy money, to charge that NL president Thomas Lynch and the league's umpires were co-conspirators in the plot. The National League expelled Fogel, and Murphy came in for sharp criticism.

During the 1912 season Murphy engaged in a public feud with Chance. While the manager was hospitalized for an operation on a blood clot, Murphy accused his players of drinking and not bearing down. Chance

defended them. Shortly thereafter, the Cubs announced that the Peerless Leader wouldn't return in 1913, though whether he resigned or was fired never became entirely clear. No longer under contract, Chance at that point talked openly with the press, claiming that Murphy refused to spend money to acquire players or improve West Side Grounds—offering to bet $1,000 that the Cubs magnate would never follow through on his oft-quoted promise to build Cub fans a new ballpark. As if to prove Chance right, Murphy started slashing payroll that winter, trading Joe Tinker to Cincinnati and Ed Reulbach to Brooklyn, and sending Mordecai Brown to the minors.

The final straw for Murphy came in his shameful handling of Johnny Evers. The respected second baseman replaced Chance as player-manager in 1913, but Murphy dismissed him after a third-place finish and shunted him off to the Boston Braves. When Evers threatened to jump to the Federal League, joining former Cub stars Tinker and Brown, AL president Ban Johnson and several National League owners pressured new NL president John Tener to do something about Murphy. In a move that was universally applauded, Tener reportedly persuaded Charles Taft to buy Murphy's stock for $500,000, and the deal was consummated on February 21, 1914. (Less than two years later, Taft sold the Cubs to former Chicago Whales owner Charles Weeghman for $503,500 as part of the settlement of the Federal League war.) As one last parting gesture before leaving Chicago, Murphy hired Hank O'Day, the umpire who'd ruled in his favor in the 1908 Merkle Game, as Cubs manager for 1914.

For years the general belief was that Murphy had been driven out of baseball; in the December 1918 issue of *Baseball Magazine*, for example, F. C. Lane wrote, "Murphy was forced out of his holdings by his unpopularity with his own associates and the general public." After reading that article, Murphy actually took the time to write a lengthy response (he was a former sportswriter, after all). "It was not hard for me to take a half-million dollars for my franchise," he wrote in an article that appeared in the February 1919 issue. "No force was required. Despite that fact I read every once in a while that I was forced out of baseball—knocked down the back steps, as it were, and kicked into the yards behind. That is simply camouflage. It is true that the Chief Executive of the National League at that time was not 'crazy' about me and that he had called a meeting to have me quartered and boiled in oil, or shot at sunrise, I don't know which. He asked me to attend the meeting and I declined to do so. I was not only ill, but thinking of how much I would likely lose in the impending Federal League war—money that I had worked hard for. Before the meeting could be held, however, I sold out to Mr. Charles P. Taft and without force, but for what every other thing of value is obtained—a price. Imagine a man being forced to take $500,000 for a baseball franchise, with a war on and money being sunk by everybody concerned in large gobs. One or two baseball politicians shouted with glee over my retirement, but I think events have since shown that the laughing was all on my side, because I got out at the psychological moment."

After leaving baseball, Murphy returned to Wilmington, the town where he'd grown up and his mother still lived, and, using some of the proceeds from his sale of the Cubs, set out in 1916 to build the "best small theater in this section of the country." To prove that luck had played no part in his business success, he chose Friday, October 13, 1917, to sign the contract for construction of his amusement palace. Nearly 200 railroad cars of material went into it, and Italian and English craftsmen worked for weeks on

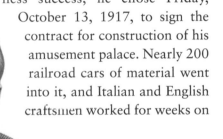

the interior. The theater featured a half-barrel foyer ceiling; carved ornamental plaster with a continuous row of Cupid heads; a lobby decorated with a sunburst chandelier, marble floors, and polished oak doors; and three painted stage curtains (one with pictures of Patrick Henry and Nathan Hale, another with Betsy Ross, and a third with a Wilmington street scene showing the courthouse). J. L. Dillon, the top decorator of the Mandel Bros. interior design firm from Chicago, proclaimed it "the prettiest thing he had ever seen."

Two years and $250,000 after the project was begun, the Murphy Theatre officially opened on July 24, 1918, to much fanfare and capacity crowds for three performances in the afternoon and evening. Speeches, singing, and music by the Wilmington Band and the regular theater orchestra preceded the movies, which starred Douglas Fairbanks and Fatty Arbuckle. Murphy sold 2,000 15-cent tickets and 1,000 10-cent tickets, donating all of the money to the Clinton County Red Cross. The next day he declared that his mother had been so overcome with emotion that she couldn't go to the opening, but his wife, Marie Louise Murphy, was there, and she called the theater "the Chicago of Southern Ohio." Speaking to the architects at the opening, Mrs. Murphy said, "You must now tell your friends at home that the reason Cincinnati does not grow faster is that it is too close to Wilmington." Charles himself was well pleased with the day and said that it was worth the entire investment to hear the children scream with delight.

Leaving Wilmington again around 1920, Charles Murphy followed the same path he'd taken as a young man, moving to Cincinnati for a while and ultimately settling in Chicago. At the age of 63, Murphy died of a paralytic stroke at his home in Chicago on October 16, 1931, leaving a $2.25 million estate to his widow and four brothers. Half of the estate represented ownership of the National League Baseball Park in Philadelphia (the Baker Bowl), which Murphy had acquired when Horace Fogel was "forced" out of baseball in 1912. The historic Murphy Theatre underwent a recent restoration and was used as a set in the 1993 movie *Lost In Yonkers*. Today kids of all ages still delight to the entertainment served up on its stage. Murphy's words when it first opened in 1918—"That's not an investment; that's a monument"—have proven apt.

LEN JACOBSON

CHICAGO

SAMUEL JAMES TILDEN SHECKARD
LEFT FIELDER 1906–12

Jimmy Sheckard was a left-handed slugger during his early years with Brooklyn, then became a master at getting on base in his later years with the Cubs. In various seasons he led the National League in triples, home runs, slugging, runs, on-base percentage, walks, and stolen bases. Sheckard also was an outstanding defensive outfielder—both SABR and STATS Inc. selected him to their retroactive Gold Glove teams for the first decade of the Deadball Era—and his career assist total is one of the highest in history for an outfielder. One sportswriter described Sheckard as "a marvelous workman in his pasture and one of the surest, most deadly outfielders on fly balls that ever choked a near-triple to death by fleetness of foot and steadiness of eye and grip." Another noted that he "did clever things in the outfield in nearly every game and was in a class by himself at trapping a ball."

"Sheckard was one of the brightest ball players in the business," proclaimed Johnny Evers, "and he was a bigger cog in the old invincible Cub machine than he ever received credit for being." One reason he received less credit than some of his more famous teammates is that, while he did many things brilliantly, he didn't always do them consistently or at the same time. Sheckard's highest batting average was .354 in 1901, but he also batted .239 in 1904 and .231 in 1908. He led the NL in 1903 with nine home runs, the same number he hit over the next six seasons combined. And his 147 bases on balls in 1911 were an NL record that stood until Eddie Stanky broke it in 1945, but in many other years his walk totals were about half that number.

Samuel James Tilden Sheckard was born on November 23, 1878, in Upper Chanceford, Pennsylvania. His full name reflected his father's admiration for New York's anticorruption governor Samuel Tilden, who lost one of the most controversial elections in history two years before Jimmy was born. In 1888 the Sheckards moved across the Susquehanna River to Columbia in Lancaster County, where Jimmy learned to play baseball. Six years later he got his first break when he filled in for an injured player on his hometown team and swatted a triple in a game against the Cuban Giants. In 1896 Sheckard pitched and played the outfield for four minor league clubs, appearing in a combined 76 games and batting .310. With Brockton the following year he played mostly shortstop and led the New England League with a .370 batting average and 53 stolen bases. The Brooklyn Bridegrooms acquired Sheckard toward the end of 1897, hoping he'd replace the aging Germany Smith, but he demonstrated that he was no shortstop by committing 19 errors in 11 games at the position.

As a left fielder in 1898, Sheckard hit .277 in 105 games for Brooklyn but was sent to the Baltimore Orioles after the season when new Bridegrooms manager Ned Hanlon brought outfielders Willie Keeler and Joe Kelley with him from Baltimore. The shuffling of personnel benefited Sheckard. Given an opportunity to play nearly every day by Baltimore's rookie manager, John McGraw, Jimmy batted .295, scored 104 runs, and led the NL with 77 steals. In the outfield he was second in the league in assists (33) and set the NL record for double plays by an outfielder (14). In 1900 Sheckard returned to Brooklyn and hit .300 as a backup to Keeler, Kelley, and Fielder Jones. When Jones jumped to the American League in 1901, Sheckard replaced him and became a star of the first order, leading the NL in slugging (.534) and triples (19), placing second in home runs (11), and third in batting average (.354), hits (196), and RBI (104).

On the verge of greatness, Sheckard showed the first signs of the inconsistency that plagued him for most of his career. After jumping to the American League's Baltimore Orioles for four games at the start of 1902, he changed his mind and returned to Brooklyn, where his batting average plummeted to .265. Sheckard bounced back with a .332 average in 1903, when he also led the league with nine home runs and tied Chicago's Frank Chance for the stolen-base crown with 67, but the following season his average fell again, this time to .239. Even though Jimmy batted a respectable .292 in 1905, reports circulated that he wasn't playing up to his potential or might even be washed up. Despite his popularity with the fans, on December 30, 1905, Brooklyn traded him to the Chicago Cubs for outfielders Jack McCarthy and Billy Maloney, third baseman Doc Casey, pitcher Buttons Briggs, and $2,000. Initially Jimmy balked at the deal—the press speculated that he'd have preferred a move to McGraw's Giants—but eventually he had a change of heart.

That transaction, along with the subsequent trade that brought Harry Steinfeldt to the Cubs, played an important part in tilting the balance of power in the National League from New York, where the Giants had won the two previous championships, westward to Chicago. Manager Frank Chance installed Sheckard in left field, moving Jimmy Slagle to center and shifting Frank Schulte to his natural position in right to complete the famous "S" outfield. Jimmy batted just .262 but established himself as a team leader who excelled at irritating the opposition—he had a "quiet way of getting a rival's goat that has never been eclipsed," noted one sportswriter. For example, he antagonized the White Sox by bragging that he would hit .400 in the 1906 World Series. Sheckard then went 0-for-21 and failed to hit a ball out of the infield. McGraw blamed Jimmy's embarrassing performance on Chance for playing the left-handed hitter against left-handed hurlers.

On June 2, 1908, Sheckard nearly lost the use of his left eye as a result of a fistfight with teammate Heinie Zimmerman. During the melee Jimmy threw something at the young infielder. Infuriated, Zimmerman picked up a bottle of ammonia and hurled it at his assailant. The bottle broke as it hit Sheckard between the eyes, spilling ammonia all over his face. Chance ran to Sheckard's assistance, but Zimmerman had the best of the manager, too, until the rest of the team intervened. The Cubs originally tried to cover up the incident, but Sheckard was sidelined for several weeks and the story eventually leaked. Jimmy batted a career-low .231 in just 115 games (his fewest since 1900).

Thanks in large part to the writings of Ring Lardner, then a beat reporter covering the Cubs, Sheckard became well-known for his horseplay with Hofman and pitcher Lew Richie. The most famous example of his flakiness occurred in a game against Pittsburgh. After Pirate hitters had been spraying the ball all around him, Sheckard stopped in the middle of left field, whirled several times, threw his glove in the air, and went over to the spot where it landed. Cubs pitcher Orval Overall couldn't figure out why Sheckard was standing only a few feet from the left-field line and motioned for his outfielder to reposition himself. Sheckard refused. The next batter, Fred Clarke, hit a liner straight into Sheckard's glove.

When there was talk after the 1910 season that the Cubs might trade Frank Schulte to the Phillies for John Titus, Schulte quipped, "They'd better pull it off quick if they want to keep me sane. It's no cinch to play in that Cub outfield and stay in your right mind." The trade never came off, and both Schulte and Sheckard enjoyed banner seasons in 1911. Jimmy led the NL in runs (121) and bases on balls (147). "Sheckard is not built according to approved models of men hard to pitch to," wrote one reporter. Officially listed at 5'9" and 175 lbs., Jimmy was "no midget," according to the reporter, "but when it comes to judging a ball to a hair line and outguessing pitchers, he is there, as his base-on-balls record shows." The reporter described Sheckard as "positively fat," but his girth was no handicap "to a man who walks to base in preference to doing the Cobb stunt." Though he led the NL in walks again in 1912 with 122, and his .392 on-base percentage was 51 points above the NL average, Sheck batted just .245. In an era obsessed with batting average, that made him expendable.

In April 1913 the Cubs sold the 34-year-old Sheckard to the St. Louis Cardinals. He batted just .199 in 52 games. The Cardinals placed him on waivers in July, and he spent the rest of the season with the Reds, for whom he batted .190 in 47 games. It was the final stop in his 17-year career in the majors. Despite an offer to join the Federal League in 1914, Sheckard remained in Organized Baseball as player-manager of Cleveland of the American Association. After the season Jimmy went home to Pennsylvania and managed Reading of the Pennsylvania State League the next season. In the spring of 1917 Sheckard played with independent teams in Brooklyn before returning to Chicago and becoming a Cubs coach. During World War I he served as athletic director at the Great Lakes Naval Training Station.

After the war Sheckard went home to Columbia, Pennsylvania, where he managed semipro ball. He discovered shortstop Les Bell, a Harrisburg native who later played for the Cardinals, Braves, and Cubs. "Jimmy was a fine man," Bell said. "Very fundamental. Bunt, hit and run, stolen base, defense—the way he played the game, from what I've been told." Sheckard remained a character. "As a manager he wore white socks and a white shirt and was always chewing tobacco," Bell remembered. "He'd hitch his pants at the knees, sit himself down and spit away. Funniest damn thing I ever saw—by the end of a game those white socks were always a distinctly brownish color."

Sheckard became the baseball coach at Franklin & Marshall College and managed the Lancaster Red Roses during their one season in the Interstate League in 1932. In the mid-'30s he declined an offer from Connie Mack to manage Federalsburg of the Eastern Shore League, a decision he later regretted. By the end of the

decade Sheckard was down on his luck. Having lost his modest savings in the 1929 stock market crash, he rose each morning to drive a truck on a four-hour trip collecting 10-gallon, 100 lb. milk cans from farmers in the Lancaster area.

On a cold Sunday in January 1947, Jimmy walked to his attendant's job at a gas station directly across from Stumpf Field, the home of the Red Roses. As he limped toward the station (he suffered from arthritis in his left foot, which doctors believed was the result of an old baseball injury), a car struck him from behind. Sheckard died of head injuries three days later. Umpire Bill Klem, who'd called the balls and strikes in many of Jimmy's games in the National League, presided over a ceremony in his honor at Stumpf Field, and the city of Lancaster erected a monument to his memory in Buchanan Park.

DON JENSEN

Orval Overall

CHICAGO

ORVAL OVERALL
RIGHT-HANDED PITCHER 1906–10, 1913

A huge man for the Deadball Era, standing 6'2" and weighing 214 lbs., Orvie Overall was a right-handed curveballer who compiled a lifetime 108-71 record and 2.23 ERA, the ninth-best ERA in major league history for pitchers with 1,500 innings. "Overall pitches his curve with a wide, sweeping overhand swing, releasing the ball over the side of the index finger as his hand turns downward," wrote Cubs teammate Johnny Evers. "His swing and curve are duplicates of those used by Adonis Terry, Jim McCormick, and some of the great pitchers of the past, and when his jerk motion at the finish of the wide swing is sharp, the curve actually darts downward." With a reputation as a "money pitcher," Overall pitched on Opening Day each year from 1906 to 1910 and compiled a 3-1 record and 1.75 ERA in four World Series.

Sometimes called the "Big Groundhog" because of his birthday, Orval Overall was born on February 2, 1881, in Farmersville, California, a small agricultural community just outside Visalia. Located in the San Joaquin Valley, about equidistant from Los Angeles and San Francisco, Visalia was a thriving community of 1,000 inhabitants. Orvie's father, Daniel, was a well-to-do businessman who owned the Palace Hotel in addition to a citrus farm, and Orvie enjoyed an upper-class upbringing. After pitching and playing first base at Visalia High School, the 19-year-old Overall enrolled at the University of California in the fall of 1900. He excelled in his studies of agricultural science at Berkeley and was elected class president.

Overall was Cal's star in both football and baseball. On the gridiron he played guard, fullback, and punter, serving as captain during his senior year. In his junior and senior years he played integral roles in victories over archrival Stanford. In baseball Orvie performed the majority of the mound work as a freshman, pitching well but suffering from occasional mental lapses. Perhaps an early indicator of the arm troubles that plagued him in later years, he missed time from pitching due to a sore arm in both his sophomore and junior years. During those times Overall played left field, first base, and catcher, though he inevitably returned to pitching as soon as his arm rounded into shape. In his junior year he entertained an offer to join the San Francisco club of the Pacific Coast League, but he elected to continue his education instead.

To his father's disappointment, Overall finally did leave the University of California to go professional in early 1904, signing with Tacoma of the Pacific Coast League for a salary of $300 a month, more than many of his veteran teammates were earning. Orvie helped Tacoma win the 1904 pennant by registering a 32-25 record. Cincinnati scout Fred Hutchinson signed the former collegian after winning a bidding war with the Chicago Cubs. Making his major league debut in Cincinnati on April 16, 1905, Overall took his regular turn throughout his rookie year and went 18-23 with a 2.86 ERA, pitching 318 innings and ranking fifth in the National League with 42 appearances. He returned to Cincinnati in 1906 but got off to a poor start, going 4-5 with a 4.26 ERA, and on June 2 the Reds traded him to the Cubs for pitcher Bob Wicker, who'd won 50 games over the past three seasons. Modern-day reference books state that the Reds also received $2,000, but contemporary sources indicate that the Cubs received the cash. Either way, many consider it the worst deal in Reds history until 1966, when they traded Frank Robinson to the Baltimore Orioles for Milt Pappas.

Having followed Overall's career closely after playing against him in California, Cubs manager Frank

Chance knew that the young pitcher's problem was overuse. Pitching less frequently in Chicago, Orvie responded by going 12-3 with a 1.88 ERA for the remainder of the 1906 season. His breakout year was 1907, when he tied Christy Mathewson for the NL lead in shutouts (8) and finished second in wins (23), third in fewest hits per game (6.74), fourth in strikeouts per game (4.73), and fifth in ERA (1.68). Overall's strong performance led the Cubs back to the World Series, this time against the Detroit Tigers, and he received the start in Game One against Wild Bill Donovan. He ended up with a no-decision in a 3-3 tie, but three days later he came back and beat Donovan in Game Four, 6-1.

Prior to the 1908 season, Orvie made a prediction: "I believe the new rule prohibiting a pitcher from soiling a glossy ball will greatly increase the hitting department of the game. You can't curve a glossy ball, and in my judgment there will be more pitchers knocked out of the box the coming season than ever before." Apparently he was the only pitcher negatively impacted; while the league's ERA fell to its lowest in history, his rose to 1.92. Overall lost his first game on May 12, snapping a personal 14-game winning streak that he'd begun on August 11, 1907. His record fell to 15-11, as he was hampered by arm trouble for much of the regular season, but he did lead the NL in strikeouts per game (6.68) and finished fifth in fewest hits per game (6.60). In the 1908 World Series, Overall matched up against the Tigers and Donovan once again, going the distance in Games Two and Five, and winning by scores of 6-1 and 2-0.

In 1909 Overall put together his finest overall season, going 20-11 while leading the NL with career bests in shutouts (9), strikeouts (205), and opponents' batting average (.198). He also finished third in ERA (1.42) and fewest hits per game (6.44), the best marks of his career in those categories as well. Despite his banner season, the Cubs failed to reach the World Series for the first time since

he joined the team in 1906. They returned to the fall classic in 1910, but by that time Overall was suffering from a sore arm, having gone 12-6 with a 2.68 ERA in just 144⅔ innings during the regular season. Though several pitchers were coming off better years, Orvie's reputation and past performance in the World Series led Chance to give him the start in Game One. He was ineffective, allowing six hits and three runs in three innings.

Overall claimed that his arm was better after visiting Bonesetter Reese during the off-season, but a contract dispute with Cubs owner Charles Murphy prevented him from testing it against major league competition. Remaining in California to work in a gold mine that he owned with Mordecai Brown, Orval stayed in shape that summer by playing semipro baseball, and while pitching for Stockton late in 1911 he felt something go in his arm. He believed that his arm would never be the same, but it did heal sufficiently over the next year to attempt a comeback in 1913. Returning to the Cubs, Overall went 4-5 with a 3.31 ERA, giving up more than a hit an inning for the first time in his career. After a short stint with San Francisco in the PCL, he decided to retire from baseball at age 32.

Overall took a job with the Maier Brewery Company, but the following year his father became ill and he took control of the family's citrus farm. In 1918 he ran for Congress but lost the election. After his father died in 1921, Orval sold off the estate's numerous holdings, making him a wealthy man. He became an appraiser and director of the First National Bank of Visalia, which later merged into the Security-First National Bank of Los Angeles. Overall continued to hold prominent positions, eventually rising to become vice-president of the bank and manager of its branch in Fresno. He died of a heart attack at age 66 on July 14, 1947, in Fresno, California.

BRIAN MARSHALL

CHICAGO

JOHN ALBERT HAGENBUSH (PFIESTER)
LEFT-HANDED PITCHER 1906–11

A side-wheeling left hander with a great pick-off move to first base that kept runners close, Jack Pfiester posted a lifetime 2.02 ERA over eight seasons, the third best all-time for pitchers with at least 1,000 innings, but he's best remembered for his seven shutouts and 15-5 career record against the hated New York Giants. "No longer will Chicago's fans struggle with the pretzel curves of the great southpaw's patronymic; no longer will it be mispronounced by seven out of every eight bugs and bugettes," wrote I. E. Sanborn of the *Chicago Tribune* after Pfiester's 2-1 victory over the Giants at West Side Grounds on August 30, 1908, his third straight win over the first-place Giants. "Pfiester, the spelling of which has been the occasion of as many wagers as its mispronunciation, will be dropped as meaningless and inappropriate, and for the rest of time and part of eternity Mr. Pfiester of private life will be known to the public and the historians as Jack the Giant Killer."

The son of Theodore and Margaret (Lynn) Hagenbush, John Albert Hagenbush was born in Cincinnati on May 24, 1878. Jack's early life was tragic. His father and mother both died in 1881, and his uncle, Fred Pfiester, took care of him and lent him his surname. In addition to his work in a wholesale leather house, Jack pitched for semipro teams around Cincinnati, jumping directly from the Shamrocks to the American League's Baltimore Orioles in 1901, though he failed to appear in an official game. In 1902 he pitched the entire season for Spokane of the Pacific Northwest League, ending up 13-15. The next year Pfiester went 19-16 and struck out 195 in 288 innings for San Francisco of the Pacific Coast League, earning a late-season tryout with the Pittsburgh Pirates. Making his major league debut on September 8, 1903, the 25-year-old southpaw lost all three games that he pitched, striking out 15 but compiling a 6.16 ERA and giving up 26 hits and 10 walks in 19 innings. Pfiester was even worse in three games with Pittsburgh in 1904; his ERA was 7.20 and he gave up 28 hits and nine walks in 20 innings, this time striking out only six. The Pirates sent him to Omaha of the Western League.

Pfiester developed into a top-notch pitcher at Omaha, leading the league with 178 strikeouts in 1904 and compiling a combined record of 49-22 in 1904-05. After his purchase by the Chicago Cubs, Jack entered the record books on May 30, 1906, by striking out 17 batters in 15 innings, setting a modern National League mark that stood until Warren Spahn struck out 18 on June 19, 1952. Pfiester went on to one of the finest rookie campaigns in history, ranking second in the NL in ERA (1.51) and fewest hits per game (6.21), fourth in strikeouts (153), fifth in winning percentage (.714), and sixth in wins (20). In that year's World Series, however, he was the losing pitcher in both of his appearances against the White Sox. Pfiester started and lost Game Three to Ed Walsh, 3-0, despite giving up only four hits and striking out nine. He also lost Game Five, giving up three hits and four runs in 1⅓ innings of relief. Pfiester's regular-season success continued into 1907, when he posted a 14-9 record and led the NL with a 1.15 ERA, the seventh lowest single-season ERA in the history of baseball. Again he placed second in fewest hits per game (6.60). This time the Cubs won the World Series, and Jack gained the victory in Game Two, 3-1, by scattering nine Detroit Tiger hits.

Pfiester put together another solid season in 1908, going 12-10 with a 2.00 ERA and developing his "Giant Killer" reputation. He is best remembered as the Cubs pitcher in the famous Merkle Game on September 23, avoiding a 2-1 loss only because Fred Merkle failed to touch second base. Few realized the extent of the pain with which he was pitching. Johnny Evers wrote, "A lump had formed on Pfiester's forearm, the muscle bunching. He could not bend his arm, and to pitch a curve brought agony." According to Evers, Pfiester threw only three curveballs the entire game, all to Mike Donlin in clutch situations. Immediately after the game Jack traveled to Youngstown, Ohio, to be treated by Bonesetter Reese. "Reese felt around, located the dislocated tendon, and snapped it back in place with his powerful fingers," wrote sportswriter Charles Dryden. "The entire diagnosis and cure occupied less than 10 minutes. Think of it, constant readers, Mr. Pfiester pitched nine full innings with a dislocated arm and held the Giants to five hits! Had Jack's neck been broken he would have shut them out."

Pfiester's performance after returning to the Cubs indicates that he might not have been cured by his visit with Reese. He started the one-game playoff against the Giants on October 8 but was knocked out in the first inning. Four days later Jack started and lost Game Three of the World Series (the Cubs' only defeat), giving up 10 Tiger hits and seven earned runs in eight innings. The 1909 season proved to be Pfiester's last hurrah; he compiled a 2.43 ERA and went 17-6 to finish fifth in the NL in winning percentage. He missed most of 1910, ending up at 6-3 with a 1.79 ERA in only 14 games. That year Jack made his final appearance in the World Series, again pitching in Game Three and scattering nine Philadelphia hits in 6⅔ scoreless innings of relief. At spring training in 1911 Pfiester suffered from stomach trouble and for a time thought his heart was weak. He pitched in only six games that season, posting a 1-4 record and 4.01 ERA.

Pfiester cleared waivers, and the Cubs sent him to Louisville in a deal for pitcher Reggie Richter. Jack went 7-12 for the Colonels over the rest of 1911, giving up 175 hits in 150 innings. Early the fol-

lowing year Chicago recalled him so they could sell him to Milwaukee, but the 33-year-old pitcher elected to retire instead. The full story of what happened didn't come out until three years later, when Pfiester filed a lawsuit against the Western Union Telegraph Company. Jack claimed that on May 3, 1912, a telegram from the Milwaukee club reading, "Will give you $300 per month," and signed "Hugh Duffy," was sent but not delivered. He claimed over $2,500 in damages as a result of his failure to secure that "profitable engagement." Pfiester won the case and was awarded $2,000.

The 38-year-old southpaw returned to baseball with Sioux City of the Western League in 1916 but went 0-4 with a 4.17 ERA, receiving his unconditional release on July 13. With his playing career now at an end, Jack and his wife, Lulu, settled north of Cincinnati in a village called Twightwee, near Loveland, Ohio. The couple had one son, Jack Jr., but the legal names of both Jack and his son were still John Albert Hagenbush until Jack had them officially changed to Pfiester in 1950. Jack Pfiester Sr. died at age 75 on September 3, 1953, of a blood ailment that had earlier required his left leg to be amputated above the knee.

STUART SCHIMLER

CHICAGO

HENRY M. STEINFELDT
THIRD BASEMAN 1906–10

Today Harry Steinfeldt is the answer to a trivia question: Who was the third baseman in the Cubs' famous Tinker-to-Evers-to-Chance infield? In his time, however, the .267 lifetime hitter was considered one of the greatest third basemen in the game. "Harry Steinfeldt, the Cubs third baseman whose glorious fielding kept the dashing Ty Cobb off the base paths in a couple of world's series, and whose lusty wallops sent many a fellow Cub scampering across home plate in the last few years, is another who was dubbed unfit by an erring leader in ill-fated Cincinnati," wrote Alfred Spink in 1910. "Harry left the haunts of the Reds, jumped in and completed Frank Chance's sterling infield, and still holds his court there, a veritable terror to seekers of base hits and stolen cushions."

The son of a German immigrant, Henry M. Steinfeldt was born in St. Louis on September 29, 1877. When Harry was five his family moved to Ft. Worth, Texas. In the early 1890s he toured with Al Field's Minstrels, playing baseball in towns in which the show was billed. Harry made his professional debut in 1895 with Ft. Worth of the Texas League. He split the next season between Ft. Worth and Galveston, batting .320 and leading all Texas League second basemen with a .989 fielding percentage. That fall Steinfeldt was drafted by Detroit of the Western League. When the Detroit president discovered that Galveston had written his name as "Steinhoff" on its reserve list, he called off negotiations and signed Harry without any compensation to the Texas League club. Justice was served the following year when the National League's Cincinnati Reds drafted both Steinfeldt and pitcher Noodles Hahn from Detroit.

Cincinnati's star-studded 1898 infield featured Bid McPhee at second base, Tommy Corcoran at shortstop, and Charlie Irwin at third. For several seasons Steinfeldt filled in when those veterans were injured or sick, establishing himself as the best utility man in club history. Manager Buck Ewing was especially impressed with Harry's quick release: "He throws better than anyone I ever saw. I don't mean his terrific throwing, particularly, but the rapidity with which he gets a ball started on a journey. The ball is hardly in his hands before he has it sailing through the air." Playing regularly after Irwin was released in midseason 1901, "Steiney" became the first third baseman to wear shin guards. His breakout season was 1903, when he batted .312 and led the National League with 32 doubles.

A leg injury hampered Steinfeldt the following year, and in 1905 he reportedly became dissatisfied and did not give the club his best efforts, prompting one observer to state that he was "all in as a player." Teammate Al Bridwell recalled a strange occourance near the end of that season. "Steinfeldt came over to me one day and said, 'Kid, you're going to be the regular third baseman pretty soon, maybe starting today,'" said Bridwell. "'What do you mean?' I asked him. 'Wait and see,' he says, 'something might happen. You never can tell in this game.' Well, about the second or third inning that day a foul ball went up off third base, near the railing, and Steiney ran over to catch it. As he did, he tumbled over the railing and hurt himself and had to leave the game. So they sent me out to play third in his place, and I finished the season at that position. That winter Steiney was traded to the Chicago Cubs for Hans Lobert [and Jake Weimer], and he became the third baseman in the famous Tinker-Evers-Chance infield."

The trade was the turning point in Steinfeldt's career. Earlier that off-season the Cubs had sent their regular third baseman, Doc Casey, to Brooklyn in the blockbuster trade for Jimmy Sheckard. The addition of Steinfeldt and Sheckard made the Cubs the greatest baseball machine in the country. Putting up the best numbers of his career, Steiney batted .327, second in the NL, and led the league with 176 hits and 83 RBI. He also led NL third basemen with a .954 fielding percentage, a statistic in which he led the league in three of his five seasons in Chicago. Steinfeldt followed up his career year in 1906 with a spectacular performance in the 1907 World Series, batting .471 to lead all players.

The Cubs rewarded Steinfeldt's efforts with a three-year contract, but from that point on his performance started to slip. In 1908 he batted a career-low .241, and though he rebounded somewhat to hit .252 in both 1909 and 1910, he tailed off significantly toward the end of the latter season. Steinfeldt's slump continued into the 1910 World Series, when he managed only two hits in 20 at-bats. Despite his poor showing, Harry remained at home in the Cincinnati suburb of Bellevue, Kentucky, when the rest of his teammates reported for spring training. He'd married a woman from Bellevue when he was playing for the Reds, and at her behest he was holding out for another three-year contract. The Cubs asked for waivers on Steinfeldt, but the waivers were recalled when both Boston and Cincinnati claimed him. Harry reported shortly thereafter, but by then Chance was so impressed with rookie Jimmy Doyle and utility man Heinie Zimmerman that the Cubs made a second attempt at waivers, and this time they were obtained. Before the start of the season Chicago sold Steinfeldt to St. Paul of the American Association. "That winds it all up," Harry told a reporter. "Don't ever think I'm going to play in St. Paul."

Steinfeldt went home to Cincinnati and worked for his father-in-law's bread-pan factory, but before long he joined St. Paul. After a good start in the American Association he received another shot at the National League with the Boston Rustlers. For 19 games Steiney was Boston's regular third baseman, now and then showing flashes of his former brilliance, but in mid-July he came down with a very serious illness. Mrs. Steinfeldt came to Boston and took him

home to Bellevue, where it was feared that he might be developing typhoid fever. According to an August report, Steinfeldt was hospitalized in Cincinnati, "suffering nervous prostration brought about through worry over his release from the Chicago team earlier in the season." The report went on to state that Mrs. Steinfeldt "is very much opposed to his playing ball any more and will urge him to retire permanently as soon as he is out of the hospital."

The lure of the baking supplies' business proved insufficient to prevent Harry's return to the diamond. In February 1912 he signed to manage Cincinnati in the new United States League, but when that circuit folded he tried out for the St. Louis Cardinals. Drawing his unconditional release before the season opened, Steinfeldt, in the words of one poetic commentator, "then tried the minors, but his heart was broken, and he could not reconcile himself to Father Time's claim." After being let go by Louisville, Chattanooga, and Meridian, he "went to his home and to bed with an illness that ended his life on August 17, 1914." The 37-year-old Steinfeldt's death certificate indicates that he died of a cerebral hemorrhage.

TOM SIMON

CHICAGO

HENRY ZIMMERMAN
INFIELDER 1907–16

A versatile fielder who could play second, third, or short—though none of them particularly well—Heinie Zimmerman rose to prominence with the Chicago Cubs during the early teens, winning the respect of fans and opposing pitchers with his aggressive batting style. The lifetime .295 hitter never fulfilled his immense potential, however, becoming one of the Deadball Era's best examples of wasted talent. "Zimmerman's disposition has not always been fortunate and his all round record hasn't been quite what it should have been," wrote F. C. Lane in 1917. "But there is no possible doubt that he is one of the greatest natural ball players who ever wore a uniform."

Henry Zimmerman was born on February 9, 1887, in the Bronx, New York, the ninth of 12 children. His father, Rudolph, a German immigrant who'd arrived in the United States in 1860, struggled to support his large family as a traveling salesman of imported furs. Several of his children sacrificed their education to earn money for the family, including Henry. "When I saw what a hard time the old man was having, I decided to get a job that was a money maker," he recalled. At age 14 Henry put away his schoolbooks and became a plumber's apprentice. Though he later claimed he'd received all the schooling he needed, others would have disagreed. Sportswriter Warren Brown described Henry as a man who "played his baseball by ear mostly" and "was no mental giant." Over time he developed a reputation for dim-wittedness that was unsurpassed, even among ballplayers.

Zimmerman first honed his baseball skills on the ultra-competitive sandlots of New York City. First at a park on the corner of 163rd Street and Southern Boulevard, and later across the Hudson River in Red Bank, New Jersey, Henry established himself as one of the metro area's finest semipros. By 1905 he was earning $20 catching and pitching on weekends, which must have seemed like a king's ransom compared to the $2 per day he took home for fixing leaky faucets in the Bronx. In 1906 Zimmerman signed on as a second baseman for Wilkes-Barre of the New York State League. The Chicago Cubs purchased him for $2,000 in the midst of his second season in Wilkes-Barre.

Only 20 years old when he arrived in the majors in August 1907, Zimmerman stood 5'11" and weighed 176 lbs., about average for his day. With an awkward, loping gait and a perpetual sneer plastered across his face, "even Franklin P. Adams would have had trouble reducing him to poetry in motion," Brown remarked. But the boy could hit. Blessed with exceptionally strong hands and forearms, the right-handed Zimmerman was one of the most aggressive hitters of the Deadball Era, known for swinging at pitches well out of the strike zone and lining them for hits.

Initially Zimmerman saw little playing time because the Cubs already featured the strongest infield in baseball. It wasn't until Johnny Evers went down with an ankle injury late in 1910 that Zimmerman got his first real opportunity in Chicago, starting every game of that year's World Series. Injuries kept Evers on the sidelines for most of 1911 as well, and Zimmerman responded with his first standout season. His .307 batting average and .462 slugging percentage both ranked among the

Top 10 in the National League, but his shaky defense infuriated manager Frank Chance. When Zimmerman muffed two chances in the early innings of an August 7 game against Boston, Chance pulled him from the field and briefly suspended him for "indifferent fielding." Zimmerman was quickly becoming one of the most potent offensive weapons in the game, a rare middle infielder who could hit for both power and average, but going into the 1912 season his status as an everday player was anything but secure.

All that changed on February 1, 1912, when the Cubs' regular third baseman, Jimmy Doyle, died suddenly from appendicitis. As a result of the tragedy, Zimmerman moved from Chance's doghouse to the hot corner, where he put together one of the Deadball Era's best offensive seasons. Teammate Cy Williams told F. C. Lane, "Zimmerman was as good a hitter that year as I ever saw. And what was he doing? He was swinging at balls a foot over his head and driving them safe. You can get away with murder when the luck is with you." Joe Tinker took the opposite view, insisting that Zimmerman was actually *unlucky* in his finest season. "Why, do you know, that fellow loses more hits through hard luck catches than I make," Tinker said. "He has the strongest pair of hands and arms that I have ever seen on a human being."

That year Zimmerman led the NL in batting average (.372), slugging percentage (.571), hits (207), doubles (41), home runs (14), and total bases (318). It was believed at the time that Zimmerman also paced the circuit with 103 RBI, which would have made him the National League's first Triple Crown winner since Hugh Duffy in 1894. Research conducted a half century later, however, determined that his actual RBI total was 99, ranking him third behind Honus Wagner (102) and Bill Sweeney (100). The year 1912 was the pinnacle of magician Harry "The Great" Houdini's popularity, and the city's sportswriters took to calling Heinie "The Great Zim." Never one for modesty, Zimmerman started referring to himself in the third person under his new nickname.

Soon The Great Zim pulled a disappearing act of his own. He enjoyed another fine offensive season in 1913, batting .313 and driving in 95 runs, but his swelled head led to confrontations with management. Acrimonious contract negotiations became an annual event. More than once Zimmerman "retired" from the game, only to un-retire once spring training rolled around. What money he did receive, he spent quickly—and often unwisely. "Zim never knew how much money he had because he made the team's secretary his banker and 'touched' the secretary for fins and sawbucks until his salary was gone, then economized until the roll was replenished," wrote one observer.

The indiscriminate spending might have been amusing if it hadn't come at the expense of his new family. In 1912 Henry married the 17-year-old Helene Chasar, who one year later gave birth to a daughter, Margaret. The marriage quickly deteriorated, and in January 1915 Chasar sued Zimmerman for alimony. "Although the wife alleges Zimmerman is paid $7,200 a year by the Chicago Club for his services," one Chicago newspaper reported, "she alleges he has not sent any money to support her in some time, excepting a five-dollar gold piece which was sent her as a Christmas present for their daughter." The couple divorced in March 1916.

The discord took its toll on Heinie's on-field performance in 1915. That year he suffered through his worst season, batting just .265 with a paltry .379 slugging percentage. For the first time, but not the last, pernicious rumors of Zimmerman's dishonesty began to surface. *The Sporting News* described him as "one of the most interesting problems of baseball," a player whose "energy [is] being misdirected and talents largely wasted." Zimmerman developed a reputation as a "bad actor," prone to sudden, inexplicable mood swings that dictated the amount of effort he put forth on any given day. The Cubs finally tired of him and dealt him to the New York Giants for Larry Doyle in August 1916. At the time of the trade, Zimmerman was under a 10-day suspension for "laying down on the job." Most managers wanted nothing to do with him, but John McGraw prided himself on his ability to rehabilitate players deemed hopeless by other teams.

The Giants were slumping toward another losing season in 1916 until the Zimmerman trade, when they suddenly caught fire and reeled off a record 26 consecutive wins. Between Chicago and New York, Zimmerman collected a league-leading 83 RBI, but his reputation preceded his accomplishments in the eyes of some observers. "Zimmerman has not, of late years, played his best game," wrote F. C. Lane. "Any time he wishes to exert himself he has the natural ability, but his temperament has been a big handicap." In 1917 Heinie responded to his critics with his best performance in four years. His .297 batting average was his highest since 1913, and his 102 RBI paced the circuit by a comfortable margin, helping the retooled Giants run away with the pennant. Zimmerman's improved performance had Lane singing a different tune: "We know nothing of Zimmerman's qualifications for alderman or a seat on the school committee, but he certainly can play third base." His triumphant season concluded in the worst manner imaginable, however, when he batted .120 and committed three errors in the Giants' loss to the Chicago White Sox in the 1917 World Series.

It was Zimmerman's role in a botched rundown in the sixth and final game that forever sealed his fate as the goat of that Series. With the game scoreless in the

top of the fourth inning, Heinie made a bad throw on an Eddie Collins grounder, allowing Collins to advance to second. Dave Robertson then dropped Joe Jackson's fly ball, putting runners at second and third with no outs. At that point Happy Felsch grounded back to the pitcher, Rube Benton, who threw to Zimmerman at third, catching Collins in a rundown. Zimmerman threw the ball to catcher Bill Rariden, but when Rariden tossed the ball back to Zimmerman, the clever Collins slipped past the catcher and sprinted for home. Both Benton and Giants first baseman Walter Holke neglected to back up the play, leaving home plate unattended. With a foot pursuit his only option, the lumbering Zimmerman tried unsuccessfully to chase down the speedy Collins, who slid across home plate with what proved to be the Series-winning run.

The play wasn't Zimmerman's fault, but that didn't matter—the press mercilessly ridiculed him. The *New York Times* called the play "Zimmerman's deathless outburst of stupidity." "The great crowd shook with laughter and filled the air with cries of derision at one of the stupidest plays that has ever been seen in a world's series," reported the *Times*. "Zim thought it was a track meet instead of a ball game and wanted to match his lumber-wagon gait against the fleetest player in the game." Collins himself exonerated the rival third baseman of all blame, but to no avail. More than a half century later, newspaper reports of Zimmerman's death carried this headline: GIANTS' HEINIE ZIMMERMAN DIES; COMMITTED 1917 SERIES "BONER."

Unfairly branded a buffoon in the papers, Zimmerman emerged from his final World Series bitter and disillusioned. In 1918 he suffered through one of his poorest seasons, his batting average falling to .272 and his RBI plummeting to 56. Lane noted a change in the former star. "He seemed to suffer from the all-round slough of discouragement which engulfed the Giants' hopes," he wrote in *Baseball Magazine*. Partly because of Zimmerman, the Giants failed to duplicate their 1917 success, and as the season progressed Zimmerman's effort started to flag. In July McGraw bawled him out in public and benched him for failing to run out a pop fly.

Before the 1919 season the Giants acquired the most notorious game thrower of all, Hal Chase. McGraw believed he could reform Chase, but instead of turning over a new leaf, Prince Hal shifted his game-fixing operations to New York, recruiting Zimmerman as his new sidekick. For the second consecutive year Heinie performed below expectations, but this time the root cause may have been something other than frustration or distraction. As the Giants limped through another disappointing campaign, Zimmerman and Chase became inseparable, often hanging out with gamblers in bars and restaurants.

In such an environment, what happened next was probably inevitable. On September 11, Zimmerman approached pitcher Fred Toney after the first inning of a game in Chicago and informed him that "it would be worth his while" not to bear down on the Cubs. One inning later, Toney asked to be removed from the game, but Zimmerman didn't stop there. That same evening, Chase and Cubs infielder Buck Herzog informed Benton that he could "make some easy money" by letting Chicago win. When Benton beat the Cubs anyway the following afternoon, Zimmerman approached him in the hotel lobby after the game and said, "You poor fish, don't you know there was $400 waiting for you to lose that game today?" A few days later in St. Louis, Chase and Zimmerman offered Bennie Kauff $125 per game to help them throw games. By that time, word of the pair's activities had reached McGraw, who promptly suspended Zimmerman. (Chase remained with the Giants for two more weeks.) At the time, McGraw's public explanation for Zimmerman's suspension was that he'd broken curfew, but shortly thereafter McGraw and Giants owner Charles Stoneham got Zimmerman to confess to his offenses.

In an earlier era Zimmerman may have been able to continue in the profession with some other club, but any such hope was forever lost with the public revelation of the Black Sox scandal. In September 1920 a grand jury was convened to investigate gambling in baseball, and it was at those hearings that Zimmerman's misdeeds came to light. McGraw and Toney both testified to Zimmerman's actions at the end of the 1919 season. In an affadavit, Zimmerman admitted to offering bribes to Toney, Benton, and Kauff, but insisted he did so only at the behest of an unnamed Chicago gambler. "He made me no personal offer, but asked me to deliver this message to these three men," Zimmerman claimed. "Although I was not to benefit by it, I went to Kauff, Toney, and Benton and delivered the message." He insisted that he'd played to win the suspect games. No one believed Zimmerman, but what he'd confessed to was damning enough. Though never officially banned, he became persona non grata throughout Organized Baseball.

In the absence of any other livelihood, Zimmerman remarried and went back to working as a plumber in the Bronx, though before long he supplemented his income through less reputable sources. In 1929-30 Zimmerman operated a speakeasy with the infamous racketeer Dutch Schultz, becoming closely connected with New York's most ruthless mobster. (In 1928 Zimmerman's brother-in-law, a top Schultz lieutenant, had been fatally shot outside a West 54th Street nightclub.) In 1935 Zimmerman was named as an unindicted co-conspirator in the government's tax evasion and conspiracy case against Schultz. The government lost the case, but a few months later Schultz was gunned down in a Newark restaurant.

Ignored and forgotten, Zimmerman reassumed the blue-collar lifestyle that was the inheritance of his childhood. In his last job he worked as a steamfitter for a construction company. Heinie died in New York City on March 14, 1969, after a brief battle with cancer. He is buried in Woodlawn Cemetery, a short drive from his boyhood home.

DAVID JONES

CHICAGO

JAMES PATRICK ARCHER
CATCHER 1909–17

Jimmy Archer was the regular catcher for the Chicago Cubs from 1911 through 1916, earning a spot on *Baseball Magazine*'s "All-America Team" each year from 1912 to 1914. Renowned for popularizing the snap throw from a squatting position, Archer enjoyed a reputation for having the best throwing arm of any catcher in the Deadball Era. "The best throwing catcher of them all was Jimmy Archer of the Cubs," said Chief Meyers, the only receiver except Archer to catch over 100 games each season from 1911 to 1913. "He didn't have an arm, he had a rifle. And perfect accuracy." Al Bridwell, who played with Archer on the 1913 Cubs, agreed. "Best arm of any catcher I ever saw," said the man who received many of Archer's snap throws. "He'd zip it down there to second like a flash. Perfect accuracy, and under a six-foot bar all the way down."

James Patrick Archer was born in Dublin, Ireland, on May 13, 1883. His family moved to Montreal when he was an infant, and by the time he was three the Archers had settled in Toronto. Jimmy played baseball at St. Michael's College and in the Toronto City League. During the winter of 1902, the 19-year-old Archer was working as a barrel maker at a Toronto cooperage when he fell into a vat of boiling oak sap, scalding his right arm and leg so badly that he was hospitalized for three months. Jimmy was in so much pain during his hospitalization that he begged for his arm to be amputated. As a result of the accident, the tendon in his right arm shrank and made his right arm shorter than his left. Jimmy always claimed that the accident was what gave him his unique ability to throw quickly and accurately from a squatting position.

Archer's career in professional baseball began when a friend, Tom Reynolds, invited him to join the team from Fargo, North Dakota, that he was managing in 1903. Jimmy batted .225 in 20 games before jumping to an independent team in Manitoba that offered more money. The following year he played in the Iowa State League with Boone, where he met his future wife, Lillian Stark. His season was briefly interrupted when he broke his collarbone by crashing into a hitching post while chasing a pop fly, but he returned in time to hit .299 in 72 games. Near the end of 1904 Archer received a September trial with the Pittsburgh Pirates. Making his major league debut on Labor Day, he appeared in seven games, all of them second games of doubleheaders, and managed three singles in 20 at-bats.

In 1905 the Pirates optioned Archer to Atlanta of the Southern Association, where he cracked his kneecap when he signaled for a fastball and Bugs Raymond crossed him up with a curve. He spent two seasons with the Crackers, hitting .254 and .224, and received a second chance at the majors with Detroit in 1907. Serving as third-string catcher behind Boss Schmidt and Freddie Payne, Archer batted .119 and caught only 17 games during the regular season, but he got the start in Game Five of that year's World Series because the Cubs were having a field day at the expense of the other two Tiger catchers. They stole three bases off Jimmy, but two came on a "walking" double steal in which no throw was made. Though hitless in three at-bats against Mordecai Brown, who pitched a shutout, Archer did manage to cut down Jimmy Slagle, Chicago's leader in stolen bases with six during the Series, at second base in the seventh inning.

In 1908 Detroit manager Hughie Jennings tried to teach Archer to step toward the base when throwing, the way most catchers do, but Jimmy preferred his natural "flat-footed" method. Concluding that the young catcher was uncoachable—and also not much of a hitter—Jennings released him, later admitting that it was the only player-release decision he ever regretted. Clark Griffith, then managing the New York Highlanders, said that he wouldn't have permitted Archer to leave the American League if he hadn't been at his ranch in Montana when Detroit requested waivers. "If I had that fellow I'd work him every day just to watch him peg," said Griffith. "There is not another man in his class when it comes to shooting the ball. He is faster than chained lightning, and he never has to take a step to get the ball to any of the bases. Kling isn't in it when it comes to keeping the runners glued to the bags."

Alas, Griffith was in Montana and Archer did clear waivers, so Jennings sent him to Buffalo, where he batted .208 in 82 games in 1908. One of those games occurred on an off-day for the Chicago Cubs as they traveled east, and manager Frank Chance was in Buffalo scouting pitcher George McConnell, a spitballer who was tearing up the Eastern League. In the fourth inning a friend asked, "Well, what do you think of the pitcher?" "Pitcher!" exclaimed Chance. "It's the catcher I've been watching." Months later the Cubs manager learned that Archer had risen from a sickbed that day because the other Buffalo backstops had refused to catch McConnell's spitter. When star catcher Johnny Kling elected to sit out the 1909 season, Chance remembered the gritty Buffalo backstop and purchased him to share the catching duties with Pat Moran.

Archer caught 80 games in 1909, improving his batting average to .230, but Kling returned in 1910 and reclaimed the starting position. Archer caught 49 games that season and spelled Frank Chance at first base in another 40, raising his batting average to .259 and showing some power (nearly one-third of his hits were for extra bases). In the 1910 World Series, Kling started at catcher for the first three games, with Archer seeing action at first base in Game Three after Chance was ejected. Archer started at catcher for the final two games, as Kling was criticized for calling too many fastballs with men on base. Jimmy played well in Game Four, the only

Cubs victory, scoring the winning run after doubling in the 10th inning, but in the decisive Game Five he allowed four stolen bases and the A's won easily.

Archer supplanted Kling as the first-string catcher in 1911, prompting the Cubs to trade the popular Kling to Boston in June. Jimmy remained the primary Cubs backstop through 1916, putting together his best season in 1912, when he batted a career-high .283 and led the National League in assists. He remained the NL's premier defensive catcher through 1914, when he broke his arm crashing into a concrete wall in Brooklyn. He shared catching duties with player-manager Roger Bresnahan in 1915 and three other catchers in 1916. The Cubs released the 34-year-old Archer in 1917 when he refused to take a pay cut. He was the last player remaining from the Frank Chance era. Jimmy helped out the Pirates during 1918 spring training but earned first-string status and started on Opening Day. Pittsburgh released him after he hit only .155 in 24 games. Brooklyn picked up Archer for nine games and then sold him to Cincinnati, where he finished his career by appearing in nine more games.

After his baseball career, Archer returned to the Chicago area and worked for Armour & Company, buying hogs. In 1931 he received a medal for reviving two workers who'd fallen unconscious from carbon-monoxide poisoning. An outstanding bowler, Jimmy served as the promotional director for the Congress of Professional Bowling Alleys. He also was commissioner of the Chicago softball league and remained active in the Old-Timer's Baseball Association. Archer died of a heart attack on March 29, 1958, in a Milwaukee hospital where he was being treated for tuberculosis. He is interred in Boone, Iowa. In 1990 Jimmy Archer was elected to the Canadian Baseball Hall of Fame.

BILL BISHOP

CHICAGO

VICTOR SYLVESTER SAIER
FIRST BASEMAN 1911–17

In an article that appeared in newspapers across the country on July 31, 1915, sportswriter Grantland Rice ranked 24-year-old Chicago Cubs first baseman Vic Saier as one of the top players in the National League. A left-handed hitter and right-handed thrower with that much sought-after combination of power and speed, Saier at the time was leading the NL in runs, RBI, doubles, and triples, and was tied for the league lead in stolen bases. He had more extra-base hits than Sam Crawford and had hit for more total bases than Ty Cobb. It must have seemed that baseball immortality was beckoning this young phenomenon, the worthy successor to the "Peerless Leader," Frank Chance. Alas, just 11 days before Rice's article was published, Saier suffered a serious leg injury sliding into the plate. He was never again the same player and was out of baseball by the age of 28.

Victor Sylvester Saier was born on May 4, 1891, in Lansing, Michigan. An outstanding athlete growing up, Vic starred in baseball and football at St. Mary's High. Stories of his prowess traveled at least as far as Chicago, because the Cubs sent scouts to see him play while he was still in high school. After graduating in 1908, Vic enrolled in St. Mary's Business College and played for a local town team, the Oldsmobile Nine. His exploits caught the attention of Jack Morrissey, a Lansing native who'd played with the 1902-03 Cincinnati Reds. Then managing the Lansing entry in the Southern Michigan League, Morrissey signed Vic for the 1910 season. Not yet 20 years old, Saier led the circuit with 175 hits and batted .339 with 42 stolen bases as Lansing tied for the pennant with

Kalamazoo. The Cubs were convinced that Saier was ready and paid $1,500 to secure his services for 1911.

Though the Cubs had won their fourth pennant in five years in 1910, Chance had begun to feel the strain of both playing and managing. Saier had a good build for a first sacker—tall, rangy, and thin (he was listed at 5'11" and 170 lbs.)—and it's probable that the 33 year-old Peerless Leader thought of Vic as his eventual successor at first base. Twenty-nine games into the 1911 season, however, Chance was hit by a pitch, essentially ending his career as a player. After veterans Solly Hofman and Kitty Bransfield were tried and failed, Saier found himself starting at first base for the reigning NL champions. How would you like to take a living legend's regular job, and have him stay on as your boss? How much more would you like it if you were only 20 years old and had started working professionally only the year before? That was the situation facing young Vic, and under the circumstances he acquitted himself well, batting .259 and fielding decently in 73 games at first base.

As the stars of the great Cub teams of 1906-10 got older, their replacements generally didn't perform as well—with the exception of Saier, whose seasons from 1912 to 1914 were at least in the same ballpark with many of Frank Chance's. Vic hit .288 in 1912 and .289 in 1913, and during the latter season he led the NL with 21 triples and added 14 home runs, 92 RBI, and 26 stolen bases. In 1914 Saier's batting average fell to .240, but his 18 home runs placed him second in all of baseball to Gavy Cravath. Four of those homers came against the great Christy Mathewson, who said that

Vic's drives were some of the hardest balls ever hit against him. The Cubs had fallen apart into warring camps—they weren't the most harmonious bunch even in the days when they were winning pennants—but in the midst of all the turmoil, the Chicago newspapers lauded Saier as "The Quiet Star." Vic had a self-effacing personality and went about his business with a minimum of fuss and bother.

Saier's leg injury in 1915 kept him out of the lineup for three weeks, and the Cubs' hopes for a surprise pennant left with him. He finished the season with a .264 average and career highs in doubles (35) and stolen bases (29), and he also hit 11 triples and 11 home runs, the last time he reached double figures in either of those categories. The 1916 season began promisingly when Vic hit a sacrifice fly to drive in the winning run in the Cubs' first game ever at Weeghman Park. But at an age at which he should have been hitting his prime, his final numbers in almost every offensive category—a .253 batting average with 25 doubles, three triples, seven home runs, and 20 steals—dropped off from 1915.

In a game against the St. Louis Cardinals on April 14, 1917, Saier tried to score from second on a single and broke his leg in a collision at home plate. His season was over after just six games. Vic might not have been ready to come back even in 1918, but we'll never know for sure because he elected to work at a defense plant to help the war effort instead of playing baseball. The Cubs sold Saier's rights to the Pittsburgh Pirates, with whom Vic attempted a comeback in 1919. His manager was Hugo Bezdek, a former Penn State football coach who didn't know much about baseball. According to Casey Stengel, who also played for the 1919 Pirates, Bezdek would turn to Saier and ask, "How did Frank Chance handle that play?" Though Saier provided veteran leadership, he hit only .223 in 58 games and was released before the season ended. Many years later his daughter said that he left the Pirates of his own accord "because he was disillusioned. He always thought of himself as a Cub."

Saier returned to Lansing, where he lived the rest of his life, returning to Chicago only to marry his wife, Felicitas. He managed the City Club for many years and moved back into the house on South Pine Street in which he'd grown up. Vic Saier died in East Lansing at age 76 on May 14, 1967.

PETER GORDON

CHICAGO

LAURANCE RUSSELL CHENEY
RIGHT-HANDED PITCHER 1911–15

Over the three-year span of 1912-14, Larry Cheney was one of the National League's most durable and effective pitchers, racking up more than 300 innings each season and joining Joe McGinnity, Deacon Phillippe, Vean Gregg, and Wes Ferrell as the only modern hurlers ever to reach the 20-win mark in each of their first three full seasons. The 6'1", 190 lb. spitballer evidently had a lot of movement on his pitches. His 26 wild pitches in 1914, double that of any other National League hurler, remain a Chicago Cubs record, and his 71 wild pitches in nearly four complete seasons in a Cubs uniform are still the team's career record. In 1915, despite pitching only half the innings of his three previous seasons, Cheney fell short by only one errant toss of leading the NL in wild pitches a record seven consecutive years. Still, Cheney led the league six times, a record he shares with Nolan Ryan and Jack Morris, and his five wild pitches in one game in 1918 has been topped only three times.

Born in Belleville, Kansas, on May 2, 1886, Laurance Russell Cheney was originally a catcher. When Larry reported to Topeka of the old Western Association in 1906, manager Dick Cooley took one look at his rocket arm and turned him into a pitcher. The transformation wasn't smooth. "I was as wild as a hawk and managers wouldn't have anything to do with me," Cheney recalled. Following a two-year stint with Bartlesville, Oklahoma, he was sold to the Chicago White Sox for $1,000. Though Cheney never pitched an official game for the Pale Hose, it was during his brief stint with the team in the spring of 1907 that he learned his money pitch from Ed Walsh, arguably the greatest spitball pitcher of all-time. The ChiSox had no patience to wait for Larry to develop his spitter, however, and returned him to the bushes.

After spending 1908 with Indianapolis of the American Association, Cheney signed with the Cincinnati Reds in 1909. Manager Clark Griffith, himself a former pitcher, wasn't a fan of spitballers, and the Reds shipped the Kansas cyclone back to Indianapolis. Injuries and illness plagued Larry's tenure with the Hoosiers. While in spring training with Cincinnati in 1911, he contracted typhoid. It was back to the minors once again after the Reds physician looked him over, but this time Larry opened eyes by winning 19 games for a Louisville team that finished deep in the American Association's basement.

Purchased by the Chicago Cubs late in 1911, Cheney made a "smash" in his first major league start. He'd struck out 10 Brooklyn Superbas and hadn't yielded a single run through 7⅔ innings when a liner off the bat of Zack Wheat forever changed his pitching style. "I just had time to throw up my hand to save my face, perhaps my life," Cheney recalled. "The ball broke the little finger on my right hand and jammed my thumb so hard against my nose, it broke my nose, too. The next year my thumb was so weak I couldn't grip the ball with it, so I developed an overhand delivery." His new delivery caused his spitball to appear to rise, making it more effective. Cheney's rookie season of 1912 was one of the best of his nine-year major league career. His 26 wins tied Rube Marquard for the NL lead, while his 28 complete games topped all pitchers.

In his sophomore season, 1913, Cheney led all major league pitchers in appearances (54) and saves (11). A four-game series with Cincinnati shows how Cubs manager Johnny Evers used him. Cheney appeared in all four games, pitching a complete-game win in game one and picking up saves in games two and three. In the final game, he gave up a two-run homer to

Johnny Bates in the eighth inning, tying the game at 5-5, but was still on the mound when the game was called in the 11th inning to permit the Cubs to catch a train to St. Louis. Cheney believed he'd get the next day off, but when the Cardinals knocked Jimmy Lavender out of the box in the seventh inning, Evers called on his workhorse yet again. The game dragged on for 17 innings, with Cheney pitching until the end. After that, Evers gave Larry two weeks off to rest his weary arm.

The Cubs ace began the 1914 season inauspiciously, walking eight, hitting two, and uncorking four wild pitches, still an Opening Day record. He quickly regained his old form, however, pitching six shutouts and a pair of one-hitters among his 20 victories. Again he led the majors in games pitched with 50. But in 1915, after three sensational seasons on the mound, Cheney's career took a turn for the worse. He began the year just as he had in 1914—wild. New Cubs manager Roger Bresnahan had little patience for pitchers who failed to find the plate, often yanking them at the first sign of wildness. Cheney quickly went from one of baseball's most durable pitchers to one who was yanked in 12 of his first 18 starts, the most incomplete games in the NL to that point of the 1914 season.

On August 31, 1915, the Cubs sent Cheney to the Brooklyn Robins. That same day Brooklyn also signed Rube Marquard, and the two acquisitions paid off the following year. Coming off a mediocre 8-11 record, the 30-year-old Cheney put together one last outstanding season in 1916, winning 18 games to help Brooklyn to its first pennant since 1900. He struck out a career-high 166, just one behind NL leader Pete Alexander, and topped all NL twirlers in lowest batting average allowed. During the World Series, however, manager Wilbert Robinson used Cheney only as mop-up, and the spitballer pitched just three innings as Brooklyn dropped the Series to the Boston Red Sox.

Larry Cheney never again equaled his exploits of previous years, though he showed occasional flashes of brilliance. In late-June 1917, for example, he tossed a beauty against the Phillies, allowing only five hits in a 1-0 loss. Cheney continued his hot pitching into July, winning four in a row and not allowing an earned run over the course of 27 innings. That August he pitched 13 innings of shutout ball, all in relief, yet didn't earn the win in Brooklyn's 22-inning, 6-5 victory over the Pirates, at the time the longest game in major league

history. During that marathon Cheney figured in one of those "believe it or not" oddities of the Deadball Era. By striking out in the 18th inning, he was the only Brooklyn batter to fan in the entire contest. After falling all the way from first to seventh in 1917, Brooklyn opened the 1918 season by dropping nine games in a row before Cheney snapped the skid by defeating the Giants. He went 11-13 that season before exiting the majors following a 3-10 mark in 1919.

After bouncing around the minors for three years, including a two-year stint in the Sally League, in which he compiled a 42-11 record, Larry gave up baseball and devoted his time to operating an orange grove. He became bitter over the ensuing years when his aspirations to return to the game as a coach or scout went unfulfilled. Sometime in the 1960s, the old warrior completed a questionnaire from the National Baseball Hall of Fame. Battling a case of pulmonary emphysema, Cheney wrote that he was retired and unable to work. The final entry on the questionnaire asked: "If you had to do it all over again, would you play professional baseball?" Cheney responded: "No." He died in Daytona Beach, Florida, on January 6, 1969.

JIM MOYES

CHICAGO

FRED "CY" WILLIAMS
CENTER FIELDER 1912–17

The National League's career home run leader until he was surpassed by Rogers Hornsby in 1929, Cy Williams is remembered today primarily for his slugging achievements with the Philadelphia Phillies during the 1920s. But the 6'2", 180 lb. center fielder started to show his potential as a power hitter while with the Chicago Cubs toward the end of the Deadball Era. In a profile of Williams entitled "The Greatest Outfielder in the National League," which appeared in the September 1916 issue of *Baseball Magazine*, Ward Mason called an already 28-year-old Williams a "great all 'round talent with a wealth of sheer natural ability which is unrivaled in the older circuit," but went on to write that "in all this there isn't so much an appreciation of what Williams has already accomplished as a vague but definite impression of what he may do when he gets good and ready."

The son of Oscar and Anna (Mead) Williams, Fred Williams was born on December 21, 1887, in Wadena, Indiana, a town of only 75 residents according to the 1890 edition of the *Indiana Gazetteer & Business Directory*. Nonetheless, two well-known baseball figures were born in Wadena within three months of each other: Williams and Doc Crandall. A tall, slender farm boy who bore a slight resemblance to Walter Johnson in face and posture, Fred acquired the nickname "Cy," commonly applied to rural-looking youngsters of the era, when he matriculated at the University of Notre Dame in 1908. He excelled in athletics in South Bend, playing backup left end on the 1910 Fighting Irish football team (Knute Rockne was the backup right end that year), and win-

ning letters in track. Williams' best events were the high hurdles and the broad jump; he did the 120-yard high hurdles in 15.6 seconds, and his best broad jump was a fraction over 22'3".

According to *Baseball Magazine*, "Williams never played even half a dozen games of baseball in his life before he went to Notre Dame, and those games were of the scrubbiest kind." During the Deadball Era the Fighting Irish baseball team frequently played exhibition games against professional teams, and during one such exhibition Cy attracted the attention of a scout from the Chicago Cubs, who wanted to sign him on the spot. "I asked him if he thought I was able to go up to high company and make good right away," Williams recalled. The scout said no. "That is what I thought," said Cy. "Now, if I sign a contract it will make me ineligible for college athletics and I should like to compete in them as long as I am here." Accepting that answer, the scout asked the young center fielder for his word that he would give Chicago first choice if he ever considered signing. "I promised," Cy recalled, "and I kept my promise, even though somewhat unusual circumstances arose after that. The scout left the employ of Cubs president Charles Murphy and joined the Cleveland club. While there he visited me again and wanted me to sign for Cleveland. But I told him I had agreed to give Murphy first choice and I would keep my word."

Just before the start of his senior year, Williams, living near Chicago, received a letter from Murphy asking him to call at the Cubs office. "Naturally I complied with this request," Cy recalled, "and while I was there

Murphy asked me to sign a contract. He said no one would know anything about it, so it couldn't possibly interfere with my participation in college athletics. Finally, after considerable persuasion, he induced me to sign. I will say that no one did know anything about this contract save Murphy and myself and that he treated me fairly throughout." After graduating from Notre Dame with a degree in architecture, Williams bypassed the minors and reported directly to the Cubs, turning down an opportunity to compete in the 1912 Olympics in Stockholm as a hurdler and broad jumper.

Making his major league debut on July 18, 1912, Cy Williams appeared in only 28 games that summer, batting .242 without a single home run. In fact, his first three seasons as a professional were fairly uneventful; he never played more than part-time, and about the only item of interest is that he played under a different manager each year. That oddity continued for each of Cy's half dozen years with the Cubs, during which he played for Tinker, Evers, and Chance. (Tinker called him "the greatest natural outfielder I ever saw.") As his career progressed, Williams served under a total of 12 different managers in his first 12 years in the majors.

Finally getting a chance to play regularly in 1915, the 27-year-old Williams batted .257 and slugged 13 home runs, good enough to rank second in the NL behind Gavy Cravath's 24. Six were inside-the-park homers, for which Cy could thank his blazing speed; a 1915 article from the *South Bend Tribune* stated that Williams was "said by many competent judges to be the fastest runner in the national game." The following year Cy improved his batting average to .279 and tied with Dave Robertson of the New York Giants for the NL lead with 12 home runs. He tailed off in 1917, however, batting .241 with just five homers. Amidst rumors of dissension between him and manager Fred Mitchell, the Cubs dealt him to the Philadephia Phillies in December for Dode Paskert.

"Williams was about the best fly catcher in the league and a fairly good batsman, but he had a fatal weakness: He possessed a poor throwing arm," wrote the Chicago correspondent to *The Sporting News* after the trade. "A great throwing outfield is one of the pet hobbies of Mitchell and it was a source of regret on his part that he couldn't boast such a combination last season." The Philadelphia correspondent wrote: "[Pat] Moran expects to develop Williams into a hitting star. Certainly the Broad and Huntingdon grounds here will help hike Williams' batting average. He always hit a million when he came here. Cy is one of the fastest outfielders in the country and he is expected to more than make good here. Williams is 29 and Paskert is 36, so about the only way the Phils can get the worst of the exchange is for the Army to draft tall Cy."

The trade proved one of the worst in Cubs history. A left-handed, dead-pull hitter (Cy admitted that he "couldn't hit a ball to left if my life depended on it"), Williams was a natural for the Baker Bowl, though it took him a couple of years before he really found his groove. Starting in 1920, he batted over .300 in six of the next seven seasons and reached double figures in home runs nine years in a row. The only year that Williams didn't bat .300 over that span was 1923, when he batted .293 and blasted 41 round-trippers to take over the NL career home run record from Roger Connor. National League managers recognized that the best defense was to play him extremely deep and around toward right field—the first "Williams shift," more than 20 years before Lou Boudreau developed a similar plan to defense Ted Williams.

Retiring from the majors with 251 lifetime homers after the 1930 season, Williams spent one year in the Eastern League as the player-manager for Richmond, Virginia, then returned to his several-hundred acre dairy farm in Wisconsin, where he worked as an architect and started a construction business. Some of the finest buildings on Wisconsin's Upper Peninsula stand today as tributes to his architectural talent. In his free time Cy hunted and fished, often engaging in those pursuits with his fellow left-handed slugger Ted Williams. Though a left-handed athlete all the way, Cy was a moderately successful artist as a right hander. In 1966 the city of Three Lakes, Wisconsin, dedicated Cy Williams Park, not far from the Lake Terrace Estates resort development designed and built by the Williams Construction Company. Cy Williams died at age 86 on April 23, 1974, in Eagle River, Wisconsin.

CAPPY GAGNON

Jim "Hippo" Vaughn
CHICAGO

JAMES LESLIE "HIPPO" VAUGHN
LEFT-HANDED PITCHER 1913–21

Remembered mainly for the double no-hitter he threw with Fred Toney in 1917, Jim Vaughn was the best left-handed pitcher in the National League from 1914 to 1920, a hard thrower with excellent control whose string of seasons in 1917-19 ranks with Carl Hubbell (1933-37), Sandy Koufax (1962-66), and Randy Johnson (1999-2002) as among the best ever by an NL southpaw. "Big Jim Vaughn used to pitch the particular kind of ball a batter liked best just to show him that he couldn't hit it," said Pete Alexander. "Nothing pleased him better than to strike a man out pitching to his strength." A large man (6'4" and between 215 and 230 lbs., though reports indicate that his weight ballooned to close to 300 lbs. late in his career) whose lumbering, side-to-side gait gave him the nickname "Hippo," Vaughn was the best left-hander the Cubs ever had. He won 20 games five times in seven years; the only other Cub southpaw who did it more than once was Jake Weimer in 1903-04.

One of eight children of Josephine and Thomas Vaughn, a stonemason, James Leslie Vaughn was born on April 9, 1888, in Weatherford, Texas, due west of Ft. Worth. Finishing school in Weatherford, Jim began pitching professionally with Temple in the Texas League in 1906. He spent 1907 at Corsicana in the North Texas League, then moved on to Hot Springs in the Arkansas State League, going 9-1 and getting a shot with the New York Highlanders. Making his major league debut on June 19, 1908, Vaughn walked four batters in 2⅓ innings and was demoted to Scranton of the New York State League, where he went 2-4 in nine games. He began 1909 with Macon in the South Atlantic League, where he threw a no-hitter and had a 1.95 ERA, yet wound up 9-16 due to sparse run support. Vaugn earned a late-season promotion to Louisville in the American Association, where he went 8-1 in nine games and threw another no-hitter.

Rejoining the Highlanders at spring training in 1910, the 22-year-old Vaughn so impressed manager George Stallings that he received the Opening Day assignment. After a rough start in which he gave up three runs in the first three innings and another in the fifth, he settled down and pitched shutout ball until the game was called on account of darkness after 14 innings with the score tied, 4-4. That game was an indication of good things to come. Though overshadowed by teammate Russ Ford's brilliant rookie season of 26-6 with a 1.65 ERA, Vaughn compiled a pretty good rookie season of his own, going 13-11 with a 1.83 ERA, 18 complete games, and five shutouts. The next two seasons were disappointments, however, and his record stood at 2-8 with a 5.14 ERA when New York sold him to Washington for the waiver price on June 26, 1912.

Even though Vaughn pitched better in Washington, going 4-3 with a 2.89 ERA, Clark Griffith sold him to Kansas City of the American Association, where he finished the year by going 2-3 and giving up 33 hits in 22⅔ innings. Returning to Kansas City in 1913, he recovered his form to go 14-13 with a 2.05 ERA, including a no-hitter against Toledo on June 23. The Chicago Cubs took a chance on him, and Vaughn responded by going 5-1 with five complete games, two shutouts, and an ERA of 1.45. Suddenly the Cubs had the best left hander in the National League, if not in all of baseball. Vaughn's 1914 season was pretty much what the next six seasons would be: 21-13 with a 2.05 ERA. Indeed, looking at his numbers for that period is like looking at Warren Spahn's over any half dozen years—17 to 23 wins, a high percentage of complete games, 260 to 300 innings pitched, good control, a decent number of strikeouts, and an ERA well below the league average.

Vaughn established himself as a dominant pitcher in 1917, going 23-13 with a 2.01 ERA and career highs in starts (38), complete games (27), and strikeouts (195). Though he didn't like talking about it, the highlight of that year came on May 2, when he and Fred Toney of the Cincinnati Reds both threw no-hitters through nine innings. Vaughn faced the minimum 27 batters (one base runner was caught stealing and two others were erased on double plays). He struck out 10 while walking two and allowing only Greasy Neale to hit a ball out of the infield. It all unraveled in the 10th, however, when Larry Kopf singled to right with one out and eventually scored. Toney retired the Cubs in the bottom half to preserve the 1-0 victory. Reds manager Christy Mathewson, who knew a bit about pitching, called it the greatest pitching performance he'd ever seen.

Responding magnificently in 1918 when new acquisition Pete Alexander was drafted into the army, Vaughn started off by beating the St. Louis Cardinals on April 18, helping himself with two hits and scoring two runs. In the Cubs home opener on April 24 he pitched a 2-0, one-hit masterpiece against the same Cardinals, allowing no one to get to second base. Hippo came down with the flu in June but returned on June 26 to beat the Cardinals again, 1-0, on another one-hitter. Though Vaughn tailed off a bit at the end, he captured the pitchers' Triple Crown in the war-shortened season, leading the NL in wins (22), strikeouts (148), and ERA (1.74). He also performed well in the World Series against the Red Sox, pitching three complete games, allowing only three earned runs—and ending up with a 1-2 record.

Almost duplicating his 1918 effort, Vaughn went 21-14 with a 1.79 ERA and 141 strikeouts, but the Cubs went 75-65 and slipped to third. In hindsight, his statistics from the 1920 season show signs that all was not

well. The Cubs continued to decline, going 75-79, so Vaughn's 19-16 record looks good in comparison, but his ERA rose to 2.54, his strikeouts fell to 131, and he gave up 301 hits in 301 innings, the first time he'd surrendered a hit an inning since 1912. The 1921 season was a flameout, as Vaughn went 3-11 with an ERA of 6.01 and left the team in June. Reports indicate that he had a sore arm, but he spent the rest of the season pitching for Beloit in the Midwest League and compiled an 11-1 record with 99 strikeouts against only nine walks.

Vaughn considered a comeback with the Cubs but never pitched more than batting practice. For the next 16 years he pitched in various minor and semipro leagues, mostly with Beloit and the Chicago–based Logan Squares, Duffy Florals, and Chicago Mills, retiring at age 49 after the 1937 season. Altogether Hippo went 223-145 in minor league and semipro ball, most of those decisions coming after he left the Cubs. Combined with his major league record of 178-137, he eclipsed the 400 mark in wins. Away from baseball, Vaughn was an assembler for a refrigeration products company. He spent the rest of his life in Chicago, dying there at age 78 on May 29, 1966.

JAN FINKEL

Claude Hendrix

CHICAGO

CLAUDE RAYMOND HENDRIX
RIGHT-HANDED PITCHER 1916–20

CIII.

A tremendous all-around athlete who was one of the Deadball Era's best at fielding his position, Claude Hendrix was a spitball pitcher who posted three 20-win seasons, each with a different team, en route to a lifetime 144-116 record and 2.65 ERA. With a batting average of .241, 14 home runs, and 97 RBI over the course of his 10 seasons, the 6'0", 195 lb. right hander was also good enough with the bat to be used frequently as a pinch-hitter. Hendrix is best remembered today, however, for his apparent attempt at throwing a game in 1920, an event that spawned the investigation that eventually led to the Black Sox Scandal.

An only child, Claude Raymond Hendrix was born in Olathe, Kansas, on April 13, 1889. His father, Price, was a prosperous bank president who became the first Democrat to be elected sheriff of Johnson County. Refining his athletic skills under the tutelage of his father, Claude excelled in sports and eventually pitched in 1908 for Fairmount College, the predecessor of Wichita State University. That year Fairmount had a powerful team, producing three players in addition to Hendrix who went on to play professionally, and in one game that spring the collegians beat the Wichita team of the Western Association. Wichita became interested in signing Hendrix, but he ended up that summer with Lincoln, Nebraska, of the higher-level Western League, compiling a 6-5 record in 13 games.

In 1909 Hendrix moved down a few rungs on the minor league ladder to Salina of the Central Kansas League, going 12-8 for a team that finished second with a 40-28 record. His breakout season came in 1910, when he pitched for an independent team in Cheyenne, Wyoming. Hendrix was 17-4 with 208 strikeouts and only 117 hits allowed in 204⅓ innings. Making the jump from semipro ball directly to the majors, Claude

debuted with the Pittsburgh Pirates on June 7, 1911, and soon befriended Honus Wagner, with whom he joined in several business deals. Hendrix finished the season with a 4-6 record, but his 2.73 ERA and 85 hits allowed in 118⅔ innings provided a hint of the performance soon to come.

In 1912, his first full season in Pittsburgh, Hendrix emerged as one of the National League's premier pitchers, placing second in strikeouts (176) and leading the league in winning percentage with a 24-9 record to go along with a 2.59 ERA. He also was spectacular at the plate, hitting .322 with a .529 slugging percentage, which would have placed him second in the NL to Heinie Zimmerman if he'd batted a sufficient number of times. Audacious enough to hold out during spring training, Hendrix returned in time to put together another solid campaign in 1913, posting a 14-15 record with a 2.84 ERA and finishing second in the NL with 5.15 strikeouts per game. He was even praised by Pittsburgh society columnist Agnes Wedgewood, who described him as "single, and oh so handsome."

Hendrix didn't remain single for long. In January 1914 he married his childhood sweetheart, Mabel Wilson, settling down with her in Kansas City. In part to be closer to his new wife, though a substantial pay increase undoubtedly affected his decision, Claude elected to sign that winter with the Federal League's Chicago Whales, for whom he enjoyed the best season of his career in 1914. The 25-year-old spitballer led the Federal League in wins (29), ERA (1.69), games (49), and complete games (34), and finished second in base runners per nine innings (8.6). Hendrix's Chifeds lost both ends of a doubleheader in Kansas City in late September, however, and finished second to the Indianapolis Hoosiers. Things were reversed in 1915—

Hendrix was a mediocre 16-15 with a 3.00 ERA despite pitching a no-hitter on May 15, and the Chifeds rallied at the end of the season to claim the last FL pennant.

The Federal League folded after 1915, and it appeared at least for a couple of seasons that so too had the once promising career of Claude Hendrix. Joining the Chicago Cubs, a team that had fallen on hard times since its last pennant in 1910, Hendrix posted an 18-28 record over the next two seasons despite ERAs of 2.68 and 2.60. His ERA actually rose to 2.78 the following season, but the Cubs turned around to win the pennant and Hendrix posted a 20-7 record to lead the NL in winning percentage. In the 1918 World Series, manager Fred Mitchell elected to alternate left handers Jim Vaughn and Lefty Tyler against the predominantly left-handed Boston Red Sox lineup. Hendrix was used as a pinch-hitter, singling in his lone plate appearance, and pitched the final inning for the Cubs in the sixth and last game of the Series.

Hendrix struggled over the next two seasons, going 10-14 with a 2.62 ERA in 1919 and 9-12 with a 3.58 ERA in 1920. He remained out of the spotlight until September 4, 1920, when the *Chicago Herald & Examiner* reported that the Cubs-Phillies game on August 31 had been fixed in favor of the last-place Phils. The newspaper revealed that Cubs president Bill Veeck Sr. had received six telegrams and two phone calls informing him that gamblers were wagering heavily on the Phillies. Veeck pulled the starting assignment from Hendrix, who'd supposedly placed a bet against the Cubs with Kansas City gambler Frog Thompson, and replaced him with star pitcher Pete Alexander, but the Chicagoans ended up losing anyway, 3-0. A grand jury was convened on September 7 to explore not only the tainted Cubs-Phillies game but the entire issue of baseball gambling in general, and the focus quickly shifted from Hendrix to the 1919 World Series. The Hendrix incident was never resolved, but the Cubs nonetheless released him at the end of the season.

Claude Hendrix returned to Kansas City, where he sold cars and played semipro ball. After his wife died in 1923, he moved to Pennsylvania to continue playing outside of Organized Baseball, first in Emmaus and later in Allentown. Hendrix purchased a successful restaurant in 1926 and lived in Allentown for the rest of his life, dying of a cerebral thrombosis on March 22, 1944, just shy of his 55th birthday.

JONATHAN DUNKLE

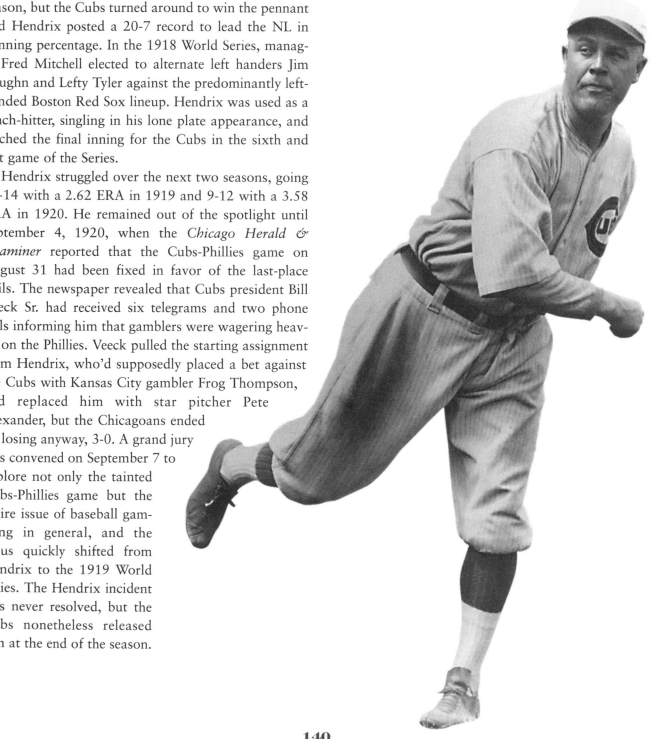

PITTSBURGH

Located on the approximate future site of Three Rivers Stadium and PNC Park, Exposition Park served as the home of the Pirates until midseason 1909.

In 1900 Louisville Colonels owner Barney Dreyfuss merged his club with the Pittsburg Pirates. Though the Colonels had finished ninth in 1899, two places behind the Pirates, Dreyfuss brought a group of talented players to Pittsburg, among them Fred Clarke, Tommie Leach, Deacon Phillippe, and Honus Wagner, who became the NL's premier player of the Deadball Era. Combined with the holdovers, which included Ginger Beaumont, Sam Leever, Jesse Tannehill, and Jack Chesbro, Clarke's Bucs finished second in 1900, the beginning of the winningest decade in franchise history.

The key to Pittsburg's success was retaining all of its top stars during the first two years of American League raids, when every other NL team lost significant players. Starting in 1901, the Pirates brought home three consecutive pennants to Exposition Park. With Wagner, Beaumont, and Clarke ranking among the NL's top hitters and Phillippe, Leever, Chesbro, and Tannehill composing one of history's greatest pitching staffs, the 1902 club finished 27½ games ahead of second-place Brooklyn, its .741 winning percentage exceeded during the 20th century by only the 1906 Chicago Cubs. The only disappointment of Pittsburg's 1901-03 dynasty was losing the first World Series to the Boston Americans, due in large part to a lack of pitching depth after Chesbro and Tannehill jumped to the AL.

WINNING PERCENTAGE 1901-1919

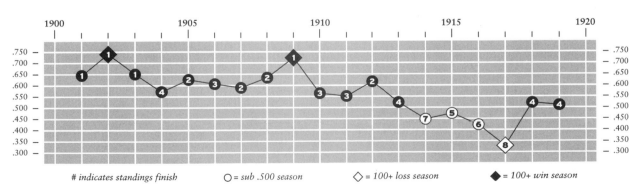

 # indicates standings finish   ○ = *sub .500 season*   ◇ = *100+ loss season*   ◆ = *100+ win season*

The Pirates fell to fourth in 1904, suffering a season-long epidemic of injuries and illnesses, but they bounced back to finish second or third behind the New York Giants and Chicago Cubs in the three-way pennant races of 1905-08. Pittsburg's fourth and final pennant of the Deadball Era came in 1909, when Dreyfuss opened a concrete-and-steel ballpark in the Oakland section of the city. He named it Forbes Field, honoring a British general who camped his army in the area during the French and Indian War. The new park was baseball's showplace, and its doublele-decked grandstand and 23,000 capacity paid off immediately when the Pirates won 110 games, the most in franchise history. Clarke, Wagner, and Leach still led the offense, while Howie Camnitz, Vic Willis, and Lefty Leifield paced the pitchers. During the '09 World Series, however, it was rookie Babe Adams who led the Bucs to victory by capturing three games.

Despite winning 24 fewer games in 1910, the aging Pirates remained competitive for three more seasons. Time caught up with them in 1914, however, and they plummeted to seventh, Dreyfuss's first appearance in the second division since arriving in the Steel City 15 years earlier. The Pirates endured three more dismal seasons before outfielder Max Carey, pitcher Wilbur Cooper, and a new crop of players returned Pittsburgh (the "h" was officially reinstated in July 1911) back to the first division in 1918.

ALL-ERA TEAM

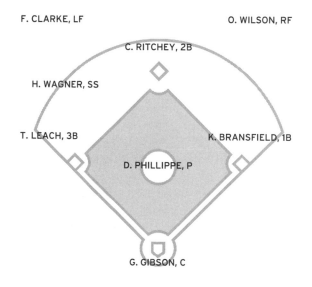

M. CAREY, CF

F. CLARKE, LF   O. WILSON, RF

C. RITCHEY, 2B

H. WAGNER, SS

T. LEACH, 3B   K. BRANSFIELD, 1B

D. PHILLIPPE, P

G. GIBSON, C

BATTING

GAMES
H. Wagner 2298
T. Leach 1523
F. Clarke 1373

RUNS
H. Wagner 1414
T. Leach 989
F. Clarke 931

HITS
H. Wagner 2766
T. Leach 1569
F. Clarke 1528

RBI
H. Wagner 1375
T. Leach 610
F. Clarke 590

DOUBLES
H. Wagner 506
F. Clarke 223
T. Leach 191

TRIPLES
H. Wagner 210
F. Clarke 144
T. Leach 137

HOME RUNS
H. Wagner 78
O. Wilson 44
T. Leach 42

STOLEN BASES
H. Wagner 601
M. Carey 392
T. Leach 263

BATTING AVERAGE
H. Wagner 325
G. Beaumont 324
F. Clarke 301

PITCHING

GAMES
B. Adams 307
S. Leever 302
D. Phillippe 292

WINS
S. Leever 157
D. Phillippe 148
B. Adams 131

LOSSES
B. Adams 94
H. Camnitz 84
L. Leifield 84

INNINGS
B. Adams 2060⅔
S. Leever 2016
D. Phillippe 2007

STRIKEOUTS
H. Camnitz 806
B. Adams 790
D. Phillippe 786

WALKS
H. Camnitz 532
L. Leifield 481
W. Cooper 458

SHUTOUTS
S. Leever 32
B. Adams 30
L. Leifield 29

ERA
V. Willis 2.08
S. Leever 2.31
L. Leifield 2.38

Pittsburg bugs congregate outside the main entrance to Forbes Field at its grand opening in 1909.

TYPICAL LINEUPS 1901–1919

1901

1. F. Clarke, LF
2. G. Beaumont, CF
3. L. Davis, RF
4. H. Wagner, SS-RF
5. K. Bransfield, 1B
6. C. Ritchey, 2B
7. T. Leach, 3B
   B. Ely, SS
8. C. Zimmer
   J. O'Connor, C

1902

1. F. Clarke, LF
2. G. Beaumont, CF
3. T. Leach, 3B
4. H. Wagner, RF-SS
5. K. Bransfield, 1B
6. C. Ritchey, 2B
7. W. Conroy, SS
8. H. Smith
   J. O'Connor, C

1903

1. G. Beaumont, CF
2. F. Clarke, LF
3. T. Leach, 3B
4. H. Wagner, SS
5. K. Bransfield, 1B
6. C. Ritchey, 2B
7. J. Sebring, RF
8. E. Phelps, C

1904

1. T. Leach, 3B
2. G. Beaumont, CF
3. F. Clarke, LF
4. H. Wagner, SS
5. K. Bransfield, 1B
6. J. Sebring, RF
7. C. Ritchey, 2B
8. E. Phelps, C

1905

1. O. Clymer, RF
2. F. Clarke, LF
3. G. Beaumont, CF
   T. Leach, 3B-CF
4. H. Wagner, SS
5. D. Howard, 1B
6. D. Brain, 3B
7. C. Ritchey, 2B
8. H. Peitz, C

1906

1. G. Beaumont, CF
2. B. Ganley, RF
3. F. Clarke, LF
4. H. Wagner, SS
5. J. Nealon, 1B
6. T. Sheehan, 3B
   T. Leach, 3B-CF
7. C. Ritchey, 2B
8. G. Gibson, C

1907

1. G. Anderson, RF
2. T. Leach, CF
3. F. Clarke, LF
4. H. Wagner, SS
5. E. Abbaticchio, 2B
6. J. Nealon, 1B
7. A. Storke, 3B
8. G. Gibson, C

1908

1. R. Thomas, CF
2. T. Leach, 3B
3. F. Clarke, LF
4. H. Wagner, SS
5. E. Abbaticchio, 2B
6. A. Storke
   H. Swacina, 1B
7. O. Wilson, RF
8. G. Gibson, C

1909

1. J. Barbeau, 3B
2. T. Leach, CF
3. F. Clarke, LF
4. H. Wagner, SS
5. D. Miller, 2B
6. B. Abstein, 1B
7. O. Wilson, RF
8. G. Gibson, C

1910

1. B. Byrne, 3B
2. T. Leach, CF
3. F. Clarke, LF
4. H. Wagner, SS
5. D. Miller, 2B
6. J. Flynn, 1B
7. O. Wilson, RF
8. G. Gibson, C

1911

1. B. Byrne, 3B
2. T. Leach, CF
3. F. Clarke, LF
4. H. Wagner, SS
5. D. Miller, 2B
6. N. Hunter, 1B
    B. McKechnie, 1B-INF
7. O. Wilson, RF
8. G. Gibson, C

1912

1. B. Byrne, 3B
2. M. Carey, LF
3. M. Donlin, RF
4. H. Wagner, SS
5. D. Miller, 1B
6. O. Wilson, CF
7. A. McCarthy, 2B
8. G. Gibson, C

1913

1. B. Byrne, 3B
2. M. Carey, LF
3. J. Viox, 2B
4. H. Wagner, SS
5. D. Miller, 1B
6. O. Wilson, RF
7. M. Mitchell, CF
8. M. Simon, C

1914

1. M. Carey, LF
2. M. Mowrey, 3B
3. J. Kelly, CF
4. H. Wagner, SS
5. E. Konetchy, 1B
6. J. Viox, 2B
7. M. Mitchell, RF
8. G. Gibson, C

1915

1. M. Carey, LF
2. Z. Collins, CF
3. D. Johnston, 1B
4. B. Hinchman, RF
5. H. Wagner, SS
6. J. Viox, 2B
7. D. Baird, 3B
8. G. Gibson, C

1916

1. D. Baird, 3B
2. M. Carey, CF
3. H. Wagner, SS
4. B. Hinchman, RF
5. J. Farmer
    J. Schultz, 2B
6. F. Schulte, LF
7. D. Johnston, 1B
8. W. Schmidt, C

1917

1. M. Carey, CF
2. C. Bigbee, LF
3. L. King, RF
4. H. Wagner, 1B
5. T. Boeckel, 3B
6. C. Ward, SS
7. J. Pitler, 2B
8. W. Fischer
    W. Schmidt, C

1918 (First half)

1. H. Caton, SS
2. F. Mollwitz, 1B
3. M. Carey, CF
4. C. Stengel, RF
5. G. Cutshaw, 2B
6. L. King, LF
7. B. McKechnie, 3B
8. W. Schmidt, C

1918 (Second half)

1. H. Caton
    R. Ellam, SS
2. C. Bigbee, LF
3. M. Carey, CF
4. B. Southworth, RF
5. G. Cutshaw, 2B
6. F. Mollwitz, 1B
7. B. McKechnie, 3B
8. W. Schmidt, C

1919

1. C. Bigbee, CF
2. Z. Terry, SS
3. C. Stengel, RF
4. B. Southworth, LF
5. W. Barbare, 3B
6. G. Cutshaw, 2B
7. F. Mollwitz
    V. Saier, 1B
8. W. Schmidt, C

Fred Clarke lectures at spring training in Hot Springs, circa 1913.

PITTSBURGH

SAMUEL LEEVER
RIGHT-HANDED PITCHER 1898–1910

With piercing blue eyes and brown hair that was thinning even early in his career, Sam Leever became known as "The Goshen Schoolmaster" as much for his appearance and serious demeanor as for his off-season profession. Leever relied on the exceptional movement of his curveball to fool batters, compiling a lifetime record of 194-100 for a .660 winning percentage, the ninth highest in major league history among pitchers with more than 2,000 innings. In an era when pitchers were listed in the newspapers each week according to winning percentage, the oft-injured right hander was the National League's "leading pitcher" in 1901, 1903, and 1905.

The fourth of Edward and Amerideth Leever's eight children, Samuel Leever was born on December 23, 1871, on a farm in Goshen, Ohio, about 20 miles northeast of Cincinnati. Like many families in that area, the Leevers were of Pennsylvania-German heritage. After graduating from Goshen High School, Sam worked there as a schoolteacher for seven years, pitching on Sundays for semipro teams in southwestern Ohio. (One of his teammates on the Norwood Maroons was Kid Elberfeld.) Lacking an impressive fastball, Leever reached the advanced age of 25 before signing his first professional contract. According to legend, the Pirates discovered him while he was playing "Anthony Over," a game that required tossing a ball over a barn to a friend on the other side; Sam supposedly curved the ball around the barn instead.

In 1897 Leever pitched for Richmond of the Atlantic League, winning 20 games and leading the league in strikeouts. He started 1898 with Pittsburgh but was soon sent back to Richmond. He won another 14 games and helped the team to the championship, returning to Pittsburgh at the tail end of that season. In 1899 Leever became the workhorse of the Pittsburgh staff, leading the NL in games (51) and innings (379) while posting a 21-23 record and 3.18 ERA for the seventh-place Pirates. The extreme workload took its toll (a sore right arm nagged him throughout the rest of his career), but he never again had an ERA as high as 3.00 or a losing record after the arrival of Honus Wagner and the rest of the Louisville gang.

In 1900-02 Pittsburgh manager Fred Clarke used a five-man rotation, anchored by a quartet of standouts: Leever, Deacon Phillippe, Jack Chesbro, and Jesse Tannehill. Though a series of mishaps prevented him from accumulating huge win totals—a line drive broke his finger on Opening Day 1900, then he developed an illness, and he almost always had a sore arm—Leever won 44 games and lost only 25 over that three-season stretch. When Chesbro and Tannehill jumped to the New York Highlanders after the 1902 season, Clarke called on Leever and Phillippe to carry a larger burden. Sam came through with a career year in 1903. In June the Pirates ran off a record six consecutive shutouts, with Leever tossing the second and sixth games of the streak—two of his league-leading seven shutouts. He also led the NL with a 2.06 ERA and finished with a 25-7 record, prompting *The Sporting News* to call him "one of the best pitchers in the world today."

Just before the 1903 World Series, however, Leever injured his shoulder in a trapshooting contest in Charleroi, Pennsylvania. With the Pirates holding a one-game advantage over the Boston Americans, Sam started Game Two in the best-of-nine series but removed himself after giving up two runs in the first inning. He took the mound again in Game Six, this time pitching a complete game but losing 6-3. Pittsburgh lost the Series in eight games largely because of Leever's ineffectiveness, and some writers accused him of cowardice or, even worse, giving less than his best effort. Several weeks after the Series, the Pittsburgh correspondent for *The Sporting News*, Ralph Davis, wrote an article defending Leever, who reportedly was still in considerable pain. "The charge that Leever 'laid' down is absurd in the extreme," wrote Davis. "There is not a more honest man in the game."

In his first regular season game the next April, Sam argued a balk call so strenuously that he was ejected and suspended for one week. He'd just married and his new bride, the former Margaret Molloy, witnessed the incident. Her verdict: it sure looked like a balk. The suspension might have cost Leever a string of four consecutive 20-win seasons; he won only 18 games in 1904, but the next two seasons he finished 20-5 and 22-7. In 1907 Leever posted a career-best 1.66 ERA but missed his regular turn in the rotation several times. He made just 24 starts and finished at 14-9.

By 1908 Leever was pitching in relief nearly half the time. With two weeks left in that season, Pittsburgh was five games behind the Giants, and some gloomy Pirates were trying to convince themselves that they still had a chance. Gloomier than most, Sam offered to sell his World Series share for "a thin dime," and Fred Clarke and Vic Willis quickly handed him nickels. The Giants began losing, and on October 4, the last scheduled day of the season, the Pirates met the Cubs at Chicago's West Side Grounds, with a win giving them no worse than a tie for the pennant. Leever escaped a lifetime of ridicule when the Cubs prevailed.

During his last two years with the Pirates, Leever pitched almost exclusively in relief; one Pittsburgh sportswriter lamented that the aging curveballer "can't stand the strain of pitching regularly." In 1909 he posted an 8-1 record but gave up more than a hit per inning for the first time since 1901. Clarke didn't pitch him in that year's World Series. The following year Sam pitched slightly better and more frequently, but his record dropped to 6-5. Clearly the 39-year-old veteran was nearing the end, yet he was insulted by the contract

the Pirates sent him for 1911 and refused to report for spring training. Barney Dreyfuss offered to sell him to a minor league team and give him a share of the proceeds, but that only insulted him more. Sam requested and received his release.

Leever ended up in the minors anyway, joining old teammate Rube Waddell with the 1911 Minneapolis Millers. He gained only seven victories even though Minneapolis racked up 99 wins en route to the American Association pennant. After a year out of baseball, Leever returned in 1913 to join Deacon Phillippe as a manager in the Federal League, which was then an independent minor league. Sam took over the franchise in Covington, Kentucky, not far from his home in Goshen, but the team moved to Kansas City in late June. He finished out the season, then retired from baseball for good.

Using Sam's savings from his career in baseball (Hugh Fullerton described him as "careful with his money," but others called him a skinflint), the Leevers purchased a 70-acre farm in Goshen, the town where The Goshen Schoolmaster continued to teach grammar school for many years. The couple never had any children. An avid outdoorsman, Sam made his own gunpowder (he claimed it was better than any available on the market) and went on many long hunting trips, often with old teammates Phillippe and Wagner. He also maintained his passion for trapshooting, firing a score of 99 out of 100 as late as age 71.

Sam eventually gave up farming and moved into Margaret's family's old house, which was closer to town and adjacent to a baseball field. Old-timers in Goshen still remember hitting foul balls into the Leevers' garden; if Sam got to the ball first, he didn't give it back. Neighbors recalled that Sam always wore a hat outdoors, and they were astonished when they saw him inside and realized he was completely bald. He often attended ball games but rarely offered advice or talked about his own career. Sam Leever died in Goshen at age 81 on May 19, 1953.

MARK ARMOUR

PITTSBURGH

Clarence Howeth "Ginger" Beaumont
Center fielder 1899–1906

In the early days of the Deadball Era, Ginger Beaumont was considered baseball's finest leadoff man, a lifetime .311 hitter who was good enough to be named by both Bill Klem and Honus Wagner as the center fielder on their all-time teams. When contemporary observers spoke of Beaumont, they focused on his surprising speed—surprising because his typical playing weight was 190 lbs. on a 5'8" frame. "He was an excellent base runner, being very fast on his feet, but nobody who saw him for the first time ambling along on his way to the batter's box would admit this," wrote one sportswriter. "A lazier or more indifferent-appearing player, emphasized by a burly body, could not be conceived. But when he hit the ball he was off like a streak, which astonished the uninitiated and made him one of the wonders of the century."

Clarence Howeth Beaumont was born to Thomas and Mary (Jones) Beaumont on July 23, 1876, in Rochester, Wisconsin. A right-handed thrower who batted from the left side, he began his baseball career in 1896 as a semipro catcher, playing with teams from Rochester, East Troy, Wampum, Burlington, and Beloit College. Connie Mack, then managing Milwaukee of the Western League, signed Clarence to his first professional contract late in 1898 when the Brewers were hit by a rash of injuries. Because Mack needed an outfielder, Beaumont made the shift from catcher to fly chaser and batted .354 with 11 stolen bases in 24 games.

That performance didn't go unnoticed by National League clubs, and Cleveland, Cincinnati, Pittsburgh, and Baltimore all expressed interest. After the season, Mack engineered a bogus sale of Beaumont to the Louisville Colonels to avoid losing him in the October draft (Barney Dreyfuss, who later became the young outfielder's employer, returned him shortly thereafter),

then traded him in December to the Pittsburgh Pirates. An account of the trade referred to Clarence as a "brilliant and promising young player" and stated that Milwaukee fans "bid farewell to Beaumont with profound regret."

Less than a year removed from semipro ball, the 22-year-old Beaumont began his big-league career primarily as a pinch-hitter and spare outfielder under manager William Watkins. That May, however, right fielder Patsy Donovan replaced Watkins. Donovan gave Clarence a chance to play regularly, and by the end of June the rookie had nailed down the center-field job. That didn't please the man he replaced, Tom McCreery, who was openly hostile to his young challenger until Donovan intervened. On July 22 Beaumont collected six hits in six times at-bat and scored six runs against Phillies left hander Wiley Piatt, a feat that remained unmatched until Shawn Green did it in 2002, 103 years later. It's even more remarkable that none of Beaumont's safeties left the infield. For the season he batted .352, sixth in the NL, and stole 31 bases, but he wasn't the best rookie on the Pittsburgh team; that honor belonged to Jimmy Williams, who batted .355 with more power.

At the end of the 1899 season Dreyfuss bought a half interest in the Pirates and merged them with the best of his players from Louisville. The result was a powerhouse and the beginning of what Beaumont later referred to as "my happiest years in baseball." Beaumont was Dreyfuss's kind of player; he didn't smoke or drink and devoted much of his free time to youth baseball in Pittsburgh. Until then the speedy outfielder was usually known as "Clarry" or "Beau," but Dreyfuss nicknamed him "Ginger" due to his red hair (though some claimed it was due to his speed and hustle), and the nickname stuck.

In 1900 Ginger Beaumont suffered through a sophomore slump, batting just .279, but for the next five years he was one of baseball's most dangerous hitters. In 1901 he finished among the NL's Top 10 in batting average (.332) and stolen bases (36), and the following year he won the NL batting title with a .357 average while finishing first in hits (193), third in runs (100) and on-base percentage (.404), and fourth in total bases (226) and stolen bases (33). Beaumont had another outstanding season in 1903, batting .341 and leading the NL with career-high marks in runs (137), hits (209), and total bases (272). Of course, the highlight of that season came on October 1 in front of 16,242 screaming fans at Boston's Huntington Avenue Grounds. Stepping in to face the great Cy Young, Beaumont lofted a fly ball to center field that was caught by Boston's Chick Stahl, thus becoming the first batter in the history of the modern World Series. For the eight-game series, Ginger batted .265 and led the Pirates with six runs.

Beaumont put together another strong season in 1904, when he batted .301 and led the NL for the third consecutive season in hits (185), but in 1905, though his .328 batting average ranked fourth in the NL, he began to suffer from knee problems that limited him to 103 games. The knee worsened in 1906, when Ginger appeared in only 80 games and batted .265 with just one stolen base. Concerned about Beaumont's physical condition, Dreyfuss traded him and fellow veterans Claude Ritchey and Patsy Flaherty to the Boston Nationals in December for infielder Ed Abbaticchio. It was a trade that clearly benefited Boston. Ginger recovered in 1907 to play in 150 games and lead the NL for the fourth time in hits (187) while finishing third in the batting race with a .322 average.

Beaumont's knee injury finally started to take its toll in 1908. The former speedster, who in his prime had legged out numerous bunts and infield hits, saw his running speed decline, and with it his batting average.

Ginger batted in the .260s in both 1908 and 1909, and Boston traded him to the Chicago Cubs in February 1910 for rookie pitcher Fred Liese and cash. Beaumont spent the 1910 season as an extra outfielder and pinch-hitter on the pennant-winning Cubs, batting .267 in 76 games. In his return to the World Series he appeared three times as a pinch-hitter, walking once and scoring a run. Ginger didn't get along well with manager Frank Chance, and the Cubs released him the following March. He finished his baseball career in 1911 with St. Paul of the American Association, batting .249 in a part-time role.

After leaving baseball, Ginger Beaumont concentrated on running his 180-acre farm in Honey Creek, Wisconsin, which he'd purchased in 1904 (probably with his pay from the first World Series) and renamed Centerfield Farm. He and his wife, Norma (Vaughan) Beaumont, whom he'd married in November 1901, enjoyed the simple life. They raised two daughters and one son and became fixtures in their community. In 1914 Ginger was elected a supervisor of Walworth County. He'd saved his money during his playing career and by all accounts was comfortably well-off. Ginger's health began to deteriorate in 1948, when he suffered a stroke. A second stroke in 1950 confined him to a wheelchair for the last years of his life. In 1951 Beaumont was inducted into the Wisconsin Athletic Hall of Fame as a charter member. Two stars of the 1903 World Series, Deacon Phillippe and Cy Young, unveiled his plaque.

Ginger Beaumont died at age 79 on April 10, 1956, in Burlington Hospital, near his Wisconsin farm. His obituary in *The Sporting News* called him "one of the game's all-time great outfielders." The Beaumont Little League in Burlington bears his name, and in 1968 the Old-Timers Athletic Club of Racine erected a flagpole and plaque in his memory. Beaumont was the subject of campaigns in the 1940s and 1980s for enshrinement in the National Baseball Hall of Fame, but at this point that supreme honor appears unlikely.

DAN GINSBURG

PITTSBURGH

BARNEY DREYFUSS
PRESIDENT 1900–32

A 5'4" German-Jewish immigrant with only a limited background in baseball, Barney Dreyfuss nonetheless became one of the most influential figures in the sport, priding himself on running the Pittsburgh Pirates without the assistance of a general manager. "Probably his greatest hobby is 'dope,'" wrote Ralph Davis in the July 1908 issue of *Baseball Magazine.* "His offices in the Farmers Bank Building are filled with volume after volume of statistics and records." Dreyfuss became known as "First Division Barney" because his Pirates finished in the first division every season from 1900 to 1913, capturing four pennants and one World Series over that 14-year span, but his greatest contributions came in 1903 when he spearheaded the effort to bring peace between the NL and AL and established the first modern World Series. The Pittsburgh franchise remained under the control of the Dreyfuss family until 1946, when it was sold to a consortium headed by banker Frank McKinney, realtor John Galbreath, and entertainer Bing Crosby.

Barney Dreyfuss was born in Freiburg, Germany, on February 23, 1865. After gaining experience at a bank in Karlsruhe, Germany, Barney immigrated to Paducah, Kentucky, in 1883 to join the Bernheim Bros. Distillery (bottlers of the famous Kentucky bourbon I. W. Harper), which was owned by his cousins Bernard and Isaac W. Bernheim. Three factors led to his emigration: he was avoiding conscription into the German army; he'd heard stories of ante-bellum America from his parents, Samuel and Fanny, who'd operated a mercantile business in Smithland, Kentucky, from 1849 to 1861; and several members of

his family had already moved to America, including his sister Rosa, who'd married Bernard Bernheim in 1882.

Though Dreyfuss once claimed that he'd started at the distillery as a bottle washer, he actually worked in the accounting office. Barney devoted long hours to studying English and working his way up at the distillery, and after a while his health began to deteriorate. His physician advised him to take up outdoor recreation, which is how he discovered baseball. Dreyfuss began playing with amateur teams in Paducah. After the Bernheim Distillery relocated to Louisville in 1888, he eventually convinced his cousins of the profit potential in owning a professional team. Using a line of credit from Isaac and Bernard Bernheim, Barney purchased an interest in the National League's Louisville Colonels in 1890. Excited about building a championship team, he left his job at the distillery and increased his ownership of the Colonels each season by buying out other shareholders. By 1899 Dreyfuss was the sole owner.

Around that time the political landscape of the National League was undergoing changes. Competition on the diamond was suffering because of syndicate ownership, and after much discussion NL magnates decided to address the issue by contracting from 12 to eight teams, folding the Louisville, Cleveland, Washington, and Baltimore franchises. Anticipating that the Colonels were headed toward extinction, Dreyfuss brokered a deal that allowed him to purchase a half interest in the Pittsburgh Pirates and, by accepting a smaller settlement from the National League ($10,000), take 14 of his Louisville players with him. Those players, which included Fred Clarke, Deacon Phillippe, Tommie Leach, and the immortal Honus Wagner, formed the nucleus of the Pirate juggernaut that finished first or second seven times in the first decade of the 20th century and ensured the financial success of baseball in Pittsburgh. Dreyfuss, in turn, ensured the financial success of his players by offering to invest their money. Though he didn't guarantee what return might be expected, he promised there would be no loss.

Within a year, and again using funds supplied by his Bernheim cousins, Dreyfuss bought out William Kerr, his principal partner in the Pirates franchise. He also dabbled in the early development of professional football, fielding a team in the Steel City in 1902. But Barney's masterstroke came in August 1903, as the Pirates were on their way to winning their third consecutive NL pennant. Loving competition as much as profit, he contacted Henry Killilea, president of the AL's front-runners, the Boston Americans, and challenged him to a post-season series between the league champions. (The previous winter Dreyfuss had played a key role in the peace negotiations between the rival leagues, mostly out of self interest: he'd secured a commitment from the AL that it wouldn't act on its threats to move the Detroit franchise to Pittsburgh.) With AL president Ban Johnson's blessing, the two magnates met in September to work out the details, and Dreyfuss stood by his challenge even though he was advised not to play the series with his pitching staff depleted by injuries. The result was the first modern World Series, a marvelous best-of-nine showdown won by Boston, five games to three.

The overwhelming success of the Pirates, both on the field and in the box office, spurred Dreyfuss on to his next big project, the building of a state-of-the-art baseball stadium. Since 1891 the Pirates had played at Exposition Park, the outfield of which was frequently underwater because of its location less than 50 yards from the Allegheny River. Dreyfuss felt that baseball was growing and patrons were no longer willing to put up with "19th-century conditions." On June 30, 1909, after just four months of construction, he opened Forbes Field, the first modern two-tiered stadium in the National League (the AL's first great ballpark of the era, Shibe Park, had opened a couple of months earlier). People laughed at Dreyfuss and commented, as John

Kieran wrote in a *New York Times* column in 1932, "Barney had sunk too much money in the steel and concrete stands." Dreyfuss laughed too, all the way to the bank. "He filled the stands three times that year and twice in later years he had to enlarge the park," wrote Kieran. "His vision brought him a fortune."

The Pirates rewarded Dreyfuss with a return trip to the World Series in 1909, and a record crowd of 29,264 turned out for Game One at Forbes Field to witness Pittsburgh defeat the Detroit Tigers, 4-1. The Series went back and forth between the teams until the Pirates prevailed in Game Seven, 8-0, as Babe Adams won his third game. It was Pittsburgh's last Series appearance of the Deadball Era. Dreyfuss's Pirates made additional trips to the fall classic in 1925 and 1927, defeating Walter Johnson and the Washington Senators in the former year and losing to Babe Ruth and the New York Yankees in the latter.

Though his team struggled during the 1910s, Dreyfuss wasn't finished contributing to the growth and success of major league baseball. Each season he was intimately involved in the scheduling process. "All other magnates relied on the experienced veteran to straighten out the schedule, and conflicts and dates, hard railroad jumps, and unequal distribution of holiday home games," wrote one reporter. When the 1919 Black Sox scandal threatened to unravel baseball's ruling structure, he led the drive to install Judge Kenesaw Mountain Landis as commissioner in 1920.

Barney Dreyfuss remained in charge of the day-to-day operations of the Pirates until 1930, when at age 65 he turned the presidency over to his son Sammy. Before the opening of the 1931 season, however, the 36-year-old Sammy died of pneumonia. Emotionally spent, Barney returned to run the Pirates for one more season. Following a glandular operation, he too contracted pneumonia while attending the National League meetings in New York City, and died at Mt. Sinai Hospital on February 3, 1932. Dreyfuss was buried in Pittsburgh's West View Cemetary two days later. "Baseball fans never tire of arguing which player should and should not be in the Hall of Fame," wrote Boston sportswriter Bob Ryan in 2003. "Is it not time for members of SABR to take up the case for Barney Dreyfuss, the most neglected of all the great administrators and patrons in baseball history?"

SAM BERNSTEIN

PITTSBURGH

FRED CLIFFORD CLARKE
LEFT FIELDER/MANAGER 1900–15

Perhaps the most successful player-manager in history, Fred Clarke was a powerful left-handed hitter, aggressive base runner, daring defender, and fearless competitor. His one weakness was going back on fly balls, but he made up for it by playing a deep left field and rushing in frequently to make spectacular diving catches. "With the possible exception of Ty Cobb and John McGraw, baseball never knew a sturdier competitor than Clarke," wrote sportswriter Fred Lieb. In his 16 seasons as Pittsburgh manager, Clarke guided the Pirates to four pennants, a remarkable 14 straight first-division finishes, 1,422 wins, and a winning percentage of .595—all of which remain franchise records.

One of a dozen children (seven girls and five boys) of William and Lucy (Cutler) Clarke, Fred Clifford Clarke was born on a farm near Winterset, Iowa, on October 3, 1872. Two years later the Clarkes moved to a farm in Cowley County, Kansas, about four miles north of Winfield, an area that Fred returned to when his baseball career ended. His brother Joshua, who briefly joined him in the Louisville Colonels outfield in 1898, was born there in 1879. That same year William Clarke uprooted his family yet again, returning to Iowa and settling near Des Moines. Fred transferred to the Dickenson public schools and delivered newspapers for the *Des Moines Leader*, whose city circulator was Ed Barrow, the future manager of the Boston Red Sox and general manager of the New York Yankees.

Clarke got his start in baseball in 1889-90 as a second baseman and substitute catcher on Des Moines amateur teams put together by Barrow. In 1891 he played for a semipro team from Carroll, Iowa. The following year Fred began his professional career with Hastings, Nebraska, batting .302 with 15 extra-base hits and 14 stolen bases in only 41 games before the Nebraska State League folded. As for his defensive play, Clarke offered this description: "They put me in the outfield and I was lucky to catch half of the drives hit to me. An old-timer told me I could improve by practice, so I went out to the field at 8 o'clock in the morning and practiced until game time in the afternoon. After a while, I got so I could catch fly balls pretty well."

In 1893 Clarke got off to a great start with St. Joseph, Missouri, batting .346 with 21 runs in 20 games, but the Western Association disbanded. Hooking on with Montgomery of the Southern League, managed by future St. Louis Cardinals manager John McCloskey, the 20-year-old outfielder again played well, batting .292 in 32 games, but the season was suspended due to an outbreak of yellow fever. Perhaps out of frustration that none of the three teams he'd played for had finished the season, Clarke decided to get out of baseball. He participated in the Cherokee Outlet Land Opening on September 16, 1893, the fourth and largest of Oklahoma's five land runs. Failing in his attempt to stake a claim, Fred returned to the Southern League in 1894 and played left field for Savannah, where he was again managed by McCloskey. This time he played 54 games before the club disbanded on June 27, but Savannah promptly sold the .311-hitting outfielder to the National League's Louisville Colonels.

Three days later Clarke enjoyed one of the greatest debuts in major league history. Facing veteran Gus Weyhing of the Philadelphia Phillies, Fred used a small, light bat to hit four singles and a triple in five trips to the plate. The rest of the season wasn't as outstanding, but the rookie still hit .268 with seven home runs and 48 RBI in 75 games. Fred probably would have done better if he hadn't tried to imitate the lifestyles of the veteran players, which involved a lot of drinking and chasing women. One day Louisville treasurer Barney Dreyfuss asked him, "Are you being fair with yourself? You will live in the major league a few years only if you continue carousing around. Then you will go back to the minors and be swallowed up, and you never will have been anyone." From that point on the young outfielder dedicated himself to baseball.

During the next two seasons Clarke established himself as one of the NL's rising stars, batting .347 and .325, but he really took off in 1897, when he batted .390 and was named player-manager in midseason. The 24-year-old "boy manager" responded well to the challenge, transforming the team into champions after the move to Pittsburgh. Clarke once told a reporter that a successful manager must know baseball, have the "shrewdness, cheek, information, and money" to get good players, and be able to mold them into "a big, happy whole, both on and off the field." He didn't want a team of rowdies, but he also didn't want players who could be pushed around. As player-manager Clarke led by example. He expected his Pirates to be gentlemen off the field, but on the field he wanted them to be as feisty as he was.

From 1900 to 1911, "Cap" Clarke not only managed the Pirates from left field and hit in the upper third of the batting order, he also batted over .300 six times and consistently ranked among the NL leaders in several offensive categories. His best season in Pittsburgh came in 1903, when he led the NL in doubles (32) and slugging percentage (.532) while finishing second in the batting race with a .351 average, four points behind teammate Honus Wagner. Clarke led the NL with 80 walks in 1909, and in that year's World Series he con-

tributed to each of the Pirates' four victories, including a three-run homer in the seventh inning of Game Five that broke open a 3-3 tie.

Because he wanted to spend more time with his wife, Annette, and two daughters, he tried to retire after the 1909 World Series. Dreyfuss wouldn't let him. Approaching his 40th birthday, Fred hung on as a regular player through 1911, when he still managed to hit .324 in 110 games. From 1912 to 1915 he led the Pirates mostly from the dugout. With Pittsburgh on the verge of finishing fifth after falling all the way to seventh in 1914, Clarke submitted his resignation in September 1915, and Dreyfuss this time accepted it. The Pirates proclaimed September 23, 1915, as "Fred Clarke Day" in Pittsburgh, and the 42-year-old manager suited up one more time, playing four innings and collecting his 2,672nd hit against Dick Rudolph.

Clarke retired to his elegant Little Pirate Ranch near Winfield, Kansas, where he became a highly successful rancher and investor whose wealth was estimated at $1 million in 1917. He was an avid hunter and fisherman, a Kansas state-champion trapshooter, and an outstanding horseman. After leaving the Pirates in 1915, Clarke returned to Pittsburgh for one brief period, coaching the 1925 World Series champions and serving as vice-president and assistant manager in 1926. He was elected to the National Baseball Hall of Fame in 1945. Clarke succumbed to pneumonia on August 14, 1960. He is buried in St. Mary's Cemetery in Winfield.

ANGELO LOUISA

Honus Wagner

PITTSBURGH

John Peter "Honus" Wagner
Shortstop 1900–1917, Manager 1917

Honus Wagner was the National League's greatest all-around player of the Deadball Era. At the time of his retirement in 1917, Wagner held the all-time major league records for games (2,792), at-bats (10,430), runs (1,736), hits (3,415), and total bases (4,862). The lifetime .327 hitter also held the all-time NL records for doubles (640) and triples (252), and his 1,732 RBI were second behind Cap Anson's 1,879. To round out the package, Wagner played every position at the major league level except catcher. "While Honus was the best third baseman in the league, he was also the best first baseman, the best second baseman, the best shortstop, and the best outfielder," said teammate Tommie Leach. "That was in fielding. And since he led the league in batting eight times between 1900 and 1911, you know that he was the best hitter, too. As well as the best base runner."

To see Wagner play was to witness raw power. Standing 5'11" and weighing 200 lbs. with a barrel chest, massive shoulders, and heavily muscled arms, he gripped his 40-something-oz. bat with huge hands several inches apart, allowing him to slap an outside pitch to right or slide his hands together and pull an inside pitch down the left-field line. "The Flying Dutchman" didn't look fast, with incredibly bowed legs that deprived him of several inches of height and any semblance of grace, but he managed to steal 722 bases (third on the all-time list as of 1917) and leg out almost 1,000 extra-base hits, whirling his arms like a berserk freestyle swimmer as he tore around the bases. Honus was a sight in the field as well. His glove seemed too small for his hand, and he made it look even smaller by cutting a hole in the palm and pulling out much of the stuffing. From his usual position at shortstop he covered most of the left side of the infield, digging out grounders and firing the ball to first along with a shower of rocks and dirt.

One of Katrina (Wolf) and Peter Wagner's five sons and four daughters, John Peter Wagner, better known as "Honus" (a diminutive of Johannes, the German equivalent of John), was born on February 24, 1874, in the tiny borough of Chartiers, just outside of Mansfield (later renamed Carnegie), six miles from downtown Pittsburgh. Like many immigrants' sons in western Pennsylvania, Honus left school early to work in the coal mines. Later his older brother Charley opened a barbershop and made him an apprentice, but baseball was Honus's real love. Albert, another older brother, began playing the sport professionally, and when his Steubenville team of the Inter-State League needed help in 1895, he suggested the 21-year-old Honus.

Wagner's first year in professional baseball was an odyssey covering five teams, three leagues, and 80 games, but he hit between .365 and .386 in each league and showed his versatility by playing every position except catcher. Ed Barrow, then wearing several hats with Wheeling, West Virginia, of the Iron and Oil League, liked what he saw and took Honus with him to his next team, Paterson, New Jersey, of the Atlantic League. Wagner rewarded Barrow's faith by playing wherever needed—first, second, third, or the outfield—and hitting .313 with power and speed, following up that performance by hitting .375 in 74 games in 1897. Recognizing that Wagner should be playing at the highest level, Barrow sold him to the Louisville Colonels, which were managed by his old friend Fred Clarke.

Making his major league debut with Louisville on July 19, 1897, Wagner batted .338 in 61 games, mostly playing center field. The next year, splitting time almost equally between the corner infield positions, he hit .299 in 151 games; he didn't see the south side of .300 again until 1914. After batting .336 in his last year at Louisville, playing mostly third base and right field, Wagner thanked Dreyfuss for taking him to Pittsburgh in 1900 by posting career highs in batting average (.381) and slugging percentage (.573). Honus owned the decade 1900-09, leading the majors in every significant category except triples (second behind Sam Crawford) and home runs (tied for fifth). A summary of his year-by-year titles shows that he led the NL in batting average seven times during that decade, on-base percentage four times, slugging percentage six times, total bases six times, doubles seven times, triples three times, RBI four times, and stolen bases five times.

During the American League player raids of 1901, Honus showed his loyalty to Dreyfuss and Pittsburgh by refusing an offer of $20,000 up-front from Chicago White Stockings manager Clark Griffith. The Pirates began a three-year stranglehold over the NL, but they still couldn't decide on a permanent position for their greatest star. Wagner played prima-

rily shortstop in 1901, but the arrival of Wid Conroy moved him to the outfield for most of 1902. Conroy was released the following year when he turned out to be an AL spy, leaving the Pirates without a shortstop entering the 1903 season. Wanting the reluctant Wagner to be his shortstop, Clarke put Leach at short and Wagner at third during spring training but instructed Leach to convince Honus to swap positions. The con game worked, and Wagner took over at shortstop on a permanent basis in 1903.

After leading the NL in hitting with a .355 mark that season, Wagner got off to a great start in the first World Series, going 5-for-13 and driving in two runs as the Pirates won three of the first four games. But the Boston Americans stormed back to win four straight, and in those games Wagner went 1-for-14 with only one RBI, suffering the ultimate humiliation of making the final out of the Series on a called third strike. Worse, the greatest player in the National League led all players in errors, with six. Several Boston writers, noting Wagner's miserable performance, implied

that he might be "yellow," a slap that haunted him for years.

From 1904 to 1907 the Pirates finished between second and fourth each year, occasionally challenging the Giants and Cubs on their runs to glory. Wagner was still Wagner, always among the league leaders, but after the 1907 season the 33-year-old superstar announced his retirement. With simple tastes and frugal living, not to mention Dreyfuss's wise investment help and some income-producing real estate, Honus was on solid financial ground. He said he was tired, that he'd suffered his share of injuries and wanted to take at least a year off, but most observers didn't take the announcement seriously. "If Wagner is going to quit anything, let him quit kidding," wrote the *Pittsburg Dispatch*. If his "retirement" was a ruse to get a hefty raise, it worked. Dreyfuss doubled his salary to $10,000 (the figure he maintained for the rest of his career), making him the highest-paid player in baseball. Honus, who hated spring training and often did anything he could to avoid or at least delay it, rejoined the Pirates a week into the 1908 season.

Wagner put together his greatest season that year. Both leagues hit just .239, but Honus didn't notice; his .354 led the NL comfortably. Settling for second in homers (10) and runs (100), he led the league in just about everything else: hits (201), doubles (39), triples (19), RBI (109), and stolen bases (53). It added up to an offensive winning percentage of .878 in Lee Sinins' *Sabermetric Baseball Encyclopedia*—the greatest single season in National League history until Barry Bonds' astounding 2001-02 seasons.

And it wasn't enough. In the closest pennant race ever, the Pirates could have forced a three-way tie by winning their finale against the Cubs, but they lost, 5-2, Wagner's two errors not helping.

A winter of brooding brought the Pirates back with a vengeance in 1909, going 110-42 for the most wins in club history. As usual, Wagner carried the team, leading the NL in hitting (.339), slugging (.489), on-base percentage (.420), doubles (39), and RBI (100). The stage was set for the World Series with the Detroit Tigers, coming off their third straight AL title, and their nominee for baseball's top player, Ty Cobb. The match-up didn't disappoint—at least not in Pittsburgh—as the Pirates won in seven games behind the pitching of Babe Adams and the hitting of ageless wonders Wagner,

Clarke, and Leach. Honus outplayed Tyrus, outhitting him .333 to .231, driving in six runs to five for Cobb, and stealing six bases to Cobb's two; the latter mark stood as the Series record until Lou Brock stole seven in 1967. The victory was particularly sweet for Wagner, who'd finally vindicated himself for 1903.

The 1910 season was a disaster, however. Wagner struggled, fielding lackadaisically and hitting well below .300 until a late-season surge got him to his accustomed territory, but his batting average of .320 was still his lowest since 1898. The Pirates attributed his subpar performance to an injury, then a lingering cold, or maybe just a slump, but the real cause was an open secret—his out-of-control drinking. Honus had some ugly confrontations with teammates and umpires, receiving several ejections and suspensions. The situation was serious enough for Clarke to have a long talk with Wagner after the season.

Perhaps the only good thing to come out of 1910 was the now famous T-206 card, one of which commanded over $1 million at auction in 2000. Pirate secretary John Gruber, making $10 on the deal, sold the American Tobacco Company a picture of Wagner to reproduce in card form to be inserted in packages of cigarettes. Though Honus smoked cigars and chewed tobacco, he supposedly didn't like cigarettes and didn't want kids buying them to get his picture. He put an end to the deal, sending Gruber a check for $10, but a few cards got out before the print run was stopped.

Wagner had his last big seasons in 1911 and 1912, winning his final batting title in the former year and leading the league in RBI for the last time in the latter. He hit .300 in 1913, the last time he reached that level. Wagner and the Pirates declined together. The team fell to seventh in 1914 and Honus batted a career-low .252, though he did collect his 3,000th hit on June 9, doubling against Philadelphia's Erskine Mayer to become the first player to achieve that milestone in the 20th century. Pittsburgh improved to fifth in 1915 with Wagner having somewhat of a last hurrah. Playing all 156 games, the 41-year-old shortstop hit .274 and legged out 32 doubles and 17 triples to go along with 78 RBI. One of the season's highlights was belting a grand slam against Brooklyn's Jeff Pfeffer on July 29, making him the oldest player to hit one.

When Clarke retired after the 1915 season, Dreyfuss brought in Jimmy Callahan to manage the Pirates.

Wagner batted .287 in 1916, good enough to rank eighth in the National League, and he ended the year on a bright note, marrying Bessie Smith on December 31. Honus was dubious about playing another year. Bessie's cooking was taking its toll on his waistline, and he wasn't playing basketball or hunting as much as he used to in the off-season. Wagner started the 1917 season fairly well, but by July it was clear that he was finished. Callahan was fired and Honus, who'd served as acting manager when Clarke was unavailable, agreed to take over. After winning his first game and losing the next four, he told Dreyfuss the job wasn't for him. Wagner batted .265 in just 74 games, making his final playing appearance on September 17, when he put in three innings at second base.

Honus Wagner's life after his playing career was a mix of highs and lows. His first child, Elva Katrina, was stillborn on January 9, 1918, causing Honus to throw himself into war work, making speeches urging Americans to buy Liberty Bonds. On December 5, 1919, the Wagners were blessed by the birth of a healthy daughter, Betty Baine. Bessie gave birth to another girl, Virginia Mae, on May 3, 1922. A doting father, Honus took his daughters everywhere, teaching them to play ball and calling them "my boys." He held political jobs—state fish commissioner and sergeant-at-arms of the Pennsylvania Legislature—and coached the Carnegie High School football team and the Carnegie Institute of Technology (now Carnegie Mellon University) basketball and baseball teams. Most prominent of his ventures was the sporting-goods store bearing his name. The business went through several weak phases, as he lacked business sense and had some less than ideal partners. Eventually Honus tried to make a go of it with Pie Traynor, an honest man as well as a great third baseman, but the poor economy in the early 1930s finally finished it off.

The Wagners were hit hard by the Depression. William Benswanger, taking over leadership of the Pirates after the death of his father-in-law, Barney Dreyfuss, heard of Honus's situation and gave him a coaching job in 1933. His first task, which he performed admirably, was to make a big-league shortstop out of the hard-hitting Arky Vaughan. Honus primarily coached the rookies, becoming a substitute father to them, and chatted with the fans. He liked to spin yarns about his past achievements, like the time he scooped up a grounder in his steam-shovel hands, along with grass, pebbles, and a rabbit that had run onto the field, and heaved the whole mess to first, nailing a fast runner—by a hare. Once shy, he became a fine after-dinner speaker and barroom raconteur.

One of the original five electees to the National Baseball Hall of Fame in 1936, Wagner held on as a Pirates coach until 1951, when age and injuries finally forced him to retire. He lived out the remainder of his years at home in Carnegie, making his customary journeys to the Elks Club and other Pittsburgh watering holes. Honus made his last public appearance on April 30, 1955, at the unveiling of the Frank Vittor statue of him that would stand in Schenley Park outside Forbes Field. Too weak to leave the car, he waved to the crowd and left before the ceremonies ended. The statue later graced the entrance to Three Rivers Stadium and now greets visitors to PNC Park. Honus Wagner died at age 81 in his Carnegie home at 12:56 A.M. on December 6, 1955. He was buried in Jefferson Memorial Cemetery in Pleasant Hills, south of Pittsburgh.

JAN FINKEL

PITTSBURGH

Thomas William Leach
Third baseman/center fielder 1900–12, 1918

Though standing just 5'6" and weighing as little as 135 lbs. at the beginning of his career, Wee Tommie Leach was nonetheless one of the leading power hitters of the Deadball Era's first decade. Over the course of his 19 years in the NL, Leach finished in the Top 10 six times each in triples, home runs, and total bases. "Sometimes they played me right in back of the infield," he recalled years later in explaining his surprising long-ball proficiency. "Every so often, I'd manage to drive a ball between the outfielders and it would roll to the fence. I was pretty fast, and by the time they ran the ball down and got it back to the infield, I'd be home. I don't ever recall getting a home run on a ball hit outside of the park." Leach was exaggerating, but not by much: of his 63 career home runs, 49 were inside-the-park, which places him second on the all-time list behind Sam Crawford's 51.

Thomas William Leach was born on November 4, 1877, in the village of French Creek, in western New York, but his family moved to an Irish neighborhood in Cleveland when he was five years old. There the Leaches were neighbors of the Delahantys, a family that produced five major leaguers. Enthusiastic about the tremendous success of Ed Delahanty, who became perhaps the greatest slugger of the 1890s, Tommie's father encouraged his son by saying, "If Ed can do it, so can you." Tommie worked as a printer's devil but played baseball constantly, and in 1896-97 he became employed as a third baseman with a succession of teams: Hanover, Pennsylvania; Petersburg, Virginia; and Youngstown and Geneva in Ohio. His big break came in 1898, when he hit .325 in 97 games for Auburn and led the New York State League in runs (85) and home runs (5). In August owner John Farrell sent Leach for a two-week trial with the New York Giants, but

Giants owner Andrew Freedman promptly returned him, saying, "Take your boy back before he gets hurt. We don't take midgets on the Giants."

That same month Louisville Colonels owner Barney Dreyfuss acquired the 20-year-old Leach for $650. Tommie served as utility man and didn't travel with the club when it was on the road. Despite spending several weeks with the Colonels, he played in just three games, making more errors (3) than hits (1). Leach started the 1899 season with Louisville but was farmed out to Worcester after making five errors in his first game. After a six-game stint in the Eastern League, Tommie returned to Louisville and batted .288 for the season, appearing in 25 games at shortstop and 80 at his preferred position of third base. When the core of the team moved to Pittsburgh in 1900, Leach became a reserve—the Pirates' incumbent third baseman was Jimmy Williams, who'd hit .355 as a rookie in 1899—and he struggled to a .212 mark in just 160 at-bats. But Williams jumped to the American League in 1901, opening up third base for Leach, and the boyish-looking speedster established himself as one of the best in the National League by batting .305 with power.

Tommie Leach became a full-fledged star in 1902. Usually batting third in the order between Ginger Beaumont and Honus Wagner, the right-handed–hitting Leach batted .278 and placed second in the NL with 85 RBI. Most impressively, he led the league with 22 triples and six home runs (the latter mark was the lowest by a home run champion in the 20th century). The triples are what established Leach as a leading power hitter. The following year, to go along with seven inside-the-park home runs (good enough to tie for second in the NL home run race), he hit 17 three-baggers, third best in the league behind Wagner's 19 and Mike

Donlin's 18. In that year's World Series he slugged four more triples, a total that hasn't been matched in any Series since. Like many of the Pirates, Tommie did most of his damage early in the Series—in Game One he ripped four hits, including two triples into the roped-off crowd at Boston's Huntington Avenue Grounds, but then went 0-for-13 in the final three games, all losses.

In July 1904 Clarke received a serious spike wound, keeping him away from the team for six weeks. When Wagner refused to serve as acting manager, the job fell to 26-year-old Leach. Tommie had two mediocre offensive seasons in 1904 and '05, hitting .257 each year. In a game against St. Louis during the latter season he suffered an injury that had a significant impact on his career. Leach laid down a bunt that was fielded by Cardinals first baseman Jake Beckley, who sailed the ball a yard over the head of pitcher Jack Taylor, covering first base. By the time Beckley retrieved the ball, the fleet-footed Leach was rounding third and heading for home. Rather than risk another lousy throw, the scatter-armed first baseman decided to race Tommie to the plate. Beckley dove head first from one direction while Leach slid feet first from the other, and in the resulting collision the diminutive Pirate sustained two broken ribs. Leach had difficulty throwing when he returned from his injury, so for the first time he began playing the outfield on a regular basis. Over the next few seasons he played both third base and center field, but beginning in 1909 he became a full-time center fielder.

In 1907 Leach topped the 100-run mark for the first time and ranked fourth in the NL in batting average

(.303) and stolen bases (a career-high 43), but his most enjoyable year came in 1909. That season he led the league with 126 runs and was second with six homers as the Pirates won another NL pennant. The 31-year-old Leach was starting to go bald, and just before the World Series he shaved his head completely and applied liniment to his scalp in an attempt to prevent his hair from falling out. Detroit Tigers third baseman George Moriarty tried to embarrass Tommie during the Series by pulling the cap right off his head, but Leach got the last laugh. Making amends for his slump in the first World Series, Tommie led the Pirates with nine hits, four doubles, and a .360 batting average as Pittsburgh took the '09 Series in seven games.

After an injury-plagued 1911 in which Leach hit .238, the Pirates dealt him and Lefty Leifield to the Chicago Cubs for Artie Hofman and King Cole in June 1912. It was common knowledge that Tommie aspired to become a manager (Cincinnati had expressed interest in making him player-manager in 1908, but the Reds and Pirates couldn't agree on compensation), and some surmised that the deal was prompted by friction over who would eventually succeed Clarke as manager, him or Wagner. Tommie played well in two and a half seasons in Chicago—he led the NL with 99 runs in 1913 and hit seven home runs in 1914—before slumping to a .224 average with the Reds in 1915, his last full season in the majors. Clarke finally resigned as manager of the Pirates at the end of 1915, and although Leach was rumored to be in line for the job, it eventually fell not to Wagner but to Jimmy Callahan. Aside from brief stints with the Pirates and Westinghouse Munitions during the Great War, Tommie spent the next seven seasons in the minors.

Leach had purchased citrus property in Haines City, Florida, in 1914, and that is where he spent the rest of his non-baseball life. In the 1920s he managed several teams in the Florida State League, and in 1935-41 he was a Boston Braves scout. Tommie had suffered tremendous personal loss during his playing days—his first wife had died of pneumonia in 1908, and he had lost a second wife to illness in 1911—but his third wife, Sara (Darling) Leach, ended up outliving him. The last surviving player from the 1903 World Series, Tommie Leach died in Haines City on September 29, 1969, a month shy of his 92nd birthday.

MARK ARMOUR

Charles Phillippe

PITTSBURGH

CHARLES LOUIS "DEACON" PHILLIPPE
RIGHT-HANDED PITCHER 1900–11

Voted by Pittsburgh fans as the greatest right-handed pitcher in Pirates history in 1969, Deacon Phillippe may have been the best control pitcher ever—his 1.25 walks per nine innings is the lowest ratio of anyone who hurled after the modern pitching distance was established in 1893. Longtime teammate Honus Wagner recalled that Phillippe "wanted to hurl against the other team's best pitcher and often worked out of turn to do it." Although he was a six-time 20-game winner, never had a losing season, and won 189 games in a 13-year major league career that didn't begin until he was nearly 27 years old, he is best remembered today as the winning pitcher in the first modern World Series game.

The son of Andrew Jackson and Margaret (Hackler) Phillippe, Charles Louis Phillippe (pronounced PHIL-uh-pee) was born on May 23, 1872, in Rural Retreat, Virginia, a tiny town in Wythe County where his family had lived for several generations. The spring that supplies the town with water to this day is still called Phillippe Springs. When Charlie was three his family moved to the Dakota Territory near the town of Athol. He grew up and learned to play baseball on the prairies of what was to become the state of South Dakota in 1889. By 1896 Charlie had moved to Minnesota, and that year he played professionally for a team in Mankato. The next two years he pitched for Minneapolis of the Western League, posting a 21-19 record in 1898, his last minor league season. The Louisville Colonels drafted Phillippe, and on May 25, 1899, he pitched a no-hitter against the New York Giants in only his seventh major league game. For his rookie season he was 21-17 in 321 innings for the ninth-place Colonels, becoming one of several Louisville stars to move to Pittsburgh in 1900.

Standing a shade over 6'0" and weighing 180 lbs., Phillippe was described as "a handsome man with a sturdy oval face, a lantern jaw, and dark hair parted a shade left of center." Though friends usually called him Charlie, he acquired the nickname "Deacon" in the early days of his major league career. Phillippe wasn't a clergyman. Though he did lead a choir during the off-season, he picked up the name because of his reticent demeanor, his humility, and the way he lived his life. In the words of one writer analyzing an upcoming season, "He will be there again, as strong and good as ever, for Phil never does anything during the winter that would result detrimentally to him." Deacon was a longtime friend and teammate of Sam Leever, a fellow right-handed pitcher with a similar disposition and a strikingly similar record.

Though the Pirates had a deep and talented pitching staff during his early years, Deacon was probably its biggest star. He won 20 or more games in each of his first four years in Pittsburgh, extending his career streak to five years. His best season was 1903, when he and Leever were asked to make up for the defections of Jack Chesbro and Jesse Tannehill to the American League. Phillippe opened the year by pitching a two-hitter to defeat the Cincinnati Reds, and he continued to do more than his share throughout that summer, finishing with a 25-9 record. When the Pirates recorded a record six consecutive shutouts that June, he pitched the first and fifth games of the streak.

Phillippe's finest hours came during the 1903 World Series. The Pirates staff was depleted by an injury to 25-game winner Leever and the nervous breakdown of 16-game winner Ed Doheny. Deacon beat Cy Young in Game One, 7-3, racking up a season-high 10 strikeouts. "Phillippe pitched in masterly style," admitted Boston manager Jimmy Collins. The Pirate ace bounced back to pitch a four-hitter to win Game Three and, after a travel day and a controversial rainout, won Game Four by a 5-4 score, after which the Pittsburgh fans hoisted him on their shoulders and carried him around Exposition Park. The best-of-nine series was tied at three games apiece when Deacon next took the mound in Game Seven. With the Pittsburgh crowd chanting "Phil, Phil, Phillippe, Phil; He can win and you bet he will," Phillippe somehow lost to Young, 7-3. Three days later he lost the eighth and final game as well, 3-0. In the eight-game series, Deacon pitched five complete games and recorded all three of his team's victories—a performance that's unlikely to be matched. To show their appreciation, Pittsburgh fans presented him with a diamond horseshoe stickpin and Barney Dreyfuss gave him 10 shares of stock in the club.

After cashing in on his fame during the offseason by playing on the Pittsburg Five, a basketball team captained by Wagner, Phillippe contracted an illness early in 1904 that settled in his eyes, causing him to be hospitalized in late May. He managed only 19 starts that year and had his least effective season, 10-10 with a 3.24 ERA. Deacon returned to form in 1905, winning 20 games again and posting a 2.19 ERA. By 1906 he was 34 years old and suffering from the chronic arm problems that plagued him the rest of his career. Over the next two seasons he started 50 games and relieved in 18 others, compiling an aggregate record of 29-21.

In 1908 Phillippe pitched only 12 innings the entire season, missing a few weeks with a sore shoulder early on and then breaking a finger on his pitching hand when struck by a line drive off the bat of the Phillies' Red Dooin on July 8. Still not ready for retirement, Deacon pitched as a spot starter and reliever for the champion 1909 Pirates, fashioning an 8-3 record with a 2.32 ERA and pitching six scoreless innings in a triumphant return to the World Series. The next season he was mainly a relief pitcher, finishing 14-2 with a 2.29 ERA. A lifetime .189 hitter, Deacon entered the record books that season when he connected for an inside-the-park grand slam, becoming the last pitcher to accomplish that feat until Mel Stottlemyre did it in 1965. He won his last 13 decisions, which turned out to be the last of his major league career.

Phillippe left the Pirates after a few ineffective appearances in 1911 but returned to base-

ball the following year as player-manager of the Pittsburgh entry of the outlaw United States League, which played its home games at Exposition Park. His team, which the press dubbed the Filipinos, finished the aborted season with the best record in the league at 16-8. In 1913 Deacon managed the Pittsburgh team in the Federal League, also called the Filipinos.

Following his retirement as an active player, Phillippe worked briefly for a steel mill, owned and operated a cigar store, scouted for the Pirates, and served as a court bailiff, all in the greater Pittsburgh area. In his later years he and his wife, Belle, lived with their only child, a daughter, in Avalon, Pennsylvania, where he died while watching television on March 30, 1952. Phillippe is buried in Pittsburgh's Allegheny Cemetery.

MARK ARMOUR

PITTSBURGH

CLAUDE CASSIUS RITCHEY
SECOND BASEMAN 1900–06

One of the unsung members of Fred Clarke's highly successful Pirates of the early 1900s, Claude Ritchey was a durable, sure-handed second baseman whose small stature (5'6½", 167 lbs.) and reputation for hitting in the clutch earned him the nickname "Little All Right." Even as late as 1964, no less an authority than Joe Reichler, editor of *The Baseball Encyclopedia*, chose Ritchey as the greatest Pirate second baseman of all time. Off the field, Ritchey could be difficult and ornery. Concerning his experimentation with a vegetarian diet, Honus Wagner biographers Dennis and Jean DeValeria wrote, "Perhaps a difficulty in locating a good salad in a world of steak eaters aggravated his already surly and unsociable disposition."

Claude Cassius Ritchey was born in Emlenton, Pennsylvania, on October 5, 1873, the son of Lucreatia Annette Ritchey (his biological father is unknown). Raised by his mother and stepfather, Amos Crum, Ritchey first played baseball in Emlenton in 1890. He later played at Parkers Landing, Pennsylvania, before beginning his professional career in his native state with Franklin in 1894. Ritchey split the next season between Steubenville-Akron, Ohio, of the Interstate League, and Warren, Pennsylvania, of the Iron and Oil League. While at Steubenville-Akron he met and befriended the great Honus Wagner, a teammate with whom he was reunited at Warren after Steubenville-Akron folded. Playing for Buffalo of the Eastern League in 1896, Ritchey contributed to the Bisons' second-place finish and caught the eye of major league scouts. The Brooklyn Bridegrooms drafted him after the season.

Ritchey's long and winding road to Pittsburgh, however, wasn't meant to go through the Big Apple. In the spring of '97 Brooklyn turned him over to Cincinnati when Tommy Corcoran, who'd been sold to the Reds, failed to report. Ritchey made his major league debut with Cincinnati on April 22, 1897. His first exposure to the National League was a mixed one. On one hand, Ritchey played in 101 games, mostly at shortstop, and hit big-league pitching at a .282 clip, 25 points lower than the league average but certainly acceptable for a rookie infielder. His fielding, on the other hand, was atrocious even by the standards of the late 1890s. Perhaps because of his defensive problems—50 errors in 100 games at five positions (shortstop, second base, and all three outfield spots)—and perhaps because Corcoran, a defensive standout, eventually did report, Ritchey was dealt to the Louisville Colonels for pitcher Bill Hill prior to the start of the 1898 campaign.

At Louisville, Ritchey was again reunited with his good friend Wagner. Unfortunately for the Colonels, the change of scenery didn't improve Ritchey's fielding much and, in fact, lowered his batting average to .254, 21 points below the league average. On July 20, 1898, Louisville's manager, feisty Fred Clarke, grew tired of the way his team was playing and rearranged his infield, in the process shifting Ritchey from shortstop to second base. The Clarke shuffle netted positive results, with the Colonels playing .639 ball the rest of the season. The impact of the move on Ritchey's career was profound. In 1899 he had one of his better seasons with the bat, hitting an even .300 with 65 runs and 73 RBI, but the most dramatic improvement came in the field. Ritchey established himself as a capable second baseman, recording 414 assists and taking part in 54 double plays. It was a modest beginning, but with time and practice Ritchey transformed himself into one of the top fielders of the Deadball Era.

When the Colonels merged with Pittsburgh in 1900, Ritchey, along with the other top Louisville players, was transferred to the Steel City. It was there, or more specifically at Exposition Park, that Ritchey became a fixture at second base for the new-look Pirates. Teaming with the likes of Clarke, Wagner, Tommie Leach, Ginger Beaumont, Deacon Phillippe, and Sam Leever, Ritchey helped propel the Pirates to three pennants and two second-place finishes in seven seasons.

During those glory years, Ritchey's personal stats were impressive. Though usually batting in the lower half of the order, he averaged 61 runs and 60 RBI while batting .277 and posting an on-base percentage of .349. As his son, John, later said, "My father got his hits when they counted." In the field, Ritchey led NL second basemen in assists twice, double plays twice, and fielding percentage four times. In addition, he demonstrated his durability by playing in 94% of the Pirate games and topping NL second basemen in games played three times. Perhaps his most memorable moment came in Game Seven of the 1903 World Series, when Ritchey established Series records for most assists (8) and total chances (13) by a second baseman in a nine-inning game. Those records have been tied but not broken.

In 1907 the Pirates traded their star second sacker, along with Ginger Beaumont and Pat Flaherty, to the Boston Nationals for Ed Abbaticchio. According to the DeValerias, Pirates owner Barney Dreyfuss agreed to the trade because he believed Ritchey's interest in the game had waned after he'd purchased some oil wells and turned a handsome profit. The deal turned out to be bad for the Pirates. Abbaticchio played only two full seasons in Pittsburgh, but Ritchey and Beaumont still had good baseball left in them. They helped an abysmal Boston squad improve by 10½ games in 1907 and another two games in 1908. Ritchey led National League second basemen in fielding percentage in 1907 and the next year paced the circuit in double plays and posted a .361 on-base percentage. When his performance declined in 1909, however, Boston released him to Providence, where he played 62 games, hit .237, and averaged 2.5 assists per game. Ritchey played two weeks for Louisville in 1910 and retired from professional baseball after a brief but dismal comeback attempt in 1912 with the Pittsburgh Filipinos of the United States League.

Outside of baseball, Ritchey held several jobs in the Emlenton area, including operating a clothing store and working for the Emlenton Refining Company (which merged with Quaker State Oil in 1931). During his leisure time he liked to pick berries and entertain his former Pirate teammates. Ritchey was married twice: in 1903 to Sophia Bayer, from whom he was divorced in 1917, and in 1924 to Kathryn Kunselman (1897-1965). By his first marriage he had one daughter; by his second, two daughters and a son. Like so many ballplayers, Ritchey suffered from alcoholism, and he died from cirrhosis of the liver on November 8, 1951. His grave can be found in the Emlenton Cemetery.

ANGELO LOUISA

Howard Camnitz

PITTSBURGH

SAMUEL HOWARD CAMNITZ
RIGHT-HANDED PITCHER 1904, 1906–13

Though his reign as one of the National League's top pitchers was short-lived, Howie Camnitz was the undisputed ace of the Pittsburgh Pirates pitching staff during their world championship season of 1909. That year Camnitz, a right-handed curveball specialist, tied for the NL lead in winning percentage (25-6, .806) and ranked fourth in ERA (1.62). "I always inspect very closely the box score of the club we are about to meet next," he once explained. "My object is to ascertain what players are doing the hitting. If a player comes up who has been clouting the ball, it may be the safest plan to let him walk." Camnitz himself was a terrible hitter, perhaps the worst of the Deadball Era's first decade, when he batted a combined .101.

Nicknamed "Rosebud" for his shock of red hair, Samuel Howard Camnitz was born in Covington, Kentucky, on August 22, 1881, the second eldest child of printer Henry Camnitz and his wife, Elizabeth. Howie's brother Harry, who was three years younger, also went on to the major leagues, pitching four innings for the 1909 Pirates and two for the 1911 St. Louis Cardinals. Growing up in bluegrass country, Howie of course learned to ride horses, a talent he later demonstrated at manager Fred Clarke's Little Pirate Ranch, but his forte was pitching a baseball. After making his professional debut with Greenville of the Cotton States League in 1902, he enjoyed a breakout season with Vicksburg in 1903, leading the CSL in winning percentage (26-7, .788) and strikeouts (294).

Camnitz started the 1904 season with Pittsburgh, but even with the powerful Pirates behind him, he posted a 1-4 record and 4.22 ERA in 10 games, eight of them in relief. The word on the Kentucky curveballer was that he didn't "protect" his best pitch: "He would curve the ball over home with such regularity that bats-men cut loose, feeling sure that the oval was there," wrote one scout. Camnitz returned to the minors with Springfield, Illinois, and tore up the Three-I League, compiling a 14-5 record and 151 strikeouts in just 19 games. He spent the next two seasons with Toledo of the American Association, topping the 300-inning mark each year and winning 22 games in 1906. Pittsburgh owner Barney Dreyfuss stopped by more than once to check on the progress of Camnitz and teammate Otto Knabe, on whom the Pirates had attached strings. Ultimately Dreyfuss recalled Cammy, losing Knabe to the Phillies in the minor league draft.

Beginning his second stint with the Pirates on September 28, 1906, the 25-year-old Camnitz fired a seven-inning shutout against Brooklyn. He'd learned to "protect" his curveball in the minors; an updated report noted that he "disguises the pitch excellently now." In 1907 Howie's career took off. Appearing in 31 games, including 19 starts, he went 13-8 with four shutouts and a 2.15 ERA. The following year Camnitz was even better, finishing with a 16-9 record, limiting NL hitters to a .210 batting average, and lowering his ERA to 1.56, fourth lowest in the NL. Howie also ranked fourth in strikeouts per game (4.49).

Camnitz saved his best work for 1909, when he led the Pirates to their first pennant since 1903. He began his banner season on Opening Day by holding the Cincinnati Reds scoreless, the first of his six shutouts that season. In July Camnitz hurled his second one-hitter of the season against the New York Giants; the opposing pitcher, Rube Marquard, broke up the no-hit bid with a sixth-inning bunt single. Pitching a career-high 283 innings, Howie held the league to a .211 batting average and a .267 on-base percentage. In early October, however, his dream season was interrupted by illness—some reports had him suffering with a throat irritation, while others said he'd fallen off the wagon. Whatever the reason, Camnitz performed dismally in the World Series. Starting Game Two, he was battered for five runs in 2⅓ innings, the last run coming when Ty Cobb swiped home against his replacement, Vic Willis. Camnitz's only other appearance came in Game Six, when he allowed a run in one inning of relief.

Though he pitched serviceably over the next three seasons, Camnitz's poor performance in the 1909 World Series marked the beginning of his decline toward mediocrity. His demise came as no surprise to Heinie Zimmerman. "Cammy is always trying and never lets down when there is an alleged weak hitter up," said the Cubs star infielder in 1909. "Howard is such a hard worker that I doubt if he will last as long as the man who occasionally eases up." Camnitz slipped badly during 1910, ending the season at 12-13 with a 3.22 ERA, almost double his ERA from the previous season. One Pittsburgh sportswriter even called him "fat" (his usual playing weight was 169 lbs.). Dreyfuss stuck with the embattled pitcher, granting him a hefty $1,200 raise, and over the next two seasons Camnitz posted back-to-back 20-win seasons, though his ERA and ratio of base runners per nine innings never came close to his 1907-09 levels.

By 1913 Howie was walking too many batters—he issued a career-high 107 free passes that year—and, ominously, his strikeouts were dropping precipitously. On August 20, following a 6-17 start, Camnitz and third baseman Bobby Byrne were dealt to the Phillies for outfielder Cozy Dolan and cash. After a season in which he combined to lose 20 games for two teams that finished in the first division, Howie signed with the Pittsburgh franchise in the newly formed Federal League. During 1914 training camp in Hot Springs, Arkansas, Dreyfuss had to obtain a court injunction to prevent Camnitz from recruiting Pirates players in the Hotel Eastman and outside the gates to Whittington Park. Honus Wagner called Howie a "troublemaker" and told him to stay away from the younger players.

Once the season started, it quickly became apparent that Camnitz's career was on the wane. Pitching in a less competitive league, Howie mustered a 14-19 record, compiling a mediocre 3.23 ERA and walking more men than he struck out. Just a few weeks into the 1915 campaign, he was accused of violating team rules and hand-

ed his unconditional release. In addition to keeping himself in poor shape, Camnitz got into an altercation with another guest at the team's New York City hotel. "We did everything in our power to protect Camnitz, and he would have continued to be a member of our club had he conducted himself properly," the club stated in a press release.

Camnitz refused to go away quietly, serving notice that he'd continue to report to the team's home field, Exposition Park, every day for the duration of his contract. In addition, he promised that he'd report to the club offices twice each month to collect his paycheck. If his pay wasn't forthcoming, Camnitz threatened a lawsuit. In a letter to club president Edward Gwinner, Camnitz wrote, "As I have been doing regularly every day, I am again reporting for duty, and tendering the club my services." Gwinner wasn't impressed. "Why, Camnitz hasn't been in condition to pitch a good game of ball this season, so I don't think he could give us his services," he remarked. With that final slap in the face, Howie Camnitz's career in professional baseball came to an end. After the 1915 season he retired to private life in Louisville. Camnitz died at age 78 on March 2, 1960, about a month after leaving the auto sales business in which he'd worked for over 40 years.

IRV GOLDFARB

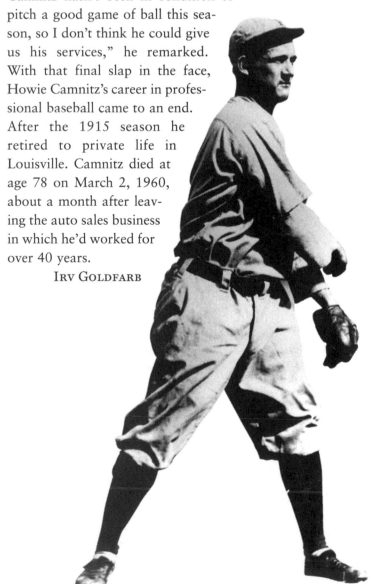

PITTSBURGH

GEORGE C. GIBSON
CATCHER 1905–16, MANAGER 1920-22, 1932-34

Over the three-year period 1908-10, George Gibson averaged 144 games behind the plate per season, an unheard-of figure for a catcher during the Deadball Era. "Wagner, Clarke, and Leach have been set above all others in allotting credit for Pittsburg's success, but there is a deep impression in many people's minds that 'Gibby' was the one best bet," wrote Alfred Spink in 1910. Though Gibson wasn't much of a hitter, as evidenced by his lifetime .236 batting average, he was generally regarded as one of the NL's premier catchers because of his deadly accurate throwing arm. When his playing days were over, the popular former backstop turned his reputation as a smart player into a moderately successful managing career, compiling a 413-344 record in parts of seven seasons as one of the first Canadians ever to manage in the majors.

The son of a bricklayer and building contractor, George C. Gibson was born on July 22, 1880, in London, Ontario. His first job was carrying buckets of water to the laborers his father employed, and though he eventually learned the bricklaying trade, his first love was baseball. George was known by several nicknames, but the most popular was "Moon." Some sources suggest that the nickname was inspired by his round, moon-shaped face, but he actually picked it up playing on a sandlot team known as the Mooneys. Gibson began his amateur career as a second baseman, but by the time he was 12 his already strong throwing arm landed him a position as a catcher on the church league's Knox Baseball Club. From there he gained additional experience with the West London Stars and the Struthers and McClary clubs.

Gibson played his first professional game in 1903 with Kingston, New York, of the Hudson River League, and that August he was purchased by the Eastern League's Buffalo Bisons, managed by George Stallings. Moon joined the Bisons on September 2, replacing the injured Buffalo first baseman, hitting a single off Baltimore's Hooks Wiltse, and successfully handling 10 putouts. "I didn't get paid much," he recalled, "but it sure beat hauling bricks!" At the end of the 1903 season, Stallings released Gibson to the Eastern League's Montreal Royals amidst rumors that the young catcher had talked back after his foul-mouthed manager chewed him out for missing a sign. After batting .290 in his second season in Montreal, the Royals sold him to the Pittsburgh Pirates in late June 1905.

The first time the 5'11½", 190 lb. Gibson walked into the Pittsburgh clubhouse, Honus Wagner took one look at him and hollered, "Here comes Hackenschmidt," a reference to George Hackenschmidt, a famous championship wrestler at the time. (Wagner's comment illustrates how the size of baseball players has changed over the last century.) In his major league debut at Cincinnati on July 2, "Hack" Gibson recorded six putouts, two assists, and one error. He explained the error in *The Glory of Their Times*: "The first time one of the Cincinnati players got on first base, he tried to steal second. I rocked back on my heels and threw a bullet, knee high, right over the base. Both the shortstop and second baseman—Honus Wagner and Claude Ritchey—ran to cover second base, but the ball went flying into center field before either of them got near it. I figured they were trying to make me look bad, letting the throw go by, because I was a rookie. But Wagner came in, threw his arms around me, and said, 'Just keep throwing that way, kid. It was our fault, not yours.' What had happened was that they had gotten so used to Heinie Peitz's rainbows that any throw on a straight line caught them by surprise."

Though he posted back-to-back batting averages of .178 in 1905-06, and allowed 13 passed balls during the latter season, Gibson steadily improved before putting together his greatest season in 1909, when the Pirates posted a 110-42 record. That year he caught 150 regular-season games for the Pirates, including a remarkable string of 134 consecutive games to set an NL record. "There is no doubt but that Gibson could have caught every game of the National League schedule had it been necessary for him to do so," wrote Spink. "However, the pennant was clinched many days before the wind-up and Clarke gave Gibson the rest he so richly deserved." He kept his streak alive despite "black and blue marks imprinted by 19 foul tips upon his body, a damaged hand, a bruise on his hip six inches square where a thrown bat had struck, and three spike cuts." George even managed to post one of his better offensive seasons: .265 with 25 doubles, nine triples, two home runs, and 52 RBI. In the midst of his streak, Gibson slugged a double for the final hit in Pittsburgh's Exposition Park on June 29, and the next day captured the Pirates' first hit (a single) in the new Forbes Field. On the eve of the World Series, press reports described him as "far and away the best catcher in the National League."

During his Pittsburgh prime, Gibson led all NL catchers in fielding percentage three times (1909, 1910, and 1912), and after injury-plagued seasons in 1912-13 he managed to hit a career-best .285 in 1914. He proclaimed, however, that "*thinking* was my real specialty." George had diligently studied the mental game of baseball under Fred Clarke's tutelage, and years after his retirement he credited Clarke with teaching him to play intelligent baseball. In August 1916 the 36-year-old Gibson was placed on waivers and claimed by the New York Giants, but he refused to report that year. John McGraw persuaded him to join the Giants as a player-coach in 1917, and the following May he accepted a coaching position with Sacramento of the Pacific Coast League. The 1918 season closed early because of the war and Gibson returned to his Ontario farm until he was hired in 1919 to coach the Toronto Maple Leafs of the International League.

Gibson spent one season in Toronto before being summoned to manage the Pirates from 1920 to 1922. George again retired to his farm after spending 1923 as a coach for the Washington Senators, but he returned to baseball in 1925 to coach the Chicago Cubs, finishing the season as manager after Rabbit Maranville was dismissed. Though he wasn't reappointed for 1926, he became a scout for the Cubs until he took over the Pirates again in 1932. During his two stints as Pittsburgh manager, Moon developed a reputation as a taskmaster and strict disciplinarian. "The Pirates have more signals than the Notre Dame football team," wrote one reporter, "and Gibson insists that every order be carried out to the letter." George was intolerant of mental mistakes, and his temperament left him ill-suited to the task of managing locker room politics. In June 1934 the Pirates replaced him with Pie Traynor.

George Gibson remained active in baseball, sponsoring amateur clubs and serving as vice-president of the Pirates' London farm club in the PONY League in 1940-41. At the end of his baseball career he retired to his Ontario farm with his wife, Margaret (McMurphy), whom he'd married in 1900. The couple had three children: George Jr., William, and Marguerite (who married catcher Bill Warwick, who'd played for her father on the 1921 Pirates). George enjoyed gardening and hunting and became an expert curler. He died of cancer at age 86 on January 25, 1967. Gibson was inducted into the Canadian Baseball Hall of Fame in 1987. In 2003 a plaque in his honor was rededicated at London's Labatt Park, with Gibson relatives present.

TREY STRECKER

PITTSBURGH

ALBERT PETER "LEFTY" LEIFIELD
LEFT-HANDED PITCHER 1905–12

Lefty Leifield won 103 games during his six full seasons with Pittsburgh in 1906-11, more than any other Pirate pitcher over that period, and his lifetime ERA of 2.47 over 12 seasons is the 28th best in the history of the game among pitchers with at least 1,500 innings. "He was one of those ain't-got-a-thing pitchers who never threw a ball where the batter wanted it," wrote *The Sporting News*. Lacking an overpowering fastball, a sharp-breaking spitter, or a truly devastating curve, Leifield relied instead on the element of surprise—throwing curves on 2-and-0 and 3-and-2 counts—and his ability to locate pitches with pinpoint accuracy.

The fourth of Henry and Margaret Leifield's nine surviving children (three children died in infancy), Albert Peter Leifield (alternately spelled Leifeld) was born in Trenton, Illinois, on September 5, 1883, at least according to most sources. Census records from Albert's childhood, however, indicate that he was born in 1882, not 1883, so it seems likely that he fabricated his date of birth. Albert was two when his father, a $65-a-month policeman, moved the family from Trenton to a flat in the Fairgrounds section of St. Louis, at the nexus of local baseball in the late 19th century: both the original Sportsman's Park and Robison Field were a few blocks away. For a time Albert attended grammar school at Holy Trinity, but his father's death in 1900 forced him to quit school and work in a shoe factory for $2.50 a week—a five-and-one-half-day week, at that.

In 1902 Leifield caught on as a pitcher with the team from nearby Alton, Illinois, of the independent Trolley League. From there he quickly ascended the rungs of the minor league ladder, pitching for Joplin of the Missouri Valley League in 1903 and Des Moines of the Western League in 1904. After going 23-8 for Des Moines in 1905, Leifield received a late-season trial with the Pittsburgh Pirates. In his major league debut on September 3, he pitched a shutout against the Chicago Cubs in a six-inning game shortened because both teams needed to catch trains. Lefty ended his month with the Pirates at 5-2 with a 2.89 ERA, earning a shot at the starting rotation for the following season.

Veteran stalwarts like Vic Willis, Sam Leever, and Deacon Phillippe led the Pittsburgh pitching staff in 1906, but the young Leifield more than held his own. He compiled a record of 18-13 with 24 complete games, finishing in the top five in the National League in ERA (1.87) and shutouts (8). Leifield's greatest game of the campaign came on the front end of an Independence Day doubleheader against the Cubs. Taking a no-hitter into the ninth inning, Lefty allowed a lone single to Jimmy Slagle, who eventually scored the game's only run with the assistance of an error. The winning pitcher, Mordecai Brown, also finished with a one-hitter, giving up just a single by Leifield.

In 1907 Leifield won 20 games while leading the Pirates in strikeouts and shutouts and posting a 2.33 ERA. The following year he shaved his ERA to 2.10 and won 15 games, one of five Pittsburgh pitchers with 15 or more victories. Lefty sometimes had a tendency to be too fine in locating his pitches, and in those two seasons he walked nearly as many batters (186) as he struck out (199). Yet he continued to post low ERAs, which he attributed to the exceptional defense of his teammates, especially his shortstop. "Hans Wagner was the grandest player that I ever looked at," Lefty said. "He could hit anything, field anything, and steal bases on any catcher or pitcher in the business. And he never made a mistake."

In 1907-08 Leifield had a knack for keeping the ball in the park—he allowed only two home runs in 504⅔ innings, a remarkable ratio even for the Deadball Era—but he lost that knack in 1910-11, when he gave up 13. "One game the first two batters, Josh Devore and Larry Doyle of the Giants, each hit the first pitch for home runs," he recalled. "[Fred] Clarke charged in from left field and said, 'I don't care if they kill you today, but you're going all the way.'" Even though the legendary player-manager could be tough on his pitchers, Lefty remembered him as open to new ideas. One year Clarke scoffed when Leifield showed up at spring training with a soccer ball. "A couple of years later, though, Clarke was convinced that kicking a soccer ball helped condition our legs and he had me and Bobby Byrne bring along some extra balls," Lefty recalled.

In 1909 Leifield enjoyed another outstanding season—a 19-8 record and 2.37 ERA—but in Game Four of that year's fall classic he was roughed up by the Detroit Tigers, lasting only four innings before being lifted for a pinch-hitter with the score 5-0 against him. Though tagged with the loss, he considered his lone appearance in a World Series as his top thrill in baseball, and 57 years later he still remembered to the penny the amount of his winner's share. "It was only $1,825.22, but it seemed like a million dollars to us," said Leifield, whose top season salary was $3,500. "There was nobody around to dig into your pockets for income tax then. You could get 14 oz. of real beer for a nickel, and six loaves of bread for a quarter."

As the Pirates plunged toward .500 over the next two seasons, so too did Leifield. He was a combined 31-29, even though his ERAs of 2.64 and 2.63 were still about a half-run better than the NL average. Lefty remained a workhorse, leading the Pirates in appearances both seasons and ranking third in the league in innings pitched (318) in 1911. But a sore arm caused him to pitch poorly in the first months of 1912, and on June 22 the Pirates traded him and Tommie Leach to the Chicago Cubs for pitcher King Cole and outfielder Solly Hofman. The trade was big news—Leifield and Cole were former 20-game winners and Leach and Hofman were highly respected veterans—but all except Leach were over the hill. Lefty pitched better with the Cubs, winning seven out of nine decisions and posting a 2.42 ERA, but before the end of 1913 he was out of baseball.

Arm troubles again were the culprit. After posting an ERA of 5.48 over six games, Leifield was sold to Atlanta of the Southern Association. He refused to report, returning to St. Louis, where he worked in a saloon and a grocery store. Before long, however, his arm regained its strength, and he returned to baseball with San Francisco of the Pacific Coast League. He pitched the next four years in the minors with San Francisco and St. Paul, finally working his way back to the majors with his hometown St. Louis Browns during the war-torn season of 1918. Now in his mid-30s, Leifield pitched mostly in relief and went 2-6 with a respectable 2.55 ERA. The following year he improved his record to 6-4, and one of his victories was a one-hitter against the Boston Red Sox (Ossie Vitt ruined the no-hit bid with a slow roller in the seventh inning). Leifield appeared to be on his way back, but in 1920 he pitched only nine innings (and was blasted for 17 hits) before the Browns released him.

Following the end of his playing career, Leifield coached for the Browns, Tigers, and Red Sox, and managed in the minors for seven years, winning an American Association pennant with St. Paul in 1931. He was highly regarded as a fungo hitter. "I'd run the boys ragged with my fungo bat in spring training and when they came north, they were in good condition," he recalled. Leifield worked in the St. Louis water department for 26 years until failing eyesight forced him to retire in 1962. Married with two daughters, Lefty spent his last years fishing, betting on horses, and taking in an occasional game at Busch Stadium. He died in Alexandria, Virginia, on October 10, 1970.

LEN JACOBSON

J. O. Wilson Sr.

PITTSBURGH

JOHN OWEN "CHIEF" WILSON
RIGHT FIELDER 1908–13

Owen Wilson is best remembered for hitting 36 triples in 1912, which is not only a major league record but also a record for all of Organized Baseball. To modern fans, that fact alone conjures up images of speedy leadoff hitters, but that isn't the type of player Wilson was. Rather, at 6'2" and 185 lbs., the left-handed–hitting slugger was powerfully built and not particularly fast (his 1912 stolen-base total of 16 was only one fewer than the career high he'd set in 1909), and he typically batted sixth or seventh in the order. Wilson blasted most of his triples over the heads of rival outfielders. "A three-base hit may usually be made only by driving the ball clear to the fence, particularly toward center field on most grounds," he said. "I made 36 triples my best year, but not a few of those long drives would probably have been homers had they not been stopped by the fence."

John Owen Wilson was born on August 21, 1883, at his family's ranch in Bertram, Texas, about fifty miles north of Austin. He was the strong, silent type—roommate Bobby Byrne recalled that "he wouldn't say two words all day." Possessed of a rifle-like throwing arm, Owen began his career in baseball as a right-handed pitcher with various independent teams before hooking on in 1905 as an outfielder with Austin of the Texas League. When that team folded on June 6, he joined the eventual pennant winner, Ft. Worth, playing there a total of two seasons. Wilson moved up to Des Moines of the Western League for the second half of 1907 and batted .323. The Western League's best pitcher that year was Denver's Babe Adams. When he joined the Pittsburgh Pirates at the end of that season, he recommended Wilson to owner Barney Dreyfuss. "I told him about this fellow playing for Des Moines who could really powder the ball," Adams recalled. "I had a lot of

respect for him, not only as a hitter but as a fielder. He had a tremendous arm."

The Pirates signed "Tex" Wilson and made him their right fielder in 1908, which is when he earned another nickname, "Chief." While attending a pre-season gala at manager Fred Clarke's ranch in Winfield, Kansas, the Texas-born rookie's ability with a lariat was so impressive that Clarke proclaimed that he looked like a "Chief of the Texas Rangers." How Wilson handled a bat was another matter: he was one of the National League's worst offensive players in 1908, batting just .227 in 144 games, and all but 18 of his 120 hits were singles. He was plagued by boos from the Pittsburgh fans, and the fact that he played every day for a team that almost won the pennant is a testament to his defense, especially his tremendous throwing arm. Wilson averaged 20 assists per season over his nine-year career, leading the NL with 34 in 1914.

In 1909 Chief Wilson played in all 154 games for the pennant-winning Pirates, gaining the fans' respect by improving his batting average to .272 and showing some power (he hit 22 doubles and 12 triples, increasing his slugging percentage by 89 points). The following year he posted nearly identical numbers—a .276 batting average and a .373 slugging percentage—but 1911 was when he finally came into his own, batting an even .300 and boosting his slugging mark to .472. That season Wilson led the NL in RBI (107) and ranked third in doubles (34) and fifth in home runs (12), setting a Pittsburgh team record that wasn't broken until Kiki Cuyler and Glenn Wright each hit 18 in 1925. In a harbinger of the season to come, he also hit three triples in a game at Forbes Field on July 24.

Wilson enjoyed an advantageous context for his record-breaking season. For one thing, 1912 was the best year ever for triples: the 683 three-baggers hit by the NL that season were more than have been hit in any National League season since, even with expansion. Second, spacious Forbes Field may have been the best ballpark ever for triples: the Pirates led the NL in that category in 31 of the 62 seasons they played there, and in 1912 they would have led the NL even without Wilson. (Owen did hit 24 of his 36 triples at Forbes Field, many of which undoubtedly would have been home runs at other parks.) Taking both year and ballpark into consideration, it's no surprise that the 1912 Pirates still hold the modern record for triples (129).

For the most part, Chief Wilson's 1912 statistics are surprisingly similar to his 1911 numbers—again he hit exactly .300, and his 11 home runs were only one fewer than the previous season's dozen. The big difference was that his doubles dropped from 34 to 19, while his triples skyrocketed from 12 to 36. Wilson wasn't feasting on the lesser pitchers, either; his 1912 triple victims included Christy Mathewson, Pete Alexander, Mordecai

Brown, Rube Marquard, and Ed Reulbach. The triples came in streaks. Wilson had 11 by the end of May and then played 14 games without one. Beginning on June 17, he hit triples in five straight games. Wilson hit his 33rd in the 118th game, a pace that would have led to 43. He then went into a triple slump, hitting only three in the last 34 games. "Wilson attempted to triple, but tapped the pellet a trifle too hard and it floated over the right-field wall," wrote the *Pittsburgh Post* on September 14.

In the ninth inning of the Pirates' final game, Owen was thrown out at home trying to leg out an inside-the-park grand slam. Instead he settled for his 36th triple, shattering the previous major league mark of 31 set by Dave Orr in 1886 and tied by Heinie Reitz in 1894. (The minor league record is 32, set by Jack Cross in 1925.) Surprisingly, the new mark received little attention in the press. The reason, according to a 1913 article by Ernest Lanigan, was that a typo in the record book had Napoleon Lajoie listed with 43 triples instead of the 11 he actually hit in 1903. Lanigan also noted that Joe Jackson similarly received no credit for establishing a new American League record in 1913 with 26 (Sam Crawford tied the AL mark two years later).

From that point onward, Owen Wilson's baseball career and life were less spectacular. In 1913 he didn't miss a single game for the third time, but his batting average fell to .266 and his triples plummeted to 14, still good enough to rank fourth in the NL. After the season the Pirates sent him to the St. Louis Cardinals in an eight-player trade. Wilson finished his nine-year major league career with three seasons in St. Louis, the first two of which were solid. In 1914-15 Wilson led all NL outfielders in fielding percentage, and his 12 triples in 1914 placed second in the league, but his hitting skills faded quickly after that. In 1916 the 33-year-old right fielder batted just .239 with a .299 slugging percentage, by far his lowest marks since his rookie year of 1908. At that point Wilson returned briefly to the Texas League, appearing in 16 games for San Antonio in 1917. After retiring from baseball, J. O. Wilson slipped back into oblivion. On February 22, 1954, he died suddenly while working on the ranch where he'd been born 70 years earlier.

MARK ARMOUR

PITTSBURGH

Chas "Babe" Adams

CHARLES BENJAMIN "BABE" ADAMS
RIGHT-HANDED PITCHER 1907, 1909–16, 1918–26

Best remembered for three victories as a rookie that helped the Pittsburgh Pirates win the 1909 World Series, Babe Adams was one of the Deadball Era's greatest control pitchers. His 1.29 walks per nine innings over 17 years in the majors ranks second on the modern list, behind only Deacon Phillippe's 1.25. To put Adams' mark in perspective, the preeminent control pitcher of today, Greg Maddux, based on his numbers after the 2003 season, would have to pitch another 209 consecutive nine-inning games without a single walk to lower his lifetime ratio to the same level.

Charles Benjamin Adams was born on a farm in Tipton, Indiana, on May 18, 1882. Charley was actually born left-handed, but he developed his right hand by throwing stones at tree stumps and rabbits after a childhood accident nearly severed the little finger of his left hand. At age 16 he went to live with Lee Sarver, a farmer in Mt. Moriah, Missouri, a tiny town in the northwest corner of the state. Encouraged by Sarver, Charley pitched for the high school and town teams. A seamstress made red velvet uniforms for him and his catcher; the others on the town team wore overalls. After Adams was beaten badly in a 1904 game against the team from Lamoni, Iowa, Walter Steckman, the opposing shortstop, showed him (in the words of a 1909 newspaper article) "how to grasp the ball for the different twists and to let loose the whirlers which had so mystified the boys." Charley practiced throwing his new curveball against a barn door. The effort paid off when a local umpire, who doubled as a talent scout, recommended him to the team from Parsons, Kansas, of the Missouri Valley League.

It was a long way from the majors, but Charley was so anxious to report for the 1905 season that he arrived in Parsons while the ground was still snow-covered; he helped build the grandstand and painted signs on the outfield fence while waiting for his teammates to arrive. He pitched a one-hit shutout in his first game and went on to win 30 games, prompting the St. Louis Cardinals to purchase his contract. Adams opened 1906 with the big-league club, making his debut on April 18. He started and lost what turned out to be his only outing for St. Louis, going four innings and giving up eight runs to the juggernaut Chicago Cubs. The Cards sent Adams to Louisville of the American Association, which immediately released him to the Western League's Denver Grizzlies. He remained with Denver through 1907, the year he led the Western League in wins (23) and winning percentage (.657). The Pirates purchased Adams' contract for $5,000 at the tail end of that season and pitched him in four games, not enough for him to shake his rookie status. Loaned back to Louisville in 1908, he went 22-12 and walked only 40 in 312 innings.

By that point Adams had been tagged with the nickname "Babe," though its precise origin remains uncertain. According to one story, Denver teammates pinned it on him in 1907 after a woman asking for his autograph told him he had a nice round face like a baby's. But James Skipper, Jr., in his book *Baseball Nicknames*, states that Adams earned the sobriquet during his 1908 Louisville stint because female fans hollered "Oh, you babe!" whenever he took the mound. The dark-featured Adams was popular with the ladies, and many hearts were broken when he married Blanche Wright, his high school sweetheart from Mt. Moriah, shortly before training camp in March 1909.

As a 27-year-old rookie, Adams both started and relieved and helped the Pirates win the pennant by compiling a 12-3 record with a stunning 1.11 ERA. Fred Clarke's decision to start him in Game One of the

World Series against the Detroit Tigers, however, came as a shock. According to legend, NL president John Heydler had seen Washington pitcher Dolly Gray hold Detroit scoreless for 18 innings in a game earlier that season and suggested to Clarke that Adams and Gray were similar in style (ignoring the fact that Babe was a right hander and Gray a lefty!). But Honus Wagner biographers Dennis and Jeanne DeValeria contend that it was simply Adams' extraordinary composure and terrific final two months of the season that led Clarke to his decision. Surviving a ragged first inning, Adams fed the Tigers a steady diet of low curves and pitched a complete-game six-hitter, winning 4-1. In Game Five he was as sharp as he had to be, giving up four runs but striking out eight in a six-hit, 8-4 victory. In the seventh and final game at Detroit's Bennett Park, Adams again yielded just six hits in an 8-0 shutout.

Adams followed up his 1909 heroics with an 18-9 season in 1910 and 20-win seasons in 1911 and 1913, establishing himself as one of the league's best pitchers. Perhaps his greatest performance came on July 17, 1914, against the Giants and Rube Marquard, when he pitched 21 innings, walked none, and still lost a 3-1 decision. The game may have had negative consequences for both pitchers; Marquard lost 22 games that year while Babe's record slipped to 13-16. The following year Adams rebounded to 14-14, but in 1916 he developed a sore shoulder and started off the season with a 2-9 record. On August 3 the Pirates released him to St. Joseph, Missouri, of the Western League. He elected not to report.

When his shoulder gained strength over the winter, Adams reported to St. Joseph and put together a stellar 1917, going 20-13 with a 1.75 ERA and just 34 walks in 308 innings. The team moved to Hutchinson, Kansas, in midseason, providing the added benefit of being close enough to Mt. Moriah to go home between starts. Hutchinson transferred Babe's contract to Kansas City of the American Association for 1918, but players like Adams, who were exempt from the draft because they were over 35, became attractive to major league clubs. Babe rejoined the Pirates and made three late-season appearances.

The Babe Adams of old had returned, his control even better than before his shoulder injury. Despite being the NL's oldest pitcher in 1920, he led the league in shutouts and allowed just 18 walks in 263 innings, the fewest ever for a pitcher with more than 250 innings. Adams remained with the Pirates through August 1926, finally being waived out of the league with a career record of 194-140 and a 2.76 ERA. He dabbled one more season in the minors, then returned to his farm in Mt. Moriah in 1928.

In the 1930s Adams became a newspaper reporter, covering local sports and serving as a war correspondent in the Pacific during World War II and in Korea until age 70. In 1958 he and Blanche moved to Silver Spring, Maryland, to live with a daughter. Babe died there at 86 after a long illness. His ashes were returned for burial in Mt. Moriah, where the citizens have erected a black marble monument in his honor on the town square. In 2002 the Missouri General Assembly renamed U.S. 136 the Babe Adams Highway.

BRIAN STEVENS

PITTSBURGH

John Bernard "Dots" Miller
Infielder 1909–13

After playing regularly for the Pittsburgh Pirates at second base for three seasons and first base for two, Dots Miller became the quintessential utility man, spending time at every infield position for the Cardinals and Phillies during the last seven years of his 12-year career. In 1915 Ring Lardner picked the lifetime .263 hitter as the utility man on his personal all-star team. "When you're picking utility guys, you want fellas that does that for a livin'," wrote Lardner. "The best utility infielder I know anything about is Jack Miller. You can't call him a regular. He's in the game every day, but he don't never play the same place two days in succession. They're a'scared he might get thinkin' the game was monot'nous and quit."

John Bernard Miller was born in New York City on September 9, 1886, the fourth of eight children of Josephine and John Mueller, a German immigrant who anglicized the family name upon arrival in America. Shortly after John's birth, the Millers moved to Kearny, New Jersey, a Newark suburb made up mostly of Scotch and Irish immigrants who worked in the thread mills. The first record of Miller playing baseball is with a team from Caldwell, but it wasn't until he began playing shortstop for Kearny's Parkway Athletic Club that he developed into a serious prospect. In 1908 he caught the eye of Larry Rutlon, the manager of Easton in the Atlantic League. Miller abandoned his day job as a stained-glass installer and signed his first professional contract, playing well enough with Easton to garner the interest of Pittsburgh. The Pirates purchased his contract and sent him to the Ohio-Pennsylvania League with McKeesport, just outside Pittsburgh.

Playing shortstop as a property of the Pirates could be seen as a dead-end proposition in the Deadball Era, but Miller performed well enough to be brought up for a workout with the big club in September 1908. When Honus Wagner was late reporting to spring training in 1909, Miller received his first extended opportunity to display his talents. The 22-year-old shortstop made all the plays, and soon the other Pirates began calling him "Hans No. 2." When Hans No. 1 finally arrived in camp, a reporter asked him, "Who's the new kid?" Wagner replied, "That's Miller." The reporter, misunderstanding, listed the young infielder as Dots Miller. Henceforth John Bernard Miller, sometimes known as Jack, sometimes Barney, was now and forever known as "Dots." In an era of colorful nicknames, Miller had one of the best.

Despite initially sharing the same position, Miller and Wagner also shared a German heritage and quickly became friends, with Honus often joining Dots on his visits home to Kearny. Soon they were side by side on the field as well. A few games into 1909 Miller replaced Ed Abbaticchio as the regular second baseman. Typically batting fifth or sixth in the lineup, the rookie drove in 87 runs, third best in the NL, while batting a respectable .279. Miller's defense was just as impressive; he led all second basemen in assists, total chances, and fielding percentage. New York Giants manager John McGraw told reporters, off the record, that Pittsburgh's double-play combination was the best in the league. In that fall's World Series, Dots batted .250 and drove in four runs, two of them in the decisive Game Seven victory over the Tigers.

In 1910 Miller fell prey to the sophomore jinx, his batting average dropping to .227 as he drove in just 48 runs. Despite his poor on-field performance, Dots' personal life flourished. Along with his brother-in-law and business partner, Joe Gunderman, Miller opened the Parkway Tavern in Kearny, an impressive establishment featuring a bar, catering hall, card and billiard room, bowling alley in the basement, and apartments on the second and third floors. Born and raised in one of those apartments was Dots' nephew Jack Tighe, who went on to manage the Detroit Tigers in 1957-58.

The following year Miller returned to his rookie form with 78 RBI and a career-best 82 runs scored, but the Pirates once again failed to challenge for the pennant. Much of the team's failure was blamed on an anemic offense, particularly a lack of production from the first-base position. To fill the breach in 1912 the club turned to Miller, whose soft hands helped him dig out low throws and whose 5'11½" figure presented infielders with an ample target. Playing 147 games at first base, Miller responded with another solid offensive campaign, batting .275 with 87 RBI. In 1913 he was even better, ranking second in the NL in triples (20) and fourth in RBI (90) and total bases (243). But while Miller thrived, the Pirates floundered. Their 78 wins that season marked their lowest total since 1899.

In December 1913 Barney Dreyfuss sent Miller to the St. Louis Cardinals in the trade for Mike Mowrey and Ed Konetchy. As it turned out, Miller rivaled Konetchy as the most valuable player in the deal, averaging 149 games and 544 at-bats for the Cardinals over the next four seasons. Some have speculated that his trade may have been prompted by an off-season scandal: according to press accounts, Dots became involved with a married woman and was implicated in the ensuing divorce suit. His indiscretion scared away neither the Cardinals nor Pearl Thoroman, whom Dots married later that year. Helping St. Louis improve on its 1913 win total by 30 games, Miller quickly won over both the fans and his new teammates. In addition to batting .290 with 88 RBI, he displayed the defensive versatility that soon became his trademark, splitting time between first, second, and shortstop.

Over the next few seasons Dots played every infield position, and eventually he was named captain of the Cardinals. After the 1917 season manager Miller Huggins left to join the Yankees, and Dots was rumored as his likely replacement. Cardinal president Branch Rickey chose Jack Hendricks, however, and Miller ended up voluntarily enlisting in the Marines, for whom he served overseas in 1918. Decorated for marksmanship, Dots returned from active duty in time to rejoin the Cardinals in 1919. After batting just .231

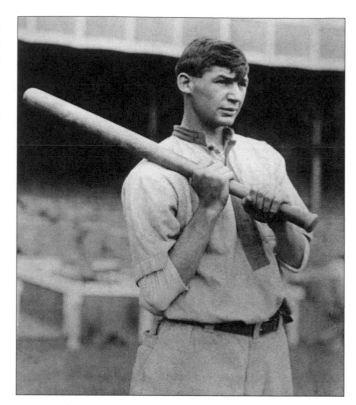

that season, Miller was sold to Philadelphia, where he spent his last two years as a player, befriending a talkative outfielder named Casey Stengel. Decades later, the Old Professor recounted tales of Uncle Dots in his heyday to Jack Tighe when he was managing the Tigers. Dots finished his playing career in style with the 1921 Phillies, batting .297.

After the season Miller accepted a job managing the San Francisco Seals of the Pacific Coast League. In his first year as manager he guided the Seals to the 1922 PCL pennant. Only in his mid-30s, Miller appeared to have a bright future. His managerial career was cut short partway through the 1923 season, however, when he was diagnosed with pulmonary tuberculosis. Dots returned immediately to Kearny. After one week at home, he was sent to the tuberculosis retreat at Saranac Lake, New York, in the Adirondack Mountains. The mountain air, theorized the doctors of the day, could aid in what was termed the "cold weather cure." In reality there was no cure for tuberculosis in 1923. With his family at his bedside, Dots Miller passed away on September 5, 1923, four days shy of his 37th birthday. His body was returned to Kearny, where he was buried in North Arlington Cemetery.

TOMMY CARRELLA

PITTSBURGH

ROBERT MATTHEW BYRNE
THIRD BASEMAN 1909–13

Standing a tad under 5'8" and weighing just 145 lbs., Bobby Byrne was the Pirates third baseman toward the end of Pittsburgh's reign as one of the National League's top teams. "Byrne is always a dangerous man for the reason that at all times he is cool, nervy and smart," wrote Alfred Spink. Perhaps his actions in a game on June 10, 1911, best illustrate the type of player he was. With Byrne at first and Fred Clarke at third, the two Pirates pulled off a double steal, with Byrne sneaking to third as Brooklyn catcher Bill Bergen argued the call at home with umpire Bill Klem. After Dots Miller walked, he and Byrne pulled off another double steal, giving the hustling leadoff hitter steals of second, third, and home in the same inning.

The fifth and last child of John and Ellen Byrne, Robert Matthew Byrne was born on New Year's Eve, 1884, in the rough Kerry Patch section of St. Louis, a neighborhood that also produced "Scrappy Bill" Joyce, "Rowdy Jack" O'Connor, and Patsy Tebeau. Though Bobby was of Scottish ancestry, both his parents were born in Ireland; John came to America at age seven in 1851, and Ellen immigrated at age 13 in 1864. As a youngster Bobby took to soccer first and was good enough to be selected to an All-St. Louis team. He played his first serious baseball with a local semipro club, the St. Louis Arcades, before embarking on a professional career as a shortstop with Ft. Scott of the Missouri Valley League in 1904.

Making stops at Springfield (Central League) in 1905 and Shreveport (Southern Association) in 1906, Byrne finally reached the majors in 1907 with his hometown Cardinals. Moved to third base by manager John McCloskey, the right-handed hitter batted .256 in 149 games during his rookie year, but the following season he slumped to .191. Byrne's average stood at .214 when the Redbirds finally gave up on him, shipping him to Pittsburgh on August 19, 1909, for cash and infielders Alan Storke and Jap Barbeau. A Pittsburgh newspaper reported that Byrne was "not a consistent hitter, but a great base runner and a fine third baseman." His acquisition proved critical down the stretch; inserted into the leadoff spot, he compiled an on-base percentage of .387 (well above his career mark of .324) and made just two errors in 46 games as the Pirates captured the pennant.

During the 1909 World Series, Byrne became involved in the biggest controversy of his career. After being hit in the shoulder by a pitch to lead off Game Seven, he reached second on a sacrifice but was thrown out trying to steal third. "I broke my ankle sliding into George Moriarty at third base and spiked the Tiger third sacker so badly that eight stitches were required to close a gash in his knee," Byrne recalled. "It all happened in the first inning and probably was the only time in Series history that the regular third sackers of the rival clubs were carried off the field on stretchers." (Byrne's recollection wasn't quite accurate; while he did indeed have to be carried off the field by teammates, Moriarty remained in the game long enough to double in the second inning before giving way to a pinch-runner.) Contemporary coverage of the incident wasn't kind to the Pirate cornerman. "Byrne and Moriarty were injured when Bobby made a needless attempt to steal third in a game in which Wild Bill Donovan, the Detroit pitcher, showed nothing," wrote one reporter. The Pirates won without Byrne, who received a big ovation when he showed up on crutches for the next day's victory celebration at Forbes Field.

Though the defending world champions slumped to third place in 1910, Byrne showed that he was fully recovered from his injury by putting together his greatest season, posting career highs in batting average (.296), runs (101), and stolen bases (36). Feasting on pitchers like never before, he led the NL in doubles (43) and tied teammate Honus Wagner for the lead in hits (178), an accomplishment he considered his greatest as a ballplayer. "That was quite a feat in those days," he boasted, "especially when you consider that we didn't have a shiny rock to hit against every time we came to the plate. The ball was usually well discolored." Byrne also might have bragged about his performance on August 25, in a game at Brooklyn, when he doubled, stole third, and then stole home, becoming the first NL player of the 20th century to steal home in an extra-inning game.

Despite going 5-for-5 and collecting five RBI in a 14-0 pasting of the Reds on Opening Day 1911, Byrne batted just .259 for the season, though he did hit a career-high 17 triples. In 1912 he bounced back to hit .288 with 31 doubles, 11 triples, and a career-high three home runs. During the off-season, a few days after Thanksgiving, Byrne was driving near his home when his car ran into a telegraph pole. Accounts of the accident called his survival "a miracle." Bobby thought

he'd escaped with merely a few scratches, but the next week he began experiencing a "jerking pain" on his right side. His doctors confined him to bed, his back wrapped in gauze to prevent further injury. Not long after he recovered from that brush with death, his mortality was tested a second time when he was struck behind the left ear by a Joe Wood fastball in a March exhibition game in Hot Springs, Arkansas. Knocked unconscious, Bobby remained in serious condition overnight but was back in action one week later.

Though Byrne batted .270 in 113 games for Pittsburgh in 1913, reporters speculated that the lingering effects of his beaning were a factor when the Pirates traded him and pitcher Howie Camnitz to Philadelphia in August for outfielder Cozy Dolan and cash. Moving to second base in 1914 to allow Hans Lobert to remain at third, Byrne batted .272 in what turned out to be his last full season as a regular. The following year new Phillies manager Pat Moran shifted him back to third, but the 30-year-old veteran broke his hand and was replaced by rookie Milt Stock. Byrne made just one pinch-hit appearance in that year's World Series. The next two years he played in a combined 61 games for the Phillies. In September 1917 the White Sox picked him up on waivers and went on to the World Series without him—Bobby batted just once for Chicago.

His playing days over at age 32, Byrne spent three years away from the game before becoming a minor league manager in 1921. After stints at Miami (Oklahoma) and Saginaw, he returned to St. Louis in 1923, working in several city positions and later for the U.S. government and the Scullin Steel Company. Bobby also owned a bowling alley and once tossed 19 consecutive strikes, including a 300 game. He and his wife, Laura, had two sons, Bobby Jr. and Bernie, both of whom played minor league baseball and became fighter pilots during World War II. After Laura passed away in 1945, Bobby spent much of his time playing golf. In his later years, his prized possession was a certificate stating that he shot a 74 at the Lakeside Golf Club in Missouri—at the age of 74. Bobby Byrne died of cancer on his 80th birthday, December 31, 1964, at the Caley Nursing Home in Wayne, Pennsylvania. He was buried in Calvary Cemetery in St. Louis.

IRV GOLDFARB

PITTSBURGH

MAXIMILLIAN GEORGE CARNARIUS (CAREY)
OUTFIELDER 1910–26

Considered the Tris Speaker of the National League for his fleet-footed base running and defensive brilliance in the outfield, Max Carey was a switch-hitting leadoff man who used his phenomenal speed and ability to hit to all fields to compile a lifetime batting average of .285. In addition to leading the NL in walks and triples twice, Carey led the league in steals 10 times from 1913 to 1925, and his 738 career stolen bases stood as the modern NL record until 1974, when it was broken by Lou Brock. He remains Pittsburgh's all-time leader in steals and ranks among the team's all-time leaders in virtually every offensive category except home runs and RBI. Carey's career represents a bridge from the bunt-and-speed game of the Deadball Era to the lug-and-slug game of the 1920s; he played regularly through 1928, making him one of the last active Deadballers.

The son of Frank and Catherine (Astroth) Carnarius, Maximillian George Carnarius made his first slide on January 11, 1890, in Terre Haute, Indiana. In Latin Max's surname means "handler of meat," but his father, who went by his middle name of August, had forgone the family's traditional occupation for a career as a soldier and swimming teacher in his native Prussia. After the Franco-Prussian war, August immigrated to the United States, where he became a contractor. Desiring a disciplined education for his son, he enrolled 13-year-old Max in a six-year pre-ministerial program at Concordia College in Ft. Wayne. The demanding program included some military training and a lot of physical education, and young Max excelled at swimming and track.

After graduating in 1909, he was sent to Concordia Seminary in St. Louis to fulfill his parents' dream and become a Lutheran minister.

Baseball got in the way during the summer of 1909, when Max attended a Central League game back home in Terre Haute. The opposing team, South Bend, had recently sold its shortstop to a higher league, and after the game Carnarius tracked down the manager, Aggie Grant, and asked if he could be the team's new shortstop, showing him a track medal as proof of his athleticism. Though baseball wasn't his best sport, Max had played the infield for Concordia College and was noted for his speed and agility. Needing to fill the hole in his lineup, Grant told the 19-year-old Carnarius to report the next day, and Max stayed in the lineup for the rest of the season despite hitting .158 with 24 errors in 48 games. At least he earned a new name out of the experience. Not wanting to risk his amateur standing by using his real name, Max asked Grant for a new name. The manager told the umpire that his new shortstop was named "Max Carney or Carey or something like that," and the umpire recorded it as "Max Carey," the name that Max went by for the rest of his life.

Carey reported to the seminary in the fall, but the damage to his parents' dream had been done. Returning to South Bend the following spring, Max asked for another chance and was told by the team's new manager that he already had a shortstop, but there was an opening in left field. In his second year in the Central League, Carey mostly played the outfield and hit .294 with 36 stolen bases, causing league president

NL in bases in balls in 1918 and 1922 and walked almost twice as much as he struck out, Carey frequently found ways to get on base, including a memorable 1922 afternoon in which he reached base nine times in one extra-inning marathon. He also had nine five-hit games in his career.

As for his defense, Carey covered both left and center field for the Pirates and excelled at both positions. Early in his career he was called "Scoops" in homage to the turn-of-the-century first baseman Scoops Carey, who was a Pittsburgh native, but some claimed that the nickname came from his ability to charge sinking liners and scoop them into his glove before they hit the grass. Using flip-down sunglasses several years before Harry Hooper made them popular, Carey recorded 6,363 putouts, an all-time NL record that it took Willie Mays to break. He retired holding a major league record of six seasons with over 450 chances accepted and led all NL outfielders in putouts nine times, range factor seven times, double plays five times, and assists four times. His 339 outfield assists remain the most for any NL outfielder since 1900. Carey also led the NL in outfield errors four times, running into miscues on plays that other outfielders wouldn't have attempted.

Max Carey achieved his greatest fame on the base paths, however. "Stealing bases is the art of picking up little things, like a spitball pitcher who never threw to first if he was going to throw a spitter to the plate," he explained. With the aid of a pair of sliding pads that his mother had sewn for him (he later patented the design, and it was still in use many years after his career ended), the former Concordia College track star led the NL in stolen bases for the first time with 61 in 1913, then repeated the achievement each year from 1915 to 1918 with totals of 36, 63, 46, and 58. After his injury-plagued 1919 season, Carey won five more titles in the six years 1920-25, compiling totals of 52, 51, 51, 49, and 46. Following Wagner's advice, Max kept his legs in condition by running regularly during the off-season. In an era when the average base stealer was thrown out roughly half the time, the 32-year-old Carey was successful on 31 consecutive attempts in 1922, ending the season with an eye-popping 96% success rate.

After watching Ty Cobb hit in a 1924 spring training game, Carey remodeled his batting stance and went on to have the most productive offensive season of his career in 1925, batting .343 as the Pirates won the

Frank Carson to recommend him to the Pittsburgh Pirates. In the waning days of the 1910 season, Max reported to Pittsburgh and went out to shortstop for infield practice in hopes of returning to his favorite position. According to a story that he loved to tell in later years, he informed Honus Wagner that he was here to be the team's new shortstop. Asking Carey to wait a minute while he went to speak with the manager, Wagner supposedly suggested to Fred Clarke that he retire from playing and let the brash rookie play his left-field position.

Carey did replace Clarke in the lineup for the final two games of 1910, picking up three hits and a couple of walks, and he remained a fixture in the Pittsburgh outfield for the next 16 seasons. At the plate he enjoyed five full seasons of averages over .300 and was on his way to a sixth when stopped by an injury in 1919; that campaign was the only one between 1911 and 1928 in which he played less than 108 games. Though he was by no means a power hitter, the 5'11½", 170 lb. Carey used his speed in roomy Forbes Field to lead the league in triples in 1914 and 1923 and reach double figures in that category nine times. A patient hitter who led the

National League pennant. He displayed all of his talents in the World Series as Pittsburgh faced off against the defending champion Washington Senators. Facing the Pirates in the decisive Game Seven was legendary speedballer Walter Johnson, who'd already won two games in the Series, but the shrewd Carey had done his homework. Acting on a tip from Detroit Tigers outfielder Bobby Veach, Max knew that whenever Johnson shortened his delivery, he tipped off his much less effective curveball. Despite playing with broken ribs, he sat on Johnson's curves and rapped out four hits, including three doubles, as the Pirates rallied to a 9-7 victory. For the Series Carey batted .458 with 11 hits and three stolen bases and undoubtedly would have been the Series MVP had such an award existed. Instead he settled for a new $16,000 contract, making him the highest-paid player on the Pirates.

The 1925 World Series proved to be Max Carey's swan song as an active player in Pittsburgh. Former manager Fred Clarke, who'd given his spot in the outfield to Carey back in 1910, was now only a stockholder in the club, but he enjoyed sitting on the bench as an "assistant" to manager Bill McKechnie, frequently second-guessing his decisions. Clarke's meddling led to dissension in the clubhouse that boiled over after a doubleheader loss in Boston on August 7, 1926. As the captain of the Pirates, Carey (along with fellow veterans Carson Bigbee and Babe Adams) called a team meeting and attempted to pass a resolution banning Clarke from the bench, but owner Barney Dreyfuss foiled Carey's uprising (which became known as the "great Pirate mutiny") by suspending and then waiving the star outfielder. Claimed by the Brooklyn Robins, he played two more seasons before retiring in 1929, the year he lost over $100,000 in the stock market crash.

In 1930 the Pirates healed old wounds by welcoming Carey back as a coach, and the next year he was announced as the successor to longtime Brooklyn manager Wilbert Robinson. One writer suggested that the nickname of Robins be replaced with "Canaries" in honor of the new manager, but the idea didn't catch on and the team reverted to its early nickname of

Carey poses for a publicity shot with players from the All-American Girls Professional Baseball League. He told anyone who'd listen that the quality of play in the AAGPBL was as high as any in professional baseball.

"Dodgers." Promising that the Dodgers would take a more "scientific" approach to the game, Carey attempted to introduce his "inside baseball" style of play, with a heavier emphasis on bunting and speed. In 1932 his system resulted in a surprising third-place finish, but the bubble burst in 1933 as age and questionable personnel moves saw the team fall to sixth. Carey spoke confidently of the coming year at spring training in Miami, but before the 1934 season opened, coach Casey Stengel replaced him as manager. Carey was bitter over his firing and later remarked that he was the first manager to be fired by the newspapers.

Retiring to his home in Miami Beach, where he'd spent off-seasons since 1920, Max and his wife, Aurelia (Behrens) Carey, raised two sons, both of whom became chemical engineers. Max consistently found jobs in baseball. He co-owned a baseball school in Ft. Lauderdale, toured Japan with an amateur team, and served as manager and general manager of the Miami franchise in the Florida East Coast League in 1940-42. In 1944 Carey managed the Milwaukee club in the All-American Girls Professional Baseball League. He took a friendly but firm approach with his players, stressing the fundamentals of his stealing and bunting techniques, and won the pennant in his first season. After that Max served as the league's president through 1950, working tirelessly to improve the level of play and promote public interest in the league. In 1946 the Racine Belles won the league championship series with a dramatic hit in the 10th inning of the final game. "I'll never forget it," Max said afterwards. "Barring none, even in the majors, it's the best game I've ever seen." Carey often invited former teammates and opponents to see his female teams play, with the intention of surprising them with their high level of ability.

During the 1950s Carey again managed in the minor leagues for a couple of seasons and spent much of his time writing, working on a self-published book on baseball strategy and tactics and authoring several magazine articles. In an article that appeared in *Esquire* in 1955 he chose his 20 greatest players of all time, ranking old teammate Honus Wagner first and listing Babe Ruth a mere 18th. Max also served as a dog-racing steward at the Miami Beach Kennel Club and was general manager of dog tracks in Key West and Colorado. After narrowly missing out on election for several years, Carey earned his highest honor when he was voted into the National Baseball Hall of Fame in 1961. The good news of his election came on the same day that he learned that he was losing his job as chief judge of the Miami dog-racing authority due to a change in state government. Undaunted, the 71-year-old Carey made a rousing speech at his induction on July 24, thanking the staff of *The Sporting News* for lobbying for his election and calling on the major leagues to expand into Florida.

Max Carey remained active in his final years, making the circuit of old-timers games and post-season banquets. He remained much in demand for his outspoken opinions and knack for story and joke telling. Carey gave a number of interviews to newspapers and frequently wrote to Hall of Fame historian Lee Allen to help with various research projects. He enjoyed corresponding with fans about the modern game and fielded a steady stream of autograph requests. After the 1959 Cuban Revolution, Carey became heavily involved in programs to assist the refugees who flooded Florida's shores, even setting up special baseball leagues for refugee children. Another of his pet issues was the lack of a pension fund for old-time players. After serving as a pallbearer for fellow Miami resident Jimmie Foxx, Carey bemoaned a system that paid modern players exorbitant salaries while allowing Foxx to live out his final years in poverty. He even dedicated some time to politics, hitting the campaign trail in 1968 in support of Richard Nixon. After suffering for years from heart-related ailments, Max Carey died of a heart attack in Miami Beach on May 30, 1976.

JOHN BENNETT

PITTSBURGH

ARLEY WILBUR COOPER
LEFT-HANDED PITCHER 1912–24

Even though his 13 years in the Steel City fell between the world championship seasons of 1909 and 1925, Wilbur Cooper was arguably the greatest pitcher in Pittsburgh Pirates history. Cooper holds the franchise's modern records for victories (202) and complete games (263). An exceptional fielder, hitter (his lifetime batting average was .239), and control pitcher who allowed only 2.2 walks per nine innings over the course of his 15-year career, Cooper was slim in stature and threw his repertoire of a fastball, curve, and changeup with a fluid delivery, causing many to mistake his stylish manner for indifference. "Nothing could be farther from the truth," wrote one reporter. "The Pirate southpaw works as hard as any other hurler, but his grace and ease of motion mislead some of the rooters."

The fifth oldest of seven children (all boys, one of whom died in infancy) of Maggie (Lough) and Jesse Cooper, Arley Wilbur Cooper was born in Bearsville, West Virginia, on February 24, 1892, 18 years to the day after the birth of his future teammate Honus Wagner. In Wilbur's youth the Cooper family moved north to Waterford, Ohio, where Jesse established a farm and worked as a schoolteacher. During his childhood Wilbur attended school and helped out on the farm, but it wasn't long before his strong left arm steered him toward a different line of work. The 19-year-old pitcher made his debut in professional baseball in the Ohio State League in 1911 with the Marion club, which was owned by newspaper publisher and future U.S. President Warren Harding. Legend has it that Harding was the person who recommended Wilbur to the Pirates, but the young southpaw made a stop between Marion and the majors, pitching for Columbus of the American Association at the tail end of 1911 and for most of 1912.

Following a 16-9 year at Columbus in 1912, Cooper received a late-season trial with Pittsburgh, making his major league debut on August 29. Eight days later he made his first start, blanking the St. Louis Cardinals, 8-0, a performance that was made all the more memorable by Honus Wagner's stellar defensive play. At the end of one inning, the rookie presciently remarked, "Mr. Wagner, if you field like that behind me, I'll stay up here a long time." Cooper wasn't always so gracious. An intense competitor, he often became visibly upset when teammates made errors, which may have been another reason (along with his youth) that observers called him the "Baby Pitcher." In any event, Cooper was nothing short of sensational in his six-game tryout, running his record to 3-0 with two shutouts and a 1.66 ERA.

On a team that was rapidly sinking in the standings, Cooper's development into a mature pitcher offered a glimmer of hope for the future. Pitching mostly out of the bullpen in 1913, he showed enough promise to warrant an offer of a two-year contract at $5,000 per season from the Federal League. Cooper turned down the Feds and turned up his performance, emerging in 1914 as the ace of the Pirates by winning 16 games and posting a 2.13 ERA in 266⅓ innings. After an inexplicably dreadful 1915 campaign—5-16 with an ERA nearly two-thirds of a run higher than the National League average—Wilbur bounced back the following year to post a career-best 1.87 ERA. Pitching for a sixth-place club in a nearly deserted Forbes Field, he received only enough offense from his teammates to compile 12 wins, while the Pirates were shut out in seven of his 11 losses. Cooper confidently referred to himself as a "star player," and his top salary of $12,500 reflected his value to the club.

As Cooper developed, he increasingly relied on pin-point control: from 1917 to 1924 he finished in the NL's Top 10 five times in fewest walks per nine innings. A fast worker, he was often in mid-windup when he received the signal from Walter Schmidt, his catcher for nine years. Wilbur and fellow quick pitcher Pete Alexander once hooked up for a game in Forbes Field that lasted only 59 minutes. As the Pirates slowly built themselves back into contenders, they leaned heavily on Cooper to consume innings and protect their otherwise mediocre staff. In 1918-22 he finished no worse than third in the NL in innings pitched each season, leading the league in 1921. During that span he led the NL in complete games twice while finishing in the top five in ERA three times. In three of those five seasons Cooper was a 20-game winner, and in the other two he finished with 19 victories. In 1919 the New York Giants offered $75,000 for him; the Pirates turned them down.

Cooper reached the 20-victory mark for the fourth and final time in 1924, leading the NL with four shutouts and helping the Pirates to a 90-63 record, just three games off the pace, the closest the club had come to a pennant in more than a decade. Pittsburgh won the World Series the next season, but the man who helped bridge the rebuilding gap for the franchise wasn't there to see it happen. On October 27, 1924, the Pirates traded Cooper, Rabbit Maranville, and Charley Grimm to the Chicago Cubs for Vic Aldridge, George Grantham, and Al Niehaus. It was one of the blockbuster deals of the 1920s, and it was a devastating blow for the 32-year-old Cooper. "I do not want to see again in baseball a spectacle like that of the lonely, homesick Cooper trying to pitch a game against his longtime teammates at Wrigley Field in Chicago," wrote longtime Pittsburgh baseball reporter Charles Doyle in 1925.

While the Pirates were winning their first pennant in 16 years, the Cubs fell to last place and Cooper fell with them, winning only 12 games and raising his ERA a full run to 4.28. After he got off to a similarly mediocre start in 1926, the Cubs sold him to Detroit for the waiver price in June. In 13⅔ innings with the Tigers, Cooper managed to lose four games and post an 11.20 ERA before drawing his release. Though his major league career was over, he continued to pitch in the minors through 1930 with Toledo of the American Association, Oakland of the Pacific Coast League, and Shreveport and San Antonio of the Texas League. Later Cooper managed McKeesport and Greensburg in the Pennsylvania State League and Jeannette in the Eastern League before retiring from baseball.

Married with three daughters, Wilbur Cooper spent his later years supporting youth baseball and working in real estate in the Pittsburgh area before moving to Southern California in 1947. In his lifetime he was named as the left-handed pitcher on the *Pittsburgh Press* All-Time Pirates Team in 1934, elected to the City of Pittsburgh Sports Hall of Fame in 1959, and recognized as a Sports Great in 1963 by the West Virginia Centennial Commission. In 1969 Cooper was voted the greatest pitcher in Pirates history in a Pittsburgh poll conducted to commemorate the 100-year anniversary of professional baseball.

Despite a lifetime record of 216-178 and a 2.89 ERA, Cooper drew little support for induction into the National Baseball Hall of Fame, receiving no more than 11 votes from the baseball writers during his period of eligibility. He remains one of only two modern NL pitchers with more than 3,000 innings and an ERA under 3.00 who are not enshrined at Cooperstown (the other is Red Ames). In one of his last letters he wrote: "I would die a happy man if they voted me into the Hall of Fame. But, if they don't, I will understand." Cooper died in Encino, California, on August 7, 1973, after suffering a heart attack.

DAVID CICOTELLO

PHILADELPHIA

This photo from the 1915 World Series shows Baker Bowl's right field fence, which accounted in large part for the Phillies' disproportionate number of Deadball Era home runs.

Some consider the turn-of-the-century Phillies to be the greatest of all Phillies teams, even greater than the club's subsequent NL champions. Despite finishing third in 1900, Philadelphia's extraordinary talent made it an inviting target for American League raiders. The Phils still placed second in 1901 after losing Nap Lajoie and pitchers Bill Bernhard, Chick Fraser, and Wiley Piatt to the Philadelphia Athletics. The roof didn't fall in until 1902, when practically every worthwhile player—hard-hitting outfielders Ed Delahanty and Elmer Flick, infielders Harry Wolverton and Monte Cross, and pitchers Al Orth, Red Donahue, and Bill Duggleby—cast his lot with the AL. While the A's won the first of

their six Deadball Era pennants, the Phils plunged to a dismal seventh, placing them at a severe disadvantage in the battle for the Quaker City's baseball patronage.

The 1905 Phillies gained 31 victories over the previous season, returning to the first division after a three-year absence. The team now featured new mainstays in catcher Red Dooin, infielders Kitty Bransfield and Mickey Doolan, and outfielders Sherry Magee and John Titus. Over the course of eight seasons, these Quakers finished consistently in the middle of the pack—as high as third once (1907); as low as fifth twice (1909 and 1912); and five times in their conventional fourth slot.

WINNING PERCENTAGE 1901–1919

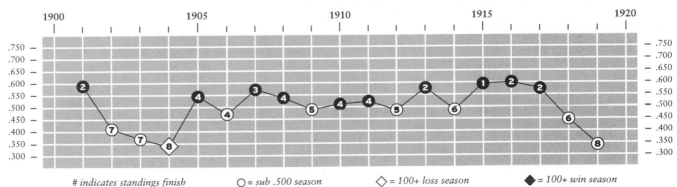

 # indicates standings finish   ○ = sub .500 season   ◇ = 100+ loss season   ◆ = 100+ win season

The Phils finally broke out of their rut in 1913, finishing second while pounding out 73 round-trippers, a Deadball Era–record. That year, the first under William Baker's ownership, two newcomers, Gavy Cravath and Fred Luderus, finished one-two in the NL home run race, with 19 and 18 respectively. Taking aim at Baker Bowl's 40'-tall fence in right field, only 272' from home plate, the Phillies led the NL in homers four times from 1911 to 1915.

Philadelphia plummeted to sixth in 1914 after losing Doolan, Otto Knabe, Tom Seaton, and Ad Brennan to the Federal League. The sudden decline prompted Baker to elevate Pat Moran from coach to manager. With Cravath blasting 24 homers, Dave Bancroft plugging the hole at shortstop, and Pete Alexander winning 31 games, the Phillies won their first-ever pennant in their first year under Moran, albeit with a .592 winning percentage, the lowest to capture the NL flag to that time. Philadelphia lost the 1915 World Series in five games to the Boston Red Sox, with all four defeats coming by a single run. The Phils just missed out in 1916-17 as well, placing second in both seasons.

With a pennant and three runners-up in five years, the Phillies had just passed through their most successful era until the late 1970s. In 1919 they plunged to the bottom of the NL, their first tailender since 1904 but the forerunner of numerous eighth-place finishes in the half-century to follow.

ALL-ERA TEAM

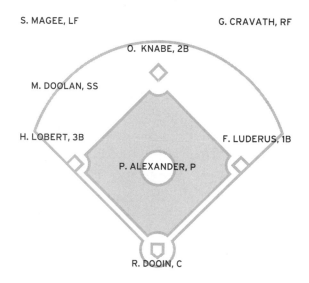

R. THOMAS, CF

S. MAGEE, LF   G. CRAVATH, RF

O. KNABE, 2B

M. DOOLAN, SS

H. LOBERT, 3B   F. LUDERUS, 1B

P. ALEXANDER, P

R. DOOIN, C

TEAM LEADERS
1901–1919

BATTING

GAMES
S. Magee 1521
M. Doolan 1302
F. Luderus 1295

RUNS
S. Magee 898
R. Thomas 654
J. Titus 649

HITS
S. Magee 1647
F. Luderus 1317
J. Titus 1209

RBI
S. Magee 886
G. Cravath 665
F. Luderus 626

DOUBLES
S. Magee 337
F. Luderus 247
G. Cravath 217

TRIPLES
S. Magee 127
G. Cravath 72
J. Titus 64

HOME RUNS
G. Cravath 116
F. Luderus 83
S. Magee 75

STOLEN BASES
S. Magee 387
D. Paskert 149
R. Thomas 149

BATTING AVERAGE
S. Magee 299
H. Wolverton 295
H. Lobert 293

PITCHING

GAMES
P. Alexander 329
T. Sparks 223
B. Duggleby 220

WINS
P. Alexander 190
T. Sparks 95
B. Duggleby 86

LOSSES
B. Duggleby 96
T. Sparks 94
P. Alexander 88

INNINGS
P. Alexander 2492
T. Sparks 1690
B. Duggleby 1621

STRIKEOUTS
P. Alexander 1403
E. Moore 651
T. Sparks 586

WALKS
P. Alexander 555
E. Moore 518
E. Rixey 410

SHUTOUTS
P. Alexander 61
T. Sparks 18
G. McQuillan 17

ERA
P. Alexander 2.12
T. Sparks 2.44
E. Moore 2.63

The 1916 Phillies, whose .595 winning percentage was the franchise's best of the Deadball Era
—three points better than the percentage of the previous season's pennant winners.

TYPICAL LINEUPS 1901–1919

1901

1. R. Thomas, CF
2. H. Wolverton, 3B
3. E. Flick, RF
4. E. Delahanty, LF
5. E. McFarland, C
6. H. Jennings, 1B
7. B. Hallman, 2B
8. M. Cross, SS

1902

1. R. Thomas, CF
2. G. Browne, LF
3. S. Barry, RF
4. K. Douglass
   H. Jennings, 1B
5. R. Dooin, C
6. R. Hulswitt, SS
7. B. Hallman, 3B
8. P. Childs, 2B

1903

1. R. Thomas, CF
2. K. Gleason, 2B
3. H. Wolverton, 3B
4. B. Keister, RF
5. S. Barry, LF
6. K. Douglass, 1B
7. R. Hulswitt, SS
8. F. Roth
   R. Dooin, C

1904

1. R. Thomas, CF
2. K. Gleason, 2B
3. H. Wolverton, 3B
4. S. Magee, RF
5. J. Doyle
   J. Lush, 1B
6. J. Titus, LF
7. R. Hulswitt, SS
8. R. Dooin, C

1905

1. R. Thomas, CF
2. K. Gleason, 2B
3. E. Courtney, 3B
4. J. Titus, RF
5. S. Magee, LF
6. K. Bransfield, 1B
7. M. Doolan, SS
8. R. Dooin, C

1906

1. R. Thomas, CF
2. K. Gleason, 2B
3. K. Bransfield, 1B
4. J. Titus, RF
5. S. Magee, LF
6. M. Doolan, SS
7. E. Courtney, 3B
8. R. Dooin, C

1907

1. R. Thomas, CF
2. O. Knabe, 2B
3. J. Titus, RF
4. S. Magee, LF
5. K. Bransfield, 1B
6. E. Courtney, 3B
7. M. Doolan, SS
8. R. Dooin, C

1908

1. E. Grant, 3B
2. O. Knabe, 2B
3. J. Titus, RF
4. S. Magee, LF
5. K. Bransfield, 1B
6. F. Osborn, CF
7. M. Doolan, SS
8. R. Dooin, C

1909

1. E. Grant, 3B
2. J. Bates, CF
3. J. Titus, RF
4. S. Magee, LF
5. K. Bransfield, 1B
6. O. Knabe, 2B
7. M. Doolan, SS
8. R. Dooin, C

1910

1. J. Titus, RF
2. O. Knabe, 2B
3. J. Bates, CF
4. S. Magee, LF
5. E. Grant, 3B
6. K. Bransfield, 1B
7. M. Doolan, SS
8. R. Dooin, C

1911

1. O. Knabe, 2B
2. D. Paskert, CF
3. H. Lobert, 3B
4. S. Magee, LF
5. F. Luderus, 1B
6. J. Titus
   F. Beck, RF
7. M. Doolan, SS
8. R. Dooin, C

1912

1. D. Paskert, CF
2. H. Lobert, 3B
3. S. Magee, LF
4. G. Cravath, RF
5. F. Luderus, 1B
6. O. Knabe, 2B
7. M. Doolan, SS
8. B. Killefer, C

1913

1. D. Paskert, CF
2. O. Knabe, 2B
3. H. Lobert, 3B
4. S. Magee, LF
5. G. Cravath, RF
6. F. Luderus, 1B
7. M. Doolan, SS
8. B. Killefer, C

1914

1. B. Byrne, 2B
2. B. Becker, LF
3. H. Lobert, 3B
4. S. Magee, LF-INF
5. G. Cravath, RF
6. F. Luderus, 1B
7. D. Paskert, CF
   J. Martin, SS
8. B. Killefer, C

1915

1. B. Byrne, 3B
2. D. Bancroft, SS
3. D. Paskert, CF
   B. Becker, LF
4. G. Cravath, RF
5. F. Luderus, 1B
6. P. Whitted, CF-LF
7. B. Niehoff, 2B
8. B. Killefer, C

1916

1. D. Paskert, CF
2. B. Niehoff, 2B
3. M. Stock, 3B
4. G. Cravath, RF
5. P. Whitted, LF
6. F. Luderus, 1B
7. D. Bancroft, SS
8. B. Killefer, C

1917

1. D. Paskert, CF
2. D. Bancroft, SS
3. M. Stock, 3B
4. G. Cravath, RF
5. P. Whitted, LF
6. F. Luderus, 1B
7. B. Niehoff, 2B
8. B. Killefer, C

1918 (First half)

1. D. Bancroft, SS
2. C. Williams, CF
3. M. Stock, 3B
4. F. Luderus, 1B
5. G. Cravath, RF
6. I. Meusel, LF
7. P. McGaffigan, 2B
8. E. Burns, C

1918 (Second half)

1. D. Bancroft, SS
2. C. Williams, CF
3. M. Stock, 3B
4. F. Luderus, 1B
5. I. Meusel, LF
6. G. Cravath, RF
7. E. Hemingway
   H. Pearce, 2B
8. B. Adams, C

1919

1. L. Callahan, RF
2. L. Blackburne, 3B
3. C. Williams, CF
4. I. Meusel, LF
5. F. Luderus, 1B
6. D. Bancroft, SS
7. G. Paulette, 2B
8. B. Adams, C

PHILADELPHIA

ROY ALLEN THOMAS
CENTER FIELDER 1899–1908, 1910–11

A place hitter and exceptional bunter who specialized in fouling off pitches and drawing walks, Roy Thomas was an exemplary practitioner of "inside baseball," but his skill package would have been useful to teams of any era. Playing mostly center field for his hometown Philadelphia Phillies, the left-handed hitter and thrower was nearly the equal of Phillies legends Billy Hamilton and Richie Ashburn, both in ability to reach base and as guardian of the middle pasture. Even though he stood 5'11", he ranks among the top players of all time in ratio of walks to plate appearances, leading the NL in bases on balls in seven of his nine full major league seasons. And on defense, Thomas led the loop's outfielders in putouts three times, assists once, and total chances per game twice.

Roy Allen Thomas was born on March 24, 1874, in Norristown, Pennsylvania, a prosperous manufacturing town on the Schuykill River. Roy's parents were primarily of Welsh descent. They raised him in a strict Christian household, and he continued to observe the Sabbath even as a professional ballplayer. (In 1904-05 Phillies manager Hugh Duffy accumulated most of his playing time on Sundays while spelling Thomas.) Roy grew up in Sheetz's Mill, just outside Norristown, and attended Norristown High School. After graduation he rode the nation's first commuter railway to nearby Philadelphia, where he attended the University of Pennsylvania. A baseball standout for the Quakers, Thomas earned his bachelor's degree from the Ivy League institution in 1894. He then played four years for the Orange Athletic Club, a semipro outfit whose roster included a number of former collegians. One of the club's frequent opponents was the Honesdale Reds, which in 1898 included a high school pitcher named Christy Mathewson.

Thomas broke into the National League in 1899 with a .325 batting average and career highs in games (150), runs (137), hits (178), walks (115), and on-base percentage (.457). Among his hits must have been numerous bunt singles; though the exact number is unknown, contemporary observers estimated that he typically attempted 200 bunts per season. Because Thomas never sacrificed more than the 23 times he did as a rookie, we can assume that bunting for a hit was a major component of his offensive arsenal. As for his amazing walk totals, his secret was fouling off pitches; the pesky leadoff hitter frequently turned lengthy at-bats into bases on balls. Thomas is purported to have fouled off as many as 27 pitches in a single at-bat.

In his sophomore season, 1900, Thomas batted .316, led the NL in runs (132) and walks (115), and may have been responsible for launching a reform in baseball rules that helped create the game's structure as we know it today. During one extended plate appearance that season he reportedly raised the ire of Brooklyn manager Ned Hanlon, a member of the NL rules committee. "Have your fun now, kid, because we're going to take care of you for next year," Hanlon yelled. Sure enough, in 1901 the NL adopted the foul-strike rule (counting the first two fouls as strikes), apparently at Hanlon's impetus.

The new rule barely inhibited Thomas's ability to draw walks: he led the NL in that category for six of the next seven seasons. In 1900 he averaged one walk for every 4.6 at-bats; over the next three seasons his ratio fell only slightly to one walk per 4.7 at-bats, a drop of only about 2%. In contrast, the NL walk rate dropped by 6% over the same period, from one for every 12.9 at-bats in 1900 to one per 13.7 at-bats in 1901-03. Thomas also maintained his batting average.

From 1899-1905 he batted no lower than .290 (which, in 1904, was his only sub-.300 average in that stretch). Significantly, he fused his ability to reach base with baseball's most crucial skill, scoring runs. Widely heralded as one of the NL's best baserunners, Thomas scored at least 100 runs in four different seasons and stole 244 bases in his career.

Thomas's decline at age 32 was precipitous. In 1906 his batting average plummeted 63 points to .254, and it sank even further to .243 the following year. Let go by the Phillies early in 1908, Thomas batted .256 in 102 games for Pittsburgh that season and .263 in 82 games for Boston the next. Roy returned to the Phillies for a 1910 swan song in which he batted .183 in 23 games. In 1911 he capped off his playing career with a noble civic gesture that cemented his place in Quaker City lore. With outfielders John Titus and Sherry Magee unavailable, Thomas temporarily came out of retirement to fill in, batting .167 in 21 games.

With his playing days over, Thomas left behind one of the most unusual statistical resumes in baseball history. His career fielding percentage of .972 was an NL record at the time of his retirement. According to Bill James, Thomas was the only major league regular to score three times as many runs as he drove in. He also had the lowest ratio of doubles to total hits of any big league regular, the highest ratio of singles to total hits, the highest ratio of on-base percentage to slugging percentage (.413 to .333, or 1.24 to 1), the highest ratio of walks to extra-base hits (6.5 to 1), and the fewest RBI for a player with at least 1,500 hits.

Off the field, Thomas was involved in several business ventures. He became part owner of a Philadelphia-area car dealership during his playing days, and he also worked for a morticians supply firm. For most of his post-playing career he worked for a Philadelphia–based coal company as a sales representative. Thomas never lost his passion for baseball. He coached the Penn baseball team in 1903 and resumed his duties there from 1909 to 1919, compiling a career record of 88-81-3. In 1928-33 he coached at Haverford College, and between his collegiate stints he worked in minor and semipro leagues around Philadelphia and New Jersey. Thomas maintained relationships with many of his former teammates, corresponding for years with players such as Elmer Flick. Throughout the 1940s and '50s he was viewed as a link to Philadelphia's baseball heritage.

Roy Thomas died at age 85 on November 20, 1959, at his home in Norristown where he lived his entire life. Bessie, his wife of four decades, had preceded him in death a decade earlier, and he was living with his son Roy Jr., one of his four children. Philadelphians remembered Thomas as a gentleman who was true to his family, his city, his Phillies, and his faith. Baseball historians remember him as a man whose batting tactics were partly responsible for a fundamental change in baseball's rules at the dawn of the Deadball Era.

BILL LAMBERTY

PHILADELPHIA

Charles Sebastian "Red" Dooin
Catcher 1902–14, Manager 1910–14

Red Dooin was an outstanding defensive backstop who caught 1,124 games for the Phillies, which is still the team record. "This writer has watched catchers from the days of Charley Farrell and Connie Mack and none could go farther for fouls or block off a runner at the plate as Dooin did," wrote a *Sporting News* reporter in 1925. "When Dooin was in his playing prime he never weighed more than 145 lbs., yet he was absolutely spike fearless and would block the swiftest and heaviest runner when there was only a small chance to retire him."

Born in Cincinnati on June 12, 1879, Charles Sebastian Dooin started out as a cloth cutter and clothing salesman but aspired to be a catcher, even though he stood only 5'6" and weighed less than 120 lbs. In 1898 he persuaded Indianapolis of the Western League to give him a break—and wound up with a broken hand in his first game. The next year he signed with Rock Island of the Western Association. This time the league, not Dooin, broke up. He hooked on with St. Paul and hit a game-winning triple in his debut, after which manager Charles Comiskey asked him if he had a trade. "I'm a tailor," Red said. The future Chicago White Sox magnate advised him to go back to tailoring. Undaunted, Dooin landed with his third team of the 1899 season, Youngstown of the Interstate League. He sassed the manager and was gone in a week. Still undaunted, Red went home to Cincinnati and joined a semipro team called "Spinney's Specials," playing through 1900 alongside another mighty mite named Miller Huggins. In 1901 St. Joe of the Western League needed a catcher and sent Dooin a contract. When Red reported, the manager took one look at him and said, "I wanted a catcher, not a jockey." Dooin managed to last the season, batting .252.

Red Dooin finally caught a good break in 1902. The new American League's raids on NL rosters created plenty of openings, and the Phillies picked up the pint-sized, 22-year-old backstop. He still weighed less than 150 lbs., but he was tough, scrappy, and fearless. One of his claims to fame remains unrecognized. By Dooin's account, one day in 1906 the Penn athletic director, Mike Murphy, took one look at Red's scarred legs and suggested that he wear shin guards. "You can't play baseball with shin guards," Dooin said. "They play football with them," said Murphy, "and they run just as fast as you." The next day Murphy brought him a pair of rattan guards. Dooin put them on under his stockings. The first time a sliding runner bounced off them, Red was sold. He had some lighter ones made from papier-mâché and continued wearing them under his stockings.

Baseball history credits Roger Bresnahan with introducing shin guards, but Dooin always maintained that Bresnahan got the idea from him in 1907. "We were playing the Giants in Philadelphia, and I blocked the Rajah as he came flying into the plate," said Dooin. "In the collision he went down and came in contact with my legs. 'Say, what have you got under your stockings?' the astonished Bresnahan asked. In the clubhouse after the game I showed the guards to Roger. Afterwards he went down to a Philadelphia sporting-goods house, where I had mine made, and purchased a pair for himself. But because of his bulk and the fact that any additional weight would slow him up if he wore the guards like I did, Bresnahan had to put aside the idea of leg protection. He continued to experiment, however, and the white cricket shinguards resulted. He only wore them behind the plate. He took them off when going to bat. I continued to wear mine under the stockings."

In 1909 Horace Fogel bought the Phillies. A promotion-minded baseball writer, Fogel wanted a feisty, colorful manager. Red Dooin was all of that. The temperamental redhead took over the helm as player-manager in 1910, but a broken ankle that season and a broken leg in 1911 ended his days as a regular player. The latter injury occurred during a game in St. Louis in which Dooin had blocked off three Cardinals at the plate in the early innings. Each time the runner probably should have scored, and Bresnahan, managing St. Louis, threatened to fine the next player who was blocked by Dooin. Later in the game, Cardinals outfielder Rebel Oakes, remembering Bresnahan's threat, charged the plate on a close play and broke one of Dooin's legs, shin guards and all.

From 1910 to 1914 the Phillies played in the shadow of Connie Mack's mighty Athletics machine, but nearly every season Dooin had them challenging the NL powers of Chicago and New York before eventually fading from the race. William F. Baker—he of the shallow pockets—replaced Fogel as club president in 1913, and the following year the Federal League cut out the heart of the Phillies. At the same time it also nearly ruined the minor league Baltimore Orioles, which almost resulted in a break for Dooin. When Mack turned down Baltimore's offer of Babe Ruth and Ernie Shore, Jack Dunn offered them, with shortstop Claud Derrick, to Dooin and the Phillies for $19,000. According to Red, "Baker nearly exploded when I reported to him that Dunn asked $19,000 for three of the most promising players in the International League. He told me he wouldn't give $19,000 for the whole International League."

It's fun to imagine how many home runs the Babe might have hit in Baker Bowl—if Baker somehow managed to hold on to him—but alas, the Ruth-less Phillies finished sixth in 1914, after which Dooin was fired. The Phillies had compiled a respectable 392-370 record over the course of his five-year tenure, but the following year they won their only pennant of the Deadball Era. Red started the 1915 season back in Cincinnati, then went to the Giants, for whom he caught and coached through 1917. He played for Rochester in 1918 and the next year caught his last game at age 40 while managing Reading of the International League.

Dooin retired to Atlantic City, where he owned several properties and had substantial money in the bank. In 1932 the banks closed and he lost all his cash, forcing him to sell off some of his real estate. Dooin had a rich baritone voice—during his playing days he'd performed on the winter vaudeville circuit as a singer and actor in addition to working in the men's department of a Philadelphia department store—so he went back to singing, in vaudeville and on the radio. Red and his wife, Julia, moved to Rochester, New York, where the former ballplayer died at age 72 on May 14, 1952. Married almost 50 years, the couple had no children.

NORMAN MACHT

PHILADELPHIA

John Franklin Titus
Right fielder 1903–12

John Titus was a strong-armed outfielder who recorded more than 20 assists for seven straight seasons, but he was better known for his mustache, quiet demeanor, selectivity at the plate, and the ubiquitous toothpick in his mouth. "Titus had one of the best batting eyes I ever saw," said Phillies teammate Pete Alexander. "He would take his position at the plate with the easiest and most confident air in the world. If the ball was an inch outside of the plate, he would watch it go by and never bat an eye lash. If it was an inch inside, he wouldn't move. He would just draw in his stomach and let the ball pass. But if you put the ball over the plate, he would whale the cover off. It used to exasperate me merely to watch him. Many a time I've said to myself, If I were pitching, Old Man, I'd knock that toothpick out of your mouth and maybe then you'd move over."

John Franklin Titus was born to Theodore and Agnes (Uren) Titus on February 21, 1876, in St. Clair, Pennsylvania, about 100 miles northwest of Philadelphia. His father was a native of Easton, Pennsylvania, and his mother was born in England. As a child John lost the tip of his right index finger in an accident. Before his career in professional baseball, he worked in the coal mines and served in the army during the Spanish-American War. At age 22 John joined Company K, 8th Regiment of the Pennsylvania Infantry. The company initially reported to Camp Hastings in Mt. Gretna, Pennsylvania, then moved on to Georgia and Virginia. A typhoid outbreak during the summer of 1898 forced the soldiers back to their home state, and by that time most of the fighting was over.

After Company K disbanded, Titus returned home and joined a basketball team in St. Clair whose players all decided to grow mustaches. He ended up keeping his throughout most of his baseball career, at a time when very few players sported facial hair, becoming the last major league player with a mustache until Frenchy Bordagaray came along in 1934. Titus played semipro baseball in nearby Pottsville and signed with Concord, New Hampshire, of the New England League in 1903. His stay in the minors was brief. In early June the 5'9", 156 lb. outfielder was tearing up the league with a .407 batting average when the Phillies purchased his contract for $1,700. He was actually 27 years old at the time, but newspaper accounts listed him as 24.

Titus made his major league debut on June 8, 1903, and saved a baseball used in that game for the rest of his life—even though he went hitless in four at-bats as the Phillies lost to the Pirates, 2-0. But the following afternoon he knocked home a fourth-inning run that snapped the Pittsburgh pitching staff's string of 56 consecutive scoreless innings. Titus went on to bat .286 in 72 games that season. "They changed his style when he joined the Phillies," wrote a Pottsville sportswriter decades later. "It was the fashion in those days to choke the bat and meet the ball with a short kick instead of the long, rhythmic swing which Jack had when he played in Pottsville. His swing here was comparable to that of Joe DiMaggio, except that Titus batted and threw left-handed."

The lifetime .282 hitter improved his batting average each of the next two seasons, putting together a career year in 1905. Titus finished in the NL's Top Five in slugging percentage (.436), total bases (239), doubles (36), RBI (89), and walks (69). Perhaps his best day as a Phillie occurred on May 25, 1907. Philadelphia trailed Brooklyn, 5-0, in the first game of a doubleheader when Titus blasted a two-run triple in the sixth inning and scored on a passed ball. Two innings later he again tripled home two runs, tying the game, 5-5, and scored the eventual winning run on an error. In the second game Titus doubled, tripled, drove in three runs and scored one himself as Philadelphia won, 7-4, sweeping the twin bill.

Though he remained a solid, dependable player, appearing in at least 143 games each year in his first seven seasons, "Silent John" garnered less attention than his more volatile and outspoken teammates. Kid Gleason once said, "He doesn't even make any noise when he spits," and it's believed that he was never thrown out of a single game in his entire career. New York Giants catcher Roger Bresnahan once tried to rattle Titus by snatching the toothpick out of his mouth and grinding it into the dirt behind home plate. John flushed with anger and spewed a loud string of obscenities. The display was so out of character for the taciturn Phillie that Bresnahan actually apologized.

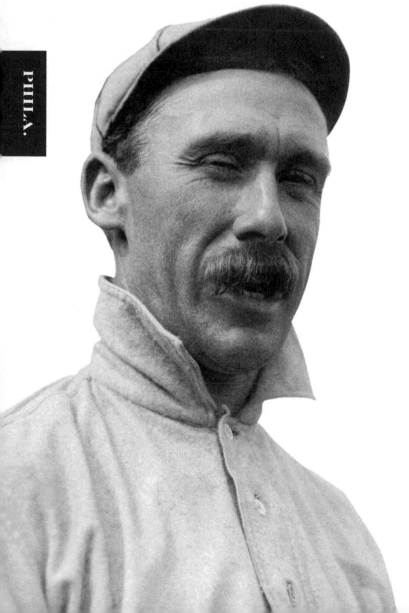

Eventually NL pitchers detected a pattern with Titus and his ever-present toothpick. He kept the sliver of wood in the corner of his mouth until he got the green light to swing at a pitch; then he'd shift it to the center of his mouth. After one alert pitcher noticed the subtle giveaway, word got around the league. Titus adjusted his mannerisms rather than abandon the toothpick. In another of his peculiarities, John ran with an unusual closed gait, prompting his teammates to make a play on his last name and call him "Tight Ass."

The Phillies led the NL in late-May 1911 when Titus broke his leg sliding into home plate in a game against the Cardinals. By the time he returned to the lineup, the Phils had sunk to third and the once fleet outfielder had lost much of his speed—after stealing more than 20 bases in each of the previous three seasons, he totaled only 18 in the next three years combined. On July 1, 1912, Philadelphia traded Titus to the Boston Braves. He finished the season strong, batting .325 in 96 games for Boston. Late that season rookie Rabbit Maranville, on his first day with the Braves, was feeling intimidated until he spotted the 37-year-old Titus during batting practice. "I said to myself, 'What is this, an old man's league, or is somebody kidding me?'" he wrote later. "After I saw him hit, I changed my mind as he was one of the best hitters in baseball." Titus began 1913 as the Braves starting right fielder but was relegated to the bench, even though he was leading the team with a .297 batting average. The Braves ended up selling him to Kansas City of the American Association after he suffered another broken leg in July.

By the 1914 season Silent John Titus was 38 years old, though the papers now said he was 31. In late April he suffered a fractured skull and remained unconscious for several hours after former teammate Bill Burns beaned him. Titus remained out of the lineup for two months. The following summer he was hitting .263 when Kansas City released him on July 22. He decided to retire. On September 15, 1915, Titus married Ethel Stone, his 17-year-old next-door neighbor in St. Clair. Little is known about his life after baseball. John Titus died at age 66 at his home in St. Clair on January 7, 1943. His wife and his brother, Harry, survived him. Local obituaries don't mention any children. Titus was buried with full military honors at a funeral attended by many local veterans of the Spanish-American War.

ALLAN WOOD

Sherry Magee

PHILADELPHIA

SHERWOOD ROBERT MAGEE
LEFT FIELDER 1904–14

Today we'd call Sherry Magee a five-tool player: he could hit, run, field, throw, and hit with power. For more than a decade he was the Phillies' greatest offensive weapon, setting the team's modern record for steals (387) and ranking among the Top 10 in almost every other category. Magee's defense was nearly the equal of his offense; sensational catches with his back to home plate were his trademark, and Pirates scout Frank Haller commented that his every throw was "on a line and right on target." He was undoubtedly the NL's most valuable player in 1910, and either he or Johnny Evers deserved the appellation in 1914. One reporter called Magee "probably the best all-around ball player in the National League," while another went a step further: "To my mind Sherwood Magee is one of the best all-around players the game has ever seen."

The son of an oil field worker, Sherwood Robert Magee was born on August 6, 1884, in Clarendon, Pennsylvania. "The Irish traits of quick wittedness, a hot temper and an aggressive love of fighting are his by birthright," wrote John J. Ward in *Baseball Magazine*. Regarding Magee's personality, one Philadelphia reporter called him "as gentle and good-natured as an old woman," but Ward described him as "a man for whom it is easy to conceive a great liking or a passionate hatred." Standing 5'11" and weighing 179 lbs., Sherry was physically imposing—"husky" and "burly" were adjectives commonly used to describe him. In addition to his baseball skills, he was a crackerjack bowler and a standout football and basketball player.

In late June 1904, Phillies scout Jim Randall was getting off a train in Carlisle, Pennsylvania, when he overheard some baseball fans raving about a kid named Magee who played left field for the local Lindner team. After checking out the kid and liking what he saw,

Randall approached him and asked if he'd be interested in playing with a league team. "What team?" asked Magee. "The Phillies," replied Randall. Sherry couldn't believe he'd heard right, and it wasn't until Randall pulled out a contract and offered him a roll of bills that he realized he wasn't dreaming. The next day he was in Philadelphia, practicing with the Phillies, and the day after that—June 29, 1904, to be exact—19-year-old Sherry Magee (listed as "McGee" in the box score) was starting in left field against the Brooklyn Superbas.

Philadelphia's strength in 1904 was its outfield—Shad Barry in left, Roy Thomas in center, and John Titus in right—but an injury to Titus caused Barry to fill his position, opening up left field for Magee. Though the nervous rookie misjudged two fly balls, both of which led to Superba runs in an 8-6 loss, he hit the ball hard in each of his four at-bats. "Magee overcame his unfamiliarity with the Philadelphia grounds and soon learned to field as became a big leaguer," wrote Ward. Three weeks later, when Titus returned to the lineup, Sherry was so firmly entrenched that the Phillies traded Barry to Chicago. Magee batted .277 for the season and led the team with 12 triples despite playing in just 95 games. Sportswriters considered his jump from the sandlots to immediate stardom in the majors to be without precedent.

Over the next several years Magee rarely missed a game, establishing himself as one of baseball's young stars. In 1905, his first full season, he was the biggest factor in Philadelphia's gain of 31 victories over 1904, scoring an even 100 runs, stealing 48 bases, and batting .299 with 24 doubles, 17 triples, and five homers. The next year he was just as good, hitting .282 with 36 doubles, eight triples, and six homers and finishing second in the NL in stolen bases with 55, a modern Phillies record that stood until Juan Samuel swiped 72 in 1984. In 1907 Magee had his best season yet, leading the NL with 85 RBI and placing second to perennial batting champion Honus Wagner with a .328 average.

As Sherry reached stardom, he also developed a reputation as a troublemaker. "On the ball field Magee is so fussy most of the time that people who do not know him naturally form the opinion from his actions that he is a born grouch," wrote one reporter. "That he is one of the most hot-headed players in either big league is admitted," wrote another reporter. "It couldn't be denied, because the records, showing how often he has been suspended for scrapping with the umpires, speak for themselves." Off the field, the young slugger could be just as difficult. The captain of the Phillies during Magee's early years was Kid Gleason, who kept an old leather belt in his locker that he used on young players who misbehaved, and on several occasions Magee literally felt the captain's wrath. Sherry also became known for "crabbing" at teammates. "Magee, like Evers, has an unusual amount of base ball gray matter and spirit," explained one reporter. "This spirit plays for victories and is easily upset when 'bones' are pulled."

In 1909 Magee slumped to .270 (still 26 points above the NL average) and played with "marked indifference," prompting rumors that he would be traded to the New York Giants for holdout slugger Mike Donlin. The Phils refused the deal because of the age difference between the two players (Donlin was six years older), and their patience paid off when Magee put together his finest season in 1910. Playing in 154 games, he broke Wagner's tenure on the batting throne by hitting .331 and led the National League with career highs in runs (110), RBI (123), and on-base percentage (.445). He walloped 39 doubles, 17 triples, and six homers to give him a league-leading .507 slugging percentage, and his 49 stolen bases ranked fourth in the league.

Sherry was enjoying another banner year in 1911, but his season was marred by his actions in the third inning of a game against St. Louis on July 10. With the Phillies leading, 2-1, Magee came to bat with one out, Dode Paskert on second, and Hans Lobert on first. With two strikes, rookie umpire Bill Finneran called Magee out on a pitch that appeared to be high, prompting Magee to turn away in disgust and throw his bat high in the air. Finneran yanked off his mask and threw him out of the game. Sherry, who had been heading to the bench, suddenly turned and attacked the umpire, clutching him for a second before hitting him with a quick left just above the jaw. With blood spurting from his face, the young umpire fell to the ground, apparently unconscious.

The field umpire, Cy Rigler, and the Phillies manager, Red Dooin, who was coaching first base, both rushed to the plate to assist Finneran; meanwhile

Paskert and Lobert ran all the way around the bases, erroneously thinking that time hadn't been called. Magee stood in front of the Phillies bench for a few seconds before teammates led him under the stands. When he came to and realized what had happened, Finneran ripped off his chest protector and tried to reach the Philadelphia bench. Rigler tried to hold him back but only partly succeeded, his shirt becoming covered with blood in the process. Kitty Bransfield intercepted Finneran and prevented him from reaching the bench. After he calmed down, he went to the hospital for treatment. The game continued with Rigler behind the plate, and the Phillies won, 4-2, after which Magee expressed regret for the incident, offering as an excuse that Finneran had called him a vile name. Dooin added that the rookie umpire had been too aggressive all season, often bragging about his ability as a fighter and threatening to lick players.

Unsympathetic to the Phillies' pleas, NL president Thomas Lynch, himself a former umpire, announced that Magee had been fined $200 and suspended for the rest of the season—the most drastic punishment meted out in the NL since 1877, when four players were barred for dishonesty. The Phillies appealed to the NL board of directors, arguing that Lynch had been too severe, especially since one regular outfielder, Titus, already was out with an injury and the club was fighting for its first pennant. The directors declined to overturn the suspension, and the Phillies went 13-16 without Magee, tumbling to fourth place, 6½ games behind the Cubs. At that point Lynch reinstated him. Magee hit seven of his 15 home runs after his return, but the Quakers climbed no higher in the standings.

In the following year's City Series against the Athletics, Magee was hit by a pitch during batting practice and broke his right wrist and forearm, putting him out for the first month of the season. He was scarcely back when he was involved in an outfield collision with Paskert. Overcoming his injuries to bat .306 in both 1912 and 1913, Sherry combined with Gavy Cravath to give the Phillies what Ward called "the greatest 'team' of extra-base specialists in existence." But despite all he'd accomplished in his decade with the Phillies, Magee remained unpopular with the infamous fans of the City of Brotherly Love. "For five years, prior to 1914, the local fans have roasted Sherwood Magee," wrote a Philadelphia reporter. "They cheered his long swats as all fans do, but still they shouted for his release." Ward agreed, attributing Magee's lack of popularity to the generally held belief that he was "a man who played for his own personal record and not for the good of the team."

That all changed, however, when Magee was named captain of the Phillies in 1914. "When he was given the captaincy everyone looked at affairs from a different viewpoint," said one veteran teammate. "Now he could talk all he liked and there would be no resentment, for that was all a part of his job. And it gave the added stimulus to Magee that made him the greatest team worker we had." After opening the season at his usual position in left field, Sherry demanded an opportunity to play shortstop in mid-May, when it became apparent that none of the players attempting to replace the departed Mickey Doolan was adequate. "I can't do any worse than some of the men that have been in there," he told Dooin. Before the Phils acquired Jack Martin in July, Magee played 39 games at Doolan's old spot, performing surprisingly well for a career outfielder. With characteristic immodesty, he even declared himself among the best shortstops in the business. "Others were more conservative in their estimate of his ability," wrote one reporter, who nonetheless acknowledged that he was not the worst of Doolan's replacements.

Due to injuries to other players, Magee also played a significant number of games at second and first base in 1914. "In spite of the constant shifting of position on a hopelessly demoralized team, he proved himself the most valuable batsman in the league," wrote Ward. Magee batted .314 and led the NL in hits (171), doubles (39), RBI (103), and slugging percentage (.509). After that kind of season, he was shocked when the Phillies passed him over and appointed Pat Moran as manager to succeed Dooin. Magee negotiated halfheartedly with the Federal League's Baltimore Terrapins, whose players included Doolan and several other former Phillies, but what he really wanted was to be traded to a winning team. "This great ball player has been hitched to losing teams for so long that with each season the desire to be with a champion has grown stronger," wrote one reporter.

On December 26, 1914, Magee received a belated Christmas present when the Phillies dealt him to the world champion Boston Braves for cash and two players to be named later. The trade had its critics in both cities. Braves manager George Stallings, who already had one crab on his hands with Evers, now had to contend with a second one in Magee. He became further dismayed when one of the Boston players in the deal turned out to be Possum Whitted, a hustling center fielder who'd been one of his favorites. And in Philadelphia, one reporter wrote, "Just when Magee becomes popular with the fans, and is playing the game of his life, the club makes another mistake by permitting him to go to a rival club." But some Philadelphians had long believed that Magee was the "jinx" that had been following the Phillies, and they were happy to see him go. What happened to Sherry in 1915—when the Phillies won their first-ever pennant—would lend evidence to their suspicions.

Reporting to spring training in Macon, Georgia, Magee was in a Braves uniform no more than 15 minutes when he stepped in a hole while shagging a fly ball. He fell and injured his shoulder. Weeks later, when it failed to improve, he saw a doctor and learned that his collarbone was broken. Magee was only 30 but never again was the same player. He had batted over .300 three years in succession and had hit 15 homers in 1914, but in 1915 he batted .280 with only two homers. Sherry was worse the following year, batting a meager .241. In 1917 he again performed poorly for Boston—in 72 games he batted .256 with only one homer—but turned around his career when the Cincinnati Reds picked him up on waivers in August. Filling in for the injured Greasy Neale, Magee batted .321 over the rest of the season. His revitalization continued during the war-shortened 1918 season, when he batted .298 and drove in an NL–leading 76 runs, becoming the only non-Hall of Famer to lead the league in RBI four times.

The next season a serious illness forced Magee out of action for two months, causing him to lose his regular position to rookie Pat Duncan. Though he batted a career-low .215, Sherry realized his long-held ambition of playing for a pennant-winning team. Appearing twice as a pinch-hitter in the 1919 World Series, he picked up one hit and was released after Cincinnati's victory, marking the end of his 16-year career as a major league player. Though he'd skipped the minors on his way up, Magee played seven years in the bushes on his way down, six of them in the American Association. His best full season came with Minneapolis in 1922,

when he batted .358, third best in the AA, and set a record that August by reaching base in 20 consecutive pinch-hitting appearances. Three years later Magee got off to an even better start, leading the AA with a .464 average, but Milwaukee released him in June after losing 16 of 18 games. In desperation Sherry begged for work from his last major league employer, Reds owner Garry Herrmann. "You know I never drank Whiskey and don't to-day and have a lot more sense than I had there before," he wrote in his letter to Herrmann. But when no job with the Reds was forthcoming, Magee signed as player-coach with Jack Dunn's Baltimore Orioles. He held on for one more season, finally retiring as an active player at the age of 42.

Sherry was ill prepared for the next phase of his life, but an inspiration came to him while presiding over exhibition games at Baltimore's 1926 training camp: he'd become an umpire. In 1927 Magee served as an arbiter in the New York-Penn League. His work attracted so much positive comment that he was named to the National League staff for the coming season by John Heydler, who'd been an assistant to President Lynch at the time of the Finneran incident in 1911. Picking up on the irony of umpire baiter turned umpire, many veteran reporters expected Magee to be a disaster. "His appointment at the time brought a reflective smile to the fans and players that recalled his ancient feuds with the umpires," wrote one scribe after the 1928 season, "but Sherry surprised the old-timers by his cool decisions on the field, the manner in which he ran his ball games and the cleverness of his work." Heydler commented that Magee had made good in his first year and was destined to become one of the game's leading umpires.

Sherry spent the 1928-29 off-season at his home in Philadelphia, working in a nearby restaurant. In early March he came home complaining of a headache and fever. A physician diagnosed that he was suffering from pneumonia, and his condition worsened over the ensuing week. At age 44, Sherry Magee died on March 13, 1929, leaving behind Edna, and his three grown children. The obituary that went out over the AP wire described him as "one of baseball's most colorful figures," "one of the greatest natural batsmen in the game," and "a master in judging fly balls, a fine base runner and full of so-called 'inside baseball.'"

TOM SIMON

PHILADELPHIA

MICHAEL JOSEPH DOOLITTLE (DOOLAN)
SHORTSTOP 1905–13

The prototype good-field, no-hit shortstop, Mickey Doolan had a remarkable ability to snap the ball accurately to first base from almost any position. Sportswriter Fred Lieb remarked that Doolan "could throw standing on his head" and favorably compared his defense to that of his elite contemporaries Honus Wagner and Joe Tinker. Lieb's comparison holds up under scrutiny. Between 1906 and 1913, Doolan led the National League in putouts four times, assists five times, double plays five times, and fielding percentage once. According to Bill James's Win Shares system, the Philadelphia captain was the NL's preeminent fielding shortstop three times.

Doolan was born Michael Joseph Doolittle in Ashland, Pennsylvania, on May 7, 1880, to James and Anna (Kennedy) Doolittle. His adopted surname was variously spelled "Doolan" and "Doolin" throughout his 71 years, and during his playing days reporters referred to him as Mike as often as Mickey. As a youngster Mickey suffered an injury to his throwing arm and had to overcome residual stiffness. Unable to make the long overhand throw from shortstop to first base, he compensated by developing a "snap" throw, wristing the ball from a sidearm to three-quarters orientation. It worked. As a teen Mickey played amateur ball throughout southeastern Pennsylvania, and in 1900-01 he played shortstop for Villanova College, where he acquired an education in dentistry and the ubiquitous nickname of Doc.

Because baseball was Doolan's passion, his off-season occupation had to take a backseat for the time being. From 1902 to 1904 he played professionally for Jersey City, which was managed by future Phillies skipper Billy Murray. In 1903 Mickey was the regular second baseman, contributing solid defense and a .287 batting average as Jersey City went 92-33 to capture the Eastern League pennant. Doolan's performance convinced Brooklyn to draft him, but the Superbas erroneously drafted Pop Dillon instead. Mickey returned to Jersey City, which subsequently sent him to the Phillies for Bill Keister and $2,500.

Becoming Philadelphia's regular shortstop in 1905, Doolan batted .254, 24 points above his career average. The three men who managed the Phillies over the next nine seasons penciled his name into the lineup nearly every day, even though he never hit much, and in 1909 he was even named team captain, a position he held through 1913. Doolan's best year at the plate was 1910, when he logged personal highs for at-bats (536), hits (141), doubles (31), batting average (.263), and on-base percentage (.315). Those modest marks represented rarefied air for Mickey, who was one of the truly bad hitters of an offense-starved era. By 1913 his batting average had plummeted to .218 and his slugging percentage to a woeful .270.

After the 1913 season Doolan agreed to join a world tour organized by Charles Comiskey and John McGraw. In an odd premonitory run-in prior to the tour's departure, the Phillies attempted to prevent Doolan from leaving unless he took out a life insurance policy for $10,000 to protect the club. A leader of the Players Fraternity, Doolan balked at the suggestion and maintained that he was legally a free agent. At the last

minute McGraw, who'd been interested in acquiring Doolan to play third base for the Giants, agreed to pay the premium on the player's behalf.

When the grand world tour docked in New York harbor at the completion of the trip, Mickey Doolan was one of two players to sign on the spot with the neophyte Federal League. The Baltimore Terrapins offered him a salary of $6,000, a huge increase on his 1913 pay. It's unknown whether Phillies owner William Baker offered any salary increase whatsoever, but his reputation spurs doubt. Mickey had received only one raise since 1908, when the Phillies hiked his salary to $3,500 prior to the 1911 season. Doolan played one full season with Baltimore, then hooked on with the pennant-bound Chicago Whales when the last-place Terrapins cut him late in the 1915 season. After the collapse of the Federal League, Doolan was awarded to the Chicago Cubs, for whom he saw limited action in 1916 before his inclusion in the midseason trade sending Heinie Zimmerman to the Giants for Larry Doyle. In McGraw's employ at last, Mickey played infrequently in New York and was back in the minors by 1917.

Signing as player-manager of the International League's Rochester Hustlers, Doolan guided the team to fifth place, an improvement of eight games and two places in the standings over the previous season, but was nonetheless let go. Returning to the NL as a second baseman for Brooklyn in 1918, he appeared in 92 games and batted .179 with just 10 extra-base hits in 308 at-bats. Following stints in the International League with Reading and Jack Dunn's powerhouse Baltimore Orioles, Mickey reemerged in the majors in 1926 as a coach for the Cubs, a role he held through 1928. After spending a year away from the game to focus on his dental practice, Doolan served three years as a coach for the Cincinnati Reds, leaving the majors for good after the 1932 season.

With his baseball career behind him, Doolan practiced dentistry until 1947. On retirement he and his wife, Emma, relocated to Orlando, Florida, where Mickey suffered a stroke in late 1949. A subsequent leg injury left him a partial invalid. Acute appendicitis beset Doolan in late October 1951; the appendix ruptured and he succumbed to peritonitis on November 1. Emma survived Mickey by just over three months. The couple left behind no children.

PAUL MITTERMEYER

PHILADELPHIA

WILLIAM EDWARD "KITTY" BRANSFIELD
FIRST BASEMAN 1905–11

At 5'11" and 207 lbs., Kitty Bransfield looked like a power hitter but owed his reputation as one of the NL's top first basemen more to his glove work. Bransfield helped form the nucleus of the juggernaut Pittsburgh Pirates that dominated the National League from 1901 to 1903. Yet in the great tradition of baseball superstitions, his departure from Pittsburgh in 1904 left such a void that the club's decades long quest for another adequate first sacker became known as "The Bransfield Curse." Kitty revived his career in Philadelphia; in his book *The National Game*, published in 1910, Alfred Spink described the big first baseman as "something unusual—a player who was almost all in and then came back stronger than ever." The lifetime .270 hitter remained with the Phillies through 1911, becoming, according to Spink (with perhaps a touch of hyperbole), "probably the most popular player in the National League."

William Edward Bransfield was born on January 7, 1875, in Worcester, Massachusetts, and spent most of his life in that city. His original nickname was "Kid," but a reporter with bad hearing thought it was "Kitty" and the nickname stuck. Bransfield began his career in baseball as an outfielder with shop teams in Worcester. In 1894 he went behind the bat, and the following year he received a tryout with the professional team in Pawtucket. Found wanting, Kitty returned to the Worcester area and played for strong semipro teams in Westboro and Grafton. In 1898 the 23-year-old backstop received another professional trial, this time with the National League's Boston Beaneaters. Already well stocked at catcher with the talented but volatile Marty Bergen, the Beaneaters looked Kitty over for five games and released him to Worcester's minor league team. After spending the 1899 season behind the plate,

Bransfield switched to first base in 1900 and led the Eastern League in hitting with a .371 average.

With the death of Tom O'Brien and the poor performance of Duff Cooley, the Pittsburgh Pirates desperately needed a new first baseman for 1901. Bransfield, whom they acquired in a straight sale from Worcester, proved to be a perfect fit. As the Pirates walked away with their first NL pennant by 7½ games over the second-place Phillies, Kitty batted .295 in 139 games and established career highs in runs (92) and RBI (91). The 26-year-old rookie was no slouch on defense, either, even though his playing style at first base was unusual for the Deadball Era. At a time when bunting was a major part of the game, Bransfield played back on the grass, so deep that he claimed he never saw shortstop Honus Wagner make more than a handful of great plays. "He would cut that ball loose for the bag, and I had to be there," Kitty remembered. "So whenever it was hit his way I was digging for the bag. I knew he would have it there, and I had to arrive as soon as the ball. I never had time to watch him field it. But if you want me to make an affidavit that he was the greatest ball player that ever lived, I'll gladly do it."

Though Bransfield batted a career-high .305 during his sophomore season, he never quite fulfilled the promise of his rookie season with Pittsburgh. His average fell to .265 in 1903, and his poor hitting in the first-ever World Series that year was another hint that his days in the Steel City might be numbered. In 1904 Bransfield became mired in a physical and mental slump, his batting average plummeting to .223. Prior to the 1905 season, Pirates owner Barney Dreyfuss shipped him to the Philadelphia Phillies along with Otto Krueger and Moose McCormick for minor league phenom Del Howard. It turned out to be one of the worst trades in

Pirates history. No fewer than 25 different players tried their hand at the initial post for the Pirates from 1905 to 1920. In 1908 four different players auditioned and were found wanting. Some claimed that Charlie Grimm finally ended the curse when he joined Pittsburgh in 1919, but others believe that it wasn't laid to rest until the arrival of Willie Stargell a half-century later.

The move to the Phils did wonders for Bransfield. From 1905 to 1910 he anchored a rock-solid defensive infield that eventually included Otto Knabe and Mickey Doolan at second and short, respectively, and Harvard Eddie Grant at third. Though known more for his glove than his bat, Bransfield in his best years was an above-average hitter during a time when good hitters were scarce. His finest year with the Phillies was 1908, when he led the team with three home runs, 71 RBI, and a .304 batting average, becoming one of only five .300 hitters in the NL that season.

Off the field, Kitty developed a reputation as a man of integrity. Years after the 1919 Black Sox scandal, teammate Red Dooin recalled an incident at the Polo Grounds during the 1908 pennant race when gamblers tried to persuade the Phillies to drop games to the Giants. "Why, gamblers opened up a satchel, must've had over $150,000 in it, told our pitchers to help themselves," Dooin recalled. "At the first game at the Polo Grounds, a big man handed me $8,000, told me there was $40,000 more waiting for me. I called big Kitty Bransfield, who threw him down the stairs." Dooin and Bransfield figured in another story involving gamblers, this one set in Philadelphia. Both were called to a house on Columbia Avenue. When they realized their hosts were gamblers, Dooin threw the pair of sports down one flight of stairs and Bransfield finished the job, transporting them to street level.

Young Fred Luderus took over at first base for the Phillies in 1911, making the 36-year-old Bransfield expendable. That September he became a Chicago Cub, ending his major league career by filling in for the ailing Frank Chance for three games. In 1912 Bransfield attempted to hook on with Louisville but was released to Montreal, where he succeeded Chick Gandil at first base and became player-manager later that season. He failed to make winners out of the Royals and was fired in the middle of the 1914 campaign.

Bransfield spent the rest of 1914 and all of 1915 working as an umpire in the New England League. The

International League was his next stop, and in 1917 he became a National League umpire. He lasted only one year. In 1918 Kitty rejoined the New England League, where he umpired through 1921. He returned to the big leagues in 1922 as a scout for the Cubs. In 1924 Bransfield took the managerial reins one last time, leading Waterbury to an Eastern League pennant.

After leaving baseball, Bransfield became supervisor of public playgrounds in his native Worcester in 1934, and he later worked as a night watchman for the Parker Manufacturing Company. During his later years he remained an active observer of the baseball scene, always noting that he still hadn't seen any player who could compare to Wagner. Kitty Bransfield died in Worcester at age 72 on May 1, 1947.

DAVID ANDERSON

E. L. Grant

PHILADELPHIA

EDWARD LESLIE GRANT
THIRD BASEMAN 1907–10

Eddie Grant was a typical Deadball Era third baseman: mediocre offensively (as attested by his lifetime .249 batting and .295 slugging averages) but defensively reliable, particularly against the bunt. "As a batter Grant was noted for his ability to sacrifice," remembered Mike Donlin, "and he could lay back near third base and still throw out the fastest runners after they had bunted." In his playing days "Harvard Eddie" was best known for his Ivy League diplomas. In an era when most of his teammates played poker while traveling by train, the intellectual Grant generally could be found smoking his pipe and reading a book. Today, however, he is remembered as the most prominent major leaguer killed in combat during World War I (others include Bun Troy and Alex Burr, both of whom were killed in France within a week of Grant).

Edward Leslie Grant was born on May 21, 1883, in Franklin, Massachusetts, 30 miles south of Boston. After graduating from the public high school in 1901, Eddie spent a post-graduate year at Dean Academy in Franklin before matriculating at Harvard College in the fall of 1902. That year he distinguished himself as the freshman basketball team's top scorer and, according to the *Harvard Crimson*, "a valuable team man and excellent left-handed batter" for the freshman baseball team. As a sophomore Eddie played varsity basketball and tried out for varsity baseball, but before the first game he was declared ineligible for having received money playing in an independent league the previous summer. With intercollegiate competition no longer an option, he joined his class team and spent the summer with St. Albans of Vermont's outlaw Northern League.

Returning to Cambridge in the fall of 1904, Grant carried a heavy course load with the intention of graduating a year early and enrolling in law school. Though ambitious, Eddie was a mediocre student at Harvard, earning an average grade of slightly above C. Classmates described him as quiet, thoughtful, unassuming, and serious. In athletics Eddie stood out a bit more. Again he played class baseball—earning a spot on the 1905 All Leiter Team, Harvard's intramural all-stars—and joined the semipro Milford club when the school year ended. That summer, in addition to fulfilling his degree requirements, Eddie got his first taste of Organized Baseball—at the major league level, no less. In early August the Cleveland Naps were in Boston, but Napoleon Lajoie was laid up with an infected leg. The best local substitute the Naps could find was Eddie Grant, who filled in at second base and collected three hits in his big-league debut.

For the next three years Grant attended Harvard Law School during off-seasons and played professional baseball during summers. While with Jersey City in 1906, his first full season in Organized Ball, Eddie played in 86 games and posted the highest batting average in the Eastern League (.322), though his 307 at-bats weren't enough to qualify as the league leader. That mark earned him a shot with the Philadelphia Phillies, for whom he split time with Ernie Courtney in 1907 before taking over as the regular third baseman in 1908. During the off-season of 1908-09 Grant received his law degree and was admitted to the Massachusetts bar, and for the rest of his baseball career he practiced law in Boston during the winter months.

Grant enjoyed his finest big league season in 1909, batting .269 as Philadelphia's leadoff hitter and finishing second in the National League with 170 hits. Before a doubleheader against the New York Giants that year, he supposedly found a domino with seven white spots. As the story goes, after joking with teammates that the domino was an omen that he would have seven hits that day, Eddie went 5-for-5 against Christy Mathewson in the first game, then batted safely in his first two at-bats against Rube Marquard in the second. The seven consecutive hits were believed to be an NL record, but Eddie remained modest. "I didn't get another hit off Matty all season," he recalled.

Grant put up similar numbers the next year, when one commentator called him "perhaps the best-hitting third baseman in the National League, barring Bobby Byrne of the Pittsburgs," but the 1910 season proved to be the apex of his career. In February 1911 he was sent to the Reds in the trade that brought Hans Lobert and Dode Paskert to the Phillies. In Cincinnati Eddie slumped to a .223 average in his final season as a regular, improving slightly to .239 as a part-timer in 1912. Many attributed his sudden decline to a tragedy in his personal life. In 1911 Eddie had married Irene Soest in Philadelphia, but she died of heart trouble less than nine months later. The Giants purchased Grant in the midst of the 1913 season. He played sparingly as New York captured its third consecutive pennant, and that fall he participated in his only World Series, appearing as a pinch-hitter and pinch-runner. Grant held on for two more seasons as John McGraw's bench coach and seldom used utilityman. Before spring training in 1916 he announced his retirement, intending to devote himself to his Boston law practice. He was 32 years old.

Grant's career as a full-time lawyer lasted barely one year. When the United States declared war on Germany on April 6, 1917, he became the first major leaguer to enlist (Hank Gowdy was the first active major leaguer). After four months of officer training in Plattsburgh, New York, Grant was commissioned as captain of Company H of the 307th Infantry Regiment and sent to Camp Upton on Long Island for several months of training with the troops he would lead. Arriving in France as part of the American Expeditionary Forces, Grant's division saw some combat before being assigned to the Meuse-Argonne offensive, the final great American drive of the war.

On October 2, 1918, the 307th Regiment launched an attack in the Argonne Forest, a rugged, heavily wooded area with thick underbrush, deep ravines, and marshes. By the morning of the third day, October 5, Eddie was exhausted. He hadn't slept since the beginning of the offensive, and some fellow officers noticed him sitting on a stump with a cup of coffee in front of him, too weak to lift the cup. One of his troops, a former policeman at the Polo Grounds, remembered: "Eddie was dog-tired but he stepped off at the head of his outfit with no more concern than if he were walking to his old place at third base after his side had finished its turn at the bat. He staggered from weakness when he first started off, but pretty soon he was marching briskly with his head up."

Later that day the 307th was moving forward when Major Jay, as he was carried past on a litter, ordered Captain Grant, the highest-ranking officer left in his battalion, to assume command. The major had hardly spoken when a shell came through the trees, wounding two of Grant's lieutenants. Eddie was waving his hands and calling out for more stretcher bearers when a shell struck him. It was a direct hit, killing him instantly.

Eddie Grant was buried in the Argonne Forest only a few yards from where he fell. Later his remains were moved to the Romagne Cemetery in France. A monument in Grant's honor was unveiled at the Polo Grounds on Memorial Day 1921, and a highway in the Bronx, a baseball field at Dean Academy (now Dean Junior College), and two American Legion posts still bear his name.

TOM SIMON

PHILADELPHIA

George Watt McQuillan
Right-handed pitcher 1907–10, 1915–16

George McQuillan was the Doc Gooden of the Deadball Era. In 1908 he enjoyed one of the best rookie seasons ever, going 23-17 for the mediocre Phillies with a sparkling 1.53 ERA in nearly 360 innings of work (in 1985 the young Gooden posted an identical ERA). An unusually fast worker even in an era of briskly paced games, McQuillan pitched with "supreme self-confidence," according to *Baseball Magazine*, becoming known as the brightest young pitcher in the game. Within three years, however, his career came crashing down in a sordid web of alcoholism, sexual escapades, and financial troubles.

George Watt McQuillan's parents, Mary (Smyth) and Robert McQuillan, were Irish immigrants living in Brooklyn when George was born on May 1, 1885. A few years later the family moved to Paterson, New Jersey, the first planned industrial city in the United States. After playing outfield for his high school team, McQuillan got his start in professional baseball in 1904 with Paterson's minor league team in the Hudson River League. On January 5, 1905, he married 19-year-old Mary Bernadine, whom he'd met at the Paterson ballpark. The couple had a son, George Jr., in 1906. After his marriage, McQuillan supplemented his baseball income by working as an electrician during winters for the Edison Electric Company in Paterson.

Abandoning the outfield for the pitcher's mound, McQuillan put together impressive minor league stints at Paterson, New Bedford, Jersey City, and Providence before joining the Phillies in 1907. He pitched well, posting a 4-0 record and 0.66 ERA in six games, earning a shot at Philadelphia's starting rotation in 1908. By almost any measuring stick, McQuillan was the second-best pitcher in the National League that season, inferior only to Christy Mathewson. *Baseball Magazine* said

he had "enough inherent ability to make him a worthy rival of Mathewson." He also bore a physical resemblance to the great Giant pitcher. At 6'0" and 185 lbs., "Big Mac" was intimidating. As one writer put it, "he looms up on the landscape like the head boss of a gang of lumber jacks or a scene shifter in a stone quarry." Thanks largely to McQuillan, who pitched in 48 games (15 more than any of his teammates), the Phillies led the league in ERA at 2.10.

McQuillan spent the winter of 1908-09 pitching for Matanzas in the Cuban Winter League, facing African American stars such as John Henry Lloyd, Pete Hill, Grant Johnson, and Bruce Petway. Mac started out 0-2, including a 4-2 loss to the legendary Cuban hurler José Méndez, who pitched for Almendares. The hapless Matanzas club, mired in last place with a 3-36 record, folded in midseason. The free-spending McQuillan, who'd been counting on a full season's paycheck, was left penniless and stranded in Havana. He borrowed $25 from a friend for passage back to the United States, a debt the friend was still trying to collect three years later. Shortly after returning from Cuba, McQuillan came down with what the media called a case of jaundice, but which probably was a venereal disease contracted in Havana. He still pitched almost 250 innings in 1909, posting a 13-16 record for the Phillies despite a 2.14 ERA.

By that time Mary McQuillan had filed for divorce and George was an alcoholic. While never overtly mentioning his alcoholism, sportswriters constantly criticized his "refusal to take care of himself"; one writer said his "careless disregard of training rules" had made him "undependable," while another said he "failed to keep in condition." McQuillan's unreliability limited him to 152⅓ innings in 1910, and the frustrated

Phillies decided to get rid of him even though he'd posted a league-leading 1.60 ERA. After the season the Phils sent McQuillan to the Reds in a mammoth deal involving eight players, all of them major league regulars.

Almost immediately after becoming property of the Reds, George McQuillan hit rock bottom. On November 24, 1910, he reported to a medical clinic in Hot Springs, Arkansas, the Reds spring training site. He was diagnosed with secondary syphilis, an advanced but not serious stage of the disease. "He must let alcohol alone and stick to his treatment and if he will do that he will come out all right," wrote his doctor, W. O. Forbes, in a letter to Reds owner Garry Herrmann, who'd reluctantly agreed to pick up the tab for the treatment. "He has made up his mind thoroughly to abstain from alcohol in all forms and this will be of great value to him the coming year. I will outline a course of treatment for him to follow during the summer which will in no way interfere with his work and, I feel sure, will keep him in A-1 condition. [We] will take good care of him and see that he *behaves*."

In addition to paying for the syphilis treatment, Herrmann also paid for McQuillan's wife, with whom the pitcher had reconciled, to join him in Hot Springs. To make amends, George bought $270 worth of jewelry on credit from a Hot Springs jeweler. The store balked at first, but after McQuillan got a respectable citizen—Senators catcher Gabby Street—to vouch for him, the store let him purchase the jewelry. Two years later the jeweler, after repeatedly failing to collect from McQuillan, was forced to appeal to the National Commission for the funds to be drawn out of McQuillan's paychecks.

Though Dr. Forbes had assured Herrmann that his pitcher would be as good as new by the start of spring training, McQuillan in 1911 bore no resemblance to the promising pitcher of a few years earlier. After watching him post a 2-6 record and 4.68 ERA in half a season, the Reds, according to one report, "jumped at the chance to let him slide to the minors when the opportunity presented itself." The Reds felt that "McQuillan's persistent refusal to take care of himself and to lead the simple life ruined a most promising career," and sold his contract to Columbus of the American Association. The move served as a wake-up call, and George became determined to make it back to the majors. "I won't be in Columbus long, let me tell

you," he told *Baseball Magazine*. "They can't keep me down in the sticks." That statement is ironic in hindsight, for McQuillan spent the rest of his life in the Ohio capital—it remained his permanent home until his death in 1940.

In the three seasons he pitched for the Columbus Senators, McQuillan compiled a 34-30 record with a 2.34 ERA. In 1913 he was hit on the head by a line drive, an injury that at first was believed to be career-threatening. He recovered quickly, however, and had a 12-4 record in July 1913 when he returned to the majors with the Pittsburgh Pirates. McQuillan had three middling seasons with Pittsburgh before the Phillies reacquired him on waivers in mid-1915. He pitched relatively well, but Philadelphia let him go in 1916. After a brief stint with Cleveland in 1918, McQuillan's major league career was over. He remained in the minors until 1924, pitching for Kansas City, Peoria, Nashville, New Orleans, Rock Island, and Columbus, the latter two of which he also managed. Soon after his retirement he found employment as manager of a furniture warehouse in Columbus, a job he held until he died of a heart attack on May 30, 1940.

ERIC ENDERS

PHILADELPHIA

FREDERICK WILLIAM LUDERUS
FIRST BASEMAN 1910–20

Though acknowledging that Fred Luderus "is not a McInnis on defense, nor a Daubert in batting, nor a Merkle on the baselines," J. C. Kofoed in the July 1915 issue of *Baseball Magazine* called the Phillies first baseman "the most underrated man in baseball today." A pure fastball hitter who feasted on pitches between his waist and shoulders, Luderus reached double digits in home runs each season from 1911 to 1914, taking as much advantage of Baker Bowl's short right field as anyone; 75% of his 83 home runs in a Phillies uniform came at home. Only a fair fielder (he led National League first basemen in errors four times) and never a streak of lightning on his feet (his nine stolen bases in 1915 were a career high), the modest Ludy became known for his dependability after his home run hitting dropped off. From 1916 to 1920 he played in 533 consecutive games, considered "the greatest streak of continuous play by a modern major leaguer."

Frederick William Luderus (pronounced loo-DARE-us) was born in Milwaukee on September 12, 1885. In his teenage years the thick-boned, heavy-muscled German American earned a reputation on the Milwaukee sandlots as a rugged first baseman, eventually signing to play in 1905 with Sault Ste. Marie of a short-lived Class D circuit called the Copper Country Soo League. The next season it became known as the Northern Copper Country League, and Luderus returned each year (with Grand Forks until that team disbanded, then with Winnipeg) until the struggling circuit folded after the 1907 season. After sitting out the 1908 season with diphtheria, Fred resumed his career in 1909 with Freeport, Illinois, and led the Wisconsin-Illinois League in hitting with a .321 average. On the recommendation of scout George Huff, the Chicago Cubs purchased his contract for $2,200.

The 24-year-old Luderus replaced the disappointing Del Howard as Frank Chance's principal backup. Setting foot in a big-league ballpark for the first time on September 23, 1909, Fred batted .297 and drove in nine runs in 11 games with the Cubs. At West Side Grounds on September 29 he connected for an inside-the-park home run, the first of his career 84 homers. Ironically, it was the only one he hit for a team other than the Phillies, and it came against the Phillies' Lew Moren. In 1910 Chance used second-string catcher Jimmy Archer as his primary backup at first base. Luderus played infrequently, batting .204 in just 54 at-bats, and in August the Cubs traded him to Philadelphia for left hander Bill Foxen. The Phillies intended to use Luderus as a temporary replacement for the ailing Kitty Bransfield, but Ludy batted .294 down the stretch with 14 RBI in 21 games, forcing manager Red Dooin to consider him as a candidate for the first-base job in 1911. At training camp the following spring, the 36-year-old Bransfield failed to regain his prowess and Luderus stole his position.

Most believed that Bransfield would win back his position once the warmer weather arrived, but the Phillies ended up releasing the popular veteran when the left-handed hitting (but right-handed throwing) Luderus started popping balls over Baker Bowl's short right-field fence. It was nearly four weeks into the campaign before the rookie hit his first homer, but he then collected five in 12 days. After another month's drought, the streaky Luderus smashed nine during a three-week period. On July 15, 1911, he became the first player in Phillies history to hit two over-the-fence home runs in a single game, in the process establishing himself as the NL leader in home runs with 14. Ludy notched just two more over the final 11 weeks, but he hit .301 for the season and his 16 circuit clouts led the Phillies and ranked second in the league behind Wildfire Schulte's 21. He finished third in the NL in RBI (99) and total bases (260).

In 1913 Luderus clubbed a career-high 18 home runs—three more than the entire St. Louis Cardinals, but one less than teammate Gavy Cravath. Out-of-town sportswriters constantly poked fun at the bumper crop of home runs in Philadelphia, blaming it on the "cigar box" the Phillies played in. To a certain extent their criticism was valid. The Phillies did hit 51 of their major league-leading 73 home runs at Baker Bowl, but they also led the majors in home runs hit on the road.

Ludy's most successful season was 1915, when new manager Pat Moran appointed him captain and the Quakers captured their first NL pennant. Though he hit only seven home runs, down from 12 the previous season, Luderus set career highs in batting average (.315) and doubles (36), finishing second in the NL behind Larry Doyle of the Giants in both categories. In that year's World Series, Fred was a shining star in defeat, batting .437 (the Phillies collectively batted .182) with a home run and six of his club's nine RBI.

Luderus's ability to hit home runs didn't return after 1915; he hit exactly five in each of the next four seasons despite not missing a single game after June 2, 1916. He received as much attention for his durability as he ever had for his slugging. On August 3, 1919, Luderus played his 479th consecutive game, breaking the modern record set only one year earlier by Eddie Collins of the White Sox. Ludy's streak had almost ended earlier in 1919. Phillies manager Jack Coombs had started another first baseman because Fred was suffering from a charley horse, but baseball record keeper Al Munro Elias was at the ballpark that day and pleaded with Coombs to get Luderus into the game. Coombs sent Fred in to pinch-hit and the streak survived. On September 24, 1919, the 525th game of the streak, the Phillies honored their dependable first baseman with a "Fred Luderus Day," presenting him with a gold watch and diamond stickpin between games of a doubleheader.

The streak continued until Opening Day 1920. Suffering from an attack of lumbago, Luderus was unable to play and the streak ended at 533 games, which remained the NL record until the otherwise unremarkable Eddie Brown broke it in 1927. Fred's back condition proved serious; he appeared in just 16

games in 1920, his last season in the major leagues. Beginning in 1921, he spent 10 of the next 13 years managing in the minors, eight as a player-manager. Ludy could still hit. In 1923 he batted .362 and led Oklahoma City to the Western League pennant. With the same club the following season Luderus reportedly taught a young Carl Hubbell how to throw the screwball. All told, he spent seven seasons managing in the Oklahoma capital.

After retiring from baseball, Luderus returned to Milwaukee and worked as the grounds supervisor at the Milwaukee Yacht Club. With professional assistance from former teammate Cy Williams, who'd become an accomplished architect, he built a house in the Three Lakes region of northern Wisconsin. Eventually he started his own toy business, developing a national market for dolls and animals made of yarn. Fred Luderus suffered a fatal heart attack at his home in Three Lakes on the evening of January 5, 1961. Survived by his wife, Emmy, and three daughters, he was buried in Milwaukee's Pinelawn Cemetery.

JOE DITTMAR

Patrick Moran

PHILADELPHIA

PATRICK JOSEPH MORAN
CATCHER 1910–14, MANAGER 1915–18

Following a lengthy playing career in the National League, mostly as a reserve catcher, Pat Moran became one of the Deadball Era's most successful managers. In a span of five years, Moran took over two mediocre franchises with little history of winning, rebuilt their rosters, and managed each to its first NL pennant. In contrast to some managers of the era, he showed that a manager could win while treating his players honestly and with respect. "As leader, it is my business to give orders, and these are always carried out," Moran explained. "Not by the 'mailed fist' method, as I do not believe in that style, but as one friend to another. The players carry them out because they have confidence in me."

Patrick Joseph Moran was born on February 7, 1876, in the mill town of Fitchburg, Massachusetts. As a youth he worked in one of the local textile mills for $3 per week, playing catcher on the company baseball team alongside teammates who were several years older. Moran was recruited by a semi-pro club in Orange, Massachusetts, where he performed well and attracted the attention of the organized minor leagues. He spent two years with Lyons in the New York State League before that club sold him to Montreal in the Eastern League, where he played two more years. In the minors Pat became known more for his excellent throwing arm than his mediocre offense.

Purchased by the NL's Boston Beaneaters in 1901, the 25-year-old Moran played his first major league season under legendary manager Frank Selee, whom he later credited for his own managerial success. Pat spent five years in Boston, playing more or less regularly after his rookie season. His best year was 1903, when he hit a career-high .262 and was one of six National Leaguers to finish second in the league with seven home runs (Brooklyn's Jimmy Sheckard led the circuit with nine). Additionally, he set the single-season record for assists by a catcher at 214, a mark that still stands. In 1906 the Chicago Cubs purchased him to back up Johnny Kling. The timing of the move proved serendipitous for Moran, who became a valuable reserve on one of baseball's greatest teams. He also met his wife in Chicago; their marriage led to two children.

Prior to 1910 the Philadelphia Phillies acquired Moran as their backup catcher. His playing time dwindled after a couple of years as the top reserve, but the Phils recognized his intelligence and ability with pitchers, and his duties evolved into those of a pitching coach. When owner William Baker jettisoned manager Red Dooin after the 1914 season, the Philadelphia players strongly backed Moran's elevation to manager. Baker agreed, naming him to the post in October but giving him only a one-year contract for $4,500. Some doubt existed as to how Moran would do with a mostly veteran club that possessed many players on long-term contracts. One reporter noted that the Phillies were "not keen for keeping the rules of training and were mighty hard to handle." But the new manager made several personnel moves that transformed the Phillies from a sixth-place club into 1915's pennant winner. Though none were celebrated at the time, one year later they were deemed "so successful they could be counted as 'once in a lifetime' affairs."

Several weeks after Moran's hiring, the Phillies purchased shortstop Dave Bancroft from the Pacific Coast League. The question of what to do with Dooin lingered, as he was still regarded as a valuable backup catcher and was threatening to jump to the Federal League. Moran traded him to Cincinnati for their starting third baseman, Bert Niehoff, then shifted Niehoff to second to plug that hole. Another forced trade shipped outfielder Sherry Magee, who was disappointed at not being named manager, to the Boston Braves for Oscar Dugey, a reserve infielder, and Possum Whitted, a 25-year-old outfielder. In his final major off-season trade, Moran sent third baseman Hans Lobert, who was past his prime, to the New York Giants for pitcher Al Demaree, 21-year-old third baseman Milt Stock, back-up catcher Jack Adams, and cash. Thus Moran replaced the second baseman and shortstop the Phils had lost to the Federal League in 1914 and added new starters at third and in the outfield.

The Phillies gained the league lead on July 14 and never looked back, winning the pennant by seven games over the defending-champion Boston Braves. After winning Game One of the World Series against the Boston Red Sox, 3-1, the Phillies dropped four consecutive one-run games, three by the score of 2-1. Baker took his time about resigning Moran, who was now without a contract. After some arduous negotiations, Moran signed a three-year contract for $25,000. Over the next few years the club essentially stood pat, making few moves to improve further as Baker exhibited his parsimonious ways. Moran led the Phillies to back-to-back second-place finishes in 1916-17, but the club fell to sixth in the war-muddled 1918 season after Baker turned to player sales as a way of making money. With his three-year contract expired, Moran must not have been too disappointed when the Phillies let him go. His good friend John McGraw snapped him up as his pitching coach at a salary of $5,000, one of the era's highest for a coach.

Moran never coached a single game for the Giants. After the 1918 season Cincinnati Reds owner Garry Herrmann, unable to determine the status of his manager, Christy Mathewson, who'd been sent to Europe with the AEF in 1918, hired Moran away from McGraw. The Reds had finished slightly above .500 in each of the previous two seasons. The team featured two of the National League's best players in center fielder Edd

Roush and third baseman Heinie Groh, and it also had the makings of a decent pitching staff, but with a few exceptions the rest of the team was mediocre.

As he had with the Phillies, Moran immediately set about recasting his new club. The Reds traded shortstop Larry Kopf and outfielder Tommy Griffith to Brooklyn for first baseman Jake Daubert. When Kopf failed to report, Moran swapped his own holdout second baseman, Lee Magee, to get his shortstop back. To fill the second base hole, Moran brought in Morris Rath from the minor leagues. The club also claimed pitcher Slim Sallee on waivers from the New York Giants; in 1919 Sallee finished second in the NL with 21 wins. Additionally, Moran installed Dutch Ruether, who'd been claimed off waivers from the Cubs in 1917, in the starting rotation; Ruether went on to lead the league in winning percentage.

The 1919 Reds won the pennant with a winning percentage of .686, the highest of any major league team since the 1912 Boston Red Sox. Cincinnati then defeated the Chicago White Sox in the World Series, five games to three. (Of course, that was the infamous Black Sox Series in which a number of the Sox conspired with gamblers to give less than their best effort.) In 1920 the Reds battled the Giants and Dodgers into September before finishing third. The next year the team slumped to sixth, but Moran worked his magic once again. His 1922 starting eight included only two players, Daubert and Roush, left over from the 1919 world champions. He also overhauled the pitching staff, in one move acquiring future Hall of Famer Eppa Rixey, whom he knew from his days with the Phillies. In 1922 and 1923 the Reds finished a strong second to a Giants club that won four consecutive pennants.

Always a heavy drinker, Moran's addiction took a turn for the worse over the winter of 1923-24 and he began skipping meals. By the time he arrived for spring training, the 48-year-old manager was already ill. His condition quickly deteriorated, and on March 7, 1924, he passed away at the Reds training camp in Orlando, Florida. The official cause of death was listed as Bright's disease, a kidney ailment. Moran left behind an impressive managerial resume: one World Series victory, two NL pennants, and four second-place finishes in only nine seasons of managing.

DAN LEVITT

PHILADELPHIA

GROVER CLEVELAND "PETE" ALEXANDER
RIGHT-HANDED PITCHER 1911–17

Pete Alexander didn't look the part of the National League's most dominant pitcher of the Deadball Era's second decade. Unlike his older contemporaries Christy Mathewson and Walter Johnson, who had a majestic, almost regal way about them, Alex carried himself with an unhurried shuffle, a uniform that never seemed to fit just right, and a cap that looked a size too small and stood on his head at a precarious tilt. But when he pitched, he was the picture of grace and efficiency— often completing games in less than 90 minutes—with a smooth three-quarter delivery and outstanding control of a sneaky fastball and devastating curve that he kept low and outside. Despite pitching half his games in tiny Baker Bowl, a graveyard for pitchers, he put together arguably the best season ever by a rookie pitcher in 1911, and each year from 1915-17 he won the pitching Triple Crown, leading the NL in wins, strikeouts, and ERA.

Grover Cleveland Alexander—called "Dode" by family and friends, and later "Old Pete" or "Alex" by teammates and the press—was born to William and Margaret (Cootey) Alexander on February 26, 1887, in the tiny farming community of Elba, Nebraska. He was one of 13 children (12 boys), the sixth of eight to survive into adulthood. Grover considered himself "an average farm boy" and described his youth as "more or less a matter of long days of work and short nights of sleep." He acquired a reputation as an excellent cornhusker, a task his father credited with giving him the powerful wrist that made his curveball so deadly. Young Dode also developed his control by throwing stones at clothespins or chickens. William Alexander hoped his son would study law, as had his presidential namesake, but Dode chose to became a lineman with the phone company so he could play ball on weekends.

In 1909 Alexander signed with Galesburg of the Illinois-Missouri League and went 15-8 with six shutouts. In late July, however, he suffered an injury that ended his first season prematurely and cast doubts about his future. Dode was running from first to second, trying to break up a double play, when the shortstop's throw hit him square in the right temple. He was unconscious for two days. Alexander awoke suffering from double vision, which he endured through the fall and winter and into the spring, when it disappeared as suddenly as it had come.

The 1910 season got off to a bizarre start for Alexander. Galesburg sold him to Indianapolis of the American Association, but the Hoosiers, having heard of his double vision and suspicious that Galesburg had been so anxious to let him go, sold him to Syracuse of the New York State League. There Alexander pitched a stretch of 87 innings in which the only run he allowed scored on an error with two outs in the ninth inning. For the season he was 29-11 with an ERA of 1.85, earning the nickname "Alex the Great." Clearly he was ready for the majors, but the Philadelphia Phillies were more interested in George Chalmers of Scranton. They got Chalmers for $3,000 and, as insurance, drafted Alex from Syracuse for $500. Chalmers struggled over seven seasons, but Philadelphia's investment in Alexander yielded a better dividend.

"You'll pitch five innings," Phillies catcher Pat Moran told the 24-year-old Alex before his first game in Philadelphia, a City Series exhibition in 1911 against the world champion Athletics. "They'll be murder, but you'll learn something." Instead it was the A's who did the learning, as the rookie from Nebraska allowed no runs, hits, or walks in his five innings, a harbinger of the greatest season ever by a rookie pitcher. Capping off his spectacular year with a 12-inning, 1-0 victory over a 44-year-old Cy Young, who was nearing retirement, Alex led the NL in complete games (31), innings (367), and shutouts (7). With a mediocre team behind him, he also led the NL with 28 wins, which remains the modern record for rookies. His 227 strikeouts, good for second in the league, stood as the rookie record until Herb Score gunned down 245 for the Indians in 1955.

From 1912-14 Alexander remained one of the league's best pitchers, ranking among the leaders each year in innings and strikeouts, but in 1915 he raised his performance to an even higher level. That year he went 31-10 to lead the NL in wins and achieve the first of his four pitcher's triple crowns, leading the league with a microscopic 1.22 ERA and a career-high 241 strikeouts. Alex also led the NL in the rest of the important pitcher's statistics in 1915: innings (376⅓), complete games (36), winning percentage (.756), and shutouts (12). The first of his four one-hitters that season, a 3-0 win in St. Louis on June 5, was the closest he ever came to a major league no-hitter; shortstop Artie Butler of the Cardinals singled past his head with two down in the ninth. In the World Series, Alexander defeated Boston's Ernie Shore in Game One, 3-1, but lost Game Three, 2-1, as Duffy Lewis singled in the bottom of the ninth to score Harry Hooper. He was too exhausted to pitch Game Five, and the Phillies lost a heartbreaker, 5-4, behind Erskine Mayer and Eppa Rixey.

Rebounding from the disappointing Series, Alexander won his second Triple Crown in 1916: 33-12, 167 strikeouts, and a 1.55 ERA. He reached career highs in innings (389), starts (45), complete games (38), and shutouts (16), becoming the only NL pitcher to reach double figures twice in shutouts and setting the modern record by three over Jack Coombs (1910) and Bob Gibson (1968). In 1917 Alex went 30-13 and led the NL in innings (388), strikeouts (200), starts (44), complete games (34), and shutouts (8). Under the rules of 1917, Alexander won the ERA title at 1.83 to give him his third pitcher's Triple Crown; under today's rules, however, the title would belong to Fred Anderson

of the Giants, who compiled his 1.44 ERA in 162 innings but with fewer than 10 complete games.

With World War I raging in Europe, on December 11, 1917, the Philadelphia front office committed one of the most cynical acts in baseball history. After Alexander informed the Phillies that he'd be drafted into the army, owner William Baker sent him and his catcher, Bill Killefer, to the Chicago Cubs for Mike Prendergast, Pickles Dillhoefer, and $55,000. Alex won two of his three 1918 decisions, all complete games, before the army finally came calling. On May 31 he married Amy Marie Arrants of Omaha, whom he'd met on a blind date several years earlier, then reported for duty at Ft. Dunston, Kansas. A sergeant assigned to the 89th Division and the 342nd Field Artillery, Alex shipped out on June 28 and arrived in Liverpool on July 9. His unit went to the front late in July.

Alexander survived the war but never fully recovered from it. He spent seven weeks at the front under relentless bombardment that rendered him deaf in his left ear. Pulling the lanyard to fire the howitzers caused muscle damage in his strong right arm. Alex caught some shrapnel in his outer right ear, an injury considered minor at the time but which may have been the progenitor of cancer almost 30 years later. He was shell-shocked. Worst of all, the man who used to have a round or two with the guys became alcoholic and epileptic, a condition possibly caused by the skulling he'd received in Galesburg in 1909. Living in a world that believed epileptics to be touched by the devil, he used alcohol to cover up his epilepsy because he knew it was more acceptable to be a drunk.

Alexander returned to the Cubs on May 9, 1919, and had to work his way back into shape, dropping his first five decisions in the process. Once he got turned around, he finished at 16-11 and led the NL with nine shutouts and a sparkling 1.72 ERA, which remains the lowest for a Cub pitcher since the team began playing in Wrigley Field. In 1920 he put together the fourth and last of his Triple Crown seasons: 27-14 with 173 strikeouts and a 1.91 ERA. From 1921 on, however,

Alexander was a different pitcher, still winning more than he lost but depending on finesse and pinpoint control, never striking out 100 batters again and posting ERAs over 3.00 for the first time in his career.

Ending his major league career in the place where it started, Alex lost all three decisions with the Phillies in 1930—his first losing record ever—and was released. The previous season he'd won nine games for the Cardinals, giving him a career total of 373, the number he believed put him ahead of Christy Mathewson's 372 and gave him the NL record. Decades later, however, researchers discovered an error in Matty's 1902 numbers, improving his record from 13-18 to 14-17 and linking the two right handers forever in the record books. Alex tried to continue with Dallas in the Texas League but was ineffective. He also pitched a few games with the House of David team.

The last two decades of Alexander's life are the picture of a man spinning out of control. He entered various sanitariums seeking help, but nothing worked. Having put up with enough, Amy divorced him in 1929, hoping to shock him to his senses, but remarried him in 1931. Alex shuffled around the country in an odyssey of odd jobs (including a stint recounting his 1926 World Series strikeout of Tony Lazzeri in a Times Square flea circus), cheap hotels, boarding houses, and the like. His poverty and inability to straighten out became an embarrassment to baseball. The Cardinals sent $50 a month to whoever was keeping Alex to dole out as necessary under the ruse that it was his NL pension.

Alexander's desperate situation found temporary relief in his election to the Hall of Fame in 1938. He pulled himself together enough to go to Cooperstown for the first induction ceremony on June 12, 1939, and thoroughly enjoyed his time with the honorees. It was bittersweet, though. As Alex put it, "I'm in the Hall of Fame, and I'm proud to be there, but I can't eat the Hall of Fame." The Alexanders divorced again in 1941 but remained close. Alex suffered a heart attack on October 15, 1946, as he was leaving Sportsman's Park after watching the Cardinals beat the Red Sox in the World Series. In 1947 he was injured in a fall during an epileptic seizure in Los Angeles. He also developed cancer on his right ear, necessitating its amputation.

Alexander made his last public appearance as a guest of the Yankees at Games Three and Four of the 1950 World Series. Back in St. Paul, Minnesota, he left his hotel room to mail a letter to Amy on November 4, telling her he was looking forward to meeting her in Kansas City. Alex went back to his room and died. He was buried with full military honors in his family's plot in Elmwood Cemetery outside St. Paul. His death certificate says he died of cardiac failure, but Amy always believed that he died in a fall from an epileptic seizure.

JAN FINKEL

PHILA.

Dode Paskert

PHILADELPHIA

GEORGE HENRY "DODE" PASKERT
CENTER FIELDER 1911–17

Fleet-footed Dode Paskert was one of the finest defensive center fielders of the Deadball Era. "It is no exaggeration to say that Paskert is one of the greatest judges of a fly ball in the game today," wrote *Baseball Magazine*'s J. C. Kofoed in 1915. "Those who have seem him circle, hawk-like, turn his back and speed outward, and then make a daring leap, with the spoiling of a three-bagger at the end of it, know how true that statement is." Paskert was an extremely patient hitter who worked pitchers deep into the count, often ranking among the National League leaders in both walks and strikeouts. A pronounced pull hitter, he choked up on the bat and found his hits by punching the ball into left field. Though used most often in the leadoff position, Paskert frequently hit for extra bases; from 1912-18 he ranked among the NL's Top 10 in doubles four times and home runs once.

George Henry Paskert was born in Cleveland on August 28, 1881, the oldest of three children of Matilda (Radermacher) and Bernard Paskert, a railroad flagman. The grandson of German immigrants, George completed two years of high school before finding work as a machinist's apprentice. He was still working in that profession in 1904 when a traveling salesman saw him pitch for a semipro club in Warren, Ohio, and recommended him and a teammate, future major leaguer Jimmy Austin, to Dayton of the Central League. Converting to the outfield, Paskert spent three seasons with Dayton before moving on to Atlanta, where he batted .290, led the Southern Association in stolen bases, and helped the team to the 1907 championship. The Cincinnati Reds purchased his contract two weeks before the end of the season. Paskert was already 26 years old, though few knew it at the time. For several years into his major league career, his birth year was incorrectly reported as 1886, leading contemporaries to believe he was five years younger than his true age.

The precise origin of Paskert's nickname (an early 20th-century moniker also applied at various times to Joe "Dode" Birmingham and Pete "Dode" Alexander) has been lost to history, but more than likely it was a dig at his perceived low intelligence. *The English Dialect Dictionary*, published in 1900, describes a "dode" as a "slow [-witted] person," and a scattering of press accounts confirm that Paskert was considered stupid. In 1911, for example, *Baseball Magazine*'s W. A. Phelon grouped Paskert with fellow center fielder Johnny Bates in that regard. "Certain critics declare that there is no choice between Bates and Paskert when it comes to intelligence," Phelon wrote, "that both of them are crowned with domes of elephant-tusk, and that if either of them ever thought quickly it must have been when deciding whether to take beer or ginger ale." Whatever its origin, the nickname didn't bother Paskert, who usually included "Dode" in his signature.

A second nickname, "Honey Boy," was more complimentary. So named because he was "such a sweet ballplayer," the 5'11", 165-lb. center fielder impressed observers from the start with his speed and superior range, though his offensive skills took longer to mature. After posting on-base percentages of .298 and .327 in 1908 and 1909, respectively, Paskert enjoyed a breakout season in 1910, when he paced all NL outfielders in putouts and finished third in the league with 51 stolen bases. Most impressively, he batted .300 and led the Reds with a .389 on-base percentage. Despite that performance, Cincinnati failed to finish in the first division for the third time in four years, prompting manager Clark Griffith to overhaul his roster. The following February, the Reds shipped Paskert to the Phillies, along with teammates Fred Beebe, Jack Rowan, and Hans Lobert, in exchange for Johnny Bates, Eddie Grant, George McQuillan, and Lew Moren. Cincinnati soon regretted the trade, as Paskert proved to be by far the most valuable of the eight players in the deal.

On April 13, 1911, in just his second game with his new club, Honey Boy made one of the sweetest catches of the Deadball Era. In the bottom of the eighth inning, Fred Snodgrass of the Giants smashed a deep line drive into the gap in left-center field at the Polo Grounds. It looked like a sure home run, but Paskert raced after the drive and at the last moment turned, dove parallel to the ground, and speared the ball with his bare hand. Years later, such experienced observers as sportswriters Fred Lieb and Jim Nasium and Phillies left fielder Sherry Magee still considered it the greatest catch they'd ever seen. It was also one of the last at the original Polo Grounds. The day after the game, the wooden park burned to the ground and was replaced two months later by the steel and-concrete edifice that hosted the Giants for the next 46 years. Four years later Paskert again drew praise for his fielding, this time on the larger stage offered by the 1915 World Series. Matched up against Boston's Tris Speaker, the concensus choice for greatest outfielder of the era, Dode outshined his rival by making several spectacular grabs. In Game Three Paskert recorded seven putouts, several of which were of the "hair-raising variety."

Paskert brought more to the Phillies than his fielding. In 1912 he enjoyed the best offensive season of his career, posting career highs in batting average (.315), on-base percentage (.420), and slugging percentage (.413). That showing convinced the Phillies to sign Paskert to a three-year contract, a rare display of confidence during the heyday of the reserve clause. But the following season his offensive production declined as he was at various times hampered by scarlet fever, a broken index finger, a dislocated middle finger, and a groin injury. Though Paskert never replicated his standout 1912 season, he remained an integral part of the Philadelphia attack for several years, finishing in the league's Top 10 in runs three times from 1913-17.

In an era when most players faded quickly after their primes, Dode impressed observers with his consistent, durable play in the face of advancing age. "Time does not dim him," wrote *The Sporting News* in 1917. "His arm is as dangerous to a base runner as ever and his hit-

ting eye does not seem to have lost any of its keenness." Jim Nasium added, "The remarkable thing about Paskert at 36 years of age is that he has lost none of the use of his legs, and is still able to pull down the hits or circle the bases at full speed without even breathing hard. He is never even attacked by charley horse, never suffers from sprained tendons, and never has to tape his legs as a result of the strain of continual service." Nasium concluded that Paskert as a fielder was still "better than Speaker in going to his left" and better than Cobb "in any direction."

Such high praise undoubtedly helped persuade the Chicago Cubs to trade their young slugger Cy Williams for Paskert following the 1917 season. The deal was one of many shortsighted exchanges in Cubs history: Williams spent the next 13 seasons in Philadelphia, winning three home run crowns, while Dode's days as an effective major leaguer were numbered. Over the next few seasons he continued to impress with his play in center field, but injuries to his wrist and back finally began to diminish his offense. In 1919 Paskert batted .196, and though he rebounded to hit .279 in 1920, that off-season the Cubs sold him to Cincinnati for the waiver price. Back where he'd started his major league career 14 years earlier, he collected 16 hits in 92 at-bats before drawing his release.

Shortly before leaving the major league scene, Paskert was hailed as a hero for his actions in rescuing three families from an early-morning fire. According to newspaper reports, Dode and a friend were walking home at 1:30 A.M. on February 23, 1921, when they spotted the blaze. While his friend pulled the alarm, Paskert made three trips up a burning stairwell, carrying out five children and directing their parents to safety. "In rescuing the families," the *Cleveland Plain-Dealer* reported, "Paskert's hands were burned badly and his face blistered by the flames." More than an act of selfless heroism, Paskert's courage also may have brought redemption. Seven years earlier, he was driving his car through a crowded Cleveland street when he ran down and gravely injured a 12-year-old delivery boy. Paskert was charged with violating the speeding ordinance and was sued by the boy's father for $12,000.

Though past 40, Paskert refused to retire when the Reds dropped him in 1921. Over the next six years he traveled the country as an itinerant minor leaguer—with Kansas City and Columbus in the American Association, Atlanta and Nashville of the Southern Association, and Erie of the Ohio-Penn League—before finally leaving the game at age 46 after the 1927 season. Dode returned to Cleveland, where he lived with his wife, Emily Belle DeKalb (whom he'd married in 1902), and their one son, finding work as an inspector for the Gabriel Snubber Company. Surviving his wife by five years, he passed away on February 12, 1959, after suffering a stroke. Paskert is buried in St. Mary's Cemetery in Cleveland.

DAVID JONES

PHILADELPHIA

WILLIAM KILLEFER
CATCHER 1911–17

A lifetime .238 hitter, Bill Killefer is best remembered today as the favorite catcher of Grover Cleveland Alexander. During the second decade of the Deadball Era, however, contemporaries praised the 5'10½", 170 lb. backstop for his astute pitch calling and lethal throwing arm. Recent statistical analysis confirms their opinion, crediting Killefer with defensive value that more than outweighs his offensive shortcomings. John Thorn and John Holway studied his effect on pitching staffs and found it to be so great that they concluded, "Some day, perhaps, Cooperstown will recognize Bill Killefer as the other, and equal, half of the Alexander-Killefer battery. When they do, we suggest they put Bill's plaque on the wall opposite Alexander, where he can grin back at Alex, just 60' 6" away."

William Killefer was born on October 10, 1887, in Bloomingdale, Michigan, the youngest of four children of William and Emma Killefer. A Civil War veteran who eventually became a probate judge, Bill Sr. turned from farming to selling insurance shortly before Bill Jr.'s birth. All three Killefer boys were avid baseball players while attending school in nearby Paw Paw. Though Bill and his brother Wade (better known as "Red") went on to lengthy major league careers, the family believed that the best ballplayer was the oldest son, Karl, who was killed in a hunting accident while in his teens.

By the time Bill graduated from Paw Paw High School in 1906, Red had already signed a professional contract to play for the nearby Kalamazoo team. Bill attended college at Sacred Heart Academy in Wisconsin, then transferred to St. Edward's College in Texas. After his freshman year he turned pro and followed his brother to Kalamazoo. Bill finished the 1907 season with Jackson, Michigan, then split 1908 between San Francisco and Austin, Texas. He began

1909 with Houston, where he caught a pitcher named Everett Hornsby. Killefer began an important friendship by passing used bats and balls along to Hornsby's younger brother Rogers.

Killefer debuted in the majors with the St. Louis Browns in September 1909 but spent the next three seasons bouncing between the high minors and the majors. In 1912 he finally became the Phillies' regular catcher when Red Dooin was injured. He played so well that player-manager Dooin accepted a backup role on his return to duty. While Killefer's hitting never became formidable, his defense was so stellar that he was soon regarded as one of the NL's best receivers. Somewhere along the line he acquired the nickname "Reindeer Bill," but the story behind its origin is murky. One account said it was because he was a fast runner (he did steal 32 bases in one minor league season), but he never stole more than six bases in a major league season, leading some to suggest that the nickname was facetious.

On January 9, 1914, Killefer signed a three-year, $17,500 contract with the Chicago Whales of the upstart Federal League. Though to that point his career batting average stood at .207, Philadelphia quickly countered by offering him a three-year contract for $19,500. After consulting with his lawyer and his father, Killefer jumped back to the National League 11 days later. The Feds sued to enforce their contract, and the case was watched eagerly. Not only would the outcome be enormously important to the Federal League, it could prove a crucial test of the reserve clause. The judge who heard the case ruled that the Feds had entered the negotiations with "unclean hands," and accordingly awarded Killefer to Philadelphia. In his ruling he made a point of chiding Killefer, describing him as an exceptionally skilled player but "a person upon whose pledged word little or no reliance can be placed and who, for gain to himself, neither scruples nor hesitates to disregard and violate his express engagements and agreements." *The Sporting News* editorialized that the catcher "was due for a spanking."

The highlight of Killefer's seven years with Philadelphia came in 1915, when his expert leadership of the pitching staff helped an average team to the pennant. Unfortunately, Killefer was injured and couldn't catch in the World Series, which Philadelphia lost to the Boston Red Sox in five games. In December 1917 the Phillies sent Alexander and Killefer to Chicago for two journeymen and a record $55,000. Alexander was drafted into the army and pitched only three games, but Killefer worked magic with the rest of the Chicago staff and led the team to the 1918 pennant. The Cubs allowed Boston only nine runs in the six-game World Series, but their bats failed and they lost to Babe Ruth's Red Sox.

By 1919, with his years as a front-line catcher starting to take their toll, Killefer began grooming Bob O'Farrell to be his successor behind the plate. In August 1921, with the Cubs mired in sixth place, Killefer was named player-manager. Though he batted a career-high .323 that year, he announced his retirement as a player at season's end to focus on managing. During Killefer's reign, his old battery mate Alexander became a mentor for the Chicago pitchers. Bill also tried unsuccessfully to acquire old friend Rogers Hornsby. Killefer piloted the Cubs to three straight winning seasons but never won a pennant and was fired midway through a disappointing 1925 season.

Hornsby, then serving as player-manager of the Cardinals, hired Killefer as a coach for 1926. Without his friend's calming influence, Alexander got into trouble in Chicago and was put on waivers. On Killefer's recommendation, the Cardinals claimed Old Pete (a nickname Killefer coined), whose pitching down the stretch helped the Cardinals capture the pennant. For the third time, and with a third different club, Alexander and Killefer again were NL champions.

Once more Babe Ruth was on the team they faced in the World Series. This time the result was different. Alexander pitched complete-game victories in Games Two and Six to force a deciding game. Called out of the bullpen in Game Seven, Alexander struck out Tony Lazzeri to get out of a seventh-inning jam. With two outs in the ninth inning of a one-run game, Ruth walked and tried to steal second. Killefer's old protégé Bob O'Farrell caught Alexander's pitch and threw to Hornsby, who tagged Ruth to end the game. With a lot of help from his old friends, Bill Killefer finally was a world champion.

His moment of glory didn't last long. Hornsby was traded after the season, and Killefer was offered the job. Stating that he wouldn't take Rogers Hornsby's job for any money, he accepted a coaching position with the crosstown Browns. In 1930 he became the Browns manager but wasn't given the resources to produce a winner. In 1933 he resigned and Hornsby succeeded him. Rumors had Killefer returning to his native state to manage the Tigers, but he never again received the opportunity to manage in the majors. He did manage Sacramento to a PCL pennant and coached for several major league teams. Killefer also worked as a scout for the Cleveland Indians; among the players he signed was Larry Doby. Bill resigned in 1955, ending nearly a half-century in professional baseball. Killefer was 72 when he died of liver failure on July 3, 1960, at the Veteran's Administration hospital in Elsmere, Delaware. He is buried in Paw Paw, Michigan.

PETER MORRIS

PHILADELPHIA

EPPA RIXEY JR.
LEFT-HANDED PITCHER, 1912–17, 1919–20

One of the lesser-known members of the Hall of Fame, Eppa Rixey merited induction not for his work during the Deadball Era—when, aside from 1916, he was generally disappointing—but during the 1920s, when he was arguably the best left hander in the game. Rixey was a finesse pitcher, using brains and guile to make batters hit his pitch. "How dumb can the hitters in this league get?" he said to roommate Rube Bressler. "When they're batting with the count two balls and no strikes, or three and one, they're always looking for the fastball. And they *never* get it. They get the change of pace every time—and they're always just as surprised to see it as they were the last time."

Eppa Rixey Jr. was born in Culpeper, Virginia, on May 3, 1891, the fourth of six children of Eppa Sr. and the former Willie Alice Walton. Whereas the typical Deadballer came from a family of farmers or laborers, Eppa's background was comparatively aristocratic. The Rixeys of Culpeper were Virginia gentility, descended from the Riccias of Italy, who'd come to America by way of England, Scotland, and France. Eppa Sr. was a banker who moved his family to Charlottesville when his namesake son was 10. After completing high school in Charlottesville, Eppa entered the University of Virginia, where he used his 6'5" height to advantage on the basketball court and the pitcher's mound.

Recognizing Rixey's talent, NL umpire Cy Rigler, a basketball and baseball coach at UVa during the off-season, tried to induce Eppa to sign with the Philadelphia Phillies. Eppa initially refused, saying he planned to be a chemist, but Rigler sweetened the deal by promising a split of whatever finder's bonus he might receive. With his younger brother in college and his father's bank enduring an economic downturn, Eppa succumbed after receiving his bachelor's degree in chemistry in 1912. Shortly thereafter, the NL passed a rule prohibiting umpires from scouting for any individual team, and neither Rigler nor Rixey ever saw a dime of any bonus.

Jumping directly from the grounds of Thomas Jefferson's university to the major leagues, Eppa Rixey was an anomaly among his lower-class, less educated teammates. Eppa wrote poetry in his spare time, particularly enjoying sonnets and triolets, and during the off-season took graduate courses in chemistry, mathematics, and Latin. Later he spent winters teaching Latin at Episcopal High School in Washington, D.C. Eppa eventually headed a clique of college-educated Phillies—in 1914 he boarded with Joe Oeschger, who'd attended St. Mary's College in California, and Stan Baumgartner, a University of Chicago graduate—but during his early years he endured a great deal of resentment and hazing.

With his Southern drawl, "Rix" was a target for comments about the Civil War, and catchers Bill Killefer and Eddie Burns frequently sang "Marching Through Georgia" when they were in his presence. On one occasion they even got a drum and paraded some of their teammates around the clubhouse and onto the field, all of them singing or humming the Sherman marching song. Eppa responded in true rebel fashion, too, tossing gloves and buckets at them—and he was really angry. His face flushed, the cords stuck out on his neck, he cussed his teammates, with "Damn Yankees" being the mildest of his uncomplimentary epithets.

On another occasion it was star left fielder Sherry Magee who antagonized Rixey. One afternoon in Cincinnati the "three collegians," all of whom were camera hounds, gathered several players in front of the Metropole Hotel for a photo. Stepping out on the fire escape on the sixth floor, Magee saw them and dropped a paper laundry bag filled with water, hitting Eppa squarely on the head. Rixey was furious. He dropped his camera, ran into the hotel, and jumped into an elevator, but Magee was gone by the time he reached the sixth floor.

No wonder, then, that Rixey's seven seasons in Philadelphia were marked by inconsistency. He reported to the Phillies in June 1912 and pitched well enough for a rookie, compiling a 10-10 record with a 2.50 ERA. But the following year Rixey's ERA increased to 3.12, and in 1914 it soared to 4.37, prompting one reporter to write that he "has been drawing down a salary that would make a successful man feel cheap, for two years, and has not pitched a nickel's worth of good ball." Even during the pennant-winning season of 1915 Rixey was only mediocre, lowering his ERA to 2.39 but mustering an 11-12 record. Manager Pat Moran still believed in him, bringing him in to relieve Erskine Mayer in the third inning of the fifth and final game of the World Series; Rixey ended up taking the loss, giving

up home runs to Duffy Lewis and Harry Hooper, the latter's bouncing into the center-field bleachers for what would be a ground-rule double today.

The following year Eppa justified Moran's confidence with perhaps the best season of his career, going 22-10 with a microscopic 1.85 ERA and a career-high 134 strikeouts. Always a good-fielding pitcher, he handled 108 chances without an error in 1917 but led the NL in losses (21) despite a 2.27 ERA. Rixey hated losing and was apt to destroy a locker room or disappear for a day or two after a tough defeat, of which he suffered many. His 251 losses are the all-time record for left handers, but his 266 victories also were an NL record for southpaws until Warren Spahn broke it in 1959. The consummate Virginia gentleman, Rixey greeted that moment with characteristic humor, saying he was glad Spahn had broken his record because it reminded everybody that he had been the one to set it.

After serving with the Chemical Warfare Division in Europe during 1918, Eppa returned for two more abysmal seasons in Philadelphia under managers Jack Coombs and Gavy Cravath, neither of whom he liked. He was happy to be reunited with Pat Moran when the Phillies traded him to the Reds for Jimmy Ring and Greasy Neale on November 22, 1920. Rixey blossomed in the Queen City, winning 100 games in his first five seasons. In 1921 he set a record that is unlikely to be equaled, serving up only one home run in 301 innings. Rixey's 25 wins led the NL in 1922.

Retiring after the 1933 season, Eppa Rixey settled in the Cincinnati area, where he worked in the insurance agency that his father-in-law had founded in 1888. He and his wife, Dorothy, had two children, Eppa III and Ann. Grandson Eppa Rixey IV is now the chief operating officer of the Eppa Rixey Insurance Agency, whose motto is "Hall of Fame Performance for Your Insurance Needs." To cap off Eppa's happy and prosperous life, he was elected to the National Baseball Hall of Fame by the Veterans Committee on January 27, 1963. "They're really scraping the bottom of the barrel, aren't they?" he joked on hearing of his election. Unfortunately, Rixey was the first honoree to die between election and induction, suffering a fatal heart attack on February 28, 1963. He is buried in the Greenlawn Cemetery in Milford, Ohio.

JAN FINKEL

PHILADELPHIA

Erskine John Mayer
RIGHT-HANDED PITCHER 1912–18

Erskine Mayer was a back-to-back 20-game winner for the Philadelphia Phillies in 1914-15 before overwork limited his effectiveness and shortened his career. Mayer had a decent fastball but relied more on control and an excellent sidearm curve, a pitch that led Wilbert Robinson to call him "Eelskine" because the pitch was "so slippery." The Southern-born, college-educated right hander was one of the skinniest pitchers of the Deadball Era at 6'0" and only 150 lbs., but his Judaism and his amazing family history are what really distinguished him from his contemporaries.

Erskine John Mayer was born under the name of James Erskine in Atlanta on January 16, 1889. His grandparents on his father's side were Jews who came from Germany, where his great-grandfather had been a buyer for Otto Von Bismarck. He disappeared one day, and it wasn't until years later that his body was discovered buried in a stable. Both paternal grandparents were musicians, a talent they passed on to Erskine's father, Isaac, who composed an opera written in Hebrew. That lineage was poles apart from Erskine's family on his maternal side. His mother, born Henrietta Frankel, could trace her ancestry back to the *Mayflower*. Her family owned land in what was then Virginia territory and today is in Kentucky. Erskine's maternal grandmother's brother, James Allen, captained a riverboat that ran from Hannibal, Missouri, to New Orleans. It was from marking twain on Captain Allen's boat that young Samuel Clemens chose the nom de plume of "Mark Twain." Erskine's maternal grandmother married a Jew named Frankel and converted to Judaism.

Isaac Mayer worked as a concert pianist and music teacher in Ohio and Georgia, where Erskine was born. Evidently unconcerned about injuring his hands, Isaac enjoyed baseball and often played catch with his three sons; one of Erskine's brothers, Sam, became a minor league outfielder who received an 11-game trial with the Washington Senators in 1915. Erskine attended the Georgia Military Academy and Georgia Tech, where he studied engineering and became the star pitcher for the baseball team. Erskine left college in 1910, his senior year, to sign with the Class D Fayetteville Highlanders. Earlier he'd been rejected by Atlanta of the Southern League because he was deemed too skinny.

Fayetteville won the championship of the East Carolina League in 1910, and Mayer led the circuit with an .882 winning percentage (15-2). After a 14-13 season the following year at Albany, Georgia, of the South Atlantic League, Erskine returned to form with Portsmouth in 1912, leading the Virginia League in wins (26) and winning percentage (.743). He made his major league debut for the Phillies on September 4, 1912, pitching two scoreless innings in a 5-2 loss to the New York Giants. Mayer pitched in seven games that September, failing to secure his first victory, but in 1913 he went 9-9, pitching mostly in relief.

Mayer enjoyed a breakout campaign in 1914, posting a 21-19 record and tossing 321 innings, fifth-best in the National League. "His ability to stand work is a source of mystery to other pitchers," wrote one reporter, who credited Mayer's durability to his easy sidearm delivery. Despite the heavy workload, Erskine posted a solid 2.58 ERA, with the season's highlight coming on July 27 when he blanked the St. Louis Cardinals on one hit, a second-inning single by Chuck Miller. Earlier that season, on June 9 at the Baker Bowl, he gave up a ninth-inning double to Honus Wagner, the Pittsburgh star's 3,000th career hit.

Erskine Mayer enjoyed his best season as a big leaguer in 1915, again winning 21 games (against 15 losses) and lowering his ERA to 2.36. A fine hitter, he batted .239 in a season when the Phillies as a team batted .247. Nonetheless Mayer was overshadowed by his pitching partner and roommate, Pete Alexander. "Every time I pitched well, Alexander topped me," Erskine remembered. Mayer also began to show signs of wear. After defeating the Braves on July 1, his record stood at 12-4 with a 1.83 ERA. For the remainder of the season he was 9-11 with a 2.89 ERA. His teammates attributed his downfall to his July 4 marriage.

Mayer's troubles continued in that year's World Series against the Boston Red Sox. After Alexander won the opener, Mayer allowed just two runs in Game Two but lost when the opposing pitcher, Rube Foster, singled in the winning run with two outs in the ninth inning. Subbing for a fatigued Alexander, Mayer got a second start in Game Five with the Phillies down three

games to one. Once again facing Foster, Mayer allowed two first-inning runs and left after only 2⅓ innings. He wasn't charged with the Phillies' 5-4 defeat.

Proving much less durable over the rest of his career, Mayer often pitched in relief and spot-starter roles. The Phils slipped to second in 1916, due in part to an off year by Mayer, who posted a 7-7 record. He was 11-6 with a 2.76 ERA in 1917 and had a 7-4 record in 1918, when Philadelphia traded him to Pittsburgh on July 1 for pitcher Elmer Jacobs. Exactly one month later, Mayer participated in one of the greatest pitching duels in history. At Braves Field in Boston, he and Art Nehf of the Braves hurled scoreless baseball for 15 innings. Wilbur Cooper finally relieved Mayer in the 16th and got the win when the Pirates pushed across two runs against Nehf in the 21st. In all, Mayer won nine games for Pittsburgh while losing only three, finishing the 1918 season with a 16-7 record, 18 complete games, and an ERA of 2.65.

The next season Mayer's record stood at 5-3 when the Pirates placed him on waivers on August 6. No NL team claimed him, but the Chicago White Sox, in the thick of the American League pennant race, picked him up for the $2,500 waiver fee. Mayer wasn't much help, appearing in six games and going 1-3 with an 8.37 ERA. The White Sox won the pennant anyway but lost the best-of-nine World Series in eight games to Cincinnati. Mayer pitched one inning in a mop-up role in Game Five, allowing one unearned run in what turned out to be his final big-league appearance. He was totally unaware that several of his teammates had accepted money in a conspiracy to lose the Series.

Mayer returned briefly to the minor leagues in 1920, pitching one game for the Atlanta Crackers before leaving his playing days behind. His revulsion when the details of the Black Sox scandal surfaced probably contributed to his decision to retire. "Erk loved baseball for the true sport it afforded," said his wife, Grace, "and he felt if a game had been thrown he was through with baseball." Mayer was operating a cigar store in downtown Los Angeles when he died of a heart attack on March 10, 1957.

LYLE SPATZ

PHILADELPHIA

CLIFFORD CARLTON "GAVY" CRAVATH
RIGHT FIELDER 1912–20, MANAGER 1919–20

Gavy Cravath was an anomaly in the Deadball Era. Employing a powerful swing and taking advantage of Baker Bowl's cozy dimensions, the Philadelphia cleanup hitter led the National League in home runs six times, establishing new (albeit short-lived) 20th-century records for home runs in a season and career. In an era when "inside baseball" ruled supreme, Cravath bucked the trend and preached what he practiced. "Short singles are like left-hand jabs in the boxing ring, but a home run is a knock-out punch," he asserted. "It is the clean-up man of the club that does the heavy scoring work even if he is wide in the shoulders and slow on his feet. There is no advice I can give in batting, except to hammer the ball. Some players steal bases with hook slides and speed. I steal bases with my bat."

Clifford Carlton Cravath was born in Escondido, California, on March 23, 1881. His father, A. K. Cravath, became the first mayor of Escondido in 1888 and later sheriff of San Diego County during the 1890s. Cliff was the catcher on his high school baseball team but is better remembered locally as captain of the Escondido football team that lost the first-ever high-school gridiron matchup in the history of San Diego County, 0-6, to San Diego High School in 1898. Following graduation, Cravath worked as a fumigator, telegraph operator, and semipro ballplayer in San Diego and Santa Ana, where his family relocated after the turn of the century.

It was during his semipro days that he gained the nickname "Gavy." There are many stories about its origin, but it's apparently a contraction for the Spanish word *gaviota*, which means "seagull." During a Sunday game in the early 1900s, Cravath reportedly hit a ball so hard that it killed a seagull in flight. Mexican fans shouted "Gaviota." The English-speaking fans thought it was a cheer and the name stuck. It's pronounced to rhyme with "savvy," so sportswriters added the extra "v," but Cravath himself spelled it G-A-V-Y. The Southern Californian also had another nickname, "Cactus" (because of his western background and prickly personality), but he didn't care for it and never included it in his signature.

Stories of Cravath's potent bat spread quickly, and in 1903 the young slugger entered the professional ranks with the Los Angeles Angels of the Pacific Coast League. Playing initially in right field and later at first base, Cravath helped the Angels claim two pennants over the next five years. At the end of 1907, based on his .303 batting average and 10 home runs, Cravath was selected team MVP and sold to the Boston Red Sox. He departed California for what was known out west as "the Eastern Leagues." Isolation on the West Coast had already cost Gavy precious years; at 27 he was old for a major league rookie.

Not fitting the mold of the stereotypical Deadball Era fly chaser, Cravath had difficulty breaking into a Boston outfield that soon became dominated by the fleet-footed Tris Speaker and Harry Hooper. Throughout his career Gavy remained sensitive about his relative lack of speed. "They call me wooden shoes and piano legs and a few other pet names," he once said. "I do not claim to be the fastest man in the world, but I can get around the bases with a fair wind and all sails set. And so long as I am busting the old apple on the seam, I am not worrying a great deal about my legs." Cravath was batting .256 with only a single home run (but 11 triples) when the Red Sox sold him to the Chicago White Sox in August 1908. A slow start in the Windy City in 1909 got him traded to the lowly Washington Senators.

Washington manager Joe Cantillon also was the owner of the Minneapolis Millers of the American Association, and he sent Gavy to Minneapolis after the new outfielder went hitless in six at-bats for Washington. The 1910-11 Millers are now recognized as the outstanding minor league team of the Deadball Era, and Cravath became the team's biggest star. Learning to hit to the opposite field to take advantage of Nicollet Park's short porch (it was a lot like Baker Bowl, running 279' down the right-field foul line with a 30' fence), the right-handed–hitting Cravath batted .326 with 14 home runs in 1910. The following year he led the Association with a .363 batting average, and his 29 home runs were the most ever recorded in Organized Baseball. At one point that season Cantillon threatened to fine Gavy $50 if he hit any more home runs over the right-field barrier; apparently he'd broken the same window in a Nicollet Avenue haberdashery three times during a single week.

Despite his impressive numbers, Cravath couldn't escape the minors, a victim of the Deadball Era's draft rules. It took a clerical error—the Millers inadvertently left out the word "not" in a telegram to Pittsburgh—to get Gavy back to the big leagues. In a controversial decision, the National Commission ruled that Minneapolis couldn't retain Cravath because of the mistake. The 31-year-old slugger received his second chance at the majors in 1912 with the Philadelphia Phillies, who purchased his rights for $9,000. This time the more experienced Cravath proved that he belonged in the big leagues, batting a respectable .284 with 11 home runs and 70 RBI in his first season with the Phillies. Displaying a strong, accurate arm, he also led NL outfielders with 26 assists.

Cravath's greatest year in the majors arguably was 1913. Though that year's Chalmers Award went to Brooklyn's Jake Daubert, most historians agree that Cravath, who led the majors with 19 home runs, 128 RBI, and a .568 slugging average, was the NL's true

most valuable player. Gavy paced the circuit with 179 hits, placed second in batting average at .341 (behind Daubert's .350), and ranked fourth in doubles (34) and triples (14). His RBI total established a modern NL record that wasn't broken until Rogers Hornsby drove in 152 in 1922. Cravath followed up that performance with another solid campaign in 1914, batting .299 with 100 RBI and winning the second of his six home run titles with 19 circuit blows—all 19 of them hit at home. Defensively, he led NL outfielders again with 34 assists.

In 1915 Cravath smacked 24 home runs, a figure that established a 20th-century record and gave him as many as 13 of the other 15 major league teams hit collectively that season. There's no question that the Baker Bowl helped him do it. With a short left-field power alley and a right-field fence only 272' from home plate, Gavy took advantage of his home park as much as any player in history—79% of his 1915 home runs and 77% of his career four-baggers came at Baker Bowl. He led the NL in home runs hit at home seven times but never turned the trick on the road; indeed, he never hit more than five on the road in any season. Despite those statistics, Gavy was defensive when reporters suggested that he owed his impressive home run totals to Baker Bowl's short right field. "That right-field fence was never any farther away than it was when I joined the club," he told F. C. Lane. "And while we are on the subject, let me make a point. That fence isn't always a friend to the home-run slugger. I have hit that fence a good many times with a long drive that would have kept right on for a triple or a home run if the fence hadn't been there. There are always two sides to every fence."

Putting aside his 24 home runs, Cravath did much more in 1915 to help the Phillies win their first pennant. For the third time in his career he was the NL's leading outfielder in assists (28), and he also led the league with 89 runs, 115 RBI, 86 walks, and a .393 on-base percentage. In the 1915 World Series the Red Sox respected Cravath's right-handed power so much that they didn't pitch their young left hander Babe Ruth, who was coming off an 18-8 season. Gavy knocked in the deciding run in the Series opener at Baker Bowl but failed to drive in another run as Philadelphia lost each of the next four games by a single run.

Cravath finished third in the NL home run race in 1916, belting 11 to finish one behind both Dave Robertson of the Giants and Cy Williams of the Cubs.

PHILA.

Had he hit one extra long ball, he would have led the NL in home runs for seven consecutive years—a feat that wasn't accomplished until Ralph Kiner did it from 1946-52. In 1917 Gavy tied Robertson for the NL lead with 12 home runs and placed second to young Rogers Hornsby in slugging average (.484 to .473) and triples (17 to 16). During the war-shortened 1918 season, it took only eight round-trippers for Cravath to win his fifth home run title, but he posted career lows in batting (.232) and slugging (.376).

Defying Father Time, the 38-year-old Cravath rebounded in 1919 to put together one last magnificent season. Playing just 56 games in the outfield, he won his sixth and final NL home run crown with 12 fence-clearing blows in only 214 at-bats. (In the American League, meanwhile, Ruth shattered the single-season mark Cravath had set in 1915 by blasting 29 circuit clouts.) Gavy also collected six hits (including two home runs) in 19 pinch-hitting appearances. "A good pinch-hitter is a valuable man to have on a ball club and can win a lot of games," he said. "The thing that handicaps him is the fact that he is usually never called upon until late in the afternoon when the sun is lower and the ball correspondingly harder to see. Besides, he has had no opportunity to face the pitcher and size him up. For all that, I rather like to hit in the pinch."

Buried at the bottom of the NL standings midway through the 1919 season, the Phillies canned manager Jack Coombs. Cravath reluctantly took his place and guided the Phils to 29 victories in 75 games over the rest of the season. Invited to return to the helm in 1920, Gavy played even less frequently than he had in 1919, though he still managed to lead the NL with 12 pinch hits. The Phillies improved, finishing with a 62-91 record, but ended up last again. When a reporter asked him about the grand jury investigation into an allegedly fixed late-season game in which his Phillies whitewashed the Cubs, 3-0,

Cravath replied, "I don't know why they gotta bring up a thing like this just because we win one. We're liable to win a game anytime."

The wins weren't frequent enough for the Phillies management, which released the nearly 40-year-old player-manager after the 1920 season. Cravath decided to retire as an active player, prompting sportswriter Robert Maxwell (the namesake for college football's Maxwell Trophy) to proclaim, "Gavvy is the greatest home run-clouter in the history of baseball and has piled up a record that might never be equaled." Cravath's career home run record of 119, however, was not only equaled but shattered by Babe Ruth the very next year, and it stood as the NL record until only 1923, when it was surpassed by Cy Williams.

Gavy Cravath managed the Salt Lake City Bees of the Pacific Coast League in 1921, then spent one year as a scout for the Minneapolis Millers, his last job in baseball. Returning to Laguna Beach, California, where he'd enjoyed his off-seasons fishing the Pacific and accumulating property, he became active in the real estate business. In September 1927 Cravath was elected magistrate judge, and for the rest of his life he enjoyed saying that he claimed the gavel quite by accident. He and two friends didn't like the sitting judge in Laguna Beach, so they drew straws to determine which of the three would run against him. Gavy drew the short straw and won the election by an almost 3:1 ratio. Lacking any formal legal training, he claimed that he based his decisions on principles of sportsmanship that he'd learned on the baseball diamond.

Well-known and widely respected, Judge Cravath was reversed only twice during his 36-year tenure on the bench. When he finally died at age 82 on May 23, 1963, few Laguna Beach residents realized that in a prior life the Honorable Clifford C. Cravath had set major league home run records that it took the mighty Babe Ruth to break.

BILL SWANK

PHILADELPHIA

DAVID JAMES BANCROFT
SHORTSTOP 1915–20

Dave Bancroft was Honus Wagner's successor as the National League's premier shortstop. A brainy on-field leader with tremendous range, Bancroft was especially adept at scooping up bad-hop grounders and cutting off outfield throws to hang up runners between bases. He believed that "the business of batting and fielding is a contention between minds," crediting his uncanny intuition to a rigorous study of opposing batters, but he also had extremely quick hands and moved gracefully in either direction. Though he batted only .248 during his five Deadball Era seasons, the switch-hitting Bancroft became known as a "timely swatter and good waiter"; he ranked second in the NL in walks in 1915 and third in 1916 and 1918.

The youngest of three children born to Ella (Gearhart) Bancroft and her husband, Frank, a truck farmer and news vendor on the Milwaukee Railroad, David James Bancroft was born on April 20, 1891, in Sioux City, Iowa. Dave attended Hopkins Grade School and Sioux City High School. During the summer after his junior year of 1909, he began his professional baseball career with Duluth, Minnesota, that year's Minnesota-Wisconsin League champion. In midseason Duluth sent the 18-year-old shortstop to Superior, Wisconsin, its rival on the south shore of St. Louis Bay. For the summer Bancroft batted .210 with only six extra-base hits in 111 games. He returned to Superior the next year and played in a league-leading 127 games, improving his average to .267, stealing 38 bases, and earning a reputation as a defensive standout. Dave remained there after the season to marry Edna Harriet Gisin. The couple, which remained childless, made the Lake Superior harbor town their lifelong home.

After hitting .273 with 41 stolen bases in his third year at Superior, Bancroft was drafted by the Portland Beavers of the Class AA Pacific Coast League in the fall of 1911. The next year he batted just .207 and was demoted to the Colts, Portland's club in the Class B Northwestern League. Two of Bancroft's teammates on the 1913 Colts—Harry Heilmann and Carl Mays—were bought by the Detroit Tigers, but the best Dave could manage after hitting .244 was a promotion back to the Pacific Coast League.

Batting leadoff in 1914, "Beauty" (a nickname he received because that's what he shouted every time his pitcher threw a good-looking pitch) hit .271 in 176 games and led the Beavers to the PCL championship, prompting fans to compare him to Roger Peckinpaugh, who'd starred at shortstop for Portland in 1911. Cleveland and the New York Giants had the first two picks of any of the Portland players. The Indians selected Bill Rodgers, Bancroft's partner in the middle infield, while the Giants, fearing Bancroft might sign with the Federal League, chose third baseman Art Kores (who ironically did jump to the Feds). Phillies scout Cap Neal stole Bancroft for a mere $5,000.

Philadelphia fans worried that the rookie wouldn't be able to replace the revered Mickey Doolan, but their fears proved unfounded. Bancroft was the sensation of the year, sparking the Phillies to their first NL pennant by batting .254 with a career-high seven home runs (six of them at the Baker Bowl) and playing spectacular defense. On August 12, for instance, he initiated a triple play against the Giants. With Larry Doyle on third and Buck Herzog on second, Dave Robertson got the hit-and-run sign and lined the ball to Bancroft, who caught the drive and whipped the ball to Bobby Byrne, catching Doyle several feet off third, and then taking Byrne's return throw to catch Herzog off second. Manager Pat Moran insisted that Dave was the difference between the pennant winners of 1915 and the sixth-place club of 1914. In the World Series the 24-year-old Bancroft hit .294, more than 100 points higher than the Phillies hit as a team.

Bancroft suffered through a sophomore slump in 1916, batting a career-low .212 with just 13 extra-base hits, and his late-season injury decimated the Phillies' pennant chances. His batting average rose consistently for the next six seasons, however, and in 1918 he led NL shortstops in chances handled for the first of four times. In five seasons in Philadelphia Bancroft established a reputation as a smart, scrappy ballplayer, well suited to the scientific game—exactly the type of player John McGraw coveted. At McGraw's suggestion, Giants owner Charles Stoneham telephoned Phillies president William Baker on June 7, 1920, and offered shortstop Art Fletcher, pitcher Wilbur Hubbell, and $100,000 for Bancroft. Baker took the next train to New York and consummated the deal, bringing along the National League attorney as a witness lest Stoneham try to back out.

When Bancroft took the field in his first game as a Giant, catcher Frank Snyder called him to a conference on the mound and offered to explain the team's signs. "Why, have they changed?" asked Bancroft. "If not, I know them already." On June 28, 1920, less than three weeks after his acquisition, the new Giant collected six hits in six at-bats. Bancroft became one of only two National Leaguers to score 100 runs that season, and although the Giants failed to capture the 1920 flag, they won the next three pennants with "Beauty" as their captain.

During the 1923 season Bancroft's legs began to bother him. In June he reported to the Polo Grounds with a high fever but insisted on playing. At the end of the game Bancroft collapsed in the clubhouse. He ended up being hospitalized with a severe case of pneumonia, earning even more admi-

ration from John McGraw. That November, reportedly as a favor to Christy Mathewson, who was then general manager of the Boston Braves, McGraw sent Bancroft and outfielders Casey Stengel and Bill Cunningham to Boston for pitcher Joe Oeschger and outfielder Billy Southworth. McGraw wanted to give his captain the opportunity to manage, but he also had Travis Jackson waiting to take over at shortstop. At age 33 Bancroft became the NL's youngest manager.

From 1924 to 1927 Bancroft managed the talent-poor Braves to a 249-363 record and four consecutive second-division finishes. He then put in two seasons with Brooklyn as a player only before returning to the Giants in 1930 as a coach under McGraw. Bancroft retired as a player after the 1930 season but remained an important presence in the Giants dugout, taking over the reins whenever his boss was too sick to manage. McGraw finally retired in June 1932 but Bill Terry was appointed player-manager to take his place. A disappointed Bancroft finished the year under Terry and retired from major league baseball. He returned to his native Midwest and managed sporadically in the minors, at various times guiding the Minneapolis Millers, the Sioux City Cowboys, and the St. Cloud Rox.

Later Bancroft spent three years managing Max Terry's traveling all-girls team, which took him across the United States and to South America and Cuba. When he finally left baseball he became a warehouse supervisor for Interprovincial Pipeline Company. Retiring in 1956 to pursue his favorite pastimes of hunting and fishing, Bancroft was inducted into the National Baseball Hall of Fame in 1971. He died in Superior on October 7, 1972, just over three years before the *Edmund Fitzgerald* left that same town on its final voyage.

TREY STRECKER

Opened in 1902, the Palace of the Fans was an intimate ballpark featuring arches, columns, and "rooter's row," field-level seats where beer could be bought, a dozen glasses for a dollar.

The Cincinnati Reds typically finished a tad under .500 during the Deadball Era, and their .374 winning percentage in 1901, placing them in last for the first time since 1880, proved to be their worst of the era. The Reds' climb to respectability started the next season, when local interests took control of the team and installed Garry Herrmann as president.

That year saw the opening of the Palace of the Fans. Along with the new ballpark came new players: rookie Bob Ewing joined ace left hander Noodles Hahn on the pitching staff, and in August Joe Kelley, Cy Seymour, and Mike Donlin jumped from the Baltimore Orioles to round out the hardest-hitting outfield in baseball. After

reaching .500 in 1902, Cincinnati posted winning records in each of the next three seasons despite losing Sam Crawford to the American League.

A disappointing sixth-place finish in 1906 caused the Reds to rebuild around speed, bringing in young talent like Dick Hoblitzell, Hans Lobert, Mike Mitchell, Dode Paskert, and Bob Bescher. Cincinnati soon returned to its familiar place in the middle of the pack, even finishing in the first division for the first time in five years with a 77-76 record in 1909.

In 1912 the Reds christened a new grandstand, dubbed Redland Field (later renamed Crosley Field), but the added seating capacity proved unnecessary over

WINNING PERCENTAGE 1901-1919

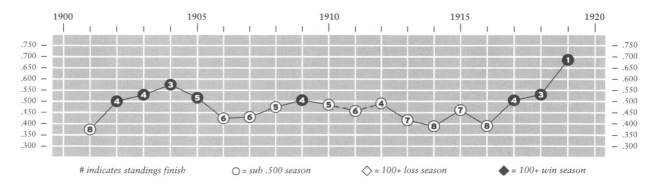

 # indicates standings finish   ○ = sub .500 season   ◇ = 100+ loss season   ◆ = 100+ win season

the next four years when the club never finished higher than seventh. Hope returned to Rhineland in 1916 when Herrmann traded player-manager Buck Herzog to the New York Giants for Christy Mathewson, who took over as manager and focused on improving the pitching. Acquiring Dutch Ruether, Jimmy Ring, Hod Eller, Dolf Luque, and Rube Bressler to supplement incumbent star Fred Toney, Matty guided the Reds to fourth in 1917 and third in 1918, the club's first back-to-back winning seasons since 1904-05.

Mathewson's enlistment in August 1918 led Herrmann to replace him for the 1919 season with Pat Moran, who four years earlier had led the Phillies to their only pennant of the Deadball Era in his first year at their helm. As in Philadelphia, Moran again inherited an up-and-coming cast, with two of the NL's greatest stars in Edd Roush and Heine Groh. During the off-season the Reds also acquired a trio of significant veterans from the New York teams: first baseman Jake Daubert from Brooklyn, and pitchers Slim Sallee from the Giants and Ray Fisher from the Yankees.

Cincinnati opened the season with seven wins and never looked back, running away with its first NL pennant and the Queen City's first crown of any sort since its American Association championship in 1882. Unfortunately, the Reds' victory in the 1919 World Series over the formidable Chicago White Sox will forever be tainted by the Black Sox scandal.

ALL-ERA TEAM

E. ROUSH, CF
B. BESCHER, LF
M. MITCHELL, RF
M. HUGGINS, 2B
T. CORCORAN, SS
H. GROH, 3B
J. BECKLEY, 1B
N. HAHN, P
L. McLEAN, C

TEAM LEADERS
1901–1919

BATTING

GAMES
H. Groh 969
M. Mitchell 857
D. Hoblitzell 850

RUNS
H. Groh 523
B. Bescher 496
M. Huggins 441

HITS
H. Groh 1041
D. Hoblitzell 897
M. Mitchell 892

RBI
M. Mitchell 420
D. Hoblitzell 409
T. Corcoran 334

DOUBLES
H. Groh 177
D. Hoblitzell 132
B. Bescher 125

TRIPLES
M. Mitchell 88
D. Hoblitzell 65
H. Groh 57

HOME RUNS
C. Seymour 26
D. Hoblitzell 24
S. Crawford 19

STOLEN BASES
B. Bescher 320
H. Lobert 168
M. Mitchell 165

BATTING AVERAGE
C. Seymour 332
E. Roush 325
J. Beckley 320

PITCHING

GAMES
B. Ewing 252
P. Schneider 200
R. Benton 167

WINS
B. Ewing 108
N. Hahn 88
G. Suggs 62

LOSSES
B. Ewing 103
P. Schneider 85
N. Hahn 64

INNINGS
B. Ewing 2020⅓
N. Hahn 1367
P. Schneider 1245

STRIKEOUTS
B. Ewing 884
N. Hahn 623
R. Benton 477

WALKS
B. Ewing 513
P. Schneider 476
R. Benton 386

SHUTOUTS
F. Toney 17
N. Hahn 16
B. Ewing 15

ERA
N. Hahn 2.31
B. Ewing 2.37
P. Schneider 2.65

The 1919 Reds compiled a winning percentage of .686, the highest in the National Leage since the 1909 Pittsburgh Pirates.

TYPICAL LINEUPS 1901–1919

1901

1. J. Dobbs, CF
2. D. Harley, LF
3. J. Beckley, 1B
4. S. Crawford, RF
5. G. Magoon, SS
6. H. Steinfeldt, 2B-3B
7. C. Irwin, 3B
8. B. Bergen, C

1902

1. D. Hoy, CF
2. J. Dobbs, LF
3. J. Beckley, 1B
4. S. Crawford, RF
5. H. Peitz, 2B
6. T. Corcoran, SS
7. H. Steinfeldt, 3B
8. B. Bergen, C

1903

1. M. Donlin, LF
2. C. Seymour, CF
3. C. Dolan, RF
4. J. Beckley, 1B
5. H. Steinfeldt, 3B
6. T. Daly, 2B
7. T. Corcoran, SS
8. H. Peitz, C

1904

1. M. Huggins, 2B
2. C. Seymour, CF
3. J. Sebring
   C. Dolan, RF
4. F. Odwell, LF
5. H. Steinfeldt, 3B
   J. Kelley, 1B
6. T. Corcoran, SS
7. S. Woodruff, INF
8. A. Schlei, C

1905

1. M. Huggins, 2B
2. S. Barry, 1B
3. J. Kelley, LF
4. C. Seymour, CF
5. T. Corcoran, SS
6. F. Odwell, RF
7. H. Steinfeldt, 3B
8. A. Schlei, C

1906

1. M. Huggins, 2B
2. J. Kelley, LF
3. F. Jude, RF
4. C. Seymour, CF
5. J. Delahanty, 3B
6. A. Schlei, C
7. T. Corcoran, SS
8. S. Deal, 1B

1907

1. M. Huggins, 2B
2. H. Lobert, SS
3. M. Mitchell, RF
4. L. Davis, CF
5. J. Ganzel, 1B
6. L. McLean, C
   A. Kruger, CF
7. M. Mowrey, 3B
8. F. Odwell, LF

1908

1. M. Huggins, 2B
2. J. Kane, CF
3. H. Lobert, 3B
4. M. Mitchell, RF
5. J. Ganzel, 1B
6. A. Schlei, C
7. D. Paskert, LF
8. R. Hulswitt, SS

1909

1. B. Bescher, LF
2. R. Oakes, CF
3. D. Egan, 2B
4. M. Mitchell, RF
5. D. Hoblitzell, 1B
6. H. Lobert, 3B
7. L. McLean, C
8. T. Downey, SS

1910

1. B. Bescher, LF
2. D. Egan, 2B
3. D. Hoblitzell, 1B
4. M. Mitchell, RF
5. D. Paskert, CF
6. H. Lobert, 3B
7. L. McLean, C
8. T. McMillan, SS

1911

1. B. Bescher, LF
2. J. Bates, CF
3. D. Hoblitzell, 1B
4. M. Mitchell, RF
5. T. Downey, SS
6. D. Egan, 2B
7. E. Grant, 3B
8. L. McLean, C

1912

1. B. Bescher, LF
2. A. Marsans, CF
3. D. Hoblitzell, 1B
4. M. Mitchell, RF
5. D. Egan, 2B
6. A. Phelan, 3B
7. J. Esmond, SS
8. L. McLean, C

1913

1. B. Bescher, LF
2. J. Bates, RF
3. H. Groh, 2B
4. D. Hoblitzell, 1B
5. A. Marsans, CF
6. J. Tinker, SS
7. J. Dodge, 3B
8. T. Clarke, C

1914

1. H. Moran, RF
2. B. Herzog, SS
3. G. Twombly, LF
4. H. Groh, 2B
5. D. Hoblitzell, 1B
6. B. Daniels, CF
7. B. Niehoff, 3B
8. T. Clarke, C

1915

1. T. Leach, CF
2. B. Herzog, SS
3. R. Killefer, LF
4. T. Griffith, RF
5. H. Groh, 3B
6. I. Wingo, C
7. B. Rodgers, 2B
8. F. Mollwitz, 1B

1916

1. H. Groh, 3B
2. B. Herzog, SS
3. E. Roush, CF
4. H. Chase, 1B
5. T. Griffith, RF
6. G. Neale, LF
7. B. Louden, 2B
8. I. Wingo, C

1917

1. H. Groh, 3B
2. L. Kopf, SS
3. E. Roush, CF
4. H. Chase, 1B
5. T. Griffith, RF
6. G. Neale, LF
7. D. Shean, 2B
8. I. Wingo, C

1918 (First half)

1. H. Groh, 3B
2. L. Magee, 2B
3. E. Roush, CF
4. S. Magee, 1B-LF
5. T. Griffith, RF
6. G. Neale, LF
7. L. Blackburne, SS
8. I. Wingo, C

1918 (Second half)

1. H. Groh, 3B
2. L. Magee, 2B
3. E. Roush, CF
4. H. Chase, 1B
5. G. Neale, LF
6. T. Griffith, RF
7. L. Blackburne, SS
8. I. Wingo, C

1919

1. M. Rath, 2B
2. J. Daubert, 1B
3. H. Groh, 3B
4. E. Roush, CF
5. G. Neale, RF
6. L. Kopf, SS
7. R. Bressler
   S. Magee, LF
8. I. Wingo
   B. Rariden, C

CINCINNATI

JACOB PETER BECKLEY
FIRST BASEMAN 1897–1903

When Jake Beckley gained election to the National Baseball Hall of Fame in 1971, most fans had no idea who he was or why he should be so honored. Beckley's reputation suffered because he never played on a pennant winner, and only one team he played for (the 1893 Pirates) finished as high as second place. Still, the colorful Beckley compiled a .308 lifetime average, hit .300 or better in 13 of his 20 seasons (including the first four seasons of the Deadball Era), and retired in 1907 as baseball's all-time leader in triples. He still stands fourth on the all-time list, behind Sam Crawford, Ty Cobb, and Honus Wagner. Beckley held the career record for games played at first base until 1994, when Eddie Murray passed him, but he still leads all first basemen in putouts and total chances.

Jacob Peter Beckley was born on August 4, 1867, in Hannibal, Missouri, the Mississippi River town that Mark Twain made famous. A left-handed batter and thrower, Jake started his baseball career with fast semi-pro teams in the Hannibal area. While pitching in the Western League in 1886, former Hannibal teammate Bob Hart recommended the 18-year-old Beckley to his manager. Jake traveled to Leavenworth, Kansas, and batted .342 in 75 games, playing mostly second base and the outfield. Though left-handed throwers still played second, short, and third in the 1880s, Jake didn't have the arm to play any position except first base. Leavenworth moved him there the following season, and that is where he remained for the rest of his career.

Beckley batted over .400 in 1887 (walks counted as hits that season), splitting the summer between Leavenworth and another Western League team in Lincoln, Nebraska. The following year Lincoln sold him to the Western Association's St. Louis Whites. Beckley played only 34 games before the Whites sold him in June 1888 to the National League's Pittsburgh Alleghenys for $4,000. Still only 20 years old, Jake batted .343 as a rookie and solidified the right side of the Pittsburgh infield. The next year he again led the club's regulars in batting and soon earned the nickname "Eagle Eye"—not for his ability to draw bases on balls (his walk totals were consistently below the league average) but for his batting skill. The hard-hitting Beckley brought a dash of excitement to the Alleghenys, and before long he became the team's most popular player.

Beckley married in 1891, but his wife Molly died after only seven months of marriage. Jake slumped badly after her death, with his batting average plummeting to a career-low .236 in 1892. He didn't marry again until his baseball career was over. "Eagle Eye" returned to the .300 mark in 1893-95, but when he slumped again in 1896, the Pirates, over the loud objections of their fans, traded him to the New York Giants for Harry Davis and $1,000. Beckley didn't hit well in New York, either, and most people thought his career was over when the Giants released him in May 1897. The Cincinnati Reds needed a first baseman and signed him a few weeks later. His bat came alive again in Cincinnati, and on September 26, 1897, Beckley belted three homers in a game against St. Louis. No other major leaguer performed that feat again until Ken Williams did it in 1922.

Jake Beckley was one of the most colorful players of the early Deadball Era. Considered a handsome man even though one of his eyes was slightly crossed, Beckley kept his impressive mustache after all but a handful of players had relinquished theirs; at the time of his retirement he was one of only three men in the majors who still sported facial hair. He also yelled

"Chickazoola!" to rattle opposing pitchers when he was on a batting tear. Despite his stocky build (he stood 5'10" and weighed 200 lbs.), he ran well enough to reach double figures in stolen bases and triples almost every year, and he also didn't mind cutting across the infield if the umpire's back was turned. One day, when umpire Tim Hurst wasn't looking, Jake ran almost directly from second base to home, sliding in without a throw. Hurst called Beckley out anyway. "You big son of a bitch," shouted Hurst, "you got here too fast!" Jake also loved pulling the hidden-ball trick and tried it on every new player who came into the league. Sometimes he hid the ball in his clothing or under his arm, and other times he hid it under the base sack and waited for the unsuspecting player to wander off first.

For seven years Beckley played first base for the Reds, batting over .300 in every season except 1898. His career nearly ended on June 14, 1901, when Christy Mathewson hit him in the head with a fastball, knocking him unconscious for more than five minutes. Beckley recovered, missing only two games, and hit .307 for the last-place Reds that season. He was "Old Eagle Eye" by then, but still a solid run producer with good range and quick reflexes on defense. His only weakness

remained his poor throwing arm; base runners always knew they could take an extra base on him. Beckley once fielded a bunt and threw wildly past first base. He retrieved the ball himself and saw the runner rounding third and heading for home. Rather than risk another bad throw, Jake raced the runner to home plate and tagged him in time for the out.

Beckley batted .327 in 1903, but manager Joe Kelley wanted to play first base himself, so in February 1904 the Reds sold the 36-year-old star to St. Louis. Jake hit well in his first two seasons with the Cardinals, but his batting declined as injuries began to slow him down. He served briefly as a National League umpire in 1906, while on injury leave from the Cardinals, and tried to play again the following spring. In May 1907 the Cardinals released Beckley, ending his 20-year career in the majors, but Jake wasn't yet finished with baseball. He signed a contract with Kansas City of the American Association and played there for three years and managed the team for one. During that time a teenage Casey Stengel saw him perform the unusual (and now illegal) maneuver of bunting with the handle of his bat. "I showed our players," said Stengel 50 years later, when he was managing the Yankees, "and they say it's the silliest thing they ever saw, which it probably is but Beckley done it."

After short stints in 1910 with Bartlesville and Topeka, Beckley returned in 1911 to his hometown of Hannibal, where he managed and batted .282 at age 44. In late 1911 he moved to Kansas City and retired from professional ball, though he played on semipro and amateur nines for several more summers. He also helped coach the team at nearby William Jewell College and umpired for the independent Federal League in 1913, the year before the circuit became a short-lived major league. Beckley operated a grain business in Kansas City after he stopped playing ball. He once placed an order with a Cincinnati company, which cabled back, "We can't find you in Dun and Bradstreet." Beckley replied, "Look in *Spalding Baseball Guide* for any of the last 20 years." Beckley suffered from a weak heart, and he was only 50 when he died in Kansas City on June 25, 1918. He was buried in Hannibal, where the townspeople erected a small monument to his memory after his election to the Hall of Fame.

DAVID FLEITZ

CINCINNATI

FRANK GEORGE "NOODLES" HAHN
LEFT-HANDED PITCHER 1899–1905

In July 1903 Noodles Hahn won his 100th game just two months after turning 24, becoming the youngest player since the pitching distance moved to its current 60'6" in 1893 to reach that milestone. In the century since, only Bob Feller, another power pitcher, managed to win 100 games at a younger age. But Hahn had already racked up over 300 innings pitched in each of his first four seasons. "I am wise enough to know that I cannot last forever and that I am greatly shortening my career by pitching as I did last season," he told *The Sporting News* after the 1901 season, in which he'd pitched a career-high 375⅓ innings. Those words proved prophetic; after achieving his 100th victory, Hahn won only 30 more games and within three years was out of baseball, a victim of a dead arm at age 26.

Frank George Hahn was born in Nashville, Tennessee, on April 29, 1879. He acquired his distinctive nickname as a youngster, though he claimed he didn't know why. "All I know is they always called me 'Noodles,'" Hahn said. But a friend claimed to recall the origin quite well. "When Hahn was a boy in Nashville," the man explained, "he always had to carry his father's lunch to him. His father worked in a piano factory, and the lunch was always noodle soup, so the nickname was a natural." Noodles was only 16 in 1895 when he joined the nearby Chattanooga team of the Southern League, moving to Mobile when the franchise was transferred there in July. The next year he pitched well enough to attract the attention of both the Detroit and St. Paul clubs of the Western League.

Detroit won out, and although neither of Hahn's two seasons with the Wolverines was particularly impressive—he finished 17-17 in his first year and 12-19 in his second while earning a reputation for a "lack of condition"—Cincinnati Reds owner John Brush purchased him on the recommendation of St. Paul owner Charles Comiskey, who'd previously managed the Reds. Not yet 20 and coming off a mediocre year, Hahn received little attention at the start of his first major league training camp. He pitched well, however, and *The Sporting News* reported that he had "terrific speed, good curves, and the best control ever displayed by a green southpaw." For the first time Noodles didn't throw as hard as he could on the first day of practice, and he was getting his arm rubbed frequently. Despite his strong spring, near the end of camp there was some doubt whether Hahn would make the team. Manager Buck Ewing reportedly favored letting him go, but Brush insisted that he open the season with Cincinnati.

Hahn burst into the National League with three straight victories, one of which set the tone for his rookie campaign. Leading 1-0 heading into the bottom of the ninth inning at Pittsburgh, Hahn surrendered a leadoff triple to Willie Clark. As the next batter stepped in, Noodles laid the ball on the ground, making it look as if he'd quit under the strain. Then, according to one reporter "with a slow motion he put his hand in his shirt pocket, pulled out a plug of tobacco, took a bite and then prepared for business." The crowd watched dumbfounded as Hahn struck out the final three batters (his only strikeouts of the game, according to the box score). Pittsburgh's Patsy Donovan "talks of the game to this day," wrote the *Cincinnati Commercial-Tribune* a year and a half later. "He will tell you that it was the greatest game he ever saw a young pitcher deliver." Hahn finished the 1899 season with a 23-8 record and a league-leading 145 strikeouts. "This year shows me what I can do when I'm not drinking," he told the *Cincinnati Enquirer*. "I'll never again indulge in any kind of strong drink."

Though his 1900 record of 16-20 paled in comparison to his phenomenal rookie year, Hahn still tossed 311⅓ innings, led the NL in strikeouts again with 132, and hurled the season's only no-hitter. The *Boston Herald* remarked at midseason that he was already generally regarded as the NL's best left-handed pitcher. The 1901 season proved to be the pinnacle of Noodles' short career. Pitching for a hapless club that finished in last place with only 52 wins, Noodles won 22 games (against 19 defeats), racking up 42% of his team's victories—the second-highest percentage in modern NL history, behind only Steve Carlton's 46% in 1972. For the third consecutive season Hahn led the NL in strikeouts with a career-high 239, and he also led the league in complete games (41) and innings (375⅓). On May 22 he became the first player since the introduction of the modern pitching distance to strike out 16 batters in a nine-inning game, a mark that wasn't surpassed until Dizzy Dean struck out 17 in 1933.

With a salary of $4,200 (a dramatic increase from his $1,800 salary of only two years earlier), making him the highest-paid player on the team, Hahn pitched well over the next two seasons as Cincinnati improved to around .500. In 1902 he went 23-12 and finished second in the NL with a 1.77 ERA. The next year he almost duplicated his won-loss record (22-12) and finished with a 2.52 ERA, still well below the National League average. Hahn started slowly in 1904, but *The Sporting News* believed he'd come around: "He has given good service for a longer period than most southpaws, but there is no reason to believe 'Noodles' will not retain his effectiveness for several seasons." Though he finished with a 2.06 ERA, the second lowest of his career, his record fell to 16-18 amidst reports that he was slipping.

Hahn hurt his arm during the 1905 season and never returned to his previous form. He did pitch a four-hitter against St. Louis in April in which his "famous jump ball played havoc with the visiting players," but by mid-August he had pitched only 77 innings. The Reds released him, their decision made easier because that he was still earning his "wartime" salary of over $4,000. "Hahn has failed to reach his old standard," reported the *Cincinnati Commercial-Gazette.* "Without his speed, he was robbed of much of his effectiveness." Noodles finished the season pitching for local semipro teams.

Opening Day 1906 found him with the American League's New York Highlanders. Manager Clark Griffith held Hahn back from starting until the weather warmed up. He pitched well in his first start in May, but through July he'd hurled only 42 innings. Deciding it was time to move on to other endeavors, he asked for and received his release.

With his major league career behind him, Hahn, who'd attended the Cincinnati Veterinary College during off-seasons, became a veterinary inspector for the U.S. government in Cincinnati. He continued to pitch semipro ball and visited Crosley Field on a regular basis. Noodles kept a locker there and frequently put on a uniform to pitch batting practice until 1946, when he was 67 years old. In the early 1950s he and his wife, Salome (Stevens) Hahn, moved from Cincinnati to Candler, North Carolina. That was where Noodles Hahn passed away at age 80 on February 6, 1960.

DAN LEVITT

CINCINNATI

AUGUST "GARRY" HERRMANN
PRESIDENT 1902–27

A self-made success in the rough-and-tumble world of Cincinnati politics, Garry Herrmann was the gregarious president of the Cincinnati Reds from 1902 to 1927 and chairman of the three-man National Commission that ruled major league baseball from 1903 to 1920. A flashy dresser who favored checkered suits and pinky rings, Herrmann became known as "The Walking Delicatessen" for his habit of taking a supply of sausages with him wherever he went. While some owners disliked his business decisions, few disliked him personally. Noted for his generosity, Herrmann often began dinner meetings with a single table but would add seating over the course of the evening, refusing to turn people away. Finally, when the last course was devoured, Herrmann invariably picked up the check.

August Herrmann was born in Cincinnati on May 3, 1859. Sometime in his early years he acquired the nickname "Garibaldi," later shortened to "Garry." His father died when he was 11, forcing him to work stuffing salt sacks and running errands. Eventually Garry became a printer's devil and started *The Law Bulletin*, the official newspaper of the courts of Hamilton County. A staunch Republican, he became a useful cog in Cincinnati's corrupt political machine run by George "Boss" Cox. Herrmann served as clerk of the courts, member of the school board, and president of the Cincinnati Water Works Commission, charged with creating the Queen City's new waterworks system. By the summer of 1902 he was important and wealthy enough to join Cox and the Fleischmann brothers, Julius (the mayor) and Max, as a minority participant in their purchase of the Reds from John T. Brush for $150,000. Never a ballplayer himself—he preferred bowling, and later became president of the American Bowling Congress—Herrmann nonetheless was given the run of the baseball operations by his co-owners.

Having sold the Reds, Brush put together $200,000 to buy the New York Giants from Andrew Freedman, who was so hated by the other NL owners that they footed a good part of the bill. Freedman was solidly connected in New York politics, however, and his absence from the ownership ranks of the NL enabled the American League to find a site for a ballpark in Gotham. Herrmann, therefore, became a part owner and president of an NL club while at the same time participating in a key solidifying event in the success of the AL—this during the bitter war raging between the two leagues. It was a typical Herrmann moment. He took care of business, saw to his own comfort, and enabled others to do well.

In fact, the agreement of January 10, 1903, that ended the battle between the two leagues became known as the "Cincinnati Peace Treaty," partly because of the role that Herrmann played by giving up his claim on the services of Sam Crawford to the AL's Detroit Tigers. Better known now as the National Agreement, it established that the major leagues would be governed by a National Commission consisting of the presidents of the two leagues and a club president agreed to by both. For the duration of its existence, that meant AL boss Ban Johnson, whoever was leading the NL at the moment, and Herrmann. The Cincinnati president's affability and instinct for compromise made him a natural choice, but some claimed that his willingness to agree with Johnson was what secured his position.

A former Cincinnati sportswriter, Johnson was indeed the dominant off-field figure in baseball during the Deadball Era, and Herrmann, despite his status as an NL owner, often sided with Johnson and the AL on controversial issues. But Herrmann scholar Kevin Grace of the University of Cincinnati takes issue with the commonly held belief that Herrmann was merely Johnson's "pliant tool." Grace points out that although the two men had known each other in Cincinnati, their friendship was only casual, "not on the order of Comiskey-Johnson before their falling out." Rather, Grace views Herrmann's selection as chairman of the National Commission as the result of his "national reputation as a fair mediator, borne of his involvement in Republican machine politics." According to Grace, Herrmann was simply the kind of person who could "get along with anyone and bring sides together."

Herrmann was responsible for some important and far-reaching compromises. For instance, he is sometimes called the "Father of the World Series." Like the old World Series of the 1880s between teams of the NL and the American Association, the first modern World Series in 1903 was an exhibition arranged between the clubs. Thus, the Giants were within their rights when they refused to play the AL champs in 1904, calling the junior circuit a bush league undeserving of major league status. Herrmann was instrumental in making the World Series an annual event with the official sanction of the National Commission, and it has been played essentially on that same basis since the 1905 World Series between the New York Giants and the Philadelphia Athletics.

Herrmann also kept an open mind to innovation. On August 24, 1908, floodlight manufacturer George Cahill and several Cincinnati businessmen, Herrmann included, created the Night Baseball Development Company with an investment of $50,000. Two towers were built and an exhibition game was foreseen. The project died when the promoters realized that they needed two additional towers, but Herrmann was enthusiastic about an idea that his fellow owners resisted as "unnatural." He saw night baseball as a moneymaker that would be good for the game. Herrmann would have been proud that Cincinnati eventually host-ed the first major league night game in 1935, four years after Herrmann's death.

More successfully, Herrmann oversaw the construction of the ballpark that eventually became known as Crosley Field, the home of the Reds until the early 1970s. The old Palace of the Fans was demolished after the 1911 season, and architect Harry Hake's new ballpark was part of the Cox machine's effort to make Cincinnati an exemplar of what historians call the "City Beautiful Movement." The huge cost of the new grandstand, coupled with poor attendance in the midteens, caused financial hardship for the Reds. Unable to meet its obligations and in danger of foreclosure, the Cincinnati Exhibition Company dissolved, and a new corporation called the Cincinnati Base Ball Club Company was formed. Stockholders were asked to buy shares in the new corporation to raise capital and keep the club solvent, but the upheaval had little impact on Herrmann personally. He remained at the helm of the club as though nothing had happened.

Herrmann faced his most serious opposition as chairman of the National Commission when NL president John Heydler refused to support his re-appointment just before the 1919 World Series. It was the best and worst of times for the Cincinnati president, whose Reds had just won their first NL pennant. Herrmann reveled in his role as host of the World Series. His generosity and appetite were on display for all to see, and he was ecstatic when the Reds finally won the world championship and restored the glory that Cincinnati had enjoyed during the early days of professional baseball. Ironically, the subsequent revelation that the White Sox had thrown the Series was the final blow that brought down the National Commission. Herrmann resigned as chairman in January 1920, and his position was never filled. The Black Sox scandal forced owners to hire Kenesaw Mountain Landis as the game's first commissioner. True to his character, Herrmann supported Landis's appointment in the belief that it was the right thing for baseball in the long run.

Herrmann continued as Reds president through the 1927 season, when poor health and increasing deafness forced him to resign and sell his shares in the club. He was 71 when he died on April 25, 1931. His wife, Anna Becker, had passed away in 1916. The couple left behind one child, Lena Herrmann Finke.

JOHN SACCOMAN

Bob Ewing

CINCINNATI

GEORGE LEMUEL "BOB" EWING
RIGHT-HANDED PITCHER 1902–09

In his prime, Long Bob Ewing—the "Long" referring to his 6'1½", 170 lb. frame—was the workhorse of the Cincinnati staff, becoming the team's winningest pitcher of the Deadball Era and the most significant spitball pitcher in the history of the franchise. Toiling for six managers in eight years on a succession of mediocre teams, Ewing led the Reds in complete games twice and victories and strikeouts three times each. He still holds the franchise record for career ERA for 1,000 or more innings. Though he never led the National League in a major statistical category, Ewing finished second in innings pitched, complete games, and strikeouts in 1907.

Born on April 24, 1873, George Lemuel Ewing—"Bob" was likely a name he adopted in preference to George—grew up on a farm in Auglaize County, Ohio. According to family lore, he started out in baseball as a boy pitching potatoes against a target on the barn. Despite his early fascination with the game, Bob got a relatively late start in the professional ranks, turning 24 before signing his first contract. Through the mid-1890s he pitched for his hometown Wapakoneta Indians against teams from other small towns in western Ohio. The competition was surprisingly brisk. In 1897 the loose network of local rivalries coalesced into the short-lived Northwestern Ohio League. Of all the players in the four-team circuit, nearly one in five eventually reached the majors: Wapakoneta had Ewing and George Rohe; St. Marys boasted Jack Harper and Topsy Hartsel; Piqua featured Nick Altrock; and Lima was led by Jim Delahanty and Roger Bresnahan.

In August 1897 Ewing signed with the Toledo Mud Hens, who were on their way to the Interstate League pennant. He made his professional debut with a 9-4 victory over Springfield. The *Toledo Commercial* reported that in spite of indifferent support, the newcomer remained "as cool as the January weather in Alaska." Over the next three seasons, Ewing pitched nearly 900 innings and won more than 20 games annually for Toledo. Promoted to Kansas City in 1901, he went 21-5 to lead the Western League in winning percentage. With Ewing, Jake Weimer, and Bill Wolfe combining for 64 victories, the Blues won the pennant.

The turning point of Bob Ewing's career came on October 10, 1901. Home from Kansas City, he hooked up with a club in Sidney, Ohio, for a couple of post-season games. When the Cincinnati Reds came to Sidney on a barnstorming tour, Ewing drew the pitching assignment. The game was called for darkness after eight innings, but he held the big leaguers to a 3-3 tie. Within two weeks he was under contract with the Reds. In his first major league game on April 19, 1902—five days before his 29th birthday—Ewing walked 10 batters, seven of them in one inning, in a 9-5 loss to Chicago. It was nearly a month before he gained his first victory, and then he missed the second half of the season with a sore arm. Bob had to fight for a place on the roster the next two seasons before establishing himself as one of the Reds' top pitchers. By late 1904 Ewing had mastered the spitball, becoming one of its first exponents in the National League. With that new weapon he enjoyed his best year in 1905, securing his 20th victory in the last game of the season. A month later he married Nelle Hunter, the daughter of a prominent Auglaize County physician.

In good times and bad, Bob Ewing earned a reputation as a hard worker and a sober, conscientious professional. He was, in the approving words of a Cincinnati sportswriter, "the most tractable of ballplayers." Though he never enjoyed so much as a taste of a pennant race in Cincinnati, he enjoyed several moments of glory:

- August 18, 1903: Ewing pitches a one-hit shutout in New York, allowing only an infield single by Jack Dunn in the eighth inning. Teammates argue that if the play had been scored correctly, Ewing would have been credited with a no-hitter.
- September 11, 1906: Ewing duels Deacon Phillippe and Vic Willis to a scoreless tie in Pittsburgh, scattering eight hits over 15 innings.
- April 11, 1907: On Opening Day, Ewing beats Pittsburgh, 4-3, as the Reds come from behind with two runs in the ninth inning.

From 1907 on, Ewing was the senior member of the Reds in time of service. The 35-year-old spitballer was also approaching an age when most pitchers of the era were used up. On January 20, 1910, the Reds traded him to Philadelphia in a two-for-two swap of pitchers—Ewing and Ad Brennan for Harry Coveleski and Frank Corridon. Observed Jack Ryder, the longtime baseball writer of the *Cincinnati Enquirer*, "Faithful followers of the Reds will be sorry to see Long Bob Ewing go, in spite of the fact that he has not been a big winner for a number of years. Bob has been very unlucky in his work for some time, pitching a lot of close games in which he lost by small scores."

In Philadelphia, Ewing was initially an afterthought in manager Red Dooin's plans. But when other pitchers faltered, Bob stepped up. The oldest regular starting pitcher in the league, he went 16-14 for a fourth-place team, leading the Phillies in complete games and pitching three games in which he allowed three hits or fewer. That, however, was Ewing's last hurrah. His arm gave out and Philadelphia dropped him in September 1911. Roger Bresnahan gave Ewing a brief look in St. Louis in 1912, after which the aging spitballer returned to the minors. He reached the end of the line in 1913, failing in a trial with Minneapolis and drawing his release two weeks after his 40th birthday.

Ewing returned home and made a few appearances with the Wapakoneta team before hanging up his glove. He lived comfortably after quitting baseball and pursued a variety of occupations: raising hogs and training harness horses, managing an assortment of businesses, and serving two terms as sheriff of Auglaize County. Long Bob Ewing died of cancer on June 20, 1947, at age 74. Nelle, his wife of 42 years, survived him by a quarter century. She also remained an avid Reds fan, living to meet Pete Rose and Johnny Bench and see the dawn of the Big Red Machine dynasty of the 1970s. She attended more than 60 consecutive Opening Days before her own death in 1972.

Bob and Nelle Ewing are buried in Walnut Hill Cemetery near New Hampshire, Ohio, under a common headstone decorated with a baseball and bat. On August 12, 2001, all eight of Ewing's surviving grandchildren were present at Cinergy Field for his induction into the Cincinnati Reds Hall of Fame.

MIKE LACKEY

CINCINNATI

JAMES BENTLEY "CY" SEYMOUR
CENTER FIELDER 1902–06

Aside from Babe Ruth, Cy Seymour is the only player in the modern history of major league baseball to pitch more than 100 games and collect more than 1,500 hits. Like Ruth, Seymour was a left-handed thrower and batter who began his career as a pitcher before switching to the outfield. But unlike the great Sultan of Swat, Seymour had the misfortune of pitching in a hitter's era and hitting in a pitcher's era. Doing the bulk of his pitching in 1897-99, when the National League batted a collective .281, he held opponents to a .244 average while compiling a lifetime 61-56 record and 3.76 ERA, including 25 victories and a league-leading 239 strikeouts in 1898. Doing the bulk of his hitting from 1901 to 1910, when the NL batted a collective .252, Seymour posted a lifetime batting average of .303, including a 1905 season that stands out as arguably the greatest offensive performance by a National Leaguer during the Deadball Era.

James Bentley Seymour was born on December 9, 1872, in Albany, New York. He preferred to be called James or J. Bentley rather than "Cy" (short for "Cyclone," the nickname sportswriters pinned on him), and he also came in for a good deal of chiding for his ostentatious dress and his insistence that he was related to the Duke of Somerset. After beginning his baseball career with the semipro Ridgeway team in his hometown of Albany, Seymour reportedly earned $1,000 per month pitching for Plattsburgh of the Northern New York League, which was supported by millionaire sportsman Harry Payne Whitney. If true, that might explain why he didn't make his debut in Organized Baseball until 1896, when at age 24 he reported directly to the National League's New York Giants.

Veteran catcher Duke Farrell provides a glimpse of the type of pitcher Seymour was when he first joined the Giants. One day in Chicago the rookie was sailing along effectively until the eighth inning, when suddenly he lost his control. "His cheeks turned red, he threw his hat off after a bad pitch, then threw his glove away after another," Farrell recalled. "Finally, Cy was worked up to such a state that after making a pitch he would run to the plate and grab the ball out of my hands, hustle back, and without waiting for my sign shoot it back. Nine Chicago runners crossed the plate before the inning ended. Seymour subsequently had many aerial flights, but nothing like his Chicago performance." Another catcher, Wilbert Robinson, claimed that he'd never seen anyone pitch quite like Cy, first throwing high around a batter's head, then dropping the next pitch around his feet. After watching Seymour in 11 early season games in which he posted a 2-4 record with a 6.40 ERA and 51 walks in 70⅓ innings, the Giants decided they'd seen enough and farmed him out to Springfield of the Eastern League. There he went 8-1 over the remainder of the season.

Returning to the Giants in 1897, Seymour started to fulfill his potential, though he still had a penchant for wildness and excitability—the *New York Times* called him "the youngster with a $10,000 arm and a $00.00 head." For the season he was 18-14 with a 3.37 ERA, finishing second in the NL in strikeouts (149) and first in strikeouts per game (4.83) and fewest hits per game (8.23), but also leading the league in walks (164). "Cy is rapidly improving," wrote the *New York Herald*. "Occasionally he gets a slight nervous chill, but by talking to himself with words of cheer and taking good self-advice, he lets the wobble pass away." In 1898 Seymour reached the apex of his short pitching career, improving his record to 25-19, lowering his ERA to 3.18, and leading the NL in strikeouts with 239, 61 ahead of the runner-up, Doc McJames. Again he led the NL with 213 walks, but he also led the Giants in wins, starts (43), and innings (356⅔), prompting some to suggest that he'd supplanted Amos Rusie (20-11, 3.03 ERA) as staff ace. It was reported that he had the best curve in the league and as much speed as Rusie ever had.

Around midseason Seymour also began to play the outfield on a fairly regular basis, batting .276 with four home runs in 297 at-bats, giving rise to speculation that he might be converted to a full-time outfielder. As with Babe Ruth two decades later, his playing the outfield had more to do with injuries and the light hitting of New York's regular outfielders than with managerial insight. New manager John B. Day, who took over the Giants in 1899, was faced with a dilemma, just as Red Sox manager Ed Barrow later was with Ruth, but ultimately he sided with William Koelsch of *The Sporting Life*, who wrote: "The suggestion that Seymour be placed in the outfield permanently is more than a rank proposition. As long as Seymour has the speed he has now he is more valuable on the slab than anywhere else."

Coming off such fine seasons, both of New York's ace pitchers expected raises for 1899. Parsimonious Giants owner Andrew Freedman had other ideas. With no raises forthcoming, Rusie chose to retire while Seymour held out for the first month of the season, not returning until May 11, when Freedman broke down and offered $2,000 for the season, $500 more than Cy had earned in 1898. Pitching for a dispirited club that finished with 90 losses, Seymour compiled a 14-18 record with a 3.56 ERA while finishing second in the NL strikeout race with 142, only three behind Noodles Hahn. Again he led the league in strikeouts per game (4.76) and walks (170), while finishing fourth in fewest hits per game (8.28).

Seymour didn't know it yet, but his days as an effective pitcher were over. Ted Breitenstein had warned him that using the "indrop ball" (screwball) would leave his arm "as dead as one of those mummies in the Art Museum," but he refused to take heed and ultimately it cost him. Seymour didn't start his first game of 1900 until eight days into the season, and then he was lifted in the second inning after giving up four runs. He started another game in mid-May but was shifted to center field after giving up 10 runs in six innings. Cy played left field in the next game, but after that he disappeared from the lineup completely except for a couple of mop-up appearances in which he was again hit hard. Seymour didn't win his first game until early June, ironically the same day the Giants announced that they were farming him out to Worcester. Then, mysteriously, the *Times* reported, "Seymour put in his appearance again at the Polo Grounds yesterday, having been refused by the Worcester management as unfit. It is likely some deal will be fixed up for his re-trading to Chicago." After that he did pitch a couple of games for Charlie Comiskey's minor league Chicago White Sox, though he remained on the Giants' reserve list.

In 1901 Cy Seymour embarked on a second career as a major league outfielder, and it proved even more successful than his career as a pitcher had been. He jumped to the American League's Baltimore Orioles, managed by John McGraw, who'd been impressed with Cy's toughness when he'd pitched three games against the Orioles in two days during the 1898 season. Years later McGraw said that no player, not even Joe McGinnity, deserved the title "Iron Man" more than Seymour. Playing mostly right field in 134 games for Baltimore, Cy emerged as a star by hitting .303 and finishing third in the National League in stolen bases with 38, but that was nothing compared to the statistics he compiled with the Cincinnati Reds when he joined that team after the break-up of the Orioles in 1902. In his first three and a half seasons in Cincinnati, Cy batted .340, .342, .313, and a remarkable .377—122 points above the league average that season, a differential that wasn't topped in the NL until Rogers Hornsby's stupendous .424 mark in 1924 placed him 141 points above the National League average.

Not even the great Honus Wagner could match Seymour's batting accomplishments in 1905. Both players met in a season-ending doubleheader. A reporter wrote that "10,000 were more interested in the batting achievements of Wagner and Seymour than the games. Cheer upon cheer greeted the mighty batsmen upon each appearance at the plate, and mighty cheering greeted the sound of bat upon ball as mighty Cy drove out hit after hit. The boss slugger got four-for-seven while Wagner could only get two-for-seven." Seymour's .377 average not only beat out Wagner by 14 points, it was also the highest batting average by a National Leaguer during the entire Deadball Era. That season Cy also led the league in hits (219), doubles (40, the most hit by an NL outfielder until Pat Duncan collected 44 in 1922), triples (21), RBI (121), and slugging percentage (.559, an NL Deadball Era record that lasted until Heinie Zimmerman slugged .571 in 1912). The only category that prevented Seymour from winning the Triple Crown in 1905 was home runs, finishing one behind teammate Fritz Odwell, who hit his ninth in his last at-bat of the season.

How did Cy Seymour put up such incredible numbers? We know that he eschewed the common practice of moving to the front of the batter's box to attempt to hit the curve ball before it broke; he preferred staying back in the box and waving his bat around, stating that it gave him "that much more time to be sure which infielder is going to cover second base [on the hit-and-run play]. A large portion of my base hits were made in this way." Seymour also used a wide variety of bats, depending on the pitcher he was facing—a practice more common today, but highly unusual in the Deadball Era. He used a light bat when facing a location pitcher and a heavier one when he was up against

a fireballer, which seems the opposite of what one might expect. But as Brooklyn Superbas manager Ned Hanlon said, "I look upon Seymour as the greatest straight ball player of the age; by that I mean he is absolutely all right if you let him play the game his own way. But if you try to mix up any science on him, you are likely to injure his effectiveness."

Something injured Seymour's effectiveness during the first half of 1906. In his first 79 games with Cincinnati he batted only .257, a 120-point drop-off from his average of the previous season. On July 14 the Reds sold him back to the Giants. The purchase price was variously reported at $10,000 or $12,000; either way, it was the largest sum ever paid for a single player. After playing one game for New York (in which he made a sensational catch), Seymour demanded a por-

tion of his sale price, claiming that Garry Herrmann had promised it to him if the deal was consummated. Seymour threatened to go on strike when Herrmann denied making any such promise, but McGraw somehow coaxed him back onto the field. On his first trip back to Cincinnati after the "trade," Seymour made front-page headlines in the *Cincinnati Post* by descending from the Giants' team carriage in a set of bright-red false whiskers and announcing to the multitude, "Cy Seymour, I am pained to relate, ladies and gentlemen, is not coming to the park today. He is afraid that the Cincinnati fans will lynch him." When he grounded out weakly in his first at-bat, he was jeered and cheered by the local fans.

Seymour bounced back to hit .320 in 72 games for the Giants, giving him a season's average of .286, still good enough to rank 10th in the NL. Though he never returned to the rarefied heights of 1905, he did hit consistently above the NL average in the next three years, including a .294 mark in 1907 that placed him fifth in the NL batting race. Seymour's best known moment with the Giants came in 1908's one-game playoff against the Chicago Cubs. In the second inning he misjudged a fly ball hit by Joe Tinker, allowing three runners to score in a game that New York eventually lost, 4-2. That incident reinforced Seymour's reputation as a poor fielder (in 1903 he'd made 36 errors, the single-season record for an outfielder since 1900), but in 1904 *The Sporting Life* claimed that he "is as speedy and graceful as ever in centre field and covers a world of ground out there, more than any other centre fielder in the National League."

During 1909 spring training Seymour took exception to a prank played on him by Arlie Latham. He beat up the 49-year-old third-base coach, causing McGraw to suspend the star center fielder for eight weeks. (Ironically, Cy had played an indirect role in Latham's hiring; while coaching third one day he tackled Moose McCormick, who'd run through his hold-up sign in an attempt to stretch a triple into a home run. From that moment on, according to Christy Mathewson, McGraw realized the need for a full-time coach.) In the first inning of the first game after his suspension, Seymour sustained a career-altering injury when he collided with right fielder Red Murray while chasing a long fly ball. After lying motionless for five minutes, Cy

appeared to have recovered and resumed his position in center field. The next Boston batter sent a fly ball to him that he caught, and as he prepared to throw home (there was a runner on third), he collapsed and had to be carried off the field. The injury to Seymour's leg, according to Mathewson, curtailed his effectiveness for the rest of his career.

Typical of aging stars of the Deadball Era, when the Giants released him in 1910, Seymour returned to the minors with the Eastern League's Baltimore Orioles. Former major leaguer Bobby Vaughn claimed that the 37-year-old outfielder still had the best batting eye of anyone in baseball and was a "conscientious ball player, whatever else may be said." But a newspaper report after Cy's 1911 release stated, "Although he played good ball, his habits were such that it was decided that he would no longer play on the team." After hitting .306 the following year in 124 games with Newark of the International League, Seymour made it back to the majors in 1913 for a brief (39 games) but unsuccessful (.178) stint with the Boston Braves. He then returned to the International League for a dozen games with Buffalo, writing to his old boss Garry Herrmann after the season to request assistance in finding a managerial position. "I may seem funny to you the way you know me," he wrote. "I am different on the inside than on the out & I know if I had half a chance I will make good."

No job came of the letter, and Seymour remained out of Organized Baseball until 1918, when at age 46 he played in 13 games for Newark. He died in New York City on September 20, 1919, after contracting tuberculosis while working in the shipyards of New York during World War I. One obituary claimed that Seymour worked on the docks because he was unfit for military service, and it was also rumored that he was penniless. He was probably an alcoholic; both Blanche McGraw and Hans Lobert described him as a hard drinker, and there was one well-reported incident from his days with the Reds when he was removed from a game because he was inebriated. Cy Seymour's burial in the Rural Cemetery of his hometown of Albany was a simple affair, with his boyhood chums acting as pallbearers. Though a large throng attended the service, there was no one present from Organized Baseball.

BILL KIRWIN

CINCINNATI

JOHN BANNERMAN "LARRY" McLEAN
CATCHER 1906–12

At 6'5" and nearly 230 lbs., Larry McLean was a large presence and a sizable talent, and he did things in a big way—including getting into trouble. Owing largely to a lifelong battle with alcohol, McLean's career was punctuated by repeated suspensions, occasional brawls, and periodic scrapes with the law. Still he spanned 15 years in the major leagues, maintaining a lifetime batting average of .262 and performing with distinction in his only World Series. McLean played his best baseball for Cincinnati, for whom he batted over .285 three times. Baseball historian Lee Allen compared him to a later Reds backstop: like Ernie Lombardi, McLean was big and slow but could hit and throw. Though he frequently drove managers to distraction, he was a favorite with writers and fans wherever he went.

Born on July 18, 1881, in Fredericton, New Brunswick, Canada, John Bannerman McLean grew up in the Boston area. His family called him Jack, but he was nicknamed "Larry" early in his career after someone detected a resemblance to Napoleon "Larry" Lajoie. McLean started his baseball career in 1899, playing in Canada with the Saint John Roses and Fredericton Tartars. He made his major league debut with the Boston Americans on April 26, 1901, smacking a pinch double off Joe McGinnity in Baltimore. Boston let him go and he returned to Canada with the Halifax Resolutes. McLean had a tryout with Cleveland in 1903 before being awarded to the Chicago Cubs in a contract dispute. He played only one game and was traded to the Cardinals in the deal that brought Mordecai Brown to Chicago. Years later *The Sporting News* recalled that McLean "did not lead an athletic life" in St. Louis.

There is a Bunyanesque quality to the stories about Larry McLean. It started, perhaps, on April 18, 1906, when McLean—who'd been demoted to the Pacific Coast League in 1905 after playing 27 games for the Cardinals—survived the San Francisco earthquake while in town with his Portland teammates. He hit .355 in 1906 and helped Portland to the PCL pennant, but already there were signs of trouble off the field; Portland withheld $200 of his salary against his promise to remain "sober and temperate," the first of many such clauses that appeared in his contracts.

Toward the end of the 1906 season Portland sold McLean to the Cincinnati Reds. Larry played in a dozen games down the stretch, then returned in 1907 and spent his first full season in the majors, appearing in 113 games and batting .289. "Cincinnati has not had a more popular idol in years than Long Larry McLean," declared *The Sporting News* correspondent Charlie Zuber. While with Cincinnati, McLean collared a murder suspect on the street and was said to have swum the Ohio River rather than arrive late to the ballpark. When the Reds visited Havana in 1908, admirers presented him with a silver-handled cane engraved "to the greatest catcher that has ever been seen in Cuba." In 1910 Larry did a turn in vaudeville—playing himself, Zuber said, "as nearly as possible."

Through it all, Larry strove to stay in line. In 1908 he pledged $1,000 that he wouldn't take a drink for one full year. McLean played under several managers with Cincinnati, and each tried a different way of dealing with him. John Ganzel was permissive. Clark Griffith challenged McLean with hard work and responsibility, naming him team captain and appointing him as acting manager for a few days in 1909 when Griffith was ill. Hank O'Day sat McLean down for heart-to-heart talks. Nothing worked for long. McLean's file at the National Baseball Library is rife with dunning notices, complaints about bounced checks, and a report from a private detective the Reds hired to follow him. Once, asked who would catch that afternoon, O'Day growled, "The big fellow—if he can see 'em."

McLean's association with the Reds nearly ended in 1910, when he ran afoul of training rules. Suspended indefinitely by the team and infuriated by newspaper accounts of his behavior, Larry wrote a letter of resignation. "When I take a trip through Chinatown, the 'boys' take particular delight in putting it in the papers, but when any of the other players get soused, the news is suppressed," he complained. "Can you blame me for wanting to get away from the Cincinnati Club?" McLean eventually returned to the Reds after a one-week suspension, but was stripped of his captaincy and forced to sign a draconian new contract. Forty percent of his salary was held back as a season's-end sobriety bonus, the entire contract to be voided if McLean touched "a single drink." When the big catcher made his first appearance before a home crowd, he was greeted with "much applause and some kidding," which he accepted "as a matter of course."

McLean remained with the Reds until September 1912, when he was suspended for failing to show up for an exhibition game in Syracuse. After the season the Reds sold him to the Cardinals. Larry broke his arm in a poolroom brawl just weeks before the start of spring training. The judge let him off with a lecture after witnesses testified that he'd been trying to break up the fight. McLean recovered and played 48 games for St. Louis before the Cardinals traded him to the pennant-bound New York Giants on August 6, 1913. Larry hit .320 in 30 games down the stretch. When Chief Meyers hurt his hand before the second game of the World Series, McLean took over as the starting catcher. He went six-for-12 against the formidable Philadelphia Athletics pitching staff and was one of the heroes of Game Two, the Giants' lone victory. He tagged out two runners at the plate in the ninth inning, then led off the 10th with a single against Eddie Plank to ignite a game-winning rally. After the Series, Giants manager John McGraw said, "McLean behaved like a man from the moment we got him. I found him easy to handle."

McGraw and McLean got on handsomely until June 1915 when McLean was again suspended for drinking. The Giants were at the Buckingham Hotel in St. Louis, where Larry decided to confront his manager. McLean accused scout Dick Kinsella of spying on him and the club of plotting to beat him out of a $1,000 bonus. Words were exchanged, McLean lunged at McGraw, and a melee ensued. A half dozen ballplayers jumped in the fracas, furniture was smashed, and McLean fled into the night. His major league career was over. Larry played some semipro ball but soon drifted out of the game.

Not much is known of McLean's life after baseball, but it's a safe bet that much of it was spent in saloons. On March 24, 1921, McLean got into an argument in a Boston speakeasy. When he attempted to climb over the bar, the bartender drew a pistol and shot him. McLean staggered outside and died on the street. He was 39 years old. After his death, the *Reach Guide* reflected that he was "a man of great size, a convivial disposition and a bad temper when under the influence of liquor, which led him into many more or less serious rows during his baseball career."

In 2000 the New Brunswick Sports Hall of Fame recognized Larry McLean as one of the province's sports pioneers. But perhaps the highest tribute came from an anonymous sportswriter at the time of his death: "He had no enemies, even among those with whom he clashed."

MIKE LACKEY

John "Hans" Lobert

CINCINNATI

JOHN BERNARD "HANS" LOBERT
THIRD BASEMAN 1906–10

Hans Lobert's game was built around speed. Aside from 1912, when an injury caused him to miss more than half the season, the stocky, bowlegged third baseman stole 30 or more bases each year in 1907-14. At a field day in Cincinnati on October 12, 1910, Lobert rounded the bases in 13.8 seconds, considered a record at the time. He also raced against—and defeated— Olympic gold medal winner Jim Thorpe, collegiate track star Vince Campbell, and even a racehorse. One reporter suggested that if Hans put his mind to it, he could be the world-record holder in the 110 and the 440. But the hard-nosed Lobert was far from one-dimensional. The lifetime .274 hitter batted over .300 four times and twice led National League third basemen in fielding percentage.

The son of a cabinetmaker, John Bernard Lobert was born in Wilmington, Delaware, on October 18, 1881. The family included six children, and John's brothers Frank and Ollie also played professional baseball. After moving to Williamsport, Pennsylvania, the Loberts eventually relocated to the Pittsburgh area, where John began playing for the Pittsburgh Athletic Club. After a 1903 game in Atlantic City, New Jersey, a vacationing Barney Dreyfuss invited Lobert to try out for the Pittsburgh Pirates that September. When John showed up in the clubhouse at Exposition Park, Honus Wagner found out that they lived near each other, that they shared the same name (Johannus in German, which was their common heritage), and perhaps recognized that they bore a slight facial resemblance—especially in their prominent noses. The great Pirates star dubbed the 21-year-old rookie "Hans No. Two," and called him that for the next 50 years.

The nickname stuck, but Lobert didn't. Having clinched the pennant, Pittsburgh manager Fred Clarke tried him out at every position in the infield except first base. Hans appeared in five games, making three errors and only one hit in 13 at-bats. He described his lone hit in *The Glory of Their Times*. According to the story, late in a game against Joe McGinnity of the New York Giants, with two strikes against him, Lobert bunted for a single. When he took his position at third base, John McGraw, who was coaching third for the Giants, asked him who taught him to bunt with two strikes. "Nobody did," Lobert replied, "but I like to bunt and nobody was looking for a busher to do that." McGraw responded, "Well, you keep it up. That's the way to keep them on their toes."

The Pirates decided Lobert needed more seasoning, so they sold him to Des Moines, Iowa, of the Western League. He played 143 games in 1904 and batted .264 with 37 stolen bases. That winter the Des Moines team changed hands, and the new owner offered Lobert a contract with a substantial cut in pay. Spurning the offer to play closer to home, Hans signed with Johnstown of the outlaw Tri-State League and batted .337 with 31 stolen bases in 115 games. Late in the 1905 season the Chicago Cubs purchased Lobert's contract from Des Moines, which still held his rights in Organized Baseball. Hans batted .196 in 14 games with the Cubs. Just before the start of the 1906 season, the Cubs traded Lobert and pitcher Jake Weimer to the Cincinnati Reds for third baseman Harry Steinfeldt. "If that trade hadn't been made, it would have been Chance, Evers, Tinker, and Lobert, I guess," Hans surmised. Even though the competition wasn't quite as stiff with the Reds, he became a utility man, batting .310 with 20 stolen bases in 79 games—35 at third base, 31 at shortstop, and 10 at second base.

In 1907 Lobert replaced the ancient Tommy

Corcoran as the Reds' everyday shortstop, batting .246 with a team-high 30 stolen bases. After starting the 1908 season at shortstop, he moved in midseason to third base, the position he played for the rest of his career. Playing in all 155 games, the 26-year-old Lobert led Cincinnati in just about every offensive category in 1908: batting average (.293), at-bats (570), runs (71), hits (167), doubles (17), triples (18), home runs (4), RBI (63), and a career-high 47 stolen bases. The next season the Reds pilfered 280 bases, running away with the National League lead in that category, but Hans slumped to a .212 batting average and only 30 steals. Despite appearing in just 93 games in 1910, Hans batted .309 and contributed 41 steals to Cincinnati's league-leading total of 310.

In February 1911 the Reds sent Lobert to the Philadelphia Phillies as part of an eight-player trade. Prior to that season, all 12 of his career home runs had been of the inside-the-park variety. In 1911, however, Hans blasted a career-high nine home runs, all of them over the fence and eight of them at Baker Bowl. He also batted .285 and led the Phillies with 40 stolen bases. Lobert endured another injury-plagued campaign in 1912, increasing his batting average to a career-high .327 but appearing in just 65 contests. Probably his best year, both off and on the field, was 1913. Hans married Philadelphia resident Rachel Campbell that year and defeated Jim Thorpe in a 100-yard dash at the Polo Grounds. He also played in 150 games, batting an even .300, leading all NL third basemen in fielding percentage (.974), and ranking third in the NL in runs (98) and stolen bases (41) and fourth in hits (172) and total bases (243).

That 1913 season proved to be the apex of Lobert's career. After one more decent season in Philadelphia—he batted .275 in 135 games and led NL third basemen again with a .943 fielding percentage—Lobert went to Chicago with the intention of sign-ing a contract with the Federal League's Chicago Whales. There he ran into his old friend John McGraw, with whom he'd barnstormed around the world during the off-season of 1913. McGraw convinced him not to sign with the Feds, then acquired him from the Phillies in January for pitcher Al Demaree, young third base-man Milt Stock, and reserve catcher Bert Adams. The Giants gave Lobert a three-year contract, matching the money the Feds had offered him. Lobert batted .251 as the regular third baseman in 1915 but tore ligaments in his knee, ending his season after only 106 games. He struggled for two more years, calling it quits when his contract expired in 1917.

With McGraw's assistance, Lobert received an appointment as baseball coach of the U.S. Military Academy at West Point, where he remained for eight years. He then became a full-time scout for McGraw, and in 1928 he joined the Giants as a coach. The fol-lowing year Lobert became the manager of Bridgeport of the Eastern League, leading the team to three consecutive second-place finishes. In 1932 he took the helm of Jersey City of the International League. Returning to Philadelphia in 1934, Lobert worked as a Phillies coach until 1942, when he spent one year as the team's man-ager. He was determined to mold the team in his own image—the Phillies even short-ened their name to the more streamlined "Phils" to add some dash—but they still fin-ished last in the NL in both stolen bases and victories. Lobert coached for the Reds for two sea-sons, then returned to the Giants.

When Connie Mack died in 1956, Hans Lobert became the man who'd been in major league baseball longer than anybody else. He continued to scout and work as an instructor for the Giants until his death in Philadelphia at age 87 on September 14, 1968.

JONATHAN DUNKLE

CINCINNATI

MICHAEL FRANCIS MITCHELL
RIGHT FIELDER 1907–12

Mike Mitchell was a strapping 6'1", 185 lb. right fielder with speed, power, and, according to noted baseball historian Bill James, the best outfield arm of the Deadball Era's first decade. In addition to stealing 107 bases from 1909 to 1911, Mitchell led the National League in outfield assists in 1907 and triples in 1909 and 1910. The right handed hitter and thrower with a career slugging percentage of .380 led the Cincinnati Reds in slugging in 1907 and each year from 1909 to 1911. "Mitchell is probably the heaviest hitter in the National League, a name which he was won because of his liking for nailing out three baggers and home runs just when a hit is needed," wrote Alfred Spink in 1910. "He is a splendid fielder, fast as lightning on the bases, and can throw with the best of them." Though Mitchell lasted just eight seasons in the majors, six of them with Cincinnati, James ranked him as the 108th best right fielder of all time.

Michael Francis Mitchell was born on December 12, 1879, in Springfield, Ohio, about 65 miles northeast of Cincinnati. He was already 22 by the time he joined an independent team from Schenectady, New York, in 1902. Mike played well enough to earn a 12-game tryout that September with Toledo of the American Association, slugging a home run and a pair of triples among his dozen hits. He made his debut in Organized Baseball with Troy of the New York State League in 1903, and the following year he split the season between Newark of the Eastern League and Syracuse of the NYSL. According to sportswriter Hugh Fullerton, University of Illinois athletic director George Huff, scouting for the Chicago Cubs, went to Syracuse that summer looking for an outfielder and discovered both Mitchell and Frank Schulte. "Both were secured, but Chicago offered Mitchell less money than he was get-

ting at Syracuse," wrote Fullerton. "He was forced to accept the offer, but openly stated he would not give his best efforts to the club, and so was lost to Chicago."

In 1905 Mitchell joined Portland of the Pacific Coast League and batted .251 in 147 games, giving little indication of the performance that was soon to come. In 1906 he put together one of the greatest minor league seasons of the Deadball Era, raising his batting average 100 points to win the PCL batting championship, and collecting 31 doubles, 12 triples, and a league-leading six homers to help Portland cop the pennant. With numbers like those, Cincinnati manager Ned Hanlon thought that Mike might provide the big bat that had been missing from the middle of his lineup since the Reds had sold Cy Seymour to the New York Giants. In his major league debut on April 11, 1907, Mitchell went 3-for-4 with a triple to lead the Reds to a 4-3 victory over the Pittsburgh Pirates. It was the beginning of a season that would earn him STATS, Inc.'s retroactive Rookie of the Year award. The 27-year-old freshman finished fifth in the NL in hits (163), sixth in triples (12) and total bases (213), and seventh in batting average (.292).

Mitchell demonstrated his athleticism on September 10, 1907, earning a gold medal and $100 during a field day in Cincinnati by winning the fungo-hitting contest; his mark of 413', 8½" was considered the world record until Ed Walsh swatted one 419'. Mitchell also set a modern record in 1907 for assists by an outfielder with 39, which stood until Chuck Klein gunned down 44 base runners in 1930. After his rookie year Mike's assist total never exceeded 23, but by then National League opponents knew better than to challenge his rifle arm. Right field at the Palace of the Fans was a notorious sun field, and Mike reportedly made one putout when a high fly that he'd lost in the sun struck him in the chest, bounced off, rolled down his arm and into his hand. Luck turned against him in 1908, however. Limited by injury to 119 games, Mitchell slumped to a .222 batting average with just one home run, a game winner in the 10th inning against Brooklyn on August 15.

Mitchell bounced back in 1909 to record his best season in the majors. In addition to his league-leading 17 triples, he ranked second in the NL in batting (.310) and slugging (.430), fourth in RBI (86) and total bases (225), fifth in on-base percentage (.378), and sixth in hits (162) and stolen bases (37). Mike maintained his outstanding performance in 1910, blasting a league-leading 18 triples, ranking second in RBI (88), and appearing in all 156 games. The following year he was even better, batting .291 with career highs in doubles (22) and triples (22), the latter figure placing him second in the NL behind Larry Doyle's 25. Mike's greatest game in the majors came on August 19, 1911, in the second game of a doubleheader against the New York Giants. In front of a crowd of 35,000 at the Polo Grounds, Mitchell hit for the cycle, stroking three of his hits against the great Christy Mathewson. His stellar performance helped Cincinnati beat New York, 7-4, snapping Matty's personal 22-game winning streak against the Reds that dated back to June 1908.

Though he was only 32 years old at the start of the 1912 season, Mitchell's best seasons were behind him. That year, his last with the Reds, he batted .283 and saw his production drop off in just about every statistical category. In December Mike became the key Cincinnati player in the blockbuster eight-player trade in which the Reds acquired Joe Tinker from the Chicago Cubs. Mitchell's career went into serious decline after leaving Cincinnati. In 1913 he switched to left field because the Cubs had their own strong-armed right fielder in Frank Schulte, Mike's old minor league teammate. Mitchell got off to a decent start in Chicago, batting .262 with four home runs and 15 stolen bases in 82 games, but on July 29 the Cubs placed him on waivers and the Pittsburgh Pirates claimed him. Fred Clarke played him in center field between Max Carey and Owen Wilson, and he finished out the season by hitting .271 in 54 games.

Mitchell started 1914 as the Pirates' right fielder after Wilson was traded to the Cardinals during the off-season, but he played his way out of the lineup by hitting just .234 in 76 games. On July 20 the Washington Senators, needing an outfielder because center fielder Clyde Milan had broken his jaw in a collision with right fielder Danny Moeller, acquired Mitchell for the waiver price. Washington manager Clark Griffith remembered Mike from their years together in Cincinnati, and Mike showed a glimpse of his former prowess by batting .285 with nine stolen bases in 55 games. Milan returned to action in 1915, however, so Griffith sold Mitchell to the New York Yankees in March. Having recently returned from a six-week vacation in Cuba, a place that he'd first discovered on a barnstorming trip with the Reds, Mike elected to retire rather than report to New York

After his baseball career, Mitchell managed pari-mutuel machines at several racetracks in the Midwest and West before retiring to Phoenix in 1954. He was 81 when he passed away in Phoenix on July 16, 1961.

MARK DUGO, DON GEISZLER & MIKE LACKEY

CINCINNATI

RICHARD CARLETON HOBLITZELL
FIRST BASEMAN 1908–14

After Dick Hoblitzell established himself as a regular at the tender age of 20, commentators mentioned him in the same breath as Ed Konetchy and Kitty Bransfield as one of the great first basemen of the National League. A perfect gentleman both on and off the field, the college-educated "Hobby" was an intelligent player whom both teammates and opponents respected. "He stands well up to the plate, takes a healthy swing at the ball, and is a long driver at opportune times," wrote one reporter. "In fact, he is looked upon by opposing pitchers as one of the most dangerous men at the bat that they are called upon to face."

Richard Carleton Hoblitzell was born on October 26, 1888, in the Ohio River village of Waverly, in West Virginia's oil region. His parents, Henry and Laura (Alcock) Hoblitzell, were of German, Swiss, French, and English descent. The exact spelling of their unusual last name was a source of confusion throughout Dick's career; Dick himself, however, consistently spelled it with two *l*'s. The family owed its middle-class existence to Henry's work in the oil fields. When Dick was eight years old, the Hoblitzells moved a short distance downriver to Parkersburg, West Virginia. He captained the Parkersburg High School football team during his freshman and sophomore years. For his last two years Dick attended prep school at Marietta Academy, playing halfback in 1905-06 for the Marietta College team. In the fall of 1907 he enrolled at the Western University of Pennsylvania (which became known as the University of Pittsburg the following year) and played end for the famous WUP football team.

Earlier that year Dick had signed a contract to play professional baseball with Clarksburg, West Virginia, of the Pennsylvania and West Virginia League. Assuming the alias of "Hollister" to protect his amateur status, the left-handed hitter and thrower played shortstop for his first two weeks when an emergency arose that forever changed the course of his baseball career. Clarksburg's regular first baseman became injured, and the 6'0", 172 lb. Hoblitzell was pressed into duty at the initial sack. Though he'd never played the position before, it became the one that he manned for all but seven of the nearly 1,300 major league contests he played in the field.

When the school year ended in 1908, Hoblitzell jumped his contract with Clarksburg to join Reading, Pennsylvania, of the outlaw Union League. When that league folded after only six weeks, he accepted an offer from Newark of the Eastern League. Before Hobby appeared in any official games, however, the National Association informed Newark that its new first baseman still belonged to Clarksburg. Hoblitzell remained in Newark for two weeks, awaiting settlement of his case. On June 30 he was informed that Clarksburg had sold him to Wheeling of the Central League. Returning to his native state, Hobby appeared in 53 games and attracted attention by batting .357.

On August 4, 1908, the Home Furniture Company, which owned the Clarksburg team, wrote the following letter to Frank Bancroft, business manager of the Cincinnati Reds: "We understand that your people are looking over young Hoblitzel now with Wheeling, Central League. This man belongs to us and we have had three offers for him, but have been trying to get more money for him. He is a very promising player with good habits and enough brains to do as he is told. If you want this man we will sell him to you for $1000, we can get this from other parties but would rather do business with you as our dealings with you in the past have been very satisfactory." The Reds purchased

Hoblitzell from Clarksburg on August 21. St. Louis Cardinals manager John McCloskey, meanwhile, had made a special trip to watch Hoblitzell play and taken the young first baseman with him to St. Louis. When word reached Cincinnati, the National Commission (through Cincinnati owner Garry Herrmann, no doubt) immediately notified the Cardinals that Hoblitzell couldn't play until title to him was resolved. Not surprisingly, the Commission ruled in Cincinnati's favor, finding that Clarksburg had allowed Hoblitzell to play for Wheeling on condition that it retained the right to sell him to another club.

Making his debut with the Reds on September 5, 1908, Hoblitzell took over at first base for player-manager John Ganzel and batted .254 over the last 32 games. The following year he appeared in 142 games and batted .308, third-best in the NL behind only Honus Wagner and teammate Mike Mitchell. Having shaved a year off his true age, Hoblitzell was considered a 19-year-old phenom whose "rise in baseball has been of the meteoric variety." Despite his sudden success, he continued his education during the off-season at the Ohio College of Dental Surgery, earning the ubiquitous nickname "Doc" along with his DDS.

Over the five-year period 1909-13, Hobby was the top run producer in a strong Cincinnati lineup. During the first half of 1914, however, he mysteriously lost his ability to hit, slumping all the way to .210 after 78 games. "The Red first baseman was as inefficient in the art of 'knocking 'em where nobody was' as an infant in a Grammar school," wrote one reporter. Hoblitzell cleared waivers, a trade with the New York Yankees fell through, and on July 16 the Boston Red Sox claimed him off the waiver wire for a mere $1,500. He rebounded during the second half to hit .319 in 69 games, plugging a hole in the Boston lineup and turning the Sox into pennant contenders. Hobby remained a Red Sox regular through 1917, serving as the team's captain and performing admirably in the World Series of 1915-16.

In March 1918 Hoblitzell passed an examination for the U.S. Army Dental Corps. With his mind on his impending military service, he got off to a horrible start and was batting .159 when he was called to duty, marking the end of his major league career. Stationed in Sheffield, Alabama, Hoblitzell rose to the rank of lieutenant before his discharge in 1920. He then played and managed in the minors for five seasons, leading the Charlotte Hornets to a Sally League pennant as player-manager in 1923. Following four years in the real estate business in Charlotte, Hoblitzell returned to the Hornets dugout in 1929 for the highest salary ever paid to a Sally League manager. He remained as player-manager through 1930, then umpired in the Piedmont and International leagues in 1932-33. After his retirement from baseball, Dick settled in Williamstown, West Virginia, the hometown of his wife, Constance, and managed a cattle farm. He died of colon cancer in a Parkersburg hospital on November 14, 1962.

TOM SIMON

CINCINNATI

ROBERT HENRY BESCHER
LEFT FIELDER 1908–13

Bob Bescher stole 428 bases even though he played regularly for only eight seasons. The switch-hitting leadoff hitter and left fielder pilfered 81 bases in 1911, still the Cincinnati Reds modern single-season record. In 1912 *Baseball Magazine*'s F. C. Lane declared him the "King of Basestealers," not only for his raw number of steals but for his steals gathered per hit, which outshone the likes of Ty Cobb and other luminaries. Bescher studied National League pitchers to help him get a good jump and always slid feet first, often eluding the tag by employing a hook slide. Judging the height of the catcher's throw by the infielder's hands, Bescher would slide to the inside of the bag if the throw was high and to the outside if it was low.

Robert Henry Bescher was born on February 25, 1884, in London, Ohio, 25 miles southwest of Columbus. His parents, Antone and Mary Bescher, with whom he lived on the outskirts of London for much of his life, were owners of a local brick factory. A brother and sister died young, essentially making Bob an only child. At age 15 he left home to attend Notre Dame, which until World War I enrolled students from first grade through graduate school. Bob prepped under the Golden Dome from 1899 to 1902, playing no varsity sports even though his status as a high school student didn't prevent him from doing so. He then spent a year punching cows at a Nebraska cattle ranch. There Bob developed skills that he employed years later while spending off-seasons at his manager Clark Griffith's ranch in Montana.

In 1904 Bescher returned to Ohio to attend Wittenberg College in Springfield, less than 20 miles from his hometown of London. In his two-year college career he used his speed and size—6'1" and about 200 lbs.—to great advantage on the gridiron, garnering all-state honors as a halfback and becoming the greatest football player in Wittenberg history. In later years Bescher went on to don the leather helmet professionally for the Dayton Oakwoods, playing even during the baseball season under an assumed name. Bob claimed he was never injured playing football—but baseball was another story. In 1907 he suffered a broken leg sliding into first on a close play, and three years later he mangled his hand on the sharp edges of the box seats while attempting to catch a foul ball. Emergency surgery prevented his hand from being reduced to a claw.

Bescher signed his first professional baseball contract in 1906 with Lima, Ohio, of the Interstate Association, batting a remarkable .539 in 39 games before the league folded in July. He finished the season with the nearby Central League team in Dayton, where he remained during his injury-plagued 1907 campaign. In Bescher's third season in Dayton he batted .305 and swiped 62 bases. The Cincinnati Reds took notice and bought his contract for $1,800. On September 5, 1908, Bob made his major league debut in Cincinnati, hitting a triple and scoring a run in a 6-5 victory over St. Louis.

Bob Bescher gained immediate stardom as one of the National League's premier base runners, leading the league in stolen bases for four consecutive seasons, 1909-12. "The London Flash"—one of several nicknames given him by newspaper reporters—enjoyed his best season on the basepaths in 1911, when he drew 102 bases on balls and posted a career-high .385 on-base percentage. That year Bescher established the modern NL record of 81 steals (breaking his own record of 70 set the previous year), a mark that stood for more than 50 years until Maury Wills swiped 104 in 1962. Even more remarkable, he reportedly was thrown out stealing only three times.

"The Speeder," to use another of his newspaper nicknames, actually got off to a rough start in 1911. After a contentious game on April 18 he was involved in a well-publicized row with Roger Bresnahan, sending the St. Louis Cardinals player-manager to the dentist's chair after Bescher landed a solid punch on his "well-developed word machine." (Though generally reserved and good-natured, Bescher could react violently when provoked; on another occasion he beat up a fellow player for throwing a bat at a friend's dog that ran onto the field during practice.) By the end of May he'd stolen a total of only 10 bases, but a spurt of 11 during the first five days of June put him on course for the record.

To understand Bescher's style of play, consider his performance against the Phillies on August 6, 1911. Early in the game he stole home on a straight double steal after stretching what should have been a routine single into a double. In the eighth inning Bescher was on first base when a teammate laid down a sacrifice bunt. Phillies second baseman Otto Knabe fielded a low throw to first behind the bag and focused his attention on preventing the batter from advancing. Bescher meanwhile never stopped running, and the warning cries from Knabe's teammates came too late—Bescher scored before the ball reached home.

In 1912 Bescher batted a career-high .281 and finished fifth in the voting for the Chalmers Award, leading the NL with 120 runs and posting an exceptional 87% success rate in his stolen-base attempts. But toward the end of the 1913 season he began to show signs of slowing up. In his last 50 games Bescher was only 13 for 23 (57%) in stolen-base attempts and also grounded into seven double plays. Though his 94 walks led the NL, his 38 stolen bases ranked sixth, well behind Max Carey, the new "King of Basestealers." On December 12, 1913, the Reds traded Bescher to the New York Giants for Buck Herzog and Grover Hartley. In 1914 "The London Flash" batted .270 and played center field for the first time in his career, but his difficulty getting along with John McGraw caused him to move on to the St. Louis Cardinals after only one year with the Giants. In three seasons in St. Louis his batting average fell from .263 to .235 to .155. Bescher wound up his major

league career by appearing in 25 games with Cleveland in 1918, then bounced around the minors for several years before retiring from baseball at age 41.

In retirement Bescher returned to London and worked as an oil inspector for the state of Ohio, mixing in frequent hunting and fishing trips. He also managed the Eagles Lodge, earning a reputation during Prohibition as a talented manufacturer of home brew. Bescher remained a local legend; for many years a London storefront displayed pictures of him and Ty Cobb, the NL and AL single-season record holders in stolen bases. Bob kept in touch with his Cincinnati roots, contacting the Reds now and then to recommend a player or express interest in a coaching position (which never materialized). Bob Bescher died prematurely on November 29, 1942, two miles west of the town where he was born, when a train slammed into the car he was driving, also killing a female passenger.

STEVE CONSTANTELOS

CINCINNATI

John Cleborn "Rube" Benton
Left-handed pitcher 1910–15, 1923–25

A hard-throwing, fast-living left hander, Rube Benton pitched professionally for 24 years, compiling a 150-144 record and 3.09 ERA in 15 seasons in the National League. Benton had a reputation for drinking, gambling, and driving too fast, all three of which combined in various ways to interrupt his major league career. He eventually died at age 50 from injuries suffered in a car crash.

One of J. J. Benton's six children, John Clebon Benton was born on June 27, 1887, in Clinton, North Carolina. A tall, lanky youth with natural athletic ability, John pitched in several independent leagues, including a 1909 stint with Lakeland in the then-semipro Florida State League. The following year he started the season 11-5 for Macon in the Sally League before the Cincinnati Reds purchased his contract for $3,500, an unusually high price for a Class C player. "Rube" (an inevitable nickname for a country boy from the South, especially one who bore so many other similarities to Rube Waddell) made his major league debut on June 28, 1910, losing to the Cubs one day after his 23rd birthday. He appeared in 11 more games, 10 in relief, finishing the season 0-1 with a 4.74 ERA.

Optioned to Chattanooga in 1911, Benton went 18-13 in the minors and returned to Cincinnati late in the season. Though his record for the Reds was 3-3, he showed great promise by finishing five of his six starts and posting a 2.01 ERA. Benton's breakout season came in 1912, when he won 18 games and led the National League with 50 appearances and 39 starts. He got off to another strong start in 1913, winning 11 of 18

decisions, but the motorcycle he was riding early one morning struck a trolley car at high speed. Unconscious when he was taken to the hospital, he suffered a broken jaw and numerous cuts and bruises. The Reds suspended him for the remainder of the season.

Already Rube was exhibiting the erratic behavior that plagued him for the rest of his life. His contract for 1914 included a clause stipulating that he'd receive a bonus if he abstained from alcohol and tobacco to an extent deemed satisfactory by manager Buck Herzog. For that one brief season Benton managed to avoid controversy, winning 16 games (including four shutouts) for a last-place club that won a total of 60.

In 1915 Rube returned to drinking and carousing. His record stood at 6-13 when Cincinnati placed him on waivers in early August. The New York Giants verbally claimed him for the waiver price, but shortly thereafter the Pittsburgh Pirates offered $4,000. The Reds accepted the Pirates' offer, prompting the Giants to file a grievance. Benton, meanwhile, reported to the Pirates and pitched on August 17 against the Chicago Cubs, which played the game under protest. He tossed a six-hitter and defeated the Cubs, 3-2. One week later, the National League's Board of Directors awarded Benton to the Giants. It ruled, however, that the Pirates had acted in good faith; rather than forfeiting the August 17 game to the Cubs, the board ordered that it be stricken from the records and replayed in September. The day after the decision, Rube pitched his first game for the Giants—against the Pirates, of all teams!—and gave up 12 hits in four innings of a 9-7 loss. He finished the season 3-5 for the last-place Giants, giving him a combined record of 9-18.

Despite his concern over his new pitcher's "inability to take the game seriously" (a common euphemism for alcohol abuse), John McGraw thought highly of Benton's pitching ability. The 6'1" left hander rewarded his manager's faith by going 31-17 over the next two seasons. In the 1917 World Series, Rube pitched Game Three, with the Giants already down two games to the Chicago White Sox, and revived his team with a brilliant 2-0 victory, becoming the first southpaw to hurl a shutout in a World Series. Benton's next start was Game Six, when Heinie Zimmerman was labeled a goat for chasing Eddie Collins across home plate, though Benton himself had neglected to cover home. Rube lasted only five innings and ended up the losing pitcher despite not giving up any earned runs. Benton's next season was cut short by the military draft. He reported to Camp Jackson, South Carolina, in May 1918 and spent an uneventful year in the army, mostly playing baseball against college and professional players. Returning to the majors in 1919, Rube won 17 games for the second-place Giants while his old team, the Reds, won the pennant and the World Series.

The following year Benton again became the center of a controversy, testifying on September 24, 1920, before a Chicago grand jury that was investigating baseball gambling. At the time he was suffering through a 9-16 season, the worst of his Giant career. Rube testified that the only game-fixing incident he knew of was an offer from Giants teammates Buck Herzog and Hal Chase to throw a game against the Cubs in September 1917. He'd refused their bribe and won the contest. Herzog didn't appreciate Benton bringing up his name before the grand jury. Claiming that Rube had carried a grudge against him since 1915, when he was managing the Reds, Herzog countercharged that Rube won $3,800 betting on Cincinnati in the 1919 World Series. He produced affidavits signed by two Boston Braves, Tony Boeckel (who, like Benton, later died in a car accident) and Art Wilson, to support his claim. The grand jury subpoenaed Benton a second time, and this time he admitted knowing that the 1919 World Series was fixed. Though Rube denied betting on the Series himself, he testified that Chase won $40,000 on the Reds, and he also named four of the Chicago players who were in on the fix. Benton's testimony proved to be crucial to the Black Sox investigation.

Rube pitched well at the beginning of 1921, compiling a 5-2 record and 2.88 ERA, but the Giants suddenly released him in midseason. There was no official explanation for his release or the failure of any big-league club to claim him, but Benton was now considered an undesirable character. The Giants assigned him to St. Paul of the American Association. In 1922 he won a total of 24 games, including the only two games the Saints took from the International League-champion Baltimore Orioles in the Junior World Series. Both the Reds and the St. Louis Browns expressed interest in Benton for 1923. AL president Ban Johnson declared Benton ineligible, however, and NL president John Heydler followed Johnson's lead, though he decided to leave the final decision to Commissioner Landis. To everyone's surprise, Landis ruled on March 8, 1923, that "Benton is eligible to play with the Cincinnati club and no one is going to keep him from doing so if that club wants him." Rube spent three more seasons with the Reds, winning 30 games and losing 29. His 2.77 ERA in 1924 ranked fourth in the NL.

After the 1925 season Benton drew his release from the Reds and returned to the American Association, pitching the next eight years for the Minneapolis Millers, a team known as "the Old Men's Home of Baseball." In 1931 Rube was returning from a hunting trip in Indiana when he swerved to avoid a hay wagon and crashed into a statue in front of a cemetery. He suffered a shattered cheekbone, injuries to his hands, and internal injuries as well. The newspaper noted that his family investigated the accident and reported that he hadn't had a drink all day. It was feared that Benton's pitching career was over, but he recovered in time to post an 18-7 record for the first-place Millers in 1932. He continued to pitch for Minneapolis through 1934, finally hanging up his spikes at age 47. Benton came out of retirement to pitch in a semipro game for Erwin, North Carolina, on June 27, 1937, his 50th birthday. On December 12 of that year he was involved in a head-on collision in Dothan, Alabama, and died of a fractured skull and chest injuries. His wife and one daughter survived him.

BILL BISHOP

CINCINNATI

ARMANDO MARSÁNS
CENTER FIELDER 1911–14

A brilliant defensive outfielder, Armando Marsáns was the first Cuban to make an impact in the major leagues. Dubbed "an aristocrat by birth, but a big league outfielder by choice," he was on the verge of stardom when his career was derailed by an ill-fated attempt to challenge the reserve clause. Marsáns was known for his aggressive base running, often stretching singles into doubles and doubles into triples. "There is not a more intelligent player in the game than Marsáns, who seems to have an uncanny knack of knowing what to do and when to do it," wrote one reporter.

The son of a well-to-do Havana merchant, Armando Marsáns was born in Matanzas, Cuba, on October 3, 1887. His family, like many wealthy Cubans, moved to New York City in 1898 to escape the Spanish-American War. Eleven-year-old Armando took to baseball, playing regularly in Central Park. He loved the game by the time his family returned to Cuba after a year and a half. In 1905 Armando signed with Almendares, a powerful team in the Cuban Winter League. Marsáns and another promising youngster, Rafael Almeida, combined to lead the team to the pennant. In 1907 Almendares won another title, defeating a Fé team that included African American stars Rube Foster, Pete Hill, Charlie Grant, and Bill Monroe.

In 1908 the Cincinnati Reds visited Cuba for a series of exhibitions against the best teams on the island. Marsáns' Almendares club won four of its five games against the Reds, thanks mostly to pitcher José Méndez, but also with contributions from Marsáns, who scored the only run in a 1-0 victory on November 13, 1908. By that time Marsáns and Almeida both were playing in the U.S. minor leagues with New Britain of the Connecticut State League. Marsáns was an outstanding player for New Britain, batting .285 over four seasons. In June 1911 Cincinnati purchased his and Almeida's contracts on the recommendation of Reds secretary Frank Bancroft, who remembered the Cuban pair from his exhibition trips to the island. At the time the sale prices were reported as $2,500 for Marsáns and $3,500 for Almeida. In Marsáns' later legal battles with the Reds, owner Garry Herrmann claimed that he paid $6,000 for Marsáns alone.

Marsáns and Almeida were the first Cubans to reach the majors since 1873, and there were whispers around baseball that they had some "Negro" blood. The Reds refuted this at length, calling Marsáns and Almeida "two of the purest bars of Castilian soap ever floated to these shores," and insisting that they were entirely of European descent. In fact, that was probably true, at least in Armando's case, as the surname Marsáns is of Catalán rather than Spanish origin. In the late 19th century about 8,000 people—Marsáns' family likely among them—emigrated from Catalonia to Cuba. Racial mixing was fairly uncommon among the light-skinned *catalanes*, who ranked at the top of Cuba's skin color based caste system.

Whatever their racial background, Marsáns and Almeida got along fine with their new teammates. "The gentlemanly deportment and fast work on the field of these boys have already made them popular with other members of the Reds," the *Cincinnati Enquirer* reported on July 1, before the pair had gotten into a single game. Only about 15,000 Cubans lived in the United States in 1911, but the Reds acquired the Cuban players in part because, according to the *Enquirer*, they were "figuring on Marsáns and Almeida being good drawing cards in New York and Philadelphia, where there are thousands of Cubans." Fans back in Cuba, meanwhile, were so enthusiastic that Marsáns and

Almeida even had their own media escort. Victor Muñoz, sports editor of *El Mundo* in Havana, accompanied the Reds everywhere they went, much as the Japanese media followed Hideo Nomo and Ichiro Suzuki nearly a century later.

On July 4, 1911, in the midst of one of the biggest heat waves ever to hit the Midwest, Marsáns and Almeida finally made their debuts against the Cubs at Chicago's West Side Grounds. The heat was so sweltering that afternoon that it caused 27 deaths in Chicago. With the Reds comfortably ahead in the first game of a traditional Independence Day doubleheader, Marsáns entered as a defensive replacement for exhausted right fielder Mike Mitchell. He went 1-for-2, and to the *Cincinnati Enquirer*'s Jack Ryder he "looked good at the bat and fast on his feet." Marsáns spent the remainder of the 1911 season as the Reds fourth outfielder.

Though there is no record of what their personal relationship was like, Marsáns and Almeida became inseparable in the public's eye after spending nearly a decade as teammates with Almendares, New Britain, and Cincinnati. But Almeida failed to impress the Reds either at bat or in the field and was dispatched to the minors after three years on the bench. Marsáns, meanwhile, became one of the brightest young stars in the National League, and one of the fastest. In 1912, his first full season, his .317 batting average and 35 stolen bases both ranked in the NL's Top 10. In 1913 he increased his stolen bases to 37 while batting .297, 35 points above the league average.

Marsáns made a strong impression on Reds manager Clark Griffith, who left after the 1911 season to take over the Washington Senators. In the spring of 1912 Griffith offered the Reds $5,000 for Marsáns but was refused. Griffith never did obtain Marsáns' services, but he did develop an affinity for Cuban players unparalleled in baseball history. During his 44 years in charge of the Washington club, 63 Cubans debuted in the majors—35 of them with the Senators.

A genteel man who spoke and wrote nearly flawless English, Marsáns was the antithesis of what later became the Latin American baseball stereotype. He reportedly attended college in the United States, though that isn't confirmed. Still, American sportswriters always emphasized that he was "of wealthy parentage and aristocratic stock." In 1912 the *Philadelphia Inquirer* noted that Marsáns and Almeida "are both large land owners in Cuba and have independent incomes, and the fact that they continue to be ball players instead of prominent men of affairs on the island is simply because that is what they prefer to be." Marsáns spent his off-seasons managing a tobacco factory that he owned in Havana, and was well liked enough by fans in Cincinnati to open a successful cigar store there. By 1914 his annual baseball earnings were $4,400, more than double what he'd earned as a rookie.

Though almost universally well liked, Marsáns was headstrong and temperamental. According to a friend, "there is really only one man who is his master, and who can reason and talk to him, and that man is his father." In 1914 Marsáns' quick temper led to the biggest scandal of his career. In June he got into a heated argument with his manager, Buck Herzog, who "said a number of things not at all to the liking of the classy outfielder." Herzog suspended Marsáns, and Marsáns demanded to be traded, a request that was refused by Herrmann. Marsáns responded by jumping his contract and leaving for St. Louis, where he was wined and dined by the owners of the Federal League's Terriers. Marsáns was offered a three-year, $21,000 contract by the Feds, which he accepted after giving the Reds 10 days' notice, the same notice a ball club was required to give before terminating a contract with a player. Cincinnati immediately filed a lawsuit in, ironically, federal court, claiming that its "property" had been jeopardized. After Marsáns had played only nine games with St. Louis, the court issued an injunction barring him from playing in the Federal League pending the outcome of trial.

The Reds also retaliated by impounding the clothing and equipment he'd left in his locker in Cincinnati. Because Marsáns owned a cigar shop there, the club also appealed to his business interests. "Marsans is very enthusiastic about his cigar business, and holds it close to his heart," a correspondent wrote to Herrmann. "If he can be made to realize that his actions with the

Cincinnati Baseball Club will not help the sale of his cigars, I am sure that he will act differently."

Marsáns' case, along with that of Hal Chase, became a cause célèbre for Federal League supporters. *Baseball Magazine* dubbed it "the sensational Marsans case, one of the series of recent legal battles which have thrown the baseball world into an upheaval, and which threaten to wreck the entire game." Unable to play while the two sides battled in court, Marsáns returned to Havana, where he spent his days shark fishing in the bay. "We are not restraining Marsans and Chase from playing, but trying to get them to play," Herrmann insisted. "It is the Federal League that is keeping them from playing, if any one is." In a bizarre twist, Marsáns' younger brother Francisco showed up in Cincinnati in September 1914, apologized to the Reds for any trouble Armando had caused them, and offered his own services to replace Armando in the outfield. The team declined.

Because the National Commission had threatened to ban any player who competed against Marsáns, he was forced to play the 1914-15 Cuban Winter League season under the assumed name "Mendromedo." In February 1915, with Marsáns still on the sidelines, his friend John McGraw visited him in Cuba, offering to trade for him if he'd return to the NL with the Giants. Marsáns would have none of it. He believed that the press, and New York writers in particular, treated him unfairly, saying that they "always thought it funny to poke jokes at me." Finally, on August 19, 1915, a federal judge in St. Louis set aside Herrmann's injunction, ruling that Marsáns could play in the Federal League until the case was decided on appeal. Marsáns returned to the Terriers the next day, and the team finished the season only percentage points out of first place.

But the legal battles had ruined Marsáns' career. After the Federal League folded, his contract was assigned to the St. Louis Browns, but he was no longer the player he'd been after being out of the majors for nearly two years. Disappointed with his performance, the Browns traded him to the Yankees for Lee Magee on July 15, 1917. *Baseball Magazine* predicted that going to New York would revitalize Marsáns, as he was "a brilliant outfielder, once a .300 hitter and even now a most dangerous man on the bases." But Marsáns had always been prone to injury, and soon after reporting to the Yankees he suffered a broken leg that ended his season. In 1918, at age 30, Marsans gave it one more try with the Yankees but batted only .236 in what turned out to be his final major league season.

In 1923, after a four-year absence from American baseball, Marsáns returned to bat .319 in a brief minor league stint with Louisville. Also in 1923 he briefly joined Martín Dihigo on the Cuban Stars of the Eastern Colored League, becoming the first player to play in both the major leagues and the formally organized Negro Leagues. In 1924, his last season in the United States, Marsáns became the first Cuban manager in the minors, serving as player-manager of the Elmira Colonels of the New York-Penn League. He batted .280 in his farewell to American baseball. Marsáns played a few more winters in Cuba before retiring there, too, after the 1927-28 season.

In all, Marsáns played on 10 pennant-winning teams in his 21 seasons in the Cuban Winter League, posting a lifetime average there of .261 in 455 games. He twice led the notorious pitchers' circuit in runs and in 1913 won the batting title with a .400 average. He also led the league in stolen bases three times. Playing most of his career in spacious Almendares Park, he hit only two lifetime home runs in 1,632 at-bats. Marsáns also was a longtime manager in the league, leading Orientales to the championship as player-manager in 1917. In the 1940s he managed Marianao, where his players included Ray Dandridge, future batting champion Roberto Ávila, and rookie outfielder Orestes "Minnie" Miñoso. He also managed Tampico in the Mexican League in 1945-47, winning championships in 1945 and 1946.

On July 26, 1939, Marsáns became one of the first 10 men inducted into the Cuban Baseball Hall of Fame. The inductees were honored with a bronze plaque placed at La Tropical Stadium in Havana, where it remains today. Little is known of Marsáns' post-baseball life. His reaction to the Cuban Revolution of 1959 is unknown, but since the rebellion's goal was to overthrow the wealthy aristocracy to which Marsáns belonged, it's hard to imagine him supporting the revolutionaries. Marsáns died in Havana a little over a year after Fidel Castro's takeover, on September 3, 1960.

ERIC ENDERS

CINCINNATI

HENRY KNIGHT GROH
THIRD BASEMAN 1913–21

Heine Groh was the National League's best third baseman of the Deadball Era. Historian Greg Gajus suggests that Groh would have won at least one MVP award (for the 1919 season) and perhaps two others (1916 and 1918), and that eight of his 12 full seasons were of All-Star quality. Groh positioned himself at the extreme front of the batter's box with both feet facing the pitcher, choking up on his peculiar bottle bat and slapping at the ball. Taking advantage of his size (5'8", 160 lbs.) to create a small strike zone and draw lots of walks, he also became adept at bunting and executing the hit-and-run. Groh led the NL in walks in 1916, hits in 1917, and runs in 1918. He also led the league in doubles twice and had a batting average of .298 or better each year from 1917 to 1921.

Henry Knight Groh was born in Rochester, New York, on September 18, 1889. Turning down an opportunity to attend the University of Rochester, Groh signed with Oshkosh of the Wisconsin-Illinois League in 1908. He played shortstop and batted .161, an average he remembered to the last decimal point—in spite of a failing memory—when interviewed more than a half century later by Larry Ritter for *The Glory of Their Times*. Groh batted .297 in back-to-back seasons at Oshkosh in 1909-10 ("I kept practicing and practicing at it, and the next year I hit about .285, and the year after that I made it to .300," was the way he remembered it), after which the New York Giants purchased his contract. In 1911 the Giants assigned Groh to Buffalo of the Eastern League, where he batted .333 and earned a promotion to the big city for 1912.

Heine Groh made his major league debut as a pinch-hitter against the Chicago Cubs on April 12, 1912. The umpire was Bill Klem, who had a long-running feud with Giants manager John McGraw. As the small and boyish-looking Groh made his way to the plate, a voice from the Cubs dugout yelled, "McGraw's sending in the batboy to show you up, Bill." The entire grandstand heard it, and most of them believed it. Klem glared at the kid and asked, "Are you under contract with the New York club?" "I am," replied Groh. The umpire let him bat, and Groh laced the first pitch for a single. Many fans left the Polo Grounds that day thinking they'd seen the batboy make a hit.

Groh earned a spot as the Giants' utility infielder in 1912 but didn't get much playing time, appearing in just 27 games and batting .271 for the NL champions. That year McGraw suggested to the diminutive infielder that he use a bat with a bigger barrel. Groh's hands were too small to grip such a bat, so he asked Spalding Sporting Goods to customize a bat for him. Most bats were gradually tapered from the barrel to the handle, but the bat Spalding created for Heine had an unusually thick barrel and an unusually thin handle, with an abrupt taper in between. As Groh told Ritter, "We whittled down the handle of a standard bat, and then we built up the barrel, and when we were finished it looked like a crazy sort of milk bottle." Thus was born the bottle bat, an innovation that will forever be associated with Heine Groh.

Desperate for pitching, the Giants traded Groh to the Cincinnati Reds on May 22, 1913, along with pitcher Red Ames, outfielder Josh Devore, and $20,000 in cash, for infielder Eddie Grant and pitcher Art Fromme, who was coming off a 16-18 season with a 2.74 ERA. Groh's inclusion was an afterthought, but he turned out to be the key player in a lopsided deal for the Reds. The move gave him an opportunity to play every day, and he entrenched himself as Cincinnati's starting second baseman. In 1915 the Reds moved

Groh to third base, which may have been the most important position in the infield during the bunt-crazy Deadball Era. "I'd get in front of that ball one way or the other," Heine said, "and if I couldn't catch it I'd let it hit me and then I'd grab it on the bounce and throw to first." Contemporaries considered Groh the NL's best-fielding third baseman, and his .967 career fielding average is the best for any third baseman that played before 1920.

With Jake Daubert ahead of him and Edd Roush behind him in the order, Groh enjoyed his finest season in 1919, ranking among the league leaders in virtually every category to lead the Reds to their first NL pennant. The Reds captured their first world championship even though Groh didn't play particularly well during the World Series, but their celebration was tainted by allegations that the White Sox had lost intentionally. Groh was one of the first to speak out against the idea of a fix, saying he didn't see anything suspicious. After the plot was confirmed, his only comment was, "I think we'd have beaten them either way."

Two years later Groh became embroiled in a bitter salary dispute with Reds owner Garry Herrmann, vowing never to rejoin the Cincinnati club. To resolve the impasse, Groh and the Reds worked out an agreement under which he'd sign a contract and immediately be traded back to the New York Giants. Fearing an "unhealthy situation if a dissatisfied player could dictate his transfer to a strong contender before he agreed to sign a contract," Commissioner Landis voided the deal and ruled that Groh could play only with the Reds for the remainder of the season. Nobody liked that solution—not the Reds, not the Giants, and certainly not Heine Groh. Once the season ended, the parties finally consummated the trade, and Groh rejoined John McGraw's Giants a decade after he'd started his big-league career with that team.

Groh's batting average plummeted to .265 in 1922, 66 points below his average of the previous season and the lowest of his career to that point. Once the World Series started, however, his bottle bat came alive. Heine hit safely in each of the five games, finishing with a Series–best .474 batting average as the Giants swept the New York Yankees. (From that point on his Ohio license plate number was 474.) Groh remained a key member of a

Giants team that won three straight pennants. Late in the 1924 season he suffered a serious knee injury. Heine was 35 by then and never again able to play regularly because of the knee, spending the next two years as a seldom used infielder. In 1927 he ended his career with Pittsburgh, playing only 14 games during the regular season and making his final big-league appearance as a pinch-hitter in the 1927 World Series.

When his playing days were over, Heine Groh remained in baseball, first as a minor league manager and later as a scout. He eventually returned to Cincinnati, where he worked as a cashier at River Downs Race Track. Groh was 78 when he died of a respiratory ailment on August 22, 1968.

SEAN LAHMAN

CINCINNATI

IVY BROWN WINGO
CATCHER 1915–26

Ivy Wingo caught 1,233 games over 17 seasons, breaking George Gibson's National League record for games caught in a career (Wingo's record eventually fell to Al Lopez in 1940). A left-handed hitter with a lifetime .260 batting average, the redheaded Georgian was known more for his offense than his catching. For a time he held the season and career records for errors by a catcher, most of which were high throws that sailed into center field on stolen-base attempts. Ivy was a multi-dimensional athlete who possessed a strong throwing arm. In an era long before statisticians tracked success rates for catchers in throwing out opposing base stealers, a rudimentary chart in the May 1914 issue of *Baseball Magazine* suggested that Wingo, who threw out an average of 0.94 base stealers per game, was among baseball's best in that facet of the catcher's duties.

Ivy Brown Wingo was born in Gainesville, Georgia, on July 8, 1890. His father, Dr. Absalom Holbrook Wingo Sr., and mother, Nancy (Smith) Wingo, moved their large family to Norcross, Georgia, a quaint village of approximately 150 residents, by the time Ivy's brother Absolom "Al" Holbrook Wingo Jr. was born there in 1898. Situated on the Chattahoochee River about halfway between Atlanta and Athens, Norcross became known in the 1920s as "the cradle of baseball players." In addition to Ivy, the tiny town produced his brother Al, who played in the majors with the Detroit Tigers from 1924 to 1928, and the Carlyle brothers, Roy (who played for three American League teams in 1925-26) and Cleo (who played 95 games for the Boston Red Sox in 1927). After making his start in baseball with the Norcross town team, Ivy entered the professional ranks in 1909 with Greenville of the Carolina Association. Late in the 1910 season the St. Louis Cardinals purchased

his contract but used him solely to warm up pitchers, since 31-year-old player-manager Roger Bresnahan shared the catching duties with Ed Phelps. Wingo didn't make his major league debut until April 20, 1911. Even then the 20-year-old bullpen catcher caught in only 18 games the entire season, as Bresnahan continued to alternate behind the plate with Jack Bliss.

Wingo claimed that he owed his big break to the sentiment of Pete Alexander. Early in the 1912 season, the great Philadelphia Phillies pitcher built up a huge lead in the first game of a doubleheader against the Cardinals. "Bliss was working, and as he would have to serve in the second game anyway, the manager thought it a good opportunity for me," Ivy remembered. "Alex knew I was a young rookie trying to make good, so when I faced him at bat, he laid the ball right over the center of the plate. I promptly hit it for two bases. The next time up he did the same thing and I responded with another two-bagger. Bresnahan, our manager, figured he couldn't very well take out a catcher who was hitting like that, so he left me in the second game. And I played pretty regularly from that time on. Alexander could, had he wished, have struck me out both times I faced him and he told me so afterwards. But he had the game won and figured I was only a rookie, so he let me hit to give me a bit of encouragement." Wingo went on to bat .265 in 100 games that season.

Ivy possessed unusual speed for a catcher. He achieved a career high with 18 stolen bases in 112 games for the Cardinals in 1913, after which he was selected to participate in a world tour led by John McGraw and Charles Comiskey. The tour featured the New York Giants and Chicago White Sox, but some players backed out after reaching the West Coast, opening up positions for Ivy and others to serve as their replacements. Wingo played in Japan, China, Australia, the Philippines, Egypt, and Europe before returning home the first week of March 1914. That season he caught only 70 games for the Cardinals as 21-year-old rookie Frank Snyder took over the bulk of the backstop duties. Wingo stole 15 bases and batted .300 for the only time in his career, and there was talk of moving him permanently to the outfield to take advantage of his athleticism and open up more playing time for Snyder.

After the 1914 season Ivy threatened to sign with the Federal League. He ended up holding out all winter. At the start of the 1915 season the cash-starved Cardinals traded him to Cincinnati for Cuban-born catcher Mike Gonzalez, who later coined the phrase "Good field, no hit." Wingo reported to the Reds, lured by a large salary increase, but his batting average plummeted to .221, 79 points below his average of the previous season. With the demise of the Federal League, the Reds considered trading Wingo to get rid of his huge contract. Management gave in, however, when Cincinnati fans signed a petition requesting that the popular catcher not be traded. It turned out to be a good decision. Wingo played more or less regularly for Cincinnati through 1925. After platooning with Bill Rariden in 1919, he helped lead the Reds to their first world championship by hitting .571 in that year's World Series.

Wingo served mainly as a coach in 1926, after which he turned down an offer of an assistant manager's job with Cincinnati to take over as manager of Columbus of the American Association, which Garry Herrmann had purchased to serve as a Reds farm club. His one season in the Ohio capital proved frustrating; the team finished in last place with a 60-108 record and he managed to get himself thrown out of the same game twice (he was ejected first for arguing and later when the umpire found him hiding in the bullpen). Wingo returned to the Reds as a coach in 1928-29, making his last major league appearance by catching one game during the latter season. In 1930 the 40-year-old backstop returned to Georgia, serving as player-coach with the

Atlanta Crackers under former Reds outfielder John Dobbs, but was released because he couldn't catch enough to please the ownership.

Wingo spent one last year as a Reds coach in 1936, after which he and his wife, Mattie May, returned to his hometown of Norcross. He lived there in retirement only a short time, passing away on March 1, 1941. Leaving behind his wife and one son, Ivy was buried in the Norcross town cemetery. Former Reds teammate Eppa Rixey eulogized him as "one of the best hustlers on the team."

JIM SANDOVAL

CINCINNATI

FRED ALEXANDRA TONEY
RIGHT-HANDED PITCHER 1915–18

Fred Toney is best remembered as the victor of perhaps the greatest pitchers' duel in major league history, a 1917 game in which he and Jim Vaughn both pitched no-hitters over the first nine innings. What is often forgotten is that Toney was one of the National League's best pitchers from 1915 to 1921. Despite little run support, the 6'1", 195 lb. right-handed fastball pitcher reached the 20-win plateau twice. Toney tried to make up for his lack of formal education with his exceptional strength. He often amazed teammates by taking two 50 lb. weights, one in each hand, and holding them out at arm's length from his body.

Fred Alexandra Toney was born on December 11, 1888, just outside Nashville in rural Davidson County, Tennessee, where he lived for the rest of his life. He started his minor league career in 1908 with Winchester, Kentucky, of the Blue Grass League. Winchester had discovered Toney while he was pitching for an independent team in Bowling Green, Kentucky, but that team disbanded and Fred had gone home before Winchester could offer him a contract. At first the big right-hander resisted the professional team's overtures, stating that he didn't want to pitch under the pressure found in Organized Baseball. At the urging of his friend Greasy Hanly, however, Toney signed a contract for $60 per month, with the stipulation that Hanly also receive a contract so he wouldn't be alone.

Reporters soon compared the young fireballer to Walter Johnson. On May 10, 1909, Toney pitched a 17-inning no-hitter against Lexington, striking out 19 batters and giving up only two walks. The Chicago Cubs purchased him from Winchester for $1,000 in August 1910—even though he'd tried to look bad in the presence of the Chicago scout. Preferring to pitch for a minor league team in the South, the 22-year-old

Tennesseean didn't report to the Cubs until 1911. Even then he didn't seem to be giving his all. Over the next two and a half seasons Toney bounced back and forth between Chicago and Louisville of the American Association.

On July 1, 1913, the Cubs finally gave up on Toney and sold him outright to Louisville, where he remained through the end of the 1914 season. After the Brooklyn Robins drafted him in the winter of 1914, the big pitcher said that he "would rather play with the Feds for cigarette money than the salary the Brooklyn club is offering." Following a false report that he'd signed with the Federal League's Pittsburgh Rebels, Brooklyn placed him on waivers and the Cincinnati Reds claimed him on February 22, 1915. That season Toney became one of the best pitchers in the National League. He went 17-6 and placed second in the NL in winning percentage and ERA (1.58). Toney's record would have been even better if he had pitched for a better team; the Reds finished in seventh place in 1915 and ranked last in the NL in runs. Pitching a team-high 300 innings in 1916, Toney posted a 2.28 ERA but continued to be plagued by a lack of run support, compiling a 14-17 record. That August he stated that he could be a 25-game winner if the Reds gave him the four runs per game he felt he deserved, instead of the 2½ runs he thought he was receiving.

Toney's first two years in Cincinnati were just a prelude for 1917, the finest season of his career. He went 24-16 with a 2.20 ERA in 339⅔ innings, placing second in the NL behind Pete Alexander in wins and innings pitched. On July 1, 1917, Toney pitched a pair of three-hitters, winning both ends of a doubleheader against the Pittsburgh Pirates, but his best performance came on May 2 against the Chicago Cubs. A crowd of only 2,500 attended that day's matchup between Toney and Jim "Hippo" Vaughn, and through the first nine innings neither pitcher allowed a hit. (Only Cy Williams had reached base off Toney, drawing walks in his first two trips to the plate.) Vaughn finally unraveled in the 10th inning. Larry Kopf singled, went to third on an error, and scored on a poorly played grounder hit by Jim Thorpe. Toney set down the Cubs in order in the bottom half, giving him the win and a 10-inning no-hitter.

Fred Toney's life took a dramatic downturn during the off-season of 1917-18. First a United States marshal arrested him for attempting to avoid the draft. It was alleged that Toney had falsely claimed his wife, child, and parents as dependants even though he hadn't lived with his wife for the three years prior to signing his draft statement. During his trial, which ended in a hung jury, it came out that he was traveling with a young woman who wasn't his wife. In April 1918 Toney was arrested again, this time for violating the Mann Act, which prevented the transportation of minors across state lines for sexual purposes.

The Cincinnati fans were merciless to Toney at the start of the 1918 season. His pitching suffered, and his record stood at 6-10 when the Reds sold him to the New York Giants on July 15. After his move to the bigger city, he rebounded to go 6-2 with a 1.69 ERA for the rest of the season. Reporting to the Giants in May 1919 after pleading guilty to the Mann Act charge and spending time in prison, Toney posted a 13-6 record with the NL's fourth-best ERA (1.84). He also proved his honesty by turning down teammate Heinie Zimmerman's offer to throw a game, reporting the bribe to John McGraw after the first inning. Zimmerman was suspended from the Giants and eventually banned from baseball. Toney pitched well for two more seasons in New York, going 21-11 in 1920 and 18-11 in 1921. In the latter year he played in his only World Series, failing to last more than three innings in either of his two starts against the Yankees.

Toney's dismal performance in the 1921 World Series signaled the beginning of his downfall as a pitcher. In 1922 he started the season 5-6 with a 4.17 ERA before the Giants sent him, Larry Benton, and $100,000 to the Boston Braves for Hugh McQuillan on July 30. On hearing the news, Fred took a train to Nashville, where he announced his retirement. "I have $50,000 and don't have to play baseball with the Braves," he said. That October the St. Louis Cardinals claimed Toney on waivers. The veteran pitcher decided to report in 1923, but he quit baseball again in the second inning of a game on June 23, 1923, after an altercation with Cardinals infielder Specs Toporcer. Toney eventually returned to finish the season, posting an 11-12 record with a 3.84 ERA. At spring training the next year he injured the middle finger of his pitching hand while bunting. Toney was unable to grip the ball properly and the Cardinals released him. He went home to Tennessee and pitched for the Nashville club in the Southern Association through 1925.

After retiring from baseball, Fred Toney farmed and operated a soft-drink and sandwich stand that was decorated with memorabilia from his baseball career. During World War II he served as a security guard at an aircraft plant near Nashville. After the war Toney worked as a court officer for the Davidson County Sheriff's Office. He held that job until his death at age 64 on March 11, 1953.

BRIAN MARSHALL

CINN.

CINCINNATI

EDD J. ROUSH
CENTER FIELDER 1916–26, 1931

A left-handed hitter with a lifetime batting average of .323 in 18 seasons, Edd Roush was the best place hitter in the National League toward the end of the Deadball Era, winning NL batting championships in 1917 and 1919 and finishing second in 1918. "Some batters, and good ones too, scoff at the whole theory of place hitting, calling it a myth," he said. "They are wrong, however." Wielding a short, thick-handled bat that weighed 48 oz., one of the heaviest in baseball, Roush snapped at the ball with his arms and placed hard line drives to all parts of the field by shifting his feet after the ball left the pitcher's hand and altering the timing of his swing. "Place hitting is in a sense glorified bunting," he said. "I take only a half swing at the ball, and the weight of the bat rather than my swing is what drives it." The Reds center fielder also was the NL's premier defensive outfielder of the late Deadball Era, combining speed with a knack for turning his back on the ball and running to the spot where it landed.

The sons of William C. Roush, a good semipro baseball player of the 1880s, Edd J. Roush and his twin brother, Fred, were born on May 8, 1893, in Oakland City, a southwest Indiana town of population 2,370 in the 1910 census. A natural left hander, Edd often threw right-handed as a youth because he didn't have access to a left-hander's glove. He began his baseball career in 1909 with the semipro Oakland City Walk-Overs, getting a shot when one of the team's regular outfielders failed to show up. "We waited for five minutes and the outfielder never did show, so they gave me a uniform and put me in right field," Roush recalled. "Turned out I got a couple of hits that day, and I became Oakland City's regular right fielder for the rest of the season." In 1911 he learned that some of the Walk-Overs were receiving $5 per game, and he wasn't one of them. In the first of his many battles over money with team management, Edd jumped to a rival team from Princeton, 12 miles due west of Oakland City. "And don't think that didn't cause quite a ruckus," he said more than a half century later. "I think there are still one or two around here that never have forgiven me to this very day."

Roush entered the professional ranks in 1912 with Evansville, about 30 miles due south of Oakland City, returning to his natural left-handed throwing after purchasing his first left-hander's glove. He batted .284 in his first year in the Kitty League and was hitting .323 in August 1913 when Evansville sold him to the Chicago White Sox for $3,000. Roush batted 10 times in about a month with Chicago, earning the first of his lifetime 2,376 hits off of Chief Bender on September 9 before being farmed out to Lincoln of the Western League. The following year the Federal League's Indianapolis Hoosiers offered him $225 a month, almost twice what he was earning at Lincoln, so he decided to jump. In his return to his native state, the 21-year-old Roush played part-time and showed his potential by hitting .325 in 166 at-bats for the Federal League champions. In 1915 the team moved to Newark, where Edd, inserted into the lineup regularly by player-manager and lifelong friend Bill McKechnie, hit .298 with 28 stolen bases.

Following the breakup of the Federal League, the New York Giants bought both Roush and McKechnie.

CINN.

Edd hated New York, and he especially hated playing for the demanding John McGraw. "If you made a bad play he'd cuss you out, yell at you, call you all sorts of names," he recalled. "That didn't go with me." Roush got off to a slow start and was hitting just .188 on July 20, 1916, when the Giants sent him to the Reds in what later became known as the "Hall of Fame trade"—in exchange for Buck Herzog and Wade Killefer, McGraw shipped Christy Mathewson, McKechnie, and Roush, all of whom were bound for Cooperstown, to the Cincinnati Reds.

"I still remember the trip the three of us made as we left the Giants and took the train to join the Reds," Roush recalled. "McKechnie and I were sitting back on the observation car, talking about how happy we were to be traded. Matty came out and sat down and listened, but he didn't say anything. Finally I turned to him and said, 'Well, Matty, aren't you glad to be getting away from McGraw?' 'I'll tell you something, Roush,' he said. 'You and Mac have only been on the Giants a couple months. It's just another ball club to you fellows. But I was with the team for 16 years. That's a mighty long time. But I appreciate McGraw making a place for me in baseball and getting me this managing job. He's doing me a favor, and I thanked him for it. And by the way, the last thing he said to me was that if I put you in center field I'd have a great ballplayer. So starting tomorrow you're my center fielder.'"

When Mathewson carried through on his promise, Roush found himself playing alongside Greasy Neale, who also was in his first year with the Reds but had been with the team since the start of the season. "The first game I played there, about three or four fly balls came out that could have been taken by either the center fielder or the right fielder," Edd recalled. "If I thought I should take it, I'd holler three times: 'I got it, I got it, I got it.' But Greasy never said a word. Sometimes he'd take it, and sometimes he wouldn't. But in either case he never said a thing. We went along that way for about three weeks. Finally, one day Greasy came over and sat down beside me on the bench. 'I want to end this, Roush,' he says to me. 'I guess you know I've been trying to run you down ever since you got here. I wanted that center-field job for myself, and I didn't like it when Matty put you out there. But you can go get a ball better than I ever could. I want to shake hands and call it off. From now on, I'll holler.'

And from then on Greasy and I got along just fine. Grew to be two of the best friends ever."

Roush hit .287 with 14 triples in 69 games for the Reds in 1916, and the trade really began to pay off for Cincinnati the next year when Edd won the first of his two batting titles, beating out Rogers Hornsby, .341 to .327. After hitting .333 and losing out by two percentage points to Zack Wheat in 1918, he earned his second batting championship in 1919 by hitting .321, edging out Hornsby by three points. Amazingly, even though it was good enough to lead the league, Roush's .321 in 1919 was his lowest batting average over the 10-year period 1917-26.

With the post–Deadball Era explosion in offense, Roush averaged .350 over a four-year period, 1921-24, but won no additional batting championships. He did lead the NL in doubles with 41 in 1923 and in triples with 21 in 1924. After the 1926 season the Giants reacquired Roush from the Reds in a trade for George Kelly. Remembering the abuse he'd received from McGraw back in 1916, Edd tried to get New York to trade him by holding out for a salary of $30,000. "I've been trying to get you back ever since I traded you away a long time ago," said McGraw. "Now you're either going to play for me or you're not going to play at all." Roush ended up signing a three-year contract worth a total of $70,000 and twice hit over .300 for the Giants, but his legs started to give out on him. He sat out the 1930 season in a salary dispute, then returned to the Reds for one final season in 1931.

Roush had invested wisely and was able to retire altogether when his playing days were through. He devoted himself to his hometown of Oakland City, serving on the town and school boards, presiding over the board of directors of a local bank, and running the cemetery where he is now buried. Edd and his wife, Essie, raised a daughter, Mary. Over the years he accepted only one baseball job, serving one year as a coach with the 1938 Reds under his best friend, Bill McKechnie, who coincidentally was inducted into the Hall of Fame in 1962, the same year as Roush. For 35 years the Roushes maintained a winter residence in Bradenton, Florida. On March 21, 1988, 94-year-old Edd Roush left us the way all great ballplayers should: he passed away just before a spring training game at Bradenton's Bill McKechnie Field.

JIM SANDOVAL

BROOKLYN

The Guinea Flats loom behind the right-field fence in this August 1912 photo of live action at Washington Park.

Named after "Hanlon's Superbas," a popular vaudeville troupe, Ned Hanlon's Brooklyn Superbas were the reigning NL champions at the opening of the Deadball Era. The team featured many of the famous Baltimore Orioles of the 1890s—Hanlon, Willie Keeler, Hughie Jennings, Joe Kelley—because in 1899 Baltimore owner Harry von der Horst purchased a controlling interest in the Brooklyn club, then stripped his Orioles to strengthen Brooklyn.

Brooklyn lost Joe McGinnity, Fielder Jones, and Lave Cross to the American League before the 1901 season, and Keeler, Kelley, and Wild Bill Donovan prior to 1903. Suddenly not so superb anymore, the Superbas

finished fifth that year, the first of 12 consecutive seasons in the second division. Throughout that dismal period, Brooklynites still flocked to Washington Park, so named because it stood in an area of South Brooklyn where George Washington's Continental Army had fought the Battle of Long Island.

For big games, especially when the opposition was the hated Giants, late arrivals had no choice but to rent space on the fire escapes or rooftop of the Guinea Flats. Saloons did a thriving business selling growlers of beer to those fans, who hauled them up on ropes. In the evenings players rarely strayed far from the park, eating, drinking, and carousing in neighborhood restau-

WINNING PERCENTAGE 1901-1919

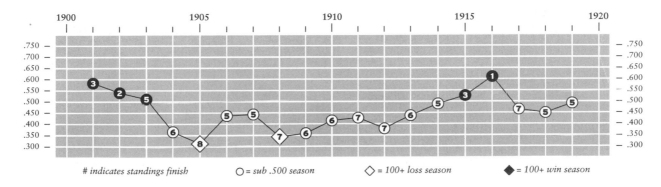

 # indicates standings finish   ○ = *sub .500 season*   ◇ = *100+ loss season*   ◆ = *100+ win season*

rants and pubs. Already Brooklyn had developed the bond between team and fans for which it became famous in later decades.

In 1910, five years after Hanlon had been fired, the team finally abandoned the "Superbas" moniker and reverted to its 19th-century nickname "Dodgers,"—short for "Trolley Dodgers," a term for Brooklyn inhabitants, whose streets had been made hazardous by their rapid-transit system. Three years later, when the team moved into Ebbets Field, Brooklyn was piecing together a competitive club. New manager Wilbert Robinson, hired in 1914, inherited talented players like Jake Daubert, Zack Wheat, Nap Rucker, and Jeff Pfeffer. A year later the team—now called the "Robins" after their popular manager—returned at long last to the first division. The team won its only pennant of the Deadball Era in 1916, with solid contributions from veterans Larry Cheney, Rube Marquard, and Jack Coombs, all of whom had been acquired by Robinson.

Despite fielding virtually the same lineup that lost the 1916 World Series to the Boston Red Sox, Brooklyn plummeted from first to seventh in 1917, the biggest drop in the standings for a pennant-winning team to that point in the NL's 42-year history. The Robins' record was even worse in 1918, when they lost most of their pitching staff to military service. The club's slight improvement in 1919 gave little indication that another surprise pennant was just around the corner.

ALL-ERA TEAM

H. MYERS, CF

Z. WHEAT, LF   H. LUMLEY, RF

G. CUTSHAW, 2B

B. DAHLEN, SS

R. SMITH, 3B   J. DAUBERT, 1B

N. RUCKER, P

O. MILLER, C

TEAM LEADERS 1901–1919

BATTING

GAMES
Z. Wheat 1374
J. Daubert 1213
J. Hummel 1139

RUNS
J. Daubert 648
Z. Wheat 635
J. Sheckard 429

HITS
Z. Wheat 1547
J. Daubert 1387
J. Hummel 973

RBI
Z. Wheat 640
J. Daubert 415
J. Hummel 390

DOUBLES
Z. Wheat 251
J. Daubert 138
J. Hummel 127

TRIPLES
Z. Wheat 107
J. Daubert 87
J. Hummel 82

HOME RUNS
Z. Wheat 51
H. Lumley 38
J. Daubert 33

STOLEN BASES
J. Daubert 187
J. Sheckard 169
G. Cutshaw 166

BATTING AVERAGE
J. Daubert 305
Z. Wheat 299
J. Sheckard 298

PITCHING

GAMES
N. Rucker 336
J. Pfeffer 190
H. McIntire 179

WINS
N. Rucker 134
J. Pfeffer 96
D. Scanlan 64

LOSSES
N. Rucker 134
H. McIntire 98
G. Bell 79

INNINGS
N. Rucker 2375⅓
J. Pfeffer 1501⅔
H. McIntire 1300⅓

STRIKEOUTS
N. Rucker 1217
D. Scanlan 574
J. Pfeffer 568

WALKS
N. Rucker 701
D. Scanlan 582
H. McIntire 450

SHUTOUTS
N. Rucker 38
J. Pfeffer 23
G. Bell 17

ERA
J. Pfeffer 2.16
N. Rucker 2.42
G. Bell 2.85

The 1907 Superbas finished 65-83, the franchise's best record during the decade between 1903 and 1914.

TYPICAL LINEUPS 1901-1919

1901

1. J. Kelley, 1B
2. W. Keeler, RF
3. J. Sheckard, LF
4. T. Daly, 2B
5. B. Dahlen, SS
6. T. McCreery, CF
7. C. Irwin, 3B
8. D. McGuire, C

1902

1. J. Sheckard, LF
2. W. Keeler, RF
3. C. Dolan, CF
4. T. McCreery, 1B
5. B. Dahlen, SS
6. T. Flood, 2B
7. C. Irwin, 3B
8. H. Hearne, C

1903

1. S. Strang, 3B
2. J. Sheckard, LF
3. J. Dobbs, CF
4. J. Doyle, 1B
5. B. Dahlen, SS
6. J. McCredie, RF
7. T. Flood, 2B
8. L. Ritter, C

1904

1. J. Dobbs, CF
2. P. Dillon, 1B
3. H. Lumley, RF
4. J. Sheckard, LF
5. S. Strang, 2B
6. C. Babb, SS
7. M. McCormick, 3B
8. D. Jordan, 2B
   B. Bergen, C

1905

1. J. Dobbs, CF
2. J. Sheckard, LF
3. H. Lumley, RF
4. H. Batch, 3B
5. D. Gessler, 1B
6. P. Lewis, SS
7. C. Malay, 2B
8. L. Ritter, C

1906

1. D. Casey, 3B
2. B. Maloney, CF
3. H. Lumley, RF
4. T. Jordan, 1B
5. J. McCarthy, LF
6. P. Lewis, SS
7. W. Alperman, 2B
8. B. Bergen, C

1907

1. W. Alperman, 2B
2. D. Casey, 3B
3. H. Lumley, RF
4. H. Batch, LF
5. T. Jordan, 1B
6. B. Maloney, CF
7. P. Lewis, SS
8. L. Ritter, C

1908

1. A. Burch, LF
   H. Pattee, 2B
2. B. Maloney, CF
3. J. Hummel, LF-2B
4. H. Lumley, RF
5. T. Jordan, 1B
6. T. Sheehan, 3B
7. P. Lewis, SS
8. B. Bergen, C

1909

1. A. Burch, CF
2. W. Clement, LF
3. T. Jordan, 1B
   J. Hummel, INF-OF
4. W. Alperman, 2B
5. E. Lennox, 3B
6. H. Lumley, RF
7. T. McMillan, SS
8. B. Bergen, C

1910

1. B. Davidson, CF
2. J. Daubert, 1B
3. Z. Wheat, LF
4. J. Hummel, 2B
5. J. Dalton, RF
6. E. Lennox, 3B
7. T. Smith, SS
8. B. Bergen, C

1911

1. B. Tooley, SS
2. J. Daubert, 1B
3. Z. Wheat, LF
4. J. Hummel, 2B
5. B. Davidson, CF
6. B. Coulson, RF
7. E. Zimmerman, 3B
8. B. Bergen
   T. Erwin, C

1912

1. H. Moran, CF-RF
2. H. Northen, RF-CF
3. R. Smith, 3B
4. J. Daubert, 1B
5. Z. Wheat, LF
6. J. Hummel, 2B-RF
   G. Cutshaw, 2B
7. B. Tooley
   B. Fisher, SS
8. O. Miller, C

1913

1. H. Moran, RF
2. G. Cutshaw, 2B
3. C. Stengel, CF
4. Z. Wheat, LF
5. J. Daubert, 1B
6. R. Smith, 3B
7. B. Fisher, SS
8. O. Miller, C

1914

1. J. Dalton, CF
2. J. Daubert, 1B
3. R. Smith, 3B
4. Z. Wheat, LF
5. G. Cutshaw, 2B
6. C. Stengel, RF
7. D. Egan, SS
8. L. McCarty, C

1915

1. H. Myers, CF
2. O. O'Mara, SS
3. J. Daubert, 1B
4. Z. Wheat, LF
5. G. Cutshaw, 2B
6. C. Stengel, RF
7. G. Getz, 3B
8. O. Miller
   L. McCarty, C

1916

1. H. Myers, CF
2. J. Daubert, 1B
3. C. Stengel, RF
4. Z. Wheat, LF
5. M. Mowrey, 3B
6. G. Cutshaw, 2B
7. I. Olson, SS
8. C. Meyers, C

1917

1. I. Olson, SS
2. J. Daubert, 1B
3. J. Hickman, CF
   H. Myers, CF-INF
4. C. Stengel, RF
5. Z. Wheat, LF
6. G. Cutshaw, 2B
7. M. Mowrey, 3B
8. O. Miller, C

1918 (First half)

1. I. Olson, SS
2. O. O'Mara, 3B
3. J. Daubert, 1B
4. H. Myers, CF
5. J. Johnston, LF
6. J. Hickman, RF
7. R. Schmandt, 2B
8. O. Miller, C

1918 (Second half)

1. J. Johnston, RF
2. I. Olson, SS
3. J. Daubert, 1B
4. Z. Wheat, LF
5. H. Myers, CF
6. O. O'Mara, 3B
7. M. Doolan, 2B
8. M. Wheat, C

1919

1. I. Olson, SS
2. J. Johnston, 2B
3. T. Griffith, RF
4. Z. Wheat, LF
5. H. Myers, CF
6. E. Konetchy, 1B
7. L. Malone
   C. Ward, 3B
8. E. Krueger, C

BROOKLYN

CHARLES HERCULES EBBETS
OWNER 1898–1925

Hard working and ambitious, Charles Ebbets worked for the Brooklyn baseball club for 42 years, serving at various times as ticket seller, clerk, bookkeeper, scorecard salesman, business manager, president, field manager, part owner, and eventually owner. Though sometimes accused of miserliness, the good-natured magnate generally was popular with the Brooklyn fans, and deservedly so; he incurred huge personal debt to purchase the team and keep it in Brooklyn when a move to Baltimore threatened, and did it again a decade later to give the fans a state-of-the-art ballpark in an era when public financing of such a facility was unthinkable. Today Ebbets is best remembered for Ebbets Field, which opened in 1913 and was razed in 1960, three years after the Dodgers moved to Los Angeles. His name lives on in the 21st century primarily because of the current trend toward building retro-style ballparks—every city seems to want its new stadiums to be a nostalgic "Ebbets Field–style" ballpark.

Charles Hercules Ebbets was born in New York City on October 29, 1859, and attended the city's public schools. Baseball was his favorite sport even though he was a much better bowler. Initially pursuing a career in architecture, Charley worked on several prominent projects, including the Metropolitan Hotel and Niblo's Garden, a famed New York amusement center. He also tried his hand at publishing, printing cheap editions of novels and textbooks that he sold door to door. Active in local politics, Ebbets served four years on the Board of Aldermen and one in the New York Assembly before an unsuccessful campaign for the New York Senate convinced him to devote his considerable talents to baseball rather than politics. Charley was 23 when he started working for the Brooklyn baseball club as clerk, bookkeeper, and scorecard salesman during its inaugural season in the Interstate League in 1883.

Ebbets' ascent in the Dodgers organization dovetailed with the history of the borough. He joined the club two weeks before the opening of the Brooklyn Bridge, the engineering feat of its day but also the death knell for Brooklyn as an independent city. Charley remained with the team as it moved to the American Association in 1884 and the National League in 1890, ascending to its presidency when his predecessor in that office, Charles Byrne, died three days after Brooklyn was incorporated into New York City in 1898. Later that season Ebbets even tried his hand as field manager, sitting on the bench in the club president's traditional top hat and compiling a 38-68 record. Ned Hanlon replaced him as manager the following season.

Having acquired his first shares of stock in the team from George Chauncey some 12 years earlier, Ebbets invested his life's savings in 1902 to buy out Ferdinand Abell, one of the club's original owners. Shortly thereafter the majority owner, Harry von der Horst, put his entire interest up for sale, and Hanlon expressed a desire to buy the team and move it to Baltimore. Tapped out but desperate to keep the team in Brooklyn, Ebbets purchased von der Horst's shares after obtaining a loan from his friend Henry Medicus, a Brooklyn furniture dealer. Now in control of virtually all of the club's stock—he bought the remnants from

Hanlon several years later—Charley reelected himself president with a raise in salary from $7,500 to $10,000, and elected Medicus and Charles H. Ebbets Jr. as treasurer and secretary, respectively.

With his background in architecture, Ebbets dreamed of constructing a magnificent concrete-and-steel baseball palace to replace outmoded Washington Park. After considering several potential sites, he finally settled on a 4½-acre garbage dump on the edge of a disreputable neighborhood called Pigtown. Located between the Bedford and Flatbush sections of Brooklyn, the land had two primary benefits: it was affordable and adjacent to the tracks of nine separate trolley lines. Without revealing his intentions, which would have driven up the price significantly, Ebbets set about acquiring the land parcel by parcel, making his first purchase in September 1908. Operating his club frugally and borrowing heavily from the bank, he eventually bought the final parcel on December 29, 1911.

When asked what he'd name his new ballpark at the groundbreaking ceremony on March 4, 1912, Ebbets' initial reaction was to continue the name Washington Park. "Washington Park, hell," said Len Wooster of the *Brooklyn Times*. "That name wouldn't mean anything out here. Why don't you call it Ebbets Field? It was your idea and nobody else's, and you've put yourself in hock to build it. It's going to be your monument, whether you like to think about it that way or not." With its proper name decided, construction on Ebbets Field continued throughout 1912, with Ebbets wielding the trowel at the ceremonial laying of the cornerstone on July 6. That August he solved his financial problems by taking on the builders, his old friends the McKeever brothers, as half partners in the club.

With an initial seating capacity of 18,000 and a final price tag of $750,000, Brooklyn's gorgeous new ballpark officially opened on April 9, 1913. The exterior featured a curved brick façade at the corner of Sullivan and Cedar streets highlighted by classical arched windows. Inside the main entrance was an ornate lobby with a domed ceiling that stood 27' high at its center.

The terrazzo floor was tiled like the stitches of a baseball, and a chandelier with 12 baseball-bat arms holding 12 baseball-shaped globes hung from the ceiling. Double-tiered stands ran along the foul lines from the right-field corner to a bit beyond third base, where a single double-decked bleacher extended to the left-field corner. At the time the park's dimensions were 419' to left, 476' to dead center, 500' to right center, but, because of Bedford Avenue, only 301' to right. Ebbets installed two long benches at the back of the grandstand, one for himself and his friends and the other for the McKeevers and their friends.

Over the years Ebbets received credit for several innovations, including the rain check and the idea that teams should draft in inverse order to their final standings in the annual minor league draft. He also was an early proponent of uniform numbers. During an exhibition game in Memphis on March 28, 1917, the previous year's World Series combatants, Brooklyn and the Boston Red Sox, wore numbers on their sleeves because Ebbets thought fans in non-major league cities would be unfamiliar with the players. In 1922 he proposed that all teams be required to put numbers on players' sleeves or caps, but the league voted to leave it to the discretion of the individual teams.

In 1923 Ebbets moved the Dodgers' training camp to Clearwater, where he'd purchased a home during the Florida land boom, and over the next several years so many Brooklyn fans attended spring training that the tiny ballpark took on many of the sights and sounds of Ebbets Field. Late in the 1923 season Ebbets began to suffer heart difficulties. On the advice of his doctor he returned to Clearwater and contemplated selling the team. In the spring of 1925, shortly after coming north from spring training, Ebbets fell ill again and his doctor ordered him to his suite at the Waldorf-Astoria Hotel. Early on the morning of April 18, 1925, 65-year-old Charles Ebbets died with his sister, his son, two daughters, and his second wife at his bedside. He left behind an estate valued at nearly $1.28 million.

JOHN SACCOMAN

BROOKLYN

EDWARD HUGH HANLON
MANAGER 1899–1905

Ned Hanlon managed 19 seasons in the major leagues—12 in the 19th century, when he compiled a .586 winning percentage, and seven in the Deadball Era, when his winning percentage fell to .449. "Foxy Ned" guided five National League pennant-winners, the 1894-96 Baltimore Orioles and the 1899-1900 Brooklyn Superbas, but never finished higher than second after 1900. Some say the game had passed him by, but another possible explanation is that he was focusing most of his attention on returning big-league baseball to his beloved Baltimore.

The son of a house builder, Edward Hugh Hanlon was born on August 22, 1857, in Montville, Connecticut, about halfway between New London and Norwich. A speedy center fielder who excelled on defense, Ned reached the big leagues in 1880 with the NL's Cleveland Blues. In 1881 the lifetime .260 hitter began an eight year stint with the NL's Detroit Wolverines, posting his most successful season in 1887 when he hit .274 with a career-high 69 stolen bases and captained a team that became world champions. After the Wolverines disbanded, Hanlon joined the NL's Pittsburgh Alleghenys in 1889, eventually being named the team's third manager of that season. He showed a glimpse of his talent for leadership by posting a 26-18 mark with a team that finished with an overall record of 61-71. Hanlon was active in the players' Brotherhood and was one of the first to jump to the Players League, serving as player-manager of the Pittsburgh Burghers in 1890. When the league folded, he became player-manager of the NL's Pittsburgh franchise, now called the Pirates. When

Hanlon got off to a 31-47 start in 1891, the Pirates demoted him to captain and named Bill McGunnigle as the new manager. Ned suffered a late-season knee injury that ended his career as a regular player.

The 34-year-old Hanlon was out of baseball when Harry von der Horst, the son of a wealthy Baltimore brewery owner, signed him in June 1892 to manage the Orioles, giving him stock in the team and full authority over baseball operations. Though Ned told his new players that they had enough talent to win, by the end of 1893 only three remained: the battery of Sadie McMahon and Wilbert Robinson and young infielder John McGraw. After finishing dead last in a 12-team league in 1892, Hanlon traded for outfielders Steve Brodie, Willie Keeler, and Joe Kelley, shortstop Hughie Jennings, and first baseman Dan Brouthers. He also acquired second baseman Heinie Reitz and catcher Boileryard Clarke from the California League. In little more than a year, "Foxy Ned" had given his team a complete makeover. It won NL pennants in 1894 and 1895 but lost the Temple Cup Series each year. Baltimore won a third pennant in 1896 and this time swept the Cleveland Spiders to capture the Temple Cup. Though the Orioles finished second in 1897, they took the last Temple Cup series, defeating the pennant-winning Boston Beaneaters.

At a meeting of National League owners in February 1899, Hanlon and von der Horst swapped stock with Brooklyn owners Gus Abell and Charles Ebbets, with von der Horst gaining a controlling interest in both teams. Hanlon became manager of the Brooklyn club, taking Keeler, Kelley, Jennings, and several other Oriole stars with him. Hanlon's Brooklyn squad, known as the Superbas after the vaudeville troupe Hanlon's Superbas, won NL titles in 1899 and 1900. "Those old Baltimore Orioles didn't pay any more attention to Ned Hanlon than they did to the batboy," said Sam Crawford. "When I came into the league, that whole bunch had moved over to Brooklyn, and Hanlon was managing them there, too. He was a bench manager in civilian clothes. When things would get a little tough in a game, Hanlon would sit there on the bench and wring his hands and start telling some of those old-timers what to do. They'd look at him and say, 'For Christ's sake, just keep quiet and leave us alone. We'll win this ball game if you only shut up.'"

Baltimore, meanwhile, was contracted out of the NL after the 1899 season. In 1901 the American League moved in, installing McGraw as manager of the new major league Orioles. Withstanding mass defections to the AL, Hanlon kept his plucky Superbas near the top of the standings in 1901 and 1902, but his heart remained in Baltimore. When the Orioles left Maryland in 1903 to relocate to New York City and become the Highlanders, Ned purchased the Eastern League's Montreal Royals and moved the team to the now-vacant American League Park, which he bought for $3,000 after it had cost $21,000 to build only two years earlier. (He also owned Union Park, but it was in disrepair after years of abandonment.) Hanlon installed Robinson as player-manager of the new minor league Orioles, and sent another old Oriole, Jennings, down from Brooklyn when the team got off to a rough start.

The Superbas fell to fifth in 1903 after Keeler jumped to the AL. That off-season Hanlon saw a great opportunity. The stock market had been unkind to von der Horst, forcing him to sell off his stock in the Superbas. Ned offered to purchase the team and move it back to Baltimore, but Charles Ebbets arranged for von der Horst to sell to local interests, himself included. After turning down many lucrative offers to manage elsewhere over the years, Hanlon felt betrayed. To make matters worse, Ebbets informed him that his salary was being lowered from $11,500 to $7,500. Despite his pledge that 1904 would be his last season in Brooklyn, Hanlon guided the Superbas to a dismal 56-97 record that season, then returned in 1905 to top the century mark in losses.

In 1906 Hanlon became manager of the Cincinnati Reds, replacing his old Oriole star Kelley, but still he dreamed about bringing big-league baseball back to Baltimore. He also felt he had a score to settle with Ebbets. One month after the close of the 1906 season, Hanlon filed two lawsuits. The first claimed that Ebbets and secretary-treasurer Henry Medicus received greater salaries than the Brooklyn club's constitution allowed. His second lawsuit called for repayment of a $30,000 loan he had given the Brooklyn club. Hanlon's resort to the legal system proved futile; the only satisfaction he received was $10,000 for the stock he still held in the Superbas.

The Reds finished sixth in 1906, giving Ned his third straight losing season. His enthusiasm for managing beginning to wane, and soon to celebrate his 50th birthday, a tired Hanlon was in Brooklyn in late July 1907 when he announced to the press that he didn't intend to return to the Reds in 1908. After the season—the Reds again finished sixth—he moved back to Baltimore where he still owned the Eastern League's Orioles. In 1909 Ned sold the team and its ballpark for $70,000 to an investment group headed by his old player Jack Dunn, who had pitched for him with the 1899-1900 Superbas. With the arrival of a Federal League franchise in 1914, Hanlon became the club's biggest individual shareholder in the Baltimore Terrapins. The Terps flopped and the league went defunct. After being denied the opportunity to buy the St. Louis Cardinals with the intention of moving the team to Baltimore, Hanlon and his partners sued Organized Baseball for violating the Sherman Antitrust Act. In a landmark 1922 decision, the U.S. Supreme Court held that baseball was not interstate commerce and was therefore exempt from regulation by acts of Congress.

Ned Hanlon spent the last 21 years of his life outside baseball, though he still showed up occasionally for events at Oriole Park, the rechristened American League Park that he used to own. In 1916 he joined the Baltimore parks board, becoming its chairman in 1931. Among his acts in that capacity was putting old Oriole Brodie on the parks department's payroll. Hanlon died in Baltimore at age 79 on April 14, 1937, and was buried in New Cathedral Cemetery, which became an eternal gathering place for old Orioles—McGraw, Robinson, and Kelley are also buried there.

ZACK TRISCUIT

William Dahlen
BROOKLYN

WILLIAM FREDERICK DAHLEN
SHORTSTOP 1899–1903, MANAGER 1910–13

Splitting his 21-year career just about equally between the 1890s and the first decade of the Deadball Era, Bill Dahlen was a solid hitter, outstanding shortstop, and scientific base runner. Though not exceptionally fast, Dahlen stole at least 20 bases in 14 seasons, taking big leads and avoiding tags by using a "straddle" or "hook" slide. As a fielder Dahlen had an excellent throwing arm and covered a lot of ground. He still ranks in the top three of all time for assists and putouts at shortstop, though he also holds the NL record for most errors. At the time of his retirement as a full-time player in 1909 (he went on to play in four games in 1910-11), Dahlen had appeared in more National League games than any other player in history, and was second only to Jake Beckley in plate appearances. He also ranked in the Top 10 in at-bats, extra-base hits, RBI, and stolen bases.

Reared in the Mohawk Valley town of Nelliston, New York, where he was born on January 5, 1870, William Frederick Dahlen was regarded as both the neighborhood "live wire" and its pest. After attending the Nelliston public schools, he entered the Clinton Liberal Institute at Ft. Plain, New York, in 1887. Bill spent three years as a member of the school's baseball team, after which he signed to play for a semi-pro club in Cobleskill, New York, for $40 a month. A year later that club entered the New York State League but folded on September 28, whereon Dahlen joined the Albany team for the final games of the season. His combined batting average of .343 was the league's second best, while his 137 hits and 18 triples were league highs. Those numbers caught the attention of Joe Battin, a former major leaguer who recommended Dahlen to his friend Cap Anson, manager-first baseman of the National League's Chicago Colts.

Dahlen became an immediate fan favorite in Chicago, playing shortstop, third base, and the outfield for two seasons before becoming primarily a shortstop in 1893. Though the Colts challenged for a pennant in only one of his eight years with the team (1891), Dahlen nevertheless established himself as one of the outstanding players of the 1890s. He put up his biggest numbers in 1894, when he batted .357 and slugged .566 with a .444 on-base percentage. That year Dahlen batted safely in 42 consecutive games, the fourth-longest streak in major league history, and still the longest ever by a National League right-handed batter. He was finally stopped on August 7, 1894, oddly enough in a game in which the Colts had 17 hits in a 10-inning, 13-11 win over the Reds. The next day he launched a new streak that lasted 28 games, giving him hits in 70 of 71 contests.

Though Dahlen served as team captain and batted .290 with 27 steals in 1898, Chicago president Jim Hart became disenchanted with his nonchalant attitude and traded him to Baltimore in January 1899. Because of syndicate ownership, however, the veteran shortstop never played for the Orioles; he was transferred to Brooklyn, along with the rest of Baltimore's best players. Dahlen spent five successful years in Brooklyn, though he never again hit as well as he had in Chicago. Along with Willie Keeler, Joe Kelley, and Hugh Jennings, who also came from Baltimore, he led the Superbas to NL pennants in 1899 and 1900.

Dahlen was less successful in the *Chronicle-Telegraph* Cup series following the 1900 season, batting just .176 (three hits in 17 at-bats), though Brooklyn managed to defeat second-place Pittsburgh, three games to one.

In December 1903, after leading NL shortstops with a .948 fielding average at the advanced baseball age of 33, Dahlen got both married and traded. His second wife (he'd been married and divorced from a woman he met while playing for Chicago) was the former Jeanette Hoglund, and his new team was the New York Giants. On December 12, Giants manager John McGraw, unsure of his ability to retain his own great shortstop, George Davis, traded journeyman right hander Jack Cronin and rookie shortstop Charlie Babb to Brooklyn to get Dahlen. It proved an excellent trade for the Giants, one that McGraw later called "the most successful deal I ever made." Babb played only two seasons and Cronin one before they were gone from the big leagues. Dahlen, meanwhile, was well at home with McGraw's style of play, and his league-leading 80 RBI helped spark the Giants to a pennant.

He followed with an 81-RBI season in 1905, well among the leaders that year and helping the Giants repeat as NL champions. Appearing in his first World Series, Dahlen played flawlessly in the field, handling 29 chances without a miscue as the Giants defeated the Philadelphia Athletics in five games. The trio of A's pitchers—Chief Bender, Eddie Plank, and Andy Coakley—completely stymied him, however, holding him hitless in 15 at-bats.

After Chicago replaced the Giants as pennant winners in 1906-07, McGraw revamped his team for 1908. His biggest move sent Dahlen, Dan McGann, Frank Bowerman, George Browne, and George Ferguson to the Boston Doves for Fred Tenney, Al Bridwell, and Tom Needham. Dahlen played well in Boston but became dissatisfied with management and, as had happened in Chicago, appeared to lose interest in playing. The Doves released him following the 1909 season, whereon Charles Ebbets brought him back to Brooklyn to succeed Harry Lumley as manager of the Superbas.

Not surprisingly, the man known as "Bad Bill" for his fiery temperament and frequent ejections during his playing days was much the same as a manager. The most memorable of his tirades was his exchange of blows with umpire Cy Rigler in a 1912 game against the Giants. Brooklyn finished in the second division in

each of Dahlen's four seasons at the helm. Despite his lack of success, Ebbets liked Dahlen and wanted to keep him on as manager. His partners, the McKeever brothers, wanted someone new, however, and replaced Dahlen with Wilbert Robinson for the 1914 season.

Bill Dahlen continued to live in Brooklyn after his managerial career ended. At various times he owned a filling station and worked as a bullpen attendant at Yankee Stadium and a night clerk in Brooklyn's main post office. He died in Brooklyn on December 5, 1950. His wife had died earlier; a daughter and a brother survived him.

LYLE SPATZ

Bill Bergen

BROOKLYN

WILLIAM ALOYSIUS BERGEN
CATCHER 1904–11

The caption beneath Bill Bergen's image in a 1908 issue of *The Sporting News* stated that he "ranks with the best receivers in modern baseball. He is an intelligent student of the points of a batsman, a true and fast thrower and is without a peer in judging and capturing foul flies." Alas, if the descriptions could stop there, Billy, as he was sometimes called, might have faded into anonymity rather than ignominy. Decades after Bergen's career ended, however, baseball historians became fascinated with his offensive ineptitude. His lifetime batting average of .170 stands as the nadir of futility; no other major leaguer with 2,500 at-bats finished his career with a batting average lower than .210. He collected only two home runs in 3,028 at-bats, which is noteworthy even for the Deadball Era. Bergen's lifetime on-base percentage is a deplorable .194, and his .201 lifetime slugging percentage is just as bad. One other peculiar statistic stands out: in 3,028 at-bats he was never hit by a single pitch, which may be indicative of his approach to hitting—and lack of success.

The second son of Michael and Catherine (Delaney) Bergen, both of whom were born in Ireland, William Aloysius Bergen was born on June 13, 1878, in North Brookfield, Massachusetts. As a youngster Bill learned the skills of catching from his brother, Martin, nearly seven years older. Marty Bergen went on to become an excellent National League backstop for the 1896-99 Boston Beaneaters. Today, however, he is remembered as the much troubled soul who tragically murdered his wife and children before taking his own life in January 1900. In sharp contrast to his brother, Bill Bergen was personable and got along well with his teammates.

Bill began his professional career in 1898 with Pawtucket of the New England League. Graduating to the Interstate League in 1899, he played the next two seasons for Ft. Wayne, Indiana. One afternoon, after Ft. Wayne had fallen into a bases-loaded, no-out predicament, Bergen reportedly demonstrated his skills behind the plate by picking off all three runners. In 1901 the 6'0", 185 lb. receiver got his first taste of major league ball when he joined the Cincinnati Reds. Bergen became the primary catcher as a rookie and again in 1902, but his batting averages of .179 and .180 convinced the Reds to give utility man Heinie Peitz most of the playing time behind the plate in 1903.

Appearing in just 58 games that season, Bergen batted .227, the only time in his 11-year career that he hit for an average higher than .190. Despite his banner season, the Reds sold him to Brooklyn in February 1904. The Superbas already had a backstop named Lew "Old Dog" Ritter, and for several seasons he and Bergen shared Brooklyn's catching duties. Despite playing part-time, Bergen earned a reputation for the NL's strongest throwing arm, so strong that his mere presence behind the plate was enough to intimidate base runners. Notes in newspapers of the day often remark on his lightning release and ability to throw to second base on a line while standing flat-footed.

On August 23, 1909, Bergen gunned down six St. Louis Cardinals attempting to steal (for years it was reported that he threw out seven, but recent research confirms that the number was six). Despite catching only 941 games, Bergen ranks in the Top 10 for career assists by a catcher. And while only six of the 13 catchers in the Hall of Fame ever amassed as many as 100 assists in a single season, Bergen accomplished that feat in nine of his 11 major league campaigns, failing only in 1903 and 1907, the two seasons he caught fewer than 60 games. He reached a high of 202 assists in 1909, making him one of only a handful of backstops ever to accumulate more than 200 in a season. And it wasn't just in throwing that Bergen excelled. His lifetime fielding average of .972 exceeded the .967 league average for catchers and he caught two no-hitters.

Bergen's offense was a different story. Though it hardly seems possible, his batting actually got worse as the years went on. In 1909 he batted .139, the lowest post-1900 mark for a batting-title qualifier. That year Bergen also put together the longest hitless streak in major league history. After singling in his first at-bat on June 29, 1909, he went 46 at-bats before singling again in his second trip to the plate in the second game of a

doubleheader on July 17. The streak breaker, appropriately, was of the infield variety. According to statistical evidence, Bergen's defensive skills were still adequate in 1911, when he compiled an NL-leading .981 fielding average. His pitiful offensive skills sank to a new low, however, even for him—a .132 batting average and just 10 RBI in 227 at-bats. With promising young catcher Otto Miller now on the Brooklyn roster, Bergen was released at the close of the season.

At age 33, Bill Bergen still had an affinity for the game. He played in the International League in 1912-13, first for Newark and later for Baltimore. Despite failing health, Bergen continued to play for Scranton of the New York State League in 1914, but his offensive numbers began to mirror his major league production: a .161 batting average in 298 at-bats. He hung on as an active player through 1917, but by 1919 his health was limiting him to managing semipro teams in the vicinity of his home in Worcester, Massachusetts, where he'd settled in 1903, the same year he wed Alice Moran.

By 1930 Bergen's baseball days were over, his activities reduced by a worsening heart condition. Little is known of the last years of his life. On December 6, 1943, Bergen's condition necessitated admission to Worcester City Hospital. Thirteen days later he succumbed; the official cause of death was listed as heart disease. His widow, Alice, survived him, as did two sisters, Margaret McAvoy and Katherine Drumgoll. There is no mention of any children in numerous obituaries. After a requiem mass in St. Paul's Church, Bill Bergen's once rifle-like throwing arm was laid to rest in St. John's Cemetery in Worcester.

JOE DITTMAR

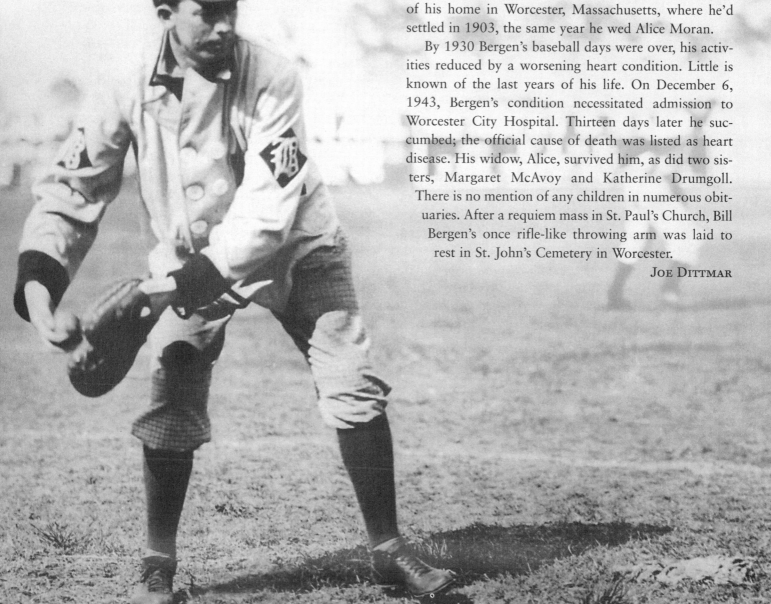

BROOKLYN

HARRY G. LUMLEY
RIGHT FIELDER 1904–10, MANAGER 1909

Harry Lumley was the Kevin Mitchell of the Deadball Era. Lumley in his prime could run the bases like a thoroughbred and more than keep up his end of the game on defense. "Some of the veteran fans hold him to be the best slugger in the history of baseball," wrote one reporter in 1907. Ring Lardner described Lumley as one of a dozen left-handed hitters "who hit fly balls or high line drives and who hit them so far that opposing right- and centre-fielders moved back and rested their spinal columns against the fence when it was these guys' turn to bat." But heavy-hitting Harry also had a tendency to put on weight, and a series of injuries cut short his major league career after only seven seasons.

Harry G. Lumley was born in Forest City, Pennsylvania, on September 29, 1880. His family moved to Lestershire (now known as Johnson City) in central New York when Harry was a child, and he and Frank Schulte were teammates on the semipro team sponsored by the Endicott-Johnson shoe factory. In 1901 Lumley batted .350 in his professional debut with the nearby New York State League franchise in Rome. After belting a league-leading eight home runs in 1902 for St. Paul of the American Association, which wasn't yet under the National Agreement, Harry jumped to Colorado Springs of the Western League for the following year. When the American Association entered Organized Baseball during the off-season, Colorado Springs was forbidden from playing him, and he was forced to leave the team after only a dozen games. Lumley spent the rest of 1903 with Seattle of the outlaw Pacific Coast League, leading the fledgling circuit with a .387 batting average. That offseason the PCL joined Organized Baseball, making the Seattle slugger eligible for the draft, and he was selected by the Brooklyn Superbas.

Harry Lumley burst into the majors with a huge season in 1904, batting .279 in a career-best 150 games and leading the National League with 18 triples and nine home runs. Eighty-two years later, those numbers earned him SABR's hypothetical NL Rookie of the Year award, but his best was yet to come. After improving his average to .293 with only a minor power drop-off in 1905, Lumley posted a career year in 1906. "The fight between Lumley and [Honus] Wagner for the leadership in National League batting has been fast and furious," a sportswriter wrote. Lumley eventually finished at .324, third behind Wagner and Harry Steinfeldt. Though rheumatism and a split finger limited him to 133 games, Lumley slashed 12 triples, third in the NL, and his nine home runs were second only to Brooklyn teammate Tim Jordan's 12. He was Brooklyn's most popular player, and commentators called him "one of the hardest hitters in the country" and "perhaps the most valuable asset in the Brooklyn organization." The Superbas refused lucrative offers for their prized slugger from six of the seven other NL clubs, including one from the Giants for $10,000.

Lumley featured prominently in a story Lardner wrote for *The New Yorker* in 1930 called "Br'er Rabbit Ball." The story centered around Ed Reulbach, who'd been assigned by Frank Chance to pitch batting practice to the Superbas because he'd been struggling with his control. "Well, we got to Brooklyn and after a certain game the same idea entered the minds of Mr. Schulte, Mr. Lumley, and your reporter, namely: that we should see the borough by night," wrote Lardner. "The next morning, Lumley had to report for practice and, so far as he was concerned, the visibility was very bad. Reulbach struck him out three times on low curve balls inside. 'I have got Lumley's weakness!' said Ed to Chance that afternoon. 'All right,' said the manager. 'When they come to Chicago, you can try it against him.' Brooklyn eventually came to Chicago, and Reulbach pitched Lumley a low curve ball on the inside. Lumley had enjoyed a good night's sleep and if it had been a 1930 vintage ball, it would have landed in Des Moines, Iowa. As it was, it cleared the fence by 10 feet and Schulte, playing right field and watching its flight, shouted: 'There goes Lumley's weakness!'"

Injuries combined with a "tendency to embonpoint," as one reporter described Lumley's proclivity for gaining weight, caused the hard-hitting outfielder's career to go steadily downhill after 1906. In 1907 he broke an ankle while sliding, ending his season after 127 games. His nine home runs to that point were enough to rank second again in the NL and his .425 slugging percentage was the circuit's third best, but his batting average plummeted 57 points to .267. Lumley was named captain in 1908, but the ankle injury continued to bother him and prevented him from getting down to playing weight. He struggled through a season-long slump, made worse by abuse from Brooklyn's fickle fans. Not satisfied with calling Lumley a "rotten has-been," one bug hurled the skeleton of an umbrella at the right fielder, and the steel rod stuck in the ground just a couple of feet in front of him. When Harry suffered a charley horse in his good leg in early August, Ebbets offered to send

him home at full pay for the rest of the season. The Superbas' game captain declined, finishing out the year with a .216 average.

Lumley's perseverance was rewarded during the off-season when Ebbets named him manager for 1909. Actually the Brooklyn magnate had promised the job in September 1908 to Bill Dahlen, the former Superbas shortstop who was then playing for the Boston Doves. After months of delay, the job fell to Lumley when Boston owner George Dovey reneged on his promise to part with Dahlen. The right fielder's appointment met with derision from some reporters, who didn't consider him to fit the Deadball Era stereotype of a brainy and aggressive manager. But within a week of taking over, Harry put his own mark on the club by waiving 13 players, including several regulars from 1908's seventh-place finishers. Appearing in only 55 games as a player in 1909 and batting .250 without a single home run, Lumley guided the Superbas to a 55-98 record, an improvement of 2½ games and one place in the standings. Ebbets nonetheless replaced him with Dahlen before the 1910 season, and the deposed manager appeared in only eight games that year before drawing his release in June.

Lumley settled in Binghamton, New York, near his hometown of Lestershire, serving as player-manager of the New York State League's "Bingoes" through 1912. Later he operated the Terminal Cafe, a tavern that stood near the current site of NYSEG Stadium, where the Eastern League's Mets play. Lumley participated in an old-timers' day at Ebbets Field in 1936, but failing health forced him to give up his restaurant the following year. A widower who never had any children, Harry Lumley died in Binghamton on May 22, 1938.

TOM SIMON

BKLYN.

BROOKLYN

JOHN EDWIN HUMMEL
UTILITY MAN 1905–15

Considered a "Methusalah" because he played for Brooklyn for an uninterrupted period of more than a decade, John Hummel was known as the "prince of utility players," appearing in 548 games at second base, 293 in the outfield, 160 at first base, and 74 at shortstop. Hummel batted .254 and stole 117 bases over the course of his dozen seasons in the majors, but his strength, according to J. C. Kofoed of *Baseball Magazine*, "is not measured by his hard hitting, nor yet his remarkable fielding or daredevil base stealing. 'Versatility' is the one word that sums up the tall Pennsylvanian's worth." The 5'11", 185 lb. utility man preferred playing first base, but his teammates thought he was best suited for the outfield. "Most of all, I would like to get settled in one spot," the reticent Hummel confided.

John Edwin Hummel was born on April 4, 1883, in Bloomsburg, a college town in central Pennsylvania. "I used to play ball in lots when I was seven years old," John recalled. "My father was a cabinet maker in Bloomsburg, and he taught me the trade. But I did not stay in the shop when I heard the other kids playing ball. When he'd start the big lathe going I'd sneak out." John got his first real baseball experience when he enrolled in the Bloomsburg State Normal School (now known as Bloomsburg University) and played second base on a standout college team that defeated Bucknell, Penn State, Carlisle, Franklin & Marshall, Gettysburg, and Villanova. Though he was still a year short of obtaining his degree, Hummel finished out the 1903 spring semester and left school for good, signing to play baseball with Wilmington, Delaware, of the outlaw Tri-State League.

"My first day on the field with Wilmington, I kicked on a decision and [teammate] Bill Everson, the old pitcher, called me 'Rowdy John,'" Hummel recalled. "The newspapers took it up and I made up my mind right then that I'd never kick again. When the papers and the players saw I was quiet, Everson called me 'Honest John' and then finally 'Silent John,' which has stuck to me ever since." The "Honest John" appellation, according to the *Brooklyn Eagle*, came because Hummel "was always striving to win, even when the lead of the opposing team was great enough to bury the hopes of the ordinary player."

After playing the outfield in Wilmington for two years, batting .307 in his first season and .292 in his second, Hummel made his debut in Organized Baseball in 1905 with Holyoke, Massachusetts, of the Connecticut League. Alternating between second and third base, he fielded well and batted .338 with 32 stolen bases in 110 games. That fall the Brooklyn Superbas acquired him for third baseman Mike "Kid" McCormick and cash. Making his major league debut on September 12, 1905, Hummel replaced second baseman Charlie Malay for the rest of the season and batted .266 in 30 games. The following year he appeared in 50 games at the keystone sack, but he also played in 21 games in the outfield and 15 at first base. Hummel batted just .199 but connected for the first of his 29 career home runs at Pittsburgh's Exposition Park on July 10, 1906.

The apex of Hummel's career was from 1908 to 1912, when he averaged 142 games per season. In 1908 he played in all 154 games, ranking second in the NL with 594 at-bats. Hummel left his mark on that season's pennant race, not to mention Larry Doyle's leg, when he spiked the star second baseman of the archrival Giants on September 8, knocking him out of the lineup for the rest of the season. "There was no excuse for Hummel cutting Doyle down," wrote Sam Crane in the *New York Evening Journal.* "He was out so far on a force play that he hadn't a show to make the bag."

The next year Silent John went back on his vow never to "kick"—he was ejected three times that season, twice when he didn't even open his mouth. On the third occasion, rookie umpire Stephen Cusack sent him to the bench even though all he did was say, "I thought I was safe." As always, Silent John remained reclusive off the field. "Hummel is a Trappist monk," wrote one reporter. "On the train after a game, this silent fellow will lean against a berth and noiselessly smoke, quickly subsiding into his strange apathy."

In 1910 Hummel finally got the chance to "settle in one spot," appearing in 153 games at second base. He made the most of the opportunity, leading all NL second basemen with a .965 fielding percentage. Though he batted only .244, he established career highs in runs (67), RBI (74), doubles (21), triples (13), home runs (5), and stolen bases (21). On the negative side, the free-swinging right-handed hitter led the National League with 81 strikeouts. The following season Hummel again played regularly at second base, improving his league-best fielding percentage to .972. He reverted to his role as utility man in 1912, however, splitting his time almost evenly between second base and the outfield.

By that season, though he'd not yet turned 30, Hummel had been with Brooklyn longer than any other player on the roster. "Practically every fan in the City of Churches believes Silent John to be a grandpa," wrote Kofoed. Despite his longevity with the Superbas, Hummel wasn't a fan favorite. That changed in 1914 when John filled in at the start of the season for Jake Daubert. "Every Brooklynite realizes that few first basemen would appear to advantage as understudy for the big fellow, but the veteran's work during Daubert's

enforced absence was more than satisfying—it was sensational," wrote Kofoed. Though he eventually tailed off to a more characteristic .264, Hummel batted .355 in his first 35 games, which is how he came to be featured in *Baseball Magazine.* "Hitherto he has not been a particular favorite of the bleacherites, for the 'sun gods' are worshippers of the blatant and spectacular," wrote Kofoed. "This season saw a decided change. Now Hummel is one of the biggest favorites on Robinson's squad, and his every appearance is greeted with vociferous cheers."

In 1915 the 32-year-old Hummel batted .230 in just 53 games, the fewest since his rookie year, and the Dodgers finally released him. He spent the offseason playing basketball in Springfield, Massachusetts, the hometown of his wife, Agnes. Reportedly turning down several lucrative offers from Federal League clubs, John played the next three seasons with Buffalo in the International League before returning to the majors in 1918 to play 22 games for the war-depleted New York Yankees. He then embarked on a career as a minor league manager, piloting teams in Saskatoon, Binghamton, Harrisburg, Scranton, Wheeling, and his adopted hometown of Springfield before retiring from baseball in 1927.

At the height of his playing days Hummel stated that his goal after baseball was to open a café and cigar store in Bloomsburg, but he ended up settling in his wife's hometown and working 26 years as a foreman for the Diamond Match Company, also managing the company baseball team. In his later years he disdained the livelier ball. "In the good old days we played heart and soul for one run, whereas now they play for 10 or 12," he said. John Hummel was 76 when he died at Springfield's Mercy Hospital on May 18, 1958. Agnes survived him, as did the couple's two children and four grandchildren.

Tom Simon

BROOKLYN

GEORGE NAPOLEON RUCKER
LEFT-HANDED PITCHER 1907–16

Nap Rucker was one of the Deadball Era's top left-handed pitchers, and also one of baseball's most famous sons of the South. In an era when the Brooklyn Superbas had a reputation for fielding bad teams, "the Rucker appendage is the only thing that has kept Brooklyn in the league," the *New York Herald* once wrote. "He was the easiest pitcher to catch, and had the best disposition of any pitcher I ever knew," said Brooklyn catcher Otto Miller. "He was faster than most people thought, even when they were looking at him, because his fastball was deceptive. It fooled the hitters not only because of the hop on it, but because it was on top of them before they realized it. When he lost much of his speed, his knuckleball was as puzzling as his fastball had been. It broke straight down, as if it rolled off a table. And his control was so good, I swear I could have caught him blindfolded."

George Napoleon Rucker was born on September 30, 1884, in Crabapple, Georgia, a small community north of Atlanta. His parents were John Rucker, a former Confederate soldier, and Sarah Hembree. Rucker's childhood, as one sportswriter later put it, "was not crowded with stirring incidents." As a red-headed, freckle-faced youth he worked as a printer's apprentice, and one day was given a headline to set in type: $10,000 FOR PITCHING A BASEBALL. That moment, Rucker always claimed, was when he decided to become a pitcher. He joined a local semipro team and caught the eye of the Atlanta Crackers of the Southern League, who signed him on a trial basis. (Many years later, Bill Nye—famous bodyguard to presidents Roosevelt, Taft, and Wilson—claimed to be the scout who recommended Nap to Atlanta.) Rucker pitched his first professional game on September 2, 1904, but he failed to impress and at season's end was farmed out to Augusta of the South Atlantic League. During his brief stay in Atlanta, though, Rucker got to know the team's official scorer, a young sportswriter whose path he would cross again in later years: former semipro shortstop Grantland Rice.

In 1905 Rucker's teammates on the Augusta team included Eddie Cicotte, Clyde Engle, and 18-year-old Ty Cobb, who was Rucker's roommate. Rucker and Cobb often went to the park early together so Cobb could practice hitting against left-handed pitching, and Rucker apparently became one of the first to experience Cobb's fury firsthand. According to a tale Rucker told years later, he and Cobb developed a routine: When they arrived home after each game, Cobb would bathe first, then Rucker. One day Rucker was knocked out of the game and left the park early. Cobb arrived home to find his roommate already in the bathtub and supposedly flew into a rage, attempting to choke Rucker. "You don't understand," Cobb seethed. "I've just got to be first—*all the time*." After compiling a 13-11 record in 1905, Rucker returned to Augusta the next year and got off to a spectacular start, prompting rumors that Connie Mack's Philadelphia Athletics were about to purchase his contract. The deal fell through, however, and Rucker finished the season in the Sally League with a 27-9 record.

That winter Charles Ebbets, acting on a recommendation from Brooklyn manager Patsy Donovan, drafted Rucker for $500, and he joined the Superbas in 1907 at a salary of $1,900 per year. As a 22-year-old rookie Rucker went 15-13, leading the fifth-place Superbas in innings (275⅓), strikeouts (131), and ERA (2.06). In 1908 he was just as good, posting a 2.08 ERA and somehow winning 17 games for a team that lost 101. The highlight of Rucker's season came on September 5, when he pitched a no-hitter at Washington Park, striking out 14 Boston Doves. (On July 22, 1911, he came close to a second no-hitter, pitching 8⅔ hitless innings against Cincinnati before Bob Bescher bounced a chopper up the middle for a single.) In 1909 Rucker was again the best pitcher on a terrible team, going 13-19 despite a 2.24 ERA and a career-high 201 strikeouts. On July 24 of that season he struck out 16 St. Louis Cardinals, tying a major league record that stood until Dizzy Dean broke it in 1933. (Rucker always claimed that he actually fanned 17, but the official scorer, Abe Yager, forgot to record one of them.) In 1910 Rucker's record improved to 17-18 as he led the NL with 320⅓ innings, 27 complete games, and six shutouts.

To supplement his income during the off-season, Rucker usually spent his winters working as a typesetter for the *Marietta Free Press*, a newspaper owned by a cousin. He also enjoyed hunting and fishing, and once nearly died on a duck-hunting trip when his boat sank. In addition, Rucker was an early aficionado of auto racing, and in 1910 was even scheduled to race Cobb at a racetrack in Savannah, but the Georgia Peach called the match off. To his managers' dismay, Rucker also spent his off-seasons eating peanuts and ice cream. Never one for vigorous training, he routinely reported to camp weighing 210 lbs., though by Opening Day he was usually down to his playing weight of 180 to 190 lbs.

Rucker opened 1911 with six consecutive losses—during which the Superbas scored a total of 10 runs—but rebounded to enjoy perhaps his best season, finishing 22-18 and topping the 20-win mark for the only time in his career. During that season he took a day off to marry Edith Wing Wood, his sweetheart from back home. Pressed by reporters, Rucker insisted that "my taking a wife will not interfere with my baseball career." Still, his baseball career did change in one important way: Manager Bill Dahlen began using him more often in relief. In 1911 and 1912, Rucker led the Dodgers not only in games started, but also in games finished as a reliever. When saves were calculated retroactively in the 1960s, it was discovered that Rucker had ranked among the NL's save leaders each year from 1911 through 1913.

Throughout his career Rucker was known as a nemesis of the New York Giants, although his lifetime record against them was a merely passable 19-24. His reputation as a Giant-beater was so great that John McGraw—undoubtedly experiencing one of his weaker moments—once touted Rucker as the finest pitcher he had ever seen. "Yes, even greater than Mathewson," he told a reporter. "Rucker is the best that ever stepped on a pitcher's mound." In 1912 the fireballer did nothing to discourage that claim, leading the NL with six shutouts and posting a 2.21 ERA, more than a run below the league average. The Dodgers again failed to support him, however, and Rucker went 18-21, losing 20 games for the only time in his career.

All of Nap's strikeouts and no-hit bids brought him acclaim as one of the fastest pitchers in the game. On October 6, 1912, Rucker and Walter Johnson became the first pitchers to have their throwing speed scientifically measured when they submitted to a test at the Remington Arms Plant in Bridgeport, Connecticut. Using copper wires placed several feet apart, the test measured the amount of time it took their fastballs to travel the distance between the two wires. The results probably underestimated the pitchers' speed: Rucker tested at 113 feet per second (77 mph), Johnson at 122 (83 mph).

In 1913 Brooklyn again played poorly, and although Rucker pitched well, his record was only 14-15. Still, an informal poll of sportswriters taken after the season named Rucker the best left-handed pitcher in baseball by a comfortable margin. Paul Shannon of the *Boston Post* wrote that he was "a steady, dependable twirler, willing to work whenever called upon, and able to hold any team in the National League in check," while Thomas Rice of the hometown *Brooklyn Eagle* lamented that "the fates have tied him up with an aggregation that has steadfastly refused to make a bid for championship honors." Rucker also received praise for what the *Cincinnati Enquirer*'s Jack Ryder called "the most perfect control ever displayed by a left-hander." Earlier in his career Rucker had been able to rely almost solely on his fastball, but in 1913 the once-great fastball began to fade, and Rucker started throwing a strange pitch that one writer called "the slowest ball in the history of the majors." Sportswriters of the day disagreed on the pitch's identity, with some calling it a slow curve and others having not the slightest idea what to call it. But Rob Neyer and Bill James, in their comprehensive study of pitching repertoires, identified the pitch as one of the earliest versions of the knuckleball. Rucker claimed to have learned the pitch with Augusta when he accidentally gripped the ball the wrong way, but another story credits its origin to an injured thumb that forced Nap to change his pitching grip in 1913. Whatever its origin, the baffling pitch struck Dan Daniel of the *New York World-Telegram* as "one of the amazing phenomena of baseball history."

In 1914 Rucker developed a sore arm, and for the last three years of his career he was able to pitch effectively only with two weeks' rest. He had a mediocre season in 1914, but succeeded marvelously as a part-time pitcher in 1915. Always respected among his teammates, the veteran now became a mentor for many of the younger Brooklyn players. "When I broke in I couldn't hit a low ball," Casey Stengel recalled in the 1950s. "Nap took me to the park every morning and fed me low balls. If it hadn't been for Nap I reckon I wouldn't be manager of the Yankees. I wouldn't have even stayed in baseball."

Rucker was always the favorite player of Charles Ebbets, who scoffed whenever other teams offered to buy the pitcher's contract. Likewise, Rucker eschewed all opportunities to leave the Dodgers. Fittingly for a rural southerner, he enjoyed life in relatively down-home Brooklyn. "It's got New York beaten by three bases," he said in 1912. "New York is more of a circus than a city. You can get a good night's rest in Brooklyn. You meet more real human beings in Brooklyn. Your life is safer in Brooklyn."

Unlike many Deadball Era players, Rucker rarely had contract squabbles. Every year after joining the Superbas he received an annual raise of between $300 and $500; by 1914 he was making $4,500 per season.

When eight of his teammates jumped to the Federal League that year, he declined to join them. In August 1915, as the outlaw league was nearing collapse, Rucker issued a stern warning to his fellow players, one that still seems relevant today: "The Feds pose as the friends of the ballplayer, yet their presence in the game has hurt public interest in the players," he said. "This loss of confidence is due to contract-jumping, purely and simply, I believe. A couple of years ago, in fact so late as last winter, the general idea among the boys was that it was all right to go out and get the money. They did not fully realize that the game with the salaries depends on their favor with the public, and that if this favor is withdrawn there will be no more high salaries and perhaps no more baseball." Perhaps in gratitude for Rucker's loyalty, Ebbets never lost an opportunity to sing his praises. "I would give a great deal of money to have my club in a World's Series if only for the honor it would bring Rucker," Ebbets told Damon Runyon in 1915. "I will always regard him as one of the greatest men the game has produced—greatest in every way."

In 1916 Ebbets got his wish. The once-hapless Robins won the pennant, and Nap Rucker finally got to pitch in the World Series. But after a decade of excellence, Rucker by 1916 was merely a spare part. He pitched in only nine games, though posting an impressive 1.69 ERA. Near season's end the Robins held "Nap Rucker Day" at Ebbets Field, featuring marching soldiers and the presentation of a handsome check from the Brooklyn club. "I will not monkey around with baseball any more," Nap said on the occasion. "I have had my day, and it has been a long one, in which I have made money and gained thousands of friends." Tellingly, with his club involved in a heated pennant race, the aging Rucker didn't even get to pitch on Nap Rucker Day. On August 1, 1916, Rucker pitched 5⅔ innings of scoreless relief against Cincinnati, earning his 134th and last major league victory. When Brooklyn faced Boston in the World Series, Wilbert Robinson gave Rucker two innings of mop-up duty in Game Four, a 6-2 Brooklyn loss. Nap pitched scoreless ball, striking out three Red Sox in his swan song as a major league pitcher.

Rucker ended his career at exactly .500, with 134 wins and 134 losses. Thirty-eight of his wins were shutouts, and 11 were 1-0 victories. Rucker won 28% of his victories by shutout, the second-highest percentage in baseball history (behind only Ed Walsh). Rucker's 2.42 career ERA was 16% better than the league average, which was 2.87 over the same span. When Rucker got the decision Brooklyn's winning percentage was an even .500, but without him the Superbas played .430 ball, losing 175 games more than they won.

After his retirement Rucker moved back to The Oaks, his plantation mansion in Roswell, Georgia, which somehow had been spared when General Sherman burned the town during the Civil War. Nap owned the local wheat mill, became an investor in the town bank, presided over two small cotton plantations populated by tenant farmers, and occasionally umpired sandlot baseball games. He also scouted the South for the Dodgers, discovering such players as Dazzy Vance, Al Lopez, and Hugh Casey. Nap served as a Dodger scout for 17 years until late 1934, when the team, presumably feeling the pinch of the Great Depression, let him go. Immediately thereafter, Rucker—who was by now one of Roswell's most prominent citizens—ran unopposed for mayor, a position that paid him $100 per year. Rucker was a segregationist Democrat; as one writer put it, "he could not be anything else politically and still be a Georgian." As mayor during the New Deal, the former pitcher was instrumental in bringing running water to Roswell, and later served as the town's water commissioner for several decades. In 1939 the Dodgers re-hired Rucker as a scout. The next year Nap's nephew, Johnny Rucker, made his debut with the rival New York Giants, for whom he played center field for seven seasons. After a brief stint working for the U.S. Government in Panama during World War II, Nap returned home to Georgia to live in semi-retirement. Nap Rucker was 86 when he died in Alpharetta, Georgia, on December 19, 1970. He was survived by his wife, Edith, and his daughter, Anne.

ERIC ENDERS

BROOKLYN

Zachariah Davis Wheat
Left fielder 1909–26

Zack Wheat remains the Dodgers' all-time franchise leader in games, hits, doubles, triples, and total bases. Though Wheat threw right-handed, he was a natural left-handed hitter who corkscrewed his spikes into the dirt with a wiggle that became his trademark. Unlike most Deadball Era hitters, he held his hands down by the knob of the bat, choking up only a little. "There is no chop-hitting with Wheat, but a smashing swipe which, if it connects, means work for the outfielders," wrote one reporter. He was an outstanding first-ball hitter, and he was also so renowned as a curveball hitter that John McGraw reportedly had a standing order prohibiting his pitchers from throwing him benders.

Even though he hit .300 each year, Wheat won as much admiration for his defense. "What Lajoie was to infielders, Zach Wheat is to outfielders, the finest mechanical craftsman of them all," *Baseball Magazine* wrote in 1917. "Wheat is the easiest, most graceful of outfielders with no close rivals." A fast runner, Zack was as close to a five-tool player as any National Leaguer of the late Deadball Era. His only weaknesses were his poor base-stealing ability and proneness to injury (his tiny size-five feet frequently caused nagging ankle injuries).

Zachariah Davis Wheat was born on May 23, 1888, at his family's farm near Hamilton, Missouri, 60 miles northeast of Kansas City. Missouri was still a wild frontier then; just six years earlier, Jesse James was murdered by a member of his own gang in nearby St. Joseph. Zack was the eldest of three sons, all of whom played professional baseball. The middle brother, Mack, spent five years as Zack's teammate with

Brooklyn, while the youngest brother, Basil, was a long-time outfielder and catcher in the minors. Their father, Basil Sr., was a descendant of Moses Wheat, one of the Puritans who fled England and founded Concord, Massachusetts, in 1635. Their mother was said to be a full-blooded Cherokee, but Zack was reluctant to discuss his Native American background. In an era that also produced Jim Thorpe, Chief Meyers, and Chief Bender, Wheat's Indian blood was thought by some to be the primary reason for his athleticism. "The lithe muscles, the panther-like motions of the Indian are his by divine right," *Baseball Magazine* wrote.

After Basil Sr. died when Zack was 16, the Wheats moved to Kansas City, Kansas, where Zack got his start as a second baseman with the semipro Union Club. With his family nearly destitute, Zack set out to make a living as a ballplayer. In 1906 he went to Enterprise, Kansas, where he earned $60 per month playing for an independent team. That was followed by minor league stops in Ft. Worth, Shreveport, and Mobile. Wheat quickly won a reputation as a top-notch defensive outfielder but was lackluster at the plate; years later he attributed his minor league batting averages of .260 in 1908 and .246 in 1909 to malaria he suffered in the southern cities. Traveling home from Mobile after the 1908 season, Zack stopped in St. Louis on September 20 to attend his first major league game. It was a doozy: the Browns' Rube Waddell defeated Walter Johnson in 10 innings, 2-1, setting an American League record by striking out 17 batters. "After seeing those two pitchers, I wondered if I wanted to be a big leaguer and have to hit against pitchers like them," Wheat remembered. As it turned out, he didn't have to worry about Waddell or Johnson; Wheat was destined for the NL.

On the advice of scout Larry Sutton, Brooklyn purchased Wheat's contract from Mobile for a reported $1,200 on August 29, 1909, and that September Zack batted .304 in 26 games for the Superbas. "He is an Indian, but you would hardly guess it except from his dark complexion," wrote one newspaper shortly after Zack's arrival in Brooklyn. "He is a very fine fellow and a quiet and refined gentleman." In 1910, his first full major league season, Wheat finally became the offensive threat he'd never been in the minors, leading the Dodgers with a .284 average while ranking among the league leaders in hits (172), doubles (36), and triples (15). "I was young and inexperienced [in the minors]," Wheat explained. "The fellows that I played with encouraged me to bunt and beat the ball out. I was anxious to make good and did as I was told. When I came to Brooklyn I adopted an altogether different style of hitting. I stood flat-footed at the plate and slugged. That was my natural style."

Nobody could argue with the results. "The beauty of Wheat's hitting is that many of his drives go for extra bases," wrote one reporter. Wheat established himself as "one of the most dreaded and murderous sluggers in the National League," ranking among the league leaders in home runs every year from 1912 to 1916. He was far ahead of his time in many aspects of hitting, adopting strategies that weren't widely accepted until decades later. Zack was sometimes criticized for his reluctance to bunt, but he argued that he was more valuable to the team by swinging away. He also came to favor a lighter bat than many, which enabled him to generate more bat speed. "I am an arm hitter," he explained to F. C. Lane. "When you snap the bat with your wrists just as you meet the ball, you give the bat tremendous speed for a few inches of its course. The speed with which the bat meets the ball is the thing that counts."

On May 13, 1912, Wheat skipped a game at Cincinnati to marry Daisy Kerr Forsman, his 25-year-old second cousin, whom he'd met only two months earlier when the Dodgers played an exhibition series in her hometown of Louisville. When the Brooklyn players found out that the couple had eloped, they decorated a "bridal suite" on the team train to St. Louis. It was the start of a tradition: in later years Wheat's family almost always accompanied him on train trips to cities around the circuit. In marrying Daisy, Zack acquired not only a wife but an agent. "I made him hold out each year for seven years," Daisy remembered, "and each time he got a raise."

In the off-season Wheat raised livestock—during World War I he sold mules to the army to serve as pack animals on the battlefields of Europe—and he used his second job as leverage in contract negotiations. "I am a ball player in the summer and a farmer in the winter, and I aim to be a success at both professions," he proclaimed. Unless Brooklyn met his demands each spring, Zack was perfectly content to stay on his farm in Polo, Missouri. Because of his annual contract difficulties, trade rumors surrounded him almost every off-season. The Dodgers never pulled the trigger, though, perhaps because Brooklynites loved Wheat so much that, as one local newspaper wrote, "they regard Zach and his wife and his two children as members of their own families." By 1926, his last year with Brooklyn, Wheat was making the grand sum of $16,000 as player and assistant manager.

Later in 1912, Wheat recommended that Brooklyn sign an old friend of his from Kansas City, a former youth basketball teammate who was showing promise as a minor league outfielder. The Superbas agreed, and Wheat and his boyhood friend—Charles Dillon Stengel, better known as "Dutch"—played together in the Brooklyn outfield for six seasons. Later Stengel gave Wheat much of the credit for his success in baseball. "I never knew him to refuse help to another player, were he a Dodger or even a Giant," Stengel said. Wheat had a mild temperament on and off the field, and it was said that he'd never been ejected. "I never saw Wheat really angry," Stengel said, "and I never heard him use cuss words." Wheat, however, did have his vices. "I smoke as much as I want and chew tobacco a good deal of the time," he once said. "I don't pay any attention to the rules for keeping in physical condition. I think they are a lot of bunk. The less you worry about the effect of tea and coffee on the lining of your stomach, the longer you will live and the happier you will be."

In 1916 Wheat had a magnificent season, batting .312 while ranking among the NL leaders in virtually every offensive category. He also set a Brooklyn record by batting safely in 29 consecutive games. For the first time in Wheat's career the Dodgers found themselves in

BKLYN.

a pennant race. In the closing weeks of the season Wheat became so excited that he was unable to sleep. "I was thinking and dreaming and eating pennants," he recalled. "I used to get up in the middle of the night and smoke a cigar so that I could calm down a little and get some sleep." Brooklyn eked out the pennant but lost the World Series handily to Boston, as Red Sox pitchers held Wheat to a .211 batting average.

In 1919 Wheat was appointed captain of the Robins, and that season marked a turning point for both Wheat and the game he loved. Over the last decade of the Deadball Era, Wheat compiled more total bases than any other National Leaguer, and in hits he ranked second only to teammate Jake Daubert. But as great a Deadball hitter as he was, Wheat's powerful stroke enabled him to take advantage of the new lively ball like few others. In 1920 he led the Dodgers to the pennant while setting new career highs in hits (191), runs (89), and slugging percentage (.463). In the first six years of the Lively Ball Era he averaged .347. In 1923-24 Wheat posted back-to-back .375 batting averages, and in 1925 he had one of the best seasons ever by a 37-year-old: a .359 batting average with 125 runs, 221 hits, and a .541 slugging percentage.

A subtle but longstanding friction existed between Wheat and manager Wilbert Robinson, stemming largely from Robinson's belief that Wheat always seemed to be pursuing the manager's job behind his back. When Ebbets died in 1925, new team president Ed McKeever pushed Robinson into the front office and named Wheat as player-manager. Newspapers confirm that Zack managed the Dodgers for two weeks. But McKeever caught pneumonia at Ebbets' funeral, dying soon afterward, and Robinson returned to the helm. In 1931 Steve McKeever, Ed's brother, hired Wheat as a coach, leading to widespread speculation that he was being groomed for the manager's spot. His job threatened by Wheat for a second time in seven years, Robinson treated his former star as coldly as ever, but Wheat never again managed in the majors, much to his disappointment. When Zack was in his 70s, a reporter asked him why he hadn't stayed in baseball. "Nobody asked me to," he replied. To add insult to injury, Wheat's 1925 managerial stint never made it into the official records.

In 1927 the Dodgers decided they no longer needed Wheat. Because of his many years of service with the team, Brooklyn was obligated to release him rather than trade him so he could negotiate his own deal with whomever he chose. After being wooed by the Giants, Yankees, and Senators, Wheat signed a $15,000 contract with the Philadelphia Athletics and batted .324 in part-time duty there. In 1928 he signed with the Minneapolis Millers of the American Association, batting .309 before suffering a bruised heel that put him on the shelf for the season and, as it turned out, forever. Wheat decided to retire from baseball in 1929. At the time, his 2,884 hits were 10th on the all-time list, while his 4,100 total bases ranked ninth.

Wheat turned to farming full-time, but the Great Depression lowered prices so dramatically that in 1932 he was forced to sell his 160 acres for just $23,000. He moved his family to Kansas City, Missouri, where he operated a bowling alley for a time before becoming a patrolman with the Kansas City Police Department. He nearly died on Easter Sunday 1936 when he crashed his patrol car while chasing a fugitive, suffering a fractured skull, dislocated shoulder, broken wrist, and 15 broken ribs. After five months in the hospital, Wheat moved with his family to Sunrise Beach, Missouri, a resort town on the shores of the Lake of the Ozarks. Wheat spent the rest of his life in Sunrise Beach. An avid hunter, he opened a 46-acre hunting and fishing resort that became a popular destination for ex-ballplayers. One of his favorite activities was turning on his radio and television simultaneously to listen to two different ball games at once. Occasionally he and Daisy drove to Kansas City or St. Louis to see a game in person.

In 1957 Wheat was voted into the National Baseball Hall of Fame by the Veterans Committee, but there was only one problem. He was ineligible for election by the veterans because he'd been retired for less than the requisite 30 years. The committee rectified the mistake at its next meeting in 1959, when it unanimously elected the newly eligible Wheat. "That makes me feel mighty proud," the 70-year-old Wheat said. "I feel a little younger, too." Zack's joy turned to sadness later that year when he lost his wife, Daisy. Zack Wheat died on March 11, 1972, at a hospital in Sedalia, Missouri. Shortly before his death he was asked if he had any advice for youngsters with ball-playing aspirations. "Yes," he said. "Tell them to learn to chew tobacco."

ERIC ENDERS

Harry "Hy" Myers

BROOKLYN

Henry Harrison "Hy" Myers
Center fielder 1909, 1911, 1914–22

Effective as a leadoff man or in the middle of the order, Hy Myers was a speedy center fielder whose unique running style made him popular with fans wherever he played. "Myers galloped with his long arms held straight down by his sides, like a man running for a train with a heavy suitcase in each hand, or an authentic Irish dancer doing his stuff," wrote *New York World-Telegram* columnist Murray Robinson in 1954. "If you see any middle-aged Brooklynites gallumping for a bus with arms held straight down, you can bet they were Hi Myers fans in their youth." Yet the genial Ohio farmer drew little national attention in his playing days, and today his name is lost in the crowd of career .280-hitting outfielders of the Deadball Era. "He does his full share of spectacular stunts, is a good hitter and has an active, energetic manner that should attract attention to him," wrote a Brooklyn reporter in 1917, "but it is a fact that he is seldom mentioned in the winter stories or the rainy day dope."

Born in East Liverpool, Ohio, on April 27, 1889, Henry Harrison Myers broke in with Connellsville in the West Virginia-Pennsylvania League in 1909. On the strength of a .304 batting average, he was sold to Brooklyn on August 2 for a reported $300. He finished the season with the Superbas, appearing in six games and collecting five hits, but Myers was too green to suit Brooklyn boss Charley Ebbets and manager Harry Lumley. One thing that made them wince was his habit of tagging up on any fly ball, whether he had to or not. One day he was leading off second when the batter hit a long double. Myers could have scored easily, but by the time he went

back to touch second, then headed home, he was out at the plate.

For the next four years the Superbas shuttled him around the minors. In 1910 they optioned him to Rochester; three weeks later he was on his way to the Sioux City Packers. The fans loved his hustle in the field and on the bases and didn't care if he had trouble tracking fly balls. Myers batted .345, stole 33 bases, and hit an impressive nine home runs as the Packers won 108 games and the Western League pennant. The following spring Brooklyn optioned him to Toronto, which bounced him back to Brooklyn by way of two other stops. In his September 1911 recall, Myers got into 13 games but still didn't impress either Ebbets or new manager Bill Dahlen. Back he went to Sioux City, where the fans were thrilled to see him. Myers batted .336 and stole 41 bases. The Dodgers recalled him on August 20 but didn't give him any playing time. Then they shipped him off to Newark of the International League, where he played all of 1913 and half of 1914.

By that point Brooklyn had yet another manager, Wilbert Robinson. Uncle Robbie liked what he saw in Myers, despite a weakness for judging and getting a jump on fly balls. It took Myers all of 1915 to gain some mastery of that art, and for the next eight years he was Uncle Robbie's center fielder. What most endeared Myers to Robinson was his hustle and alertness. With a man on second, Myers occasionally would sneak in to take a throw from the catcher to try to catch an unwary base runner; he earned at least one putout that way in 1916. In another game that year, Robinson recalled, the ball was being thrown "all over creation, and three or four men were running at once. When the big play came at the plate, whoever had the ball fired it to the man at the pan, and when the dust had settled, the Superbas were as much astonished as the newspaper men to find that Hi had taken care of the pan."

Brooklyn won the 1916 pennant but lost the World Series to the Red Sox. In Game Two Myers hit an inside-the-park home run in the first inning off Boston lefty Babe Ruth. The Red Sox tied it in the third, and with the game still tied in the last of the ninth, Boston had men on first and third with no outs. A fly ball was hit to Myers, whose throw to the plate got Hal Janvrin trying to score from third. The double play postponed Boston's 2-1 victory and prolonged the game to 14 innings, still the longest in World Series history.

Myers' best years at the plate were 1919 and 1920; he led the league in triples both years and in slugging percentage (.436) and RBI (73) in the 140-game 1919 season. Brooklyn won another pennant in 1920 and Myers led the team with 80 RBI. He had two hits in Game Five of the World Series against Cleveland but wasn't involved in the unassisted triple play made by Indians second baseman Bill Wambsganss. "I was sitting in the dugout at the time," Myers recalled in a 1962 interview. "I can remember the play very vividly. There was a big hush over the fans. The crowd was stunned. Our players just stood there. No one left the field. It seemed like minutes before anyone realized what had happened."

In the winter of 1923, Cardinals manager Branch Rickey needed an outfielder and had a good first baseman, Jacques Fournier, to trade. According to contemporary accounts, Robinson gave Rickey a choice: Hy Myers or Zack Wheat. Myers would soon turn 34, and Wheat was 35. Rickey chose Myers. "Give Rickey Credit For This Good Deal" headlined the hometown *Sporting News*. Myers hit .300 in 96 games, .210 in limited service in 1924, and retired after appearing in five games in 1925. (Wheat batted .375 each of the next two years and was still hitting above .300 in 1927.)

After his baseball career, Myers went back to his farm in Kensington, Ohio. He ran an automobile agency, then worked as a guard in a steel mill, and later as a cashier at the Kensington State Bank. In 1958 he moved to the nearby town of Minerva, where he suffered a fatal heart attack on May 1, 1965. He was survived by his wife of 53 years, Elsie (Kibler) Myers, one son, two grandchildren, and one great-grandchild.

NORMAN MACHT

BROOKLYN

Jacob Ellsworth Daubert
First baseman 1910–18

J ake Daubert was the National League's greatest all-around first baseman of the Deadball Era, as demonstrated by his selection to *Baseball Magazine*'s All-America team seven times from 1911 to 1919. A speedy, left-handed chop-hitter who also was the NL's best bunter (his 392 career sacrifices are still the all-time NL record), Daubert won back-to-back batting championships in 1913-14 and hit over .300 in 10 of his 15 seasons in the major leagues. He was also an outstanding fielder. In an era when a first baseman's defensive ability was as important as his offense, F. C. Lane wrote that Daubert "is easily one of the greatest infielders baseball has ever seen." Critics frequently compared him to his American League counterpart, Hal Chase. "Flashing and sensational like Chase, Daubert is, unlike Chase, never erratic, never prone to sudden error, never sulky or indifferent in his play," wrote Lane.

Jacob Ellsworth Daubert was born in Shamokin, Pennsylvania, on April 7, 1884, the same coal mining town that produced Harry and Stan Coveleski. His father, Jacob Sr., was a mine worker for 57 years, and older brothers Irwin and Calvin followed in their father's footsteps, with Calvin losing his life in a mine accident. At age 11 Jake started working as a breaker boy, separating slate and other impurities from the coal. In 1905 he escaped the mines by joining a semipro baseball team from Lykens, Pennsylvania, starting out as a left-handed pitcher but soon moving to first base. The following year he played for Kane, Ohio, of the Class D Interstate League, making Jake a full-fledged professional.

When Kane disbanded on July 16, 1907, Daubert completed the season with Marion of the Ohio-Pennsylvania League. The following spring he went to training camp with the Cleveland Naps but was farmed out to Nashville of the Southern Association, which he led in home runs with six (tied with Harry Lord of New Orleans). After hitting just .186 in 35 games with Toledo of the American Association at the start of the 1909 season, Daubert returned to the Southern Association with Memphis. Experimenting with different stances to improve his offense, he bounced back to hit .314 over the second half. Scout Larry Sutton recommended him to the Brooklyn Superbas, who purchased his contract in the fall of 1909.

As a rookie in 1910 Daubert batted only .264, the second-lowest average of his long major league career, but he slugged 15 triples and eight homers, good enough to rank in the NL's top five in both categories. His power numbers were more attributable to his speed than strength; seven of his home runs were of the inside-the-park variety, and years later a question-and-answer column in *The Sporting News* stated that early in his career, before his legs went bad, Daubert was faster than Eddie Collins. In any event, it was a season to celebrate—which Jake did when he returned home in early November. According to *TSN*'s "Caught on the Fly" column, "Jake Daubert, the star first baseman of the Brooklyn National team, gave a banquet to a number of amateur base ball players of Schuykill county, former teammates at Pottsville, Pa., last week and presented each with a souvenir baseball of last season's National League games."

After back-to-back .300-plus seasons in 1911-12, Daubert batted a career-high .350 in 1913 to win not only his first batting championship but also the Chalmers Award as the NL's Most Valuable Player. He later admitted his success that season was due to his beating out an unusual number of infield hits. Jake also avoided extended slumps by employing a simple philosophy: "If you can't hit, bunt. Keep on bunting until you find you can hit once more." Daubert usually bunted down the third-base line; batting second in the order, he often advanced the runner even if he failed to beat out the bunt—and received credit for a sacrifice (and no time at-bat). "Jake Daubert was the greatest bunter I ever saw," said Phillies third baseman Milt Stock. "In his prime he could bunt almost at will. I don't know exactly what he did to the ball, but he seemed to put reverse English on it some way so that it would stop just where he wanted it to stop."

Daubert won his second batting championship in 1914 with a .329 average. Again he frequently relied on the bunt; on August 15, 1914, he set two records, one for most sacrifices in a game (4) and another for most sacrifices in a doubleheader (6). Often Jake bunted with two strikes when the opposition wasn't expecting it. "In 1914 when I led the League I bunted a third strike in three straight games," he remembered. "The first

was against the Giants. There was a man on first at the time I bunted the third strike. I advanced the runner to second and beat out the throw to first. The next man up hit safely, scoring the winning run from second base. Next day, with no one on and two strikes on me, I beat out a bunt and finally scored the winning run. That night we went to Boston. Next day Bill James was pitching and had a lot of stuff. I laid down a bunt that was just about right on a third strike but it rolled foul."

With all his on-field success, the modest, polite Daubert became a fan favorite, popular enough in Brooklyn to be nominated for alderman—though he lost the election. Respected by his teammates as well, Jake served as captain of the Brooklyn club in 1916, when it captured its first NL pennant of the Deadball Era. Sportswriters liked him because he could converse on a variety of subjects beyond baseball. Even opposing players respected Daubert, electing him to the board and vice-presidency of the Baseball Players Fraternity.

In 1917 the 33-year-old Daubert snapped a run of six consecutive .300-plus seasons, dropping 55 points from his average of the previous season to finish at .261. "It was a big slump," Jake recalled. "The papers figured I was nearly through. What was the real trouble? I had a lot of money invested in things that weren't turning out especially well, and I was worried. I had sickness in my family and that bothered me. I couldn't get these things out of my mind, and got run down and off my feed generally. I was lucky to hit .261." Daubert owned a variety of businesses, among them a poolroom, a movie house, a cigar store, an ice business, and a coal washery, and it was said that he made so much money that he didn't need to play baseball. "Nevertheless, knowing what I do of the endless troubles which business affairs cause a ball player," Jake said, "if I could begin where I began years ago with Brooklyn and someone should offer me a gold bar worth $1,000 for 10¢, I'd be strongly tempted to refuse the offer because I wouldn't want to let anything get me interested in outside affairs."

Rebounding to hit .308 with an NL-leading 15 triples during the war-shortened 1918 season, the savvy first baseman sued Brooklyn owner Charles Ebbets when the owners decided to end the season early and release their players without pay, claiming that Ebbets owed him the money because he was under a multiyear contract. The case was settled out of court, but Ebbets had the final say, trading Daubert to the Cincinnati Reds for outfielder Tommy Griffith in March 1919. The Reds named him captain and he led them to their first world championship that season, but he suffered a strained leg tendon and his batting average fell to .276. "My bad leg in itself is enough to account for most of my batting slump," Daubert said. "I have always been successful in beating out bunts and infield hits. Naturally in doing so I use a good degree of speed. If your speed is cut down even a little, you will be thrown out at first on the close ones. My bad leg has cut my batting average at least 30 points."

Daubert's leg recovered sufficiently to allow him to bat over .300 each year in 1920-22. Still with the Reds early in the 1924 season, the 40-year-old veteran suffered a serious beaning—one of at least eight in his career—on an Allen Sothoron fastball. "Either I am getting old, or a few rivets have worked loose in my skull, or Sothoron put more steam on that ball than I thought," Jake said when he was back in uniform. "Anyway, this eighth experience of mine was the worst of the lot. For several hours I couldn't see. And when my sight did return, it kept coming and going like switching an electric light on and off. Besides, blood oozed out of my ears and I developed a first-class headache that lasted for three weeks. I tried various remedies, but the thing that seemed to produce the best results was a simple massage." Jake batted .281 despite missing a good chunk of the season.

Already in a weakened condition because of the beaning, Daubert began suffering from what doctors thought was appendicitis and gallstones. When the season ended, he underwent surgery and a blood transfusion. Jake never recovered, passing away on October 9, 1924. He is buried in the Charles Baber Cemetery in Pottsville, Pennsylvania. Among the pallbearers who helped lay him to rest were Reds manager Jack Hendricks and teammates Rube Bressler, Edd Roush, Eppa Rixey, and, ironically, Carl Mays, who had thrown the beanball that fatally injured Cleveland shortstop Ray Chapman in 1920. Jake was survived by his wife, Gertrude, and two children, George and Louisa. Years later George started experiencing the same symptoms his father had in 1924. He was found to be suffering from a hereditary spleen condition, one that is easily controlled with modern medicine.

JIM SANDOVAL

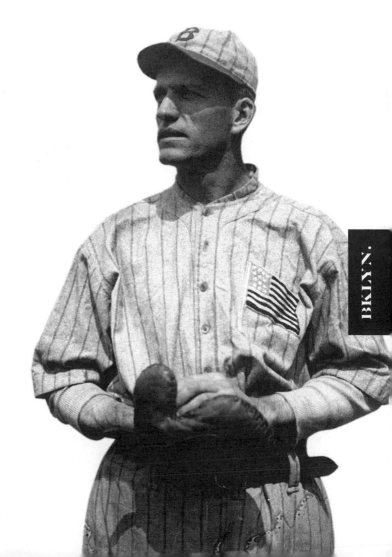

BROOKLYN

Charles Dillon "Casey" Stengel
Outfielder 1912–17

Casey Stengel is best remembered for his managerial accomplishments with the juggernaut New York Yankees of the 1950s and the bumbling, beloved New York Mets of the early '60s, but decades earlier he was a hard-hitting outfielder who compiled a .284 batting average over 14 NL seasons. Planting his right foot closer to the plate than his left, as if peering at the pitcher over his right shoulder, the left-handed Stengel held his hands down at the end of the bat and took a healthy swing. That enabled him to post a higher slugging percentage than most Deadball Era players, but it also made him susceptible to off-speed pitches. Perhaps the best aspect of his game was his defense; he excelled at playing the sun field and spent long hours practicing caroms off the unusual right-field fence at Ebbets Field.

Descended from German and Irish immigrants, Charles Dillon Stengel was born in Kansas City, Missouri, on July 30, 1890. His father made a steady living selling insurance, and Charley—known as "Dutch," a nickname that followed him to the majors—had an enjoyable childhood, much of it spent playing sandlot baseball. He was a star athlete at Central High School, leading the basketball team to the city championship and pitching the baseball team to the state championship. In 1910 Charley signed with the local Kansas City Blues of the American Association, perhaps the fastest minor league then going. His pitching skills weren't up to the level of competition, however, so manager Danny Shay moved him to the outfield. To give him some seasoning, Kansas City optioned Stengel to the Class D team in Kankakee, Illinois, where he batted .251 before the

Northern Association folded in July. For the rest of the season he hit .221 in the Blue Grass League.

When the season ended, Charley followed a friend to Western Dental College in Kansas City, using his potential career as a dentist to negotiate a raise for the 1911 season. The Blues assigned him to Aurora, Illinois, where he led the Wisconsin-Illinois League with a robust .352 average. Brooklyn's premier scout, Larry Sutton, liked what he saw in Stengel. The Dodgers bought him in the August draft and assigned him to Montgomery of the Southern Association for 1912.

At Montgomery Stengel fell under the tutelage of Kid Elberfeld, a veteran major leaguer who schooled the 21-year-old outfielder in the art of place hitting and other tactics of the "inside game." Charley started developing his reputation for eccentricity in the Southern Association; Senators scout Mike Kahoe called him a "dandy ballplayer, but it's all from the neck down." In one game he hid in a shallow hole in the outfield, covered by a lid; peeking out from under the lid, he suddenly popped out of the hole just in time to catch a fly ball that came his way. Stengel also took care of business, hitting .290 and leading the league in outfield assists. Brooklyn summoned him to the majors when the Southern Association season ended.

Stengel made an auspicious major league debut on September 17, 1912. Starting in center field, he singled four straight times, drew a walk, drove in two runs, and stole three bases as the Superbas beat the Pirates, 7-3. The next day Charley joined a poker game as the players waited out a rain delay. When he finally won a hand, one of his teammates said, "About time you took a pot, Kansas City." The other players caught on, calling the rookie "KC." After one week in the big leagues, Stengel had a new nickname, a .478 batting average, nine RBI, and a tremendous home run to right field that was said to be the longest hit in Brooklyn all season. Though Casey eventually cooled off, he still ended the season with a .316 batting average in 17 games.

Stengel held out until March 13, 1913, before Charles Ebbets finally sent him a contract that he found satisfactory. It didn't take Casey long to round into form. In an exhibition game against the crosstown Yankees on April 5, he became the first Brooklyn player to bat at Ebbets Field, and five innings later he hit the first home run at the park. A few weeks later Casey also hit the first regular-season home run. Suffering from a sprained ankle and a sore left shoulder that hindered his throwing, Stengel proved streaky and briefly lost his starting job to Bill Collins. He reclaimed center field by season's end, however, and finished the year at .272 with seven home runs and a career-high 19 stolen bases.

With newspapers reporting that the Federal League's Kansas City franchise was interested in the hometown star, Ebbets offered Stengel a three-year contract at almost double his previous salary. Casey opted for a one-year deal instead, believing that he'd have more bargaining power if he stayed healthy in 1914. In January he went to Mississippi to rehabilitate his sore shoulder and assist his old Central High coach, William Driver, who was coaching baseball at the University of Mississippi. (That stint with the college team, incidentally, is how Casey originally came to be called "Professor.") New manager Wilbert Robinson moved Stengel to right field and eventually platooned him, first with Joe Riggert and later with Hy Myers. Playing only against right-handed pitching, Casey improved his

average to .316 and led the NL with a .404 on-base percentage. The Robins rewarded him with a two-year contract and a substantial raise.

Stengel reported to training camp in March 1915 at 157 lbs., 20 pounds below his usual playing weight. The official explanation was typhoid fever, but sportswriters later hinted that it was actually a venereal disease. Casey was in the starting lineup on Opening Day 1915 but was still weak. His batting average dipped as low as the .150s before he finally broke out of his slump in July, finishing at .237, the lowest average of his career. Stengel rebounded in 1916, and teammate Chief Meyers in *The Glory of Their Times* said he deserved credit for winning the pennant. In a late-season showdown with the second-place Phillies, Stengel homered off Pete Alexander to lead Brooklyn to victory. Platooned with Jimmy Johnston in right field, Casey ranked third on the club in batting (.279), runs (66), and RBI (53) and led Brooklyn with a .364 average during the World Series.

Despite his and the team's success, Stengel found himself locked in another contract dispute with Ebbets. The Brooklyn owner became infuriated when Casey returned his contract unsigned with a note stating that he must have been sent the clubhouse attendant's contract by mistake. Stengel ended up signing just two weeks before the season. Playing in a career-high 151 games, he led the Robins in runs (69), RBI (73), doubles (23), triples (12), and homers (6). Nevertheless, on January 9, 1918, Ebbets, weary of Stengel's annual holdouts, traded him and second baseman George Cutshaw to the Pirates for pitchers Burleigh Grimes and Al Mamaux and infielder Chuck Ward.

Stengel quickly became disenchanted with Pittsburgh. During his first return to New York, his old teammate Leon Cadore told him about military life. Casey decided to enlist and spent the remainder of the war at the Brooklyn Navy Yard, running its baseball team. When the war ended, he became embroiled in another salary dispute, this time with Pirates owner Barney Dreyfuss. Casey unsuccessfully argued that he deserved a raise despite appearing in only 39 games and batting just .246 the previous season. He got off to a good start in 1919, his average hovering near .300 when the Pirates arrived in Brooklyn in May. During a Sunday game Casey was having a rough time—he struck out twice and missed a long fly that allowed three runs to score—and the crowd was letting him have it. On his way to the bench at the end of the sixth inning, he saw his old friend Cadore in the bullpen, holding a sparrow. Casey placed the bird in his cap, and when he came to bat in the top of the seventh he acknowledged the crowd's boos by tipping his cap— and releasing the sparrow.

Dreyfuss wasn't amused. On August 9 he traded Stengel to the Philadelphia Phillies for Possum Whitted. Predictably, Casey demanded a salary increase from the Phillies owner, returning home to Kansas City and spending the rest of the year barnstorming when his demand was refused. Stengel finally reported to the Phillies in 1920 and put together a solid season, batting .292 with a career-high nine home runs in 129 games. In 1921 he began to be plagued by injuries, particularly to his legs; by June 30 he'd batted only 59 times. When the trainer handed him some papers, Casey thought he was being sent to the minors. Instead he read that he'd been traded to the New York Giants.

Stengel served mainly as a pinch-hitter for the Giants in 1921, but injuries to two outfielders made him the regular center fielder in June 1922 and he batted .368 in 84 games. In 1923 his average stood at .379 on May 7 when he was suspended for 10 games for brawling with Phillies pitcher Phil Weinert. For two months Casey saw little action, but in July he got another opportunity to play center field because Jimmy O'Connell was slumping. He hit safely in 20 of the next 22 games and won the starting position. For the third straight year the Giants won the pennant and met the Yankees in the World Series. Stengel's inside-the-park home run in the ninth inning won Game One, and his home run in Game Three was the only run scored. It was his last hurrah as a Giant—one month later he was traded to the Boston Braves.

Stengel batted .280 in 131 games in 1924, but in 1925 he was hitting only .077 when the Braves sent him

to Worcester, Massachusetts, as player-manager. For the next six years he managed the Toledo Mud Hens, playing sporadically and mostly concentrating on managing. Released after the 1931 season, Casey signed on as a coach with his old Pirate teammate Max Carey, who'd just been named to replace Wilbert Robinson as Brooklyn manager. Two years later Casey became manager when Carey was fired. He lasted three years, never finishing higher than fifth, and was let go at the end of the 1936 season. Casey spent 1937 traveling. He returned to baseball the next year as manager and part-owner of the Boston Braves. Casey stayed until 1944, then managed in the minors for four more years.

The baseball world was shocked by the announcement that Casey Stengel would manage the New York Yankees in 1949. Though he had piloted the Oakland Oaks to the Pacific Coast League championship in 1948, he was widely regarded as a clown and a failure as a manager, never finishing in the first division in his nine years at the helm of a big-league club. All Casey did was win 10 pennants and seven World Series before his firing at age 70 in 1960. Turning down an offer to manage the Detroit Tigers, Stengel seemed headed for retirement until George Weiss, also released by the Yankees, invited him to manage the expansion New York Mets. On July 24, 1965, Stengel fell at a party at Toots Shor's restaurant and broke his hip. Following the advice of his wife, the former Edna Lawson (whom he'd married in 1924), Casey decided it was finally time to retire. He was elected to the National Baseball Hall of Fame in 1966 and returned to Cooperstown every year for the induction ceremonies. By 1975 he had slowed considerably and was diagnosed with a form of lymphatic cancer. Casey Stengel died on September 29, 1975, in a hospital in Glendale, California. He and Edna are buried together in a Glendale cemetery.

BILL BISHOP

BKLYN.

BROOKLYN

Edward J. Pfeffer

EDWARD JAMES "JEFF" PFEFFER
RIGHT-HANDED PITCHER 1913–21

Jeff Pfeffer—not to be confused with his older brother Big Jeff Pfeffer, who also pitched in the big leagues but won 127 fewer games—possessed many of the qualities of Jim Jeffries, the heavyweight boxer who inspired his nickname. An intimidating presence at 6'3" and a listed (though likely much greater) weight of 210 lbs., Pfeffer refused to let opposing hitters dig in at the plate. He beaned a total of 50 batters in 1915-17, leading the National League twice in that category. After nearly ruining Chick Fewster's career by hitting him in the head in an exhibition game, Pfeffer was hardly apologetic. "It was a very unfortunate affair, but as I certainly had no intention of hitting this batter, I could not blame myself," he said. "It was merely my bad luck to be mixed up in such an accident."

The youngest of seven sons, Edward James Pfeffer was born in Seymour, Illinois, on March 4, 1888. All seven of the Pfeffer boys were athletes—at one time four of them started for a local semipro baseball team—but the last two went on to the greatest athletic achievements. Francis X. Pfeffer, who was six years older than Edward, won 31 games over five seasons with Boston and Chicago in the National League. He is best remembered for throwing a no-hitter against the Cincinnati Reds on May 8, 1907, a feat that his more successful younger brother never accomplished. Frank also was the first of the Pfeffers to be called "Jeff" because of a striking resemblance to Jim Jeffries. The similarly featured Edward didn't receive the nickname until he pitched for the St. Bede's College team in 1907.

Leaving college after only two years, Edward "Jeff" Pfeffer became an 18-game winner in his first year as a professional with La Crosse of the Minnesota-Wisconsin League in 1909. He moved up to Ft. Wayne of the Central League in 1910, winning a combined 29 games over the next two campaigns. The St. Louis Browns purchased Pfeffer's contract near the end of 1911 and pitched him in 10 innings. Unimpressed with his 7.20 ERA, the Browns sold him to Denver, which in turn sent him back to the Central League with Grand Rapids. There Pfeffer blossomed into a star in 1913, winning 25 games and gaining the attention of New York Giants scout Dick Kinsella. "Sinister Dick" passed on Jeff, however, preferring his teammate Cy Pieh, who went on to win a grand total of nine big-league games. Brooklyn took advantage of Kinsella's gaffe, signing Pfeffer on August 6, 1913. He pitched in five games over the balance of that season and lost his only decision.

The Brooklyn team that Pfeffer joined was gradually coalescing into a contender. Though the Robins remained in the second division in 1914, the 26-year-old right hander posted a 23-12 record and 1.97 ERA in 315 innings as both a starter and reliever, establishing himself as the ace of a pitching staff that had previously been headed by veterans Nap Rucker and Ed Reulbach. The next year Brooklyn finished third, thanks in large part to Pfeffer's 19-14 mark and the 14-8 record of rookie left hander Sherry Smith, a former minor league teammate whom Jeff had recommended to the Robins. On October 3, 1916, Smith started a potential pennant clincher against the Giants but was knocked from the box in the early going. Jeff came through with a strong relief performance, earning Brooklyn the NL championship with a 9-6 win. That game capped off Pfeffer's greatest all-around season: he ranked second in the NL in wins (25), complete games (30), innings pitched (328⅔), and shutouts (6); third in winning percentage (.694); and fifth in ERA (1.92). He even batted .279, 73 points above his lifetime average.

In the 1916 World Series Wilbert Robinson refused to start Pfeffer in either of the first two games in Boston, preferring to go with left handers. Relegated to the bullpen, Jeff pitched only one inning in the first two games and was passed over again when Robinson chose veteran Jack Coombs to start Game Three in Brooklyn. Pfeffer did play a crucial role in that game, relieving Coombs in the seventh with the Robins clinging to a 4-3 lead. He shut down the Red Sox in order the rest of the way, striking out three of eight hitters and saving Brooklyn's only victory of the Series. In Game Five, with Brooklyn facing elimination, Robinson finally started his ace. Pfeffer pitched admirably for seven innings, limiting Boston to just six hits in a 4-1 defeat.

During his years in Brooklyn, Jeff Pfeffer could be ornery—decades later George Daubert, the team's bat-boy and son of first baseman Jake Daubert, revealed that Pfeffer terrorized him by chasing him out of the dugout following defeats—but he wasn't humorless. During a heated card game, a left-handed teammate wisecracked that one of Brooklyn's southpaws had played a hand poorly, or "just like a right hander." Without looking up from his cards, Pfeffer asked, "So, you think left handers are pretty smart, do you?" The teammate replied, "Well, you don't see any of them digging a ditch, now do you?" Pfeffer quietly answered, "That's because they want the ditches dug straight."

In 1917 Pfeffer slumped to 11-15 despite posting a 2.23 ERA. After the season he announced that he planned to join the Navy. As a token of gratitude, Brooklyn owner Charles Ebbets took money from a fund he'd set up for dependents of ballplayers in the military and bought the big pitcher an engraved wristwatch. At the 1918 training camp in Hot Springs, however, Ebbets was surprised and angered to see Pfeffer in a Brooklyn uniform, proudly displaying the watch; the pitcher had opted for a more convenient post in the Naval Auxiliary Reserves. As it turned out, Pfeffer pitched in only one game in 1918—a 2-0 shutout over the eventual pennant-winning Cubs—before his unit was activated. He returned to the Robins and won 33 games in 1919-20, but Ebbets held his grudge.

Just as in 1916, Robinson again passed over Pfeffer in the 1920 World Series (he made only one three-inning relief appearance), and Jeff actively lobbied for a trade that winter. Returning to Brooklyn in 1921, Jeff won only one of his first six decisions and was bounced from the rotation by Memorial Day. With the watch incident reportedly still in his memory, Ebbets dealt his former ace to St. Louis on June 18, 1921, for pitcher Ferdie Schupp and infielder Hal Janvrin. Pfeffer experienced a rejuvenation with the Cardinals, finishing 1921 with a 9-3 record and winning 19 games in 1922 while making a career-high 44 appearances.

That season was Pfeffer's major league swan song. After slipping to 8-9 in 1923, he was released to Pittsburgh in May 1924 and was out of the majors for good by the following spring. After pitching three seasons in the minors with the San Francisco Seals (1925) and Toledo Mud Hens (1926-27), Jeff remained in baseball for several seasons as an umpire in the American Association. He then returned to farm in his native Illinois, and also took a turn as a restaurant owner in the Chicago area. A quiet man, Pfeffer lived a solitary bachelor life, enjoying the outdoors as an avid hunter and fisherman. His later years were spent as a security officer at the Drake Hotel in Chicago. Pfeffer passed away on August 15, 1972.

JOHN BENNETT

Wilbert Robinson

BROOKLYN

WILBERT ROBINSON
MANAGER 1914–31

Though an outstanding catcher for the Baltimore Orioles during the 1890s, Wilbert Robinson is best remembered as the jovial, rotund "Uncle Robbie" who managed the Brooklyn Robins to two National League pennants and a 1,375-1,341 record from 1914 to 1931. His congeniality and happy-go-lucky attitude made him one of the most beloved characters in baseball, but on the diamond he was a never-say-die competitor who specialized in getting the most out of his pitchers. "It is doubtful that baseball ever produced a more colorful figure than the esteemed Robinson," wrote John Kieran in the *New York Times*. "Like Falstaff, he was not only witty himself but the cause of wit in others. His conversation was a continuous flow of homely philosophy, baseball lore, and good humor."

One of seven children of Henry and Lucy Robinson, Wilbert Robinson was born on June 29, 1863, in Bolton, Massachusetts. Wilbert (then known as "Billy Rob") inherited his father's butcher shop in 1883 but his heart was in baseball, not beef. Following in the footsteps of his older brother Fred, who played three games for Cincinnati of the Union Association in 1884, 22-year-old Billy Rob signed with Haverhill of the Eastern New England League in 1885. He batted .269 in a league in which nobody hit .300 and demonstrated his natural leadership ability. "Robinson was a great catcher from the first day we placed him behind the bat, but to my mind his greatest quality was, and is, his personality," recalled Haverhill manager William Prince. "His good nature was a sure remedy to drive away all the blues, and he drew us together as a sociable, harmonious club."

The following year Robinson joined the Philadelphia Athletics of the American Association. Strapped for cash toward the end of 1890, the Athletics sold him and star pitcher Sadie McMahon to the Baltimore Orioles. After batting just .216 in his first full year as an Oriole, the 29-year-old backstop raised his average to .267 in 1892. On June 10 of that season Robbie enjoyed one of the finest offensive games in the history of baseball, driving in 11 runs and racking up seven hits in seven at-bats, a record that has been matched only once—by Rennie Stennett in 1975. Over the next seven seasons in Baltimore, the 5'8", 215 lb. catcher hit .312, including a career-high .353 in 1894.

During his years with the Orioles, Robinson developed a close and long-lasting friendship with teammate John McGraw, who was 10 years younger. The two men eventually went into business together, opening the Diamond Café, a Baltimore billiards parlor that included a bar, dining room, and bowling alley. Under a joint ownership arrangement, Baltimore manager Ned Hanlon and star players Joe Kelley, Willie Keeler, and Hughie Jennings moved to Brooklyn in 1899, but Robinson and McGraw insisted on staying behind. When the season ended and they again refused to move to Brooklyn, they were traded to the St. Louis Cardinals. Robinson and McGraw spent 1900 in St. Louis, then returned to Baltimore in 1901 to play for the new Orioles of the AL, with McGraw serving as player-manager. After hitting .301 during the AL's inaugural season, Robbie took over the reins as manager on July 8, 1902, when McGraw left to manage the New

301

York Giants. The big catcher batted .293 in 91 games during his final season as a major league player.

Robinson remained in Baltimore, tending to his business affairs and catching for Baltimore's Eastern League franchise through July 1904. In 1909, after four and a half years away from baseball, he accepted an invitation to go to spring training with McGraw's Giants and work with the pitchers. Robbie did the same thing in 1910, and in midseason the following year he signed on as a full-time coach. His main duties were keeping the club loose, jockeying the opposition, and developing the pitching staff—pet projects included Rube Marquard, Jeff Tesreau, and Al Demaree. Robinson remained with the Giants through 1913, though he and McGraw quarreled throughout that last season. At a reunion with some old-time Orioles at a New York saloon after the last game of the 1913 World Series, McGraw got drunk and criticized Robinson's third-base coaching in that day's 3-1 loss to the Athletics. Robinson snapped back that McGraw's managing had been pretty lousy, too. "This is my party. Get the hell out of here," snarled McGraw. Robbie showered him with a glass of beer on the way out.

About a month later Robinson signed to manage the Brooklyn Dodgers, which soon became known as the Robins. He managed the club for the next 18 years, winning pennants in 1916 and 1920 but finishing in the second division 12 times. Developing a great rapport with his players, "Uncle Robbie" seemed to get the most out of unproven youngsters and over-the-hill castoffs, sometimes challenging for pennants when nobody expected him to. But even during the bad years, Robbie gained some measure of satisfaction if his club helped prevent McGraw's Giants from winning the pennant; though the two old friends shook hands for cameramen, neither made any effort to mend the rift between them.

The single incident for which Robinson is most famous occurred during Brooklyn's 1915 training camp in Daytona Beach, Florida. A female aviator, Ruth Law, was making daily flights in the area, dropping golf balls as a publicity gimmick for a local golf course, and eventually the talk in camp turned to the idea of catching a baseball dropped from the plane. Though none of his players was brave enough to try, Robinson, three months shy of his 52nd birthday, accepted the challenge. On the big day, Law forgot the baseball back in her hotel room. At the last minute she substituted a grapefruit from the lunch of one of her ground crew. The grapefruit landed in Robinson's mitt and exploded, knocking him down and drenching him in its juice. Thinking he was covered in his own blood, Robbie called for help. The players rushed over and began laughing when they realized what had happened. Robinson always suspected that Casey Stengel or trainer Fred Kelly had played a prank on him, and Casey later claimed that he'd been the one to drop the grapefruit, but Law herself told the true story in an interview published in 1957.

When Brooklyn owner and president Ed McKeever passed away in 1925, his heirs held a directors meeting and voted to give Robinson a new three-year contract as manager and president, along with a hefty raise in salary. Wilbert held both positions for the next five years, a period during which the Brooklyn team became known as the "Daffy Dodgers." Apocryphal stories abound from that period, tending to portray Robinson as the tolerant, easygoing Uncle Robbie or, worse, as some sort of comic buffoon. In reality he was still a sound baseball man who was simply overwhelmed by the responsibilities of his dual roles. Robbie probably felt relief when the Robins replaced him as president in 1929, allowing him to focus on managing.

Robinson and McGraw finally reconciled at the National League winter meetings in December 1930, ending their 17-year feud. Robbie remained on as Brooklyn manager through the end of the 1931 season, after which he left for his hunting camp, Dover Hall, near Brunswick, Georgia. He wasn't there long when he received word that the Dodgers had replaced him with Max Carey. In 1932 Robbie became president of the Atlanta Crackers of the Southern Association, serving for two seasons.

In early August 1934 Robinson fell in his hotel room, hitting his head on the bathtub and breaking his arm. While being administered to, he uttered his most famous line: "Don't worry about it, fellas. I'm an old Oriole. I'm too tough to die." He was wrong. Having suffered a brain hemorrhage, Wilbert Robinson succumbed in Atlanta on August 8, 1934, with his wife at his bedside. It was just five months and 11 days after the death of McGraw. The two old Orioles are buried at New Cathedral Cemetery in Baltimore.

ALEX SEMCHUCK

BROOKLYN

Ivan Massie Olson
Infielder 1915–24

Sportswriter Murray Robinson described Ivy Olson as "a spike-scarred, swarthy veteran with a barrel chest, high shoulders, a sharp nose and chin, and piercing black eyes. All he needed to make him look like a pirate of old was a bandana on his head, a patch over one eye, and a cutlass instead of a bat." An erratic fielder and lifetime .258 hitter without much power or speed, Olson tried to make up for what he lacked in natural ability with an overdeveloped sense of spirit and aggressiveness. "I believe that spirit is more important than mechanical ability," Ivy said. "Let a player hit only .200, let him make more mechanical errors than anybody else on the team, but so long as he has the nerve and determination to win, give him to me in preference to some other fellow with twice his natural talent but without his heart."

Of Swedish descent, Ivan Massie Olson was born on October 14, 1885, in Kansas City, Missouri. One of his schoolmates, though five years younger, was Charles Dillon Stengel, who later became his teammate with the Brooklyn Robins. Casey remembered Ivy as a dominant bully, the toughest kid in school. Olson ran a game of reverse tug-of-war in which two teams lined up along a wooden fence and pushed, and if he felt a boy wasn't pushing hard enough, he'd pull him out and shove another in his place. In addition to being a force on the playground, Ivy also was a tough semipro baseball player. In 1906 he made his debut in Organized Baseball with Muskogee, Oklahoma, of the South Central League. Receiving a midseason promotion to Webb City, Missouri, of the Western Association, Olson batted .136 in 44 games at third base. For some reason Webb City gave him a second chance in 1907, and he batted .221 while committing 66 errors in 133 games at shortstop.

Olson improved his batting average to .254 in his third year in the Western Association, earning a promotion to the Portland Beavers of the Pacific Coast League for 1909. He played in 415 games over the next two seasons, averaging nearly 800 at-bats per year, but the rest of his statistics weren't nearly as impressive. Nonetheless Ivy received an invitation to spring training with the Cleveland Naps.

Ivy Olson became Cleveland's regular shortstop in 1911, batting .261 but committing 73 errors in 140 games. The following year manager Harry Davis named him captain. The 26-year-old Olson was so confident of his own abilities that he advised Nap Lajoie on how to field grounders and Joe Jackson on how to improve his batting. After convening a secret meaning, his not-so-endeared teammates demanded a change. The next day center fielder Joe Birmingham was named captain, and he subsequently replaced Davis as manager. Olson held on with Cleveland for a total of four seasons. He played a significant number of games at all four infield positions, but each year his batting average fell slightly, as did his playing time.

After the 1914 season, in which Olson batted .242 in 89 games, the Naps sold his contract to the Cincinnati Reds. Announcing the acquisition, one reporter wrote that he was "one of the best infielders and general utility men in the business. He is not a very hard hitter, but a dangerous one. As a base runner he is neither fast nor slow, but is a good man on the sacks. He is a very smart ballplayer and is always out to win. Manager Herzog made a strong play in securing him." Could there be a more muddied description of mediocrity? As if to live up to his billing, Olson batted .232 in 63 games with the Reds before the Brooklyn Robins picked him up on waivers on July 17, 1915. Ivy played

303

in only 18 games over the rest of the season, batting .077 with a .909 fielding percentage. His love-hate affair with the Ebbets Field natives had begun.

"In the sphere of inverted love, no hometown butt was ever denounced more passionately and fondly than Olson," wrote John Lardner. "In Ivy the fans saw themselves and the humble fortunes of the team as a whole. Booing him was part of Brooklyn's way of life." Ivy had an interesting way of dealing with the jeers and cheers of the Flatbush faithful: he stuffed his ears with cotton. When he made a terrific play, he'd take the cotton out to hear the huzzahs, then stuff it back in again with a grin—which endeared him to the crowd even more. In another of his idiosyncrasies, Olson reportedly carried a rulebook in his back pocket in each of his 1,574 games in the majors. During an umpire's oration, he'd take out the book and rifle through the pages with a flourish, often getting ejected before he could reach the appropriate reference.

Olson replaced Ollie O'Mara as Brooklyn's regular shortstop in 1916. One week into the season he engaged in a classic battle with Rabbit Maranville, who tried to knock the ball out of his glove on a tag play. "Olson resented this and promptly began to bang Maranville on the shins with the ball," the *New York Times* reported. "This was the signal for the real fun, Maranville's punch for the head missing its mark but striking Ivan on the knee. Then Ivan's return sweep whizzed past the Rabbit's head. Umpire Rigler, who had followed the play, jumped after Olson, grabbing him about the neck and pulling him away, while half a dozen ball players made a circle around Maranville. Both men wanted to continue, but Rigler evidently figured that the gate was too small and the 800 fans had had enough for their money."

Ivy's fire helped spark the Robins to the 1916 NL pennant, but in that year's World Series he committed four errors in five games. Olson's defense became a running joke among the Red Sox; from the bench they chanted, "when in doubt, hit it to Ivy." In the third inning of Game Six Olson fumbled a grounder, allowing Hal Janvrin to reach base; then he threw the ball to second when there was no one covering the bag, allowing the runners to advance. Though others have made three errors in one World Series game, only Ivy and Willie Davis in 1966 have the distinction of making two on the same play. (Olson remained notoriously error prone during his nine and one-half seasons in Brooklyn; one newspaper account notes that one of his errant throws hit manager Wilbert Robinson in the paunch as he dozed in the dugout, waking him up.)

Brooklyn lost again in the 1920 World Series against the Cleveland Indians, but Olson redeemed himself by batting .320 without a single error in any of the seven games against his former team.

Ivy Olson enjoyed his best season in 1919, when he batted a career-high .278 and led the NL with 164 hits. He remained Brooklyn's regular shortstop until partway through the 1922 season, when he switched over to second base. Olson played sparingly in 1924, his last year in the majors as an active player. After sitting out the 1925 season, he served as player-manager for Sarasota of the Florida State League in 1926 and Pocatello of the Utah-Idaho League in 1927 before returning to Brooklyn as a coach through 1931. Ivy coached third base for the Giants during the first half of the 1932 season but was let go in July.

At that point Olson and his wife and daughter moved to the West Coast. Along with 14 other members of the 1916 Robins, Ivy went back to Brooklyn for the 1949 World Series to see his old team play the New York Yankees, who were managed, of course, by former teammate Stengel. The still swaggering 64-year-old loved the attention and cheers of the Ebbets Field faithful. Ivy Olson lived almost 16 more years, passing away in Inglewood, California, on September 1, 1965.

BRIAN STEVENS

BOSTON

Located near the Charles River on what is now the campus of Boston University, Braves Field hosted National League baseball from 1915 to 1952.

Having won five pennants from 1891 to 1898, the Boston Nationals entered the Deadball Era as one of baseball's most successful franchises. The 1901 squad retained some of those champion Beaneaters—Frank Selee, Billy Hamilton, and Kid Nichols—but during the prior off-season Jimmy Collins, Buck Freeman, and Chick Stahl had all jumped to the fledgling Boston Americans. The Americans placed second in 1901 while the Nationals fell to fifth, after which Selee was fired and his aging team broken up.

By the end of 1904 the Nationals had tumbled all the way to seventh, their lowest finish in 29 years in the NL, but the worst was yet to come. Boston finished last in 1906, 66½ games behind the pennant-winning Cubs, and from 1909 to 1912, leading the league in errors and losing 100 or more games in each of those seasons. During that dismal stretch the team went through three nicknames—"Doves," in reference to owner George Dovey; "Rustlers," an even shorter-lived moniker honoring owner William Russell; and finally "Braves," a term for members of the Tammany Hall machine, inspired by owner James Gaffney, a New York contractor with Tammany connections.

In addition to inspiring a permanent nickname for the franchise, Gaffney made another significant contribution by hiring George Stallings as manager in 1913.

WINNING PERCENTAGE 1901–1919

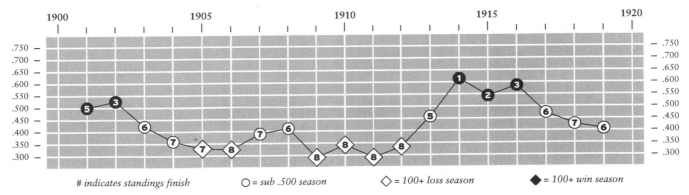

# indicates standings finish ○ = sub .500 season ◇ = 100+ loss season ◆ = 100+ win season

Stallings inherited young talent like Rabbit Maranville, Hank Gowdy, and Lefty Tyler, and to them he added pitchers Bill James and Dick Rudolph. In his first year the Braves improved to fifth, their highest position in 11 seasons.

Expectations ran high for 1914, especially after Boston acquired Johnny Evers during the off-season, but the Braves quickly fell to last with 18 losses in their first 22 games. That's where they remained until July 19. At that time they took off on one of the greatest pennant drives in baseball history, snapping the New York Giants' string of three straight NL championships. To complete their dream season, the "Miracle Braves" won the World Series by sweeping the heavily favored Philadelphia Athletics, who'd won four AL pennants in five years.

Some considered the Braves "fluke champions," but they remained competitive after moving from the decrepit South End Grounds to spacious Braves Field in 1915. Despite the illness of James, who proved to be a "one-year wonder," and injuries to Evers and newly acquired slugger Sherry Magee, Stallings kept his scrappy club around the top of the standings for two more seasons. In 1917 the Braves sank toward the bottom again, where they'd spent most of the Deadball Era, and 1914's miracle pennant was the last until 1948 for Boston's once proud NL franchise.

ALL-ERA TEAM

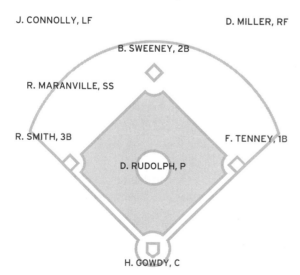

G. BEAUMONT, CF

J. CONNOLLY, LF   D. MILLER, RF

B. SWEENEY, 2B

R. MARANVILLE, SS

R. SMITH, 3B   F. TENNEY, 1B

D. RUDOLPH, P

H. GOWDY, C

TEAM LEADERS 1901–1919

BATTING

GAMES
F. Tenney	1062
R. Maranville	913
B. Sweeney	902

RUNS
F. Tenney	589
R. Maranville	396
B. Sweeney	396

HITS
F. Tenney	1125
B. Sweeney	902
R. Maranville	855

RBI
B. Sweeney	350
R. Smith	314
R. Maranville	304

DOUBLES
B. Sweeney	139
F. Tenney	131
R. Smith	124

TRIPLES
R. Maranville	57
F. Tenney	39
B. Sweeney	35

HOME RUNS
R. Maranville	20
P. Moran	16
D. Brain	15

STOLEN BASES
B. Sweeney	153
R. Maranville	143
F. Tenney	128

BATTING AVERAGE
D. Miller	.299
J. Connolly	.289
G. Beaumont	.288

PITCHING

GAMES
D. Rudolph	249
L. Tyler	247
V. Willis	206

WINS
D. Rudolph	116
L. Tyler	92
V. Willis	89

LOSSES
V. Willis	109
D. Rudolph	95
L. Tyler	92

INNINGS
D. Rudolph	1909⅓
L. Tyler	1687⅔
V. Willis	1685⅓

STRIKEOUTS
V. Willis	828
L. Tyler	827
D. Rudolph	747

WALKS
L. Tyler	678
T. Pittinger	491
V. Willis	483

SHUTOUTS
D. Rudolph	26
L. Tyler	22
V. Willis	18

ERA
D. Rudolph	2.53
V. Willis	2.70
T. Pittinger	2.90

BOS.

Braves manager George Stallings is flanked by his 1914 pitching stalwarts Bill James and Dick Rudolph.

TYPICAL LINEUPS 1901–1919

1901

1. J. Slaglc, RF
2. F. Tenney, 1B
3. G. DeMontreville, 2B
4. D. Cooley, LF
5. B. Hamilton, CF
   F. Murphy, LF
6. B. Lowe, 3B
7. H. Long, SS
8. M. Kittridge, C

1902

1. B. Lush, CF
2. F. Tenney, 1B
3. D. Cooley, LF
4. P. Carney, RF
5. E. Gremminger, 3B
6. G. DeMontreville, 2B
7. H. Long, SS
8. M. Kittridge
   P. Moran, C

1903

1. C. Dexter, CF
2. F. Tenney, 1B
3. D. Cooley, LF
4. P. Carney, RF
5. P. Moran, C
6. E. Abbaticchio, 2B
7. E. Gremminger, 3B
8. H. Aubrey, SS

1904

1. P. Geier, CF
2. F. Tenney, 1B
3. E. Abbaticchio, SS
4. D. Cooley, LF
5. J. Delahanty, 3B
6. F. Raymer, 2B
7. R. Cannell, RF
8. T. Needham
   P. Moran, C

1905

1. E. Abbaticchio, SS
2. F. Tenney, 1B
3. C. Dolan, RF
4. J. Delahanty, LF
5. H. Wolverton, 3B
6. R. Cannell, CF
7. F. Raymer, 2B
8. P. Moran
   T. Needham, C

1906

1. A. Bridwell, SS
2. F. Tenney, 1B
3. D. Brain, 3B
4. J. Bates, CF
5. D. Howard, LF
6. C. Dolan, RF
7. T. Needham, C
8. A. Strobel, 2B

1907

1. A. Bridwell, SS
2. F. Tenney, 1B
3. D. Brain, 3B
4. G. Beaumont, CF
5. J. Bates, RF
6. N. Randall, LF
7. C. Ritchey, 2B
8. T. Needham, C

1908

1. G. Browne, RF
2. G. Beaumont, CF
3. J. Bates, LF
4. D. McGann, 1B
5. C. Ritchey, 2B
6. B. Dahlen, SS
7. B. Sweeney, 3B
8. F. Bowerman
   P. Graham, C

1909

1. R. Thomas, LF
2. B. Becker, RF
3. D. Shean, 2B
4. G. Beaumont, CF
5. B. Sweeney, 3B
6. F. Stem, 1B
7. J. Coffey, SS
8. P. Graham, C

1910

1. B. Collins, LF
2. B. Herzog, 3B
3. B. Sharpe, 1B
4. D. Miller, RF
5. D. Shean, 2B
6. B. Sweeney, SS
7. F. Beck, CF
8. P. Graham, C

1911

1. B. Sweeney, 2B
2. F. Tenney, 1B
3. B. Herzog, SS
4. M. Donlin, CF
5. D. Miller, RF
6. S. Ingerton, 3B
7. A. Kaiser, LF
8. B. Rariden
   J. Kling, C

1912

1. E. McDonald, 3B
2. V. Campbell, CF
3. B. Sweeney, 2B
4. G. Jackson, LF
5. J. Titus, RF
6. B. Houser, 1B
7. F. O'Rourke, SS
8. J. Kling
   B. Rariden, C

1913

1. R. Maranville, SS
2. H. Myers, 1B
3. J. Connolly, LF
4. B. Sweeney, 2B
5. J. Titus, RF
6. A. Devlin, 3B
7. L. Mann, CF
8. B. Rariden, C

1914

1. L. Gilbert, RF
2. J. Evers, 2B
3. J. Connolly, LF
4. R. Maranville, SS
5. B. Schmidt, 1B
6. C. Deal, 3B
7. L. Mann, CF
8. H. Gowdy, C

1915

1. H. Moran, RF
2. J. Evers, 2B
   E. Fitzpatrick, 2B-OF
3. J. Connolly, LF
4. S. Magee, CF
5. B. Schmidt, 1B
6. R. Smith, 3B
7. R. Maranville, SS
8. H. Gowdy, C

1916

1. R. Maranville, SS
2. J. Evers, 2B
3. J. Wilhoit, RF
4. S. Magee, LF
5. E. Konetchy, 1B
6. R. Smith, 3B
7. F. Snodgrass, CF
8. H. Gowdy, C

1917

1. R. Maranville, SS
2. R. Powell, CF
3. W. Rehg, RF
4. J. Kelly, LF
5. E. Konetchy, 1B
6. R. Smith, 3B
7. J. Rawlings, 2B
8. W. Tragesser, C

1918 (First half)

1. J. Rawlings, SS
2. B. Herzog, 2B
3. R. Powell, CF
4. A. Wickland, RF
5. R. Smith, 3B
6. E. Konetchy, 1B
7. W. Rehg
   J. Kelly, LF
8. A. Wilson, C

1918 (Second half)

1. B. Herzog, 2B
2. R. Taggert, LF
3. R. Massey
   C. Chadbourne, CF
4. Z. Terry, SS
5. R. Smith, 3B
6. E. Konetchy, 1B
7. A. Wilson, C
8. J. Rawlings, RF

1919

1. J. Riggert, CF
2. B. Herzog, 2B
3. R. Powell, RF
4. W. Cruise, LF
5. W. Holke, 1B
6. T. Boeckel, 3B
7. R. Maranville, SS
8. H. Gowdy
   A. Wilson, C

In the midst of a streak in which they won 61 of 77 games, the 1914 Braves smile for a September 15 photo.

BOSTON

FREDERICK TENNEY
FIRST BASEMAN 1894–1907, 1911, MANAGER 1905–07, 1911

In terms of glove work, the consensus was that Fred Tenney ranked behind only Hal Chase among first basemen of the Deadball Era. Considered the originator of the 3-6-3 double play, Tenney also developed the modern style of playing deep and well off the bag. "Tenney's way is far different from that of other first baseman," wrote a *Chicago News* reporter in 1897. "He reaches his hands far out for the ball, and stretches his legs, so that he is farther out from the bag on every throw than any other first baseman in the league." With his unconventional methods, the 5'9", 155 lb. first sacker led the NL in putouts in 1905 and 1907-08 and assists each year from 1901-07, setting a major league record with 152 in 1905 that lasted until Mickey Vernon topped it in 1949. As for his offense, Tenney was a masterful bunter and exceptional place hitter who batted over .300 seven times in his 17-year career, retiring in 1911 with a .294 lifetime average.

Grandson of a former Massachusetts state treasurer and son of a Civil War veteran, Frederick Tenney was born in Georgetown, Massachusetts, on November 26, 1871. Fred's nickname, the "Soiled Collegian," came from his aggressive playing style and his degree from Brown University, where he was a left-handed catcher. On June 15, 1894, the night of his senior dinner, he received a telephone message from Boston manager Frank Selee, who was in urgent need of a fill-in for his injured catchers. After going to bed at 4:00 A.M., Fred caught the morning train from Providence to Boston. That afternoon he made his NL debut, catching the entire game even though a foul tip fractured the index finger on his throwing hand in the fifth inning. The Beaneaters offered him a contract despite the injury, and the 22-year-old rookie rejoined the team a month later, batting .395 in 27 games.

Tenney spent short stints in the minors in each of the next two seasons. He hit well enough during his time in Boston, especially in 1896, when he batted .336, but the problem was his defense; Selee thought his throwing arm from behind the plate was too erratic. Tenney didn't become a regular until 1897, when Selee switched him to first base. The Beaneaters won the first of two consecutive pennants with a 93-39 record, and Tenney batted .318 while leading the league in at-bats. That year he also started what is believed to be the first-ever 3-6-3 double play. "We were playing Cincinnati in Boston when the batter hit the ball over first," Fred recalled. "I grabbed it and threw to [shortstop Herman] Long, then hurried to the bag and took Long's throw for a double play. It seemed that you could have heard a pin drop for 10 seconds, and then the crowd just let out a roar. It had seen something new."

A left-handed hitter, Tenney topped the .300 mark in four of the next six seasons, including a career-high .347 in 1899. His performance in an exhibition game at Portsmouth, Ohio, provides a glimpse of his offensive strategy. Tenney's first time up, the Portsmouth shortstop was crowding second base. "You're too far over; I'll hit the ball through the hole," Fred said. The shortstop just laughed, so Tenney singled through the hole. His next time up, the shortstop was playing in the hole. "Now you're too far the other way," said Fred. He promptly singled over second base. "We'd be willing to lose every day," a Portsmouth reporter wrote, "if Tenney would only come back and hit some more balls through the infield." In addition to his skill as a place hitter, Fred was a magnificent bunter who led the NL with 29 sacrifices in 1902, when he also finished in the Top 10 in batting average (.315), on-base percentage (.409), walks (73), and runs (88).

Having established himself as one of the NL's leading stars, Tenney received lucrative offers from the St. Louis, Cleveland, and Detroit Americans throughout the 1901-02 seasons; the Tigers reportedly offered to raise Fred's $2,500 salary to $7,000. Speculation that he'd jump became rampant after he got into a brawl with Pittsburgh's Fred Clarke on May 15, 1902—"Clarke called me names, then I twisted his nose, and he kicked me in the stomach," Tenney said—prompting a fine and a 10-game suspension. But Tenney stuck with the Nationals, mainly because of his friendship with longtime Boston co-owner Arthur Soden, and his loyalty was rewarded when he was named captain in 1903 and manager in 1905. He received no additional pay for managing but was promised a bonus if the club didn't lose money.

With a three-year record of 158-295, Tenney lasted as manager because the owners cared more about breaking even financially than winning games. In addition to his managerial duties, Fred served as first baseman, field captain, and even business manager, handling baggage, hotels, and receipts, going into the stands to retrieve fouls, and taking tickets on Sundays (for most of his career he refused to play on the Sabbath). On August 7, 1906, Tenney and umpire Bill Klem made headlines with their fracas over unused baseballs. Accounts differ, but as Klem prepared (or declined) to return extra balls after the game, Tenney started searching Klem's pockets, whereon the two exchanged punches, leading to what *Sporting Life* called "the most turbulent scene ever witnessed on a Boston ballfield." Tenney received a two-game suspension but earned his bonus and soon became a part owner of the penny-pinching franchise. Perhaps due to his investment, Fred played on Sundays for the first time in 1907, a season in which Boston finished 58-90—not good, but easily the top mark of Tenney's three-year tenure as manager.

On October 7, 1907, Boston sent Tenney to the New York Giants in an eight-player trade even though he still owned stock in the Boston franchise, a conflict of interest that somehow escaped notice. Free of his managerial duties, the 36-year-old first baseman enjoyed his last productive season in 1908. "He is like wine—he improves with age," wrote the *New York Evening Journal*. Though he batted just .256, he led the NL in runs (101) and ranked second in walks (72). Tenney also started 156 of the team's 157 games at first base, but the one game he missed due to a back injury allowed Fred Merkle his day of infamy, ultimately costing the Soiled Collegian his only chance at a World Series.

Battling leg woes in 1909, Tenney batted a career-low .235 in 101 games, drawing his release after the season. After playing and managing for Lowell of the New England League in 1910, he reluctantly returned as Boston's player-manager in 1911—a condition on which the team's new management insisted before buying back his shares of stock. With a record of 12-41 in mid-June, Tenney remained as manager but lost his captaincy to Johnny Kling, who ultimately replaced him as manager in 1912. Because he had a two-year contract, however, he got paid not to manage in 1912, an ironic conclusion to a managerial career that initially saw him manage without receiving additional pay.

Tenney worked in Boston for the Equitable Life Insurance Society for more than three decades. When friends introduced him as "the best first baseman who ever lived," he typically replied, "Thank you, but you know as well as I do that there was only one first baseman—Hal Chase." During his playing days Tenney served as a correspondent for *Baseball Magazine*, the *Boston Sunday Post*, and the *New York Times*, and he returned to writing in his post-baseball career, typically describing the strengths of pre-Deadball stars without suggesting that the game had declined in the years since. Fred Tenney died at age 80 on July 3, 1952, at Massachusetts General Hospital in Boston, just a few miles from the South End Grounds.

MARK STERNMAN

BOSTON

Victor Gazaway Willis
Right-handed pitcher 1898–1905

A 6'2", 205 lb. workhorse who came right at batters with a powerful overhand delivery, Vic Willis was one of the most dominant pitchers of the first decade of the Deadball Era. "Willis has speed and the most elusive curves," reported the *Boston Sunday Journal*. "His 'drop' is so wonderful that, if anyone hits it, it is generally considered a fluke." Over 13 seasons in the National League, the big right hander topped the 300-inning mark eight times, including an astonishing 410 innings in 1902, the second-highest total in modern NL history. Though he pitched part of his career for second division clubs, Willis compiled a 249-205 record and 2.63 ERA, good enough to earn his induction into the National Baseball Hall of Fame in 1995.

Victor Gazaway Willis was born on April 12, 1876, in Cecil County, Maryland. Soon afterward his family moved just across the state line to Newark, Delaware, which is how Vic came to be known as the "Delaware Peach." Willis played baseball at Newark Academy and Delaware College. In 1895 he joined Harrisburg of the Pennsylvania State League, pitching in 16 of the 37 games the club played before it folded in June. Willis caught on with Lynchburg of the Virginia League, and the following year he moved up to Syracuse. Vic started 10-6 but fell ill and left the team on July 31. He returned in 1897 and went 21-16 as Syracuse won the Eastern League championship. The Boston Beaneaters acquired him for $1,000 and catcher Fred Lake on the recommendation of Syracuse catcher Jack Ryan, who'd previously caught for Boston.

The 1898 Beaneaters were fresh off their fourth pennant in seven years, but Willis was expected to help the team immediately. The rookie saw his first action on April 20, eight days after his 22nd birthday, entering a game against Baltimore in the sixth inning with the Beaneaters behind, 10-3. He gave up eight runs, three walks, and two hit batsmen over the final three innings. Nine days later Vic rebounded to win his first start, 11-4. He went on to go 25-13 as Boston won another NL pennant. Though the Beaneaters slipped to second in 1899, Willis emerged as the ace of a staff that included Kid Nichols. He posted a 27-8 record, leading the NL with five shutouts, ranking second in ERA (2.50), and pitching the only no-hitter of his career on August 7. After his triumphant season, Vic married Mary Minnis in February 1900, a union eventually blessed with a daughter and a son born 15 years apart. The following year, however, Willis slumped to 10-17 for a Boston team that finished fourth with its first losing record since 1886.

In 1901 Willis agreed to jump to the American League's Philadelphia Athletics before changing his mind, probably because Boston sweetened the pot. He turned in another good season, pitching over 300 innings and finishing 20-17 with the fourth-best ERA in the league (2.36). In 1902 Willis enjoyed his best Deadball Era season, tossing 45 complete games (still the modern National League record) and leading the NL with 225 strikeouts. Against the Giants on May 28 he struck out a league-high 13 batters. The AL came calling again in midseason; the Detroit Tigers offered him a large cash advance on a two-year contract worth $4,500 per season. Vic initially accepted but again reneged after Boston matched the offer. His services remained in dispute until after the season, when he was awarded to Boston as part of the peace settlement between the two leagues. Over the next three years Willis averaged over 300 innings but won only 42 games for a rapidly deteriorating club. In 1904 he finished with a league-high 25 losses, but his 18 wins represented one-third of Boston's total of 55. For 1905 the Beaneaters offered Willis only $2,400. He threatened to jump to an outlaw league in Pennsylvania, but in the end he rejoined Boston and again led the NL with 29 losses, a modern record that may never be broken.

Pittsburgh Pirates owner Barney Dreyfuss tossed Willis a lifeline after that wreck of a season. Scrambling to stay competitive with the Giants and Cubs, he traded third baseman Dave Brain, first baseman Del Howard, and pitcher Vive Lindaman to Boston for a pitcher who the newspapers claimed was washed up. "Don't believe those tales you hear about my being all-in," Willis wrote to Dreyfuss. "Wait until you see me in action for your team and then form your opinion of my worth. I assure you that I am delighted to be a Pirate and that I will do my best to bring another pennant to the Smoky City." The Pirates restored Vic's $4,500 salary and he quickly repaid them by pitching three straight shutouts early in the 1906 season. Back with a winning club, Willis won 23, 21, 23, and 22 games in his four years with the Pirates, never losing more than 13.

Vic pitched several of the most important games in the history of the Pittsburgh franchise, and the fact that he didn't win any of them may have played a part in delaying his Cooperstown enshrinement. In the Pirates' final game of the famous 1908 NL pennant race, manager Fred Clarke chose a well-rested Willis to face the Cubs at Chicago's West Side Grounds in front of 30,247, at the time the largest crowd ever. A victory would have given the Pirates the pennant, but Vic surrendered a tie-breaking base hit to the opposing pitcher, Mordecai Brown, and went on to lose, 5-2. The next year Willis again pitched before a record-setting crowd at the grand opening of Forbes Field. "Never, perhaps, in the history of the Old World or New—not excluding the assemblages in the Roman and Grecian amphitheaters and stadiums—was a scene more spectacular presented," gushed the *Reach Guide*. Once again the Cubs were the opposition, and they won, 3-2, even though Willis limited them to four hits.

Willis played a key role in the success of the 1909 Pirates by winning 11 in a row at one point in the season. In the World Series he pitched in two games. Willis relieved Howie Camnitz in the third inning of Game Two. Ty Cobb promptly stole home and Vic gave up two runs over his 6⅔ innings as the Tigers won, 7-2. With the Pirates up three games to two, Clarke gave Willis a chance to win the Series in Game Six. Despite being staked to a three-run lead in the first inning, he couldn't hold the Tigers and was pulled after five innings with Detroit ahead, 4-3. The Pirates lost, 5-4, but came back to win Game Seven two days later. Before the 1910 season Pittsburgh released Vic amid rumors that he was a disciplinary problem.

When the St. Louis Cardinals claimed Willis, *The Sporting News* reported that he "should have a year or two of high-class work left in him if he will behave himself." The 34-year-old veteran went 9-12 with a 3.35 ERA in 1910, after which the Cardinals waived him. Following some confusion over the waiver rules, Willis was awarded to the Cubs but elected to retire instead. The Delaware Peach returned to his hometown of Newark where he operated the Washington House Hotel. Vic Willis was 71 when he died in Elkton, Maryland, on August 3, 1947, the victim of a stroke.

DAN LEVITT

BOSTON

WILLIAM JOHN SWEENEY
INFIELDER 1907–13

Bill Sweeney's eight-year major league career was bookended by dramatic moves between two cities, but it was always his unhappy fate to be in the wrong place at the wrong time. During his rookie season of 1907, Sweeney was traded from Chicago to Boston just as the Cubs were about to win back-to-back world championships. Later, at the tail end of his career, the Braves returned him to Chicago just prior to their miracle season of 1914. In between, Sweeney served as Boston's captain in 1910-13 and became the lone stalwart in one of history's most unstable infields.

William John Sweeney was born in Covington, Kentucky, on March 6, 1886. His family moved across the Ohio River to Cincinnati, then returned to Newport on the Kentucky side, where Bill grew up. After playing shortstop at Xavier College, he made his professional debut with Toledo of the American Association in 1904. Sweeney hit only .225 and was demoted to Rock Island of the Three-I League, where he improved to .301. He served as Rock Island's captain in 1905, and on September 1 of that season he joined Portland of the Pacific Coast League. The Beavers had lost 12 of their last 14 games, but they started winning after Sweeney's arrival. Returning to Portland for the earthquake-shortened 1906 season, Sweeney pounded out a .276 average, stole 51 bases, and led all shortstops in total chances per game as the Beavers compiled a .657 winning percentage, a PCL record that stood until 1934. That winter Frank Chance's Chicago Cubs beat out several other clubs to draft him.

Sweeney's new team, of course, was coming off a pretty good season of its own. Joining a corps of infielders that included Harry Steinfeldt at third and the legendary double-play combination of Tinker to Evers to Chance meant the best he could hope for was a back-up position. Bill's off-season efforts to keep in shape by roller skating backfired when he cracked a bone in his foot as a result of lacing his skates too tightly. The unusual injury delayed his major league debut until June 14, when Joe Tinker suffered a charley horse. Sweeney took his place at shortstop and made a throwing error that led to two runs in a 4-2 Chicago win. The next day he made his first start but played too far back and committed four errors, including a critical ninth-inning miscue that forced the Cubs to play 11 innings to win. The rookie started again the following day and made only one error, but Chance had seen enough. On June 24, less than two weeks into his major league career, Sweeney was traded to the Boston Doves.

After filling a utility role for the rest of 1907, Sweeney endured two position changes in Boston over the next four years: after two seasons as a regular at third base, he shifted to shortstop in 1910; then, after one season there, he moved permanently to second base. The latter move was fortuitous. Sweeney threw with an unusual sidearm motion, which caused him to lead the NL in errors at his position for five straight seasons, but he also led the NL three times in total chances per game. Playing second base allowed him to flash his outstanding range but put less pressure on his erratic throwing arm. According to *Total Baseball*'s fielding ratings, Sweeney was an average shortstop and an above-average third baseman—and he was an outstanding second baseman.

At the plate, Sweeney's strategy was "to swing straight at the ball and send it out on a line, just over the infielders' heads." In his first three seasons his batting was competent for a Deadball Era infielder: .254, .244, and .243. Midway through 1910, however, he switched from a light bat to one of the heaviest in the majors. The result was a .267 average and a career-high five home runs. In 1911 Sweeney took his game to an even higher level, fashioning a 31-game hitting streak from May 24 to July 1 en route to a .314 average. Cincinnati offered Boston $10,000 for his contract that winter, intending to install the local boy as player-manager. Bill was excited about the prospect and held out when Boston refused the deal.

After finally coming to terms, Sweeney enjoyed the finest season of his career in 1912, ranking third in the NL in batting (.344) and second in hits (204). He also placed second in RBI with 100, an astonishing total considering that he batted leadoff for the first 25 games and was among the NL leaders in sacrifice bunts. Sweeney's fielding was equally brilliant; he set an NL record for putouts by a second baseman that stood for 21 years. Despite lacking a regular shortstop partner, he led the NL in assists and double plays. Though Boston lost 100 games for a fourth consecutive year, Sweeney finished sixth in the Chalmers Award voting for the NL's most valuable player. The winner was Larry Doyle, second baseman for the pennant-winning Giants, whose numbers were similar to Sweeney's.

Boston's fortunes began to revive under new manager George Stallings in 1913, but Sweeney's batting average fell off precipitously to .257 as he played through nagging injuries to his wrist and throwing hand. Still he tied for 13th in the Chalmers Award balloting, perhaps in recognition that he'd filled the role of acting manager in midseason when Stallings returned home because of an illness in his family. Meanwhile Sweeney's former team, the Cubs, were

headed in the opposite direction. Though still a first-division club, Chicago had won fewer games each year since its last pennant in 1910. Charles Murphy was dumping holdovers from the team's glory days, and in 1914 he jettisoned player-manager Johnny Evers, who ended up with Boston.

Evers, of course, was a second baseman, which left Sweeney in a dilemma. Stallings offered his captain a choice between moving to first base or becoming a free agent. Sweeney was reluctant to make yet another position change, but after six full seasons he'd laid down roots in Boston. In 1911 he'd married Katherine Leonard, the sister-in-law of Braves treasurer Fred Murphy, and the couple had settled in Cambridge, where Bill had built up an insurance business in the off-season. After a month of wrestling with the decision, Sweeney decided to accept the Cubs' offer of a three-year contract with a 50% raise and a sizeable signing bonus, leaving the Braves without a single player who'd been with the club since the start of the 1911 season. Undoubtedly Bill anticipated finally playing for a pennant contender. Instead, Chicago spent the year struggling to stay above the .500 mark while Boston pulled off one of baseball's most miraculous turnarounds, winning the 1914 pennant and World Series.

Sweeney's career was now in serious decline. He was Chicago's regular second baseman for all of 1914 but batted just .218, causing speculation that his mind was more on policies and premiums than baseball. Only 28 and two years removed from finishing sixth in the NL's MVP voting, Sweeney received his unconditional release. He went to spring training with the Red Sox in 1915 but was released again. There was talk that he might sign with Detroit or Cincinnati, but instead he announced his retirement. Sweeney coached the Boston College baseball team in 1916, the same year he sold the Braves a $500,000 accident insurance policy from which his premium was said to be more than a season's baseball salary. That seems to have ended his active connection with baseball. Thereafter Bill devoted his attention to his insurance business and raising his five children. He died in Cambridge on May 26, 1948.

PETER MORRIS

BOS.

314

George A. "Lefty" Tyler

BOSTON

George Albert "Lefty" Tyler
Left-handed pitcher 1910–17

Lefty Tyler was the third of the Miracle Braves' "Big Three," the only one who didn't win a 1914 World Series game (though the Braves won his only start). During the astonishing run from last to first, Tyler was, according to sportswriter Tom Meany, "untouchable when he had to be, which was most of the time." He was especially known for his grit in low-scoring games—30 of his 127 major league victories were shutouts, 10 of them 1-0 squeakers. Also known for his great "slow ball" (changeup), Lefty employed an overhand crossfire delivery (prior to 1940 pitchers weren't required to make their first forward step within the width of the pitcher's plate). His unorthodox style allowed him to hide the ball longer, making his fastball more effective and aiding his sweeping curve.

George Albert Tyler, the second of John and Martha (McCannon) Tyler's four sons, was born on December 14, 1889, in Derry, New Hampshire. His father worked in the local shoe shops. All four Tyler boys played baseball; Bill was good enough to pitch in the low minors, while Fred briefly joined his brother on the Braves in the final days of the 1914 season. George pitched for St. Anselm College and various sandlot teams in 1906. During the following season he took the mound in almost every game played by the semipro Derry Athletic Association, the roster of which included his brothers Arthur and Fred. In 1909 George ran off a string of 34 consecutive shutout innings for the DAA, including a 17-strikeout game. Those feats attracted the attention of former major league pitcher Alexander Ferson, who recommended him to Lowell of the New England League.

Tyler made his professional debut with Lowell on July 2, 1909, leaving in the fifth inning with a deficit but escaping with a no-decision. He went on to post a 5-5 record, splitting time between starting and relieving. Lefty's 19-16 record in 1910 earned him a late-season look with the Boston Nationals. He made two late September relief appearances without a decision. The next spring Tyler pitched well enough to break training camp with Boston. Rube Waddell was toiling in the minors, making Lefty the only big-league pitcher who used the overhand crossfire delivery. With a last-place club behind him, he went 7-10 with a 5.06 ERA in 1911 and 12-22 with a 4.18 ERA in 1912, leading the majors in losses during the latter season.

Things changed for Tyler in 1913. Off the field, he married Lillian McCarthy of Lowell on January 29. On the field, he led the National League with 28 complete games while lowering his ERA to 2.79 and posting a 16-17 record for new manager George Stallings. Tyler went 16-13 with a 2.69 ERA during the great 1914 season, putting together a string of 23 consecutive shutout innings during the second-half stretch run. In the final week Lefty's brother Fred was recalled from Jersey City. Many sources erroneously include the Tylers on lists of major league brother batteries; Lefty's final regular-season appearance came on October 2, but Fred didn't make his major league debut until the following day. To give catcher Hank Gowdy a rest before the World Series, Stallings had Fred Tyler catch both games of three consecutive season-ending doubleheaders, the full extent of his major league career. Lefty started Game Three of the World Series sweep. He was lifted in the bottom of the 10th inning for a pinch-hitter with his team down, 4-3. The Braves tied the game and later won it in the 12th.

Lefty Tyler's fine 1916 season of 17-9 with a 2.02 ERA and twice as many strikeouts as walks was sandwiched by seasons of finishing just over .500 with near equal walk/strikeout ratios and ERAs at or above the league average. In 1916 he also ended the Giants' record winning streak at 26 when he beat them, 8-3, in the second game of a doubleheader on September 30.

On January 4, 1918, former Braves coach Fred Mitchell, then managing the Chicago Cubs, acquired Tyler in exchange for second baseman Larry Doyle, catcher Art Wilson, and $15,000. It was a steep price to pay, but Lefty made the trade worthwhile by posting the best season of his career, going 19-8 with a 2.00 ERA. On July 17 he tied the existing NL record by pitching 21 innings to beat the Phillies, 2-1. The war-shortened season likely cost Tyler his only 20-win year, but the Cubs took the pennant. In the 1918 World Series Mitchell started only left-handed pitchers (Tyler and Hippo Vaughn each started three games) to keep Babe Ruth out of the Red Sox lineup when he wasn't pitching. Lefty won Game Two, 3-1, on a complete-game six-hitter, helping himself with a two-run single. He left Game Four for a pinch-hitter with the Cubs down, 2-0, in the eighth inning. Chicago tied the game but Boston scored in the bottom of the inning and held on for the win. With the Cubs down three games to two, Tyler lost a 2-1 heartbreaker in the deciding sixth game. Both Boston runs were unearned.

Tyler noticed soreness in his shoulder during spring training in 1919. He insisted on pitching through the pain and took a no-hitter into the seventh inning against St. Louis on April 27 before finishing with a complete-game, four-hit win. Lefty made his next start on May 2 and beat Pittsburgh, 4-2, but pain forced him from the game. Mitchell rested him until May 16, when he tossed a four-hitter in a losing cause against the Giants. He appeared in relief four days later but couldn't complete the inning. After a month's rest, Tyler allowed six hits and three walks in a complete game 2-0 loss to Cincinnati on June 24. He pitched again on June 28 but couldn't retire a single batter. It was his last appearance of the 1919 season.

The Cubs sent the 29-year-old Tyler to the Mayo Clinic where he was declared to be in perfect health except for very bad teeth. He was never again the same pitcher despite having all but three of his teeth extracted. Returning to the Cubs in 1920, he posted an 11-12 record and was released the next season after going 3-2 in 10 games. He finished the 1921 season at Rochester of the International League, going 4-1 but with a 5.01

ERA. The Braves signed Tyler in February 1922, but he never pitched again in the majors. In 1925-26 he played for Lawrence in the New England League. No statistics are available for 1925, but in 1926 he was 3-3 in eight games as a pitcher and batted .280 in 72 games as a first baseman.

After his playing days, Tyler umpired from 1928 to 1930 in the New England League and 1931-32 in the Eastern League. He worked for the New England Power Company for a time, then as a shoe cutter in the mills around Lowell. Lefty died of a heart attack on September 29, 1953—exactly 39 years from the day the Miracle Braves clinched the pennant.

WAYNE McELREAVY

BOSTON

HENRY MORGAN GOWDY
CATCHER 1911–17, 1919–23, 1929–30

Best known today as the first active major leaguer to enlist for service in World War I, Hank Gowdy was a "fair-haired skyscraper" (he stood 6'2" and weighed 180 lbs.) who caught more than 100 games in only three of his 17 seasons in the majors. Gowdy turned up as a prime actor in some of baseball's most dramatic scenes. He was key to the Boston Braves' amazing 1914 season, starring in their famous World Series victory, but in 1924, while playing for the New York Giants, he was blamed for the loss of another legendary World Series. His misplay in Game Seven of that Series is a primary reason why coaches now teach young catchers to hold onto their masks until they know exactly where the ball is before tossing them well out of the way.

The son of Horace and Carrie (Burhart) Gowdy, Henry Morgan Gowdy was born on August 24, 1889, in Columbus, Ohio. As a youngster Hank sold peanuts at Columbus's Neil Park and played football, basketball, and baseball at Hubbard Elementary School and North High School. After a failed tryout with the Columbus Senators, he began his professional career in 1908 as a first baseman with Lancaster of the Ohio State League, remaining there for two seasons. In 1910 Gowdy enjoyed a breakout year with Dallas, leading the Texas League in batting (.312), doubles (44), and home runs (11) while stealing 29 bases. John McGraw signed him for the New York Giants and gave him a seven-game tryout that September. With 21-year-old Fred Merkle firmly entrenched as the Giants first baseman, McGraw advised Gowdy to take up catching if he hoped to remain in the major leagues.

The following year Gowdy had appeared in only four games when the Giants traded him and Al Bridwell to Boston for Buck Herzog on July 22. Thereafter he became the Doves' semi-regular first baseman, batting .289 in 29 games as a fill-in for player-manager Fred Tenney. Following McGraw's advice, Gowdy made the switch to catcher in 1912 but spent most of the season on the Boston bench, appearing in only 22 games behind the plate as a third-stringer behind Bill Rariden and new player-manager Johnny Kling. To that point he'd never played an entire season at catcher, so in 1913 yet another new Braves manager, George Stallings, sent him to Buffalo of the International League, where Stallings had managed the previous season. Gowdy batted .317 in 104 games, earning a late-season call-up. In 1914 the gawky 24-year-old became Boston's regular catcher, appearing in a career-high 128 games, 115 of them at catcher. Stallings himself stated that his mild-mannered backstop was his most valuable player during that season's miracle pennant drive.

A lifetime .270 hitter who batted just .243 in 1914, Gowdy claimed that he should have hit .300 that year: "I hit just as hard during the season as I did during the Series, except that during the season they were going right at somebody while in the Series they were going safe." In Game One of the World Series he was 3-for-3 with a single, a double, and a triple, and he and first baseman Butch Schmidt, the two slowest men on the team, executed a successful double steal. In Game Three at Fenway Park, which the Braves borrowed from the Red Sox for the Series, Boston was down by

Note that in this circa 1914 photo, Gowdy has already discarded his mask as he sets out after a foul pop. That practice came back to haunt him in the 1924 World Series.

two runs when Gowdy led off the 10th inning with a blast into the center-field bleachers. It was the only home run of the Series, and it ignited a rally that tied the score. In the 12th Gowdy got his third hit and second double of the game, a bullet to left field. Running for him, Les Mann scored the winning run on a wild throw. For the Series, Gowdy batted .545 with an extraordinary 1.273 slugging percentage.

Over the next couple of years Hank Gowdy remained a Boston mainstay behind the plate, catching an average of 115 games per season. In 1917 he took the step that, despite his 1914 heroics, assured his lasting fame. The United States entered World War I in April, and on June 1 Gowdy became the first active major leaguer to enlist, joining the Ohio National Guard. (Eddie Grant had enlisted in April, but he'd already retired as a player.) The big catcher reported for duty six weeks later and was overseas by early 1918. Gowdy served with distinction in the famed Rainbow Division, so named by General John "Black Jack" Pershing because it had the uncanny luck of being surrounded by rainbows during its heaviest combat. Arriving in the Lorraine region of France in March, Gowdy endured the brutality of trench warfare as the Germans made their fierce and final effort to overrun the Allies on the Western Front. He carried the colors for the Fighting 42nd and returned to the United States a genuine hero, as popular in Boston as the mayor himself.

Turning down an offer of $1,500 a week for 30 weeks to tour the country and speak of his heroics, Gowdy returned to the Braves and on May 23, 1919, he hit the first big-league pitch he'd seen for almost two years for a single. He went on to catch 74 games and bat .279, a 65-point improvement on his last prewar season. In 1920 Gowdy was behind the plate for the 26-inning classic in which Boston's Joe Oeschger and Brooklyn's Leon Cadore locked up for a 1-1 tie. In the 17th inning he played a key role—actually two key roles—in what one reporter called "the most remarkable double play ever seen in Boston." With the bases loaded and one out, Brooklyn catcher Rowdy Elliot tapped back to Oeschger, who fired to Gowdy to force Zack Wheat at the plate. Gowdy's throw to first base was low and Walter Holke bobbled it. Big Ed Konetchy, running from second, tried to score on the fumble.

Holke's return throw was off to Gowdy's right. He reached for it, grabbed it, then "threw himself blindly across the plate to meet Konetchy's spikes with bare fist," a vivid snapshot of the Deadball game. That season Gowdy batted just .243, but in each of the next two post–Deadball Era seasons he established new career highs by hitting .299 and .317.

In June 1923, with Stallings gone, the Braves once again mired in mediocrity, and Gowdy off to a miserable .125 start, McGraw brought the veteran catcher back to the Giants in a four-player deal. Though he never played more than part-time, Hank posted the best offensive statistics of his career in his two-year stint in New York, batting consistently in the .320s and establishing a career high with four home runs in 1924. He also played in two more World Series. In the 12th inning of Game Seven of the 1924 fall classic at Griffith Stadium, Gowdy stepped into the spotlight again—this time as a goat. With one out and no one on base, Washington's Muddy Ruel popped up what looked like an easy foul. Gowdy tore off his mask, tossed it to the ground, and promptly stepped in it. "It held me like a bear trap," Gowdy recalled. He staggered around and couldn't reach the ball, which dropped to the ground. Given new life, Ruel doubled and later became Washington's winning run when Earl McNeely made his famous "pebble hit" over Freddy Lindstrom's shoulder at third. Sportswriters, calculating the difference between the winners' and losers' shares, called Gowdy's misplay "a $50,000 muff."

Partway through the 1925 season the Giants released Gowdy even though he was batting .325. He spent the next three seasons in the high minor leagues before returning to Boston as a coach in 1929-30. Gowdy celebrated his 40th birthday in 1929 but still managed to hit .438 in 16 at-bats for the Braves that season. He went on to coach for the Giants and the Cincinnati Reds during the 1930s and 1940s. During World War II Gowdy joined the Army again, becoming the chief athletic officer at Fort Benning, Georgia, where the baseball diamond is now called Hank Gowdy Field. He died at age 76 on August 1, 1966, in his hometown of Columbus. Though married for many years, Hank and his wife left no children.

Frank Ceresi & Carol McMains

BOSTON

WALTER JAMES VINCENT "RABBIT" MARANVILLE
SHORTSTOP 1912–20, 1929–35

Standing only 5'5" and weighing a good deal less during the Deadball Era than his listed playing weight of 155 lbs., Rabbit Maranville compiled a lifetime batting average of just .258, but his outstanding defense kept him in the big leagues for 23 seasons and eventually earned him a plaque in Cooperstown. "Maranville is the greatest player to enter baseball since Ty Cobb arrived," said Boston Braves manager George Stallings. "I've seen 'em all since 1891 in every league around the south, north, east, and west. He came into the league under a handicap—his build. He was too small to be a big leaguer in the opinion of critics. I told him he was just what I wanted: a small fellow for short. All he had to do was to run to his left or right, or come in, and size never handicapped speed in going after the ball."

The third of five children, Walter James Vincent Maranville was born on November 11, 1891, in Springfield, Massachusetts. His mother was Irish, but his father and the Maranville name were French. Walter (then known as "Stumpy" or "Bunty") attended the Charles Street and Chestnut Street grammar schools and played catcher during his one year at Technical High School. His father, a police officer, allowed him to leave school if he apprenticed for a trade, so at age 15 he quit to become a pipe fitter and tinsmith. To his father's dismay, Walter devoted more attention to baseball than his apprenticeship. He was playing shortstop for a semipro team in 1911 when Tommy Dowd, manager of the New Bedford Whalers, signed him to a contract for $125 per month. The 19-year-old shortstop batted .227 and committed 61 errors in 117 games.

Maranville acquired his distinctive nickname during his second season in the New England League. Some say that it came from his protruding ears, but he told a different story: "I was very friendly with a family by the name of Harrington. One night I was down to their house having dinner with them when Margaret, the second oldest daughter, asked me if I could get two passes for the next day's game, as she wanted to take her seven-year-old sister to see me play. I said, 'Sure, I'll leave them in your name at the Press Gate.' She said, 'And come down to dinner after the game.' I left the two passes as promised and after the game I went down to their house for dinner. I rang the door bell and Margaret came and opened the door and said, 'Hello Rabbit.' I said, 'Where do you get that Rabbit stuff?' She said, 'My little seven-year-old sister (Skeeter) named you that because you hop and bound around like one.'"

Maranville improved his batting average to .283 during his second year with New Bedford, and the Boston Nationals purchased his contract for $1,000. Reporting to the club on September 4, Rabbit got into 26 big-league games and made 11 errors while batting .209. "The fall of 1912 my fielding was above the average, but my hitting was not so good," he recalled. "However, I was the talk of the town because of my peculiar way of catching a fly ball. They later named it the Vest-Pocket Catch. Boston wasn't drawing any too good, but it seemed like everyone that came out to the park came to see me make my peculiar catch or get hit on the head." Maranville settled himself under pop-ups with what seemed to be total unconcern, arms at his side. As the ball plummeted towards earth, apparently ignored, he suddenly brought his hands together at waist level and let the ball fall into the pocket of his glove. "Many of the players passed different remarks about my catch that wouldn't go in print," Rabbit said. "I do, however, remember what Jimmy Sheckard said: 'I'll bet you he don't drop three balls in his career, no matter how long or short he may be in the game. Notice the kid is perfectly still, directly under the ball, and in no way is there any vibration to make the ball bounce out of his glove.'"

At training camp in the spring of 1913, new manager George Stallings scheduled two-a-day practices, one in the morning and one in the afternoon. "The players would dress after the first workout and return to the hotel where they'd loaf for an hour or so," Rabbit recalled. "Seizing the opportunity that was before me, I got a dozen kids to pitch to me before the next session, sometimes to the point that I was groggy." Despite his hard work, Maranville still couldn't crack the starting lineup. "Coming from the park after our afternoon session, I was walking with a big first baseman by the name of Gus Metz. He said, 'Rabbit, did you see where they have the ballclub picked?' I said, 'No, who have they decided on for shortstop?' He said, 'Art Bues, Stallings' nephew.' I said, 'If I couldn't play ball better than that guy I'd quit.' Walking behind us was Stallings, and he overheard what I said unbeknown to us. That evening after dinner I was loafing around the lobby of the hotel when Stallings came along and said, 'I want to talk to you.' We went over to a sofa and sat down. Stallings said, 'You don't like my selection of Bues for shortstop over you.' I said, 'No, I don't.' 'Well,' Mr. Stallings said, 'you have a lot to learn and I'm running this club and I'll make my own selections no matter what you or anybody else thinks.' I said, 'That's okay with me; I'm not trying to run your ballclub, but if I'm not a better ballplayer than that relative of yours, I'll quit.' He said, 'No, you will not; I'll keep you until we get back to Boston, then use you in a trade if I have the opportunity.'"

Maranville sat on the bench during the 1913 exhibition season until the Braves arrived in Atlanta on Easter Sunday. After going to church that morning, he put on his uniform in his hotel room and boarded the team bus. "Going up Peach Tree Boulevard on our way to the park, a player who I don't remember right off hand told me I was to play shortstop that after-

noon as Bues came down with a sore throat," Rabbit recalled. "We left Bues in Atlanta as he was a very sick boy and came into New York to open the season with the Giants. Game time came along and Stallings yelled down the bench at me, 'Rabbit, you're playing shortstop today.' I said, 'Yes, and you will never get me out of there.'" Maranville picked up three hits against Jeff Tesreau on Opening Day as the Braves won, 8-0. He went on to hit .247 in 143 games that season and remained the regular shortstop for Stallings' entire tenure in Boston.

Maranville appeared in 156 games during the miracle season of 1914, driving in 78 runs out of the cleanup spot even though he batted only .246. He came up with many big hits during the Braves' pennant drive, but none more important than the game-winning home run he belted in the 10th inning on August 6—even though he was suffering from a severe hangover from drinking too much champagne at a dinner party the night before. "In the clubhouse while I was undressing Stallings came over to me and said, 'You go back to choking up; you are no home-run hitter,'" Rabbit remembered. "Truthfully, I never did see the ball I hit, and years later Babe Adams, who was the pitcher that day, asked me if it was a curve or a fastball I hit over the fence. I told him I never saw it and he said, 'I know darn well you never did.'"

Maranville's greatest contributions came with the glove. Boston had purchased second baseman Johnny Evers from the Chicago Cubs during the previous winter, and he and Rabbit gave the Braves the best middle infield in baseball. Though no sportswriter ever penned a poem about Maranville-to-Evers-to-Schmidt, that combination turned more double plays in 1914 than Tinker, Evers, and Chance ever did in any one season. "It was just Death Valley, whoever hit a ball down our way," Rabbit recalled. "Evers with his brains taught me more baseball than I ever dreamed about. He was psychic. He could sense where a player was going to hit if the pitcher threw the ball where he was supposed to."

Evers' omniscience paid off in a big way during Game Two of the World Series. Heading into the bottom of the ninth, the Braves led, 1-0, but the Athletics had men on first and second and only one out. The batter was Eddie Murphy, a fast left-handed hitter who Maranville claimed hadn't hit into a double play all season. Rabbit was already playing only 10 feet from second base, but Evers looked over and told him to move closer. The young shortstop followed orders, moving only five feet from the bag. Bill James was about to deliver his pitch when Evers called time and instructed Rabbit to move even closer. Maranville moved within one yard of second base. On James' first pitch, Murphy hit a rifle shot between the pitcher's legs. Rabbit was practically standing on second when he fielded the grounder and fired the ball to first to complete a game-ending double play. "If it hadn't been for Evers insisting I play closer to second base, I would never have made the play, which seemed almost impossible to make from the spectators' point of view," he said.

Evers and Maranville finished one-two in the 1914 Chalmers Award voting, and that off-season they were approached by Bill Fleming, a scout for the Federal League's Chicago Whales. "We met him and he laid down $100,000 in front of Evers and $50,000 in front of me as a bonus with a three-year contract to play for the Chicago Feds," Rabbit recalled. "Evers refused and so did I." Maranville remained a fixture in the Braves infield for another six years, though he missed nearly all of 1918 when he served as a gunner in the Navy aboard the U.S.S. *Pennsylvania*. On November 10, 1918, Rabbit told his shipmates that they would get big news the next day. "Everyone kept asking me what the big news was going to be," he remembered. "I said, 'Wait until tomorrow; I will tell you then.' At 6:30 the next morning we got word that the armistice had been signed. That afternoon I was called to the captain's quarters. The captain said to me, 'How is it you knew the armistice was going to be signed today?' I said, 'I didn't know anything about the armistice being signed. The reason I said the big day is tomorrow and they would hear great news is that today is my birthday.'"

In January 1921 the Braves traded Maranville to the Pittsburgh Pirates for Billy Southworth, Fred Nicholson, Walter Barbare, and a sum of money said to be $15,000. Rabbit remained with the Pirates through 1924, giving them their first reliable shortstop since the retirement of Honus Wagner. He then spent one season with the Chicago Cubs, serving as player-manager for a short time, and another with the Brooklyn Dodgers, drawing his release in August 1926. An alcoholic by his own admission, Maranville was considered washed up as a big leaguer, but he swore off booze at Rochester in 1927 and returned to the NL in 1928 as the starting shortstop for the St. Louis Cardinals. He appeared in the World Series that year and batted .308, the same average he'd posted in the 1914 World Series.

Maranville returned to Boston in 1929 for a second stint with the Braves, playing regularly at shortstop for three years and second base for two. Legendary sportswriter Grantland Rice thought of Rabbit at that point in his career "as the link between the old days and the new in baseball. He broke in with the hard-bitten crew in Boston and wasn't exactly a sissy, reveling in the atmosphere in which he found himself. For years he was a turbulent figure on the field, fighting enemy ball players and umpires—and even the players on his own team when he found it necessary." Then in his early 40s, Maranville still played with the same old hustle. In a 1934 spring exhibition against the Yankees, with Boston down by a run, Rabbit attempted to score even though the catcher was blocking the plate. When the dust cleared, Maranville lay in agony, a bone jutting out of his ankle.

After missing the entire 1934 season, Rabbit tried to come back in 1935 but played only 23 games before giving up. He managed at Elmira in 1936, Montreal in 1937, Albany in 1939, and back home in Springfield in 1941. When he finally left Organized Baseball for good, Rabbit worked for youth baseball programs in Rochester, Detroit, and finally New York City. As director of the *New York Journal-American* sandlot baseball school after World War II, he taught thousands of kids how to play the game in clinics at Yankee Stadium and the Polo Grounds. Among his pupils were future big leaguers Whitey Ford, Bob Grim, and Billy Loes. Rabbit Maranville died at age 62 of coronary sclerosis on January 5, 1954, just a few weeks before his election to the National Baseball Hall of Fame. He is buried in St. Michael's Cemetery in his hometown of Springfield.

DICK LEYDEN

BOSTON

GEORGE TWEEDY STALLINGS
MANAGER 1913–20

A dignified, fastidious Southerner who managed in street clothes and nervously slid up and down the bench so much that he frequently wore out his trousers, George Stallings compiled an 879-898 record and won only one pennant in 13 seasons as a major league manager, yet that single gonfalon was enough to ensure his undying fame as "The Miracle Man." Indeed, the amazing ascension of his Boston Braves to the 1914 National League flag, followed by their sweep of Connie Mack's heavily favored Philadelphia Athletics in the World Series, still may be the most unlikely triumph in baseball history. The captain of those 1914 Braves, Johnny Evers, wrote that Stallings "will crab and rave on the bench with any of them," yet he also wrote, "Mr. Stallings knows more base ball than any man with whom I have ever come in contact during my connection with the game."

The son of William Henry and Eliza Jane (Hooper) Stallings, George Tweedy Stallings was born in Augusta, Georgia, on November 17, 1867 (not on November 10, 1869, as his tombstone says). He attended Richmond Academy, and it's often reported that he graduated from the Virginia Military Institute in 1886 and attended the College of Physicians and Surgeons in Baltimore. His name doesn't appear on VMI alumni rolls, however, and there's also no record that he actually attended medical school. Stallings married Bell White on April 2, 1889, in Jones County, Georgia. They had two sons before Bell divorced him in 1906. Stallings later married Bertha (Thorne) Sharpe, major leaguer Bud Sharpe's widow, with whom he had one son.

If Stallings' reputation depended solely on his playing career, no one would remember him. He made his big-league debut with the NL champion Brooklyn Bridegrooms in 1890, appearing in four games and going hitless in 11 at-bats before receiving his release. Stallings also appeared in three games while managing the Phillies in 1897-98. His entire major league playing career consisted of two hits in 20 at-bats. Stallings had more success in the minors; an 1897 publication claimed that he "was probably a member of more champion clubs than any other player of the present day." The Phillies discovered him in 1886 while he was catching for an amateur team in Jacksonville, Florida. In need of seasoning, Stallings spent the next four years bouncing around the minors. After his short stint with Brooklyn, he switched to the outfield in 1891 "to give the [San Jose] team the benefit of his speed in the game every day" and led the California League in stolen bases that year.

Stallings' managerial career began in 1893, when he managed his hometown team, Augusta of the Southern League. During the off-season he also served as the first baseball coach at Mercer College in Macon, Georgia, where he was succeeded in 1897 by Cy Young. In 1894 Stallings split the season between Kansas City of the Western League and Nashville of the Southern League, and the following year he managed Nashville to a second-place finish. After guiding Detroit of the Western League to fourth place in 1896, he was tapped to take over the Phillies. Stallings' first tenure as a major league manager gave no hint of future success. The Phillies lurched to a 55-

77 record in 1897, finishing 10th in the 12-team NL. In 1898 they got off to an even poorer start (19-27), and Stallings was fired in mid-June.

George returned to the helm in Detroit in 1899 and was still managing there in 1901, after the Western League had renamed itself the American League and declared itself a major league. The Tigers finished that first big-league season third with a 74-61 record, but Stallings ran afoul of AL president Ban Johnson, who claimed that the manager had tried to sabotage the new circuit by selling the Tigers to NL interests. Stallings later insisted that he couldn't have sold the Tigers even if he'd wanted to, because Johnson himself owned 51% of the club's stock. Nevertheless, he didn't return to Detroit. Stallings managed in the Eastern League with Buffalo in 1902-06 and Newark in 1908. He was out of baseball in 1907, tending to the peaches and cattle he raised on his plantation, The Meadows, in Haddock, Georgia, just outside Macon.

In 1909 Frank Farrell asked Stallings to take over his troubled New York Highlanders, who'd staggered home dead last during a dissension-torn 1908 season. Under Stallings the Highlanders improved to 74-77 in 1909. They were playing even better in September 1910 when Highlanders star Hal Chase, with an assist from Ban Johnson, convinced Farrell to fire Stallings and install Chase as manager. The club was 78-59 (.569) at the time. The Highlanders won 10 of their last 14 games under Chase to finish second, but they fell back to sixth in 1911. George, meanwhile, spent 1911-12 back in Buffalo before James Gaffney summoned him to replace Johnny Kling as skipper in Boston. Stallings took over the bedraggled Braves after the team had posted four straight last-place finishes. His first glimpse of his new charges wasn't encouraging: "I have never seen any club in the big leagues look quite so bad," he later recalled. Managing the 1913 Braves, who led the NL with 273 errors, must have been a trying experience for a man who could fly into a rage at the drop of a pop fly, yet the team won 17 more games than it had in 1912 and rose to fifth place.

No one expected the Braves to finish in the first division in 1914. Sure enough, Boston was in last place on July 15, though only 11½ games behind the league-leading Giants. From that point on, however, the Braves proceeded to win 61 of their last 77 games and finished the season with a 94-59 record, 10½ games ahead of New York. Stallings was profoundly superstitious—if his team mounted a rally he would freeze in position until the rally ended—and it's fun to imagine what his antics must have been like during the Braves' incredible run. Once, or so the story goes, he happened to be leaning over to pick up a pebble when the Braves started a rally; after it was over, he was so stiff he had to be helped off the field. Stallings abhorred peanut shells and pieces of paper on the field, much to the delight of mischievous opponents. The stalwart pitching of Bill James, Dick Rudolph, and Lefty Tyler, and the solid play of Johnny Evers and Rabbit Maranville had more to do with accomplishing the "miracle" than the 44-year-old manager's superstitions, but many of his players freely attributed their success to his guidance. Stallings is credited with pioneering the use of platoons to maximize the Braves' feeble offense (only one regular topped .300, and no Boston outfielder accumulated even 400 at-bats), but his ability to persuade his players that they were winners was as important as his strategic decisions.

Following the remarkable 1914 season, Stallings managed the Braves to second place in 1915 and third in 1916. Beginning in 1917, however, the team finished in sixth or seventh for each of the next four seasons, and their record got worse each year. Stallings resigned after the 1920 season. He guided Rochester of the International League from 1921 until he resigned in July 1927. George signed on to manage Montreal in 1928 but spent much of the year hospitalized for heart disease in Macon and Atlanta. When a doctor asked him if he knew why his heart was so bad, he supposedly replied, "Bases on balls, you son of a bitch, bases on balls." George Stallings died on May 13, 1929, and is buried in Macon's Riverside Cemetery.

MARTIN KOHOUT

BOSTON

WILLIAM LAWRENCE JAMES
RIGHT-HANDED PITCHER 1913–15, 1919

At the end of the 1914 season, 22-year-old Bill James stood on the cusp of baseball stardom. He'd just pitched his Boston Braves to the most improbable pennant in baseball history, and followed up on that performance by beating the mighty Philadelphia Athletics twice in three days during that year's World Series. He was such a uniquely gifted pitcher that John Ward of *Baseball Magazine* predicted, "The further acquisition of experience should make him one of the greatest all-round pitchers in history." When he wrote those words, Ward probably couldn't have imagined that this talented pitcher, with 32 major league wins behind him, had but five more in front of him.

William Lawrence James was born on March 12, 1892, in Iowa Hill, California, the third of four children of William and Emma James. Located 30 miles northeast of Sacramento, Iowa Hill was gold-mining country, and that is how James's father supported the family. When Bill was 11 years old, the family moved 50 miles north to Oroville, where the senior James found work as the manager of a dredge mining company. Bill's parents wanted a similar future for their son and encouraged him to study mining engineering at the University of California, but Bill had other ideas. During his three years at Oroville Union High School he matured into a 6'3", 195 lb. pitching prodigy blessed with an exceptional fastball. After high school Bill briefly acquiesced to his parents' wishes and attended classes at St. Mary's College in Oakland. But when Seattle of the Northwestern League offered him a contract prior to the 1912 season, he left school for good.

In Seattle James added a spitball and change of pace to his arsenal. The impressive results that followed hastened his development into the most touted prospect in all of baseball. James pitched Seattle to the pennant in 1912, at one point reeling off 16 consecutive victories. At season's end, his 26-8 record and 2.17 ERA landed him a contract with the National League's Boston Braves. It also left him with the nickname "Seattle Bill," a moniker designed mostly to avoid confusion, as the 1912 Cleveland Naps already featured a "Big Bill" James and a William "Lefty" James. "Seattle Bill" joined a Boston club that was the most wretched franchise in all of baseball. Going into 1913 the Braves had neither enjoyed a single winning season since 1902 nor finished within 50 games of first place since 1908. The team showed modest improvement during James's rookie season, climbing to fifth in the standings and moving to within 31 games of first place. James performed well, posting a 2.79 ERA while splitting time between the starting rotation and bullpen.

The Braves' stunning reversal of fortune in 1914 has long since entered baseball annals as the most unlikely championship run in history, but the critical role James played in the Boston uprising has undeservedly faded into obscurity. From July 9 until the end of the season, he went 19-1 with a 1.51 ERA. His only loss came on August 22 in Pittsburgh, when he was beaten 3-2 in 12 innings. Without that setback, James would have ended his season with a record-breaking 20-game winning streak. With it, he still assembled the best season of any pitcher in the National League. James led the NL in winning percentage (.788), and he finished in the top five in wins (26), ERA (1.90), innings pitched (332⅓), and strikeouts (156).

In Game Two of that year's World Series, James matched up against Philadelphia's Eddie Plank in a classic pitchers' duel at Shibe Park. Plank pitched brilliantly, surrendering seven hits and holding the Braves scoreless until Boston pushed across a single run in the ninth inning. James was even better, allowing just two hits, fanning eight, and coaxing a game-ending double play with the tying and winning runs on base to preserve the 1-0 victory. Two days later James was called into action again when Game Three stretched into extra frames. Pitching on one day's rest, James held the Athletics hitless in the 11th and 12th innings before Boston scored the winning run in the bottom of the 12th on a Joe Bush throwing error. In a span of three days, James had won two games, pitched 11 innings, and allowed just two hits. The Braves completed their sweep of the Athletics the following afternoon.

Despite his success and status as a World Series hero, James expressed ambivalence about life in the major leagues. "I like the game well enough," he told *Baseball Magazine* after the Series, "but I can't get used to the long jumps from one city to another. It looks nice from the outside to think of traveling around the country, but one sweep of the circuit is enough. After that it becomes hard and disagreeable work." Ironically, he got his chance to see major league baseball from the outside soon enough.

James reported late to camp the following spring after a brief holdout induced the Braves to double his salary, but it soon became apparent that he was a mere shadow of the pitcher who'd dominated the league the previous year. From the start of the season James complained of chronic arm fatigue. Initially the press took a dim view of the injury, dismissing his protests as the petulant whining of an overpaid athlete. By June, however, reduced velocity and flagging endurance forced James out of the starting rotation. After a poor relief appearance on July 30, he was shelved for the rest of the season.

The Braves hoped that a long winter's rest would restore strength to James's right arm, but it was not to be. In late March 1916, teammate Johnny Evers signaled the end was near when he admitted to reporters: "His arm is gone. Bill knows it and we know it." Shortly thereafter the 24-year-old pitcher was placed on the voluntary retired list. The press described the injury as a "dead arm," but in all likelihood James suffered a torn rotator cuff, a condition that the medicine of the day was powerless to correct.

Nonetheless, the man who'd once bemoaned the transient life of a professional baseball player attempted several comebacks. After undergoing numerous

shoulder operations, James tried to return to the Braves in 1918, but the comeback was aborted before the start of the regular season. After serving in the 63rd Infantry during World War I, James pitched one game in relief for the Braves in 1919. He then spent several years bouncing around the Pacific Coast League as a player and coach before concluding his career with Sacramento in 1925.

In retirement Bill James lived in Oroville with his wife, Harriet Newman, whom he'd married in 1924. The couple had one daughter, Janet, born in 1926. James worked as a truck driver for an oil company for several years and later as an assessor for Butte County. Despite the premature end to his once promising baseball career, he wasn't bitter. Spending his last days in an Oroville nursing home, James often watched baseball on television with a radio cradled in his lap, so he could follow two games simultaneously. He died of a stroke on March 10, 1971, two days shy of his 79th birthday, and is buried in Memorial Park Cemetery in Oroville.

DAVID JONES

BOSTON

RICHARD RUDOLPH
RIGHT-HANDED PITCHER 1913–20, 1922–23, 1927

Though he stood only 5'9½" and weighed just 160 lbs., Dick Rudolph was a large component of George Stallings' "Big Three" that helped lead the 1914 Boston Braves to their miraculous pennant and World Series sweep. "He was the bellwether of the pitching staff," said Braves coach Fred Mitchell, "and being a little fellow, I believe his success had much to do with big Bill James and George Tyler putting out that little extra effort to keep pace with the cocky kid from the Bronx." Unlike the hard-throwing James and Tyler, Rudolph was a "pitching cutie" who relied on a great curveball and spectacular control. He also threw a spitball, but "about the best you could say for it was that it was wet," recalled catcher Hank Gowdy.

Richard Rudolph was born in New York City on August 25, 1887. Late in the summer of 1905 he mailed a letter to Garry Herrmann, owner of the Cincinnati Reds, stating: "According to the league schedule your team will be in New York and Brooklyn the latter part of this month. I would like to have a chance to pitch against the Brooklyn team for your club to show my ability, as I would like to be with your team next year. Or if preferable against the New York National League team. It don't make any difference to me. All I want is a chance to show what I can do." Ignored by Herrmann, and in spite of his poor grammar, young Rudolph enrolled that fall at Fordham University and played on the baseball team the following spring. When he learned that the independent Northern League had sent collegians like Ed Reulbach and Jack Coombs to the majors, he headed to Vermont to pitch for a Rutland team that also included Eddie Collins. When that team folded, Rudolph joined New Haven of the Connecticut State League. He did well enough to decide not to return to Fordham.

Ed Barrow signed Rudolph to a 1907 Eastern League contract with Toronto. "Baldy" was a fine minor league pitcher, posting 77 wins in four seasons, including back-to-back 23-win seasons in 1909-10. Back in New York, his brother, who worked at the *New York Press*, kept his name in the local newspapers by planting stories of the "It's a crime that Rudolph doesn't get called up" type. At the close of the 1910 season the New York Giants gave him a shot, probably at the behest of Toronto manager Joe Kelley, John McGraw's old Baltimore Orioles teammate. "He has terrific speed, good control, is a quick thinker and mixes up his 'assortment' as well as any twirler in the big leagues," Kelley said. "I look for him in a few years to be as great as Mathewson."

As it turned out, Matty had no immediate worries. Rudolph mopped up in two Giant wins, then got the starting assignment of which he'd dreamed. It was a nightmare. The Phillies pounded him for 15 hits and the Giants lost, 8-2. The *Press* was forced to change its tune: "Dick Rudolph, from the wilds of the Bronx, found his path strewn with base hits when he made his first local appearance [in a major league uniform]." Rudolph was again hit hard in an April 1911 appearance, and that was enough for McGraw. Back in Toronto, Dick posted 18- and 25-win seasons, good enough to lead the International League in victories and winning percentage in the latter season. It's been said that Rudolph's size and prematurely thinning hair (making his real age appear suspicious) contributed to McGraw's decision not to bring him up again, despite his great success in Toronto.

Convinced that he had to get back to the majors soon if at all, the 25-year-old Rudolph returned to his old strategy of self-promotion. He found a sympathetic ear in Fred Mitchell. "I was going south in 1913 to join the Braves, who were training at Macon, Georgia," Mitchell recalled. "A young fellow got on the train in New York. Apparently he knew me, but I didn't know him. After a while he came over to my seat and asked if I was a ballplayer. I told him I was a coach for the Braves. He told me he was Dick Rudolph of the Toronto club, but was thinking about quitting if he wasn't sold to the major leagues. Well, I had a talk with him and found he had a good record in Toronto, but John McGraw hadn't given him much of a look. I told him not to be too hasty about quitting. I advised him to get in shape and maybe the Braves would be interested in his services. He did as he was instructed. After he was beaten by the Newark club, 1-0, in his opening game, he turned in his uniform and said he was through. He then got in touch with me again. I got in touch with Jim McCaffrey, the Toronto owner, and asked what he wanted for Rudolph. Jim (for whom I'd previously played) said, 'Oh, he'll be back in a couple of days.' I

told him he wouldn't, and he better sell him to the Braves. Well, after a couple of days when Rudolph failed to return, McCaffrey got in touch with us and agreed to let us have him for $5,000 and a pitcher named Brown."

Rudolph became an immediate success in Boston, posting a 14-13 record and 2.92 ERA in 1913. Mitchell attributed the rookie's solid performance to his brains and cunning. "He was one of the smartest pitchers who ever toed the rubber," said the Braves coach and future manager. "He wasn't fast but had a good curve ball, which he mixed with a spitball, and he could almost read the batter's mind. I've often sat on the bench with him and heard him tell whether a batter would take or hit. He made a real study of the profession." During the miracle season of 1914 Rudolph won a total of 26 games, including 12 consecutive victories. On Labor Day he beat Mathewson, 5-4, in the first game of a morning-afternoon doubleheader to move the Braves into first place. In the World Series sweep, Rudoph beat Chief Bender, 7-1, in Game One, and Bob Shawkey, 3-1, in Game Four.

Over the three-year period 1914-16, Rudolph was one of baseball's best and most durable pitchers, hurling over 300 innings each season. His performance in 1916 may have been even better than 1914; though he won seven fewer games, he lowered his ERA from 2.35 to a career-best 2.16 and led the NL with 8.9 base runners per nine innings. Dick developed arm trouble in 1918, limiting him to just 154 innings. Though he bounced back with one more workhorse season in 1919, he pitched in only 26 games over the next eight years, when he was more of a coach than a pitcher. Rudolph left the Braves after the 1927 season, retiring with a career record of 121-108 and a 2.66 ERA.

The following year Rudolph and the Braves traveling secretary bought the Waterbury, Connecticut, club in the Eastern League. They lasted one losing season. Dick joined his brother for a few years in an undertaking business in Nyack, New York. He returned to baseball as the supervisor for Stevens Brothers Concessionaires at Yankee Stadium and the Polo Grounds. Closing the circle of his baseball career, he returned to Fordham as a volunteer freshman baseball coach. Rudolph died of a heart attack in the Bronx on October 20, 1949, and is buried in Woodlawn Cemetery.

DICK LEYDEN

Joseph Francis Connolly
Left fielder 1913–16

Joey Connolly (*Total Baseball* lists him as "Joe," but family members insist that he went by "Joey") was the offensive star of the Boston Braves during their most successful period of the Deadball Era. A left-handed batter who played predominantly against right-handed pitching, Connolly usually batted third and compiled a .288 average over his four seasons in the major leagues. As for his defense, the *Boston Sunday Post* wrote that he "is fairly fast, the possessor of a strong wing and he covers a good extent of territory."

The ninth of 11 children of Irish immigrants, Connolly was born on his family's farm in the Sayles Hill section of North Smithfield, Rhode Island, but disagreement exists over his middle name and his exact date of birth. *Total Baseball* lists his full name as Joseph Aloysius Connolly and his birth date as February 12, 1886, but records in the North Smithfield Town Hall indicate that his middle name was Francis and he was born on February 1, 1884, which is consistent with records at the state archives. To add more confusion, his baptismal record at St. James Church in Manville, a section of Lincoln, Rhode Island, lists his date of birth as February 2, 1884 (he was baptized eight days later). Given Connolly's Roman Catholic background, the most plausible explanation for Aloysius is that he accepted that name when he received the sacrament of Confirmation on September 21, 1902. As for the birthdate controversy, Connolly's children admit that he lied about his age to advance his baseball career, but even they thought his actual birthday was February 12.

Joey was a quiet young man who didn't smoke, chew tobacco, or drink alcohol, possibly because some of his older brothers suffered from alcoholism. He began his baseball career as a right-handed pitcher, twirling primarily for an independent club from Putnam, Connecticut. In 1907 the "Manville Boy" (also known as the "Sayles Hill Boy") impressed John Rudderham, a major league umpire from Providence, who considered Connolly's curveball to be the best he'd ever seen. Rudderham recommended the young pitcher to Little Rock manager Michael Finn, whose team included another player who was destined to make his mark as a Boston outfielder: Tris Speaker. Finn started Joey in a 1908 spring training contest against the New York Giants. The new pitcher hurled a complete game in a 4-0 loss to Christy Mathewson.

After Connolly spent two months in the Class A Southern Association, Little Rock sent him to Zanesville of the Class B Central League, where he hit .333 in 78 at-bats—the first hint that his future lay in hitting baseballs instead of pitching them. In 1909 Joey pitched briefly again at Little Rock before returning to Zanesville, where Central Leaguers nicknamed him "Ol' Herkey Jerkey" because of his unusual delivery. He compiled a 23-8 record and played some outfield when he wasn't pitching, hitting .308 for the season. Still with Zanesville the following year, pitching for a club that finished 16 games below .500, Connolly went 16-17, hurling a no-hitter, a one-hitter, a two-hitter, and four three-hitters. One reporter wrote that a "fine assortment of speed and curves made him a cracker jack hurler," but two factors were hindering his progress: scouts thought he was too small (he stood only 5'7½"), and he was experiencing arm trouble.

His major league ambitions in jeopardy, Joey returned to Zanesville in 1911 and insisted on playing the outfield full-time—a dramatic change at age 27. Manager Joe Raidy resisted the request. Financial problems eventually forced Zanesville to sell Connolly to Central League rival Terre Haute. In his first few games

there he "misjudged flies and booted grounders like a rank amateur." Joey persevered and won the batting crown with a .355 average, adding 27 stolen bases. It proved to be his big break. The Chicago Cubs signed him and then traded him to Montreal of the International League, where he hit .316 in 1912. Clark Griffith drafted Joey for the Washington Senators, with whom he had an impressive training camp in 1913. Griff was set in the outfield, so he sold Connolly to the Boston Braves.

Joining the Braves was a homecoming for Connolly. On Sundays, when professional baseball was banned in Massachusetts, teammates often visited his Rhode Island farm. Manager George Stallings made Joey his regular left fielder in 1913. Though his season ended prematurely when he broke his ankle sliding, the 29-year-old rookie led all Braves regulars in runs (79), RBI (57), triples (11), batting average (.281), and slugging percentage (.410). He also showed an ability to adapt to a pitcher's style. When he first faced Pete Alexander, Connolly was outmatched by the great pitcher's "baffling hooks." He adapted by rushing forward and swinging before the ball broke, prompting Pete to yell, "Listen, kid, if this ball isn't coming at you fast enough, just let me know." From that day on Alexander threw him only fastballs, which was exactly what Connolly wanted him to do.

The 1914 Miracle Braves owed much of their success to Joey Connolly, the only regular to hit .300. He was also the team leader in doubles (28), home runs (9), and slugging average (third in the NL at .494). Stallings held Joey in such high regard that he reportedly bet several suits that Connolly would hit better than Home Run Baker in the World Series. That didn't happen (Connolly batted .111, while Baker batted .250), but the Braves swept the Athletics in four games. As a member of the world champions, Joey was feted with banquets throughout Rhode Island.

The Braves challenged for the pennant in 1915 and Connolly hit .298, only eight points lower than his average of the previous season, but his slugging percentage dropped nearly 100 points to .397. The following year his production and playing time decreased even more significantly; he batted .227 in just 110 at-bats. Boston's offer to Connolly for 1917 slashed his salary in half. When the outfielder refused to sign, the Braves sold him to Indianapolis. Realizing that his combined income from farming and playing semipro ball would exceed his American Association salary, he decided to retire from Organized Baseball.

On October 25, 1916, Joey began a new phase in life, marrying Manville resident Mary Delaney at St. James Church. The couple had three children: Doris, Joseph, and Edward. Besides farming, Connolly played semipro baseball in the Blackstone Valley until 1928. He also coached on the sandlot, semipro, and college levels and was active in Catholic Youth Organizations. An ardent sportsman, Joey became the founder and first president of the Sayles Hill Rod & Gun Club. On the political front, even though North Smithfield was a Republican enclave, Connolly won election to the town council and to the state legislature in 1933-34 as a Democrat. He also served as a state senator in 1935-36. After his term in office, Joey worked as an investigator for the Rhode Island Board of Milk Control.

On September 1, 1943, the lifelong Sayles Hill resident was stricken by a heart attack and died at his home. JOEY CONNOLLY CALLED OUT BY 'GREAT UMPIRE,' was the headline in the local newspaper. The local Carney Sandlot Baseball League, which he helped found, suspended play for several days in his honor. Connolly was buried at St. Charles Cemetery in Woonsocket.

DENNIS AUGER

Robison Field burns during the 1901 season. The rebuilt grandstand served the Cardinals until 1920, when they became tenants of the St. Louis Browns at Sportman's Park.

John McGraw blamed the weather: "A St. Louis ballclub, because of the city's summer climate wearing down the players, must be 25% stronger than any other major league club to win." More likely it was a combination of the team's limited resources and just plain mismanagement—what else would you call trading Mordecai Brown or selling Babe Adams after their rookie seasons? Whatever the reason, the St. Louis Cardinals were the only National League team not to win a pennant during the Deadball Era. In fact, they never placed higher than third.

The new century started on a deceptively promising note: in 1901 St. Louis finished fourth with a .543 win-

ning percentage. Three years earlier, in an egregious example of "syndicate ball," Cleveland Spiders owner Frank Robison had purchased the NL's struggling St. Louis Browns from Chris Von Der Ahe and transferred all of his best players from Cleveland to St. Louis. The "Cardinals"—so named after Robison changed the color of the team's stockings and uniform trim to vivid red—were a dramatic improvement on the Browns.

Though Cy Young had jumped to the Boston Americans, the 1901 team still featured former Cleveland stars such as Jesse Burkett, Bobby Wallace, and Jack Powell. But during the off-season that followed, the American League's Milwaukee Brewers relo-

WINNING PERCENTAGE 1901–1919

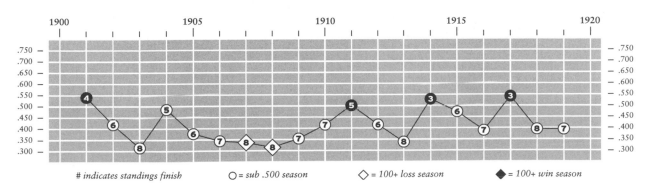

cated to St. Louis, stealing the Cardinals' old nickname and all of those former Spiders. All told, Robison lost five regulars and three starting pitchers to the American League in 1902.

It took a long time to recover; for the next dozen seasons the Cardinals failed to finish in the first division even once. During that stretch the most excitement in the vicinity of League Park came in 1911, when Roger Bresnahan kept a young team, led by Ed Konetchy, Steve Evans, Bob Harmon, and Slim Sallee, above .500 and in the pennant race until August. Three years later, under the leadership of Miller Huggins, the Cardinals finally returned to the first division with a third-place finish, thanks mainly to Bill Doak (19-6 with a league-leading 1.72 ERA). The success was short-lived, however, as St. Louis spent the next two seasons in its customary position near the bottom of the standings.

The Cardinals made their third and final first-division appearance of the era in 1917. That year their MVP was Rogers Hornsby, a slugging 21-year-old shortstop in his second full season as a regular. It also marked the beginning of Branch Rickey's quarter century stewardship of the franchise. Due mainly to the efforts of Hornsby and Rickey, St. Louis enjoyed its first pennant and world championship in 1926 and sustained success in the decades that followed, causing fans in the Mound City to forget about the Cardinals' futility during the Deadball Era.

ALL-ERA TEAM

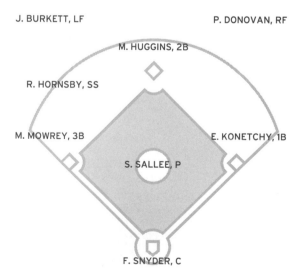

H. SMOOT, CF

J. BURKETT, LF   P. DONOVAN, RF

M. HUGGINS, 2B

R. HORNSBY, SS

M. MOWREY, 3B   E. KONETCHY, 1B

S. SALLEE, P

F. SNYDER, C

TEAM LEADERS 1901–1919

BATTING

GAMES
E. Konetchy 982
M. Huggins 803
D. Miller 697

RUNS
M. Huggins 507
E. Konetchy 501
H. Smoot 297

HITS
E. Konetchy 1013
M. Huggins 740
H. Smoot 706

RBI
E. Konetchy 476
S. Evans 303
D. Miller 275

DOUBLES
E. Konetchy 158
S. Evans 100
H. Smoot 94

TRIPLES
E. Konetchy 94
R. Hornsby 52
T. Long 49

HOME RUNS
E. Konetchy 36
R. Hornsby 27
S. Evans 16

STOLEN BASES
M. Huggins 174
E. Konetchy 151
R. Oakes 91

BATTING AVERAGE
P. Donovan 314
R. Hornsby 310
H. Smoot 292

PITCHING

GAMES
S. Sallee 317
B. Doak 224
B. Harmon 200

WINS
S. Sallee 106
B. Doak 87
B. Harmon 68

LOSSES
S. Sallee 107
B. Doak 98
B. Harmon 79

INNINGS
S. Sallee 1905⅓
B. Doak 1512
B. Harmon 1284⅓

STRIKEOUTS
S. Sallee 652
B. Doak 629
F. Beebe 605

WALKS
B. Harmon 594
S. Sallee 467
B. Doak 466

SHUTOUTS
B. Doak 20
S. Sallee 17
J. Lush 9

ERA
B. Doak 2.63
S. Sallee 2.67
L. Meadows 3.00

Player-manager Miller Huggins sits in the front row, third from left, in this photo of the 1915 Cardinals.

TYPICAL LINEUPS 1901–1919

1901

1. J. Burkett, LF
2. E. Heidrick, CF
3. D. McGann, 1B
4. P. Donovan, RF
5. D. Padden, 2B
6. B. Wallace, SS
7. O. Krueger, 3B
8. J. Ryan, C

1902

1. J. Farrell, 2B
2. H. Smoot, CF
3. G. Barclay, LF
4. P. Donovan, RF
5. O. Krueger, SS
6. R. Brashear, 1B
7. F. Hartman, 3B
8. J. Ryan
   J. O'Neill, C

1903

1. J. Farrell, 2B
2. P. Donovan, RF
3. H. Smoot, CF
4. D. Brain, SS
5. G. Barclay, LF
6. J. Burke, 3B
7. J. Hackett, 1B
8. J. O'Neill, C

1904

1. J. Farrell, 2B
2. S. Shannon, RF
3. J. Beckley, 1B
4. H. Smoot, CF
5. D. Brain, SS-3B
6. G. Barclay, LF
7. J. Burke, 3B
   D. Shay, SS
8. M. Grady, C

1905

1. J. Dunleavy, RF
2. S. Shannon, LF
3. H. Smoot, CF
4. J. Beckley, 1B
5. H. Arndt, 2B
6. G. McBride, SS
7. J. Burke, 3B
8. M. Grady, C

1906

1. A. Burch, RF
2. P. Bennett, 2B
3. S. Shannon, LF
4. H. Smoot, CF
5. J. Beckley, 1B
6. H. Arndt, 3B
7. G. McBride, SS
8. M. Grady, C

1907

1. B. Byrne, 3B
2. S. Barry, RF
3. E. Konetchy, 1B
4. J. Burnett, CF
5. E. Holly, SS
6. R. Murray, LF
7. P. Bennett, 2B
8. D. Marshall, C

1908

1. A. Shaw, CF
2. C. Charles, 2B-SS
3. R. Murray, RF
4. J. Delahanty, LF
5. E. Konetchy, 1B
6. B. Ludwig, C
   P. O'Rourke, SS
7. B. Byrne, 3B
8. B. Gilbert, 2B

1909

1. B. Byrne, 3B
2. R. Ellis, LF
3. E. Phelps, C
4. E. Konetchy, 1B
5. S. Evans, RF
6. J. Delahanty, CF-2B
7. R. Hulswitt, SS
   A. Shaw, CF
8. C. Charles, 2B-SS

1910

1. M. Huggins, 2B
2. R. Ellis, LF
3. R. Oakes, CF
4. E. Konetchy, 1B
5. S. Evans, RF
6. E. Phelps
   R. Bresnahan, C
7. M. Mowrey, 3B
8. A. Hauser, SS

1911

1. M. Huggins, 2B
2. A. Hauser, SS
3. R. Ellis, LF
4. E. Konetchy, 1B
5. S. Evans, RF
6. M. Mowrey, 3B
7. R. Oakes, CF
8. J. Bliss
   R. Bresnahan, C

1912

1. M. Huggins, 2B
2. L. Magee, LF
3. M. Mowrey, 3B
4. E. Konetchy, 1B
5. S. Evans, RF
6. A. Hauser, SS
7. R. Oakes, CF
8. I. Wingo, C

1913

1. M. Huggins, 2B
2. L. Magee, LF
3. R. Oakes, CF
4. M. Mowrey, 3B
5. E. Konetchy, 1B
6. S. Evans, RF
7. C. O'Leary, SS
8. I. Wingo, C

1914

1. M. Huggins, 2B
2. L. Magee, CF
3. C. Dolan, LF
4. D. Miller, 1B
5. O. Wilson, RF
6. A. Butler, SS
7. F. Snyder, C
8. Z. Beck, 3B

1915

1. M. Huggins, 2B
2. A. Butler, SS
3. B. Bescher, LF
4. T. Long, RF
5. O. Wilson, CF
6. D. Miller, 1B
7. B. Betzel, 3B
8. F. Snyder, C

1916

1. B. Bescher, LF
2. R. Corhan, SS
3. T. Long, RF
   J. Smith, CF
4. D. Miller, 1B
5. R. Hornsby, 3B
6. O. Wilson, RF-CF
7. M. Gonzalez, C
8. B. Betzel, 2B

1917

1. T. Long, RF
2. J. Smith, CF
3. D. Miller, 2B
4. R. Hornsby, SS
5. W. Cruise, LF
6. G. Paulette, 1B
7. D. Baird, 3B
8. F. Snyder, C

1918 (First half)

1. R. Smyth, RF
2. J. Smith, CF
3. D. Baird, 3B
4. R. Hornsby, SS
5. W. Cruise, LF
6. G. Paulette, 1B
7. F. Snyder, C
8. B. Betzel, 2B

1918 (Second half)

1. G. Anderson, RF
2. B. Betzel, 2B-3B
3. G. Paulette, 1B
4. R. Hornsby, SS
5. D. Baird, 3B
   R. Fisher, 2B
6. A. McHenry, LF
7. C. Heathcote, CF
8. M. Gonzalez, C

1919

1. J. Smith, RF
2. C. Heathcote, CF
3. M. Stock, 2B
4. R. Hornsby, 3B
5. A. McHenry, LF
6. V. Clemons, C
7. D. Miller, 1B
8. D. Lavan, SS

These Cardinals helped in the rescue effort when their train derailed near Bridgeport, Connecticut in July, 1911, killing 14.

ST. LOUIS

PATRICK JOSEPH DONOVAN
RIGHT FIELDER 1900–03, MANAGER 1901–03

A fleet-footed slap hitter who perennially topped the .300 mark, Patsy Donovan entered the Deadball Era as one of the game's most consistent stars. Standing 5'11" and weighing 175 lbs., Donovan was a singles hitter whose speed, coupled with a strong, accurate throwing arm, made him a fine right fielder. Though his days as a regular player were winding down, he went on to become a much traveled manager and longtime scout. One sportswriter called him an "excellent judge of the ball player in the raw." Indeed, Donovan's greatest accomplishment may have been convincing the Boston Red Sox to purchase a talented young left hander named George Ruth in 1914.

The second oldest of seven children of Jeremiah and Nora Donovan, Patrick Joseph Donovan was born in County Cork, Ireland. Most sources list March 16, 1865, as his date of birth, but it's probable that he later falsified his birth date to appear younger—census records from his childhood place his birth in 1863. Patrick immigrated with his family to Lawrence, Massachusetts, when he was three. After completing elementary school, Donovan, like many of the Irish immigrants in his neighborhood, went to work in Lawrence's cotton mills, a career choice that promised little other than long hours and low wages.

A gifted athlete, Donovan got his start in professional baseball in 1886 as an outfielder with Lawrence of the New England League. From there he ascended the rungs of the minor league ladder, playing with Salem in 1887 and London, Ontario, in 1888-89. In Patsy's first year in London his .359 batting average paced the International Association. Making his big-league debut with the Boston Beaneaters on April 19, 1890, Donovan spent his first two seasons in the majors bouncing around the National League and the American Association with Boston, Brooklyn, Louisville, and Washington. Halfway into the 1892 campaign he was shipped to Pittsburgh, where he spent the next seven seasons patrolling right field and consistently batting around .300.

In a decade that was infamous for rough play and rowdyism, Donovan was most admired for his quiet dignity and work ethic. Recognizing his leadership potential, the Pirates installed him as manager for 1897. In a theme that was repeated throughout his managerial career, Patsy was given little to work with and the club slumped to a 60-71 record, finishing eighth in the 12-team NL. Replaced at season's end, he was reinstated midway through 1899 and piloted Pittsburgh to a 69-58 record. Despite that improvement, Donovan once again was shown the door. Prior to the 1900 campaign, new Pirates owner Barney Dreyfuss installed Fred Clarke as player-manager. Soon after his hiring, Clarke cemented his authority by orchestrating Donovan's sale to the St. Louis Cardinals.

The Cardinals already had St. Louis native Patsy Tebeau handling the managerial duties, allowing Donovan to concentrate on his on-field performance. The new century witnessed the emergence of a new style of play, and Donovan's reliance on speed over brute strength translated well. From 1900 to 1903 he batted over .300 each season while placing even less emphasis on the extra-base hit than he had in the 1890s. In 1900, for example, he connected for only 11 doubles and one triple but batted .316 and led the NL with 45 stolen bases. The Cardinals slumped to the second division, however, leading to Tebeau's firing and Donovan's installation as manager in 1901.

Under Donovan the club improved to fourth place with a 76-64 record. The new manager received much of the credit, earning a reputation for treating his players honestly and fairly. As one writer noted, Donovan "teaches his men, and then expects them to retain their lessons. He understands his men and shows every confidence in them." But any hope for prolonged success was lost when Jesse Burkett, Bobby Wallace, Emmet Heidrick, Jack Powell, Jack Harper, and Willie Sudhoff jumped to the American League's St. Louis Browns. The mass defection caused Donovan's Cardinals to plummet to 56-78 and a sixth-place finish in 1902. They fell even further the following year, when Patsy's $8,800 salary reportedly made him the highest-paid player in all of baseball. St. Louis finished last with a nightmarish 43-94 record, 46½ games out of first place.

Let go by the Cardinals, Donovan spent the rest of the decade managing some of the worst teams of the Deadball Era. After his 1904 Washington Senators won only 38 games, the lowest total in the history of that unfortunate franchise, Donovan took a year off before accepting the manager's job with the Brooklyn Superbas in 1906. Over three seasons in Brooklyn, Donovan failed to lift the team out of the second division and was let go after a 53-101, seventh-place finish in 1908. "I did as well as could be expected of any manager with the material at hand," he explained to Reds president Garry Herrmann in a November 1908 letter inquiring about a managerial opening in Cincinnati. "Before leaving baseball I would like to have the opportunity of handling a club where I would have free rein and financial backing to secure talent."

Donovan got his opportunity when he was appointed manager of the Boston Red Sox prior to the 1910 season. Taking over a young, promising outfit that had finished third with 88 wins in 1909, Donovan didn't lift the club into contention during his two-year stewardship and was replaced by Jake Stahl, who led Boston to a world championship in his first year. His days as a player having long passed, Donovan continued in the Boston organization as a scout. In that capacity in 1914 he made his most important contribution to the success (and later sorrow) of the franchise by convincing owner Joseph Lannin to purchase Babe Ruth from the minor league Baltimore Orioles. Donovan never claimed to have discovered Ruth—the young left hander was too talented for his exploits to go unnoticed—but after watching the pitcher belt a grand slam against the Montreal Royals, Patsy rushed back to Boston and recommended Ruth's purchase "at any price."

Saddled with a lifetime .438 winning percentage, Donovan never received another opportunity to manage in the big leagues, but over the next 13 years he accepted several minor league offers. In 1915-16 he skippered the Buffalo Bisons, which included Charlie Jamieson, Joe McCarthy, and Joe Judge, to back-to-back International League pennants. After three years in Buffalo, Donovan went on to manage Syracuse, Newark, Jersey City, Springfield, and Providence without ever finishing higher than fourth. His last managing job came in 1928, when he led Attleboro of the New England League to a second-place finish. Donovan worked as a scout for the New York Yankees until 1950, finally ending a 64-year career in Organized Baseball.

Throughout his travels Donovan continued to call Lawrence home. In 1910 he married Teresa Mahoney, and the couple had three sons and one daughter. Patsy died at age 88 (or 90) on Christmas Day, 1953, after a long illness. He was buried in St. Mary's Cemetery in Lawrence.

DAVID JONES

ST. LOUIS

HOMER VERNON SMOOT
CENTER FIELDER 1902–06

Homer Smoot is the only player in history to play five seasons in the majors and collect no fewer than 500 at-bats in each of them. No other player is even close: Joe Cassidy (1904-05) is the runner-up, and he played only two seasons. Smoot's unusual career began with a .311 season, good enough to earn him retrospective designation by SABR as the National League's best rookie in 1902. He batted .311 again in 1905, but the following year he slumped to .252, and the year after that he was banished to the minors. The abrupt end to Smoot's playing days is somewhat mysterious. One source blames his diminishing eyesight, while some claim that he was slowed by muscular rheumatism.

When their son was born on March 23, 1878, Luke and Rebecca Smoot presciently named him Homer Vernon Smoot. Homer spent his childhood in the village of Galestown on the Eastern Shore of Maryland. One of his elementary-school classmates was Geneva Gordy, who became his wife in 1901. Homer crossed the Delaware state line to attend prep school at Wesley Collegiate Academy in Dover. Later he enrolled at Washington College in Chestertown, Maryland, where he played baseball and football. Smoot is listed as a member of the Class of 1897, but he continued to play for the college as late as 1899. In those same years he also played semipro baseball for Cambridge and Salisbury in his native state, and for Purcell and Laurel in Delaware.

In 1900 Smoot signed his first professional contract with the Allentown Peanuts of the Atlantic League. When that circuit folded on June 12, Homer caught on with the Worcester Farmers of the Eastern League. He returned to Worcester in 1901 and led the EL with a .356 batting average. The ongoing war between the two major leagues assured that such proficiency wouldn't go unnoticed, and the St. Louis Cardinals signed him to fill one of the gaping holes in their outfield. The Worcester correspondent to *The Sporting News*, H. T. Brewer, was skeptical of the signing. Though acknowledging that Smoot had "whacked the ball viciously," Brewer wrote that the Eastern League's batting champion should return to Worcester because "he can neither run bases nor throw."

Forced to turn to other untried youngsters in 1902, the Cardinals became known as the "kindergarten team," and the young club staggered out of the gate with five straight losses. On April 25, however, Homer lived up to his name by clubbing two home runs, the second one in the 10th inning, lifting St. Louis to a dramatic 9-8 win. Smoot's heroics were all the more surprising considering that fewer than 100 home runs were hit in the NL that year, with the Cardinals managing only 10. Homer hit only one more that season but batted a robust .311, combining with Patsy Donovan (.315) and George Barclay (.300) to give the Cardinals their last .300-hitting outfield of the Deadball Era. Smoot also disproved the criticism that he was a one-dimensional player by stealing 20 bases and tying for the NL lead in putouts.

In 1903 Smoot hit a solid .296 with four home runs, half of the club's season total. One of the homers was particularly memorable. On July 22 Smoot hit a three-run shot on a two-strike pitch with two out in the bot-

sonable to expect that he'd bounce back and achieve the stardom that had seemed likely only a year earlier. Instead, his contract was sold to Toledo of the American Association, and he never again appeared in the majors. One source claims that Smoot's diminishing eyesight caused his demotion. His obituary, however, claims that his batting eye remained "undimmed," but he was slowed by muscular rheumatism. His daughter claimed that Smoot never had eye problems, but his rheumatism was so bad by his career's end that he sometimes had to stay in bed until noon so he could have the strength to play ball in the afternoon. That Smoot stole only three bases in 1906 after averaging 20 steals in his first four seasons seems to support the rheumatism theory. Finally, it's possible that Smoot was still good enough to play in the majors but never was given a chance. In 1910 Albert Spink wrote that Smoot was "still pounds better than many outfielders in the major leagues."

Smoot spent three seasons with Toledo, batting .312 in 1907, .301 in 1908, and .270 in 1909. He split the 1910 season between Louisville and Kansas City but hit a lackluster .236. Smoot started the 1911 season with Kansas City and seemed to regain his old form. In July he was hitting a splendid .379 when his contract was sold to Wilkes-Barre of the New York State League, where he won the only pennant of his professional career. He began 1912 as an assistant manager and weekend player for Wilkes-Barre, but in June his rheumatism became so severe that he retired.

Smoot declined offers to manage in Organized Baseball, returning to the Eastern Shore of Maryland with his wife, Geneva, to raise their two sons and three daughters. He became head baseball coach at his alma mater, Washington College, but left after only one season. Homer spent the next decade farming, raising chickens, and operating a feed business in Salisbury. In 1925 he returned to baseball as manager of the local minor league club, the Salisbury Indians of the Eastern Shore League, but again lasted only one season. Two years later, his oldest son, Roger, signed with the Cardinals farm system. Homer Smoot died of spinal meningitis on March 25, 1928. He was posthumously elected to the Washington College and Eastern Shore halls of fame.

PETER MORRIS

tom of the ninth to lift the Cardinals to an 8-7 victory. Though his average dipped to .281 in 1904, he drove in a career-best 66 runs, only 14 off the NL lead. Smoot enjoyed his best season in 1905, when he matched his rookie average of .311 and posted career highs in runs (73), on-base percentage (.359), and slugging percentage (.433). His 16 triples ranked fourth in the NL. In 1906, however, Smoot struggled. He was hitting a disappointing .248 on July 25 when he was traded to Cincinnati for outfielder Shad Barry. The change of scenery didn't do much good, and he finished the season with a .252 average.

Smoot was only 28 and had been a regular for five years. Despite his disappointing season, it seemed rea-

Edward J Konetchy

ST. LOUIS

Edward Joseph Konetchy
First baseman 1907–13

Variously called the Candy Kid, the La Crosse Lulu, and the Big Bohemian—but known in box scores simply as "Koney"—Ed Konetchy was a 6'2", 195 lb. first baseman who led the National League in fielding eight times and batted .281 over 15 seasons. His 2,150 hits included 344 doubles, 182 triples (15th all-time), and 74 home runs. Koney was a right-handed hitter who almost always batted cleanup, stood straight up at the plate, choked up on his bat, and sent liners to the outfield fences. Popular with both teammates and opponents, he was known as the kind of player that even the umpires liked. "I not only play baseball for the salary connected with it, but I really and truly love the game," Ed said, "and like to fan just as much now as I did in the old days back in La Crosse, when we used to get the pictures of the athletes out of cigarette boxes."

One of seven children, Edward Joseph Konetchy (CONE-uh-chec) was born to immigrant Bohemian parents on September 3, 1885, in La Crosse, Wisconsin. "I know I tried to play baseball as soon as I was big enough to raise a bat from the ground," he said. "I used to play all the time that I could get a chance with some little scrub team or other, but the first real serious experience I had along this line was after I'd gone to work." After attending school until age 14, Ed began working in a La Crosse candy factory. "I used to get up and walk the two miles to the factory, carrying my dinner pail, and work 10 hours," he recalled. "After that we'd all get together and walk two miles in another direction to the ball field. There we'd play baseball until it was too dark to see, and then we'd walk home. We did this not once or twice, but five times a week on average. Sunday we'd gather the club together and go off to some one-horse place maybe three or four hours' ride away on a slow train to play baseball with some other club."

It wasn't until Konetchy was 16 that he joined the factory team. "They needed someone to play left field and I was willing to fill the gap," he said. "It never occurred to me that I might play another position, and I was so anxious to get on the team somewhere I didn't care especially where I played." At 20 Ed tried out for the local La Crosse team of the Wisconsin State League. Told that Konetchy was a local boy, manager Pink Hawley said, "Well, he is a better player at that than some that we have on our payroll right now." Ed made the team and played left field for a while before moving to first base, where he remained for the rest of his career. In 1907 St. Louis Cardinals manager John McCloskey sent scout Jack Huston to find a new first baseman. Huston heard that La Crosse was harboring "the next Hal Chase." After watching Konetchy in person, Huston advised McCloskey of his find, and the Cardinals purchased the 21-year-old for $1,000.

After signing Konetchy for $275 per month, McCloskey told reporters that he'd "just signed a tall Greek from the tall timbers." Koney made his major league debut on June 29, 1907, getting his first hit in a 4-3 loss to the Cincinnati Reds. Three days later, when the Cardinals played in Pittsburgh, a delegation of Greeks approached home plate with a band, a large stand of flowers, and a gold watch. "I wondered what it was all about, as I was asked to the plate," said Konetchy. "One of the fellows stepped forward, shook my hand and greeted me cordially. Then he began speaking in what I later found out was Greek. I stopped him and told him that I was very sorry, but that I happened to be Bohemian. He looked puzzled, then disappointed. He glanced at me, then the big floral piece, which was fully as tall as I am, and said, 'You take it, kid, and the best of luck to you.'"

Konetchy established himself as a regular for the Cardinals, hitting .251 in 91 games and winning praise for his glove work from managers around the circuit. John McGraw, who later made several attempts to acquire the young first baseman, declared, "Konetchy is worth the whole [St. Louis] team. With a little coaching on batting and base running, this player has the makings of the grandest man in the business at first sack." Frank Chance concurred, predicting, "This Konetchy someday is going to be the greatest first baseman in the business." Ed began to fulfill that promise in his sophomore season, 1908, when he played in all 154 games, leading NL first basemen in assists and placing second in putouts despite a patchwork St. Louis infield that included eight different shortstops. "Koney has had to handle more weird throws in two years than any two National League guardians of the initial corner," wrote a St. Louis reporter. "But he dug up and pulled down so many of them that patrons who marveled at these extraordinary performances have come to take them as a matter of course."

Aside from leading NL first basemen in both putouts and assists in 1909, Konetchy led the Cardinals in every offensive category except walks and finished in the NL's top five in hits (165), runs (88), total bases (228), triples (14), and RBI (80). When asked how he improved his batting, Ed replied, "Hard work. I made it my business to study closely the pitchers who bothered me most, particularly Nap Rucker's high fastball." He asked teammates to throw him only high fastballs during batting practice, until he was able to "whale the stuffing out of it." Konetchy also started hitting to the opposite field on the advice of new manager Roger Bresnahan. "He said I was hitting the ball to left field too often, as the fielders knew where to play me," Ed said. "I changed my stance and started poking the ball in other directions."

In 1910 Konetchy put together a 20-game hitting streak and batted over .300 for the first time. He also won the triple crown in fielding, leading NL first basemen in fielding percentage, putouts, and assists. As the season came to an end, he was selected to play on an All-National team on a barnstorming tour with an All-American team. Cardinals ownership refused to allow it, however, and a showdown was averted only when the tour was cancelled. Instead Ed spent the off-season playing indoor baseball. He was the star pitcher for his team, once striking out 21 batters. "I suppose every player had the ambition to be a pitcher, and it may be that I might have had some chance to succeed if I'd ever tried," he said. Konetchy did pitch three games in the majors, appearing twice in relief (earning his only victory in 4⅔ innings in 1913) and once as a starter, hurling a complete game and allowing 14 hits in an 8-0 loss in 1918.

During Koney's first four years in St. Louis, the Cardinals never won more than 63 games. Finally, in 1911, they got off to a good start. Bresnahan had the Cards only three games out of first place in early July when the team was involved in a train wreck on its way from Philadelphia to Boston. A dozen passengers were killed and 47 injured. Due to a pre-trip change in the location of their car to the rear of the train, the Cardinals sustained no serious injuries. Konetchy and Bresnahan led the rescue effort, carrying many passengers to safety. The team never recovered from the incident, finishing a distant fifth despite posting their first winning season since 1901. Konetchy led the National League with 38 doubles and his own team with six home runs and 88 RBI. In February 1912 he met with Bresnahan in a St. Louis hotel bar to talk contract. The negotiation turned into a drinking contest that lasted from the time the bar opened that morning until late in the afternoon. Amidst a table of empty beer bottles, Konetchy finally agreed to terms. That year he batted .314, the second-highest average of his career, but the following year his average fell to .276.

Being the star player on a second-division team, Konetchy was the frequent subject of trade rumors throughout the early part of his career. "I'm the most traded man in baseball without getting anywhere," he said. Philadelphia reportedly offered Sherry Magee, Fred Luderus, and Earl Moore for him, while other teams offered up to $20,000. When interviewed in 1938, Konetchy wondered "what kind of tag they'd have on me in this high-pressure era. One thing is certain, I was born 23 years too soon." During the off-season of 1913-14, the Cardinals' manager, Miller Huggins, finally traded Konetchy, along with Mike Mowrey and Bob Harmon, to Pittsburgh for five players. It was said that Pittsburgh manager Fred Clarke had been so eager to acquire Konetchy that he even considered trading Honus Wagner for him.

After winning 15 of their first 17 games, the 1914 Pirates fell apart, finishing seventh. Throughout the season Pittsburgh owner Barney Dreyfuss berated his players for their poor performance, particularly Konetchy, who batted only .249. At season's end, Dreyfuss refused Konetchy's demand for a three-year contract at $7,500 per year. Despite his teammates' attempts to dissuade him, Konetchy jumped to the Pittsburgh Rebels of the Federal League, which granted his contract demands. Ed's wife reportedly received $1,000 for helping convince him to sign. In his only season in the Federal League, Konetchy set career highs in batting average (.314, percentage points higher than his 1912 mark), hits (181), and triples (18), finishing in the top five in almost every offensive category while winning his second fielding triple crown. He referred to the Federal League as the "best league I have ever been connected with," even going so far as to write a scathing letter to the editor of The Sporting Life to deny a report that he'd told former teammate Bobby Byrne

that he was "sorry he had left Organized Base Ball and longed to get back with them." But the Federal League folded at the end of the season, and Konetchy was sold to the Boston Braves, along with two other players, for $18,000.

After three years with the Braves, Konetchy was sold on the eve of the 1919 season to the Brooklyn Robins. On June 28 he began an incredible streak, knocking out two singles and a double. The following day he collected four singles and a triple, followed by two more singles the next day, giving him a streak of 10 hits in consecutive at-bats, tying a record set in 1897. In 1920, his 14th season in the majors, Koney—who had once said, "The happiest moment of my life would be on a pennant-winning team"—finally got to play in a World Series. Despite only four hits in seven games, he established a Series record for most chances accepted in a game by a first baseman with 19. Midway through the 1921 season, Koney was released on waivers to the Phillies, where he finished his final year in the majors with a .299 average, a career-high 11 home runs, and a record five unassisted double plays in one season. When told that he was the NL's oldest player in terms of service, he replied: "Ed Koney's still a kid first baseman, just getting limbered up. You tell 'em."

Konetchy's playing days, in fact, were far from over; he remained active in the minors until 1927. After a year with Toledo of the American Association, he became player-manager of Omaha of the Western League in 1923. The following year he played for Petersburg of the Virginia League, leading the circuit in home runs and finishing the season as manager. In 1925, while playing for the Ft. Worth Cats, the 40 year-old Konetchy batted .345 and led the Texas League with 41 home runs and 166 RBI. After a brief stint managing Brownsville of the Texas Valley League, he returned to his boyhood home of La Crosse and managed the team to the Wisconsin State League championship in 1940. The league broke up in 1942, and Ed returned to his adopted home of Ft. Worth, becoming a foreman at the Convair plant. He also owned a restaurant and chicken farm and worked as a scout for the St. Louis Cardinals. Ed Konetchy died from heart disease on May 27, 1947. He was posthumously inducted into Wisconsin's Athletic Hall of Fame in 1961.

PAUL SALLEE & ERIC SALLEE

ST. L.

ST. LOUIS

Arthur Lawrence "Bugs" Raymond
Right-handed pitcher 1907–08

New York Giants manager John McGraw considered Bugs Raymond one of the greatest pitchers he ever managed—or tried to manage. "What a terrific spitball pitcher he was," reminisced teammate Rube Marquard. "Bugs drank a lot, you know, and sometimes it seemed the more he drank the better he pitched. They used to say he didn't spit on the ball; he blew his breath on it and the ball came up drunk." But after two successful seasons—1908, when he was the ace of the dreadful St. Louis Cardinals, and 1909, when he went 18-12 for the Giants—Raymond drank himself out of the National League in 1911. One year later he was dead at age 30.

Arthur Lawrence Raymond was born in Chicago on February 24, 1882. His nickname was short for "bughouse," a slang term for insane asylum. Raymond worked as a pressman before beginning his professional baseball career in 1903 with an independent team in Appleton, Wisconsin. The next year he made his debut in Organized Baseball with Waterloo, Iowa, of the Iowa State League, winning nine straight games and compiling a 19-7 record. Bobby Lowe, then managing the Detroit Tigers, signed Raymond that fall and pitched him in five games. After the season the Tigers sold his contract to the Atlanta Crackers of the Southern Association. Lowe reportedly discarded him when he heard rumors that the pitcher had a drinking problem.

Peeved at his demotion, Raymond reported late to Atlanta in 1905 and did little but gain notoriety for his clowning, sometimes walking to and from the pitcher's mound on his hands. He started well for the Crackers in 1906 but was suspended after being accused of throwing a game. Savannah manager Wilson Matthews signed the out-of-condition Raymond, who promised his new team a pennant. Bugs made good, contributing 18 victories to Savannah's championship season.

The next spring, while toiling for Jackson, Mississippi, of the Cotton States League, Raymond unveiled his spitball. In an exhibition against the New York Highlanders he struck out Willie Keeler three times. New York manager Clark Griffith wanted Raymond, but the deal fell through and Bugs ended up rejoining Matthews in Charleston later in 1907. He appeared in 51 games, pitching a no-hitter and compiling a 35-11 record in another championship season, but his erratic behavior continued. On one occasion an unconscious Bugs was seen being chauffeured by Matthews in a wheelbarrow. Nonetheless, the St. Louis Cardinals purchased his contract, and he appeared in eight games at the end of 1907, finishing with six complete games and a 2-4 record.

In his first 1908 appearance Raymond pitched a one-hitter against the Chicago Cubs. By then he'd mastered another new pitch, an underhand slow ball. Plagued by control problems and bad luck—St. Louis was shut out 10 times in games he started—Raymond lost a league-high 25 games for the last-place Cardinals, but he also threw five shutouts and finished second in the NL in fewest hits per nine innings (6.55), tied for second in appearances (48), and fourth in strikeouts (145). Though required to stay sober only on days he was scheduled to pitch, Raymond didn't always oblige. On one occasion he telephoned manager John McCloskey to inform him that he couldn't make his start due to a toothache. Bugs was drunk when he showed up but still defeated the Cubs without even warming up.

McGraw acquired Raymond after the 1908 season as part of a three-way trade with St. Louis and Cincinnati that sent catcher Roger Bresnahan to the Cardinals. Confident of his ability to manage strong personalities, the legendary Giants manager believed he could reform Raymond. Though Bugs arrived penniless at the Giants' 1909 spring training camp, McGraw gave him pocket money only and forbade him from purchasing alcohol. Instead, the Giants paid Raymond's salary and fines directly to his wife, who was obligated by contract not to send money to her husband. Bugs enjoyed a good season in 1909, missing out on a chance to become a 20-game winner only because he quit the Giants a month before the season ended. He still won 18 and finished with a 2.47 ERA.

Raymond's career went into rapid decline beginning in 1910. At spring training McGraw insisted on buying the alcoholic pitcher a suit of clothes, rather than trusting him to do it himself. Raymond returned the suit in exchange for a cheaper model and spent the seven dollars he saved on alcohol. Next McGraw cut off all funds to Bugs and forbade the other Giants from lending him money. In response, as the team barnstormed north, Raymond wrote out free passes to the Giants' exhibitions and gave them to bartenders in exchange for drinks. By the time the team reached New York, McGraw was denying Bugs unopened packs of cigarettes to prevent him from reselling them for money to buy booze. The manager also hired former New York City policeman Dick Fuller to keep track of Raymond. Their relationship began well but ended in a fistfight in St. Louis, with Bugs receiving a black eye. Fuller quit in disgust after the incident, and Bugs finished the season with a 4-11 record.

Before the 1911 season the Giants arranged for Raymond to receive treatment for his alcoholism at the famous Keeley Institute in Dwight, Illinois, but Bugs was expelled from the program for excessive horseplay. For a while his behavior and physical appearance improved, despite two lapses during spring training that McGraw tried to hide from the press. "McGraw told Bugs the next time he didn't show up on time that would mean the end," recalled teammate Fred Snodgrass. "The next day we were supposed to be at the park at noon, and by 2:00 Bugs still hadn't shown up. Finally we saw him in civilian clothes, walking across the field. McGraw met him at the clubhouse door. 'Bugs,' he said, 'you're through in baseball. Here's your uniform.'" When the team got back to New York, Bugs' uniform was hanging in the window of a saloon near the Polo Grounds, with a sign that read, BUGS RAYMOND TENDING BAR HERE."

Raymond started the 1912 season in the United States League, but by that point he had little left. In one game he hit four men with pitches in less than two innings. None of the batsmen were seriously hurt, a scribe noted, because Bugs could no longer throw hard enough to injure them. When the league collapsed, Raymond received his reinstatement from the National Commission and applied to McGraw to get his old job back. Mugsy wired back a terse rejection: "I have enough troubles."

Discarded by the Giants, separated from his wife, and with his five-year-old daughter recently dead from influenza, Bugs drifted back to Chicago, where he played semipro ball and again worked as a pressman. At midday on September 7, 1912, a maid entered Raymond's shabby room in the Hotel Veley and found him dead. A coroner's physician found that he'd died from a cerebral hemorrhage due to a fractured skull. The police arrested a man, Fred Cigranz, who admitted to beating up Bugs several days earlier during a sandlot game, but that was only part of the story. Raymond also had been in a brawl three weeks earlier in which he'd been hit several times in the head with a baseball bat. When he received word of Raymond's passing, McGraw said "That man took seven years off my life."

DON JENSEN

ST. LOUIS

HARRY FRANKLIN "SLIM" SALLEE
LEFT-HANDED PITCHER 1908–16

Standing 6'3" and weighing just 148 lbs., Slim Sallee was one of the Deadball Era's most unusual pitchers. With his cap usually yanked low over his eyes and employing a slow-motion windup that hypnotized batters and exasperated umpires, the left-handed Sallee finished his follow-through on the extreme first-base side of the pitcher's mound, delivering the ball from every conceivable angle. Batters constantly complained that it looked as if the ball was arriving from first base, but Roger Bresnahan claimed that the crossfire pitcher had "the best control of any southpaw that ever curved a ball over the plate." Over the period 1908-21, Sallee ranked first in relief appearances, second in saves, third in games, fourth in innings, and seventh in wins among all major league pitchers. *Baseball Magazine* attributed his success to an "imperturbable calm which nothing can disturb, faultless control, and back of all a scheming, crafty brain wise to all the quirks and twists of the pitcher."

Harry Franklin Sallee (suh-LEE) was born in the tiny Ohio River village of Higginsport, Ohio, on February 3, 1885. His lanky build later inspired monikers like "Slim," "Scissors," or "Slats," but his nickname as a youth was "Scatter" because he knocked cans and bottles off fence posts with rocks. Harry got his start in serious baseball when the pitcher for the Higginsport town team failed to show up for a much anticipated game against Augusta, Kentucky. Searching for a replacement, the Higginsport manager reportedly stumbled on young Sallee, the best of the town's kid ballplayers, sleeping on a soapbox in a livery stable. Wearing a torn flannel shirt and bored to death, "Scatter" agreed to pitch and won the game.

As Sallee's reputation grew, the team from nearby Georgetown, Ohio, began borrowing him for important contests. In 1904 Pittsburgh Pirates pitcher Charlie Case, a Georgetown resident, recommended the young left hander to Dick Kinsella, the famous scout. Kinsella got Sallee a job with a semipro team in Clinton, Iowa, but it folded in July and Sallee returned to Georgetown. That fall Birmingham Barons manager Harry Vaughn, a resident of the Georgetown area, signed the lanky left hander for his Southern Association team.

In his first professional start during 1905 spring training, the 20-year-old Sallee hurled an 11-inning complete game, allowing only two hits over the final eight innings to defeat the Cleveland Naps. Napoleon Lajoie "thought Sallee's action in delivering a ball when there was a runner on first was a balk, but when he looked it over, he declared it was something marvelous."

A few weeks later a broken hand forced Sallee to sit out a month. Sent to Meridian, Mississippi, to work his way into shape, he was leading the Cotton States League with 10 wins when the league shut down due to a yellow-fever epidemic. Another eight victories for Birmingham over the rest of 1905 gave Sallee an overall mark of 18-10 for his first year in Organized Baseball. Returning to Birmingham in 1906, he won 17 games to help the Barons claim their first Southern Association pennant. Sallee was drafted by the New York Highlanders and spent the final week of the season in the American League, though he failed to appear in a single game. The next spring the Highlanders released him to Williamsport, where he led the Tri-State League with a 22-5 record.

After his purchase by the St. Louis Cardinals, Sallee pitched extremely well in spring training, even hurling seven innings of a combined no-hitter. Nonetheless, his first major league start didn't come until May 23, 1908, when he shut out the New York Giants on four hits. Sallee again defeated the Giants in his third start, earning a "Giant Killer" reputation, but he won only one more game over the rest of the season, finishing with a 3-8 record. The 1908 Cardinals not only led the NL in errors, besting the next highest team total by 94, but also scored the fewest runs. During a four-week period St. Louis scored only five runs in 45 innings that Sallee pitched. In two consecutive duels against Christy Mathewson, the 23-year-old rookie lost both games because of infield errors, one in the 12th inning of a 2-2 game, the other resulting in a 1-0 loss.

During 1908 Sallee's drinking and poor training habits began to affect his career. When the drudgery of practice became unbearable, he often left Robison Field and walked across the street to a social club known as the "Grass Eaters," which was located 100 feet behind the Cardinals clubhouse. A clubhouse boy claimed that during games he lowered a bucket over the fence on a rope to a confederate, who filled it with beer at the social club. Sallee then found it necessary to "change shirts," walking to the clubhouse in center field.

The Cardinals were counting on more from Sallee in 1909. During his first start he demonstrated his incredible control by throwing a first-pitch strike to every batter in a four-hit victory over the Cubs. Later that season, however, Slim disappeared for a week (it was later reported that he'd been a mere two blocks away the entire time), prompting Bresnahan to suspend him. Pitching poorly after his return, including two consecutive games in which he failed to hold large leads, Sallee quit the team. "I'll admit that I've done a few things I shouldn't have done, but who hasn't?" he told a friend. "It was bad enough for them to suspend me, but when they bunched that with the fines of almost $600 this season, why, I come to the conclusion that I'm almost through with the gang. I have several offers to play elsewhere and may possibly take one of them if I can get released honorably by Bresnahan. I'm going up to Higginsport, and I'll stay there the rest of this season. And what is more, I'll never go back to St. Louis."

"Never" lasted only until the next season, but his troubles continued. After showing up a week late, Sallee severely twisted an ankle and missed most of spring training. Just before Opening Day he disappeared for over a week. On his return Slim defeated the Giants in his first start. Later in July he deserted the team for two days and was again suspended, but once again he was reinstated in time to defeat the Giants. Bresnahan tried desperately to trade the exasperating pitcher. "Sallee is a great pitcher, but he has very bad habits and for this reason I could not be induced to have him on my team," said Pittsburgh manager Fred Clarke, "not even if Bresnahan would give him to me for nothing." (The following season Slim beaned Clarke in the head, essentially ending the Hall of Famer's playing career.) Two weeks later Sallee was

missing again and was finally placed on indefinite suspension. He picked up a living by pitching games for local teams around St. Louis and helping a huckster sell vegetables from a cart.

Sallee returned to the Cardinals in 1911 and posted his best season yet, his 15-9 record helping St. Louis to its first winning record since 1901, but it could have been even better. While in New York in late August, Sallee again "fell off the water wagon" and was unable to pitch. He was fined and suspended for the remainder of the season. Sallee showed up for 1912 spring training with a new attitude. Bresnahan named him assistant manager and sent him with a squad of pitchers and catchers for early workouts in Hot Springs, Arkansas. Claiming he "never felt so nearly perfect this early in the season," Sallee finally lived up to his ability, pitching a career-high 294 innings and winning 16 games. He also established himself as a "rescue artist" with four relief wins and a league-leading six saves.

The 1944 book *Kings of the Mound: A Pitcher's Rating Manual* ranked Sallee's 1913 season as one of the finest in history. He won 19 games for a last-place team that won only 51 and finished last or next to last in the NL in every offensive category. Sallee pitched in 50 games and had an ERA of 2.71, well below the league average. In addition, he slugged the only two home runs of his career and even stole home, to this day the last Cardinal pitcher to accomplish that feat.

By 1914, when he went 18-17 with a 2.10 ERA and a league-leading six saves, Sallee was the only remaining member of the 1908 Cardinals. For all his troubles in St. Louis, he managed to outlast everyone, playing for two different ownership groups, myriad team presidents, and three managers. During his eight and a half years with the Cardinals, Sallee won 106 games and compiled a .498 winning percentage, almost 100 points better than the team's when he didn't factor in the decision. His 2.67 ERA is the lowest in Cardinals history (minimum 1,000 innings), and he ranks among the team's top 20 pitchers of all time in games, innings, and complete games.

Finally Sallee got tired of losing. On June 16, 1916, while in New York, he tore up his $6,000 per year contract and announced that he'd no longer play for the Cardinals, claiming to be "through with baseball." Slim went home to Higginsport. No one took his retirement seriously, figuring he was trying to force the Cardinals

to trade him. The St. Louis owners insisted that they wouldn't be forced into a trade, but a few weeks later they sold him to the New York Giants for $10,000. While St. Louis manager Miller Huggins claimed he knew of no wrongdoing, it was widely believed that Giants manager John McGraw tampered with Sallee. "No other deal like that will be sanctioned while I am in office," declared NL president John Tener, and rules were established to prevent a player from retiring to force a trade. Joining New York in late July, Sallee contributed several wins to the Giants' 26-game winning streak, finishing 9-4 with a microscopic 1.37 ERA.

As one of the Giants' "big three" left-handed starters that dominated the NL in almost every statistical category in 1917, Sallee won 18 games, including 10 in a row, and again led the league with four saves. He had the honor of pitching the pennant-clinching game on September 24, defeating his old Cardinal teammates, 2-1. After losing Game One of the 1917 World Series to Chicago White Sox ace Eddie Cicotte, 2-1, Sallee was beating Cicotte in Game Five, 5-2, when he tired in the seventh inning and the Sox tied the score. McGraw stayed with him in the eighth, a decision that became widely criticized when the Sox scored three runs. The Giants went on to lose the game and the Series.

In 1918 an aging Sallee developed lower back pain that eventually forced him to quit for the year after only 132 innings. During the off-season he rehabilitated by hunting and working his tobacco farm near Higginsport. Sallee even built a new house "with all modern conveniences, including electric lights and other features usually found only in city homes." He became so comfortable in Higginsport that he refused to sign with the Giants for 1919, stating that the only team he'd consider playing with was Cincinnati, which would allow him to commute from his Ohio farm. The Giants reluctantly granted Sallee's wish, and the Reds purchased him via the waiver route.

Sallee re-injured his back in his first spring training outing with the Reds and didn't return to action until May 4. Despite the late start, he won 21 of the 29 games in which he appeared. In 227⅔, innings Slim walked a mere 20 batters while striking out only 24, becoming the third 20-game winner in the modern era with more wins than walks in a season. On "Sallee Day" in late September 1919, he threw a record 65-pitch nine-inning complete game in only 55 minutes. It was the perfect example of Sallee's pitching philosophy: "My whole system is to make them hit, and keep them hitting, and try never to give the batter what he wants. It makes no difference how much speed a man has or what curves he has mastered. These things do him no good if he can't get the ball over the plate. It doesn't take any more exertion to put the ball over the plate than it does to miss it by a foot."

Ironically, the Reds beat out the Giants for the NL pennant. When McGraw was asked why he didn't re-sign Sallee, he replied, "I knew what a good pitcher he was, but he wouldn't play with me, so what could I do?" Facing the Chicago White Sox in the World Series for the second time in three years, Sallee pitched Game Two, defeating Lefty Williams, 4-2, and Game Seven, losing to Eddie Cicotte once again, 4-1. The Reds upset the highly favored White Sox, five games to three.

In 1920, two days after giving a lengthy interview in which he expressed his objection to baseball's new rules regarding foreign substances on the ball, Sallee was ejected from a game for using rosin and subsequently suspended 10 days. After being released by Cincinnati in August, Slim signed on again with McGraw's Giants, pitching exclusively in relief in 1921 when he led the NL in relief wins with six. He didn't pitch in that year's World Series, bringing his 14-year major league career to a close. At the time Sallee was second only to ex-Cardinal teammate Ed Konetchy in consecutive years of NL service. His former Cardinals manager Roger Bresnahan, then owner of Toledo in the American Association, convinced the 37-year-old to pitch one final season in 1922. Sallee was released in July after staggering to a 2-9 record.

Returning home to Higginsport, Sallee channeled his baseball savings into various successful business enterprises, including a soda bottling company, an icehouse, and a restaurant. He also served as a village councilman. Slim kept in touch with baseball by attending Reds games and becoming active in a Cincinnati social group called the Ballplayers of Yesteryear. In 1937 the great Ohio River flood wiped out Higginsport and all of Sallee's businesses, inducing financial hardship. In 1942 he and his wife, Catherine, moved to Cincinnati, where Slim took a job as a bartender. They returned to

Higginsport five years later, and in 1947 Slim coached the Higginsport town team to an undefeated season and the county baseball championship. To this day the photo of that 1947 team adorns the walls of several establishments in the sleepy Ohio River town.

Catherine Sallee died in 1948. The couple never had any children so Slim's sister Mary helped him with his daily affairs. On March 22, 1950, at the age of 65, Harry "Slim" Sallee passed away after suffering a heart attack in his Higginsport home. Eppa Rixey, Rube Bressler, Bubbles Hargrave, Billy Campbell, Larry Kopf, Tommy Griffith, Roy Golden, and Billy Maloney—all members of the Ballplayers of Yesteryear— attended the funeral. Sallee was buried in Confidence Cemetery in Georgetown. In 1995 the town of Higginsport renamed its baseball diamond Harry Franklin "Slim" Salee Field, and in 1999 Salee was honored with induction into the Ohio Baseball Hall of Fame.

PAUL SALLEE & ERIC SALLEE

ST. LOUIS

ROGER PHILIP BRESNAHAN
CATCHER-MANAGER 1909–12

Roger Bresnahan was the Deadball Era's most famous catcher, as well-known for his innovations in protective equipment as for his unusual skill package that made him one of the first catchers ever used regularly at the top of the batting order. Most catchers batted eighth in his era, but Bresnahan was adept at reaching base (his .419 on-base percentage ranked second in the NL in 1906) and possessed surprising speed despite his 5'9", 200 lb. frame. Like his close friend and mentor, John McGraw, the .279 lifetime hitter had a quick temper and was inherently tactless. One reporter described Bresnahan as "highly strung and almost abnormally emotional," but he also had a soft heart. During his five years as a big-league manager, he reportedly fined more players and took less money than any of his peers.

The seventh child of Michael and Mary (O'Donohue) Bresnahan, Roger Philip Bresnahan was born on June 11, 1879, in Toledo, Ohio. Early in his baseball career he acquired the nickname "Duke of Tralee" due to a frequently repeated inaccuracy that his birthplace was Tralee, Ireland; both his parents had immigrated to the United States from Ireland in 1870. Roger developed his enthusiasm for baseball while attending Catholic grade school in Toledo. In 1895 the stocky 16-year-old got his first paying job with a semipro team from Manistee, Michigan. The following year, after graduating from Toledo's Central High School, Roger turned professional with Lima of the Ohio State League, playing catcher but occasionally pitching.

Bresnahan pitched a six-hit shutout against the St. Louis Browns in his major league debut with the Washington Nationals on August 27, 1897. He went on to bat .375 and win all four of his 1897 pitching decisions, but the following spring Washington released the 19-year-old rookie when he held out for a higher salary. After splitting 1898 between Toledo of the Interstate League and Minneapolis of the Western League, Bresnahan returned to the National League in 1900 and appeared in two games for Chicago.

Joining the Baltimore Orioles of the fledgling American League in 1901, Roger was warming up on the sidelines one day under the watchful eye of manager John McGraw. Bresnahan grew frustrated as the team's second-string catcher was having problems handling his deliveries. "Why don't you get us a catcher?" he asked McGraw. "If you're so smart, get in there and catch yourself," the manager supposedly growled. Roger accepted the challenge, catching Joe McGinnity's complete-game victory that day. He served as McGraw's utility man for the next season and a half, playing a significant number of games at catcher, third base, and the outfield. When McGraw and several Oriole teammates jumped to the NL's New York Giants in midseason 1902, Bresnahan went with them.

Roger Bresnahan spent the next six seasons in New York, becoming one of baseball's biggest stars. In 1903 he was the Giants' regular center fielder, establishing career highs with a .350 batting average (only five points behind league leader Honus Wagner), a .443 on-base percentage (second in the NL behind Roy Thomas's .453), and 34 stolen bases. Though he continued to play the outfield on occasion, Bresnahan became New

York's first-string catcher in 1905. In that year's World Series, Bresnahan caught and batted leadoff in all five games; his .313 batting average was the highest among all Series participants.

It was during his years with the Giants that Bresnahan made his contributions to the development of playing equipment. After a hospital stay necessitated by a beaning, he experimented in 1905 with the Reach Pneumatic Head Protector, which was essentially a leather football helmet sliced in half to protect the left side of a right-handed hitter's head. More influential were his efforts with shin guards. After discovering in a home-plate collision that Red Dooin of the Phillies

wore papier-mâché protectors under his stockings, Bresnahan showed up on Opening Day 1907 wearing a huge pair of shin guards modeled after a cricketer's leg pads. At first Roger's innovation met with ridicule and protest—Pirates manager Fred Clarke insisted the guards posed a danger to sliding baserunners—but by 1909 a less bulky version was in general use. In another innovation that remains in use to this day, around 1908 Roger added leather-bound rolls of padding to the circumference of his wire catcher's mask to help absorb the shock of foul tips.

At the end of the 1908 season, in which Bresnahan caught a career-high 139 games, St. Louis owner Stanley Robison expressed interest in obtaining Roger to serve as player-manager of the Cardinals. McGraw didn't want to stand in the way of his 29-year-old protégé—as long as the Giants benefited in the process. On December 12, 1908, New York traded Bresnahan to St. Louis for the Cardinals' best pitcher, Bugs Raymond, their best hitter, Red Murray, and a replacement catcher, Admiral Schlei, whom the Cards had obtained from Cincinnati at the Giants' insistence for promising pitchers Art Fromme and Ed Karger. Appearing in just 72 games as a player, his fewest since establishing himself in the majors in 1901, Roger batted a disappointing .244 and the Cardinals finished seventh, a slight improvement over their last-place finishes of the prior two years. The Cards finished seventh again in 1910, when Bresnahan batted .278 in 88 games.

In 1911 Robison died, and control of the team passed to his niece, Helene Robison Britton. In one of her first interviews after claiming her inheritance, Britton told a reporter that she viewed Bresnahan as a good manager. "I like his system," she said. "Indeed, I adore it, even if it has not been climbing toward the first division." Shortly thereafter she told another reporter, "My great aim will be not to interfere with, but rather to further the system Mr. Bresnahan already has in effect." That first year under Britton's ownership, Roger had the Cardinals in contention for most of the season before they faded to fifth. Pleased with the club's resurgence, Britton rewarded him with a new five-year contract worth $10,000 per year and 10% of the club's profits.

When the Cardinals slipped back to sixth in 1912, however, trouble erupted between the fiery Irishman and his firmly independent boss. According to contem-

gling, the National League declared him a free agent and he received a $25,000 signing bonus from the Cubs. Eventually he settled a lawsuit against Britton for another $20,000. Serving as Jimmy Archer's backup in 1913, Bresnahan continued gathering a healthy salary even though his playing abilities had slipped. In 1915 the Cubs named him player-manager, but that year he batted a career-low .204 and was released.

With the savings he'd amassed over the years, Bresnahan purchased the former Toledo Mud Hens, which had been transferred to Cleveland in 1914 to prevent the renegade Federal League from taking over League Park. He brought them back to his hometown, serving as owner and player-manager of the American Association club. Roger provided the last baseball jobs for many of his former teammates on the downside of their playing careers. He played sparingly, finally hanging up his catcher's gear for good after the 1918 season—though at age 42 in 1921 he was pressed into emergency duty for five games and batted .417 with two stolen bases.

The Mud Hens proved a poor investment, and Bresnahan sold the team before the 1924 season. He then secured a job through his old friend McGraw as a Giants coach from 1925 to 1928. Reportedly a millionaire at one time (almost certainly an exaggeration), Roger was hit hard by the stock market crash. After a coaching stint with the Detroit Tigers in 1930-31, he went to work as a guard at the Toledo Workhouse. As times worsened, the former minor league magnate performed manual labor for the forerunner of the WPA. Eventually Roger acquired a job as city salesman for Toledo's Buckeye Brewing Company, working in that position for his remaining years. Early in 1944 he entered politics as the Democratic candidate for county commissioner. The old ballplayer lost the election by a few hundred votes.

At age 65 Bresnahan suffered a heart attack and died at his Toledo home on December 4, 1944. He never achieved one of his greatest ambitions—to give Toledo an American Association pennant—but the city mourned the passing of a man whose heart always lay in his hometown. Survived by his wife, Gertrude, and sister, Margaret Henige, Bresnahan was laid to rest in Toledo's Calvary Cemetery. The following year he was inducted into the National Baseball Hall of Fame.

JOAN THOMAS

porary reports, the two argued frequently. A story in *The Sporting News* stated that Bresnahan wanted to buy the club from Britton, and he continued to press the issue time and again even after she turned him down. The final confrontation occurred after a loss to the Cubs, when Helene criticized Roger's decision on a certain play. According to one report, "he pulled his derby down over his ears and stomped out, declaring: 'No woman can tell me how to play a ball game!'" At the end of the season, amidst rumors that Bresnahan hadn't fielded his strongest lineup in a key game against the Giants to help McGraw win another pennant, Britton fired him as manager and sold him to Chicago.

Financially, it turned out to be the best thing that ever happened to Bresnahan. After some legal wran-

ST. LOUIS

Louis Richard "Steve" Evans
Right fielder 1909–13

According to some observers, Steve Evans never took baseball seriously enough to fulfill his great potential, though he did bat .287 over his seven full seasons in the majors (two of them in the Federal League). A light hearted, cheerful right fielder with a reputation as one of the Deadball Era's greatest flakes, Evans batted and threw left-handed, of course, and had an unusual talent for being hit by pitched balls. He led the NL in that category each year from 1910 to 1912, setting a modern single-season record in 1910 that stood for 61 years before it was finally broken by Ron Hunt.

Born in Cleveland on February 17, 1885, Louis Richard Evans (how he came to be called Steve remains a mystery) spent his youth playing on the local sandlots, signing his first professional contract in 1907 with Dayton of the Central League. In midseason Dayton sold him to Fairmont, West Virginia, where he played first base for the eventual champions of the Western Pennsylvania League. It was in Fairmont that New York Giants scout Dan Brouthers, himself a former first baseman, discovered Evans and recommended him to John McGraw.

With Fred Tenney and Fred Merkle ahead of Evans at first base, manager John McGraw wanted to send Steve to Montreal of the Eastern League for more seasoning. At 1908 spring training, each time McGraw and the Montreal magnate approached him, Evans ran for a ball in the other corner of the field, ignoring calls to him by the Giants manager. After following him all over the field, the two officials finally gave up and Steve opened the season with the Giants, appearing in both ends of a doubleheader on April 16 and picking up his first major league hit in the second game. Despite his dodging, Evans ended up in Montreal anyway, hitting .292 and leading the Eastern League in doubles.

The St. Louis Cardinals purchased a newlywed Evans (his wife's name was Anna Campbell) from New York before the 1909 season. Steve later claimed that the Giants dumped him after only two games because he hit into the most damaging double play in history during the 1908 pennant race, but he never hit into a twin killing with the Giants, nor was he even with the team past April. In any event, Evans signed with St. Louis for $1,800 per season. With Cardinals star Ed Konetchy blocking his way at first base, the 24-year-old rookie opened the 1909 season as the regular right fielder and batted .259 in 143 games, leading the club in walks (66) and finishing second to Konetchy in doubles (17) and RBI (56).

Evans was the NL's first player to be hit by a pitch in 1910. It was a harbinger; when the season ended he'd been beaned 31 times, still the record for left-handed batters (the record would have been 32, but an umpire took one away from Evans, claiming that he'd "walked into a slow one" with the bases loaded). On one occasion Steve was hit in the jaw ("while the fans were certain his jaw had been broken, he merely laughed," wrote one reporter), and on another he set a record by being hit three times in a single game.

The next year Evans enjoyed his best NL season, leading St. Louis in hitting (.294) and triples (13), and ranking second behind Konetchy in home runs (5) and RBI (71). Before a 1911 game against the Giants, the Cardinals honored an odd fellow named Charles Faust, who claimed a fortune teller had told him that he would lead the Giants to the pennant. As both teams gathered on the field for the ceremony, Evans made a short speech and presented Faust with a gift box containing a pocket watch. When Faust opened the watch, it exploded and the parts went everywhere.

Steve Evans was the club's prankster and comedian, always keeping his teammates laughing. On a hot summer day in St. Louis, Evans tried to escape the oppressive sun by playing right field rather deeply, allowing him to stand in the shade of the grandstand. The crowd began to ride him, however, after several Texas leaguers dropped in front of him for base hits. When the Cardinals again took the field, Steve went to his position with a Japanese parasol slung over his right shoulder. (Umpire Hank O'Day forced him to put it down before allowing the game to continue.) On another occasion, after missing a ball he dove for, Evans looked up to see that center fielder Rebel Oakes hadn't even backed him up. He got up and retrieved the ball, all the while spewing his displeasure. The next fly ball that came to Oakes, Steve raced over and ran circles around the center fielder to make a point.

Evans put together one last solid season for St. Louis in 1912, when he batted .283 and finished second to Konetchy again in doubles (23), triples (9), home runs (6), and RBI (72), but in 1913 his batting average fell to .249 and he played in only 97 games. Discontent with his salary and the seeming impossibility of reaching the World Series with the Cardinals, he played out the season and hoped to secure a big contract with the Federal League.

Despite his lackluster play in 1913, Evans received and accepted an invitation to join the Chicago White Sox on their postseason world tour with the Giants. When the tour reached Egypt, he stood on one side of the Sphinx to receive a baseball thrown over the monument by strong-armed catcher Ivy Wingo. One of the best dancers on the team, Evans joined teammate Buck Weaver in demonstrating how to tango for a crowd at a fancy Egyptian hotel. He also was part of a singing group and was president of a shipboard shuffleboard league.

On his return to New York on the *Lusitania*, Evans immediately signed with the Federal League. That night he celebrated all over New York and was seen flashing three $1,000 bills in his wallet. With his new team, the Brooklyn Tip Tops, Evans enjoyed the greatest year of his career in 1914, leading the league in triples (15) and slugging (.556) while finishing second in batting (.348), doubles (41), and RBI (96) and third in homers (12). Splitting the 1915 season between the Tip Tops and the Baltimore Terrapins, he put together another strong year, hitting .308 and leading the league with 34 doubles. For its retroactive Federal League all-star teams, STATS Inc. selected identical outfields for both seasons: Evans, Bennie Kauff, and Dutch Zwilling.

Evans remained a prankster during his Federal League years. On a post-season hunting trip with Elmer Knetzer and Jack Lewis of the Pittsburgh Rebels, the ballplayers found themselves one morning at an all-night restaurant in Prairie Du Chein, Wisconsin. When the waitress asked him why they were out so early, Evans told her that they were there to rob the town bank, and that she must not tell anyone. After the players left the restaurant and made their way back to their hotel, the bell in the town hall began ringing and an armed posse, along with the sheriff and his deputies, raided the players' hotel room. Only after a lengthy explanation did the sheriff realize that the waitress was another in a long line of victims of Steve's pranks.

After the Federal League collapsed in 1916, Evans unaccountably failed to catch on with another major league team. He ended up signing with Toledo of the American Association, reuniting with his old Cardinals manager Roger Bresnahan, and again put up outstanding numbers: a .298 batting average, 101 runs, 33 doubles, 16 triples, and 10 home runs. Retiring from baseball after 1917, Evans returned to his Cleveland home and worked as a supervisor for the state of Ohio until his death on December 28, 1943.

PAUL SALLEE & ERIC SALLEE

ST. LOUIS

Harry Harlan "Mike" Mowrey
Third baseman 1909–13

Though nearly forgotten today, Mike Mowrey was considered one of the best third basemen in baseball during the mid-Deadball Era. A lifetime .256 hitter with a reputation for being particularly dangerous in the pinch, Mowrey was best known for his unorthodox fielding style—instead of catching a hard smash in his glove, he'd knock the ball to the ground and then pick it up to throw out the runner. Defending against the bunt was a corner infielder's primary responsibility back then, and in that aspect of his duties the 5'10", 180 lb. redhead excelled. In 1910 Alfred Spink called Mowrey "the best fielder of bunts in either league."

Jacob Mowrey's fourth son, Harry Harlan Mowrey, was born on April 20, 1884, near Chambersburg, Pennsylvania, a town of 7,000 citizens situated just north of the Mason-Dixon Line. Two decades earlier the town had been torched by Confederate General John McCausland, but by 1884 it was a hotbed of baseball activity. Town historians claim that the first night game in history occurred on May 16, 1883, opposite the Chambersburg train station, with lights placed on railroad cars. Like many railroad towns, Chambersburg had a problem with hobos. Jacob Mowrey was the town's sheriff, and he often housed the tramps in his jail cell overnight. Young Harry became particularly friendly with one tramp, prompting one of his brothers to nickname him "Mike the Hobo." The name stuck.

Mike grew up playing baseball with school and town teams in the Chambersburg area. By the turn of the century he was a husky third baseman for Chambersburg Academy, playing well enough in 1902 to earn a shot with an independent team from Chester, Pennsylvania, just south of Philadelphia. Mike returned to central Pennsylvania with Williamsport of the outlaw Tri-State League in 1904, the same year he married Nannie Hammel (the couple remained married until his death 43 years later). In 1905 the 22-year-old Mowrey joined the ranks of Organized Baseball with Savannah of the South Atlantic League. His .285 batting average and flashy defensive play at third base so impressed the Cincinnati Reds that they purchased his contract.

Mike made his big-league debut on September 24, 1905, playing both ends of a doubleheader. In total he appeared in seven games during his late-season tryout, batting .267 but making seven errors at third base. That off-season the Chicago Cubs reportedly tried to acquire Mowrey from the Reds but wound up with veteran Harry Steinfeldt instead. Steinfeldt went on to lead the Cubs in batting average in 1906 and become a key member of one of the greatest clubs of all time. Mowrey, meanwhile, spent most of 1906 on loan to Baltimore of the Eastern League, which was owned by Cincinnati manager Ned Hanlon. The Reds recalled him in August to avoid losing him in the minor league draft, and Mike hit a robust .321 in 21 games to give him the inside track on a starting position for next year.

Mowrey did win the regular third-base job in 1907, playing in 138 games and hitting .252, a comfortable nine points above the league average. He also slugged the first of his seven lifetime home runs, an inside-the-park job against Joe McGinnity on August 14. Mike regressed in 1908, however, hitting only .220 and losing his starting position to Hans Lobert. He hurt his knee in 1909 and was hitting just .191 when the Reds traded him to the Cardinals on August 22 for infielder Chappy Charles. Returning to regular duty with the Cardinals in 1910, Mowrey enjoyed the best season of his 13-year career, hitting .282 (26 points over the NL average) with two home runs, a career-high 70 RBI, and 21 stolen bases. He remained the Cardinals' regular third baseman through the end of 1913, collecting at least 400 at-bats each year and hitting between .255 and .268.

During the 1913 season George Stallings tried to acquire Mowrey for the Braves. When asked by Cards manager Miller Huggins if he wanted to go to Boston, Mike replied that he preferred to stay in St. Louis rather than uproot his family, though he had no objection to moving there after the season. Instead the Cardinals sent him to the Pirates on December 12, 1913, in a blockbuster trade that became known as the "three-for-five deal." St. Louis traded Mike, first baseman Ed Konetchy, and pitcher Bob Harmon to Pittsburgh for infielders Dots Miller and Art Butler, outfielders Owen Wilson and Cozy Dolan, and pitcher Hank Robinson. Hampered by injuries, Mowrey played in only 79 games for the Pirates before drawing his unconditional release. He played with independent teams to finish out the 1914 season.

In 1915 Mowrey remained in Pittsburgh with the Federal League's Rebels, hitting .280 and leading all Fed third basemen with a .959 fielding percentage. He also established career highs in games (151), hits (146), and stolen bases (40), ranking second in the Federal League in the latter category. After the Feds folded, Wilbert Robinson signed Mowrey for his veteran team in Brooklyn. In a 1916 photo, Mike's mashed nose and the lines in his unsmiling face create the perfect image of an experienced veteran of the Deadball wars. That year he batted .244 without a single home run in 144 games, but his career-best .965 fielding percentage led NL third basemen and the Robins won the pennant. Appearing in his first World Series, Mike hit a paltry .176 in Brooklyn's losing effort.

In 1917 the 33-year-old third baseman held out for more money, not reporting until April 10. Whether he was unprepared or suddenly got old, Mowrey batted just .214, his worst average since his abysmal 1909, and the Robins released him in August. At that point he joined the war effort, working in a steel plant and playing in the Steel League alongside other ex-professional players. After the war Mike became a player-manager for minor league teams in the Chambersburg area. In 1920 he batted .342 and led the Hagerstown Hubs to the championship of the newly organized Blue Ridge League. Hagerstown fell to the cellar the following season, and in 1922 Mike managed his hometown club in

the same league. Though he batted .351 in the 75 games he played, Chambersburg finished next to last. Mowrey also managed Rochester in the International League and Scottdale, Pennsylvania, in the Middle Atlantic League, but at some point during the 1920s he got fed up with professional baseball and returned to Chambersburg.

Mowrey lived there for the rest of his life. He bought some farmland and supplemented his farm income by working as a night watchman at Wilson College. During World War II Mike worked at the Letterkenny Ordnance Depot and coached its baseball team. He passed away from heart disease on March 20, 1947. Two months later, over 1,000 people attended a memorial service for Mike held at Henninger Field after a Letterkenny game. According to the eulogy, "He was our Grand Old Man of Baseball, who started as a sand-lotter and went to the top in baseball to become one of the greatest third basemen the game had known."

PETER GORDON

ST. LOUIS

MILLER JAMES HUGGINS
SECOND BASEMAN 1910–16, MANAGER 1913–17

Though best remembered today for his run-ins with Babe Ruth when he managed the New York Yankees during the 1920s, Miller Huggins spent 13 seasons in the National League as a gutsy second baseman and switch-hitting leadoff hitter who specialized in getting on base. Known as "Mighty Mite" for his size (he stood 5'6" and weighed 140 lbs.), "Rabbit" for his speed, and "Little Everywhere" for his range in the field, the lifetime .265 hitter was an outstanding bunter who led the NL in bases on balls in 1905, 1907, 1910, and 1914. Taking over as St. Louis's player-manager in 1913, Hug guided the lowly Cardinals to two third-place finishes in five years before jumping to the American League to take over the Yankees in 1918.

The third of James and Sarah (Reid) Huggins' four children, Miller James Huggins was born in Cincinnati, Ohio, on March 27, 1879. His father was a grocer who had emigrated from England and attended public schools in Cincinnati. Though a former cricket player himself, James Huggins didn't want his son to become a professional baseball player. They struck a compromise: Miller enrolled in law school at the University of Cincinnati (and eventually earned his degree and was admitted to the bar), even though he had no desire to become a lawyer. One day he asked one of his law professors who enjoyed the sport if he should choose law or baseball. The professor, William Howard Taft, told him that he seemed more enthusiastic to play baseball and therefore recommended it. "When you do, keep your head high and never take a backward step," added the future President of the United States.

In 1899, while Miller was still attending the University of Cincinnati, he and his brother Clarence were teammates with Mansfield, Ohio, of the Interstate League; Clarence was a talented shortstop, while Miller (under the pseudonym of William Proctor to hide his baseball playing from his father) was an outfielder with trouble catching fly balls. One day Clarence slipped and ripped his trousers, causing Miller to fill in at shortstop, and he ended up spending the rest of the season there and at third base.

The next year Miller became the second baseman for Max and Julius Fleischmann's Mountain Athletic Club, a top semipro team based in Fleischmanns (formerly Griffin's Corners), New York, near the summer resorts of the Catskills. *The Sporting News* reported that the 1900 Mountaineers "lost but four games in 60 played." The Fleischmanns were Cincinnati-based distillers and yeast manufacturers who (along with Garry Herrmann and George "Boss" Cox) purchased the Reds two years later, and their players were reported to "receive sufficient compensation to keep them from joining other clubs in minor or major leagues." They recruited many of their players from Cincinnati; in addition to Huggins, other Cincinnati natives and future major leaguers on the 1900 club were catcher Red Dooin and infielder George Rohe. Because he was so talkative—and was still playing under the name of Proctor—Miller's teammates dubbed him the "Proctor Knott of Baseball," a reference to J. Proctor Knott, a Kentucky governor and U.S. congressman who was famous for his oratory.

Playing under his legal name, Huggins joined St. Paul of the Western League in 1901. Aware of his small stature and relative lack of strength, especially on the left side of his body, he used pulleys to develop his forearms and went through a daily series of muscle-building exercises for his left leg. Though Miller struggled to a .210 average in his first season, he returned to St. Paul in 1902 and improved his average to .328, giving him the confidence to inform his father that baseball, not law, would be his profession. The next year Huggins batted .309 and stole 48 bases, prompting his hometown Cincinnati Reds to purchase his contract for

$3,000. In a telegram to Reds president Garry Herrmann, St. Paul owner George Lennon wrote, "It's my opinion in Huggins you have secured the greatest all-around ball player in America as well as a perfect gentleman in every respect."

On May 10, 1904, less than one month into his major league career, Huggins connected for his first home run, an inside-the-park grand slam against Brooklyn's Ed Poole. Though he was anything but a power hitter—he never hit more than two home runs in a season and his lifetime slugging percentage was .314, far below his career on-base percentage of .382—the rookie accomplished another unusual feat on October 8 by slugging three of his season's total of seven triples in a single game. The following year Hug improved his batting average 10 points to .273 and led the NL with 103 walks, enabling him to score a career-high 117 runs. He remained Cincinnati's regular second baseman until 1909, when a sore arm and a batting slump (he finished at a career-low .214 in only 57 games) caused him to lose his job to the undistinguished Dick Egan. In February 1910 the Reds dealt Huggins, outfielder Rebel Oakes, and pitcher Frank Corridon to the Cardinals for pitcher Fred Beebe and infielder Alan Storke.

Hug struggled at the beginning of his first season in St. Louis. "In a short time, the fans had changed my nickname from 'Little Everywhere' to 'Always in the Way,'" he recalled. But he rebounded to hit .265 with a career-high 116 walks and, according to no less an expert on the history of St. Louis baseball than the founder of *The Sporting News*, Alfred Spink, "was pronounced by experts the best second baseman that had played in a St. Louis professional team since the days of [Fred] Dunlap." In late August 1912, with Hug en route to a career-high .304 batting average, Cardinals manager Roger Bresnahan reportedly wanted to trade him back to Cincinnati (along with outfielder Rube Ellis) for outfielder Mike Mitchell and shortstop Tex McDonald. Owner Helene Britton, in the words of one newspaper, "put her French heel down on it." The following year she appointed Hug as Bresnahan's replacement, raising his salary to $8,000 (still $2,000 less than Bresnahan had earned).

The responsibilities of managing were supposed to have a detrimental effect on a player-manager's on-field performance, but Huggins put together one of his finest seasons in 1913, leading the NL with a .432 on-base percentage and the circuit's second basemen with a .977 fielding percentage. The Cardinals won only 51 games and finished dead last, however, requiring Hug to plead with Britton for another chance. She gave it to him, and she also gave him absolute authority to build the team to his liking. The next year, after a series of transactions, Huggins shocked the baseball world by guiding the Cardinals to a third-place finish, their highest ever. "There are few stars on the Cardinals, but we don't need stars," he told one reporter. "Give me a team that has learned the lesson of cooperation and has a few good pitchers and I'll beat a so-called star aggregation

any time." Britton rewarded her successful manager with a three-year contract worth a total of $25,000.

St. Louis fell to sixth in 1915, after which the 36-year-old Huggins decided to concentrate just on managing. The Cardinals dropped to seventh, and Hug appeared at second base in only seven games in 1916, his last year as a player. After the season Britton offered him an opportunity to purchase the club. While Hug was off in Cincinnati trying to raise money (one of his backers reportedly was Max Fleischmann, his old sponsor from his semipro days), club attorney James Jones put together a coalition of St. Louis businessmen and purchased the team. Though peeved at what he regarded as a fast shuffle, Huggins led the Cardinals to another third-place finish in 1917, prompting *The Sporting News* to call him a "miracle worker."

Over in the American League, meanwhile, the New York Yankees had two new owners, Colonel Jacob Ruppert and Colonel Til Huston. While Huston was in France serving as an Army engineer, Ruppert fired manager Bill Donovan. Huston sent a telegram demanding that Wilbert Robinson be hired as Donovan's replacement, but Ruppert instead turned to Ban Johnson for advice. The American League president recommended Miller Huggins. Hug was more than qualified, but Johnson had an ulterior motive: a year earlier the Cardinals had stolen Branch Rickey from the St. Louis Americans, and this was his way of getting revenge. On his next trip to St. Louis, Johnson asked his friend J. G. Taylor Spink of *The Sporting News* to sound out the little manager. With a reduced role in player acquisitions now that Rickey was running the Cardinals, Huggins indicated a willingness to meet with Ruppert and eventually signed with the Yankees in January 1918.

The rest is baseball history. The Yankees finished fourth in 1918 and third in 1919, but in 1920 Babe Ruth arrived and the Deadball Era departed. Huggins won the first of his six AL pennants in 1921, and two years later he won the first of his three world championships. On September 20, 1929, he showed up at Yankee Stadium with an ugly red blotch under his left eye. Turning the team over to coach Art Fletcher, Huggins checked in to a New York City hospital and died of erysipelas five days later. The lifelong bachelor was buried in his native Cincinnati, leaving behind an estate worth $250,000.

STUART SCHIMLER

Bill Doak

ST. LOUIS

WILLIAM LEOPOLD DOAK
RIGHT-HANDED PITCHER 1913–24, 1929

Spittin' Bill Doak still ranks second in career shutouts for the St. Louis Cardinals, behind only Bob Gibson. In 1914, his first full season in the majors, Doak came out of nowhere to lead the National League in ERA as the Cardinals achieved third place, their best finish ever. He followed with solid but unspectacular seasons over the rest of the Deadball Era, earning 87 of his 169 career wins before 1920. A slow and deliberate worker who used a huge red handkerchief to wipe his brow a few times each game, Doak relied on good control and an effective "slow drop" (curveball) to go along with his signature spitball. Today Bill Doak is best known for his namesake glove, an innovative design that remained in the Rawlings line for decades.

William Leopold Doak was born in Pittsburgh on January 28, 1891. He was modest, unassuming, and "so silent as to be almost an enigma," according to *Baseball Magazine*. In later years *The Sporting News* called Doak "the only strictly moral man on the Cards," noting that he taught a Sunday school class before going to the ballpark. His father, a civil engineer, wanted him to become a mining engineer, but Bill had other ideas. He spent his first two years in professional baseball, 1910-11, with Wheeling of the Central League, averaging almost 300 innings a year with an ERA close to 3.00. After starting 1912 with Columbus, Doak spent most of the season with Akron of the Interstate League and pitched well, earning a brief try-out with the Cincinnati Reds late in the season. After seeing Bill pitch for only two innings, Reds manager Hank O'Day wasn't impressed and released him, after which Bill returned to Akron.

The next summer the Cardinals purchased Doak for $500 on the recommendation of scout Eddie Herr. The blonde six-footer was frail-looking and put so much

effort into each pitch that rookie manager Miller Huggins suggested he take up the spitball, which required less exertion. Bill followed Huggins' advice and turned himself almost overnight into one of the NL's top pitchers, posting an ERA a full run below the league average in 1914. His 19 victories included seven shutouts and two wins over Christy Mathewson, one over Pete Alexander, and a big win over the Pirates at Forbes Field on "Bill Doak Day" before hometown family and friends. *Baseball Magazine* was so impressed that it dubbed him a prodigy.

Neither Doak nor the Cardinals built on the promise they'd shown in 1914. The team didn't contend for the pennant the rest of the decade, a period during which Doak experienced only one more winning season. Bill nonetheless enjoyed many glorious moments. In 1917 he pitched two complete-game victories over the Brooklyn Robins on one day, winning 2-0 and 12-4. Three times he pitched one-hitters, and each time he lost the no-hitter because he failed to cover first base quickly enough on an infield grounder. "Lumbago Bill," as he was called, was hampered by back problems from early in his career, which might explain why he was so slow in leaving the mound.

In 1919 Bill Doak approached the Rawlings Sporting Goods Company of St. Louis about improving the design of the baseball glove, which to that point was meant mainly for hand protection, not functional fielding. Working with Rawlings production chief William Whitely, Doak came up with a revolutionary new design that became a prototype of gloves for years to come. Bill explained what made it special: "By enlarging the thumb, bringing it up even with the first finger, a larger pocket is formed and many balls are caught on the very tips of the thumb and first finger."

Rawlings Famous Bill Doak Glove

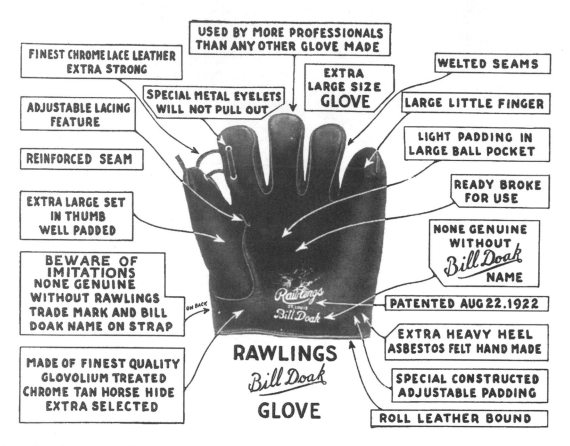

USED BY MORE PROFESSIONALS THAN ANY OTHER GLOVE MADE

FINEST CHROME LACE LEATHER EXTRA STRONG

EXTRA LARGE SIZE GLOVE

WELTED SEAMS

ADJUSTABLE LACING FEATURE

SPECIAL METAL EYELETS WILL NOT PULL OUT

LARGE LITTLE FINGER

REINFORCED SEAM

LIGHT PADDING IN LARGE BALL POCKET

READY BROKE FOR USE

EXTRA LARGE SET IN THUMB WELL PADDED

NONE GENUINE WITHOUT *Bill Doak* NAME

BEWARE OF IMITATIONS NONE GENUINE WITHOUT RAWLINGS TRADE MARK AND BILL DOAK NAME ON STRAP

ON BACK

PATENTED AUG 22. 1922

EXTRA HEAVY HEEL ASBESTOS FELT HAND MADE

MADE OF FINEST QUALITY GLOVOLIUM TREATED CHROME TAN HORSE HIDE EXTRA SELECTED

SPECIAL CONSTRUCTED ADJUSTABLE PADDING

RAWLINGS *Bill Doak* GLOVE

ROLL LEATHER BOUND

This catalog advertisement illustrates Doak's namesake glove, which remained in the Rawlings line for more than three decades.

Rawlings sold the first model for $10 as the "Premier Players' Glove" in 1920.

After the 1920 season Doak played an active role in the successful campaign to grandfather pitchers like himself who already used the spitball from the new ban against "freak" pitches. Initially spitballers were to receive only one transition year, 1920, to use their wet delivery, but the owners reversed their stance and allowed Doak and 16 others to use the pitch for the remainder of their careers.

In 1920-21 Doak had a combined 35-18 record and led the NL in ERA in 1921, once again a full run below the league average. After the Cardinals traded him to Brooklyn in June 1924, he helped the Robins make a tremendous but ultimately unsuccessful pennant drive, reeling off 10 consecutive victories from July to September. On September 6, 1924, he pitched his second two-hitter in three days, giving the Robins their 15th straight win and putting them in first place, if only

for a few hours. Bill later claimed that it was his greatest thrill as a ballplayer. After spending 1925-26 out of baseball, selling real estate during the Florida land boom, Doak came out of retirement and went 11-8 for the 1927 Robins. He ended his playing career back with the Cardinals in 1929.

Bill retired to Bradenton, Florida, where he owned a candy store called Bill Doak's Sweet Shop. He was active in amateur baseball, coaching Bradenton High School to the state championship. He also coached and sponsored boys club, midget, and American Legion teams. Doak was a golf professional and his son Bobby won the Florida Amateur Championship. The Bill Doak model glove, which had a profound impact on fielding, was a best-seller for years, earning Bill as much as $25,000 in royalties in a single year. It was still in the Rawlings line when Bill passed away in Bradenton on November 26, 1954.

STEVE STEINBERG

ST. LOUIS

HELENE ROBISON BRITTON
OWNER 1911–18

In March 1911, with women's suffrage a popular topic in the newspapers, a major league baseball club owner's death caused a stir in the worlds of both sports and society. Stanley Robison's will bequeathed controlling interest in the St. Louis Cardinals to his niece, Helene Robison Britton. The remaining shares went to Helene's mother, the widow of former club co-owner Frank DeHass Robison, Stanley's brother. Early reports dismissed the notion that a woman—or women—would maintain ownership, least of all control, of a baseball franchise. But Helene, a young wife and mother of two small children, surprised the male-dominated world of baseball by not only refusing to sell her acquisition but taking an active role in its operation for the next six years, becoming the first woman in history to own a major league baseball club.

Born in 1879, Helene Hathaway Robison spent her youth at her family home, a mansion on a bluff overlooking Lake Erie in the Cleveland suburb of Bratenahl. Her father and uncle owned a Cleveland streetcar business in addition to that city's National League baseball team, the Spiders. Helene's relatives encouraged her to become familiar with sports. Though refined and well educated, she adopted an especially keen interest in baseball through the family enterprise. Learning to keep score while attending Spiders games, Helene described that activity as a "better mental exercise than anything." In 1899 Stanley and Frank Robison purchased the NL's St. Louis Brown Stockings and arranged the two rosters to favor St. Louis. As a result, the Spiders ended up with the poorest record in baseball history and became one of four clubs eliminated in 1900, leaving Helene without her hometown team. She nonetheless maintained her interest in baseball, joining her family on road trips with the St. Louis club.

In 1901 she married Schuyler Britton, a Cleveland attorney employed in a printing business, and was living with him, their two children, and her mother at her family home by the lake at the time of Stanley Robison's death in 1911. Reports indicate that Helene and her mother initially considered selling the Cardinals to Charles Weeghman of Chicago, but they decided to keep and operate the club as its late owner had requested. Assuming her role as baseball magnate, or "magnette" as some called her, Helene endured with dignity a great deal of media gibing—one newspaper cartoon jokingly suggested that the players' uniforms might soon include bloomers. Some stories described Mrs. Britton as a militant suffragette, but interviews portray her more as soft-spoken, intelligent, and strong-willed than militant. During her years in baseball she never criticized her female detractors when she overheard their spiteful remarks. In an interview held at the ballpark, she once told a female reporter that those same women could excel in other traditionally male-dominated fields if given a chance.

On assuming ownership of the Cardinals, Helene expressed admiration for manager Roger Bresnahan. When asked what she would rather have, a team of good hitters or a team of fair batsmen with a good corps of pitchers, she told a *St. Louis Post-Dispatch* reporter, "Certainly there will never be a pennant prospect for the Cardinals until they have both. And I am satisfied that Mr. Bresnahan intends to get them for me." When the Cardinals moved up to fifth place during her first year as owner, Helene rewarded Bresnahan with a new five-year contract worth $10,000 a year and 10% of the club's profit. The team didn't fare as well the next season, and the resolute "magnatess" met head-on with the pugnacious manager. One report states that Bresnahan went into a tirade at the Britton home while defending himself against accusations of throwing games to the Giants. He also persisted in offers to buy the franchise after she refused to sell. Arguments kept erupting between the two, and at the end of the 1912 season she finally fired him after he angrily told her, "No woman can tell me how to run a ball game!"

Though her Robison predecessors lived in Cleveland even after purchasing the Cardinals, Helene wanted to be closer to her operation. In 1913 she moved with Schuyler and their children to a mansion on Lindell Boulevard in St. Louis. That year, with Helene's influence, the bespectacled, cigar-smoking Schuyler was elected president of the Cardinals—much to the relief of the NL's other owners (for two years Helene had insisted on attending and participating in their previously men-only meetings herself). But Schuyler was a figurehead; time revealed that Helene was controlling the operation. It was her decision to lure women to games by introducing a Ladies Day, when all "fanettes" accompanied by male escorts were admitted to the grandstand free. She also hired a crooner to perform between innings. In an era when following baseball and attending games unescorted were considered unladylike, Helene abated society's misgivings while encouraging her own gender to develop an interest in the sport.

Mrs. Britton staunchly maintained her ownership despite numerous difficulties. A lack of funds to renovate the Cardinals' deteriorating ballpark (originally called New Sportsman's Park, then Robison Field), the club's fall to last place in 1913, and the birth of the Federal League in 1914 failed to dampen her resolve. St. Louis's Federal League team, the Terriers, snatched some of her club's talent. Additionally, she contended with competition from the AL's Browns, who played a couple of blocks away. Despite those obstacles the Cardinals rose to third in 1914, the club's highest finish since its purchase by the brothers Robison.

In January 1916, at a peace conference over the disposal of the Federal League, Helene held her ground when the NL attempted to force a sale of her club. Reportedly Helene had already named a price when the other owners demanded that she sell for the "good of the game." At that point she called in her selling option and returned home still in possession of the club and its park. The caption over her photo in a newspaper article said "Never Tell Her She Must," suggesting that her gender accounted for her refusal to sell.

Helene also was dealing with domestic problems. She separated from Schuyler several times in 1916, the year she replaced him as club president. Filing for divorce in 1917, she alleged that he was an alcoholic who frequently struck her. Her original divorce petition stated that he absented himself from her for long periods, refused to provide support for her and the children, and incurred huge bills on his personal account and compelled her to pay them, squandering her fortune.

Finally in 1918 Mrs. Britton sold the Cardinals and their ballpark for $350,000 to a local investment group headed by Sam Breadon, who went on to become club president. The Robison brothers' original investment of $40,000 had netted a handsome profit for their descendant, but years later Helene said that she loved baseball and regretted her decision to sell. She remarried to Charles Bigsby, an appliance dealer from Boston who eventually predeceased her by 15 years. Helene Robison Bigsby died at age 70 on January 8, 1950, in Philadelphia, where she lived with her daughter, Marie. Her son, Frank DeHaas Britton, also lived nearby, as did her four grandchildren.

JOAN THOMAS

ROGERS HORNSBY
INFIELDER 1915–26, 1933, MANAGER 1925–26

By the end of the Deadball Era, Rogers Hornsby was the best player in the National League, on the verge of putting up the mind-boggling numbers that lead many to consider him the greatest right-handed hitter of all time. Though remembered today as a second baseman, Hornsby in his Deadball years mostly played the other infield positions: 353 games at shortstop, 155 at third base, 20 at first base, and only 26 at second. The young slugger already was so self-centered that he alienated most everyone around him. "I'm too good a ballplayer to be sliding for a tail-end team," he remarked during a season when the Cardinals lacked much other talent.

Rogers Hornsby, the great-grandson of well-known Texas pioneer Reuben Hornsby, was born in Winters, Texas, on April 27, 1896. He was the youngest of six children whose oft-misread first name was his mother's maiden name. While Rogers' hard-bitten personality is sometimes ascribed to his rural roots, he was really the product of an urban environment. His father died when he was two, and by the time he was six his mother had moved the family to Ft. Worth, where several of his siblings went to work in the packing houses. By 1911 the 15-year-old Rogers was playing baseball in the Ft. Worth industrial leagues. His brother Everett, 12 years older, was a spitball pitcher who went on to a career in professional baseball.

While pitching for Dallas of the Texas League, Everett arranged a tryout for his kid brother in 1914. The Steers signed Rogers but released him two weeks later without playing him in a single game. He caught on with Hugo in the Texas-Oklahoma League, but the team folded and his contract was sold to Denison. Rogers finished the 1914 season there, appearing in 113 games, batting .232, and committing 45 errors. He was Denison's regular shortstop again in 1915, improving his batting average to .277 in 119 games but this time committing 58 errors. Despite the lanky teenager's erratic fielding, the St. Louis Cardinals, who'd first seen him when they played some exhibition games against Denison that spring, purchased him in September and gave him an 18-game tryout. Hornsby wasn't much of a prospect, but St. Louis wasn't much of a team, either on the field or in the ledgers. With the Federal League wars raising salaries and draining talent, players like Hornsby, who could be had cheap, were attractive to the Cardinals.

In the minors Rogers had always used an open stance, standing well off the plate and striding into the pitch. With the Cardinals, however, manager Miller Huggins tried to convince him to choke up on the bat and crowd the plate, very much the style at the time. Using the new technique, Hornsby hit .246 in 57 at-bats with only two doubles. After spending the off-season on his uncle's farm, working, hunting, and eating, Rogers reported to 1916 training camp 30 lbs. heavier and returned to his old batting style, swinging a 36", 38-40 oz. bat. That year he earned himself a regular job, playing 83 games at third base and 45 more at shortstop. Hornsby finished second in the NL in triples (15) and was fourth in batting (.313) and slugging (.444). By the end of his first full season, the 20-year-old was suddenly a young star, and several clubs were interested in acquiring him.

In 1917 Hornsby missed part of the season because of family crises. His mother, with whom he was very close, had serious health problems, and his brother William was shot and killed in a bar. Despite those distractions, Hornsby became a star of the first order, leading the NL in triples (17), total bases (253), and slugging (.484). He was second in batting (.327) and on-base percentage (.385), third in home runs (8), and fourth in runs (86). That winter Huggins resigned as manager. Hornsby hated his replacement, Jack Hendricks. The young shortstop put up his worst full-season performance in 1918, though his .281 batting average and .416 slugging percentage (third-best in the NL) would have constituted a career year for most.

When the government issued its "work or fight" order, Hornsby was reclassified despite being the sole support for his mother and sister. He found a job at a shipyard in Wilmington, Delaware, and reported there at the end of the season. He stayed through November, heading home to Texas when the war ended. During that off-season Branch Rickey replaced Hendricks as the Cardinals manager. Hornsby got along with Rickey and in 1919 was back to his old form, batting .318 and ranking between second and fourth in the NL in almost every major statistical category. After the season John

McGraw tried hard to acquire Hornsby for the Giants. Rickey was interested in Giants rookie infielder Frankie Frisch, but the deal wasn't made.

A quick glance at Hornsby's numbers might lead one to believe that he first became a superstar in 1920, with the introduction of the lively ball, but by then he was already the NL's premier hitter. In 1916-19 he batted 66, 78, 27, and 60 points over the league average. His continued improvement as a hitter and the Cardinals' move to Sportsman's Park (more hitter friendly than Robison Field) produced a .370 average in 1920 and Hornsby's first batting title. From there he went on to his unprecedented and still unequaled batting feats in the '20s. He was the best hitter in the league throughout the decade, winning seven batting titles, six of them consecutively, and Triple Crowns in 1922 and 1925. He also won MVP awards in 1925 and 1929.

In 1925-26 Hornsby was player-manager of the Cards, winning the World Series in '26 (the Cardinals' first). He was then traded in successive years to the Giants (finally, the trade for Frisch), the Braves, and the Cubs. He was player-manager for both the Braves and Cubs. He subsequently managed the Browns (1933-37, 1952) and Reds (1952-53). He also won minor league pennants in Beaumont (1950) and Seattle (1951). Like many stars, the hard-driving Hornsby had difficulty relating to players of lesser talent and intensity (which was almost everyone) and wasn't considered a successful manager, finishing below .500 for his career.

Hornsby's most famous quirk was his avoidance of movies and newspapers, fearing that they'd ruin his batting eye. He also shunned liquor and tobacco and carefully watched his diet. The only two things that interested Hornsby, and the only two things he liked to talk about, were baseball and horse racing. The former provided his income, and the latter took it away. He was a baseball man to the end, coaching and scouting for the Mets in 1961-62. Sixty-six-year-old Rogers Hornsby died of heart failure in Chicago on January 5, 1963. He was survived by his third wife, Marjorie, and his son Bill. Another son, Rogers Jr., an Air Force navigator, was killed in a plane crash in 1949. Hornsby is buried in the family cemetery in Hornsby's Bend, Texas.

PAUL ANDRESEN

CREDITS

Photographs are used with permission from the following collections:

Cover, Library of Congress Prints and Photographs Division (Pan Subject – Sports, No. 179); p. 15, New York Historical Society Collections (ref. no. 47579); p. 16, Transcendental Graphics; pp. 20-21, *The Sporting News*; p. 23, National Baseball Hall of Fame, Cooperstown, NY; pp. 24-25, *The Sporting News*; pp. 27-34, National Baseball Hall of Fame, Cooperstown, NY; p. 36, Historic Saranac Lake; p. 38, Chicago Historical Society (SDN-003776); pp. 39-41, National Baseball Hall of Fame, Cooperstown, NY; p. 43, Chicago Historical Society (SDN-003755); p. 44, National Baseball Hall of Fame, Cooperstown, NY; p. 46, Chicago Historical Society (SDN-003760); pp. 48-49, National Baseball Hall of Fame, Cooperstown, NY; p. 50, Chicago Historical Society (SDN-003767); pp. 54-55, National Baseball Hall of Fame, Cooperstown, NY; p. 57, Chicago Historical Society (SDN-003778); p. 59, Chicago Historical Society (SDN-053180); p. 60, National Baseball Hall of Fame, Cooperstown, NY; p. 61, Chicago Historical Society (SDN-054363); p. 64, Chicago Historical Society (SDN-058772); p. 66, National Baseball Hall of Fame, Cooperstown, NY; p. 67, Chicago Historical Society (SDN-058773); pp. 70-78, National Baseball Hall of Fame, Cooperstown, NY; p. 80, Chicago Historical Society (SDN-058763); pp. 82-85, National Baseball Hall of Fame, Cooperstown, NY; p. 87, Chicago Historical Society (SDN-007231); p. 89, National Baseball Hall of Fame, Cooperstown, NY; p. 90, Chicago Historical Society (SDN-006868); p. 92, National Baseball Hall of Fame, Cooperstown, NY; p. 93, The George Brace Collection; p. 96, Chicago Historical Society (SDN-004342); p. 97, National Baseball Hall of Fame, Cooperstown, NY; p. 98, Chicago Historical Society (SDN-059678A); p. 99, Chicago Historical Society (SDN-053122); p. 101, National Baseball Hall of Fame, Cooperstown, NY; p. 103, Chicago Historical Society (SDN-053479); p. 105, Cindy Thomson; p. 106, Chicago Historical Society (SDN-058796A); p. 108, Chicago Historical Society (SDN-058863); pp. 110-112, National Baseball Hall of Fame, Cooperstown, NY; p. 115, Chicago Historical Society (SDN-005315); p. 117, Chicago Historical Society (SDN-057617); p. 118, The George Brace Collection; p. 120, National Baseball Hall of Fame, Cooperstown, NY; p. 122, Chicago Historical Society (SDN-007718); pp. 124, *The Sporting News*; pp. 125-127, National Baseball Hall of Fame, Cooperstown, NY; p. 128, Chicago Historical Society (SDN-060004); pp. 130-131, National Baseball Hall of Fame, Cooperstown, NY; p. 132, Chicago Historical Society (SDN-058070); pp. 134-146, National Baseball Hall of Fame, Cooperstown, NY; p. 148, Chicago Historical Society (SDN-002559); pp. 149-152, National Baseball Hall of Fame, Cooperstown, NY; p. 154, Chicago Historical Society (SDN-001694); p. 156, Chicago Historical Society (SDN-054782); pp. 158-160, National Baseball Hall of Fame, Cooperstown, NY; p. 162, Chicago Historical Society (SDN-

002564); pp. 164-174, National Baseball Hall of Fame, Cooperstown, NY; p. 176, The George Brace Collection; pp. 177-179, National Baseball Hall of Fame, Cooperstown, NY; p. 182, Chicago Historical Society (SDN-058243); pp. 183-185, National Baseball Hall of Fame, Cooperstown, NY; p. 186, The SABR Collection; p. 188, Chicago Historical Society (SDN-003949); p. 190, National Baseball Hall of Fame, Cooperstown, NY; p. 192, Chicago Historical Society (SDN-003956); pp. 194-213, National Baseball Hall of Fame, Cooperstown, NY; p. 214, Chicago Historical Society (SDN-058449); p. 216, National Baseball Hall of Fame, Cooperstown, NY; p. 218, Chicago Historical Society (SDN-060732); pp. 220-223, National Baseball Hall of Fame, Cooperstown, NY; p. 224, Chicago Historical Society (SDN-057695); p. 226, National Baseball Hall of Fame, Cooperstown, NY; p. 227, Road West Publishing; p. 229, National Baseball Hall of Fame, Cooperstown, NY; p. 230, Chicago Historical Society (SDN-061909); p. 232, Chicago Historical Society (SDN-001732); pp. 234-235, National Baseball Hall of Fame, Cooperstown, NY; p. 238, Chicago Historical Society (SDN-002901); p. 240, National Baseball Hall of Fame, Cooperstown, NY; p. 241, Chicago Historical Society (SDN-001726); pp. 244-246, National Baseball Hall of Fame, Cooperstown, NY; p. 248, The George Brace Collection; pp. 250-261, National Baseball Hall of Fame, Cooperstown, NY; p. 263, Chicago Historical Society (SDN-061484); p. 264, National Baseball Hall of Fame, Cooperstown, NY; p. 265, Charles M. Conlon/*The Sporting News*; pp. 267-275, National Baseball Hall of Fame, Cooperstown, NY; p. 276, Transcendental Graphics; p. 278, National Baseball Hall of Fame, Cooperstown, NY; p. 279, Chicago Historical Society (SDN-003262); pp. 280-284, National Baseball Hall of Fame, Cooperstown, NY; p. 286, Chicago Historical Society (SDN-060719); pp. 287-291, National Baseball Hall of Fame, Cooperstown, NY; p. 292, Chicago Historical Society (SDN-060700); p. 293, National Baseball Hall of Fame, Cooperstown, NY; p. 294, Chicago Historical Society (SDN-056870); p. 295, Chicago Historical Society (SDN-061466); p. 296, National Baseball Hall of Fame, Cooperstown, NY; p. 297, Library of Congress Prints and Photographs Division (LC-USZ62-71745DLC); p. 298, National Baseball Hall of Fame, Cooperstown, NY; p. 300, Chicago Historical Society (SDN-060693); pp. 301-310, National Baseball Hall of Fame, Cooperstown, NY; p. 312, Chicago Historical Society (SDN-001441); pp. 314-330, National Baseball Hall of Fame, Cooperstown, NY; p. 331, Tom Crabtree; p. 333, National Baseball Hall of Fame, Cooperstown, NY; p. 334, Bridgeport Public Library; pp. 335-337, National Baseball Hall of Fame, Cooperstown, NY; p. 338, Chicago Historical Society (SDN-003417); pp. 340-343, National Baseball Hall of Fame, Cooperstown, NY; pp. 344-347, Eric and Paul Sallee; pp. 348-349, National Baseball Hall of Fame, Cooperstown, NY; p. 350, Chicago Historical Society (SDN-056549); p. 352, The George Brace Collection; p. 354, Patty K. Sites; pp. 355-356, National Baseball Hall of Fame, Cooperstown, NY; p. 359, Chicago Historical Society (SDN-059437); p. 360, Rawlings Sporting Goods Company; p. 362, *The Sporting News*; p. 363, National Baseball Hall of Fame, Cooperstown, NY; p. 364, Chicago Historical Society (SDN-067851).